The Neo-Kantian Reader

The latter half of the nineteenth and the early part of the twentieth century witnessed a remarkable resurgence of interest in Kant's philosophy in Continental Europe, the effects of which are still being felt today. *The Neo-Kantian Reader* is the first anthology to collect the most important primary sources in Neo-Kantian philosophy, with many being published here in English for the first time.

Sebastian Luft, together with other scholars, provides clear introductions to each of the following sections (to the authors as well as to each text), placing them in historical and philosophical context:

- The Beginnings of Neo-Kantianism: including the work of Hermann von Helmholtz, Otto Liebman, Friedrich Lange, and Hermann Lotze
- The Marburg School: including Hermann Cohen, Paul Natorp, and Ernst Cassirer
- The Southwest School: including Wilhelm Windelband, Heinrich Rickert, Emil Lask, and Hans Vaihinger
- Responses and Critiques: including Moritz Schlick, Edmund Husserl, Rudolf Carnap, and the "Davos dispute" between Martin Heidegger and Ernst Cassirer.

The Neo-Kantian Reader is essential reading for all students of nineteenth- and twentieth-century philosophy, philosophy and the history of science, and phenomenology, as well as to those studying important philosophical movements such as logical positivism and analytic philosophy and its history.

Sebastian Luft is Professor of Philosophy at Marquette University, USA. He is the author of *Subjectivity and Lifeworld in Transcendental Phenomenology* (2011), and is editor (with Søren Overgaard) of *The Routledge Companion to Phenomenology* (2013).

The Neo-Kantian Reader

Edited by

Sebastian Luft

LONDON AND NEW YORK

First published 2015
by Routledge
2 Park Square, Milton Park, Abingdon, Oxon, OX14 4RN

and by Routledge
711 Third Avenue, New York City, NY 10017

Routledge is an imprint of the Taylor & Francis Group, an informa business

© 2015 Sebastian Luft, editorial and selection matter; individual chapters, the contributors
The right of Sebastian Luft to be identified as the author of the editorial material, and of the authors for their individual chapters, has been asserted in accordance with sections 77 and 78 of the Copyright, Designs and Patents Act 1988.

All rights reserved. No part of this book may be reprinted or reproduced or utilised in any form or by any electronic, mechanical, or other means, now known or hereafter invented, including photocopying and recording, or in any information storage or retrieval system, without permission in writing from the publishers.

Trademark notice: Product or corporate names may be trademarks or registered trademarks, and are used only for identification and explanation without intent to infringe.

British Library Cataloguing in Publication Data
A catalogue record for this book is available from the British Library

Library of Congress Cataloging in Publication Data
A catalog record for this book has been requested

HBK ISBN13: 978-0-415-45252-6
PBK ISBN13: 978-0-415-45253-3

Typeset in Bembo and Bell Gothic by Saxon Graphics Ltd, Derby

Kant verstehen, heißt über ihn hinausgehen.
To understand Kant means going beyond him.
— Wilhelm Windelband

Contents

Permissions		x
Chronology		xiii
Editor's Introduction		xx

PART 1
Beginnings
1

	INTRODUCTION: HERMANN VON HELMHOLTZ (1821–1894)	1
1	On General Physical Concepts (before 1847)	6
2	On the Origin and Significance of Geometrical Axioms (1876)	12
3	The Origin and Meaning of Geometric Axioms (1878)	27
	INTRODUCTION: OTTO LIEBMANN (1840–1912)	37
4	Kant's Chief Doctrine and his Chief Mistakes, from *Kant and the Epigones* (1865)	40
	INTRODUCTION: FRIEDRICH ALBERT LANGE (1828–1875)	63
5	The Standpoint of the Ideal, from *The History of Materialism* (1873)	66
	INTRODUCTION: RUDOLF HERMANN LOTZE (1817–1881)	79
6	The World of Ideas, from *Logic* (1874)	82

viii CONTENTS

PART 2
The Marburg School 93

INTRODUCTION: HERMANN COHEN (1842–1918) 93

7 Introduction to *The Principle of the Infinitesimal Method and its History* (1883) 101

8 The Synthetic Principles, from *Kant's Theory of Experience* (1885) 107

9 The Relationship of Logic to Physics, from the Introduction, with Critical Remarks, to the Ninth Edition of Lange's *History of Materialism* (1914) 117

10 The Discovery of Man as Fellowman, from *Religion of Reason out of the Sources of Judaism* (1919) 137

INTRODUCTION: PAUL NATORP (1854–1924) 158

11 On the Objective and Subjective Grounding of Knowledge (1887) 164

12 Kant and the Marburg School (1912) 180

13 The Problem of a Logic of the Exact Sciences, from *The Logical Foundations of the Exact Sciences* (1921) 198

INTRODUCTION: ERNST CASSIRER (1874–1945) 214

14 Hermann Cohen and the Renewal of Kantian Philosophy (1912) 221

15 Euclidean and non-Euclidean Geometry, from *Einstein's Theory of Relativity* (1921) 236

16 The Place of Language and Myth in the Pattern of Human Culture, from *Language and Myth* (1925) 246

17 The Problem of the Symbol and Its Place in the System of Philosophy (1927) 254

PART 3
The Southwest School 265

INTRODUCTION: WILHELM WINDELBAND (1848–1915) 265

18 Critical or Genetic Method? (1883) 271

19 History and Natural Science (1894) 287

20 Introduction to *A History of Philosophy With Special Reference to the Formation and Development of Its Problems and Conceptions* (1900) 299

21 Philosophy of Culture and Transcendental Idealism (1910) 317

	INTRODUCTION: HEINRICH RICKERT (1863–1936)	325
22	Concept Formation in History, from *The Limits of Concept Formation in Natural Science: A Logical Introduction to the Historical Sciences* (1902)	331
23	Knowing and Cognizing. Critical Comments on Theoretical Intuitionism (1934)	384
	INTRODUCTION: EMIL LASK (1875–1915)	396
24	Announcement of *The Logic of Philosophy and the Doctrine of Categories* (1910)	399
25	The Logic of the Ontological Categories, from *The Logic of Philosophy and the Doctrine of Categories* (1911)	401
26	The Boundlessness of Truth, from The *Logic of Philosophy and the Doctrine of Categories* (1911)	422
	INTRODUCTION: HANS VAIHINGER (1852–1933)	428
27	General Introduction to *The Philosophy of the As-If* (1911)	431
28	The Atom as Fiction, from *The Philosophy of the As-If* (1911)	440
29	Things-in-Themselves [as Fiction], from *The Philosophy of the As-If* (1911)	442

PART 4
Responses and Critiques   445

	INTRODUCTION: MORITZ SCHLICK (1882–1936)	445
30	Critical or Empiricist Interpretation of Modern Physics? (1921)	447
	INTRODUCTION: RUDOLF CARNAP (1891–1970)	457
31	Space as a Condition of Experience, from *Der Raum* (1922)	459
	INTRODUCTION: EDMUND HUSSERL (1859–1938)	461
32	A Critique of Windelband and Rickert on the Classification of the Sciences from *Nature and Spirit* (1927)	463
	INTRODUCTION: MARTIN HEIDEGGER (1889–1976) & ERNST CASSIRER	477
33	The Davos Dispute (1929)	479
	Main Neo-Kantian Works in German	486
	Translation of Neo-Kantian Works in English	489
	Index	492

Permissions

The publisher and the editor wish to thank all those who translated material for inclusion in this volume, and the third parties who granted permission to reprint material under copyright. Every effort has been made to trace and contact copyright holders but this may not have been possible in all cases. Any omissions brought to the attention of the publisher will be remedied in future editions.

On General Physical Concepts: untitled manuscript from before 1847, reprinted in Königsberger, Leo. 1903. *Hermann von Helmholtz*. 3 vols. Vol. 2. Braunschweig: Vieweg, pp. 126–138.

On the Origin and Significance of Geometrical Axioms: from *Popular Lectures on Scientific Subjects, Second Series*. London: Longmans, Green, and Co. 1908. Reproduces verbatim the bulk of the paper as it appeared in *Mind* Volume 1 (No. 3) 1876, pp. 301–321.

The Origin And Meaning of Geometric Axioms: from *Mind* Volume 3 (No. 10) 1878: pp.212–225.

Kant's Chief Doctrine and His Chief Mistakes: from Chapter 1 of Liebmann's *Kant und die Epigonen* [*Kant and His Epigones*]. Stuttgart: Carl Schober, 1865, pp. 20–69. Translated into English for the first time by Brian A. Chance.

The Standpoint of the Ideal, from The History of Materialism: from *Geschichte des Materialismus*, by F.A. Lange (1866, 1873). Published in English as *The History of Materialism*, trans. Ernest Chester Thomas. London: Routledge & Kegan Paul, 1950, pp. 513–534.

The World of Ideas, from Logic: from *Logik*, by Rudolf Hermann Lotze (1874). Published in English as *Logic*, trans. Bernard Bosanquet. New York: Garland, 1980, pp. 201–222.

Introduction from The Principle of the Infinitesimal Method and Its History: from *Das Prinzip der Infinitesimalmethode und seine Geschichte*, by Hermann Cohen (1883). Berlin: Dümmlers, 1883, pp.1ff. Translated into English for the first time by Lydia Patton and David Hyder.

The Synthetic Principles: from *Kants Theorie der Erfahrung*, by Hermann Cohen (1885). 2 edn. Berlin: Dümmlers, 1885, Chapter 12, "Die synthetischen Grundsätze," pp. 406–422. Translated into English for the first time by David Hyder.

The Relationship of Logic to Physics: from the Introduction to *History of Materialism*, by F.A. Lange (1914): from reprint, 1928. *Hermann Cohen's Schriften zur Philosophie und Zeitgeschichte*, Albert Görland and Ernst Cassirer, eds. Berlin: Akademie Verlag, pp. 231–267. Translated by Lydia Patton.

The Discovery of Man as Fellowman, from *Religion of Reason Out Of the Sources of Judaism*, by Hermann Cohen (1919). Trans. Simon Kaplan, Atlanta: Scholars Press, 1995, Ch. 8, pp. 113–143.

On the Objective and Subjective Grounding of Knowledge: from "Über objective und subjective Begründung der Erkenntniss", by Paul Natorp (1887). Published in *Philosophische Monatshefte* xxiii (1887), pp. 257–286. Trans. Lois Phillips and David Kolb.

Kant and the Marburg School: from "Kant und die Marburger Schule," *Kant-Studien* 17 (1912): pp. 193–221. Translated into English for the first time by Frances Bottenberg.

The Problem of a Logic of the Exact Sciences: first published as "Das Problem einer Logik der exakten Wissenschaften" by Paul Natorp in: *Die Logischen Grundlagen der exakten Wissenschaften* (Leipzig/Berlin: Teubner, 1st edn., 1910, 2nd edn. 1921), pp. 1–34. Translated into English for the first time by Frances Bottenberg.

Hermann Cohen and the Renewal of Kantian Philosophy: from "Hermann Cohen und die Erneuerung der Kantischen Philosophie," *Kantstudien* 17 (1912), pp. 252–73. Published in English, in: *Angelaki* 10.1. (2005), pp. 95–108. Trans. Lydia Patton. © 2005 Taylor and Francis Group and the Editors of *Angelaki*.

Euclidean and non-Euclidean Geometry: from *Einstein's Theory of Relativity* by Ernst Cassirer (1921). Trans. William Curtis Swabey and Marie Collins Swabey. Chicago: Dover, 1943, pp. 430–444.

The Place of Language and Myth in the Pattern of Human Culture: from *Language and Myth* by Ernst Cassirer (1925). Trans. Susanne K. Langer. New York: Dover, 1953, pp. 1–16.

The Problem of the Symbol and Its Place in the System of Philosophy: from *Zeitschrift fur Aesthetik und allgemeine Kunstwissenschaft* 21 (1927), pp. 295–322. Published in: English in *Man and World* 2 (1978), trans. J.M. Krois, pp.411–428 : 'The problem of the symbol and its place in the system of philosophy' by Ernst Cassirer. © Springer 1978. Reproduced with kind permission from Springer Science+Business Media B.V.

Critical or Genetic Method?: first published as "Kritische oder genetische Methode?" by Wilhelm Windelband (1883), in: *Präludien. Aufsätze und Reden zur Philosophie und ihrer Gescheichte*, Mohr/Siebeck: Tübingen, 1921, Vol. II pp. 99–135. Translated into English for the first time by Alan Duncan.

History and Natural Science: first published as "Geschichte und Naturwissenschaft" by Wilhelm Windelband (1894), in: *Präludien. Aufsätze und Reden zur Philosophie und ihrer Geschichte*. Tübingen, 1924, Volume II, pp. 136–160. Published in English in: *History and Theory*, 19/2, May 1980, Trans. Guy Oaks, pp. 169–185. Reproduced with kind permission of the translator and Blackwell Publishing Ltd.

Introduction: from *A History of Philosophy with Especial Reference to the Formation and Development of Its Problems and Conceptions* by Wilhelm Windelband (1900). Trans. James H. Tufts. New York/London: MacMillan, 1926, pp. 1–22.

Philosophy of Culture and Transcendental Idealism: from "Kulturphilosophie und transzendentaler Idealismus" by Wilhelm Windelband (1910), in: *Präludien*, Vol. II, pp. 279–294. Translated into English for the first time by Alan Duncan.

Concept Formation in History: from "Die Historische Begriffsbildung" by Heinrich Rickert (1902), in: *Die Grenzen der Naturwissenschaftlichen Begriffsbildung: Eine logische Einleitung in die historischen Wissenschaften*. Ed. Paul Tillich. Tübingen, 1902. Ed. and trans. Guy Oakes. Cambridge/New York: Cambridge University Press, 1986, pp. 61–138. English translation © Cambridge University Press 1986, reproduced with permission.

Knowing and Cognizing. Critical Comments on Theoretical Intuitionism: from "*Kennen und Erkennen. Kritische Bemerkungen zum theoretischen Intuitionismus*" by Heinrich Rickert (1934), in: *Kant Studien* 39 (1934), pp. 139–155. Translated into English for the first time by Jon Burmeister.

Announcement of *The Logic of Philosophy and the Doctrine of Categories*: from "Selbstanzeige," in: *Sämtliche Werke*, vol. I. Wuppertal: Dietrich Scheglmann Reprintverlag, 1910, pp. 330–332. Translated into English for the first time by Arun Iyer.

The Logic of the Ontological Categories: from *The Logic of Philosophy and the Doctrine of Categories by* Emil Lask (1911), in: *Gesammelte Werke*, vol. II, pp. 23–49. Translated into English for the first time by Arun Iyer.

The Boundlessness of Truth: from *The Logic of Philosophy and the Doctrine of Categories by* Emil Lask (1911), pp. 105–111. Translated into English for the first time by Arun Iyer.

General Introduction: from *The Philosophy of the As-If* by Hans Vaihinger (1911). Trans. K. Ogden, London: Routledge, 1965, pp. 1–16.

The Atom as Fiction: from *The Philosophy of the As-If* by Hans Vaihinger (1911). Trans. K. Ogden, London: Routledge, 1965, pp. 70–72.

Things-in-Themselves [as Fiction]: om *The Philosophy of the As-If* by Hans Vaihinger (1911). Trans. K. Ogden, London: Routledge, 1965, pp. 74–76.

Critical or Empiricist Interpretation of Modern Physics?: from 'Kritizistische oder empiristische Deutung der neuen Physik?' by Moritz Schlick, in: *Kant-Studien* 26 (1921), pp. 96–111. Translated by Peter Heath.

Space as Condition for Experience: from *Der Raum*, by Rudolf Carnap (1922). Published in English in: *The Collected Works of Rudolf Carnap, Volume 1: Early Writings*, Open Court Publishing Company, 2009. Edited by A.W. Carus, Michael Friedman, Wolfgang Kienzler, and Sven Schlotter. Trans. Michael Friedman and A.W. Carus. Reproduced with the kind permission of Open Court Publishing Company.

The Classification of the Sciences According to Windelband's and Rickert's Methods": from *Natur und Geist* by Edmund Husserl (1927), in: *Vorlesungen Sommersemester* 1927. Ed. M. Weiler. *Husserliana* 32. Dordrecht: Kluwer Academic Publishers, 2001, pp. 78–102. Reproduced with kind permission from Springer Science+Business Media B.V. Translated into English for the first time by Elizabeth A. Behnke.

The Davos Dispute: from "*Arbeitsgemeinschaft Cassirer-Heidegger*", a discussion between Ernst Cassirer and Martin Heidegger (1929), in: Guido Schneeberger, *Ergänzungen zu einer Heidegger-Bibliographie*, Bern, 1960, pp. 17–27), translated by Frances Slade, in: N. Langiulli (ed.), *The Existential Tradition: Selected Writings*. New York: Doubleday, 1971, pp. 192–203.

Chronology

1815	End of the Napoleonic Wars; Congress of Vienna
	Foundation of the German Confederation
1817	Rudolf Hermann Lotze born
1821	Hermann von Helmholtz born
1828	Friedrich Albert Lange born
1831	Hegel dies
1840	Otto Liebmann born
	Friedrich Adolf Trendelenburg, *Logische Untersuchungen* [*Logical Investigations*]
1842	Hermann Cohen born
1844	Alois Riehl born
	Søren Kierkegaard, *Philosophical Fragments*
1846	S. Kierkegaard, *Concluding Unscientific Postscript to* Philosophical Fragments
1848	Wilhelm Windelband born
	Karl Marx, *Das Kommunistische Manifest* [*The Communist Manifesto*]
	March Revolution and Opening of the National Assembly [*Nationalversammlung*]
1849	**1848 Revolution is defeated; a period of political repression starts.**
1854	Schelling dies
	Paul Natorp born
	F.A. Lange, habilitation in Bonn [1854]
1855	Heinrich von Helmholtz, *Über das Sehen des Menschen* [*On Man's Seeing*]
	Ludwig Büchner, *Kraft und Stoff* [*Force and Matter*]
1859	K. Marx, *Zur Kritik der politischen Ökonomie* [*On the Critique of Political Economy*]
	Charles Darwin, *On the Origin of Species and Natural Selection*
	Arthur Schopenhauer, *Die Welt als Wille und Vorstellung* (final edition) [*The World as Will and Representation*]

	Edmund Husserl born
1860	Kuno Fischer, *Immanuel Kant*
1862	Eduard Zeller, *Über Bedeutung auf Aufgabe der Erkenntnistheorie* [*On the Meaning and Task of Epistemology*]
	Otto von Bismarck becomes *Ministerpräsident* of Prussia
1863	Heinrich Rickert born
1865	O. Liebmann, *Kant und die Epigonen* [*Kant and the Epigones*]
	O. Liebmann, habilitation in Tübingen
	F.A. Lange, *Die Arbeiterfrage* [*The Question Regarding the Working Class*]
1866	F.A. Lange, *Die Geschichte des Materialismus* [*History of Materialism*]
	Prussian–Austrian War. Foundation of the North Germanic Confederation
1867	K. Marx, *Das Kapital* I
1869	Jonas Cohn born
1870	A. Riehl, habilitation in Graz (Austria)
	German–French War
1871	H. Cohen, *Kants Theorie der Erfahrung* [*Kant's Theory of Experience*]
	Proclamation of the German Empire; Wilhelm I becomes German Emperor
1872	F.A. Lange, Ordinarius in Marburg
1873	W. Windelband, habilitation in Leipzig
	H. Cohen, habilitation in Marburg
1874	Ernst Cassirer born
1875	Emil Lask born
	Richard Hönigswald born
	F.A. Lange dies
1876	W. Windelband, Ordinarius in Zürich
	H. Cohen, Ordinarius in Marburg
	A. Riehl, *Der philosophische Kritizismus*, Vol. 1 [*Philosophical Criticism*]
	O. Liebmann, *Analysis der Wirklichkeit* [*Analysis of Reality*]
1877	Bruno Bauch born
	H. Cohen, *Kants Begründung der Ethik* [*Kant's Grounding of Ethics*]
	W. Windelband, Professor in Freiburg
1878	A. Riehl, Ordinarius in Graz
	O. Liebmann, Ordinarius in Strasbourg
	W. Windelband, *Geschichte der neueren Philosophie*, Vol. 1 [*History of Modern Philosophy*]
	Attempted Assassination of the German Emperor and the Socialist Laws (*Sozialistengesetze*)
1879	A. Riehl, *Der philosophische Kritizismus*, Vol. 2 [*Philosophical Criticism*]
	Gottlob Frege, *Begriffsschrift*
1880	W. Windelband, *Geschichte der neueren Philosophie*, Vol. 2 [*History of Modern Philosophy*]
1881	P. Natorp, habilitation in Marburg
	R.H. Lotze dies
1882	W. Windelband, Professor in Strasbourg

	O. Liebmann, Professor in Jena
	A. Riehl, Professor in Freiburg
	Friedrich Nietzsche, *Die fröhliche Wissenschaft* [*The Gay Science*]
1883	H. Cohen, *Das Prinzip der Infinitesimalmethode* [*The Principle of Infinitesimal Method*]
	Wilhelm Dilthey, *Einleitung in die Geisteswissenschaften* [*Introduction to the Human Sciences*]
	F. Nietzsche, *Also sprach Zarathustra*
1884	W. Windelband, *Praeludien*
1886	F. Nietzsche, *Jenseits von Gut und Böse* [*Beyond Good and Evil*]
1887	A. Riehl, *Der philosophische Kritizismus*, Vol. 3
1888	**Wilhelm II seizes the Throne**
1889	H. Cohen, *Kants Begründung der Ästhetik* [*Kant's Grounding of Aesthetics*]
	Martin Heidegger born
1890	**Dismissal of Bismarck**
1891	H. Rickert, habilitation in Freiburg
1892	W. Windelband, *Lehrbuch der Geschichte der Philosophie* [*Compendium to the History of Philosophy*]
	H. Rickert, *Der Gegenstand der Erkenntnis,* 1st ed. [*The Object of Cognition*]
1893	P. Natorp, Ordinarius in Marburg
1894	H. von Helmholtz dies
	P. Natorp, *Religion innerhalb der Grenzen der Humanität* [*Religion within the Boundaries of Humanity*]
	W. Windelband, "Geschichte und Naturwissenschaften" ["Natural Science and History"]
1895	A. Riehl, Professor in Kiel
1896	H. Rickert, Ordinarius in Freiburg
	J. Cohn, *Geschichte des Unendlichkeitsproblems in abendländischen Denkens bis Kant* [*The Problem of Infinity in Western Thought up to Kant*]
	H. Rickert, *Die Grenzen der naturwissenschaftlichen Begriffsbildung*, Vol. 1 [*The Limits of Concept-Formation*]
	F. Stammler, *Wirtschaft und Recht nach der materialistischen Geschichtsauffassung* [*Economy and Right According to the Materialistic Conception of History*]
1897	J. Cohn, habilitation in Freiburg
1898	A. Riehl, Professor in Halle
1899	F. Staudinger, *Ethik und Politik* [*Ethics and Politics*]
	P. Natorp, *Sozialpädagogik* [*Social Pedagogy*]
	Eduard Bernstein, *Die Voraussetzungen des Sozialismus* [*Socialism's Presuppositions*]
	Erich Haeckel, *Die Welträtsel* [*The Riddle of the Universe*]
	H. Rickert, *Kulturwissenschaft und Naturwissenschaft* [*Cultural Science and Natural Science*]
1900	Sigmund Freud, *Die Traumdeutung* [*The Interpretation of Dreams*]
	Max Planck, *Quantenhypothese* [*The Quantum Hypothesis*]

1900/01	E. Husserl, *Logische Untersuchungen* [*Logical Investigations*]
1902	H. Cohen, *Logik der reinen Erkenntnis* [*Logic of Pure Cognition*]
	E. Cassirer, *Leibniz' System in seinen wissenschaftlichen Grundlagen* [*Leibniz' System in its Scientific Foundations*]
	E. Lask, *Fichtes Idealismus und die Geschichte* [*Fichte's Idealism and History*]
	H. Rickert, *Die Grenzen der naturwissenschaftlichen Begriffsbildung*, Vol. 2 [*The Limits of Concept-Formation*]
1903	W. Windelband, Professor in Heidelberg
	B. Brauch, habilitation in Halle
	P. Natorp, *Platons Ideenlehre* [*Plato's Doctrine of Ideas*]
1904	H. Cohen, *Ethik des reinen Willens* [*Ethics of Pure Willing*]
1905	A. Riehl, Professor in Berlin
	E. Lask, habilitation in Heidelberg
	Albert Einstein, *Spezielle Relativitätstheorie* [*Special Theory of Relativity*]
	Max Weber, *Die protestantische Ethik und der Geist des Kapitalismus* [*The Protestant Ethic and the Spirit of Capitalism*]
1906	E. Cassirer, *Das Erkenntnisproblem*, Vol. 1 [*The Problem of Cognition*]
	R. Hönigswald, habilitation in Breslau
	E. Cassirer, habilitation in Berlin
1908	J. Cohn, *Voraussetzungen und Ziele des Erkennens* [*Presuppositions and Goals of Cognition*]
	E. Cassirer, *Das Erkenntnisproblem*, Vol. 2 [*The Problem of Cognition*]
	Hugo Münsterberg, *Philosophie der Werte* [*Philosophy of Values*]
1909	P. Natorp, *Philosophie und Pädagogik* [*Philosophy and Pedagogy*]
1910	E. Cassirer, *Substanzbegriff und Funktionsbegriff* [*Substance and Function*]
	P. Natorp, *Die logischen Grundlagen der exakten Wissenschaften* [*The Logical Foundations of the Exact Sciences*]
	W. Windelband, *Die Erneuerung des Hegelianismus* [*The Renewal of Hegelianism*]
1911	B. Bauch, Professor in Jena
	P. Natorp, *Die Philosophie, ihr Problem und ihre Probleme* [*Philosophy, Its Problem and Its Problems*]
	Rudolf Stammler, *Theorie der Rechtswissenschaft* [*Theory of Jurisprudence*]
	Karl Vorländer, *Kant und Marx*
	E. Lask, *Die Logik der Philosophie und die Kategorienlehre* [*The Logic of Philosophy and the Doctrine of Categories*]
	H. Kelsen, *Hauptprobleme der Staatsrechtslehre* [*Basic Problems of Constitutional Law*]
	E. Husserl, "Philosophie als strenge Wissenschaft" ["Philosophy as Rigorous Science"]
1912	O. Liebmann dies
	H. Cohen, *Ästhetik des reinen Gefühls* [*Aesthetics of Pure Feeling*]
	P. Natorp, *Allgemeine Psychologie nach kritischer Methode* [*General Psychology According to Critical Method*]
	E. Lask, *Die Lehre vom Urteil* [*The Doctrine of Judgment*]

1913	R. Hönigswald, *Prinzipienfragen der Denkspsychologie* [*Principal Questions of Thought-Psychology*]
	E. Husserl, *Ideen zu einer reinen Phänomenologie und phänomenologischen Philosophie*, Vol. 1 [*Ideas for a Pure Phenomenology and Phenomenological Philosophy*]
	Max Adler, *Marxistische Probleme*
1914	W. Windelband, *Einleitung in die Philosophie* [*Introduction to Philosophy*]
	O. Radbruch, *Grundzüge der Rechtsphilosophie* [*Foundations of the Philosophy of Right*]
	O. Liebert, *Das Problem der Geltung* [*The Problem of Validity*]
	Outbreak of World War I
1915	E. Lask dies
	W. Windelband dies
	H. Cohen, *Der Begriff der Religion im System der Philosophie* [*The Concept of Religion in the System of Philosophy*]
1916	H. Rickert, Professor in Heidelberg
	E. Cassirer, *Freiheit und Form* [*Freedom and Form*]
1917	B. Bauch, *Immanuel Kant*
1918	H. Cohen dies
	E. Cassirer, *Kants Leben und Lehre* [*Kant's Life and Thought*]
	R. Hönigswald, *Über die Grundlagen der Pädagogik* [*The Foundations of Pedagogy*]
	Oswald Spengler, *Der Untergang des Abendlandes*, Vol. 1 [*The Decline of the West*]
	P. Natorp, *Deutscher Weltberuf* [*Germany's Vocation for the World*]
	World War I ends; Wilhelm II abdicates and Germany becomes a republic
1919	R. Hönigswald, Ordinarius in Breslau
	E. Cassirer, Ordinarius in Hamburg
	H. Cohen, *Religion der Vernunft aus den Quellen des Judentums* [*Religion of Reason from the Sources of Judaism*]
	Treaty of Versailles
1920	E. Cassirer, *Das Erkenntnisproblem*, Vol. 3 [*The Problem of Cognition*]
1921	P. Natorp, *Selbstdarstellung* [*Self-Portrait*]
	R. Hönigswald, *Grundfragen der Denkpsychologie* [*Basic Questions of Thought-Psychology*]
	H. Rickert, *System der Philosophie*, Vol. 1 [*System of Philosophy*]
1922	Max Weber, *Gesammelte Aufsätze zur Wissenschaftslehre* [*Collected Essays on the Theory of Science*]
	Ernst Troeltsch, *Der Historismus und seine Probleme* [*Historicism and its Problems*]
1923	J. Cohn, *Theorie der Dialektik* [*Theory of Dialectics*]
	Martin Buber, *Ich und Du* [*I and Thou*]
	B. Bauch, *Wahrheit, Wert, Wirklichkeit* [*Truth, Value, Reality*]
	E. Cassirer, *Die Philosophie der symbolischen Formen*, Vol. 1: Die Sprache [*The Philosophy of Symbolic Forms, vol. 1: Language*]

xviii CHRONOLOGY

1924   P. Natorp dies

A. Riehl dies

H. Cohen, *Jüdische Schriften*, 3 Vols. (ed. by E. Cassirer & Franz Rosenzweig) [*Jewish Writings*]

1925   P. Natorp, *Vorlesungen über praktische Philosophie* [*Lectures on Practical Philosophy*]

E. Cassirer, *Die Philosophie der symbolischen Formen*, Vol. 2: Das mythische Denken [*The Philosophy of Symbolic Forms, vol. 2: Mythical Thought*]

1926   B. Bauch, *Die Idee* [*The Idea*]

J. Cohn, *Befreien und Binden* [*Freedom and Bondage*]

1927   M. Heidegger, *Sein und Zeit* [*Being and Time*]

1928   H. Cohen, *Schriften zur Philosophie und Zeitgeschichte*, 2 Vols. [*Essays on Philosophy and Intellectual History*]

E. Husserl, *Zur Phänomenologie des inneren Zeitbewusstseins* [*Phenomenology of Inner Time-Consciousness*]

1929   E. Cassirer, *Die Philosophie der symbolischen Formen*, Vol. 3: Phänomenologie der Erkenntnis [*The Philosophy of Symbolic Forms, vol. 3: Phenomenology of Knowledge*]

Siegfried Marck, *Die Dialektik in der Philosophie der Gegenwart* [*Dialectics in Contemporary Philosophy*]

M. Heidegger, *Kant und das Problem der Metaphysik* [*Kant and the Problem of Metaphysics*]

E. Husserl, *Formale und transzendentale Logik* [*Formal and Transcendental Logic*]

Black Friday and the Beginnings of the Great Depression

1930   S. Freud, *Das Unbehagen in der Kultur* [*Civilization and its Discontents*]

H. Rickert, *Die Logik des Prädikats und das Problem der Ontologie* [*The Logic of the Predicate and the Problem of Ontology*]

1931   S. Marck, *Die Dialektik in der Philosophie der Gegenwart*, Vol. 2 [*Dialectics in Contemporary Philosophy*]

R. Hönigswald, *Grundfragen der Erkenntnistheorie – Selbstdarstellung* [*Basic Questions of Epistemology – Self-Portrait*]

E. Husserl, *Méditations Cartésiennes* [*Cartesian Meditations*]

H. Gödel, *Über formal unentscheidbare Sätze der Principia Mathematica und verwandter Systeme* [*On Formally Undecidable Propositions of the Principia Mathematica and Related Systems*]

1932   J. Cohn, *Wertwissenschaft*, 2 Vols. [*The Science of Values*]

E. Cassirer, *Die Philosophie der Aufklärung* [*The Philosophy of the Enlightenment*]

1933   **Hitler appointed Chancellor of Germany; Nazi takeover.**

Hönigswald, Cohn, Marck and Cassirer are either dismissed from their university positions due to the new Nazi civil service law, which declares Jews as non-Germans (*Gesetz zur Wiederherstellung des Berufsbeamtentums*), or leave voluntarily.

R. Hönigswald, *Geschichte der Erkenntnistheorie* [*History of Epistemology*]

1934	H. Rickert, *Grundprobleme der philosophischen Methodologie, Ontologie, Anthropologie* [*Basic Problems of Philosophical Methodology, Ontology, Anthropology*]
1935	B. Bauch, *Grundzüge der Ethik* [*Essentials of Ethics*]
1936	H. Rickert dies
1937	R. Hönigswald, *Philosophie und Sprache* [*Philosophy and Language*]
1938	**Reichskristallnacht**
	R. Hönigswald, *Denker der italienischen Renaissance* [*Thinkers of the Italian Renaissance*]
1939	H. Rickert, *Unmittelbarkeit und Sinndeutung* [*Immediacy and Sense-Interpretation*]
	German attack on Poland starts the Second World War
1940	J. Cohn, *Wirklichkeit als Aufgabe* [*Reality as Task*]
1941	**German attack on the Soviet Union; USA enters the war.**
1942	B. Bauch dies
	E. Cassirer, *Zur Logik der Kulturwissenschaften* [*On the Logic of the Cultural Sciences*]
1944	E. Cassirer, *An Essay of Man*
1945	E. Cassirer dies
	Death of Hitler; end of the Second World War; Nuremberg trials
1946	E. Cassirer, *The Myth of the State*
	J. Cohn dies
1949	**Foundation of the Federal Republic of Germany and the German Democratic Republic**

Editor's Introduction

THE NEO-KANTIAN READER aims to make accessible to the English-speaking reader a representative selection of translations of primary readings of the Neo-Kantian tradition, which is without a doubt the most broadly influential movement of European philosophy between approximately 1850 and 1918.[1] The Neo-Kantian Movement was inspired by the battle cry "back to Kant," mainly to counter scientific positivism and *weltanschaulich*[2] materialism in the mid-nineteenth century. Both tendencies had entered the cultural mainstream and seemed to suggest an abolition of philosophy altogether and a general decline of culture and its values.[3] Coming after the so-called collapse of German Idealism and on the heels of the rampant scientism, the Neo-Kantians wanted to revive the spirit of Kant by going back to Kant. Going back to Kant, however, meant "going beyond" him. Going beyond the founder of the critical method was motivated by the scientific and socio-political developments of the present, which necessitated, in turn, an updating of Kant's original position in the light of these novel developments.

Soon after an opening era that is rather hard to characterize in its varied tendencies, two "power centers" emerged in Marburg and in Germany's Southwest (Freiburg and Heidelberg), which brought forth such thinkers as Hermann Cohen, Paul Natorp and Ernst Cassirer (the Marburg School) and Wilhelm Windelband, Heinrich Rickert and Emil Lask (the Southwest or "Baden" School). The "imperial reign" (as Habermas once puts it) of Neo-Kantianism in German-speaking areas lasted from approximately 1860 until 1918. In the interim period after the Great War, Neo-Kantianism became identified as a staid, conservative philosophy that was attached, both intellectually as well as philosophically, to the German *Kaiserreich* and its stale values. Neo-Kantianism remained the philosophical paradigm during the 1920s, while newer movements such as phenomenology ascended.[4] Its final deathblow occurred in 1933, when the last living representatives of an erstwhile domineering philosophical community were forced to leave Germany.

The readings selected here offer a representative selection of these thinkers. The choice of readings is intended to lead the reader through the main stages in the development of Neo-Kantianism. The selections are taken from the key works of the Neo-Kantian philosophers, starting from the polymath Heinrich Helmholtz to arguably the last Neo-Kantian, Ernst Cassirer, who died in 1945, though debates about when *exactly* Neo-Kantianism began and ended will no doubt continue.

Classical Neo-Kantianism: Attempt at a Brief Definition

What *is* Neo-Kantianism? Who *are* the Neo-Kantians? Let us begin with a brief (attempt at a) definition of Neo-Kantianism. In trivial terms, Neo-Kantianism is a philosophy that attempts to revive Kant's philosophy. Immediately, several questions may ensue. What is *Kant's* philosophy about? Why would his philosophy be in need of a revival? What does it *mean* to revive Kant's philosophy? It is fair to say that within the group of thinkers whom nineteenth- and twentieth-century historiography has grouped, somewhat randomly, into this category, these were the questions that were debated. But it is also clear that there were then, and are now, no unified answers to these questions. Indeed, the entire Neo-Kantian movement can be seen as discussing and emphatically disagreeing on possible answers to these (and other) questions. Even the term Neo-*Kantianism* was contested. As in most -isms, one needs to bear in mind that it is, for the most part, a label appended to these thinkers by *others*, mostly critics. Seen in this light, many of those whom we consider staunchly embedded in the Neo-Kantian movement, did not see themselves as furthering *Kant's* philosophy at all, and they would have rejected this label outright. Other titles were used by representatives we now group under the label Neo-Kantianism; some other titles were (Neo-)Criticism, value theory (or value-theoretical philosophy), and others. Other labels were used by the bystanders, for instance, Neo-Fichteanism. Within the Neo-Kantian movement there were at least two different "camps" (in Marburg and the Southwest), not to mention isolated "satellites," who disagreed on their interpretations of Kant and stood for very different philosophical directions.

Given the "imperial reign" of Neo-Kantian philosophers, it is perhaps best to call the *period* between approximately 1860 and 1918, in terms of philosophical historiography, the *age or era of Neo-Kantianism*. Its representatives were the most important thinkers of their day, both within academia and in terms of admiration bestowed upon them by a learned public, the German *Bildungsbürgertum*, who adored their "Mandarins," to use a term famously coined by Fritz Ringer to describe the German professoriate, with almost religious devotion.

Often slandered as "*Professorenphilosophie*" or "*Kathederphilosophie*" ("philosophers' philosophy" or "lectern philosophy"), one formally defining, albeit completely extraneous, trait of Neo-Kantianism deserves to be emphasized. All Neo-Kantians were academics, i.e., they held positions of some sort within German academia (unlike the academic failures, intentionally or not, such as Schopenhauer, Nietzsche, Marx, or Kierkegaard). As such, the Neo-Kantians were quite successful career philosophers who were influential within higher education in Germany and beyond, for instance in political debates of the day, and they were altogether quite comfortable in their bourgeois setting.[5] In this capacity, they influenced and in some cases defined academic politics (esp. with respect to philosophy) at universities guided by the Humboldtian ideal (the unity of research and teaching). In this sense, a defining feature of the Neo-Kantians was certainly the image of the typical academic of the nineteenth century: male (on this more below), bespectacled, with impressive beards and gold-chained pocket watches adorning their equally impressive midsections. As Mandarins, they preached their philosophies from the lectern with a stern Teutonic demeanor.[6] In hindsight, they appear as ultra-conservative defenders of the German *Kaiserreich*, despite the fact that politically, most of them were left-leaning liberals and socialists (or perhaps better, "social-idealists").

Thus, despite this formal commonality, when we speak of "Neo-Kantianism" and "*the* Neo-Kantians" today, the current reader should be aware that one is dealing with anything but a unified school or a unified group of philosophers who have some sense of agreement amongst themselves as to what they stand for. On the other hand, their stronghold in the academic (not just philosophical) scene of their time was hard-earned and not accidental; thus, what the reader can expect is a plethora of extremely interesting, original, and thought-provoking material that has relevance for today as well. When people nowadays use the term "Neo-Kantians" and mean

Christine Korsgaard or Jürgen Habermas, they should be aware that this practice has a tradition reaching back some one hundred years, in that Husserl or Heidegger referred to their contemporaries in the same way. For the intellectual development of European thought in the nineteenth and twentieth centuries, an understanding of the positions and figures of Neo-Kantianism is close to being indispensable for understanding the transition from German Idealism to nineteenth-century scientific positivism to phenomenology, existentialism, hermeneutics, logical positivism, and beyond. Having been almost completely neglected for some half century, the Neo-Kantians are the great missing link in this historical trajectory. Nobody who wants to claim acquaintance with the history of modern philosophy and Western intellectual history can dispense with at least a certain amount of knowledge of this period and its thinkers. This anthology should be able to supply an initial introduction to this body of knowledge.

In the following, I will trace, in briefest terms, the developmental stages of Neo-Kantianism to give the present reader a certain historical map to orient herself (cf. also the timeline see pages ix–xvii).

Early History (1845–1871)

The stages of Neo-Kantianism are certainly debated and that is a good thing, as different perspectives will order the stages differently. Given the text selections of this Reader, I have opted to call this period, ranging somewhere from 1845–1871, the "early history" of Neo-Kantianism. This early period is bookended on the one side by Helmholtz's early texts and, on the other, by the publication of Cohen's first edition of *Kants Theorie der Erfahrung* (1871), which ushers in the flowering of the two schools in Marburg and the Southwest.

Prior to, and concurrent with, this period fall the writings of late Idealists or early Neo-Kantians, depending on how one wants to label them (figures such as the younger Fichte, Fries, Herbart), though I have chosen to extend this period to include Helmholtz, Liebmann, Lange, and Lotze. Especially the inclusion of Lotze in this group of thinkers shows how debatable these decisions are. Lotze is certainly not philosophically close to Liebmann and Lange, though he clearly has had an enormous influence on the Southwest School's theory of value. Liebmann and Lange certainly belong to the group of outspoken Neo-Kantians, with Liebmann's battle cry of "back to Kant" resonating with many thinkers at the time, and with Lange serving as the first Neo-Kantian professor in philosophy at the University of Marburg and being responsible for the contentious hiring of Cohen, a Jew, as his successor.

Philosophically, this early period is marked by a specifically naturalistic or psychologistic reading of Kant, especially in Helmholtz and the early Cohen, who published his first writings in the *Zeitschrift für Völkerpsychologie und Sprachwissenschaft* (*Journal for Folk Psychology and Linguistics*), a journal that offers (in the words of Edgar), "an anthropological investigation of the origins of cultural products such as art and literature"[7]. A common interpretation of Kant involved the rejection of the synthetic a priori in favor of a naturalistic interpretation of anthropological commonalities, such that one can speak of this first period as a *physiological Kantianism*. This characterization of the period is supported by the fact that it is a common trait in the transition to the flowering of the Neo-Kantian movement that the vast majority of major Neo-Kantians (with the exception, perhaps, of Alois Riehl) went on to *reject* any physiological or naturalistic Kant interpretation as constituting a retreat into subjectivism or psychologism. Indeed, Cohen came into his own, one can say, through a radically anti-subjectivistic reading of Kant in his 1871 *Kants Theorie der Erfahrung*, a reading that will become only stronger in subsequent editions. Likewise, the texts selected from Lange, Liebmann, and Lotze are already a reaction to the physiological interpretation of Kant that they encountered in the writings of their contemporaries. Thus, one can speak of "Neo-

Kantianism" in a more substantial sense of the term as the rejection of a psychologistic Kant interpretation, which thinkers such as Helmholtz found attractive, and as the only way one could remain a "Kantian" in light of the current developments in the sciences.

Flowering (1871–1914). The Formation of the Two Schools in Marburg and the Southwest

The latter quarter of the nineteenth century is without doubt *the era of Neo-Kantianism*, in the sense that it had established a stronghold in professional and academic philosophy. This era lasted until the beginning of the Great War. The two emerging power centers were in Marburg and the Southwest. Let us begin with the Marburg School.

The Marburg School, as a school with a distinct philosophical orientation, began historically with Cohen's arrival in Marburg in 1873 and his assumption of the chair left vacant by Lange's death in 1876. As already suggested, arranging for the Jewish Cohen to assume this professorship was quite the "coup" at the time, in light of the more or less open anti-Semitism in German academia. He was joined by Natorp in 1881, who first worked in the university library, assuming a professorship in 1893 (dedicated to philosophy and also pedagogy). The two can be seen as the "twin stars" of the Marburg School, exerting a wide-ranging influence in Marburg and beyond. The term "Marburg School" became an established term in German-speaking academia around 1900, where the idea of a *school establishment* (*Schulbildung*) was very much part of the philosophical "profile." This meant that there was a clear distinction between Cohen, who was the undisputed (intellectual as well as emotional) leader of the school, and Natorp, as the undisputed "second in command,"[8] surrounded by a group of young novices whose task was to "sign on" and carry further the banner of the school after their teachers' demise.[9] Ernst Cassirer was never a novice in this sense and was more of a distant satellite, though philosophically he can be seen as part of the Marburg School. The school's bloom was between 1900 and 1910, with some crises between then and the beginning of the Great War. In 1918, Cohen left Marburg to live in Berlin, while Natorp was left to fend for himself. Once Heidegger came to Marburg in 1922, the fox was in the chicken coop, so to speak, though it speaks to Natorp's honesty that he was in favor of Heidegger's move to Marburg. Natorp died in 1924 and left no students behind; none at least who would have been able to carry on the school tradition. In 1929, after the famous Davos Dispute between Cassirer and Heidegger, it was the general impression that Neo-Kantianism in the form of the Marburg School had been "finished off." In 1933, Cassirer left Germany altogether and the last remnants of the Marburg School had been all but obliterated.

Philosophically, the school can be subsumed under two key notions: the "transcendental method" as the general method utilized by the school, and the overall project of a *philosophy of culture*. The transcendental method was the method of starting out from a *factum* to begin the work of transcendental philosophy (following the analytic method Kant had used in the *Prolegomena*), with the important addition that this *factum* had to be the *factum of science* (*das Faktum der Wissenschaft*). Thus was Cohen's reading of Kant's first Critique: the notion of experience Kant had in mind was the experience of modern scientists, who "experience" nature not as a brute fact, but as obeying and standing under mathematical-physical laws. Hence, the transcendental method had to inquire into the conditions of the possibility of this Newtonian physical science, not as a psychological or historical investigation, but as an inquiry into the conceptual work that is underway as science produces its results, which are laws and concepts. This was the main "work" on the part of the Marburg School and it had its greatest impact here. It is for this reason that the Marburg School had come to be identified with critical or transcendental philosophy of science.

The second hallmark of this school – namely, its project of developing a philosophy of culture – is extremely misleading in light of the Marburg School's self-interpretation, although the overall reception of this school as offering mainly a theory of natural science might, in the end, be justified. For the overall goal of the School was to apply the transcendental method to all spheres of culture, following Kant's canonical distinction between logic, ethics, and aesthetics. Accordingly, the transcendental method had to be applied to each respective *factum* of science of each cultural sphere, and so to morality (legality) and aesthetics, in addition to science and cognition.[10] Thus, the ambition was to account philosophically for each part of reality that is created by the human being and according to the latter's creative capacities, in short, for culture writ large. It might seem obvious that a philosophy of culture that began with the different *facta* of the sciences – for example, in Cohen's system, with jurisprudence as the science of ethics, and with art history as the science of aesthetics – could be conceived as problematic by their contemporaries, and it was for this reason that the Marburg School's ambition beyond logic and theory of cognition was for the most part ignored. When Cassirer famously declares in Volume I of *The Philosophy of Symbolic Forms* that "the critique of reason turns into the critique of culture," he was echoing the basic stance of his teachers, yet his success as a philosopher of culture lay, arguably, in his making a decisive break with the transcendental method as it had been conceived and practiced by Cohen and Natorp.

Other areas of work in the Marburg School included Natorp's writings on psychology, whose main influence lay in paving the way for Husserl's later phenomenology in a transcendental register, and Natorp's works in social and pedagogical philosophy, which all stood under the banner of "idealism" (hence "Social-Idealism" and "Social Pedagogy").

The Southwest School derived its name from its locations in Freiburg and Heidelberg, in the southwest of Germany, a two-hour train ride apart. Because it was located in the State of Baden (which was combined with Württemberg after World War II, to form the State of Baden-Württemberg), it was also called the Baden School of Neo-Kantianism. Due to its philosophical orientation, it was called – to contrast with the "criticism" of the Marburgers – the "value-theoretical" (*werttheoretische*) school of Neo-Kantianism. Its first representative – not quite with the nimbus of Cohen – was Windelband, who taught first at Freiburg and later (with stops in between) in Heidelberg. His most famous pupil was Rickert, who succeeded Windelband both in Freiburg and later, after Windelband's death, in Heidelberg. Though arguably more original and profound than Windelband, Rickert attracted fewer students due to a psychological impairment (agoraphobia). The "poster child" of the Southwest School was the younger Lask, whose premature death in the trenches of the Great War certainly helped to enshrine him in the pantheon of geniuses who died young. Lask was by all accounts an original thinker who took his philosophy in a more radical direction than his teachers, though, not having attained a professorship at the time of his death, was seen as academically dependent on Rickert (as well as Max Weber) in Heidelberg.

The overall philosophical tendency of the Southwest School is rightfully indicated with the term "value theory." Its philosophical predecessor is clearly Lotze in his "transcendental" reading of the Platonic theory of the Forms, which are more aptly to be described in their ontological status as "validities." It is in this "third realm" that values are to be located. Once again rejecting a psychologistic interpretation of ideal entities, such a reading was to be utilized as a bulwark against the threatening moral relativism that had been diagnosed, famously, by Nietzsche in his trope of the death of God. Thus, as a universal value theory, the Southwest interpretation was, like the Marburg School though with some decisive differences, to culminate in a philosophy of culture. In addition to a theory of values, the Southwesterners contributed to the general discussion at the time (especially in critical discussion with Dilthey) surrounding the theory of (value-free) natural sciences and (value-laden) *Geisteswissenschaften*, i.e., the human or cultural sciences. This latter concern grew organically out of their concern with values, since it is the human sciences that deal with cultural values. Critically rejecting Dilthey's distinction between natural sciences as explanatory and the human sciences as interpretive, Windelband famously called for a methodological distinction between two different ways of attending to the object of cognition, either by way of singling out its individualities or seeing the individual object as a representative of universal laws (idiographic versus nomothetic sciences). Rickert's theory concerning the *object of cognition* is a more ambitious theory based on Windelband's more innocuous distinction. Nevertheless, with the focus on a theory of values in conjunction with the methodological distinction between individualistic and general sciences, the Southwest School displays thereby a distinctive profile vis-à-vis the Marburg School and other competing attempts at grasping the distinct character of the non-natural sciences, and thereby defending the status of philosophy itself. Lask took the latter problem into a new dimension when he set out to write a logic of philosophy itself and its *sui generis* doctrine of categories.

Decline and Late Neo-Kantianism

The decline of the late Neo-Kantian movement can most appropriately be told from the perspective of those who constructed for themselves, as Crowell puts it (quoted in note 4), a "liberation narrative," which would consist in calling out the shortcomings and mistakes on the part of the Neo-Kantians. This story can be best left to the heirs of the initial liberators. But from the perspective of the Neo-Kantian establishment, it was obvious that there were hardly any successors left after the Great War and that the remaining Neo-Kantians had a rather pessimistic view of the future of their movement. For instance, Heidegger, who had been a promising student of Rickert's, soon came under the sway of the phenomenologist Husserl and abandoned the ship. In Marburg, there were no pupils left who had the power to gain larger-scale influence[11], and with the two power centers coming apart, the scattered Neo-Kantians left (in places such as Munich or Göttingen) were not able to sustain school unity or a unified movement. Too strong were the novel philosophical forces that began chipping away at the foundations of what was once a Continent-wide movement. The Great War, which did away not only with Germany's political hegemony in Europe but its values and morals as well, is not to be overlooked in doing its part in Neo-Kantianism's demise. Indeed, in hindsight, the new crop of students flocking to the universities and attempting to find grounding in philosophical thought, were utterly disappointed by the seemingly empty gestures of the remaining Neo-Kantians. That some of them had been enthusiastic supporters of the Great War, such as Natorp, certainly did not help the movement. Hence, the Neo-Kantians who remained to carry its banner forward were perceived as backward-looking and incapable of providing any remedy to the rampant "crisis" all around. Not only were they incapable of providing help; worse, they were perceived as part of the old system that was held accountable for the catastrophe of the Great War and its devastating aftermath.

Thus, the interwar period has little to offer to the philosophical historian of Neo-Kantianism (though it is a most fruitful period for the historian of phenomenology). It was populated by (mostly second-rate) pupils of the great names, who have more or less rightfully been forgotten. The history of this short period is beset by political infighting, as detailed, in the case of Marburg, by Sieg, where the themes discussed can only be understood in historical hindsight. For instance, the skirmishes fought vehemently between "Aryan" and Jewish representatives of Neo-Kantianism – ridiculous debates over whether Jews could adequately understand Kant and could consequently be counted as part of the German cultural heritage – are uncannily prescient looking back at this period knowing what happened in Germany as of 1933.

The great schism came in 1933, when many Jews left Germany, among them many philosophers who had some relation to the Neo-Kantians (such as Cassirer or Hönigswald), and most philosophers remaining in Germany were either incapable of resisting the national-socialist "pull," or, in the case of Heidegger, actively furthered it. It is, in this context, not surprising that Neo-Kantianism came to be identified and vilified by many Nazi "philosophers" as a philosophy of the *Kaiserreich*, both degenerate and inherently "Jewish" in its substance. But apart from the unfair identification of "Neo-Kantian" and "Jewish," it would be indeed an unwritten chapter of the philosophy of the twentieth century, which, were one to speculate on how it might have been written, would have had to assess what would have happened to the Neo-Kantian movement had someone like Cassirer lived some more years in the US and established a following. It perhaps would have completely re-shaped the philosophy of the second half of the twentieth century, had some Neo-Kantians prevailed in the New World after being driven from the European continent. As it was, Neo-Kantianism was dead in Europe, never caught on in the New World, whereas others who fled, such as Strauss, Arendt, Carnap and others, went on to become extremely influential, and the only philosopher to speak of who remained standing in Germany was Heidegger.[12] Imagining what could have happened had history played itself out differently is speculation, of course, but such speculation may be permitted a century after Neo-Kantianism's peak.

Reception and Legacy

Especially after their demise, the reception of Neo-Kantianism was for the most part critical and even destructive. It became fashionable to pit one's own attempts against the backdrop of Neo-Kantianism. This is especially true for the budding Phenomenological Movement, whose defining characteristic – "to the things themselves!" (not "back to Kant") – is a battle cry directed, in critical rejection, at the Neo-Kantian obsession with "empty speculation" and "ego metaphysics." The emphasis on the role of the subject and the individual and her existence is a direct reaction to the "logicist" position of the Marburg School and the Southwest theory of values, which seem to float in some heaven inaccessible to the individual. More recent research reveals that this "dialectical" image of the new emerging philosophies, as negating in different ways the position of the Neo-Kantians, is certainly exaggerated and can only be understood in hindsight, and much more work must be done to fully uncover the many filiations and overlaps between the Neo-Kantians and their contemporaries.[13]

As for the legacy of Neo-Kantianism, it would lead too far afield to spell this out here[14], but it bears mentioning that Kant scholarship in the twentieth century, including in the Anglo-American world, would have been impossible without the prior work done by the classical Neo-Kantians. If one defining project, among others, of Neo-Kantianism was its project of a philosophy of *culture*, then one must emphasize that today's cultural studies, both empirical as well as philosophical, owe a great deal to the Neo-Kantians. Finally, today's philosophy of science has discovered the interesting approaches especially of the Marburg School. Contemporary history of science has also come to the realization that the Neo-Kantian era is a nearly untapped resource for its work. Moreover, the theory of philosophical historiography has, as of late, sparked newer reflections. Perhaps reflecting a weariness with the many forms and shapes of contemporary historiography (history of effects, history of reception, postmodern subversive historiography etc.), there is a growing interest today in the time-honored history-of-problems approach (*Problemgeschichte*) that was developed, practiced, and executed with high historical fidelity and sensitivity by most Neo-Kantians. Finally, an important debate at the time, in which the Neo-Kantians were involved, was over the status and methodology of the cultural or human sciences vis-à-vis the natural sciences, predating the famous debate regarding the "two cultures." In light of current debates over the humanities, the dialogue between the "two cultures" defining academia, and the overall project of naturalizing everything "spiritual" or "mental," the Neo-Kantians developed a whole arsenal of arguments and views on these issues, which will be interesting for the philosophical historian as well as theorists of science and the philosopher of mind.

One further issue deserves mentioning, especially in today's climate: namely, the absence of women in Neo-Kantianism. *There are no women represented in this entire movement.* Indeed, one feature that made newer philosophical movements attractive, especially phenomenology, was that they actively welcomed women into their circles. Indeed, women abounded in phenomenological circles, even to the extent that it irritated the traditional founding father, Edmund Husserl.[15]

Organization of this Volume

There are several ways in which one can present historical material of this sort, which are most likely equally justifiable. To list a few (non-exhaustive) options:

- One could make a selection *topically*, that is, based on certain philosophical canonical topics, such as epistemology, moral philosophy, social and political philosophy, aesthetics. Although many Neo-Kantians thought along these canonical divisions, the reason I have refrained from this organization is that selecting texts in this manner would have obscured the manner in which these thinkers themselves wished to present their work. Many of the conceptual and systematic distinctions they employ make it clear that these canonical divisions do not work for their system, or that they want to overcome, modify or subvert them.
- Another would be an organization according to problems and discussions *at the time when the Neo-Kantians lived*. Thus, following Beiser's latest presentation of "philosophy after Hegel," one could present the main discussions at the time, such as the materialism controversy and the *ignorabimus* debate, and select texts in which the Neo-Kantians contributed and reacted to them. The drawback here is that it would obscure the "positive" and original work, the systematic intentions, on the part of the Neo-Kantians and would present them simply as making contributions, among other intellectuals from other schools or outside of academia altogether, to these ongoing debates. They would be perceived as simply a voice within a larger choir. That historically this might have been the way the Neo-Kantians were heard is uncontested. The reason I have not opted for this principle of organization is due mainly to the fact that it would not have allowed the Neo-Kantians' positive contributions to come fully to the fore.
- The principle here was to select texts *in temporal succession* and according to *Schools*. Accordingly, the two main sections, II and III, feature a selection of the main members of the two schools in Marburg and Southwest Germany, respectively. The advantage was that in this way the two "blocks" could be most clearly discerned in their styles and intentions. Cohen and Natorp in Marburg, and Windelband and Rickert in Southwest Germany, not only collaborated especially closely, their philosophical contributions are not understandable without their partners. Moreover, the schools also saw themselves in competition, such that a great portion of their work is tacitly or overtly directed at their opponents in the other "camp." This way of presentation may certainly be contested in light of the two other options listed above, but so be it. Ideally, of course, the texts presented here will be read with a deep appreciation of the philosophical canon, especially since its reconception in Kant, and with a sensitivity to historical context.

Philological Note to the Present Selection

In taking on this project, I thought it would be a fairly easy job. After all, all(!) one had to do is select the relevant texts, scan them, write little introductions, *et voilà*. The reality of the project has proven to be much different and indeed more difficult than I anticipated, and completing this Reader has been, *mehercle*, a daunting job that has taken far too long. Indeed, over the years, I have received many queries as to when the book would finally be on the market, and all I could say was that the project was delayed for many reasons, some out of my control, some within my control, but impossible to get around. Thus, in finally presenting the public with this textbook, I apologize to all for its delay. I hope that the old German saying *Was lange währt, wird endlich gut* [Long in coming, but worth the wait] may be true of this project as well.

Not to list further excuses, but to give scholars willing to enter this area a sense of what they are in for and what future work awaits them, a few words of explanation are in order regarding the situation in which I found myself in undertaking this anthology. There is no doubt that the whole area called "Neo-Kantianism" is, for various reasons, one big "mess." Let us begin with the situation in German scholarship. First, as explained above, it is not clear what exactly Neo-Kantianism is and which philosophers or scientists fall under it. In many cases, the "-ism" suffix is intended to denigrate or critique an author. This is no different with respect to the label "Neo-Kantianism." Hence, identifying who exactly counts as a Neo-Kantian requires historical and philosophical judgment that may or may not be entirely fair with respect to a certain author. Hence, certain decisions had to be made, some of which were purely pragmatic and which may meet with approval or not, but so be it. When it comes to this area of philosophy, it is impossible to satisfy everyone.

Philologically, the situation is made worse by the sheer output on the part of the Neo-Kantians. Not only did they write entire books at the pace by which normal scholars today produce articles; also, it was common at the time to re-edit one's own previous books, but in re-editing them also partially to re-write them, noting more recent scholarship and commenting on the latter while revising one's own text, all the while revising one's very own position (cf., for instance, Natorp's "Metacritique" of his book on Plato, which nearly reverses his earlier position). Hence, to get a clear line on any philosopher's trajectory is nearly impossible to achieve, given the additional fact that of the, say, five editions a book has received, not all are available any longer in libraries. Thus, part of the reconstruction of this historical situation is guesswork at best or would require extensive research in university archives.

The situation becomes even worse when one looks at the situation on the side of the English language. Translations of Neo-Kantians are scarce and their quality very uneven. Some Neo-Kantians have been translated well – not always those one would recognize as standing out today, but important and popular at the time, such as Vaihinger. Of others, nothing or nearly nothing has been translated, or else only tangential pieces, as in the case of Cohen and Lask. Of the existing translations, figuring out exactly which edition of the German was translated has been an additional challenge. And of these existing translations, the quality of them varies greatly, including the manner in which they dealt with the scholarship cited by the original (again, some translated, some not). I tried to render the texts in as unified a way as possible, since the dates of translation (and accordingly standards of philological rigor) lay wide apart. I have also added some (hopefully helpful) footnotes, which, however, I attempted to keep to a minimum, sticking to the maxim that what I was producing was a *Reader*, not a critical edition (as much as the latter may be necessary). Although it might have been desirable, it was impossible to redo the older translations without further delaying publication. Most of them are good, even excellent, esp. in capturing the tone of voice of the philosophers of the Wilhelmian era; some, however, leave much to be desired. But in the hopes of giving a fair presentation of the individual philosophers, I have had to "bite the bullet" when it came to using existing though perhaps questionable translations, rather than omitting important texts.

However, I did not content myself with just reprinting older and existing translations, since this would have rendered this Reader a collection that completely misrepresents the philological as well as philosophical situation. Instead, I had to commission new translations to deliver a more well-rounded image of the Neo-Kantian movement. Though the translators have done admirable work, I did have to go through each new translation several times and consult with the respective translators to ensure consistency.

It is my hope that the result will prove satisfactory; yet, the texts produced here will not and cannot replace a study of the original German, nor is this collection in any way a complete rendering of the Neo-Kantian movement. Indeed, what I was able to select from existing translations and in addition managed to get translated represents, of course, only a snippet of the works of these philosophers. In the case where little or nothing was translated so far, I tried to make an even-handed selection (e.g., Cohen, with the help of Hyder and Patton[16]). In the case where a good amount of works has been translated, e.g., Cassirer (though the existing older translations leave much to be desired as well), I tried to pick texts that move off the beaten path.[17]

The resulting bottom line is that, after many years of research in this area, this Reader can only be a start for further work that will have to be carried out by others. Far from an *Editio Critica*, I would like to refer to it as an *Editio Minima*, with the intention of pointing the reader to where more can be found. It is my hope that this Reader will not only be received with charity, as merely a first stab at this nearly untapped area of European philosophical history, but that a novel wave of interest in the Neo-Kantians will ensue within English-speaking scholarship, which will finally give the Neo-Kantian movement – a movement more vilified and slandered than perhaps any other in the history of modern philosophy – its full due. To the perceptive eye, this is a philosophical movement rich in innovative and original thought, profound in its scholarship, and vast in its scope.

A note of thanks goes to the following people:

Special thanks go to Tony Bruce from Routledge for commissioning this project, and for having the patience and confidence in me to complete this Reader. It has been long in the making and long overdue, and has suffered several setbacks. For this I apologize to him and to all those who have been waiting for me to finish it. I thank Adam Johnson at Routledge for shepherding this volume through from beginning to end, including all the little things involved in such a venture, such as rights, scanning, and so on. I also thank Peter Murray, my copyeditor at Routledge, for his swift and attentive work.

This Reader could also not have been possible without the constant input and help from a number of people. I would like to thank the following scholars who have helped me in the selection of texts and, in some cases, in writing the introductory texts: Michael Friedman, David Hyder, Lydia Patton, and Andrea Staiti. Michael Friedman, David Hyder, and Lydia Patton were also involved, partly or wholly, in translating some hitherto untranslated pieces, in addition to the other translators, Elizabeth Behnke (Husserl), Frances Bottenberg (Natorp), Jon Burmeister (Rickert), Brian Chance (Lange), Alan Duncan (Windelband), and Arun Iyer (Lask). Other scholars who have helped me with their expertise in making my final editorial decisions were Frederick Beiser, Steven Crowell, Scott Edgar, Massimo Ferrari, Peter E. Gordon, Helmut Holzhey, Rudolf A. Makkreel, Dermot Moran, Guy Oakes, and Ulrich Sieg. Research Assistants at Marquette University who have worked hard in helping me assemble material and proofread were: Kimberly Engels, Dana Fritz, Matthew Zdon, and Clark Wolf. I owe them, too, a great amount of gratitude. Finally, I thank the participants in my undergraduate seminar "nineteenth Century German Philosophy" in the Fall of 2014 at Marquette University, who were the first brave readers of the texts of this volume. It is, in closing, my hope that the way courses such as this one will be taught will be changed through the availability of English translations of philosophers who were the dominant voices in philosophy in the nineteenth century.

Milwaukee, Fall of 2014
Sebastian Luft

Notes

1. A previous plan was to include a selection of French Neo-Kantians, but this would have exploded the confines of the present selection, both thematically as well as in length. A selection of French Neo-Kantian texts can be found in *The Philosophical Forum* of 2006 (37[1]).
2. "*Weltanschauung*" is the term for a worldview, oftentimes ideologically charged.
3. There are different timelines and different narratives by which one can define classical Neo-Kantianism. Cf. especially the work by Beiser on this movement, but cf. also Crowell 1998 and Friedmann 2000. The narrative given here is meant to be as open and inclusive as possible. The purpose of this collection and its introduction is not to steer interpretations in any particular direction, but rather to make this material available to the English-speaking reader.
4. As Crowell aptly puts it, regarding this interwar period, the treatment of Neo-Kantianism becomes part of "liberation narratives" (Crowell 1998, p. 185); "here, Neo-Kantianism is the *terminus ad quem* of a 'liberation from the unbreakable circle of reflection' toward recovery of the 'evocative power of conceptual thinking and philosophical language'. It thus enters the lore of Continental philosophy as the father who had to be slain in order that philosophy might live" (ibid.; the quotations stem from Gadamer in his recollections in *Philosophical Apprenticeships*).
5. That is, with the exception of the Jewish representatives of Neo-Kantianism, such as Cohen or Cassirer, who suffered from anti-Semitic attacks throughout their careers.
6. Many a philosophy professor to this day is a caricature of this ideal, or self-consciously emulates it, though it has certainly also become the prime target of the revolutionary students of the 1960s, when they declared that "*Unter den Talaren, Muff von tausend Jahren*" (under the robes [there is] a thousand-year-old fustiness).
7. Edgar 2012.
8. Cohen also referred to himself as "minister of the exterior" (since he liked to travel and escape the small university town of Marburg) and Natorp as the "minister of the interior."
9. Holzhey details this school formation and its activities in Holzhey 1986/I & II.
10. Religion is conspicuously absent from Cohen's *System of Philosophy*, although the philosophy of religion, especially the philosophical assessment of Judaism, became a dominant part of his later work.
11. Cassirer, who was recruited to the University of Hamburg in 1919, was seen as a representative of Neo-Kantianism, and arguably the most important one, as becomes clear in the Davos Debate in 1929, but he himself distanced himself somewhat from his Marburg teachers philosophically.
12. This qualification pertains to the philosophers of that generation. Certainly, a new crop of original thinkers emerged, although they did not become famous until much later. I am thinking of names such as Hans-Georg Gadamer, Dieter Henrich and Jürgen Habermas.
13. Cf. Makkreel, Rudolf and Sebastian Luft, *Neo-Kantianism in Contemporary Philosophy*. Bloomington/Indianapolis: Indiana University Press, 2010.
14. Cf., however, the 2010 essay collection edited by Makkreel and Luft, and the new essay collection, dealing directly with this legacy, edited by Staiti and De Warren (forthcoming).

15 Husserl had Edith Stein as his assistant for some time and also other female students who wrote their dissertations under him. He discouraged them, however, from pursuing a university career. In the case of Stein, he blocked her *habilitation*, the traditional entry gate to an academic career, in Göttingen, and wrote a negative letter when she applied elsewhere. For a list of female phenomenologists, cf. the page of the *North American Society for Early Phenomenology*, *http://nasepblog.wordpress.com/2014/03/08/the-women-early-phenomenology/*.
16 The help I received from other scholars is credited visibly at the outset of each reading.
17 A new translation of Cassirer's *Philosophy of Symbolic Forms* (all three volumes) is in the works, to be published by Routledge (translated by Stephen Lofts).

Bibliography

The following bibliography only lists literature referred to in this Introduction. For more literature, cf. the respective introductions to the primary texts.

Beiser, Frederick C., *After Hegel. German Philosophy 1840–1900*. Princeton & Oxford: Princeton University Press, 2014.
— —, *The Genesis of Neo-Kantianism, 1796–1880*. Oxford: Oxford University Press, forthcoming.
Crowell, Steven, "Neo-Kantianism," in: *A Companion to Continental Philosophy*, ed. Simon Critchley & William R. Schroeder. Oxford: Blackwell, 1998, pp. 185–197.
Edgar, Scott, "Hermann Cohen," *The Stanford Encyclopedia of Philosophy* (Winter 2012 Edition), Edward N. Zalta (ed.), available online at http://plato.stanford.edu/archives/win2012/entries/cohen/ (accessed 16 March 2015).
Friedman, Michael, *A Parting of the Ways: Carnap, Cassirer, and Heidegger*. Chicago/La Salle: Open Court, 2000.
Holzhey, Helmut, *Cohen und Natorp*. Vol. I: Ursprung und Einheit. Die Geschichte der 'Marburger Schule' als Auseinandersetzung um die Logik des Denkens; Vol. 2: Der Marburger Neukantianismus in Quellen. Zeugnisse kritischer Lektüre. Briefe der Marburger. Dokumente zur Philosophiepolitik der Schule. Basel/Stuttgart: Schwabe, 1986.
Makkreel, Rudolf and Sebastian Luft, *Neo-Kantianism in Contemporary Philosophy*. Bloomington/Indianapolis: Indiana University Press, 2010.
Ringer, Fritz K., *The Decline of the German Mandarins. The German Academic Community, 1890–1933*. Hanover and London: Wesleyan U Press, 1969.
Sieg, Ulrich, *Aufstieg und Niedergang des Marburger Neukantianismus. Die Geschichte einer philosophischen Schulgemeinschaft*. Würzburg: K & N, 1994.
Staiti, Andrea and Nicolas De Warren, *The Legacy of Neo-Kantianism*. Cambridge: Cambridge University Press, forthcoming.

PART 1

Beginnings

*Hermann von Helmholtz, Otto Liebmann,
Friedrich Albert Lange, Rudolf Hermann Lotze*

Introduction: Hermann von Helmholtz (1821–1894)

AT THE HEIGHT OF HIS POWERS, Hermann von Helmholtz was seen to be one of the last true polymaths [*Universalgelehrten*], publishing on medicine, physiology, physics, mathematics, and philosophy. He accumulated substantial political and academic power in Prussia, and was sometimes referred to as the "Chancellor of Physics." Helmholtz was born in Potsdam in 1821, where he attended the Gymnasium, whose director was his father. In 1838, he matriculated in medicine in Berlin, though his interests lay mainly within physics. He finished in 1842 with a dissertation in microscopic anatomy and became a doctor at the Berlin Charité clinic. Beginning in 1843, he served in the army as a military doctor, completing only three years of his eight-year service, due to the recommendation of Alexander von Humboldt. After teaching anatomy for a while, he became professor of physiology in Berlin, then moving to Königsberg to assume a professorship in physiology and pathology in 1849. Since his wife suffered from the harsh climate in Prussia, Helmholtz moved to the University of Bonn (in the milder Rhineland) in 1851 and, a keen negotiator, he took up a highly paid professorship in Heidelberg in 1858. Wilhelm Wundt was his assistant there between 1858 and 1863. In 1870, Helmholtz became a member of the Prussian Academy of Science and received a call to a professorship of physics at the University of Berlin. The recipient of numerous accolades and honors, he was knighted in 1883 and served as president of the university 1877/78. Helmholtz died from his second stroke in 1894, after witnessing the death of his son Robert, his son-in-law Werner von Siemens, and his student Heinrich Hertz.

On General Physical Concepts (before 1847) by David Hyder

This untitled early fragment on the philosophy of science most likely dates from the years before the 1847 publication of *The Conservation of Energy*, while the young Dr. Helmholtz was trying to break out of his day job as a military doctor in Potsdam to make his mark as a professional scientist back in Berlin. Thematic similarities suggest it may stem from early versions of the philosophical introduction to that monograph, which Helmholtz revised many times and indeed considered suppressing. The *Conservation* was intended to facilitate the extension of physics into the organism by Helmholtz and his circle in the *Physikalische Gesellschaft zu Berlin*. Their research programme was a conscious violation of Kant's restriction, in the *Metaphysical Foundations*, of "strict" and mathematical science to the inanimate domain.

The manuscript provides a priori foundations for the physics that will make this unification possible. Helmholtz derives basic physical principles by applying a redacted table of categories to the conditions of perceptual change, which is shown to require the existence of the relational structures of time and space. He then derives basic kinematic principles from the concepts of rigid body displacement and "stable" (uniform) motion. While both the aim and methods of this text and the Introduction to the *Conservation* overlap with the *Critique* and the *Metaphysical Foundations of Natural Science*, there are fundamental differences. These are typical of the philosophy of science developed by Helmholtz's mentor at the Friedrich-Wilhelm University in Berlin, the physiologist Johannes Müller, and his friend and colleague Friedrich Trendelenburg, Professor of Philosophy at the same university.

Trendelenburg's realist version of Kant was articulated in his lectures on the philosophy of science, published in (1840) as the *Logical Investigations*. He drew heavily on Müller's work on sense-physiology, and rejected a number of Kant's key theses. Space and time need not be exclusively ideal; they are dependent "factors of motion," the basic phenomenon common to both the animate and the inanimate, meaning that a mathematical investigation of living organisms, including psychological processes, is possible. The task of philosophy of science is to produce "a priori objects out of motion and matter" by relating formal logic to these two empirical domains. Consequently, spatial magnitudes should be defined kinematically, the approach Helmholtz follows here.

Further Reading

DiSalle, Robert, "Kant, Helmholtz, and the Meaning of Empiricism," in *The Kantian Legacy in Nineteenth-Century Science*, edited by Alfred Nordmann. Cambridge, Mass.: MIT, 2006, pp. 123–39.

Hyder, David, "Time, Norms and Structure in 19th Century Philosophy of Science," in *The Oxford Handbook of the History of Analytic Philosophy*, edited by M. Beaney. Oxford: Oxford University Press, 2013, pp. 250–279.

Torretti, Roberto. *Philosophy of Geometry from Riemann to Poincaré*. Dordrecht: Reidel, 1978.

Trendelenburg, Friedrich Adolf. *Logische Untersuchungen*. Vol. 1. Berlin: Bethge, 1840.

On the Origin and Significance of Geometrical Axioms (1876) and The Origin and Meaning of Geometric Axioms (1878) by David Hyder

Helmholtz's four papers on non-Euclidean geometry put the topic on the front burner of nineteenth-century theory of science, both academic and popular. The following selections have a complicated publication history. Both are popular presentations of the technical results of Helmholtz's two 1868 papers on the quantification of space by means of rigid-body transformations.[1] In these papers, Helmholtz had applied the transformational mathematics of Kant's and Euler's "pure theory of motion"[2] directly to the spatial magnitudes. He eventually called this fusion of geometry and kinematics *physical geometry*, arguing that one could not say in advance which physical geometry of constant curvature would provide a suitable foundation for physics.

Helmholtz had all but completed the two papers before learning of Riemann's earlier and more general treatment in his Habilitation lecture, "On the Hypotheses Underlying Geometry" (1854). By contrast, Helmholtz's 1868 papers referred not to the *hypotheses*, but to *facts* or *factual bases* underlying geometry, where the term *fact* meant "empirical regularity." In the 1870s, Helmholtz defended himself against epistemological objections raised against these earlier works in two papers intended for "the wider circle of non-mathematicians" (1896, v).

The first was originally delivered as a lecture to Gymnasium teachers in 1870, and a summary thereof was published, in English only, in *The Academy* (1870). Helmholtz completely rewrote the article for a collection of his papers (1876), to counter "the unbelievable misunderstandings and distortions suffered by Riemann's and my work in the philosophical polemic" (1896, v). For example, a widely-read article by Otto Liebmann, "On the Phenomenality of Space" (1871/1872), had argued that, while analytic descriptions of alternative geometries were logically admissible, it appeared to be a brute fact that our intelligence is bound to a flat three-dimensional faculty of spatial intuition. This "pure spatial form, the blank space-schema," which is the prior condition of visual and perceptual space, "is nothing other than the pure space of geometry," and Kant's claims regarding its metric remained valid.[3] Thus Helmholtz devoted some effort to showing that there is no obstacle to *imagining* non-Euclidean geometries, using now-standard examples of fun-house mirrors and beings on curved surfaces.

Helmholtz also used the occasion to discuss the results of further technical developments showing that non-Euclidean geometries of constant curvature were consistent with the known laws of mechanics (Lipschitz 1869, 1870). An explanation of the source of our flat space is therefore required, he concluded, since it does "not follow from the general concept of an extended magnitude of three dimensions." This source was our observations of the behaviour of rigid bodies. Not, Helmholtz emphasized, in the sense that "mankind first arrived at space-intuitions, in agreement with the axioms of Euclid, by any carefully executed systems of exact measurement... rather a succession of everyday experiences... led to the rejection, as impossible, of every geometrical representation at variance with this fact."

But this explanation of the source of geometry left open the possibility that a "strict Kantian" might *insist* on a particular geometry, at which point Helmholtz returned to the scientific fold. Since the role of geometry in physical science is to provide laws for the quantification of spatial magnitudes, such a Kantian faces a dilemma: if one stipulates that Euclidean geometry is fundamental, its propositions are analytic, because they follow from definitions of rigid-body motion expressed in the terms of analytic geometry; if, on the other hand, they are synthetic and depend on features of our intuitive faculty, it remains an open question whether a stipulated geometry will satisfactorily play this role. Either way, a bad choice of a basic geometry could force us to deny "that the mechanical and physical properties of bodies and their mutual reactions are, other circumstances remaining the same, independent of place." And such "milieu-dependence," as Einstein later called it, is all but impossible to square with the Kantian thesis that space is a passive form of intuition.[4] Thus in physics, geometrical axioms are either analytic or they can be refuted by experience.

The simultaneous English publication of Helmholtz's 1876 version in *Mind* provoked a further response from the Dutch philosopher J.P.N. Land. For Land, the central question was "whether any sort of space besides the space of Euclid be capable of being imagined" without embedding it in a higher-order Euclidean manifold (Land 1877, 41). Helmholtz answered with the second paper excerpted here, whose German original was printed as Appendix III to his *The Facts in Perception* under the title "The Applicability of the Axioms to the Physical World."[5] Helmholtz here introduced the crucial notion of a "physical geometry" and repeated the dilemma from the earlier paper. The purpose of geometry is to establish "physically equivalent magnitudes," namely ones in which the same processes occur in the same time (compare the first selection), and a *stipulated* theory of rigid-body motion might fail to determine such an equivalence-class.

The exercises in imaginability directed at orthodox Kantians, along with Helmholtz's background in physiology, have led to the stock neo-Kantian criticism that Helmholtz's arguments were *physiological* and not *transcendental*. Because he took Kant to be advancing a theory of perception, "Helmholtz failed to see that Kant intended the conclusions of his Transcendental Aesthetic to set a condition on...all possible experience of space, including measurements undertaken in physics."[6] Seen from this point of view, Helmholtz's references to the law of inertia, physical geometry, and physically equivalent magnitudes appear as afterthoughts. But as the preceding selection shows, Helmholtz was already trying, in 1847, to reformulate Kant's theories of space, time, and quantity in kinematic terms. By 1876, Helmholtz had been professor of physics in Berlin for six years, during which period the questions raised by Riemann's and his papers had spawned an entire research programme, as exemplified by Klein's and Neumann's journal, *Mathematische Annalen*. His technical work, such as the 1868 papers, never departed from these foundational problems raised by Kant's theory of mathematical physics.

Notes

1. The first of those two simultaneous papers is generally dated 1866, due to a printing error in Helmholtz's *Wissenschaftliche Abhandlungen*.
2. For the relation between Kant and Euler, and the latter's work on transformations, see Hyder 2014.
3. P. 348. Liebmann claimed that both Gauß and Helmholtz held the view that extra-mental reality had more than three dimensions, indeed that Helmholtz had told him this personally. This would agree with Helmholtz's later claim that "Space Can Be Transcendental Without the Axioms Being So," as well as with the arguments of the final sections of his 1878 paper. In contrast to Liebmann, Helmholtz held that spatial relations are intrinsically kinematic, and that space has no metrical characteristics whatsoever in the absence of motion. See the introductory remarks to the preceding selection for the source of this view in Trendelenberg and Müller. Liebmann's phenomenalist position is today called the "phenomenological" reading, and is indeed very close to Kant's actual, yet untenable position.
4. See Einstein 1924, 86f., translated in Saunders and Brown 1991.
5. See Cohen's "The Synthetic Principles" in this volume. A translation of the full paper is in Helmholtz 1977.
6. Hatfield 1990, 224. See Sully (1878a, 1878b) for a contemporary survey of the physiological literature published in tandem with Helmholtz's papers.

Further Reading

Einstein, Albert, "Über den Äther," in: *Verhandlungen der Schweizerischen naturforschenden Gesellschaft* 105, 1924, pp. 86–93.
Hatfield, Gary, *The Natural and the Normative. Theories of Spatial Perception from Kant to Helmholtz*. Cambridge: MIT Press, 1990.
Helmholtz, Hermann von, "The Axioms of Geometry," in: *The Academy* (4) 1870, pp. 128–130.
Helmholtz, Hermann von, *Populäre wissenschaftliche Vorträge*. Braunschweig: Vieweg, 1876.
Helmholtz, Hermann von, *Vorträge und Reden*. 4 ed. 2 vols. Vol. 2. Braunschweig: Vieweg, 1896.
Helmholtz, Hermann von, *Epistemological Writings: the Paul Hertz/Moritz Schlick Centenary Edition of 1921*. Translated by M. F. Lowe. Edited by R. S. Cohen and Y. Elkana, *Boston Studies in the Philosophy of Science*. Dordrecht: Reidel, 1977.

Hyder, David, "Review of Michael Friedman, *Kant's Construction of Nature*," in: *Isis* 105 (2) 2014, pp. 432–434.

Land, J.P.N., "Kant's Space and Modern Mathematics," in: *Mind* 2 (5) 1877, pp. 38–46.

Liebmann, Otto, "Über die Phänomenalität des Raumes," in: *Philosophische Monatshefte* 7 (8) 1871/1872, pp. 337–359.

Lipschitz, Rudolf, "Untersuchungen in Betreff der ganzen homogenen Functionen von n Differentialen," in: *Journal für die reine und angewandte Mathematik* 70 (1) 1869, pp. 71–102.

Lipschitz, Rudolf, "Fortgesetzte Untersuchungen in Betreff der ganzen homogenen Functionen von n Differentialen," in: *Journal für die reine und angewandte Mathematik* 72 (1) 1870, pp. 1–56.

Riemann, Bernhard, "Über die Hypothesen, welche der Geometrie zu Grunde liegen," in: *Bernhard Riemanns gesammelte mathematische Werke*, edited by H. Weber. Leipzig: Teubner, 1854.

Saunders, S., and H.R. Brown, eds., *The Philosophy of Vacuum*. Oxford: Clarendon Press, 1991.

Sully, James, "The Question of Visual Perception in Germany I", in: *Mind* 3 (9) 1878, pp. 1–23.

Sully, James, "The Question of Visual Perception in Germany II", in: *Mind* 3 (10) 1878, pp. 167–195.

Chapter 1

[On General Physical Concepts] (before 1847)[1]

TRANSLATED BY DAVID HYDER

The object of natural science is that content of our representations which we intuit as not produced through the self-activity of our faculty of representation; in other words, that which is perceived as actual[2]. Either it simply gives an ordered overview of everything empirical (natural history and experimental physics), in which case only the order is constructed for a purpose, and is, in other words, scientific. Or it tries to deduce the grounds of the facts; that is, it searches for concepts from which individual determinate empirical perceptions may be derived; thus it tries to understand the actual (scientific physics).

These natural concepts are derived in part from the mere fact alone that there are [any] determinate perceptions at all that are not produced by our own activity, and in part from the individual determinate empirical perceptions themselves. The system of the first of these yields the general or pure natural sciences (theory of time[3], geometry, pure mechanics), and the system of the second yields theoretical physics. The common feature of the general physical concepts will be that they and their consequences are the basis of all natural intuition[4], thus that they are in this regard the general and necessary form of natural intuition. Therefore the certainty of their propositions is an absolute one, whereas the certainty of the specific natural concepts only ever extends so far as to say that all facts known up until now agree to them. Furthermore, the general concepts, derived only from the possibility of any natural intuition, may not restrict the possibility of any empirical combination of perceptions, i.e. no empirical fact or law may be derivable from them, rather they can yield only a norm for our explanations.

Lemmata. The possibly thinkable connections of the representational objects under consideration fall under the general categories of possible thought-connections in general[5]. They are the following:

I) Relation of a representation-object to the faculty of representation (Modality; Objects perceived or represented)
II) Relation of an object to another. This relation is posited
    1) as something externally actual, independent of our representing (Causality)
    2) as something only represented (Comparison)

a)   of homogeneous objects (Quantity)
b)   of non-homogeneous (Quality)

An object is *equal*[6] to another in a relation if it can be substituted for the other everywhere where the result of a combination is considered only with respect to this relation.

[The objects are] *homogeneous* in a relation if both can be decomposed into simple[7] parts that are equal with respect to this relation.

An object regarded with respect to quantity is called a magnitude; accordingly, every object which can be *thought* as divided into equal or homogeneous parts can be considered a magnitude. Measuring means determining the set[8] of these parts; a determinate set is called number, an individual part, the unit of measure.

Magnitudes are thinkable either such that a continued division leads to parts that can no longer be divided into homogeneous ones (aggregated magnitudes), or such that no limit to division exists (continuous magnitudes). There is no logical contradiction in infinite divisibility, for this should be thought of only as possibly, not as actually carried out, for which indeed an infinite time would be required, just as little as [such a contradiction lies] in the thought of a continuous growth through infinitely many, infinitely close degrees.

The science of the connection of magnitudes according to quantity is arithmetic; it is developed following the laws of general logic from the concepts established here. It leads to the familiar numerical forms of positive and negative, whole and fractional (including the irrational, that is, the fractional with an infinitely long denominator), real and imaginary numbers, of which only the last cannot be reduced to determinate numerical values.

The General Physical Concepts

Perception is becoming conscious of a determinate sensation, that is, a determinate state of our organs. A sensation can only be determined in opposition to another; thus there must be representations of other opposing sensations present. And since it is not thinkable that a single and indivisible perception contain opposed qualities in it, so there must be distinct parts (acts) of perception, which, aside from the qualitatively determined content, are distinct, as if according to a relation of difference in the kind of perception itself. This relation we call time. Amongst these distinct acts of perception, we call that which is accompanied by the sensation we oppose to the others the *present perception*, and the others the *past ones*. If now they are all ordered in a sequence, such that each one is preceded by all its past ones, we thus obtain a completely determined sequence with a determinate direction of progression, all of whose members, aside from their qualitative differences, are distinct from one another according to this necessary relation of difference in the perception of time.

Therefore, since this relation should contain all possible previously existing and coming cases of perceptions and their transitions, its concept must be determined so as to fit all thinkable cases.

Time is:

1)   extended and divisible in homogeneous parts; the first insofar as it should contain the entire series of perceptions; [second] each one is contained in a part of time, and since all that comes into consideration about these parts is the containing of a perception, and not the qualitative difference of the latter, so they are to be posited as homogeneous;
2)   unboundedly extended, because the number of perceptions to be contained has no necessary boundary;

3) unboundedly divisible, because continuous changes of the perceptions are thinkable, and each of the infinitely many levels of change must be contained in time. Each part of time therefore contains still smaller parts in it; if a time-determination should be internally indifferent, thus completely determined (time-point), then it must be thought as not extended; such is the boundary between the individual parts of time.
4) The direction of procession in time is a determinate one, and only one, so that through the one determination of how much earlier or later something is than something else known, the time-point is also completely determined.

If time is considered as a magnitude, so it must be thought as growing from zero to positive infinity, through all positive whole and rational numbers. But since each time-point can be conceived as infinitely removed from the beginning of time, so time-determinations in determinate numbers are only possible by giving the positive or negative difference of the time sought from some other [time] presupposed as known, so that time is to be thought as growing continuously from negative to positive infinity. [It is given] according to quantity through an equation of determination, that is to say as dependent from a variable, or from the first dimension, if we call an extensive magnitude determined by n determinations one having n-dimensionality.[9]

Parts of time in which the same changes take place under the same circumstances are to be posited as equal.[10]

The perceptions are furthermore posited as independent of our self-activity, thus they must be posited as caused by something other, external to us, which we call *matter* insofar as it is just there, and *force* insofar as it acts on us, that is to say is the ground of changes.

Therefore the external, insofar as it is just matter, is eternally the same without qualitative difference, thus also without qualitative change. Regarded with respect to quantity, [it is] mass. But since it must act on us variously, the various parts of matter must have various forces. The forces in themselves, since they have qualitative differences, may be thought of as variable with respect to time, and a further force must be thought of as the ground of their change, and so one must go ever further back until one comes to temporally constant forces of determinate parts of matter (chemical elements).[11]

Thus the external, the ground of our sensations, is to be posited as composed of matters with various forces, thus it cannot be a single and indivisible being. Various [things] should be simultaneous; therefore, still another relation must occur in the simultaneously existing, according to which objects, aside from their qualitative differences, can be different, because a single indivisible being cannot be endowed with various qualities. This relation is space, in which the various objects are to be thought as ordered. The members of this order, since their essential characteristic is simultaneity, do not progress in a determinate direction, therefore the procession need not be a simple one, as in the case of time, but can possibly be multiple.

Space, like time, must be posited as extended and divisible into homogeneous parts, indeed as infinitely extended and infinitely divisible, because neither the number nor the divisibility of the objects contained in it are bounded a priori. Every extended part of space therefore contains still other different ones within it, a spatial determination without extension is called a point. Because the point cannot contain a real object, and is therefore not representable as matter, one wanted to declare it an unreal magnitude, but it is no less real than space itself, which is also not an actual thing.

Since the direction of procession in space is not determinate, a point is not yet given by the datum of the distance between it and some other one. Rather, more determinations are necessary, which means, according to the above definition of the concept dimension, that space is a continuously growing magnitude of several dimensions—we will assume of n, that is to say that each point is given through n determinables[12]. If there are also conditions [holding] between these determinables such that, given certain values for some of them, only certain others are possible for the rest, then individual points can also be given through fewer determinations; and, conversely, the others might follow identically from various determinations, so that the point would only apparently be given by n determinations. Thus, generally, when it is said that a point is given through n equations of determination, then the various equations holding between certain values of the variables are themselves to be factored in, and those equations which follow identically from the others are to be omitted. As with time, the measurement of space cannot begin at an initial point, because there is no such thing, rather it must depart from determinate points, which are presupposed as known.

Parts of space, which may be called spatial magnitudes, have either just as many dimensions or less—to the extent that they are further divisible, that is to say are not points. A point lying in an a-dimensional spatial magnitude will be given through a determinations, whereas in space it is so only through n, thus $n - a$ further determinations must derive from the properties of the given spatial magnitude. In other words, a spatial magnitude of dimension a is given through $n - a$ equations of determination. That of the first dimension is called a line, and that of the second, a surface.

If an a-dimensional spatial magnitude should be taken not in its whole extension, as it is given through its $n - a$ equations of determination, but instead only up to certain points, so that for each value of the $n - 1$ coordinates, the nth does not go above or below a certain value, which is given by an equation, then those points, whose totality is called a limit, are determined by $n - a + 1$ equations, and thereby form a spatial magnitude of $a - 1$ dimensions.

Now we must first ask how it is possible to determine a point against another. The only spatial magnitude that may be determined by two points is, however, the line. So the length of a particular kind of line must be given. The length of a possibly drawn line has no maximum, for it can run through infinitely distant points, and it cannot be 0, thus it must have a positive minimum. We call the length of one or several shortest lines through two points or spatial magnitudes *distance*.

If the point p_1 is distant from p_n by a, but by b from p_m, then p_n can never be less distant from p_m than $a - b$, and never more than $a + b$ (because otherwise there would be a shorter path from p_1 to p_m, or p_n to p_m, than their distance).

These are all the determinations of space, insofar as it should contain[13] all possible given material objects, and indeed since a finitely limited space (a finite spatial magnitude of dimension n) is to be posited as one that contains a finite number of finite masses, finite masses can therefore only be contained in spatial magnitudes of the highest dimension, and are called, as such, material bodies; whereas the spatial magnitudes that contain them are [called] mathematical bodies. In material bodies one can once again distinguish points, lines, etc., which then must be called material points, etc.

But the concept of space must further be determined in such a way that it can contain all possible changes of matter, which obviously are of concern here only insofar as they are changes of spatial relations, that is to say locomotions.

1) If a material object is moved, then it is perduringly present in some part of space; however, it is thinkable that the individual parts of the body keep their position with respect to one another unchanged (rigid bodies). Then the individual points, lines, etc. of every new mathematical object containing it will stand [in relation] to one another just as those of the first [mathematical object]. And in this sense one can say that the mathematical body itself, its points, lines, etc. move with the matter. In this sense, one should understand by a rigid system of points such movable points as always preserve

their relative determinations when in motion; spatial magnitudes are therefore to be regarded as continuous rigid systems.

Rigid systems such that can be moved onto the other, so that all the points of the first coincide with points of the second, are congruent. Pairs of equally distant points are congruent.

2) Matter should be movable, quite aside from all of its particular forces; but then the only remaining characteristic of a determinate piece of matter is the particular space in which it is contained. But since even this characteristic is taken from it in motion, we can only affirm its identity if we can intuit the transition from one space to another; that is, motion must be continuous with respect to space.

So if a spatial magnitude of a dimensions is thought as moved, I get $n - a$ equations, with continuously transitioning values of the $n - a$ coordinates to be solved for, given constant assumed values for the a's. I could pick an arbitrary value for one of the continuously varying ones, and would thereby obtain the appropriate value for the others. Thus the path of a spatial magnitude of dimension a is generally a spatial magnitude of dimension $a + 1$.

The values of the unknowns to be solved for do not necessarily have to change, if, that is, every point of the moved magnitude only ever passes into ones that lay in it before. We call such movement [parallel] translation[14]; the first we call lateral translation[15].

Thus line = path of a point,

surface = path of a line

3) Since spatial determination in relation to absolute space is absolutely impossible, its change, that is to say locomotion, can only take place with respect to determinate points or systems, and a point can be simultaneously at rest and in motion with respect to different ones. Rest and motion are therefore not in themselves different states of matter, but only relative ones.

Now since matter is posited as persisting in its state so long as no forces act on it, it must also be posited that its rest and motion be constant until they are changed by motive forces. Thus one must look for the determinations of the motion I will call stable motion, which is to be derived completely from that very, always constant, state of motion in which a moving body finds itself.

The concept of direction is obviously that determination of a motion through which those points along which the motion extends itself, so long as it continues undisturbed, are laid down. Thus [direction] will have to be called always constant in a stable motion.

A motion, however, is completely determined when, at any given time, those points in which the points of the body in motion are to be found are determined. If I consider only the motion of a single point, then its position is determinable if (1) the path itself is known, and (2) how much of the path it covers in each part of time, that is to say when one knows the relation between the space covered and the time taken to do so. If it is constant, I can take an arbitrarily large space, $c = s/t$, thus $s = ct$. If it is variable, then I must take an infinitely small space, in whose extension the relation is to be considered as constant, that is the differential quotient ds/dt, or $d\underset{t}{s}$.

Since in a stable motion all determinations must remain the same, c must be constant.

Now concerning the form of the path, it is first of all clear that it must always remain the same, that is, that every piece of it must be congruent to every other equally long one. Furthermore, according to our demand above, [the form] must be completely derivable from the state of motion the body finds itself in, which we are to think of as the ground of its progressing. The latter acts only in the direction of the path and obviously cannot have different effects in lateral directions. Thus no differences in the bearing[16] of the path in lateral directions can be present. In other words, since a surface is produced by lateral motion of a line, and since a point lying on the former can be completely given through determinations relative to two of its lines, and since such determinate points are equally well possible in all continuously transitioning lateral directions, [it follows that] all points on the line must conduct themselves identically with respect to all points that are given through such determinations. This therefore means: no external point may be completely determined by means of determinations of n points on a straight line; instead, $n-2$ determinations only ever yield the same points that the first two yielded on their own; or, when a point outside such a line is determined relative to two points on it, it is determined relative to all. Thus, in addition, if two points on such a line are determined with respect to external coordinate-points, so are all the others; that is, such a line is completely given through two points; we call it a *straight* line.

From this definition it follows immediately that only one straight line is possible between two points, that equally long straight lines are congruent, thus that a straight line can be measured directly by applying one of the parts of it that has been taken as a unit of measure, and which also may be used to determine the position of a point with respect to another. We shall call the length of the straight line between two points the straight distance between the two.

Straight spatial magnitudes of dimension a are ones in which a straight spatial magnitude of dimension $(a-1)$, lying only within the first magnitude, may pass through any a arbitrary points. (A plane, or straight surface, is so; any two points of it can be connected by straight lines lying entirely within it.)

Angle is the spatial relation of two straight lines to one another, the spatial magnitude to be limited by lines must be a surface, and indeed a determinate one, thus the angle is measured by the piece of a plane that lies between these sides; congruent angles are to be posited as equal....

Notes

1 Untitled manuscript reprinted in Königsberger, Leo. 1903. *Hermann von Helmholtz*. 3 vols. Vol. 2. Braunschweig: Vieweg, pp. 126-38. Original manuscript in the BBAW Nachlassabteilung. – Trans.
2 *wirklich*
3 *Zeitlehre*
4 *Naturanschauung*
5 *überhaupt*
6 *gleich*
7 *lauter*
8 *Menge*
9 Compare both Riemann's and Helmholtz's later definitions of a manifold. – Trans.
10 Compare Helmholtz's definition of "physically equivalent magnitudes" in the concluding sections of his last (1878) paper on geometry. – Trans.
11 Compare the introduction to Helmholtz's *Conservation of Energy*. – Trans.
12 *Bestimmungsstücke*
13 *umfassen*
14 *Verschiebung*
15 *Seitenbewegung*
16 *Verhalten*

Chapter 2

On the Origin and Significance of Geometrical Axioms (1876)[1]

The fact that a science can exist and can be developed as has been the case with geometry, has always attracted the closest attention among those who are interested in questions relating to the bases of the theory of cognition. Of all branches of human knowledge, there is none which, like it, has sprung as a completely armed Minerva from the head of Jupiter; none before whose death-dealing Aegis doubt and inconsistency have so little dared to raise their eyes. It escapes the tedious and troublesome task of collecting experimental facts, which is the province of the natural sciences in the strict sense of the word; the sole form of its scientific method is deduction. Conclusion is deduced from conclusion, and yet no one of common sense doubts but that these geometrical principles must find their practical application in the real world about us. Land surveying, as well as architecture, the construction of machinery no less than mathematical physics, are continually calculating relations of space of the most varied kind by geometrical principles; they expect that the success of their constructions and experiments shall agree with these calculations; and no case is known in which this expectation has been falsified, provided the calculations were made correctly and with sufficient data.

Indeed, the fact that geometry exists, and is capable of all this, has always been used as a prominent example in the discussion on that question, which forms, as it were, the centre of all antitheses of philosophical systems, that there can be a cognition of principles destitute of any bases drawn from experience. In the answer to Kant's celebrated question, 'How are synthetic principles *a priori* possible?' geometrical axioms are certainly those examples which appear to show most decisively that synthetic principles are *a priori* possible at all. The circumstance that such principles exist, and force themselves on our conviction, is regarded as a proof that space is an *a priori* mode of all external perception. It appears thereby to postulate, for this *a priori* form, not only the character of a purely formal scheme of itself quite unsubstantial, in which any given result experience would fit; but also to include certain peculiarities of the scheme, which bring it about that only a certain content, and one which, as it were, is strictly defined, could occupy it and be apprehended by us.[2]

It is precisely this relation of geometry to the theory of cognition which emboldens me to speak to you on geometrical subjects in an assembly of those who for the most part have limited their mathematical studies to the ordinary instruction in schools. Fortunately, the amount of geometry taught in our gymnasia will enable you to follow, at any rate the tendency, of the principles I am about to discuss.

I intend to give you an account of a series of recent and closely connected mathematical investigations which are concerned with the geometrical axioms, their relations to experience, with the question whether it is logically possible to replace them by others.

Seeing that the researches in question are more immediately designed to furnish proofs for experts in a region which, more than almost any other, requires a higher power of abstraction, and that they are virtually inaccessible to the non-mathematician, I will endeavour to explain to such a one the question at issue. I need scarcely remark that my explanation will give no proof of the correctness of the new views. He who seeks this proof must take the trouble to study the original research.

Anyone who has entered the gates of the first elementary axioms of geometry, that is, the mathematical doctrine of space, finds on his path that unbroken chain of conclusions of which I just spoke, by which the ever more varied and more complicated figures are brought within the domain of law. But even in their first elements certain principles are laid down, with respect to which geometry confesses that she cannot prove them, and can only assume that anyone who understands the essence of these principles will at once admit their correctness. These are the so-called axioms.

For example, the proposition that if the shortest line drawn between two points is called a *straight* line, there can be only one such straight line. Again, it is an axiom that through any three points in space, not lying in a straight line, a plane may be drawn, i.e. a surface which will wholly include every straight line joining any two of its points. Another axiom, about which there has been much discussion, affirms that through a point lying without a straight line only one straight line can be drawn parallel to the first; two straight lines that lie in the same plane and never meet, however far they may be produced, being called parallel. There are also axioms that determine the number of dimensions of space and its surfaces, lines and points, showing how they are continuous; as in the propositions, that a solid is bounded by a surface, a surface by a line and a line by a point, that the point is indivisible, that by the movement of a point a line is described, by that of a line a line or a surface, by that of a surface a surface or a solid, but by the movement of a solid a solid and nothing else is described.

Now what is the origin of such propositions, unquestionably true yet incapable of proof in a science where everything else is reasoned conclusion? Are they inherited from the divine source of our reason as the idealistic philosophers think, or is it only that the ingenuity of mathematicians has hitherto not been penetrating enough to find the proof? Every new votary, coming with fresh zeal to geometry, naturally strives to succeed where all before him have failed. And it is quite right that each should make the trial afresh; for, as the question has hitherto stood, it is only by the fruitlessness of one's own efforts that one can be convinced of the impossibility of finding a proof. Meanwhile solitary inquirers are always from time to time appearing who become so deeply entangled in complicated trains of reasoning that they can no longer discover their mistakes and believe they have solved the problem. The axiom of parallels especially has called forth a great number of seeming demonstrations.

The main difficulty in these inquiries is, and always has been, the readiness with which results of everyday experience become mixed up as apparent necessities of thought with the logical processes, so long as Euclid's method of constructive intuition is exclusively followed in geometry. It is in particular extremely difficult, on this method, to be quite sure that in the steps prescribed for the demonstration we have not involuntarily and unconsciously drawn in some most general results of experience, which the power of executing certain parts of the operation has already taught us practically. In drawing any subsidiary line for the sake of his demonstration, the well-trained geometer always asks if it is possible to draw such a line. It is well known that problems of construction play an essential part in the system of geometry. At first sight, these appear to be practical operations, introduced for the training of learners; but in reality they establish the existence of definite figures. They show that points, straight lines, or circles such as the problem requires to be constructed are possible under all conditions, or they determine any exceptions that there may be. The point on which the investigations turn, that we are about to consider, is essentially of this nature. The foundation of all proof by Euclid's method consists in establishing the congruence of lines, angles, plane figures, solids, etc. To make the congruence evident, the geometrical figures are supposed to be applied to one another, of course without changing their form and dimensions. That this is in fact possible we have all experienced from our earliest youth. But, if we proceed to build necessities of thought upon this assumption of the free translation of fixed figures, with unchanged form, to every part of space, we must see whether the assumption does not involve some presupposition of which no logical proof is given. We shall see later on that it does indeed contain one of the most serious import. But if so, every proof by congruence rests upon a fact which is obtained from experience only.

I offer these remarks, at first only to show what difficulties attend the complete analysis of the presuppositions we make, in employing the common constructive method. We evade them when we apply, to the investigation of principles, the analytical method of modern algebraic geometry. The whole process of algebraic calculation is a purely logical operation; it can yield no relation between the quantities submitted to it that is not already contained in the equations which give occasion for its being applied. The recent investigations in question have accordingly been conducted almost exclusively by means of the purely abstract methods of analytical geometry.

However, after discovering by the abstract method what are the points in question, we shall best get a distinct view of them by taking a region of narrower limits than our own world of space. Let us, as we logically may, suppose reasoning beings of only two dimensions to live and move on the surface of some solid body. We will assume that they have not the power of perceiving anything outside this surface, but that upon it they have perceptions similar to ours. If such beings worked out a geometry, they would of course assign only two dimensions to their space. They would ascertain that a point in moving describes a line, and that a line in moving describes a surface. But they could as little represent to themselves what further spatial construction would be generated by a surface moving out of itself, as we can represent what would be generated by a solid moving out of the space we know. By the much-abused expression 'to represent' or 'to be able to think how something happens' I understand—and I do not see how anything else can be understood by it without loss of all meaning—the power of imagining the whole series of sensible impressions that would be had in such a case. Now as no sensible impression is known relating to such an unheard-of event, as the movement to a fourth dimension would be to us, or as a movement to our third dimension would be to the inhabitants of a surface, such a 'representation' is as impossible as the 'representation' of colours would be to one born blind, if a description of them in general terms could be given to him.

Our surface-beings would also be able to draw shortest lines in their superficial space. These would not necessarily be straight lines in our sense, but what are technically called *geodetic lines* of the surface on which they live; lines such as are described by a tense thread laid along the surface, and which can slide upon it freely. I will henceforth speak of such lines as the *straightest* lines of any particular surface or given space, so as to bring out their analogy with the straight line in a plane. I hope by this expression to make the conception more easy for the apprehension of my non-mathematical hearers without giving rise to misconception.

Now if beings of this kind lived on an infinite plane, their geometry would be exactly the same as our planimetry. They would affirm that only one straight line is possible between two points; that through a third point lying without this line only one line can be drawn parallel to it; that the ends of a straight line never meet though it is produced to infinity, and so on. Their space might be infinitely extended, but even if there were limits to their movement and perception, they would be able to represent to themselves a continuation beyond these limits; and thus their space would appear to them infinitely extended, just as ours does to us, although our bodies cannot leave the earth, and our sight only reaches as far as the visible fixed stars.

But intelligent beings of the kind supposed might also live on the surface of a sphere. Their shortest or straightest line between two points would then be an arc of the great circle passing through them. Every great circle, passing through two points, is by these divided into two parts; and if they are unequal, the shorter is certainly the shortest line on the sphere between the two points, but also the other or larger arc of the same great circle is a geodetic or straightest line, i.e. every smaller part of it is the shortest line between its ends. Thus the notion of the geodetic or straightest line is not quite identical with that of the shortest line. If the two given points are the ends of a diameter of the sphere, every plane passing through this diameter cuts semicircles, on the surface of the sphere, all of which are shortest lines between the ends; in which case there is an equal number of equal shortest lines between the given points. Accordingly, the axiom of there being only one shortest line between two points would not hold without a certain exception for the dwellers on a sphere.

Of parallel lines the sphere-dwellers would know nothing. They would maintain that any two straightest lines, sufficiently produced, must finally cut not in one only but in two points. The sum of the angles of a triangle would be always greater than two right angles, increasing as the surface of the triangle grew greater. They could thus have no conception of geometrical similarity between greater and smaller figures of the same kind, for with them a greater triangle must have different angles from a smaller one. Their space would be unlimited, but would be found to be finite or at least represented as such.

It is clear, then, that such beings must set up a very different system of geometrical axioms from that of the inhabitants of a plane, or from ours with our space of three dimensions, though the logical powers of all were the same; nor are more examples necessary to show that geometrical axioms must vary according to the kind of space inhabited by beings whose powers of reason are quite in conformity with ours. But let us proceed still farther.

Let us think of reasoning beings existing on the surface of an egg-shaped body. Shortest lines could be drawn between three points of such a surface and a triangle constructed. But if the attempt were made to construct congruent triangles at different parts of the surface, it would be found that two triangles, with three pairs of equal sides, would not have their angles equal. The sum of the angles of a triangle drawn at the sharper pole of the body would depart farther from two right angles than if the triangle were drawn at the blunter pole or at the equator. Hence it appears that not even such a simple figure as a triangle can be moved on such a surface without change of form. It would also be found that if circles of equal radii were constructed at different parts of such a surface (the length of the radii being always measured by shortest lines along the surface) the periphery would be greater at the blunter than at the sharper end.

We see accordingly that, if a surface admits of the figures lying on it being freely moved without change of any of their lines and angles as measured along it, the property is a special one and does not belong to every kind of surface. The condition under which a surface possesses this important property was pointed out by Gauss in his celebrated treatise on the curvature of surfaces.[3] The 'measure of curvature,' as he called it, i.e. the reciprocal of the product of the greatest and least radii of curvature, must be everywhere equal over the whole extent of the surface.

Gauss showed at the same time that this measure of curvature is not changed if the surface is bent without distension or contraction of any part of it. Thus we can roll up a flat sheet of paper into the form of a cylinder, or of a cone, without any change in the dimensions of the figures taken along the surface of the sheet. Or the hemispherical fundus of a bladder may be rolled into a spindle-shape without altering the dimensions on the surface. Geometry on a plane will therefore be the same as on a cylindrical surface; only in the latter case we must imagine that any number of layers of this surface, like the layers of a rolled sheet of paper, lie one upon another, and that after each entire revolution round the cylinder a new layer is reached different from the previous ones.

These observations are necessary to give the reader a notion of a kind of surface the geometry of which is on the whole similar to that of the plane, but in which the axiom of parallels does not hold good. This is a kind of curved surface which is, as it were, geometrically the counterpart of a sphere, and which has therefore been called the *pseudospherical surface* by the distinguished Italian mathematician E. Beltrami, who has investigated its properties.[4] It is a saddle-shaped surface of which only limited pieces or strips can be connectedly represented in our space, but which may yet be thought of as infinitely continued in all directions, since each piece lying at the limit of the part constructed can be conceived as drawn back to the middle of it and then continued. The piece displaced must in the process change its flexure but not its dimensions, just as happens with a sheet of paper moved about a cone formed out of a plane rolled up. Such a sheet fits the conical surface in every part, but must be more bent near the vertex and cannot be so moved over the vertex as to be at the same time adapted to the existing cone and to its imaginary continuation beyond.

Like the plane and the sphere, pseudospherical surfaces have their measure of curvature constant, so that every piece of them can be exactly applied to every other piece, and therefore all figures constructed at one place on the surface can be transferred to any other place with perfect congruity of form, and perfect equality of all dimensions lying in the surface itself. The measure of curvature as laid down by Gauss, which is positive for the sphere and zero for the plane, would have a constant negative value for pseudospherical surfaces, because the two principal curvatures of a saddle-shaped surface have their concavity turned opposite ways.

A strip of a pseudospherical surface may, for example, be represented by the inner surface (turned towards the axis) of a solid anchor-ring. If the plane figure *aabb* (Figure 1) is made to revolve on its axis of symmetry AB, the two arcs *ab* will describe a pseudospherical concave-convex surface like that of the ring. Above and below, towards *aa* and *bb*, the surface will turn outwards with ever-increasing flexure, till it becomes perpendicular to the axis, and ends at the edge with one curvature infinite. Or, again, half of a pseudospherical surface may be rolled up into the shape of a champagne-glass, with tapering stem infinitely prolonged. But the surface is always necessarily bounded by a sharp edge beyond which it cannot be directly continued. Only by supposing each single piece of the edge cut loose and drawn along the surface of the ring or glass, can it be brought to places of different flexure, at which farther continuation of the piece is possible.

In this way too the straightest lines of the pseudospherical surface may be infinitely produced. They do not, like those on a sphere, return upon themselves, but, as on a plane, only one shortest line is possible between the two given points. The axiom of parallels does not, however, hold good. If a straightest line is given on the surface and a point without it, a whole pencil of straightest lines may pass through the point, no one of which, though infinitely produced, cuts the first line; the pencil itself being limited by two straightest lines, one of which intersects one of the ends of the given line at an infinite distance, the other the other end. [See Figures 1 and 2.]

ORIGIN AND SIGNIFICANCE OF GEOMETRICAL AXIOMS 17

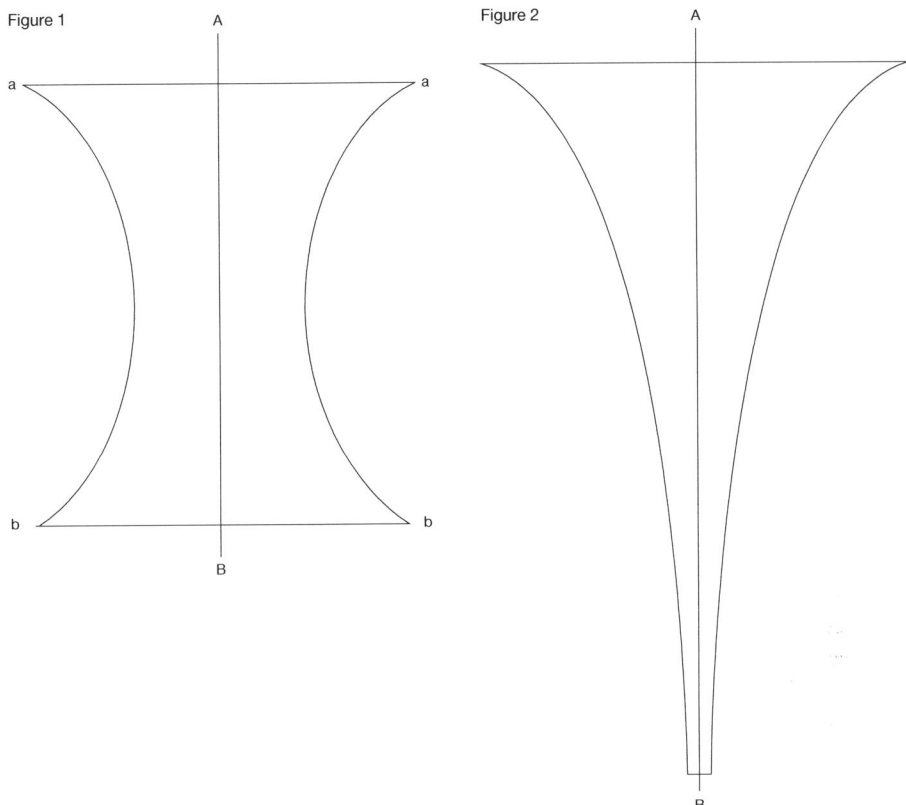

Figure 1

Figure 2

Such a system of geometry, which excluded the axiom of parallels, was devised on Euclid's synthetic method, as far back as the year 1829, by N.J. Lobachevsky, professor of mathematics at Kasan,[5] and it was proved that this system could be carried out as consistently as Euclid's. It agrees exactly with the geometry of the pseudospherical surfaces worked out recently by Beltrami.

Thus we see that in the geometry of two dimensions a surface is marked out as a plane, or a sphere, or a pseudospherical surface, by the assumption that any figure may be moved about in all directions without change of dimensions. The axiom, that there is only one shortest line between any two points, distinguishes the plane and the pseudospherical surface from the sphere, and the axiom of parallels marks off the plane from the pseudo-sphere. These three axioms are in fact necessary and sufficient, to define as a plane the surface to which Euclid's planimetry has reference, as distinguished from all other modes of space in two dimensions.

The difference between plane and spherical geometry has been long evident, but the meaning of the axiom of parallels could not be understood till Gauss had developed the notion of surfaces flexible without dilatation, and consequently that of the possibly infinite continuation of pseudospherical surfaces. Inhabiting, as we do, a space of three dimensions and endowed with organs of sense for their perception, we can represent to ourselves the various cases in which beings on a surface might have to develop their perception of space; for we have only to limit our own perceptions to a narrower field. It is easy to think away perceptions that we have; but it is very difficult to imagine perceptions to which there is nothing analogous in our experience. When, therefore, we pass to space of three dimensions, we are stopped in our power of representation, by the structure of our organs and the experiences got through them which correspond only to the space in which we live.

There is however another way of treating geometry scientifically. All known space-relations are measurable, that is, they may be brought to determination of magnitudes (lines, angles, surfaces, volumes). Problems in geometry can therefore be solved, by finding methods of calculation for arriving at unknown magnitudes from known ones. This is done in *analytical geometry*, where all forms of space are treated only as quantities and determined by means of other quantities. Even the axioms themselves make reference to magnitudes. The straight line is defined as the *shortest* between two points, which is a determination of quantity. The axiom of parallels declares that if two straight lines in a plane do not intersect (are parallel), the alternate angles, or the corresponding angles, made by a third line intersecting them, are equal; or it may be laid down instead that the sum of the angles of any triangle is equal to two right angles. These, also, are determinations of quantity.

Now we may start with this view of space, according to which the position of a point may be determined by measurements in relation to any given figure (system of co-ordinates), taken as fixed, and then inquire what are the special characteristics of our space as manifested in the measurements that have to be made, and how it differs from other extended quantities of like variety. This path was first entered by one too early lost to science, B. Riemann of Göttingen.[6] It has the peculiar advantage that all its operations consist in pure calculation of quantities, which quite obviates the danger of habitual perceptions being taken for necessities of thought.

The number of measurements necessary to give the position of a point is equal to the number of dimensions of the space in question. In a line the distance from one fixed point is sufficient, that is to say, one quantity; in a surface the distances from two fixed points must be given; in space, the distances from three; or we require, as on the earth, longitude, latitude, and height above the sea, or, as is usual in analytical geometry, the distances from three co-ordinate planes. Riemann calls a system of differences in which one thing can be determined by n measurements an '$n$fold extended aggregate' or an 'aggregate of n dimensions.' Thus the space in which we live is a threefold, a surface is a twofold, and a line is a simple extended aggregate of points. Time also is an aggregate of one dimension. The system of colours is an aggregate of three dimensions, inasmuch as each colour, according to the investigations of Thomas Young and of Clerk Maxwell,[7] may be represented as a mixture of three primary colours, taken in definite quantities. The particular mixtures can be actually made with the colour-top.

In the same way we may consider the system of simple tones[8] as an aggregate of two dimensions, if we distinguish only pitch and intensity, and leave out of account differences of timbre. This generalisation of the idea is well suited to bring out the distinction between space of three dimensions and other aggregates. We can, as we know from daily experience, compare the vertical distance of two points with the horizontal distance of two others, because we can apply a measure first to the one pair and then to the other. But we cannot compare the difference between two tones of equal pitch and different intensity, with that between two tones of equal intensity and different pitch. Riemann showed, by considerations of this kind, that the essential foundation of any system of geometry, is the expression that it gives for the distance between two points lying in any direction towards one another, beginning with the infinitesimal interval. He took from analytical geometry the most general form for this expression, that, namely, which leaves altogether open the kind of measurements by which the position of any point is given.[9] Then he showed that the kind of free mobility without change of form which belongs to bodies in our space can only exist when certain quantities yielded by the calculation[10]—quantities that coincide with Gauss's measure of surface-curvature when they are expressed for surfaces—have everywhere an equal value. For this reason Riemann calls these quantities, when they have the same value in all directions for a particular spot, the measure of curvature of the space at this spot. To prevent misunderstanding,[11] I will once more observe that this so-called measure of space-curvature is a quantity obtained by purely analytical calculation, and that its introduction involves no suggestion of relations that would have a meaning only for sense-perception. The name is merely taken, as a short expression for a complete relation, from the one case in which the quantity designated admits of sensible representation.

Now whenever the value of this measure of curvature in any space is everywhere zero, that space everywhere conforms to the axioms of Euclid; and it may be called a *flat* (*homaloid*) space in contradistinction to other spaces, analytically constructible, that may be called *curved*, because their measure of curvature has a value other than zero. Analytical geometry may be as completely and consistently worked out for such spaces as ordinary geometry can for our actually existing homaloid space.

If the measure of curvature is positive we have *spherical* space, in which straightest lines return upon themselves and there are no parallels. Such a space would, like the surface of a sphere, be unlimited but not infinitely great. A constant negative measure of curvature on the other hand gives *pseudo-spherical* space, in which straightest lines run out to infinity, and a pencil of straightest lines may be drawn, in any flattest surface, through any point which does not intersect another given straightest line in that surface.

Beltrami[12] has rendered these last relations imaginable by showing that the points, lines, and surfaces of a pseudospherical space of three dimensions, can be so portrayed in the interior of a sphere in Euclid's homaloid space, that every straightest line or flattest surface of the pseudospherical space is represented by a straight line or a plane, respectively, in the sphere. The surface itself of the sphere corresponds to the infinitely distant points of the pseudospherical space; and the different parts of this space, as represented in the sphere, become smaller, the nearer they lie to the spherical surface, diminishing more rapidly in the direction of the radii than in that perpendicular to them. Straight lines in the sphere, which only intersect beyond its surface, correspond to straightest lines of the pseudospherical space which never intersect.

Thus it appeared that space, considered as a region of measurable quantities, does not at all correspond with the most general conception of an aggregate of three dimensions, but involves also special conditions, depending on the perfectly free mobility of solid bodies without change of form to all parts of it and with all possible changes of direction; and, further, on the special value of the measure of curvature which for our actual space equals, or at least is not distinguishable from, zero. This latter definition is given in the axioms of straight lines and parallels.

Whilst Riemann entered upon this new field from the side of the most general and fundamental questions of analytical geometry, I myself arrived at similar conclusions,[13] partly from seeking to represent in space the system of colours, involving the comparison of one threefold extended aggregate with another, and partly from inquiries on the origin of our ocular measure for distances in the field of vision. Riemann starts by assuming the above-mentioned algebraic expression which represents in the most general form the distance between two infinitely near points, and deduces therefrom, the conditions of mobility of rigid figures. I, on the other hand, starting from the observed fact that the movement of rigid figures is possible in our space, with the degree of freedom that we know, deduce the necessity of the algebraic expression taken by Riemann as an axiom. The assumptions that I had to make as the basis of the calculation were the following.

First, to make algebraic treatment at all possible, it must be assumed that the position of any point A can be determined, in relation to certain given figures taken as fixed bases, by measurement of some kind of magnitudes, as lines, angles between lines, angles between surfaces, and so forth. The measurements necessary for determining the position of A are known as its co-ordinates. In general, the number of co-ordinates necessary for the complete determination of the position of a point, marks the number of the dimensions of the space in question. It is further assumed that with the movement of the point A, the magnitudes used as co-ordinates vary continuously.

Secondly, the definition of a solid body, or rigid system of points, must be made in such a way as to admit of magnitudes being compared by congruence. As we must not, at this stage, assume any special methods for the measurement of magnitudes, our definition can, in the first instance, run only as follows. Between the co-ordinates of any two points belonging to a solid body, there must be an equation which, however the body is moved, expresses a constant spatial relation (proving at last to be the distance) between the two points, and which is the same for congruent pairs of points, that is to say, such pairs as can be made successively to coincide in space with the same fixed pair of points.

However indeterminate in appearance, this definition involves most important consequences, because with increase in the number of points, the number of equations increases much more quickly than the number of co-ordinates which they determine. Five points, A, B, C, D, E, give ten different pairs of points

AB, AC, AD, AE,
BC, BD, BE,
CD, CE,
DE,

and therefore ten equations, involving in space of three dimensions fifteen variable co-ordinates. But of these fifteen, six must remain arbitrary, if the system of five points is to admit of free movement and rotation, and thus the ten equations can determine only nine co-ordinates as functions of the six variables. With six points we obtain fifteen equations for twelve quantities, with seven points twenty-one equations for fifteen, and so on. Now from n independent equations we can determine n contained quantities, and if we have more than n equations, the superfluous ones must be deducible from the first n. Hence it follows that the equations which subsist between the co-ordinates of each pair of points of a solid body must have a special character, seeing that, when in space of three dimensions they are satisfied for nine pairs of points as formed out of any five points, the equation for the tenth pair follows by logical consequence. Thus our assumption for the definition of solidity, becomes quite sufficient to determine the kind of equations holding between the co-ordinates of two points rigidly connected.

Thirdly, the calculation must further be based on the fact of a peculiar circumstance in the movement of solid bodies, a fact so familiar to us that but for this inquiry it might never have been thought of as something that need not be. When in our space of three dimensions two points of a solid body are kept fixed, its movements are limited to rotations round the straight line connecting them. If we turn it completely round once, it again occupies exactly the position it had at first. This fact, that rotation in one direction always brings a solid body back into its original position, needs special mention. A system of geometry is possible without it. This is most easily seen in the geometry of a plane. Suppose that with every rotation of a plane figure its linear dimensions increased in proportion to the angle of rotation, the figure after one whole rotation through 360 degrees would no longer coincide with itself as it was originally. But any second figure that was congruent with the first in its original position might be made to coincide with it in its second position by being also turned though 360 degrees. A consistent system of geometry would be possible upon this supposition, which does not come under Riemann's formula.

On the other hand I have shown that the three assumptions taken together form a sufficient basis for the starting-point of Riemann's investigation, and thence for all his further results relating to the distinction of different spaces according to their measure of curvature.

It still remained to be seen whether the laws of motion, as dependent on moving forces, could also be consistently transferred to spherical or pseudospherical space. This investigation has been carried out by Professor Lipschitz of Bonn.[14] It is found that the comprehensive expression for all the laws of dynamics, Hamilton's principle, may be directly transferred to spaces of which the measure of curvature is other than zero. Accordingly, in this respect also, the disparate systems of geometry lead to no contradiction.

We have now to seek an explanation of the special characteristics of our own flat space, since it appears that they are not implied in the general notion of an extended quantity of three dimensions and of the free mobility of bounded figures therein. *Necessities of thought*, such as are involved in the conception of such a variety, and its measurability, or from the most general of all ideas of a solid figure contained in it, and of its free mobility, they undoubtedly are not. Let us then examine the opposite assumption as to their origin being empirical, and see if they can be inferred from facts of experience and so established, or if, when tested by experience, they are perhaps to be rejected. If they are of empirical origin, we must be able to represent to ourselves connected series of facts, indicating a different value for the measure of curvature from that of Euclid's flat space. But if we can imagine such spaces of other sorts, it cannot be maintained that the axioms of geometry are necessary consequences of an *a priori* transcendental form of intuition, as Kant thought.

The distinction between spherical, pseudospherical, and Euclid's geometry depends, as was above observed, on the value of a certain constant called, by Riemann, the measure of curvature of the space in question. The value must be zero for Euclid's axioms to hold good. If it were not zero, the sum of the angles of a large triangle would differ from that of the angles of a small one, being larger in spherical, smaller in pseudospherical, space. Again, the geometrical similarity of large and small solids or figures is possible only in Euclid's space. All systems of practical mensuration that have been used for the angles of large rectilinear triangles, and especially all systems of astronomical measurement which make the parallax of the immeasurably distant fixed stars equal to zero (in pseudospherical space the parallax even of infinitely distant points would be positive), confirm empirically the axiom of parallels, and show the measure of curvature of our space thus far to be indistinguishable from zero. It remains, however, a question, as Riemann observed, whether the result might not be different if we could use other than our limited base-lines, the greatest of which is the major axis of the earth's orbit.

Meanwhile, we must not forget that all geometrical measurements rest ultimately upon the principle of congruence. We measure the distance between points by applying to them the compass, rule, or chain. We measure angles by bringing the divided circle or theodolite to the vertex of the angle. We also determine straight lines by the path of rays of light which in our experience is rectilinear; but that light travels in shortest lines as long as it continues in a medium of constant refraction would be equally true in space of a different measure of curvature. Thus all our geometrical measurements depend on our instruments being really, as we consider them, invariable in form, or at least on their undergoing no other than the small changes we know of, as arising from variation of temperature or from gravity acting differently at different places.

In measuring, we only employ the best and surest means we know of to determine, what we otherwise are in the habit of making out by sight and touch or by pacing. Here our own body with its organs is the instrument we carry about in space. Now it is the hand, now the leg, that serves for a compass, or the eye turning in all directions is our theodolite for measuring arcs and angles in the visual field.

Every comparative estimate of magnitudes or measurement of their spatial relations proceeds therefore upon a supposition as to the behaviour of certain physical things, either the human body or other instruments employed. The supposition may be in the highest degree probable and in closest harmony with all other physical relations known to us, but yet it passes beyond the scope of pure space-intuition.

It is in fact possible to imagine conditions for bodies apparently solid such that the measurements in Euclid's space become what they would be in spherical or pseudospherical space. Let me first remind the reader that if all the linear dimensions of other bodies, and our own, at the same time were diminished or increased in like proportion, as for instance to half or double their size, we should with our means of space-perception be utterly unaware of the change. This would also be the case if the distension or contraction were different in different directions, provided that our own body changed in the same manner, and further that a body in rotating assumed at every moment, without suffering or exerting mechanical resistance, the amount of dilatation in its different dimensions corresponding to its position at the time. Think of the image of the world in a convex mirror. The common silvered globes set up in gardens give the essential features, only distorted by some optical irregularities. A well-made convex mirror of moderate aperture represents the objects in front of it as apparently solid and in fixed positions behind its surface. But the images of the distant horizon and of the sun in the sky lie behind the mirror at a limited distance, equal to its focal length. Between these and the surface of the mirror are found the images of all the other objects before it, but the images are diminished and flattened in proportion to the distance of their objects from the mirror. The flattening, or decrease in the third dimension, is relatively greater than the decrease of the surface-dimensions. Yet every straight line or every plane in the outer world is represented by a straight line or a plane in the image. The image of a man measuring with a rule a straight line from the mirror would contract more and more the farther he went, but with his shrunken rule the man in the image would count out exactly the same number of centimetres as the real man. And, in general, all geometrical measurements of lines or angles made with regularly varying images of real instruments would yield exactly the same results as in the outer world, all congruent bodies would coincide on being applied to one another in the mirror as in the outer world, all lines of sight in the outer world would be represented by straight lines of sight in the mirror. In short I do not see how men in the mirror are to discover that their bodies are not rigid solids and their experiences good examples of the correctness of Euclid's axioms. But if they could look out upon our world as we can look into theirs, without overstepping the boundary, they must declare it to be a picture in a spherical mirror, and would speak of us just as we speak of them; and if two inhabitants of the different worlds could communicate with one another, neither, so far as I can see, would be able to convince the other that he had the true, the other the distorted, relations. Indeed I cannot see that such a question would have any meaning at all, so long as mechanical considerations are not mixed up with it.

Now Beltrami's representation of pseudospherical space in a sphere of Euclid's space, is quite similar, except that the background is not a plane as in the convex mirror, but the surface of a sphere, and that the proportion in which the images as they approach the spherical surface contract, has a different mathematical expression. If we imagine then, conversely, that in the sphere, for the interior of which Euclid's axioms hold good, moving bodies contract as they depart from the centre like the images in a convex mirror, and in such a way that their representatives in pseudospherical space retain their dimensions unchanged,—observers whose bodies were regularly subjected to the same change would obtain the same results from the geometrical measurements they could make as if they lived in pseudospherical space.

We can even go a step further, and infer how the objects in a pseudospherical world, were it possible to enter one, would appear to an observer, whose eye-measure and experiences of space had been gained like ours in Euclid's space. Such an observer would continue to look upon rays of light or the lines of vision as straight lines, such as are met with in flat space, and as they really are in the spherical representation of pseudospherical space. The visual image of the objects in pseudospherical space would thus make the same impression upon him as if he were at the centre of Beltrami's sphere. He would think he saw the most remote objects round about him at a finite distance,[15] let us suppose a hundred feet off. But as he approached these distant objects, they would dilate before him, though more in the third dimension than superficially, while behind him they would contract. He would know that his eye judged wrongly. If he saw two straight lines which in his estimate ran parallel for the hundred feet to his world's end, he would find on following them that the farther he advanced the more they diverged, because of the dilatation of all the objects to which he approached. On the other hand, behind him, their distance would seem to diminish, so that as he advanced they would appear always to diverge more and more. But two straight lines which from his first position seemed to converge to one and the same point of the background a hundred feet distant, would continue to do this however far he went, and he would never reach their point of intersection.

Now we can obtain exactly similar images of our real world, if we look through a large convex lens of corresponding negative focal length, or even through a pair of convex spectacles if ground somewhat prismatically to resemble pieces of one continuous larger lens. With these, like the convex mirror, we see remote objects as if near to us, the most remote appearing no farther distant than the focus of the lens. In going about with this lens before the eyes, we find that the objects we approach dilate exactly in the manner I have described for pseudospherical space. Now anyone using a lens, were it even so strong as to have a focal length of only sixty inches, to say nothing of a hundred feet, would perhaps observe for the first moment that he saw objects brought nearer. But after going about a little the illusion would vanish, and in spite of the false images he would judge of the distances rightly. We have every reason to suppose that what happens in a few hours to any one beginning to wear spectacles would soon enough be experienced in pseudospherical space. In short, pseudospherical space would not seem to us very strange, comparatively speaking; we should only at first be subject to illusions in measuring by eye the size and distance of the more remote objects.

There would be illusions of an opposite description, if, with eyes practised to measure in Euclid's space, we entered a spherical space of three dimensions. We should suppose the more distant objects to be more remote and larger than they are, and should find on approaching them that we reached them more quickly than we expected from their appearance. But we should also see before us objects that we can fixate only with diverging lines of sight, namely, all those at a greater distance from us than the quadrant of a great circle. Such an aspect of things would hardly strike us as very extraordinary, for we can have it even as things are if we place before the eye a slightly prismatic glass with the thicker side towards the nose: the eyes must then become divergent to take in distant objects. This excites a certain feeling of unwonted strain in the eyes, but does not perceptibly change the appearance of the objects thus seen. The strangest sight, however, in the spherical world would be the back of our own head, in which all visual lines not stopped by other objects would meet again, and which must fill the extreme background of the whole perspective picture.

At the same time it must be noted that as a small elastic flat disk, say of india-rubber, can only be fitted to a slightly curved spherical surface with relative contraction of its border and distension of its centre, so our bodies, developed in Euclid's flat space, could not pass into curved space without undergoing similar distensions and contractions of their parts, their coherence being of course maintained only in as far as their elasticity permitted their bending without breaking. The kind of distension must be the same as in passing from a small body imagined at the centre of Beltrami's sphere to its pseudospherical or spherical representation. For such passage to appear possible, it will always have to be assumed that the body is sufficiently elastic and small in comparison with the real or imaginary radius of curvature of the curved space into which it is to pass.

These remarks will suffice to show the way in which we can infer from the known laws of our sensible perceptions the series of sensible impressions which a spherical or pseudospherical world would give us, if it existed. In doing so, we nowhere meet with inconsistency or impossibility any more than in the calculation of its metrical proportions. We can represent to ourselves the look of a pseudospherical world in all directions just as we can develop the conception of it. Therefore it cannot be allowed that the axioms of our geometry depend on the native form of our perceptive faculty, or are in any way connected with it.

It is different with the three dimensions of space. As all our means of sense-perception extend only to space of three dimensions, and a fourth is not merely a modification of what we have, but something perfectly new, we find ourselves by reason of our bodily organisation quite unable to represent a fourth dimension.

In conclusion, I would again urge that the axioms of geometry are not propositions pertaining only to the pure doctrine of space. As I said before, they are concerned with quantity. We can speak of quantities only when we know of some way by which we can compare, divide, and measure them. All space-measurements, and therefore in general all ideas of quantities applied to space, assume the possibility of figures moving without change of form or size. It is true we are accustomed in geometry to call such figures purely geometrical solids, surfaces, angles, and lines, because we abstract from all the other distinctions, physical and chemical, of natural bodies; but yet one physical quality, rigidity, is retained. Now we have no other mark of rigidity of bodies or figures but congruence, whenever they are applied to one another at any time or place, and after any revolution. We cannot, however, decide by pure geometry, and without mechanical considerations, whether the coinciding bodies may not both have varied in the same sense.

If it were useful for any purpose, we might with perfect consistency look upon the space in which we live as the apparent space behind a convex mirror with its shortened and contracted background; or we might consider a bounded sphere of our space, beyond the limits of which we perceive nothing further, as infinite pseudospherical space. Only then we should have to ascribe to the bodies which appear to us to be solid, and to our own body at the same time, corresponding distensions and contractions, and we should have to change our system of mechanical principles entirely; for even the proposition that every point in motion, if acted upon by no force, continues to move with unchanged velocity in a straight line, is not adapted to the image of the world in the convex-mirror. The path would indeed be straight, but the velocity would depend upon the place.

Thus the axioms of geometry are not concerned with space-relations only but also at the same time with the mechanical deportment of solidest bodies in motion. The notion of rigid geometrical figure might indeed be conceived as transcendental in Kant's sense, namely, as formed independently of actual experience, which need not exactly correspond therewith, any more than natural bodies do ever in fact correspond exactly to the abstract notion we have obtained of them by induction. Taking the notion of rigidity thus as a mere ideal, a strict Kantian might certainly look upon the geometrical axioms as propositions given, *a priori*, by transcendental intuition, which no experience could either confirm or refute, because it must first be decided by them whether any natural bodies can be considered as rigid. But then we should have to maintain that the axioms of geometry are not synthetic propositions, as Kant held them; they would merely define what qualities and deportment a body must have to be recognised as rigid.

But if to the geometrical axioms we add propositions relating to the mechanical properties of natural bodies, were it only the axiom of inertia, or the single proposition, that the mechanical and physical properties of bodies and their mutual reactions are, other circumstances remaining the same, independent of place, such a system of propositions has a real import which can be confirmed or refuted by experience, but just for the same reason can also be gained by experience. The mechanical axiom, just cited, is in fact of the utmost importance for the whole system of our mechanical and physical conceptions. That rigid solids, as we call them, which are really nothing else than elastic solids of great resistance, retain the same form in every part of space if no external force affects them, is a single case falling under the general principle.

In conclusion, I do not, of course, maintain that mankind first arrived at space-intuitions, in agreement with the axioms of Euclid, by any carefully executed systems of exact measurement. It was rather a succession of everyday experiences, especially the perception of the geometrical similarity of great and small bodies, only possible in flat space, that led to the rejection, as impossible, of every geometrical representation at variance with this fact. For this no knowledge of the necessary logical connection between the observed fact of geometrical similarity and the axioms was needed; but only an intuitive apprehension of the typical relations between lines, planes, angles, etc., obtained by numerous and attentive observations – an intuition of the kind the artist possesses of the objects he is to represent, and by means of which he decides with certainty and accuracy whether a new combination, which he tries, will correspond or not with their nature. It is true that we have no word but *intuition* to mark this; but it is knowledge empirically gained by the aggregation and reinforcement of similar recurrent impressions in memory, and not a transcendental form given before experience. That other such empirical intuitions of fixed typical relations, when not clearly comprehended, have frequently enough been taken by metaphysicians for *a priori* principles, is a point on which I need not insist.

To sum up, the final outcome of the whole inquiry may be thus expressed:

1) The axioms of geometry, taken by themselves out of all connection with mechanical propositions, represent no relations of real things. When thus isolated, if we regard them with Kant as forms of intuition transcendentally given, they constitute a form into which any empirical content whatever will fit, and which therefore does not in any way limit or determine beforehand the nature of the content.[16] This is true, however, not only of Euclid's axioms, but also of the axioms of spherical and pseudo-spherical geometry.

2) As soon as certain principles of mechanics are conjoined with the axioms of geometry, we obtain a system of propositions which has real import, and which can be verified or overturned by empirical observations, just as it can be inferred from experience. If such a system were to be taken as a transcendental form of intuition and thought, there must be assumed a pre-established harmony between form and reality.

Notes

1 Reprinted from 1908, *Popular Lectures on Scientific Subjects, Second Series*. London: Longmans, Green, and Co., which reproduces verbatim the bulk of the paper as it appeared in 1876, *Mind* 1 (3), pp. 301–321. – Trans.

2 In his book. *On the Limits of Philosophy*, Mr. W. Tobias maintains that axioms of a kind which I formerly enunciated are a misunderstanding of Kant's opinion. But Kant specially adduces the

axioms, that the straight line is the shortest (*Kritik der reinen Vernunft*, Introduction, v. 2nd ed. p. 16); that space has three dimensions (*Ibid*, part i. sect. i. § 3, p. 41); that only one straight line is possible between two points (*Ibid*, *part* ii. sect. i. 'On the Axioms of Intuition'), as axioms which express *a priori* the conditions of intuition by the senses. It is not here the question, whether these axioms were originally given as intuition of space, or whether they are only the starting-points from which the understanding can develop such axioms *a priori* on which my critic insists.

3   Gauss, *Werke*, Bd. IV. p. 215, first published in *Commentationes Soc. Reg. Scienti. Gottengensis recentiones*, vol. vi., 1828.

4   *Saggio di Interpretazione della Geometria Non-Euclidea*, Napoli, *1868.*—*Teoria fondamentale degli Spazii di Curvatura costante, Annali di Matematica*, Ser. II. Tom. II. pp. 232–55. Both have been translated into French by J. Hoüel, *Annales Scientifiques de l'Ecole Normale*, Tom. V., 1869.

5   *Principien der Geometrie*, Kasan, 1829–30.

6   Ueber die Hypothesen welche der Geometrie zu Grunde liegen, Habilitationsschrift vom 10 Juni 1854 (*Abhandl. der königl. Gesellsch zu* (Göttingen, Vol. XIII.).

7   Helmholtz's "The Recent Progress of the Theory of Vision," pp. 156–57.

8   Helmholtz's, "On the Physiological Causes of Harmony in Music," p. 62.

9   For the square of the distance of two infinitely near points the expression is a homogeneous quadric function of the differentials of their co-ordinates.

10   They are algebraic expressions compounded from the coefficients of the various terms in the expression for the square of the distance of two contiguous points and from their differential quotients.

11   As occurs, for instance, in the above-mentioned work of Tobias, pp. 70, etc.

12   *Teoria fondamentale, etc., ut sup*.

13   Ueber die Thatsachen, die der Geometrie zum Grunde liegen (*Nachrichten von der königl. Ges. d. Wiss. zu Göttingen*, Juni 3, 1868).

14   'Untersuchungen über die ganzen homogenen Functionen von *n* Differentialen' (Borchardt's *Journal für Mathematik*, Bd. lxx. 3, 71; lxxiii. 3, I); 'Untersuchung eines Problems der Variationsrechnung' (*Ibid*. Bd. lxxiv.).

15   The reciprocal of the square of this distance, expressed in negative quantity, would be the measure of curvature of the pseudospherical space.

16   Compare the preceding selection, "On General Physical Concepts." – Trans.

Chapter 3

The Origin and Meaning of Geometric Axioms (1878)[1]

My article on "The Origin and Meaning of Geometric Axioms" in *Mind*, No. 3, was critically examined by Professor Land in No. 5, and I shall now try to answer his objections. We differ substantially on two points. I am of opinion that the recent mathematical investigations – or, as they have been called, meta-mathematical investigations[2] – as to further kinds of geometry have established the following propositions:

1) Kant's proof of the a priori origin of geometric axioms, based on the assumption that no other space relations are conceivable, is insufficient, the assumption being at variance with fact.

2) If, in spite of the defective proof, it is still assumed hypothetically that the axioms are really given a priori as laws of our space intuitions, two kinds of equivalence of space magnitudes must be distinguished: *subjective equality* given by the hypothetical transcendental intuition, and *objective equivalence* of the real substrata of such space relations, proved by the equality of physical states or actions existing or occurring in what appear to us as congruent parts of space. The coincidence of the second with the first could be proved only by experience; and as the second alone concerns us in our scientific or practical dealings with the objective world, the first, in case of discrepancy, must be discounted as a deceptive appearance.

For the rest, it is a misunderstanding on Professor Land's part if he thinks I wished to raise any objection to the notion that space is for us an a priori and necessary, or (in Kant's sense) transcendental, form of intuition. I had no such intention. True, my view of the relations between this transcendental form and reality, as I shall set it forth in the third section of this paper, does not quite coincide with that of many followers of Kant and Schopenhauer. But space may very well be a form of intuition in the Kantian sense and yet not necessarily involve the axioms. To cite a parallel instance, it undoubtedly lies in the organization of our optical apparatus that everything we see can be seen only as a spatial distribution of colors. This is the innate form of our visual perceptions. But it is not in the least thereby predetermined how the colors we see shall coexist in space and follow one another in time. And just so, in my view, the representation of all external objects in space relations may be the only possible form in which we can represent the simultaneous existence of a number of discrete objects, though there is no necessity that a particular space perception should coexist with or follow upon certain others; e.g., that every rectilineal equilateral triangle should have angles of 60°, whatever the length of the sides.

According to Kant, indeed, the proof that space is an a priori form is based essentially on the position that the axioms are synthetic propositions a priori. But even if this assertion with the dependent inference is dropped, the space representation might still be the necessary a priori form in which every coextended manifold is perceived. This is not surrendering any essential feature of the Kantian system. On the contrary, the system becomes more consistent and intelligible if the proof of the possibility of metaphysics derived from the evidence of geometric axioms is seen to break down. Kant himself, as is well known, limited the scope of metaphysical science to the geometric and physical axioms. But the physical axioms are either of doubtful validity, or they are mere consequences of the principle of causality, that is to say, of our intellectual impulse to view everything that happens as conforming to law and thus as conceivable. And as Kant's *Critique* is otherwise hostile to all metaphysical reasoning, his system seems to be freed from inconsistency, and a clearer notion of the nature of intuition is obtained, if the a priori origin of the axioms is abandoned and geometry is regarded as the first and most perfect of the natural sciences.

I pass accordingly to the proof of the two theses enunciated above.

I

Kant's proof of the a priori origin of the geometric axioms is based on the assertion that it is impossible to form a mental representation of space relations at variance with Euclid's geometry. But the metamathematical investigations reviewed in my former paper have shown that it is quite possible to devise and consistently work out systems of geometry which differ from Euclid's both in the number of space dimensions and in their axioms, with their related systems of mechanics. I myself have tried to show what would be the sensible appearance of objects in spherical or in pseudospherical space. The mathematical correctness of those geometric deductions (carried out for the most part analytically) is, as far as I can see, beyond question, and the same may be said as to the perfect validity of the corresponding systems of mechanics, which afford the same degree of free mobility for solid bodies and the same independence of mechanical and physical processes from mere position that are presupposed in the Euclidean geometry.

Nor is there the least difficulty or uncertainty as to the nature of the space perceptions that human beings would have in these other circumstances. In particular, Beltrami's discovery of the way of representing pseudospherical space in a sphere of Euclidean space shows directly what would be the appearance of visual images in pseudospherical or spherical space. Every visual image of objects at rest as seen by a spectator at rest would, in fact, be exactly the same as that of the corresponding representation in Beltrami's sphere as seen from the center (supposing always that the distance of the two eyes may be neglected in comparison with the imaginary radius of curvature of the space). There would be a difference only in the order of succession of the images, according as the observer or the solid objects moved. Nothing would be changed but the rule for inferring what images would succeed others in case of movement. And, as I have maintained, such differences are not necessarily considerable, nor need they excite attention.

Men lived for a long time on what they thought was the flat earth before they discovered its spherical form, and they struggled long enough against this truth, just as our Kantians at the present day will not listen to the possibility of representing pseudospherical space. The discrepancies in pseudospherical space would be of a somewhat similar kind and not necessarily more striking (if the measure of curvature tallied) than are those betrayed by the spherical surface of the earth to an observer whose movements are limited to a few miles.

In discussing the question whether space relations can be imagined in metamathematical spaces, the first thing to settle is the rule by which we shall judge the imaginability of an object that we have never actually seen.

I advanced a definition to this effect – that we need the power of fully representing the sense impressions which the object would excite in us according to the known laws of our sense organs under all conceivable conditions of observation and by which it would be distinguished from other similar objects. I am of opinion that this definition contains stricter and more definite requirements for the possibility of imagination than any previous one; and as far as I can see, Professor Land does not contend that these requirements cannot be satisfied for objects in spherical or pseudospherical spaces. At the same time, the representation of objects that we have often perceived, or that resemble such in whole or in parts, will necessarily be superior in one respect to the representation of objects of which this cannot be said, namely, in the swiftness and ease with which we can imagine beforehand the various aspects of the objects under different conditions of observation or run them over in memory. This ease and swiftness in the imagination of an object never actually seen will be wanting, just in proportion as the observer has more rarely perceived and less carefully apprehended anything like it.

We have absolutely never had before us constructions of three dimensions in spherical or pseudospherical space. The geometrician, however, who has trained himself in the power of representing surfaces that can be bent without stretching and without change of their measure of curvature, as well as the figures that can be drawn upon them, finds relations in these that are closely analogous to the relations in those other spaces. The physiologist, too, who has studied the combinations of sense impressions under every possible variety of conditions, including those which never occur in daily experience, is more practiced in representing unusual (yet strictly determinate) series of sense impressions than one who has never had the same training. I may perhaps be pardoned, then, if I do not see why the fact that I come "fresh from the physiology of the senses" to epistemological inquiries should be a positive bar to my dealing with such questions as the one before us.

Since, then, the metamathematical space relations have never been actually perceived by us, we must not expect to have that power of swift, easy representation of the varying aspects of objects in them that can come only from daily experience and practice. The utmost we can expect is to arrive by slow steps and careful reflection at a full, consistent representation of the corresponding series of sense impressions. But in point of fact, we strike upon similar and equally great difficulties of representation when we seek to picture to ourselves the course of an intricately knotted thread, or a many-sided crystal model, or a complex building that we have never seen, although the possibility of imagining all these is proved by the fact of actual perception.

Unfortunately, Professor Land does not say whether he has any objection to my definition of imaginative representation, nor does he himself offer any other, though he several times hints that he means something different by "imaginability." Thus he says: "We do not find that they [the non-Euclideans] succeed in this [making metamathematical spaces imaginable], unless the notion of imaginability be stretched far beyond what Kantians and others understand by the word." At the same place, he asserts that only that which can be connectedly constructed in our space can be regarded as "imagined." He adds: "Non-Euclideans try to make imaginable that which is not so in the sense required for argumentation in this case." If by "argumentation" is here meant the discussion of the question whether our conviction of the actual validity of Euclid's axioms in our objective world justifies a conclusion as to their a priori origin, I am of opinion that my definition of imaginability is the only one that can decide the question. If we should define thus: "Nothing is to be held as imaginable in space, of which we cannot actually construct a model with existing bodies," all discussion of the question in dispute is, no doubt, cut short. But this imaginability, ascribed by the definition to Euclid's space alone, affords not the least ground for deciding whether its origin is to be sought in a law of the objective world or in the constitution of our minds. Accordingly, I do not believe that Professor Land means to postulate this, though his words bear the interpretation.

I can only suppose him to object to my definition of imaginability that it does not include a reference to the apparently spontaneous readiness with which the various aspects of any common object are represented when we have sensible experience of some one of them. But we know that such an association of different impressions can be acquired and strengthened by frequent repetition – notably, for instance, between the sound of a word and its meaning. I therefore do not see that we have the right to consider this readiness of suggestion as essential to imaginability. The fact, moreover, that Lobachevsky by pure synthesis – that is to say, by actual geometric constructions – worked out a complete system of pseudospherical geometry, agreeing exactly with the results of analytical inquiry, shows that such a geometry can be grasped in all its details by the imagination.

As regards the use of analytical methods in metamathematical inquiries, this is justified by the circumstance that we have here to do with the representation of an object which has never been perceived – an object whose notion, or (so to speak) architectural plan, has first to be developed, to be shown inherently consistent, and to be elaborated in sufficient detail that for every particular case it is made clear what the corresponding sensible impression would be in the circumstances. This ideal development of the ground plan is best attained by the methods of analytic geometry, securing as these do most effectively universality and completeness of demonstration. No doubt a manipulation of notions by means of the calculus does not suffice to prove the existence of the object so treated, but the process is sufficient to the extent of proving the possibility of a consistent series of sensible pictures, whence it follows that the space relations actually perceived in a real world by organs analogous to our own might correspond with a geometry different from Euclid's.

Since the relations obtaining in metamathematical spaces of three dimensions satisfy the conditions of imaginability required by my definition – and more cannot be demanded in the case of objects never actually perceived – Kant's proof of the transcendental character of the axioms and their a priori origin must be pronounced insufficient.

II

In this second section I will start from the position that Kant's hypothesis of the transcendental origin of the geometrical axioms may be correct though not proved, and will consider of what value this immediate knowledge of the axioms would be in judging of relations in the objective world. I will also, in the first instance, adhere to the realistic hypothesis and speak its language, assuming that our sensible impressions are caused by things really existing in space and acting upon our senses. My object in so doing is merely to take advantage of the simple and intelligible speech of common life and of physical science. I regard this view of things, however, expressly as hypothetical, and I mean afterwards to drop the realistic hypothesis in my third section, when I will repeat my exposition in abstract language, without any assumption as to the nature of real existence.

First of all, we must distinguish between equality or congruence of space-magnitudes as dependent on the assumption of transcendental intuition, and their equivalence as determined by measurement with physical instruments.

I call *physically equivalent* those space-magnitudes in which under like conditions and within like periods of time like physical processes take place. The process most commonly employed, with due precautions, for the determination of physically equivalent space-magnitudes is the transference of solid bodies from one to the other, that is to say, measurement with compass and rule. Otherwise, experience teaches us generally that all space-magnitudes that have been proved equal by a sufficiently exact method of physical measurement, manifest equivalence under every other kind of physical treatment. Physical equivalence of two space-magnitudes is thus a perfectly definite objective attribute of the two, and clearly there is nothing to hinder us from investigating experientially how physical equivalence of one pair of magnitudes is dependent on physical equivalence of other pairs. This would yield a kind of geometry which, in distinction from the geometry founded on the supposed transcendental intuition of space, I will for the time being call *physical geometry*. This in its procedure would have all the character of a physical science.

As soon as we have found the proper physical means for determining whether the distances of any two pairs of points are equal, we shall also be able to distinguish the case where three points, a, b, c, lie in a straight line, because then there will exist no point distinct from b having the same distances as ab and bc from a and c.

We should then be able to seek three points, A, B, C, equidistant from one another as angles of an equilateral triangle, and upon the rectilineal sides, AB and AC, two other points, b and c, equidistant from A. Upon this the question would arise whether the distance $bc=Ab=Ac$. Euclidian geometry answers, yes. *Spherical* geometry would say that $bc > Ab$, when $Ab < AB$; *pseudospherical* geometry would say the opposite. Here then, at our first steps, we should find we had to settle our axioms.

I have chosen this example because the question is only about equality or inequality of distance between pairs of points or, in the case of the three points in one line, about the determinateness or indeterminateness of their position, and no complex construction has to be imagined. That the supposed transcendental knowledge of axioms cannot be brought to a decision in this case, because it involves the behaviour of physical bodies, is granted by my opponent.

But my opponent is of opinion that besides this *physical geometry* which takes account of the physical (as well as the geometrical) properties of bodies, there is also a *pure geometry* grounded solely on transcendental intuition – that we have, apart from experience, a representation of geometrical bodies, surfaces, lines, that are absolutely rigid and immovable, and yet may stand in the relation of equality and congruence. I add that we are bound to claim absolute exactness for this transcendental representation of straight lines, equal distances or equal angles; otherwise, we could not say whether two straight lines prolonged to infinity will intersect once only or twice, or whether every straight line that cuts one of two parallels must also cut the other lying in the same plane. Now, supposing we had satisfied ourselves, on stronger grounds than have ever yet been adduced, that we do possess intuitions of this kind, we should in fact be in a position to work out a transcendental geometry, and then insure its physical applicability to the space-relations of physical bodies, provided it could be determined that the magnitudes which appear to us as equal in transcendental intuition are also to be recognised as physically equal. It is evident, however, that this question cannot be decided by pure space-intuition. Perhaps then by experience? But how? When we rely directly on our sense-perceptions, we are very clumsy in our comparison of lengths or in estimating faint curvatures of line, and since our ability in both kinds of appreciation increases with practice, it is probable that to a great extent, if not wholly, it has been acquired by previous training and by the use of physical means. The retina, in fact, or the hand, is like a compass that we carry about with us.

There would still remain the application of geometrical reasoning, based upon the axioms, whereby we might infer the equality of two lengths or angles not directly measured.

But to be able to apply the transcendental axioms we must already have established the equality of a number of lengths or the straightness of a number of lines, which could be done again only with the help of physical instruments; and we must thus, in reasoning from the physical equality of some magnitudes to the abstract geometrical equality of others, employ the very proposition we wish to prove.

Supposing physical geometry had discovered as laws of nature a number of universal propositions exactly corresponding with the transcendental axioms, the most that could be maintained respecting the assertion that space-magnitudes equal to one another in transcendental intuition are also physically equivalent, would be that it was an hypothesis that led to no contradiction. But this would not be the only hypothesis that could be made. The correspondence would also hold if (as I showed in my previous article) physical space were taken as the image of transcendental space in a convex mirror.

That physical geometry and the supposed transcendental geometry need not be in correspondence, is clear from the fact that we can represent them as not corresponding. The way to make apparent the incongruence is implied in my former exposition. Let us suppose physical measurements in correspondence with a pseudospherical space. The sensible appearance of such a space, observer and objects both being at rest, would be the same as if we had before us in Euclidian space Beltrami's spherical model with the observer at the center. But with every change of the observer's position, the center of the projection-sphere would necessarily keep pace, and the whole projection would be dislodged. An observer, therefore, whose space-perceptions and judgments of magnitudes either depended on transcendental intuition or were the result of past experience in the sense of Euclidian geometry, would have the impression, as he moved, of seeing all objects changing position in a determinate way, and expanding or contracting differently according to the difference of direction. In like manner, though the quantitative relations are different, we see even in our actual world the apparent relative position and size of objects vary with the difference of distance as we move. Now, as a matter of fact, we are able to judge from the varying visual pictures that the objects about us do not change their relative position and size, so long as the perspective transpositions correspond exactly with the law we have found to hold in all previous experience for objects at rest; we are able also, on the other hand, to infer a motion of the objects whenever there is a departure from this law. And just so, I, who accept the experiential theory of perception, believe that anyone who could pass from Euclidian into pseudospherical space would at first indeed think he saw apparent movements, but very soon would learn to accommodate his judgment of space-relations to the new conditions.

I am quite aware, however, that this assumption is one that is formed by mere analogy from what we otherwise know of sense-perception, and cannot be experimentally proved. So let us suppose that the judgment of space-relations could not possibly become modified in such an observer, from the fact of its being connected with native forms of space-intuition. Nevertheless he would quickly discover that the motions he believed he saw were only apparent motions, because they would always be reversed when he returned to his first position; or a second observer would be able to declare that everything remained at rest while the other changed his place. Thus scientific inquiry at all events, if not immediate perception, would quickly determine what were the physically constant space-relations, just as by scientific investigation we know that the sun stands still and the earth revolves, although the sensible appearance of the earth standing still and the sun going round in twenty-four hours remains.

What I have said up to this point would, if I rightly understand him, be assented to by Prof. Land, for he himself, following out the example of 'Dr. Mises,' adduces a case of a similar sort. But then it will follow that the supposed transcendental intuition *a priori* becomes reduced to an *objectively false show*, from which we have to free ourselves and which we must try to forget, as in the case of the apparent movement of the sun. There would then be an insuperable contradiction between spacial equivalence as it appears to the native intuition and that which is manifested in objective phenomena. Our whole scientific and practical interest would be centered in the latter. The transcendental form of intuition would exhibit physically-equivalent space-relations only in the way that a map exhibits the surface of the earth – small pieces and strips correctly, larger pieces of necessity falsely. There would not then be a question only as to *manner of representation*, which necessarily implies some modification of the subject represented, but the relations between the appearance and the reality would be such that, while there was agreement within certain narrow limits, the representation would be *false* on a larger scale. In Prof. Land's example of dwellers on a spherical surface, he escapes this conclusion by falling back on Euclidian space of three dimensions. But in the case of pseudospherical space of three dimensions, if we wish to figure limited portions of it in a non-curved space, we must betake ourselves to a non-curved space of four dimensions, and must in any case one way or the other transgress the geometry of Euclid.

From these considerations my conclusion is as follows: – If we really had an innate and indestructible form of space-intuition involving the axioms with it, their objective scientific application to the phenomenal world would be justified only in so far as observation and experiment made it manifest that physical geometry, grounded in experience, could establish universal propositions agreeing with the axioms. And this condition coincides with Riemann's postulate, that the measure of curvature of our space must be determined empirically, by measurement. All measurements as yet have shown no deviation from zero in the value of this measure-of-curvature. We can therefore regard the Euclidian geometry as objectively valid within the limits of our present powers of exact measurement.

III

The discussion in the second section has been confined to the objective sphere, and conducted from the realistic point of view of natural science, whose aim is to comprehend or grasp conceptually the laws of nature. Towards this end perceptive knowledge is either only a mere help or, as the case may be, a false show to be got rid of.

Now Professor Land thinks that in my exposition I confused the notions of "objectivity" and "reality"; that when I asserted that geometrical propositions could be tested and verified by experience, I assumed without foundation "that empirical knowledge is acquired by simple importation or by counterfeit, and not by peculiar operations of the mind solicited by varied impulses from an unknown reality" (*Mind* 5., p. 46). If Professor Land had been acquainted with my different writings upon the Theory of the Senses, he would have known that I myself have always been combating the very assumption he would ascribe to me. I did not refer in my article to the difference between "objective" and "real,"[3] because it seemed to me to be of no importance for the investigation in hand. To justify this opinion of mine, let us now drop out of sight the hypothetical element in the realistic view and show that there still is a perfectly sound meaning in seeking for a physical equivalence of space-magnitudes, and in deciding by experience as to the truth of propositions that correspond in import with the axioms.

The only assumption we still maintain is that of the law of causation, to the effect, namely, that all mental states having the character of perception that come to pass in us do come to pass according to fixed laws, so that when different perceptions supervene we are justified in inferring therefrom a difference of the real conditions determining them. As regards these conditions – the reality proper that underlies the phenomena – we know nothing: all opinions we may entertain on the subject are to be regarded only as more or less probable hypotheses. But the assumption is the fundamental law of our thinking: if we surrender it, we abandon the very notion of comprehending things at all. I lay stress, then, upon the fact that no assumptions are made here as to the nature of the conditions under which the mental presentations arise. The hypothesis of subjective idealism is equally admissible with the realistic view, the language of which we have been employing.

We might assume that all our perceiving is but a dream, only a thoroughly coherent dream, in which presentation after presentation is evolved according to strict laws. In this case, the reason of the appearance of any new mental state having the character of perception would have to be sought in the fact that certain other perceptions, joined perhaps with a consciousness of certain voluntary impulses, had gone before in the dreamer's mind. What we call laws of nature on the realistic hypothesis would on the idealistic be laws governing the succession of mental states having the character of perception. And here, with reference to the question treated above in my first section, I will farther observe that in dreams we fancy ourselves perceiving as well as thinking; that is to say, some of our states arise with the constraining character of perception, others without this as a free play of representation (so far as in the waking state this may be called free). The question, therefore, whether by giving rein to the imagination we might call forth such a series of representations as would correspond, in perception, to a pseudospherical space, retains its full meaning on the idealistic hypothesis.

Now we find, as a fact of consciousness, that we think we perceive objects occupying determinate positions in space. If an object appears thus in one particular part of space and not in another, this must depend on the kind of real conditions that evoke the presentation. We must conclude that other real conditions might have existed fitted to produce a perception of the like objects in a different position. In the world of reality there must be some causes or aggregates of causes determining at what particular place in space an object shall appear to us. These I will designate, for shortness, *topogenous moments*, i.e., circumstances determining space-perception. We know nothing of their nature; we know only that the occurrence of spatially different perceptions involves a difference of topogenous moments. Also there must be different causes in the sphere of the real, when at the same place we think we perceive substances with different qualities. I will call these *hylogenous moments*, i.e., circumstances determining the perception of material things. New names are chosen in both cases, to avoid the misleading associations of current expressions.

If now we perceive and affirm anything that involves space-relations, the real meaning of our words no doubt is nothing more than that between certain topogenous moments, the nature of which is unknown to us, a certain relation holds, whose nature also is unknown. Hence Schopenhauer and many followers of Kant have been led to the improper conclusion that there is no real content at all in our space-perceptions, that space and its relations are purely transcendental and have nothing corresponding to them in the sphere of the real. We are, however, justified in taking our space-perceptions as *signs* of certain otherwise unknown relations in the world of reality, though we may not assume any sort of similarity between the sign and what is signified. But if only so much stands fast – that to unlike signs there correspond unlike objects and to like signs there correspond objects that are like in a certain relation or complex of relations, although we may not be able to define it at the time – this will suffice to yield us a real content. The same holds for space-perceptions as for qualities of sensation. Blue and red are qualities of sensation only; nevertheless we are justified in maintaining that a blue surface is physically different from a red surface. When we observe that the most diverse physical processes may go on during equal periods of time in similar fashion at different, but congruent, parts of space, the real meaning of such a perception is, that there may be in the sphere of reality equal sequences and aggregates of hylogenous moments combining with certain distinct groups of topogenous moments, which latter we then call *physically-equivalent*. We may thus discover by observation what special figures appearing in our perception correspond with physically-equivalent topogenous moments; and experience tells us that they are equivalent for all physical processes.

Now in the case of the equilateral triangle, above, the question is only about (1) equality or inequality of distances, i.e., physical equivalence or non-equivalence of the systems of topogenous moments corresponding with these, and (2) determinateness or indeterminateness of the position of a point, i.e., of its topogenous moments. These notions of determinateness and equivalence in relation to particular sequences we can, however, apply also to objects of unknown character. And I thence infer that the science which I have called physical geometry consists of propositions of real content and that its axioms are determined by relations that hold in the sphere of the real.

Nevertheless, a geometry based on transcendental intuition is conceivable also. We have only to assume that, without physical measurement, the intuition of the equality of two space magnitudes is developed immediately by the manner of action of the topogenous moments upon our consciousness, and that the magnitude of the apparent distance of every pair of points depends by the same formula on any three functions of the topogenous moments of each of the points, as the distance in Euclidean space (according to the Pythagorean proposition) depends on the three right-angled co-ordinates of each point. If such a law were given immediately for the perceived distance, our intuitions of space would necessarily satisfy the axioms of Euclid, however the topogenous moments of the separate points might be in the sphere of the real; for the whole of Euclid's geometry may be developed from that formula for the distance of two points. But then the question would arise whether the equality of the perceived distance and the physical equivalence of the distance depend on the same function of the topogenous moments or not. That is a question that goes beyond the province of space-intuition, and can be decided only by physical investigation. If there is agreement, the fact would have to be signalised as a law of nature, or, as I called it in my former paper, a pre-established harmony between intuition and the real world.

Thus I think I have sufficiently proved that the propositions put forward by me in that paper rest upon no confusion of the "objective" and the "real". By way of conclusion I will bring my results once more together: –

1) There exists in any case the science that I have called *physical geometry*, and its general propositions are products of experience.
2) The assumption of a knowledge of axioms by transcendental intuition apart from all experience is (a) an *unproved* hypothesis, and (b) an *unnecessary* hypothesis, since it explains nothing in our actual knowledge of the outer world that cannot equally be explained without its help: also, as regards our objective knowledge, (c) a wholly *irrelevant* hypothesis, since the propositions it includes can be applied to the relations of the objective world only after their objective validity has first been independently proved.

The presumed transcendental knowledge of axioms can thus have at the most an educational value, as helping to a first notion of space-relations.

Notes

1. Reprinted from *Mind* 3 (10): 212–225. – Trans.
2. The name has been given by opponents in irony, as suggesting *metaphysical;* but as the founders of "non-Euclidean geometry" have never maintained its objective truth they can very well accept the name.
3. The German word used by me, and translated "real" in the English, was "*wirklich*," that which works or acts. "*Wirklich*" has not the implication of "independent existence" that "real" has.

Introduction

Otto Liebmann (1840–1912)

OTTO LIEBMANN WAS BORN 1840 IN LÖWENBERG, Silesia. Due to his father's participation in the National Convention in Frankfurt, the family moved there in 1848. They then moved to Berlin in 1849, where Liebmann attended the Friedrich-Wilhelm Gymnasium, whose Principal, Ranke, was a brother of the famous historian Ranke. By 1859, Liebmann had studied philosophy and mathematics in Jena, Leipzig, and Halle. His teachers were Kuno Fischer and Gustav Fechner, among others, and he was also impressed by the historian Heinrich von Treitschke. In 1866, Liebmann took his Habilitation in Tübingen. He volunteered for the Franco-Prussian War (1870–71). Immediately thereafter, he became *Professor Extraordinarius* at the newly founded University of Straßburg in the recently annexed province of Alsace. In 1882, he moved to the University of Jena, where he taught until 1911. He died in 1912.

Liebmann's first and undoubtedly most famous work was his *Kant und die Epigonen* [*Kant and His Epigones*], which he published in 1865 at age 25, and which many consider the beginning of the neo-Kantian movement (more on this work shortly). But his *oeuvre* spanned a wider scope than Kant exegesis and Kant scholarship. For instance, he kept a journal of his time in the Franco-Prussian War, which was published anonymously in 1871 (*Vier Monate vor Paris* [*Four Months Before Paris*]). His philosophical *magnum opus* was his *Analysis der Wirklichkeit* [*Analysis of Reality*], published in 1876, which received three more editions, each time in increasingly expanded versions. His trademark, however, was the short, carefully crafted essay, in which he developed smaller points, rather than drafting grand systems. His interpretation of Kant was intended to indicate a method for developing a sustainable *Weltanschauung* out of the critical philosophy, a tendency that would be important especially for the Southwest School. Though he was influential as a teacher for, among others, Wilhelm Windelband and Bruno Bauch, Liebmann's overall *oeuvre* remained small, and he referred his students at all times to a thorough study of Kant's philosophy. Students remembered that each lecture was crafted "like a small piece of art." In this position as influential teacher, he has been described as "the vanguard of the great army that has written the name 'Neo-Kantianism' on its flags,"[1] and he is recognized, in this sense, as someone who launched the two great schools of Neo-Kantianism in Southwest Germany and Marburg.

Kant's chief doctrine and his chief mistakes

Liebmann's *Kant und die Epigonen* traces the development of Kant's philosophy into the nineteenth century. The title already names the main thesis of the book: contrary to the way they are usually seen, Liebmann considers such post-Kantian philosophers as Fichte, Schelling, Hegel, Herbart, Fries, and Schopenhauer to be mere epigones of Kant. They were, in other words, uninspired repetitions of Kant without any special originality, or worse, repetitions of his main mistakes. What made the book especially famous, and which is why it has been widely viewed as the beginning of the Neo-Kantian movement, is Liebmann's recommendation, at the end of each chapter, to go back to Kant: "*es muss auf Kant zurückgegangen warden*" ["it is necessary to return to Kant"] is a phrase that is repeated almost verbatim at the end of each chapter dealing with the epigones. It is for this reason that the philosophers following Liebmann's battle cry to return to Kant gradually came to be called "Neo-Kantians," though the way they returned to Kant bore in most cases little resemblance to Liebmann's original program. So to call Liebmann the first Neo-Kantian in any substantial way (besides, e.g., the physicist Helmholtz) is in a certain sense arbitrary, for one could equally have mentioned earlier philosophers, such as Fries or Trendelenburg. Nor were all "Neo-Kantians" as close to Kant as the title might suggest; certainly many Neo-Kantians were influenced by Fichte or Hegel in a way that Liebmann might have deemed unacceptable, just as in many respects the label "Neo-Kantianism" *in general* is misleading and highly ambiguous. In terms of the "standard narrative," however, Liebmann may rightfully be considered the first "outspoken" Neo-Kantian with a clear vision that future philosophy, if it was to make any headway, had to stage a return to Kant – whatever that meant for a particular thinker.

Indeed, Liebmann's thesis for why the post-Kantian philosophers were, to his mind, epigones was quite an original one. His thesis was that the latter followed Kant in believing in the existence of a thing in itself, and to hold in the first place that such a thing existed, was Kant's *proton pseudos,* his initial mistake, repeated blindly by his epigones. Hence, the passage selected from this work is Chapter One, in which Liebmann critiques Kant's notion of the thing in itself. In this discussion, Liebmann's initial rejection of the Kantian concept is laid out in detail. Liebmann maintains that the notion of a thing in itself violates the very tenets Kant had set up in his Transcendental Aesthetics. Namely, we can only cognize objects in space and time; there are, for us, no things outside of space and time, such a "thing" could only be construed as an *Unding,* a non-thing. To consider the possibility of such a non-thing would open philosophy back up to a mysticism or a romantic "philosophy of feeling." Liebmann traces the development of Kant's initial mistake, in a reconstruction of Kant's philosophy from the first to the second edition of the *Critique of Pure Reason* and with the careful attention to textual details that would become a trademark of the Neo-Kantians. In the end, the verdict is: "The Kantian 'thing in itself' is the failed attempt of the abstract intellect to find a concept that would be the transcendent answer to an unanswerable question, where we can only be helped by another kind of satisfaction of feeling that eliminates the occasion for our question. When the intellect makes these attempts to realize this unthinkable idea, it falls into the contradiction of wanting to think the unthinkable – it commits a *metabasis eis allo genos* [category mistake] in the eminent sense." It is this initial mistake that the post-Kantian epigones unquestioningly go along with; accordingly, their answers are all vulnerable, in Liebmann's judgment, to the charge of committing a *metabasis*. But the fate of Kant's philosophy, fortunately, does not depend on defending a problematic thing in itself alone; indeed, it is the task of the philosophers who want to go back to Kant, to "separate the genuine content of Kant's doctrine from the impure dross."

Note

1   Quoted in Ollig, *Der Neukantianismus,* p. 14.

Further Reading

Köhnke, Klaus Christian, *The Rise of Neo-Kantianism: German Academic Philosophy between Idealism and Positivism.* Trans. R.J. Hollingdale. Cambridge: Cambridge University Press, 1991.
Ollig, Hans-Ludwig, *Der Neukantianismus.* Stuttgart: Metzler, 1979, pp. 9–15.
Willey, Thomas A., *Back to Kant. The Revival of Kantianism in German Social and Historical Thought, 1860–1914.* Detroit: Wayne State University Press, 1978.
Windelband, Wilhelm, "Otto Liebmanns Philosophie," in: *Kant Studien* 15 (1910), pp. III ff.

Chapter 4

"Kant's Chief Doctrine and his Chief Mistakes" from *Kant and the Epigones* (1865)[1]

TRANSLATED BY BRIAN A. CHANCE

Many a judgment is accepted out of habit, or connected through inclination: but since no reflection preceded or at least critically succeeded it, it counts as one that has received its origin in the understanding. (Kant, *Critique of Pure Reason* A 260-1/B 317-7)

Our task is to separate the genuine content of Kant's doctrine from the impure dross. In order to do this, it is above all necessary that we remind ourselves of the primary points of his reasoning in their connection to one another; and we must therefore ask permission to present the reader in short, compact sentences something with which he has long been familiar. Let us put ourselves as one does in epics immediately *in medias res!* The following is the primary doctrine, the quintessence, of the critique of pure reason.

★ ★ ★[2]

All our representing consists in intuiting and thinking, and each representation is intuitive or abstract. But all intuiting takes place in space and time and cannot take place outside of them. All thinking, further, can in itself (as a function of the intelligible subject) only occur in time and is always related to something given in intuition (thus, in space and time). *Therefore, space and time are forms and conditions of all representing*.

Space and time are not abstracted from intuitions since they must rather already be present if any intuition is to be subjectively or objectively possible. Hence, although we could remove in thought everything existing in space and time, we absolutely could not remove space and time. For if we could, both the empirical world and even our self (our "I") would be eliminated, and the self would have removed itself in thought, which is impossible.[3] Further, mathematical propositions only express determinations of space and time that are not acquired from experience (cognized *a posteriori*) but are rather independent of experience and purely in virtue of the laws of our intellect (*a priori*) are declared to be incontrovertibly certain, that is, absolutely *universal* and *necessary*. Finally, space and time are not discursive but intuitive representations, for they relate to representations subordinate to them (different spaces and times) not as a genus does to a species, but as a whole does to its parts. *Therefore, space and time are necessary, pure* a priori *intuitions (functions of the intellect)*.

Space and time are, however, only necessary to the extent that they are "conditions of the possibility of all internal and external experience." If we abstract from experience and representing in general, then space and time are nothing; that is, *space and time have empirical reality and transcendental ideality*.

★ ★ ★

This is the content of the "Transcendental Aesthetic," which contains the proper foundation and what is truly new and epoch-making in the Kantian philosophy. In regards to the content of the subsequent "Transcendental Analytic," as the first part of the "Transcendental Logic," we want to note that the table of categories as well as other things are both in need and capable of significant simplification. Without going into the unessential particulars of this portion of the *Critique*, therefore, we now present the essentially universal elements.

★ ★ ★[4]

The manifold of elements of experience given in space and time (the matter of representing) can only become genuine experience or present itself to consciousness as a connected world of intuitive objects when it is connected to our intellect (categories) by means of certain syntheses. We cannot, as *Hume* rightly noted, acquire these syntheses from experience since experience only provides us with a multiplicity of *successive and coexisting* impressions of (internal and external) sense but never a *necessary connection* of these impressions. *Therefore, just as space and time are functions of the cognizing subject*[5], *so too are the categories; that is, they are necessary* a priori *representations*. And since they can only be thought in space and time, they relate only to spatial and temporal objects; that is, they have validity only within our intellect.[6]

★ ★ ★

Accordingly, the following reciprocal relationship exists with certainty:

1) *Our intellect only cognizes the elements of experience that are given in space and time and connected by the categories as an object.*[7]
2) *Everything that is given in space and time, that is, everything to which the categories are applicable, has validity only in relation to the intellect and is therefore nothing if independent of the intellect.*[8]

The situation, therefore, is as follows:

The external sensible world of corporeal things, as well as the inner world of our mental properties and abilities (thus the objects of inner and outer experience, i.e., everything given in space and time) is in no way robbed of its existence and reality (empirical reality); rather, it exists just as surely as I, the representing subject, exist.[9] But just as certain as this fact is that the material and mental world disappear when I annihilate this subject with its intellectual functions (space, time, and the categories) because it only exists in and through the forms of the intellect.[10] This means, therefore, that the subject and object of cognition are connected so intimately and necessarily by these transcendental forms of existence common to both of them, that they can only exist *with* each other, are necessary correlates, and stand or fall together. – But since I, the cognizing subject, do not stand supreme over these two inseparable factors of the world that is in fact represented (that is, the empirical world), but rather, eternally confined to the limits of my subjective intellect, am identical to one of these factors, I express the dependency of both factors of cognition in such a way that I attribute unconditional dependence on the existence of my intellect (transcendental ideality) to the empirical world (the object of experience) despite its factive existence (empirical reality).[11]

By following this train of thought with the closest attention, we find everything developed into its parts with such exacting, ruthless consistency and such deep clarity of thought that it can only convince us that as it were the scales fall from our eyes and we feel like the world after the discoveries of *Columbus* and *Copernicus*. From the transcendental ideality of space and time and the limitation of the categories to the data, given in both, of internal and external experience follows the thorough-going dependence of the actual, empirically-real world on the cognizing subject and *vice versa*. The standpoint of transcendental idealism, which involves empirical realism *de facto*, is developed completely validly; and up to this point, *Kant's* philosophy is irrefutable. Of course, in order to extract the pure gold of truth we have already had to strip and throw away a good deal of impure dross along the path we have followed. To this extent, we have taken an independent course since we have separated thoughts in this divorce that are unified in Kant's work. We have looked only at the truth and turned our backs to falsehood. – Now we must identify the inconsistency that, while it was omitted in our presentation, is combined with the truth almost at the beginning in Kant. This unfortunate inconsistency which is already a disruptive presence in the opening chords of the critical philosophy rises to a screeching, unbearable dissonance in its further development and all but destroys the in-itself grand and sublime impression of the whole work. It will be our task not only to lay bare and eliminate this lamentable mistake but also to examine the conditions from which it was able to grow. –

It has long been known that *Kant* did not stay completely true to his original doctrine. And this fact has been more generally noticed since *Arthur Schopenhauer* carefully identified the differences between the first edition of the *Critique of Pure Reason* and all subsequent editions, *Rosenkranz* presented them to the public in his synoptic edition, and *Kuno Fischer* addressed them in such a brilliant and beautiful manner.[12] But while a kind of infidelity to himself certainly lies in the changed deduction of the categories and the critique of idealism[13] patched into the second and subsequent editions, something much worse that has lain hidden in the *first form* of Kant's doctrine, like a worm in fruit, has been almost entirely overlooked. It entered because he made a concession to dogmatic philosophy and in so doing brought into question the existence of his own philosophy. In general, the inconsistency consists in this: Although it *follows necessarily* from the Transcendental Aesthetic and the fact, emphasized and often repeated by Kant himself, that the theoretical intellect may only cognize within its forms of cognition – that is, by means of its functions – and that anything whatsoever that is thought to exist outside and be independent of them can be nothing to the intellect, that something extra-spatial and extra-temporal absolutely cannot be represented or thought, Kant agrees from the beginning to recognize such an object that is emancipated from the forms of cognition and thus irrational; that is, he agrees to represent something that cannot be represented – a wooden piece of iron. He does this *gradatim*[14] in an order that is just as interesting to observe more closely as it is useful for the completion of our task.

First, he calls the manifold data of internal and external experience given in space and time *appearances*. How does he arrive at this? What justifies him to do so? The world may and, indeed, must disallow this title; for through it she will suffer the loss of her dignity, her already acknowledged empirical reality, that is, her actuality. It would obviously lie in the title *appearance* that something is presupposed that *appears* – namely something that appears as the empirical world. But if everything that is given in space and time is "appearance," then that which appears, the ostensible substrate of appearance, must *not* be in space and time. And since space and time are necessary forms of the intellect, this would be something that our intellect was not able to grasp and about which it could therefore not speak. A thing that lies outside of space and time is, once and for all, *nonsense*. Even if the spatial-temporal world were only "appearance", it would not be so *for the intellect* since it is absolutely unable to compare the world in space and time with anything else because this world is precisely *everything. Consequently, it cannot be given the title "appearance."*

Let us take notice of this and proceed further!

We already find the consequence of this *proton pseudos* in the Transcendental Aesthetic. For there a "thing in itself" enters at the appropriate time that "*may ground the appearances*"[15]. Now this should be precisely the extra-spatial and extra-temporal substrate of the world whose impending arrival has already been quietly announced to us in the unjustified title "appearance."

Da seht, dass Ihr tiefsinnig erfasst.
Was in des Menschen Hirn nicht passt. (Faust I, lines 1950–1)[16]

Concerning this superfluous appendage it is later said on page 286 and 290: *it is problematic, indeed it is something about which we can neither say it is possible or impossible.*[17] Now I indeed want to know how one can talk at all about a thing when one isn't even sure about its possibility or impossibility. To speak clearly, this is a problematic something without content about which we can know absolutely nothing, that is, only an obscure phrase in place of the simple, honest "*nothing.*"

Unconcerned by this, he speaks on page 358 of the "thing in itself" as something that "is the ground of appearance" and on page 538 "must be the ground." We thus see how the stranger that was at first quietly tolerated has the impudence to push forward from the sphere of the *problematic* through the sphere of the *assertoric* to *apodictic* validity.[18] What a parasite!

In the *Prolegomena* and the later writings, the necessary existence of the "thing in itself" is assumed as a fact that is known and raised above all doubt (*Prolegomena*, pp. 104, 141). And to top it all off, it is ultimately "not wanting to assume things in themselves is declared an absurdity" (p. 163)[19].– This is now the worst one can imagine; the parasite has now become indispensable. *Honny soit qui mal y pense!*[20] –

But with this the *critical philosophy* is indeed taken to its grave and *dogmatism* triumphs. Now consider that between these expressions the same man includes expressions such as: "the character of something's existence cannot be found in the mere concept of a thing".[21] (But perhaps in the *non-concept*?) Further, "One cannot sense anything outside of oneself but only in oneself, and the whole of self-consciousness therefore provides nothing other than merely our own determinations".[22] Indeed, in the second and subsequent editions these expressions remain quietly standing next to those, *toto caelo* contrary expressions. – One might ironically call this "the antinomy of Kantian reason." –

With this the clear, naked inconsistency is brought to light as a fact. If we were malicious, or opponents of Kant, we close the books here with "*Sapienti sat!*"[23] and leave the cart stuck in the mud. But since we, in the first place, greatly esteem and recognize with unfeigned reverence what is grand, pure, and true in the master's doctrine and, further, have begun this entire investigation not to criticize him but to understand the systems of his successors on the basis of his correctly understood principles and consistently developed thoughts and, in this way, to find the path to further advancement of science, we cannot be satisfied with this state of affairs but must instead direct the following question to ourselves.

What caused Kant to make such an obvious mistake? What brought him to incorporate a "thing in itself" into his philosophy, which leaves no place for such a thing? For we certainly require an explanation of why such an (it appears) easily avoidable mistake could have gotten by such a master in the field of speculative thought. The answer to this question will be a kind of deduction of the thing in itself; not an objective one (in which the validity of this concept would be demonstrated), but rather a subjective one (in which the possibility that and how such a thought could occur in this system will be presented). Such a deduction, which resembles in its essentials the astronomical explanation of an eclipse by calculating an existing constellation, can begin from different points. In particular, one either proceeds psychologically by identifying the conditions of the human mind under which he could have fallen into the said mistake; or, by working from the prior developmental process of philosophy, one emphasizes historically the doctrines of previous systems that appear to be antecedents, forefathers, or ancestors of the "thing in itself." One could call the former a biography or a deduction *a priori*, the latter a genealogy or a deduction *a posteriori* of the "thing in itself." – It is obvious that these two considerations do not stand without connection next to one another but internally complement, condition, and explain one another and therefore that the deduction will only be complete when we take both into consideration; and this will also happen. But when, despite belonging together, we separate these considerations, beginning with the historical and only after further intermediary investigations allowing the psychological to follow, there is good reason for this since in our opinion Kant himself was aware of the first but not the second, and since the second, more thoroughgoing consideration will also contain our final, objective judgment concerning the entire issue. –

In proceeding now with this historical deduction, we must allow ourselves to reach back further than we might otherwise; for what is most important to us is to be convincing, which is not possible in the present case without being detailed.

All philosophy is, according to its essence, a consideration of the world as a whole – that is, a consideration of the world in its material and spiritual parts; its object is the *cosmos*, and, in particular, the *macrocosm* that we extend far beyond all fixed stars and nebulae, and the *microcosm* in our own self that we pursue into the obscure regions of anticipation and feeling, what *Herbart* called "the threshold of consciousness" and *Leibniz* "*petites perceptions*." As different as the successive and simultaneously arising systems of all thinkers, peoples, and times have been in their principles and inferences, their fundamental ideas and their execution, they have all addressed this object. Philosophy will not passively accept the object of cognition and representation or let itself be dictated to, as does the common human understanding; it wants to *comprehend* this object, grapple with it and only then let it be regarded as comprehended. Just as the general end, the fundamental idea, of all philosophers is shared, so too in a certain sense is their means or organon. But what is this means? How does philosophy pursue its end, to achieve a comprehensible reproduction of the cosmos? Poets, painters, and composers also press into the depths of nature and the human soul and make both comprehensible by reproducing them. But how does the comprehension of an artist differ from that of a philosopher? What is the specific difference between artistic and philosophical reproduction? – This difference is decisive.

The artist grasps his object in imagination and reproduces it as something intuitively beautiful; the philosopher comprehends it in reason and thinks it as an abstract truth. – He who is unable to remain with the multiplicity of sensible particular things understood as individuals that is forced upon us, but is rather driven by a desire for knowledge and seeks the unity in multiplicity, the condition of the conditioned, the cosmos in nature, he philosophizes. But this is only possible if one forms general representations. In forming these, I must look away from what is not homogenous, and thus relatively indifferent, in a number of objects; I must *abstract*. *Abstract representation* is the means, the organon of *philosophical* cognition, as opposed to the *intuitive* cognition of the *artist*.

It is in this way that different philosophers on the path of abstract thinking attempted to come closer to the essence or ground of the world. Whether they preferred to begin as empiricists with the material data of experience or as rationalists with mental data, they followed *this* goal with *these* means. But not only the means and end but also (what may seem stranger) the *results* of all different systems agree, despite their sharp differences, in one *essential determination*; and this is precisely what is significant for us. – Namely, let them begin from ever so different principles, seek the ground of the world on ever so different paths; in the end they all end up *on one point, where thinking stops*; they hit upon a very general something, whether of mental or material nature, which they declare cannot be investigated further and is therefore the ultimate ground or inner essence of the world. The entire manifoldness of the world is then reduced to or deduced from this final essence or ultimate ground; and then – the curtain falls. Whether this final and highest thing is the fluid element, as Thales thinks, or as Spinoza asserts, substance, or as Hegel claims, the dialectic of absolute spirit – *this* is common to them all: that they stop with this kind of most general something, do not analyze it further, and claim to explain *everything* from just this *one thing*. Even those philosophers like Democritus, Leibniz, and Herbart who seek the primal ground of the world not in a unity but in a multiplicity agree with them that they must stop with such an ultimate ground (consisting of a multiplicity). – If we allow each his respective ultimate ground, it may be that everything in the world can be strictly and consistently deduced from it, and everything may appear quite beautiful and uplifting. Reason has done its part, and reason can – go to bed. But that unfortunately is nothing! For we can always find curious questioners who would gladly like to know more, unwilling to recognize that ultimate ground as something final, and are even spiteful enough to call sleeping reason a *ratio ignava*[24] and the ultimate ground an *asylum ignorantiae*[25].

Usually one quickly finds relevant responders for these questioners, who refer the general something that previously passed as the ultimate ground back to something yet more general and thereby believe they have found the deeper ground and then rest on their laurels as well. In so doing they have obviously forgotten to note that they have *further extended* the border *but not eliminated* it, that their gain is completely relative, and that they will therefore quickly have to repeat the same process of questioning and answering. – This is equally true, as I have said, of all approaches to philosophy, of transcendental idealism as well as materialism. The latter, for example, regards its doctrine as quite plausible because it begins with *matter* as the most solid basis that everyone can grasp with his hands. But one only needs to ask, "Yes, but what is this matter?" and materialism is already at the end of its wisdom; for it becomes apparent that it only knows the *predicates* of matter, the sensible relations, while the subject (i.e., matter), which is supposed to be the ground for all sensory impressions as *ekmageion*[26], is in fact nothing but a completely unknown ultimate ground, an empty, thoroughly relative, concept, in short an empty shell. –

Because this process in the development of philosophy repeated itself again and again, human reason appeared to be like a child that would like to run through a rainbow and is astonished that he will never succeed in doing so. It in fact appeared increasingly, as Jacobi rightly noted, that "instead of approaching human beings, truth was fleeing us"[27]. Taken aback by this appearance, men (skeptics) have often arisen who want to bring philosophy to its senses (i.e., to reason[28]) by telling it that it will never achieve its goal. These men are like those who tell the child "the rainbow is too far." – In response to this, the child will certainly give up his effort, but it will not be persuaded of the impracticality of its enterprise. It could only become convinced when an expert informed it that the colored phenomenon is not something solid, not some curved figure affixed to the vaulted arch of the sky, but rather the reflection of the sun's rays in raindrops falling in front of them and that it must always escape us as long as the wall of rain hovers *in front of* our eyes and the sun stands *behind* us in the sky, etc. Given this information, a clever child would abandon its fruitless endeavors because it would then see that they are foolish and without success and that the object yearned for is something completely different from that for which it was held to be (namely, something solid, palpable) but is instead merely a visible relation. – Such an intelligent and informative man has now been found for the philosophical human spirit; unfortunately, he has admittedly not informed this spirit completely but only in part and thus not completely eradicated the foolishness, but he has given us a considerable piece of pure, genuine truth. This man is *Immanuel Kant*. –

Kant was first engaged with the *Leibniz-Wolffian* philosophy. In this philosophy, as in all previous ones, there is also something final and most universal that is not further justified. It treats this something, presupposing the principles of logic, under the heading "Ontology" and calls it "thing" (*ens*). By turning first to the Leibniz-Wolffians in order to teach them, he was naturally forced to speak their language to be intelligible to them, and he was also (and indeed primarily) forced to address the "thing." But because he was forced, in conformity with his principles, to explain each and every object as a correlate of a subject and the Wolffians understood by "thing" not such a correlate but something absolutely independent, general, and also empty, he called it the "thing in itself" in order to express this alleged independence even from a subject of cognition and its universal and necessary forms. Now, in the beginning he tolerated this "thing in itself" as a doctrine foreign in his philosophy. But after he had, in the initial sketches of his great thoughts, exhausted that boldness of thought that does not shy away from seeming paradoxical and is not afraid to say something that is a slap in the face to general opinion in order to triumph in the end, he initially lets the "thing in itself" run along in the background but subsequently (as we have seen above) concedes increasingly more validity to it instead of repudiating and forgetting it in accordance with Seneca's motto:

Etiam oblivisci interdum expedit.[29]

Instead of this, he rather expels it with increasing inconsistency from the forms of our intellect (space, time, and the categories) and in the process falls into the contradiction of representing the unrepresentable. This concept or rather the non-concept is once fixed by the word, and now the wooden piece of iron has been taken into the graces of the theory more and more for benefit of dear dogmatic humdrum until it at last became indispensable and reached apodictic certainty. In doing this, Kant took the final, ultimate step in denying the critical philosophy, just as Galileo denied the Copernican system of the world. – For not only was a false and unthinkable concept incorporated into his doctrine through the "thing in itself," but it also brought into question the insight reached in the Transcendental Aesthetic concerning universality and necessity, that is, the apriority of the forms of all intuition, space and time, which was really the epoch-making thought of his magnificent worldview. He thereby abandons his most important thought and confirms the words of Demosthenes: *pollakis dokei to phulaxai tagatha tou ktesasthai chalepoteron einai.*[30]

Everything he says about this non-concept he has smuggled in is obscure and contradictory. First it is "neither possible, nor impossible," then something that "must be thought," then "an X about which one can say nothing," etc. One can already conclude from this vacillating and unclear way of speaking that Kant has no pure conscience when it comes to this point:

Ce que l'on conçoit bien, s'énonce clairement.[31]
                                       Boileau

But now he has to wear it like a dogmatic pigtail, one that always annoys and brushes up against him, is always the subject of argument, and can never be argued away:

Er dreht sich rechts, er dreht sich links,
Der Zopf der hängt ihm hinten.[32]

And despite all this, none of Kant's successors have seen that this "thing in itself" is a foreign drop of blood in the critical philosophy[33], which would not have even been *mentioned* if its given principles had been developed consistently. *Fichte*, for example, seemingly eliminates it from his *Science of Knowledge* although it is only moved to another place. *Schopenhauer* believes that it is "a correct conclusion from false premises" that was only introduced in an illegitimate way, although it appears to be precisely the opposite: a false conclusion from two premises each of which taken by itself is correct.[34] The inference is the following:

> Everything conditioned is necessarily connected to something external to it as its cause.
> The empirical world of space and time is conditioned.
> Thus, etc.

As long as one takes a *dogmatic* point of view, this syllogism is completely right. But when one has gained the *transcendental* insight that space and time are universal and necessary forms of intuition given *a priori* and that, therefore, nothing exists *outside* and *everything* exists *in* them, one notices the sophism of the *fallacia falsi medii*[35]. The world in space and time is certainly "conditioned" but not by something *outside* of it (for there is nothing outside of it; it is everything), but rather by its *immanent* conditions and necessary forms: space, time, and the categories. Thus, had one defined the predicate "conditioned" more precisely, one would have noticed that it has a different sense in each of the premises and therefore that there is a *quaternio terminorum*[36]. – By the way, Kant himself has expressed this (if we ignore the mode of expression already affected by his mistake) when he says "we are never justified in making a leap from one member of the empirical series, whichever it may be, outside of the connections of sensibility, just as if these members were things in themselves [etc.]"[37] and "that the concepts of the understanding can never be of transcendental but always only of *empirical* use."[38] – –

The foregoing is the *historical* deduction, as we have called it above. Everyone is likely aware that the puzzle has not been solved by it and that we therefore cannot let ourselves be satisfied by it; and for this reason, we refer the reader to the *psychological* deduction, which should give us the key to, and provide complete insight into, the true origin of this remarkable mistake. Before we turn to these considerations, however, let us give ourselves a problem whose solution will be more important to our final goal than it may appear at first.

Namely, it is well known that, not long after the emergence of the critical philosophy, a series of dangerous attacks were undertaken against the *Critique of Pure Reason*, which, by mercilessly laying bare actual and alleged mistakes of Kant, did not destroy his reputation, but allowed the development of new philosophical doctrines, and in so doing hampered a genuinely thorough examination of this excellent system. One of the most astute of Kant's opponents, G.E. Schulze, in his *Aenesidemus*, turned himself against the master and his apostle Reinhold simultaneously and, because he believed that in addition to Kant's real and chief mistake he had also destroyed doctrines that are irrefutable, is partially to blame for the fact that Kant was thought so precipitously to have been conquered.[39] This has created a great deal of harm!

I will now endeavor to demonstrate that, to the extent they are of any importance, all of Aenesidemus' attacks are directed against the consequences of the "thing in itself" and that they collapse into nothing when directed against the pure and genuine critical philosophy. Therefore, do not think that the following section is an arbitrary intermezzo. It is an organic part of our examination.

The relevant passage is Aenesidemus page 108ff. The skeptic begins with a "Brief Account of Humean Skepticism." As well he should! For Kant was, as he himself says, "awakened from his dogmatic slumber" by Hume.[40]

There we read (page 108):

If it is true, Hume says, that our representations originate either directly or indirectly from the affective power of existing objects on our minds or to a certain extent consist of copies of originals found outside us and that what is real in our representations is founded on them, then in order to be real, the concepts of cause, effect, [etc.] must arise *directly or indirectly* from the impressions *on us* of objects existing outside of us.

The form of this inference is *hypothetical*. If the presupposition does not stand, the inference is invalid. Concerning the *content* of the presupposition, we know (something that Hume, of course, did not consider) that external objects exist only to the extent that given sensations are combined in intuition by the intellect's universal forms of combination (categories) and, in general, that everything objective is an inseparable correlate of the subject of cognition. Further, this connection of cause and effect is not a representation of an *object* but of a *relationship* among objects. Since the presupposition mentions the copies of *objects* in representations but not their connections and relations, the causal nexus does not belong here.

After it is required (page 109) that two things supposed to stand in the relation of cause and effect to each other, first, border and touch each other, second, are temporally contiguous to another and, third, stand in necessary connection to each other, we find (page 111) further: "But if we had cognition of the power of the object or, in other words, of that in virtue of which it is the cause of certain effects, then it would have to be possible for us to pronounce and determine immediately upon observation of an object what would follow from it; for the cognition of an inner constitution includes that cognition of everything that necessarily belongs to and constitutes a component of it." – In opposition to this, one must recall that the effect is not a "component" of the cause but is "determined" by it. As a pure concept, the causal nexus requires only *that* something follow; in order to know *what* will follow, we would have to have thoroughly complete cognition of all the governing conditions. Although it will be difficult for the latter ever to be the case, we are still convinced with each apprehended constellation of empirical conditions that something must proceed from it in the same way we are convinced that something must precede it as cause. This unconditional conviction, which we harbor whether we want to or not, is precisely what lends the causal nexus the character of a category. In assuming the universality and necessity of this relationship everywhere and always, although we only perceive the temporal succession, the *post hoc*, and never the necessity of succession, the *propter hoc*, we recognize that the causal nexus is supposed by and independent of all experience. – In conformity with the false supposition of existing objects independent of our representations we now find (page 115): "The necessary connection that belongs to the essence of cause and effect therefore does not exist in the objective objects but merely in the series of *our representations* of them."[41] But now it is precisely this summit of Humean doubt that is the point of departure for the triumph of the *critical philosophy*. For in proving that we can only speak of and know objects in representation but never those *outside of representation*, he restricts the use of the categories to the field of representation. – Bacon, who was certainly no idealist, still said: "*Omnes perceptiones, tam Sensus quam Mentis, sunt ex analogia Hominis, non ex analogia Universi. Estque Intellectus humanus instar specula inaequalis ad radios rerum, qui suam naturam Naturae rerum immiscent, eamque distorquet et inficit*"[42]. Thus, he at least recognizes the *collaboration* of our intellect in the development of representation of sensible objects. But I would still like to meet the man who had ever seen "originals" to the alleged "mirror images" in our intellects and could therefore verify that we are only given "copies" in representation and cognition. Indeed, he must have come to know this through a *supernatural revelation*, or he must have been successful in completing an action with respect to the mind that one in the popular way of speaking calls "going out of one's skin". –

In reference to the justification of the Humean views given on page 117–22, we can only repeat that the proposition "The category of causality is a synthetic judgment *a priori*" means exactly the same thing as "It is a necessary feature of my intellect to assume an effect for every cause and *vice versa*." Both propositions are tautological. And it will be difficult for anyone to dispute the content of the latter proposition, once he has understood its sense. A person whose ears are punched unexpectedly turns himself to the person who hit them and responds appropriately. How would he be able to do this if he did not in accordance with category of causality and on the basis of the spatial proximity, gestures, etc. of the person standing next to him assume that he was the cause of the affront he experienced? –

After thoughts that are partly ancillary and partly already dealt with are presented on pages 118–130, the elaboration of the chief question begins on page 130: "*Has the critique of reason really refuted Hume's skepticism?*"

"The answer to the question posed above will depend," so it says on page 131, "chiefly on our enquiring whether the grounds that Mr. Kant gives for the claim that necessary synthetic judgments originate in the mind and the inner source of representations itself, and constitute the form of experiential cognition, are such that David Hume could have held them to be sufficient and compelling." – We reply: It does not depend on whether David Hume, by recognizing the arguments of his opponent, declares himself to be defeated (we are really quite indifferent to this) but on whether *Kant* has evidently *refuted* him to the extent that he in general *wants to refute* him. Further, all Kant wanted to say by demonstrating the existence of synthetic *a priori* judgments was that all empirical cognition or experience (also the inner, psychological experience) is held together by certain general connections (categories) that cannot be explained through experience itself; however, it did not occur to him to claim that the mind (subject) was the *cause* of these categories or that it brought them forth, which Fichte was the first to do. The categories are functions of the intellect by which the subject *as well as* the object of cognition are conditioned. The apriority of the categories can be most simply presented as follows.

It is a fact and, indeed, as Aenesidemus page 122 expressly emphasizes, an *undeniable* fact that we have experiences. But experience would be impossible without the syntheses of cause and effect, etc. (categories). Consequently, the *existence* of categories is *at least* an *undeniable* fact too. Further, these categories can arise either from experience (internal or external), that is, be given *a posteriori* or not arise from experience but be presupposed by it as its conditions, that is, be given *a priori*. They do not arise from experience, as *Hume* was completely right to claim and *Aenesidemus* notes on page 110. Consequently, *the categories are given* a priori. QED

Aenesidemus is perpetually caught up in the mistake that "given *a priori*" means the same as "brought forth by the mind (subject)". This is why he now argues against Kant that while he presents human reason as "the source or real ground" of necessary synthetic judgments in our experience, "we merely *think* that the faculty of representation is the ground of these judgments but cannot infer from this that it really is this ground." All these attacks are punches in the air because the presupposition from which one begins is completely false and a misunderstanding of Kant's doctrine. –

Kant calls these forms of cognition, that are in fact present in all cognition, and without whose presence and existence all cognition and representing in general would fall apart and, indeed, be destroyed, and that therefore must be assumed in all experience, without in any way being able to know from whence it arises – *cognitions a priori*. There can be no talk of their *origin* or *real ground*. For *they are already there, given* as soon as we represent or cognize something. The intelligible I or subject of cognition moves perpetually in them, as in its element, like a fish in water. If it were at all possible that this subject of cognition could inexplicably come out of these intellectual forms (space, time, and the categories) like the fish comes out of the water into air, then that which somehow remained would be as completely foreign and unintelligible for the intellect as rays of light broken by air are to a fish. But *omne simili claudicat*[43]. Such a metamorphosis, such an emergence of the subject from its intellectual forms is an impossible case about which we should not even speak since it contradicts and insults the actual laws of our reason.

Although Aenesidemus stands far below the level of Kant's perspective on the world, he always presupposes that *Kant* wants to thoroughly refute *Hume* and demands on page 133 that the critique of reason should either prove the opposite of Hume's claims or reduce them to absurdity. But the critique of reason will not think to do this at all since it is of course in agreement with the best of Hume's claims. Hume says namely: "The necessary connection between cause and effect is not derived from experience". – "Entirely correct", Kant replies. – "Thus," Hume continues, "this connection is without meaning and must be denied in the object". "Absolutely not," replies the critique of reason. The causal nexus would be something merely subjective and without application to objects only if we acknowledged objects *outside* of our representations, as you have assumed in your *petitio principii*. But since it is really a contradiction to speak of objects besides those that are given in representation, your inferences do not follow". –

Further, when Kant is in general criticized for applying the categories in his thought in his discovery of them, this is just as absurd as if one wanted to criticize an optician for using his optic nerve, retina, pupils, etc. in his investigations.[44] Such an objection is only possible when one misinterprets Kant's doctrines in an empirical way and has no understanding of its *transcendental* perspective. And that the latter is indeed the case for *Aenesidemus* can be seen clearly first in the syllogism on page 140 that is alleged to be the summation of the critique of reason, which shows no recognition that for Kant "being empirical" and "being a representation" are the same and that cognitions *a priori* are the presupposition of all representing. This ignorance comes out almost comically in the naïve comment (page 182) "that indeed something which *at the present stage of culture* can only be thought in this one way (apriority of the categories), *might be able to be explained differently at a different later stage of culture.*"

The extent to which Aenesidemus is not up to the task of comprehending the Kantian depths can be seen further from the following passage (page 143): "It is incorrect that, as it is supposed in the critique of reason, the *consciousness of necessity* that accompanies certain synthetic propositions constitutes an *infallible* indication of its origin *a priori* from the mind. Notwithstanding their empirical origin, there is a consciousness of necessity connected with the real impressions of the external senses, e.g. those that even according to the critical philosophy are not supposed to arise from the mind with respect to their matter but from things outside of us. When an impression is present in us, we must recognize it as present". – Again the admonished misunderstanding of "*a priori*". For this "must be recognized as present" of the impression present in us is not an expression of metaphysical necessity and universality, but of empirical compulsion. But what compels us to do this? Have we perceived something compelling us? No! Rather, in accordance with the category of causality we presuppose an object that is the cause of the present impression in us and arrive in this way at the empirical necessity of compulsion. But what would remain from this "must," from this empirical necessity, if our representing were not governed and directed by this category, i.e., if we removed the metaphysical necessity of the *nexus causalis*? Nothing but the proposition: "As long as an impression is present to our consciousness, it is present to it." A sentence that with regard to its content is an empty, superfluous tautology and with regard to its form is *assertoric*, but not *apodictic*. – When the mathematician says, "All plane triangles that have ever existed, exist now, and will ever exist must have interior angles equal to two right angles, and the contrary is unthinkable" or the philosopher says, "All events in the world must have a cause and would be impossible without one," they carry within themselves with these propositions that inner conviction of the necessity of the same that cannot be taken from experience, but must be given *a priori*. But the individual impressions, e.g., the impression of the piece of paper lying before me, could fall away completely or be exchanged with others without thereby altering the nature of our consciousness and our intellect. This is the difference between cognitions *a posteriori*, whose content is not valid for the laws of cognition, and cognitions *a priori*, which cannot be thought away without simultaneously destroying the intellect – a difference that Kant discovered and Aenesidemus did not comprehend. –

Until now the skeptic has been completely mistaken because he directed his attacks against the incontrovertible truths of the critical philosophy. But he henceforth turns against the "thing in itself" and what he says against this is so correct and on target that we can even endorse it. "When," as it says in page 286, "the discussion concerns *things in themselves*, one understands by that in general a Something that is supposed to exist *realiter* outside of our representations, does not first arise with our representations or cease to exist with them, but would rather be there if we were not there at all. If one asks, e.g., whether a thing in itself is the ground of the representation of a tree that one sees while awake and in healthy mental condition, the question is not whether among the many other marks that, taken together, make up the representation of the tree, there is also the mark of a relation and a relationship of the representation to an object found outside of us or whether we do not have to represent the tree as something that is independent from us; but rather whether something is objectively present that stands in connection with the intuition of the tree and has determined the content of the intuition in such a way that if this Something were not as it is in itself and real outside of us (in the same way the representation of the tree is real in us) and did not stand in a real connection with our mind, we would not have any representation of the tree. The critical philosophy certainly claims that such things in themselves exist objectively and that they are the real ground of the content of our cognitions of experience. *However, it claims this without any justification and has through its doctrines concerning the nature and determination of the principles of pure reason completely destroyed any attempt to prove these claims.* For while it is true, as the critical philosophy claims to have proven apodictically, that cognition of the thing in itself completely outstrips all the abilities of our faculty of representation and that this thing is completely unknown to us with respect to what it objectively is, *the claim of this philosophy that this thing is a condition under which we have the possibility of possessing all cognitions of experience simply makes no sense because, in order to be able to claim that things in themselves are the ground of the representations in our minds, one must at least know that things in themselves exist* realiter *and that they can be the cause of something*. When one supposes further that the principle of causality may not be applied to things in themselves but has validity only in relation to that which as experience is merely subjectively present in us (as the critical philosophy claims to have completely shown), the possibility of presenting the connection of certain parts of our cognition with things that do not belong to this is thereby given up; *and if the principle of causality is invalid beyond experience, it is a misuse of the laws of the understanding when one applies the concept of* **cause** *to something that is supposed to be beyond our experience and completely independent of it.* Therefore, although the critical philosophy does not explicitly deny that things in themselves exist and are causes of the matter of empirical cognition, *it must, in virtue of its own principles, actually deny all reality and truth to the supposition of such a transcendental cause of the matter of our empirical cognition; and not only the origin of the matter of empirical cognition but also the [transcendental] reality of this cognition (or its actual relationship to something beyond our representations) are, according to its own principles, completely uncertain and for us* = x." The last words of this passage (which, although we cannot approve of its *tendency*, we adopt completely with respect to its *content*) should have been formulated more sharply by writing "unthinkable and absurd" in place of "uncertain and for us = x". –

The goal of this episode (if one wants to call it that) has herewith been accomplished. We now pick up the thread of our earlier investigation again. –

If it is clear from what has gone before that Kant contradicted the true spirit of his own doctrine by supposing a thing in itself that existed outside of the boundaries (that is, the necessary and universal forms) of our intellect (space, time and the categories); and if we have further seen the historical conditions, the antecedents in the order of development of philosophical systems, to which this "thing in itself" owes its illegitimate existence; and if we have finally come to the conviction that this non-concept has above all others given justified cause for attacks against the Kantian philosophy and that, when it is removed, this philosophy stands unrefuted and irrefutable in its chief propositions – a last question still remains, the answer to which will be of essential interest to us and at the same time, through consideration of the entire problem, provide us with a deep insight into our mental nature. This question is:

What are the subjective, psychic conditions under which Kant was able to arrive at the supposition of his "thing in itself"?

The answer to this question will contain the previously promised deduction *a priori* of the "thing in itself". –

On the basis of the principles of the critical philosophy developed at the beginning of the chapter, we came to the following results: The subject and object of cognition stand in thoroughgoing relation to each other and are inseparable factors and necessary correlates of cognition. Therefore, there is neither something independently subjective (I in itself), nor is there something independently objective (thing in itself). Subject and object are connected to each other through the universal and necessary forms of representing and cognizing: space, time, and the categories. It is within the domain of these forms that the intellect moves and the world, the cosmos, develops; a *different* domain is not only *unknown* but also *unthinkable*. How, we ask, is it still possible that an intellect so constituted strives to go beyond its necessary forms, given that it cannot at all represent any others? This is the question or rather the puzzle. Here too we will begin with the most universal, simple, and general facts as Kant and Socrates are in the habit of doing.[45] –

If you go walking with a child in the fresh air, the child will direct this and that question to you about the many objects it notices. For to him the vast, manifold world is not yet, as it is to us, an old acquaintance whose peculiarities one has, if not become acquainted with, at least learned to observe neutrally through many years of interaction. For example, the child sees the great disk of the full moon gleaming red just over the horizon. Since it has never perceived this appearance, it will ask: "What is that?" You will answer, "That is the moon", and it will accept this instruction with child-like wonder. – Or someone rides quickly across a stone path in front you in such a way that the impact of the horse's hooves make sparks fly up from the stone. The child asks, "Whence does that arise?", and you will answer, "That arises because iron sprays glowing pieces when it is stuck on stone". – In response to these questions, the following happens in the soul of the child: the low-hanging, larger than usual, red moon is identified with the high-hanging, smaller, silver moon through the common name. Thus "the moon" has acquired a wider meaning for the child and has become the common owner of the state previously known to him as well as the one he now perceives, a substance which partakes in or is capable of different and changing properties. In short, the *category of substantiality is applied* in the soul of the child to the moon in relation to those different appearances or states. – In the second case it has learned a universal rule that sparks arise from the meeting of stone and iron, that the stone and iron are related to the sparks as a cause is to its effect, that is, that the *category of causality has come into application* in relation to this event.

Now the more awakened the child becomes, the less it is satisfied by these initial answers. It will, for example, confused about the different ways the moon appears, further ask what grounds these differences or even what the moon really is. Or in the other case, it will want to know how it happens that the iron is able to strike off glowing pieces of stone and what kind of hidden essential parts and properties lie hidden in the stone and iron, etc. – By considering these mental activities in the soul of the child, you are able to take a look into your own intellectual past, to the genesis of your own level of mental formation, and become aware *that you have reached the height of your total state of knowledge*[46] *by means of a step-wise increasing exchange of interrelated questions and answers*. Certainly, a person at our level of development tends with age to ask fewer questions (whose *actual goal is instruction*) to other people but seeks answers all the more in books, his *own understanding* of the *immediate objects of nature and art*. But all mental development is at its core nothing more than that exchange of questions and the finding of answers[47], and the more quickly, tenaciously, eclectically, and tirelessly this asking of questions and finding of answers occurs in a subject, the more intelligent that person should be regarded.

We should now note that, on analogy with the child's two previous questions (as long as we are dealing exclusively with *objective certainty* and *theoretical cognition*), two things are always asked: "What is that?" and "Whence does it come?" Translated into the philosophical manner of speaking, this means *that the human intellect moves perpetually in the categories of substantiality and causality*.[48] I am here prepared for the objection that one cannot introduce necessary and universal forms of the understanding (synthetic *a priori* judgments) by empirical-inductive means. However, it is not at all our intention to provide a *justification of the doctrine of the categories*. The question of the categories is here, as we will see, of secondary interest; it is only a means to lead us to an answer to our primary question.[49] What interests us here is only this: (1) that the categories, as universal synthetic forms of cognition, are not extended without motivation from the subject to the object, but rather that they are first set in motion, at first unconsciously, by the need for cognition and knowledge, and then brought concretely to consciousness only gradually by practice and habit, until they are finally separated and grasped as abstract concepts from live representation; (2) that regardless of the motive pursued by the question they come to intuitive validity in the answer; but (3) that abstract cognition is not the first fact of the mind, but rather that it is awakened and brought forth from the domain of immediate representation, the ineffable sensation.

The question therefore is prior to the act of cognition that gives us the answer. In what does this question consist? When someone directs a question to us about some point, we must presuppose that he is uncertain about the point and further that he finds this uncertainty uncomfortable and wishes to drive it out with certainty. If he formulated the result of these subjective feelings in abstract representations, in words, the question arises with which he turns to the place where he expects an answer, regardless of whether it is a human being, a physical experiment or some other thing. It is not important where he turns, but that in all cases of cognition a question is advanced which is then followed by an answer that satisfies it. – When we isolate and conceptually analyze this psychic process that should be regarded as the immediate ground of cognition, the following elements emerge:

1) The feeling of uncertainty (Socratic *agnoia*)
2) Uneasiness about this (Platonic *thaumazein*)
3) Striving for elimination of the cause of uneasiness by attainment of knowledge (*philosophia*)

From these arise the formulated *question*. *This is the source of all cognition*.

Now this manner of cognition, which one tends to call philosophy, has the peculiar feature that the objects that it asks for and strives to cognize are the most universal ideas and not relatively indifferent particulars; further that it aims for the inner unity of the world-whole, the cosmos, and that therefore the aforementioned psychic process occurs on a large scale. – This is the one truth, which I do not at all pretend to have presented for the first time; but no one has yet to clearly and concisely grasp, think, express, and analyze it in all its conceptual particulars. Plato said, *"mala gar philosophou touto to pathos, to thaumazein*[50]; *Kant* gave practical reason "primacy" in relationship to theoretical reason or the intellect; *Fichte*, *Schelling*, and *Schopenhauer* regard the intellect as something secondary. In all of these, the truth resonates darkly, one-sidedly, and in half measure like an incomplete echo; but nowhere has this been followed to its ground; nowhere has it been shown how it is that the mind proceeds from the immediate and dumb silence of intuitive representing to cognition in general, to abstraction and thought. But we have seen that the occasion for this development is given by the aforementioned psychic process, the immediate expression of which is the *question*. No answer (i.e., cognition) is possible without a proceeding question; and without it the entire manifoldness of inner and outer experience (microcosm and macrocosm) would pass us by indifferently, as on a mirror that reflects nothing; indeed, we would not even, as can easily be shown, be able to arrive at self-consciousness. – The *maieutike techne* of Socrates in his philosophical conversations and Plato's entire dialogical representation, in particular the metaphorical claim that all learning is recollection (*mathesis anamnesis*), are also founded on this. By expecting everyone to ask himself in thought the questions directed to him, the sage in these dialogues takes over the role of the questioner and promotes the thought process of the student (which, as we have said, consists of a series of questions and answers strung together into a monologue) by using an appropriate sequence of questions to neither let him tire as time passes nor lose his direction so that the obtuseness and obscurity of thought are simultaneously eliminated and it is demonstrated to the student *ad oculos*[51], how he is able to produce thoughts from within himself of which he previously had not the slightest inkling by purposeful and persistent exercise of his monologue in thought. –

If we set aside the relatively indifferent questions of daily life, which for the most part arise not from speculative, but from practical, motives and are of ephemeral interest, and consider only those that are asked purely for the sake of cognition and knowledge and answered in science, we discover that there are only two most universal (purely theoretical) questions, which have already been directed to us by the simplicity of a childlike mind, namely:

1) What is that?
2) Whence does it come?

By trying to answer these questions completely, theoretical reason will be driven from level to level, from particular to universal; it seeks an ever higher "what" and an ever deepening "whence." It is precisely this that Kant expresses as follows: "When the condition is given, so too is the entire series of conditions subordinated to one another," and "the proper principle of reason in general is: to find the unconditioned of the conditioned cognitions of the understanding, with which the unity of the understanding is made complete".[52] It is in precisely this respect that *Schopenhauer* neither understood the *Kantian philosophy* nor explained nor even improved it but rather unjustifiably scolded it.[53]

But what is characteristic of the theoretical intellect is that, when any domain of knowledge has been investigated and cognized by an exchange of questions and answers, it *ultimately does not stop with an answer but always with more questions.* – Let us observe this in an example. There is a tree in front of me. I first observe it simply as a sum of its sensible parts and properties from the side of "what" and as something developed entirely from dispositions and seeds from the side of the "whence." But this will hardly satisfy me in the long run; I can ask further questions and investigate more deeply; I will be able to follow the physical, chemical biological laws, powers, processes that are active in this product of nature and, in addition to the seed from which it arose, have been active in the incalculable past. But even if I were to succeed in attaining exhaustive insight into the elements and the inner workings, whose product and whole appear to me to be this tree – would I be able to satisfy myself with this? Would I here not, rather, after the long exhausting scientific investigations, again fall precisely into that feeling of uncertainty, the *agnoia* and the *thaumazein*, which is the source of the question, the subjective motive of all cognition? Demanding that the mind stand still will not help here; it drives the mind onward from question to answer, and it would remain with a question even when it knew that no answer was to be expected. For the dictum of Bacon applies in this respect as well: *Incogitabile est, ut sit aliquid extremum aut extimum Mundi, sed quasi necessario occurrit, ut sit aliquid ulterius.*[54] – It is obvious that my investigation will stop here with the question: "Yes, but what is the deeper ground, the higher unity that connects all of these physical, chemical, biological powers, laws, and processes and that forces them to unite for the production of this individual tree? How does it bear fruit, out of which things identical to it can arise? – And finally – what is the whole, the unending, sublime nature, of which this tree is an unimportant part, and how does it act?" – If it is honest with itself, the theoretical intellect must here shrug its shoulders and admit: "*Non possumus!*[55] I don't know the answer!" –

It is this way throughout all intellectual pursuits and in the sciences in particular. Opticians, for example, assume certain undulations of aether as an explanation of the visible sensible qualities of light and colors. Here one must first consider that the undulations of the aether, even if they were proven, would not be *alone* sufficient to explain the existence of these qualities in sensation but that the *eye* as correlate must be added to this, without which the vibrations of the aether would never give rise to "color." It is only from the cooperation of the eye and the vibrations of the aether that blue, red, light, dark, etc. would arise; and if one were to take away either the eye or the hypothetical vibration of the aether, these qualities would disappear into *nothing*. Let us proceed. These vibrations of parts of the aether and the aether itself, which one assumes as the correlate to the subjective organ, the eye, in visual appearances – *have I perceived them?* No! Rather, I have *added them in thought*. But suppose it would be possible at some higher stage of science to demonstrate the undulation of aether. What fundamentally would be gained? The question of the "what" and "whence" would immediately arise anew, and I would then endeavor to find a new hypothetical correlate as a possible answer to it. *The investigation would always end with a question.* Let us further consider the following: If instead of the eye, which is an organ for visual appearances, we had another organ with the ability to perceive *magnetic powers* in immediate sensation, that is, if we had a *magnetic eye* instead of a *light eye*, the sensible world would change entirely. Light and color qualities would disappear, and in their place a series of different sensations and qualities would appear, the nature of which we now have no conception. And so we stand in the end again and again by the questions we asked in the beginning: "What is that really? Whence does this totality arise?" In this way, the intellect digs and seeks increasingly deeper causes, more universal substrata, helps itself with hypotheses and endeavors to confirm them – and then:

Encheiresin naturae nennt's die Chemie
Spottet ihrer selbst und weiß nicht wie. (Faust I, lines 1940–1)[56]

But finally when we have now come with Kant to the deep insight that space, time, and the categories are functions of the intellect and that the entire world, this empirically real world, is not something independent, but is rather the inseparable correlate of the subject of cognition, then this uncertainty, this astonishment will put the quickest and most embarrassing end to the question. The known world will then appear like a thoroughgoing puzzle to us; and it will seem to us, as *Arthur Schopenhauer* aptly puts it, that we are like "someone who, although he doesn't know how, has come across a completely unknown group of people, whose members each present themselves as the friend and relative of the person they are next to and, in this way, introduce themselves sufficiently to him. In the meantime, as he assures he is pleased to meet the next person, the question is always on his lips: How the devil did I come across this group?"[57]

In short, we see that *our knowledge can only end with an unanswered question*. Despite all the insight we have acquired, we find ourselves in the end, after so much and such long questioning, investigating, answering, cognizing, again and again in the place we began: in the *agnoia* or, as the astute theological skeptic *Nicholas of Cusa* aptly called it, in the "*docta ignorantia.*"[58] The question is the end of knowledge, just as it was its beginning.

But when we are not honest with ourselves, when we do not admit our inability to find ultimate answers and want to create for the questioner the illusion that we could identify something positive as the deepest ground of the cosmos acting and expanding in time and space, then our intellect creates an X that is not spatial, not temporal, not ordered and cognizable through the categories and is thus not capable of being represented at all by us, a thing that we do not recognize as a thing – in short, a *"thing in itself."* –

There we have it! The "thing in itself" is nothing less than the absurdity[59] that the intellect, which terminates in questions dreams up for itself in the end, an empty, unending grasping for some fantasy that eternally retreats from the human spirit's desire for knowledge, like the apple from the mouth of Tantalus.[60]

In general one can make the absurdity of this empty pseudo-concept clear (to use a jocular analogy) by observing that by using the thought of the thing in itself as the condition of that through which the abstract intellect itself is first *kat' energeian*[61] conditioned, *the intellect emerges as its own grandfather*. But if we look closer at the conceptual elements of this, I ask myself: *What is one supposed to understand by something that is neither spatially extended, nor is found at any location; neither lasts for a period of time, nor is either present, past, or future; nor, finally, is either the effect of a cause, nor the cause of an effect?* Such a thing is nothing less than a *knife without a blade or handle*. That is, it is not an *empty* concept but *no concept at all*. –

Had Kant even begun to seriously analyze this pseudo-concept instead of always groping around it, he would have had to discard it as we have done here. In this way, he verifies what he himself said: "I note that it is not at all unusual, either in common discussion or in writings, when one compares the thoughts that an author has made concerning his work, to understand him even better than he himself did *because he did not sufficiently determine his concepts and hence at times spoke or thought contrary to his intentions*"[62] That fits perfectly! –

Incidentally, Kant was dimly aware that his doctrine was not on sure footing here. This is why it did not occur to him to deduce the *categorical imperative* from the "thing in itself"; rather he allows it to enter with a flash as a *deus ex machina* from the world of feeling without introduction. This is also why he calls the "thing in itself" a *negative* concept, a border concept, and at first acts as if he only wanted to use it "to limit the pretensions of sensibility".[63] But apart from the fact that this "negative concept" subsequently contains a very positive one, *the final and ultimate goal of our intellect cannot be a concept at all but only an unanswered question, an unsolved puzzle*. From a *concept*, one can always move inferentially into the domain beyond; but not from a *question*. Indeed, strictly speaking, the intellect may not (one should say) even formulate a question when it stands on its eternal borders (space, time, and the categories) because it would have to be convinced *a priori* that the question is idle and unanswerable; it must remain in *agnoia* and *thaumazein*. In fact, this is what it will do. It is Kant's great, disastrous mistake that at this decisive point he has insulted the nature of the human intellect and his own doctrines. –

As one can see, the *historical* and *psychological* deductions of Kant's great mistake meet in the end. In the former, we found inductively in all systems the concept of a final, most universal ground of the world that is always pushed further back and is for this reason empty, and deduced from this concept that the critical philosophy arrived at the *transcendental non-concept* of the "thing in itself" by supposing this *empty concept* after it had correctly fixed the final and ultimate limit of human cognition in cognition *a priori*. On the other hand, we have now inductively found the final subjective agent of cognition in the psychic process of questioning and deduced from it how the intellect, when it extends these questions transcendentally beyond the borders of its ability, deceives itself with precisely this "thing in itself" as an alleged answer.

Our problem has now been solved. On the one hand, the conditions under which Kant arrived at this inconsistency have been completely developed; on the other, the *limit of a properly consistent critical philosophy* has been presented, and in this way the criterion for the evaluation of his predecessors has been provided. Nevertheless, we must not fail to add a few short remarks, which will complete our investigation insofar as they will to a certain extent identify the metaphysical location of the abstract intellect.

Cognition begins and ends with a question. Now for the abstract intellect a question is certainly something unsatisfying, unfinished, *even negative*. But the human mind consists so little in purely abstract cognition and reflection that something unmediated in objective sensation and subjective feeling must rather precede it before it can come to questions, cognition, and abstract knowledge. But when the final, transcendental border-question forces the abstract intellect to declare itself bankrupt, this painful confession is foreign to *feeling*. For because it provides the occasion for the question, even for the final, ultimate question, but is also *toto genere* different from abstract cognition, it can find for itself, in the place where thought must doubt its possibility, a concept as answer, a *surrogate*, and give as it were a *felt answer*, which it is of course impossible to capture or think in words. – Thought there tries to grasp

was die Welt
Im Innersten zusammenhält.[64] (Faust I, lines 382–3)

But thought discovers that it is locked in time, space, and categories. *Feeling*, in contrast, finds inner contentment and reconciliation in something positive, ineffable, in something that cannot be thought or expressed but must be felt. Here it confronts, as it were, the *theos arretos*[65] of the Gnostics, i.e., that Thing of what is it said:

Ich habe keinen Namen
Dafür! Gefühl ist Alles.[66] (Faust I, lines 3455–6)

This is what is most proper and essential to human nature, the puzzle in our breast, the sanctum of our soul, that which finds its intelligible, symbolic expression in art and religion. It is the same thing that allows the abstract intellect to strive and wrestle for conceptual truth in philosophy that, on the other hand, always returns in the most glorious and profound works of art of the greatest minds. – It is that which in *Beethoven's* Ninth Symphony electrifies and invigorates our most inner being and – after the strained, desperate struggle for reconciliation has degenerated into a wild, fruitful dissonance in the last movement – first in quiet, deep tones forebodingly permeates us, then rising and growing in ever fuller chords lifts us up, until finally the struggling soul triumphantly and with titanic power shakes off the earthly burden and in limitless, heavenly, transcendent jubilation moves to the celebration of eternal world peace. – It is that which *Rafael*, after lifting the curtain before the needy gaze of humanity, allows to shine forth in the Sistine Madonna, in the glory of an anticipated beyond, in the holy, timid eyes of the virgin. It is that which *Goethe's* Faust *everywhere* seeks in vain, what he could find neither in the realm of thought nor in the lower spheres of sensual pleasure, and what is finally, after a long life's struggle, sung to him in a calming and reconciliatory way:

Alles Vergängliche
Ist nur ein Gleichniß;
Das Unzulängliche
hier wird's Ereigniß
Das Unbeschreibliche
hier ist's getan.[67] (Faust II, lines 12,104–9)

Here we can find what we seek: not in *concepts*, not by means of the *abstract intellect*. – When we deepen ourselves into one of these masterpieces, the joyful, reconciliatory light appears to our inner gaze; – then the hasty curiosity of enjoyment fades and disappears in front of the deep, hallowed seriousness of understanding; aesthetic pleasure becomes ethical work. For we feel that this most deep something has been expressed, for which our most inner being longs, that comforts and lessens our longing, about which our abstract intellect investigates and queries in vain, because it is only something felt, not effable or even conceivable. It is precisely for this reason that we feel ourselves lifted after the enjoyment of such a masterpiece, or better still, more purified – and then subdued again – a mood of the soul that seems oddly to be a mixture of bliss and sorrow because we are on the one hand really internally satisfied, but on the other feel painfully inhibited by our inability to *cognize* that which we enjoy, that is, to understand it by using the medium of the questioning intellect.

The abstract intellect must silence itself here. It stands there helpless with its question to the world-spirit. It has the question, but as for the answer, the world-spirit speaks a language different from it. Should it ever give him an intelligible answer, it would say:

Du gleichst dem Geist, den Du begreifst,
Nicht mir![68] (Faust I, 512–13)

But one should certainly protect oneself from a so-called "philosophy of feeling" *á la Jacobi, Baader, etc.* Philosophy should *cognize* and *know*; and feeling is not the organon of cognition. Cognition has that as its object which can be represented abstractly, grasped with concepts, thought, therefore always something universal. Feeling will be satisfied by the ineffable, nameless, absolutely individual. But a "cognizing feeling" or a "philosophy of feeling" is analogous to a "listening eye" or a "seeing ear". –

The Kantian "thing in itself" is the failed attempt of the abstract intellect to find a concept that would be the transcendent answer to an unanswerable question, where we can only be helped by another kind of satisfaction of feeling that eliminates the occasion for our question. When the intellect makes these attempts to realize this unthinkable idea, it falls into the contradiction of wanting to think the unthinkable – it commits a *metabasis eis allo genos* in the eminent sense. –

This is the significance and fate of the Kantian "thing in itself."

Notes

1 This is chapter 1 of Liebmann's *Kant und die Epigonen* [*Kant and His Epigones*]. Stuttgart: Carl Schober, 1865, pp. 20–69. This is the first translation into English, translated by Brian A. Chance. – Ed.

2 What follows is Liebmann's summary of the Aesthetic. In the original, it is presented with half-indention, which makes it look misleadingly like a quote. I have added the "★ ★ ★" to make the separation from the main part of the text clear. – Trans.

3 *Herbart* claims (*Psychology as Science*, § 114) that the *Kantian* proof rests on a *quaternio terminorum*. Kant argues as follows:
What experience teaches never contains the mark of necessity.
Space and time are necessary representations.
Therefore, space and time are not learned from experience.
According to Herbart, "necessity" has a different meaning in each of the premises. Space and time are necessary only insofar as one cannot think them away; but this is true only because they are what first make the *corporeal world* possible, which is actual for us, and because one must always represent that which is the condition of the possibility of something actual as necessary. But for this reason, the major premise is false. For in *this* sense *experience* certainly teaches us something *necessary*. In response to this objection, one should reply as follows. First, that one *declares* the conditions of the possibility of something we recognize as actual as *necessary* is not something experience *teaches* us, but rather something *we demand according to the subjective laws of thought*. Second, space and time are not necessary only because the corporeal world would be impossible without them but *primarily* because our *own intelligence, the subject of cognition, my own ego* would be impossible without them. It is not only that we cannot represent *Nothing* without space and time; we cannot represent *at all* without them; they are perpetually present in all mental activities, etc. In short, if one wants to bring the Kantian argumentation into the form of a syllogism, it would be the following:
Everything that I cannot think away from the subject of cognition without simultaneously destroying the subject is essential to it, that is, *a priori*.
I cannot think away space and time from the subject of cognition without simultaneously destroying it.
Therefore, etc.
Since this entire doctrine has recently been attacked by V. *Kirchmann* (*Philosophy of Knowledge*, vol. 1, pp. 418–420), and H. *Lotze* (*Microcosm: Ideas for a Natural History and History of Mankind*. Vol. 3, p. 485) is at least not satisfied with the proof, we now refer to the argument that one finds on pp. 24 and 31 of the first edition of the *Critique of Pure Reason*. This should destroy any doubt.

4 These set-off a similar paraphrase. – Trans.

5 *Critique of Pure Reason*, p. 253. We always cite according to the *first edition*.

6 Ibid., p. 246.

7 Ibid., pp. 48, 49, 246, 253.

8 Ibid., p. 42. Cf. *Prolegomena to Any Future Metaphysics* (1783), p. 62.

9 *Critique of Pure Reason*, pp. 370, 371, 379.

10 Ibid., p. 383.

11 Ibid., pp. 371, 378.

12 Schopenhauer, *The World as Will and Representation*, 3rd. edition vol. 1, p. 515; Fischer, *History of Recent Philosophy*, vol. 3, preface p. XIV, p. 278. Cf. Ueberweg, *De priore et posteriore forma Kantianea criticae rationis purae* (Berolini: Typis Mittler et Filii, 1861).

13 Kant, *Critique of Pure Reason*, second edition p. 274.

14 By degrees – Ed.

15 *Critique of Pure Reason*, second edition, p. 49 (Liebmann's emphasis).

16 "Here see that you grasp with profundity what does not fit into man's brain." – Ed.

17 Not a direct quotation. – Tr.

18 Kant clearly becomes *transcendent* in this passage (p. 539) as well by applying the category of causality, which according to his own utterly correct explanation is only applicable to spatial and temporal objects, to this unrepresentable, supersensible, "thing in itself" or *noumenon*.
19 The quotation has some paraphrase. – Tr.
20 "Shamed be he who thinks evil of it." – Ed.
21 *Critique*, p. 225 and p. 272 in the second edition.
22 Ibid., p. 378.
23 "This is enough for the sage." – Ed.
24 Lazy reason – Ed.
25 Asylum of ignorance – Ed.
26 Imprint – Ed.
27 F.H. Jacobi, *David Hume: A Dialogue* (Breslau: Gottl. Loewe, 1787), p. 79.
28 *zu Vernunft bringen* – Trans.
29 "It is sometimes expedient to forget." Also rendered as "etiam oblivisci quod sis interdum expedit" ("it is sometimes better to forget what one knows"). – Ed.
30 "It seems that good things are often harder to keep, than to get." Demosthenes, *Olynthiac*, I.23 – Ed.
31 "What can be conceived well can be clearly formulated." – Ed.
32 "He turns right, he turns left, but the pigtail, it always hangs behind him." From "Tragische Geschichte," a poem by Adalbert von Chamisso (1781–1838), German poet and botanist. – Trans.
33 Schleiermacher, in a most interesting little essay on the Spinozistic system ("A Short Account of the Spinozistic System", in *History of Philosophy*. Berlin: Reimer, 1839, p. 283 ff.), comes close to what has been proven by us here, but does not completely reach it. In particular, in comparing *Spinoza* with *Kant*, he comes to the conclusion that the noumenon or thing in itself arose because of "an inconsistent residue of old dogmatism" in the critical philosophy. But this apt, justified scolding is not pursued far enough to provide occasion to lay bare the truly critical foundational thoughts and to repudiate the fundamentally false and misleading views that, unfortunately, from this mistake of Kant's have overgrown the sprouting seed of truth and threaten to suffocate it like weeds. Schleiermacher was afraid to grasp the dangerous nettle forcefully, suffocate them, pull them out, and throw them away as we have now done. He was satisfied to explain "that *Kant* in this piece is *mutatis mutandis* Spinozist," but while the nagging inconsistency of the critical philosophy is touched by this, it is certainly neither explained nor rejected. Thus, the attack lacks its force and the weapon its point.
34 Schopenhauer, *The World as Will and Representation*, vol. 1, p. 597.
35 Fallacy of false disjunction – Ed.
36 Fallacy of four terms – Ed.
37 *Critique of Pure Reason*, p. 563.
38 Ibid., p. 246.
39 *Aenesidemus oder über die Fundamente der von H. Prof. Reinhold in Jena Elementarphilosophie. Nebst einer Verteidigung des Skeptizismus gegen die Anmaßungen der Vernunftkritik.* 1792.
40 Kant, *Prolegomena*, p. 13.
41 Not a direct quotation, italics added – Tr.
42 "All perceptions, those of the senses as well as the mind, are from analogy with the human being, not from analogy with the universe. And indeed, the human intellect is comparable to a mirror that is unequal to the rays of things and which [for that reason] admixes *its* nature to the nature of things, thereby distorting and influencing [them]." Bacon, *New Organon*, I, 41 (italics added by Liebmann – Ed.).
43 "No simile runs on all fours." – Ed.
44 Here is the place for Hegel's comparison of Kant with a scholastic philosopher who "sets about to learn how to *swim before he dares to go in the water*" (Hegel, *Encyclopedia of the Philosophical Sciences*. 1827, Introduction, §10). This false, utterly inaccurate analogy has already been given its due by a competent person. Cf. Kuno Fischer, *History of Recent Philosophy*, vol. 3, p. 21.
45 "His own—that is, the Socratic—method of conducting a rational discussion was to proceed step by step from one point of general agreement to another," Xenophon. *Memorabilia* IV. 6.15

46   *Gesamtbildung* – Ed.
47   One only needs consider Plato's *Theaetetus*, so important for the theory of knowledge, which will not become outdated as long as people think. There we find the following noteworthy passage: "Socrates: Do you define thought as I do? Theaetetus: How do you define it? Socrates: As the talk which the soul has with itself about any subjects which it considers. You must not suppose that I know this that I am declaring to you. But the soul, as the image presents itself to me, when it thinks, is merely conversing with itself, asking itself questions and answering, affirming and denying." *Theaetetus* 189–190. Cf. *Sophist*, 263.
48   A third question is "To what end?" The answer to this contains the concept of a purpose. But because this is a category that belongs in the domain of the practical, we will set it aside.
49   A deduction or justification of the categories lies entirely outside the domain of this essay, which has only a critical goal. Parenthetically, this goal is the following. What Kant understood as apriority is the conviction of necessity of these universal syntheses given independently of experience, and what gives them this character of "category" has already been noted. But all synthesis rests on intuitions. Now space and time are given as universal forms of intuition. Inert coexistence lies in the character of space, and in time lies restless, flowing succession. In their combination, the following cases are the most common: I seek either something spatial that persists necessarily through temporal change – *substantiality*; or I seek the necessary temporal succession in what persists spatially – *causality*.
50   "Wonder is the only wonder of philosophy." *Theaetetus* 155d. Cf. Aristotle, *Metaphysics* 1.2: "It is through wonder that men now begin and originally began to philosophize."
51   "to his eyes" – Ed.
52   *Critique of Pure Reason*, p. 307.
53   Arthur Schopenhauer claimed in his critique of Kantian philosophy that Kant was incorrect here and that "the principle of *sufficient* reason always demands only the completion of the next condition, *never the completion of the series*". *World as Will and Representation*, vol. 1, p. 572. This claim sounds more or less like someone who wanted to say: "In order to stand at this height above the ground, the architrave only needs a capital". This is a short-sighted, or at least an incomplete manner of expression. The architrave and capital would both collapse if the latter were not supported by the pedestal and it again by the ground. One might formulate the above proposition of Kant's better as follows: "It is a postulate of reason, that it *fully* find the series of other-conditioning states in a *regressus in indefinitum*, whose result is the present, to the extent it is able to extend its reach backwards". But he who in accordance with Schopenhauer's method would always be satisfied with the *next* condition would indeed be *unbelievably limited*, a *true monstrosity of small-mindedness*.
54   "It is unthinkable that there be something at the end of the world or outside it, which nonetheless exists upon the condition that there be something farther out." *New Organon*, I.48.
55   "We cannot." – Ed.
56   "Chemistry calls it *encheiresin naturae* [grasp of nature], mocks itself and knows not how." – Ed.
57   Schopenhauer, *World as Will and Representation*, vol. 1, p. 117.
58   Learned ignorance – Ed.
59   "Unding" (literally, a "non-thing") – Ed.
60   Sensing this, the Platonic Socrates says: "We graciously conceded this point, without considering that it is impossible for anyone to somehow know those things that one does not know at all." (Charmides, 175c)
61   "Due to its potentiality" – Ed.
62   *Critique of Pure Reason*, p. 314 [Liebmann's emphasis].
63   *Critique of Pure Reason*, p. 255.
64   "What holds together the world in its innermost heart." – Ed.
65   "The ineffable God." – Ed.
66   "I have no name for it. Feeling is everything." – Ed.
67   "All that must disappear
Is but a parable;
What lay beyond us, here
All is made visible;

Here deeds have understood
Words they were darkened by;
Eternal Womanhood
Draws us on high." (Trans. David Luke, Liebmann omits the last 2 lines). – Ed.

68 "You are in the image of the spirit that you grasp, not in mine." – Ed.

Introduction

Friedrich Albert Lange (1828–1875)

FRIEDRICH ALBERT LANGE'S LIFE WAS SHORT BUT EVENTFUL. He was as much a philosopher as a pedagogue, journalist, and social activist. Born in 1828 in Wald close to the industrial town of Solingen, the Langes moved to Zurich in 1840, where Lange's father, a minister, took up a professorship in theology, replacing David Friedrich Strauß, who had been removed from his position due to his infamous book *Das Leben Jesu* [*The Life of Jesus*]. From 1847 till 1851, Lange studied theology, philosophy, classical philology, and, later, mathematics in Bonn, where he finished with a dissertation on "*Quaestiones metricae.*" In 1855, he took the Habilitation on a pedagogical topic and was a reader in pedagogy for three years, already then exerting a significant influence as a teacher. In 1858, he switched to the Gymnasium in Duisburg, mainly for financial reasons. It was at this time that his interest in political and economic issues arose. Due to reprimands from the school district, he quit his job in 1862 and became active as a journalist, founding a press himself and joining local unions. At this time, he began publishing articles dealing with the fate of the working class. As a founder of the *Neue Rheinische Zeitung,* he attempted to recruit Karl Marx and Friedrich Engels as writers, though he resisted their Marxist brand of socialism (more on this below). Frustrated by the Prussian government and its lagging reforms, he accepted a position as a Gymnasium teacher once again in Switzerland. There, in Zurich, he took his Habilitation in philosophy and in 1870 became professor of "inductive philosophy." Despite suffering from colon cancer beginning in 1870, he accepted a position at the University of Marburg in 1872, where he taught with great success, despite severe pain, until his untimely death at age 47 in 1875. Since he facilitated the hiring of Hermann Cohen to be his successor in Marburg, he is often seen as the founder of the Marburg School, which is true only from an historical standpoint. Lange's philosophical interests remained mostly in the realm of social-political philosophy. His most famous books were *Die Arbeiterfrage in ihrer Bedeutung für Gegenwart und Zukunft* [*The Question of the Working Class in its Meaning for the Present and the Future*] (1865) and his *Die Geschichte des Materialismus und Kritik seiner Bedeutung in der Gegenwart* [*The History of Materialism and a Critique of its Contemporary Meaning*] (1866, later expanded into two volumes), from which the present text has been selected. Three weeks before his death, he completed his *Logische Studien*

[*Logical Studies*], which was published posthumously in 1877. There, he defended the objective status of logical laws against a psychologistic interpretation.

The Standpoint of the Ideal (1873)

As mentioned, Lange's status as the founder of the Marburg School is disputed from a philosophical point of view. Indeed, his influence in recruiting Hermann Cohen to be his successor – Cohen being the first Jew to hold the position of *Ordinarius* in a German university – speaks to his political interests and instincts. His philosophical work had little to do with what later would become the Marburg brand of Neo-Kantianism. Instead, his interests lay in the question of the working class and the threat of "materialism," to which he felt Marx and Engels had succumbed in their historical materialism. In this sense, the work for which he is most remembered, *The History of Materialism,* is a critique of materialism, as the "lowest, but also comparatively the firmest stage in philosophy." Naturalism, as a reductive worldview (of reducing everything worldly to natural laws), is a consequence of materialism. Instead, Lange propagates the "standpoint of the ideal" against this rampant materialism. The selection below is the central chapter of this book.

What kind of standpoint is this? In the words of the philosophical historian Lehmann, the standpoint of the ideal is a "quite peculiar doctrine that is understandable from the historical situation and at first appears to be fairly tangential but not unimportant for the further development of Neo-Kantianism; a doctrine, with which Lange, in an attempt to satisfy his aesthetic-religious needs, wanted to give to faith what science was unable to give him".[1] In this attempt, he argued for the completion of material reality through an ideal world created by humanity with an irreducible validity, thus influencing the value theory of Southwest Neo-Kantianism. Rejecting a materialist interpretation of the world, which is inherently "pessimistic," he embraces the aesthetic image of the world, which is, to him, optimistic: "Not only poetry, but speculation, too, however it may appear to be directed to knowledge only, has essentially aesthetic, and through the attractive force of the beautiful, also ethical intent." The rejection of metaphysics, which Lange shares with Kant, must not, however, rule out the creation of "an ideal world of [man's] own creation." Any such hope, to Kant, was limited to the assumption of a "kingdom of ends" as an infinite ought. Instead, Lange sides with the Kantian Schiller in his powerful vision of humankind as "emanations of a truly religious elevation of the soul to the pure and troubled sources of all that man has ever worshipped as divine and supermundane." Lange, thus, promotes a non-theistic, quasi-religious faith in eternal values, which may equally not fall prey to political ideologies. Lange's vision reaches its climax in a call to action, which recommends revolution for the sake of the ideal: "Let knowledge be spread, let truth be proclaimed in every street and every tongue, let come of it what may; but let the battle for emancipation ... be directed against the points where the menacing of liberty, the hindering of truth and justice have their roots – against the secular and civil institutions by which ecclesiastical societies secure a corrupting influence, and against the enslaving power of a perfidious hierarchy that systematically undermines the freedom of the peoples." Lange's lasting legacy might be precisely the laying out of the possibility of a socialism guided by the standpoint of the ideal, or as Natorp will later call it, as a contrast to Marxism, for a "social idealism."

Notes

1   Ollig, op. cit., p. 19.

Further Reading

Knoll, J.M. & H. J. Schoeps, eds., *Friedrich Albert Lange, Leben und Werk*. Duisburg: Braun, 1975.
Ollig, Hans-Ludwig, *Der Neukantianismus,* op. cit., pp. 15–21.
Stack, George G., "Kant, Lange, and Nietzsche: Critique of Knowledge." Ed. Keith Ansell-Pearson. *Nietzsche and Modern German Thought*. London: Routledge, 1991, pp. 30–59.
Teo, Thomas, "Friedrich Albert Lange on Neo-Kantianism, Socialist Darwinism, and a Psychology without a Soul," in: *Journal of the History of the Behavioral Sciences*, 38 (2002), pp. 285–301.

Chapter 5

"The Standpoint of the Ideal" from *The History of Materialism* (1873)[1]

Materialism is the first, the lowest, but also comparatively the firmest stage in philosophy. Starting immediately from natural knowledge, it becomes a system by looking beyond the limits of this knowledge. The necessity that rules in the sphere of the natural sciences lends to the system which is most immediately based upon them a considerable degree of the uniformity and certainty of its separate parts. A reflection of this certainty and necessity falls also upon the system as such, but this reflection is deceptive. Precisely what makes Materialism a system, the fundamental hypothesis which elevates the particular branches of natural knowledge by a common bond into a whole, is not only its most uncertain part, but is, in fact, untenable before a deeper-going criticism. But exactly the same relation is repeated in the particular sciences upon which Materialism is based, and therefore, too, in all the separate parts of the system. The certainty of these parts is, rightly considered, nothing but the certainty of the facts of the science, and this is always greatest for the immediately given particular. The unity which makes the facts into a science and the sciences into a system is a product of free synthesis, and springs therefore from the same source as the creation of the ideal. While, however, this deals quite freely with the materials, synthesis in the province of science has only the freedom of its origin from the speculative mind of man. It is, on the other hand, tied to the task of establishing the utmost possible harmony between the necessary factors of knowledge, which are independent of our will. As the artisan, in the case of an invention, is tied to its purpose, while at the same time the idea of it springs freely from his mind, so every true scientific induction is at once the accomplishment of a given task and a product of the speculative mind.

Materialism more than any other system keeps to reality, i.e., to the sum total of the necessary phenomena given to us by the compulsion of sense. But a reality such as man imagines to himself, and as he yearns after when this imagination is dispelled, an existence absolutely fixed and independent of us while it is yet known by us – such a reality does not exist and cannot exist, because the synthetic creative factor of our knowledge extends, in fact, into the very first sense-impressions and even into the elements of logic.[2] The world is not only *idea*, but also *our* idea; a product of the organisation of the *species* in the universal and necessary characteristics of all experience; of the *individual* in the synthesis that deals freely with the object. We may also say that the reality is the phenomenon for the species, while the delusive appearance, on the contrary, is a phenomenon for the individual, which only becomes an error by reality, i.e., existence for the species, being ascribed to it.

But the task of producing harmony among phenomena, and of linking the manifold that is given to us into unity, belongs not merely to the synthetic factors of experience, but also to those of speculation. Here, however, the connecting organisation of the species leaves us in the lurch: the individual speculates in his own fashion, and the product of this speculation acquires importance for the species, or rather for the nation and contemporaries, only in so far as the individual creating it is endowed with rich and normal talents and is typical in his modes of thought, while by his intellectual energy he is called to be a leader.

The conceptual poesy of speculation is, however, not even so completely free; it still strives, like empirical research, after a unitary exhibition of data in their connection, but it lacks the guiding compulsion of the principles of experience. Only in poesy, in the narrower sense of the word, in poetry, is the ground of reality consciously abandoned. In speculation, form has the preponderance over matter; in poetry it is completely dominant. The poet creates in the free play of his spirit a world to his own liking, in order to impress more vividly upon the easily manageable material a form which has its own intrinsic value and its importance independently of the problems of knowledge.

From the lowest stages of synthesis, in which the individual still appears completely bound by the characteristics of the species, up to its creative dominance in poetry, the essence of this act is always directed to the production of unity, of harmony, of perfect form. The same principle which rules absolutely in the sphere of the beautiful, in art and poetry, appears in the sphere of conduct as the true ethical norm which underlies all the other principles of morality, and in the sphere of knowledge as the shaping, form-giving factor in our picture of the world.

Although, therefore, the very picture of the world which the senses give us is involuntarily formed upon the ideal within us, yet the whole world of reality, as compared with the free creations of art, appears inharmonious and full of perversities. Here lies the source of all Optimism and Pessimism. Without comparison we should not be able to form a judgment as to the quality of the world. But when from some elevated point we regard a landscape our whole nature is attuned to ascribe to it beauty and perfection. We must first destroy the powerful unity of this picture by analysis, in order to remember that in those huts, peacefully resting on the mountain slope, there dwell careworn men; that behind that little sheltered window perhaps some sufferer is enduring the most terrible torments; that beneath the murmuring summits of the distant forest birds of prey are rending their quivering prey; that in the silvery waves of the river a thousand tiny creatures, scarcely born to life, are finding cruel death. To our sweeping glance the withered branches of the trees, the blighted cornfields, the sun-scorched meadows, are only shadows in a picture which delight our eye and cheers our heart.

Thus the world appears to the optimistic philosopher. He praises the harmony which he himself has introduced into it. As compared with him, the Pessimist a thousand times is right; and yet there could be no Pessimism of all without the natural ideal of the world which we carry within us. It is only contrast with this that makes reality bad.

The more freely synthesis exerts its function, the more aesthetic becomes the image of the world, the more ethical is its reaction upon our activity in the world. Not only poetry, but speculation too, however it may appear to be directed to knowledge only, has essentially aesthetic, and through the attractive force of the beautiful, also ethical intent. In this sense we might indeed say, with Strauss, that every genuine philosophy is necessarily optimistic. But philosophy is more than mere imaginative speculation; it embraces also logic, criticism, the theory of knowledge.

We may call those functions of the senses and of the combining intelligence, which produce reality in us, individually low as compared with the lofty flight of spirit in freely creative art; but as a whole, and in their combination, they may not be subordinated to any other mental activity. Little as our reality may be a reality after our own hearts, it is nevertheless the firm basis of our whole intellectual existence. The individual grows up from the soil of the species, and general and necessary knowledge forms the only safe basis for the elevation of the individual to an aesthetic apprehension of the world. If this basis is disregarded, speculation too can no longer be typical, no longer be full of significance; it loses itself in fantasies, in subjective caprice and puerile frivolity. But, above all, is the most genuine possible conception of reality the whole basis of daily life, the necessary condition of human intercourse. The community of the species in knowledge is at the same time the law of all interchange of ideas. But it is even more than this: it is also the only way to the mastery of nature and its forces.

However much the modifying influence of the psychical synthesis reaches down to our most elementary ideas of things, of an object, yet we have the conviction that something lies at the bottom of these ideas and of the world arising from them that does not spring from ourselves. This conviction rests essentially upon the fact that we discover between things not merely a *connection*, which might indeed be just the plan upon which we have conceived them, but also a *co-operation*, which goes on irrespective of our thought, and which acts upon us ourselves and subjects us to its laws. This strange element, this 'non-ego,' of course only becomes again 'object' for our thought by being conceived by each individual in the universal and necessary forms of knowledge of the species; yet it does not therefore consist merely of these forms of knowledge. We have before us in the laws of nature not merely laws of our knowledge, but also evidences of *something else*, of a power that now compels us and now is dominated by us. In our commerce with this power we are exclusively dependent upon experience and upon reality, and no speculation has ever found the means of penetrating by the magic of pure thought into the world of things.

The method, however, which leads equally to the knowledge and to the mastery of nature, demands nothing less than a continual disintegration of the synthetical forms under which the world appears to us, so as to eliminate every subjective element. Withal indeed the new knowledge that better harmonised with the facts could in its turn only attain to form and stability by means of synthesis; but science found itself driven to simpler and ever simpler views, until at last it had to halt at the principles of the mechanical theory of the world.

Every falsification of reality attacks the bases of our spiritual existence. As opposed to metaphysical imaginations, which make pretensions to penetrate into the essence of nature and to determine from pure notions what only experience can teach us, Materialism as a counterpoise is therefore a real benefit. Moreover, all philosophemes which tend to regard reality alone must necessarily gravitate towards Materialism. On the other hand, Materialism lacks relations to the highest functions of the free human spirit. It is, apart from its theoretical inadequacy, unstimulating, barren for science and art, indifferent or inclined to egoism in the relations of man to man. It can hardly close the circle of its system without borrowing from Idealism.

If we observe how Strauss decks out his universe that we may be able to adore it, the thought presents itself that in truth he is not so very far removed from Deism. It seems almost a matter of taste whether we adore the masculine 'God,' the feminine 'Nature,' or the neuter 'All.' The sentiments are the same, and even the mode in we which conceive the object of these sentiments offers no essential difference. In theory, indeed, 'God' is no longer personal; and in the rapt elevation of the soul even the 'All' is treated as a person.

Natural science cannot lead to this. All natural science is analytical and clings to the particular. The particular discovery delights us; method compels our admiration, and by the continual succession of discoveries our glance is perhaps conducted to an infinite perspective of ever more perfect insight. Yet with this we are already quitting the ground of strict science. For the universe, as mere natural science enables us to comprehend it, we can as little feel enthusiasm as for an 'Iliad' spelt out letter by letter. But if we embrace the whole as a unity, then in the act of synthesis we bring our own nature into the object, just as we shape the landscape that we gaze at into harmony, however much disharmony in particulars may be concealed by it. All comprehension follows aesthetic principles, and every step towards the whole is a step towards the Ideal.

Pessimism, which likewise clings to the whole, is a product of reflection. The thousand contrarieties of life, the cold cruelty of nature, the pains and imperfections of all creatures, are collected in their individual features, and the sum of these observations is contrasted with the ideal picture of Optimism as a terrible indictment of the universe. A complete picture of the universe, however, is not reached in this way. Only the Optimist picture of the world is destroyed, and this involves a great service, if Optimism is inclined to become dogmatic and to pass itself as the representative of truth and reality. All those beautiful ideas of the individual disharmony which is resolved into the harmony of the great whole, of higher, divine contemplation of the world, in which all riddles are solved and all difficulties disappear, are successfully destroyed by Pessimism; but this destruction affects the dogma only, not the ideal. It cannot do away with the act that our mind is so constituted as ever anew to produce within itself a harmonious picture of the world; that here as everywhere it places its ideal beside and above the reality, and recreates itself from the struggles and necessities of life by rising in thought to a world of all perfections.

This ideal effort of the human spirit acquires now fresh strength through the knowledge, that our reality also is not absolute reality, but appearance; for the individual conclusive and corrective of his casual combinations, in the species a necessary product of its disposition in co-operation with unknown factors. These unknown factors we conceive to ourselves as things which exist independently of us, and which, therefore, would possess that absolute reality which we have just declared to be impossible. But the impossibility remains; for even in the notion of the thing, that stands out as a unity from the infinite coherency of existence, there lies that subjective factor which, as a constituent part of our human reality, is quite in place, but beyond it only helps to fill up, on the analogy of our reality, the gap for that which is absolutely inconceivable, but which must at the same time be assumed.

Kant has abandoned metaphysical inquiry into the true bases of all existence because of the impossibility of a certain result, and has limited the task of metaphysic to the discovery of all *a priori* given elements of experience. It is, however, questionable whether this new task is not equally impracticable; and it is no less questionable whether man, on the strength of the natural impulse to metaphysics which Kant himself maintains, will not continually make fresh efforts to break through the barriers of experience, and to build up into empty air brilliant systems of a supposed knowledge of the absolute nature of things. The sophisms by which this is possible are indeed inexhaustible; and while sophisms cunningly elude the position of criticism, a splendid ignorance easily breaks through all barriers with a still more brilliant success.

One thing is certain, that man needs to supplement reality by an ideal world of his own creation, and that the highest and noblest functions of his mind co-operate in such creations. But must this act of intellectual freedom always keep on assuming the deceptive form of a demonstrative science? In that case Materialism, too, will always reappear, and will destroy the bolder speculations with an attempt to satisfy the instinct of the reason towards unity by a minimum of exaltation above the real and demonstrable.

We may not doubt of another solution of the problem, especially in Germany, since we have in the philosophical poems of Schiller a performance which unites with the noblest vigour of thought the highest elevation above reality, and which lends to the ideal an overpowering force by removing it openly and unhesitatingly into the realm of fantasy. This must not be taken to mean that all speculation must also assume the form of poetry. Schiller's philosophical poems are more than mere products of the speculative instinct. They are emanations of a truly religious elevation of the soul to the pure and troubled sources of all that man has ever worshipped as divine and supermundane. May Metaphysics ever continue its efforts towards the solution of its insoluble problem! The more it continues theoretical, and tries to compete in certainty with sciences of reality, the less will it succeed in obtaining general importance. The more, on the other hand, it brings the world of existence into connection with the world of values, and tries to raise itself by its apprehension of phenomena to an ethical influence, the more will it make form predominate over matter, and, without doing violence to the facts, will erect in the architecture of its ideas a temple of worship to the eternal and divine. Free poetry, however, may entirely leave the ground of reality and make use of myth in order to lend words to the unutterable.

Here then we stand too before an entirely satisfactory solution of the question as to the immediate and more distant future of religion. There are only two ways which can permanently call for serious consideration, after it has been shown that mere Rationalism loses itself in the sands of superficiality, without ever freeing itself from untenable dogmas. The one way is the complete suppression and abolition of all religions, and the transference of their functions to the State, Science, and Art; the other is to penetrate to the core of religion, and to overcome all fanaticism and superstition by conscious elevation above reality and definitive renunciation of the falsification of reality by mythus, which, of course, can render no service to knowledge.

The first of these ways involves the danger of spiritual impoverishment; the second has to deal with the great question whether, at this very time, the core of religion is not undergoing a change which makes it difficult to apprehend it with certainty. But the second difficulty is the lesser one, because the very principle of the spiritualisation of religion must facilitate and lend a more harmonious form to every transition rendered necessary by the intellectual requirements of a progressive age.

There is the additional difficulty, whether the abolition of all religion, however desirable it may appear to many well-meaning and thinking men, is at all possible. No reasonable man will entertain the notion of a sudden or even violent step. He will rather descry in this principle primarily a maxim for the attitude of the more highly cultured, somewhat in the sense of Strauss, whose residuum of religion is here little concerned. But next an effort will be made to employ the State and the School in order gradually to withdraw the ground from under religion in the life of the people, and systematically to prepare the way for its disappearance. If we suppose such a course of proceeding, it would be very doubtful whether it would not necessarily produce, in spite of scholastic enlightenment, a popular reaction in favour of a thoroughly fanatical and narrow-minded conception of religion, or whether ever fresh, perhaps wild, but at the same time vigorous, shoots would not spring up from the roots that had been left behind. Man seeks the truth of reality and hails the extension of his knowledge so long as he feels himself free. But let him be chained down to what can be attained by the senses and the understanding, and he will revolt, and will give expression to the freedom of his imagination and his spirit, perhaps, in still cruder forms than those which have been successfully destroyed.

So long as men sought the core of religion in certain doctrines on God, the Human Soul, the Creation and its Order, it was inevitable that every criticism which began by separating upon logical principles the chaff from the wheat must end in complete negation. The sifting process went on till nothing was left.

If, on the other hand, we descry the core of religion in the elevation of our souls above the real and in the creation of a home of the spirit, then the purest forms may produce essentially the same psychical processes as the charcoal-burner's creed of the uncultured masses, and all the philosophical refinement of ideas will never bring us to zero. An unrivalled model of this is the way in which Schiller, in his 'Realm of Shadows,' has generalised the Christian doctrine of redemption into the idea of an aesthetical redemption. The elevation of the soul in faith here becomes the flight into the idea-land of beauty, where all labour finds its rest, every struggle and every want their peace and their reconciliation. But the heart which is terrified by the awful power of the law which no mortal can resist, opens itself to the divine will, which it recognises as the true essence of its own will, and thus finds itself reconciled with Deity. If these moments of elevation are but fleeting, yet they work with freeing and purifying effect upon the soul, and in the distance appears the perfection which no one can any more deprive us of, figured under the image of Herakles mounting to the skies.

This poem is a product of a time and a sphere of culture which were certainly not inclined to concede too much to what was specifically Christian; the poet of the 'Gods of Greece' does not conceal himself; everything here is in a sense pagan; and yet Schiller here stands nearer to the traditional life of Christian faith than the rationalistic dogmatism which arbitrarily maintains the notion of God and abandons the doctrine of redemption as irrational.

Let us accustom ourselves, then, to attribute a higher worth than hitherto to the principle of the creative idea in itself, and apart from any correspondence with historical and scientific knowledge, but also without any falsification of them; let us accustom ourselves to regard the world of ideas, as figurative representation of the entire truth, just as indispensable to all human progress as the knowledge of the understanding, by resolving the greater or less import of every idea into ethical and aesthetic principles. This advice will indeed appear to many an old or even new believer, as if we were to draw the ground from beneath his feet and ask him to remain standing as though nothing had happened; but the question is, what is the ground of ideas, whether it is their ordering into the whole of the world of ideas on ethical considerations, or the relation of the conceptions in which the idea finds expression to empirical reality? When the revolution of the earth was demonstrated, every Philistine believed that he must fall unless this dangerous doctrine were refuted, much as nowadays many a man fears that he will become a barber's block, if Vogt can prove to him that he has no soul. If religion is worth anything, and if its lasting worth lies in its ethical, and not in its logical content this must, of course, have been so earlier also, however much we might like to regard literal belief also as indispensable.

If this state of affairs had not been clearly present in the consciousness of the wise, and at least dimly in the consciousness of the people also, how could the poet and the sculptor in Greece and Rome have ventured to shape the course of the living myth and to give new forms to the ideal of deity? Even Catholicism, rigid as it appears, handled dogma at bottom only as a powerful clamp to hold together in its unity the gigantic fabric of the Church, while the poet in legend, the philosopher in the profound and daring speculations of Scholasticism, dealt as they pleased with the material of religion. Never indeed, never since the beginning of the world, has a religious dogma been held by people who could rise above the standpoint of the rudest superstition as true in the same manner as a piece of sensible knowledge, a result of calculation or of a simple inference of the understanding, even though perhaps never down to the latest times has there prevailed entire clearness as to the relation of these 'eternal truths' to the invariable functions of the senses and the understanding. We can always with the most orthodox zealots, discover in their sayings and writings the point where they obviously pass into symbol, and reproduce the plastic representation of a subjective development of the religious idea, with the same expressions and the same emphasis, with which they can so sensuously and concretely exhibit the relatively objective doctrines, that are admitted by a wide community, and are regarded by individuals as inexpugnable. If these truths of the universal doctrine of the church are prized as 'higher,' and put above all other knowledge, even that of the multiplication-table, yet there is always present at least a suspicion that this superiority does not rest upon greater *certainty*, but upon a greater *value*, against which neither logic, nor touch of the hand, nor sight of the eye, can avail, because for it the idea, as form and essence of the constitution of the soul, may be a more powerful object of longing, than the most real matter. But even where the greater certainty, the higher sureness and trustworthiness of religious truths are vaunted in express terms, these are only the periphrastic expressions or confusions of an exalted mind for the stronger impulse of the heart towards the living source of edification, of strengthening, of fresh life, which flows down from the divine world of ideas, as compared with the sober knowledge which enriches the understanding with small change, for which we happen to have no employment. Carried away to the height of this spiritual condition, Luther, though he himself, by this destructive force of his conviction, threw down an edifice that had stood a thousand years, rises to the point of cursing the reason that opposes itself to what he with all the might of his glowing spirit has conceived as the idea of a new epoch. Hence, too, the value which really pious minds have always given to inward *experience* as an evidence of faith. Many of these believers, who own their peace of soul to a fervent wrestling in prayer, and hold spiritual communion with Christ as with a person, know theoretically very well that the same emotional processes are found also with the same success and with the same authenticity in connection with entirely different articles of faith, nay, among the adherents of entirely foreign religions. The opposition to these and the equivocal character of an evidence which equally well supports contradictory ideas, they do not as a rule realise, since it is rather the common opposition of every belief against unbelief that stirs their minds. Does it not here become manifest that the essence of the thing lies in the form of the spiritual process, and not in the logical and historical content of the particular views and doctrines? These may well be connected with the form of the process, as are in the corporeal world chemical composition and crystalline form; but who is there to demonstrate to us this connection, and what phenomena of isomorphism shall we only here find exhibited?

This predominance of the form in belief betrays itself also in the remarkable trait that the believers in varying and even mutually hostile confessions, show more agreement with each other, betray more sympathy with their most eager opponents, than with those who appear indifferent in matters of religious controversy. The most peculiar phenomenon of religious formalism, however, lies in the *philosophy of religion*, as it has shaped itself in Germany, especially since Kant. This philosophy is a formal translation of religious into metaphysical doctrines. A man, who was so far removed from the charcoal-burner faith in regard to unhistorical traditions and scientific impossibilities as the Materialists could ever be, Schleiermacher, brought about, by dwelling on the ethical and ideal content of religion, a real torrent of religious revival. The mighty Fichte announced the dawn of a new historical epoch by the outpouring of the Holy Spirit upon all flesh. The Spirit, of which it is prophesied in the New Testament that it shall lead the disciples of Christ into all truth, is no other than the Spirit of Science, which has revealed itself in our days. It teaches us in revealed knowledge the absolute unity of human existence with the divine, which was first preached to the world by Christ in a parable. The revelation of the kingdom of God is the essence of Christianity, and this kingdom is the kingdom of liberty, which is won by the absorption of our own will into the will of God – death and resurrection. All doctrines of the resurrection of the dead in the physical sense are only misunderstandings of the doctrine of the kingdom of heaven, which is in truth the principle of a new constitution of the world. Fichte was entirely in earnest with his requirement of a transformation of the human race by the principle of humanity itself in its ideal perfection as opposed to the absorption of the individual in self-will. Thus the most radical philosopher of Germany is at the same time the man whose feelings and thoughts form the profoundest contrast to the interest-maxims of political economy and to the whole dogmatic theory of Egoism. It is not, therefore, without significance that Fichte was the first in Germany to raise the Social Question, which would, indeed, never exist if self-interest were the only spring of human actions, if the, abstractly considered, perfectly correct rules of political economy, as the only ruling laws of nature, everlastingly and invariably guided the machinery of human toils and struggles, without the higher idea ever asserting itself, for which the noblest of mankind have for thousands of years suffered and wrestled.

"No, abandon us not, sacred palladium of mankind! comforting thought, that from our every labour and our every suffering there results for our brother men a new perfection and a new delight; that we labour for them and do not labour in vain; that on the spot where we now exhaust ourselves and are trodden underfoot, and – what is worse than this – grossly err and fail, there will in the future flourish a race that may always do what it wills, because it will will nothing but what is good; while we from loftier regions rejoice over our descendants, and find developed in their virtues each germ that we implanted in them, and know them for our own. Arouse us, prospect of this time, to the sense of our dignity, and show it to us at least in our disposition, though our present state is at variance with it. Shed boldness and high enthusiasm upon our undertakings, and if we are crushed beneath them, while we are sustained by this thought, 'I have done my duty,' let us be invigorated by this other thought, 'No seed that I have sowed is lost in the moral world; in the day of ingathering I shall see its fruits and weave me from them immortal garlands.'"[3]

The poetical fervour with which Fichte wrote these words had seized him not on occasion of a vague religious contemplation, but in regard to Kant and the French Revolution. So intimately fused with him were life and teaching; and while the word of life was perverted by the hirelings of the Church to the service of death, of ignorance, of the prince of this world, there arose in him the spirit of the breaker of all chains, and loudly confessed that the fall of society in France had at least brought forth something better than the despotic governments whose aim is the degradation of mankind.

It is remarkable how, on a closer inquiry, the views and efforts of men often group themselves very differently from the common notion of them. It is a trivial saying that extremes meet; but it is far from being always true. Never, never will the decided free thinker feel any sympathy with rigid ecclesiasticism and the dead worship of the letter; but he may feel much with the prophetic enthusiasm of a pious soul, in which the word has become flesh, and which bears witness of the spirit that has taken possession of it. Never will the enlightened dogmatist of Egoism feel sympathy with the quiet souls who in their humble closets seek upon their knees a kingdom that is not of this world; but he may well feel it with the rich rector who can valiantly defend his creed, maintain his dignity, and prudently manage his property, and who drinks with him in champagne, if he sits near him at some luxurious christening dinner, or at the festive inauguration of a new railway.

Because it is the form of spiritual life that determines the inmost character of the man, so too their attitude to those who differ from them is a genuine touchstone of minds, whether they be of the truth or not. He must be a bad disciple of Christ, in the strictest sense of the religious, who cannot conceive that when the Lord appears in the clouds to judge the quick and the dead, He may place an Atheist like Fichte on His right hand, while thousands go to His left who cry, with the righteous, 'Lord, Lord!' He must be a bad friend of truth and justice who despises a man like A. H. Franke as an enthusiast, or treats the prayer of a Luther as idle self-delusion. In fact, so far as religion in its inmost essence forms an antithesis to Ethical Materialism, it will always retain friends amongst the freest and most enlightened minds, and the only question is whether in religion itself the principle of Ethical Materialism, of 'secularisation' as theologians call it, is not gaining such ascendancy that our better consciousness must tear itself free of all its previous forms and strike out new paths. In this point, in the relation of existing religions to the collective aims of our present civilisation, lies the true secret of their modifications and their persistence, and all attacks of the critical understanding, however justified and irresistible they may be, are yet not so much the cause as rather only the symptoms of their decay, or of a great fermentation in the whole spiritual life of their adherents. Hence it is, also, that even the conservative tendency which religious philosophy took with Hegel, accompanied by very similar modifications to those of Fichte, has borne no lasting fruits, either for the Church or for Philosophy. It can no longer be permitted that knowledge of the unveiled truth should be reserved for the philosophers alone, while the masses are forced back into the solemn twilight of the old symbols. As in politics the doctrine of the reasonableness of the actual state of things has done unholy service to the cause of Absolutism, so Philosophy contributed, chiefly through Hegel and Schleiermacher, to promote a tendency which, deserted by the naïve innocence of the old mysticism, attempted to save religion by a negation of negation. What protected the dogmas of religion against the teeth of criticism in the ages when the cathedrals grew up, or when the mighty melodies of worship arose, was not the anti-criticism of ingenious apologists, but the reverent awe with which the soul received the mysteries, and the holy fear with which the believer shrank from approaching in his inmost soul the border where truth and poesy separate. This holy fear is not the *consequence* of the fallacies which lead to the belief in the supernatural, but rather their *cause*, and perhaps this relation of cause and effect runs back to the earliest ages of undeveloped civilisation and undeveloped religions. Why, even Epikuros, besides fear, regarded the sublime dream-images of the gods as amongst the sources of religion!

What will become of the 'verities' of religion when all piety has disappeared, and when a generation grows up that has never known the deep emotions of religious life, or that has grown weary of them and has turned away from them? Every young fool triumphs over its mysteries, and looks down with self-complacent disdain on those who can still believe this silly stuff. So long as religion stands in its full strength, it is not always its most paradoxical principles that are the first to be doubted. Theological critics exert themselves by the application of the greatest acuteness and the most extensive erudition to correct tradition in some point or other far enough removed from the core of faith; men of science find reason to refer some particular miracle to a physically intelligible phenomenon. At such points the process of boring is continued, and when all the arts of attack and defence have been exhausted, as a rule the nimbus of venerableness and inviolability that enwrapped religious tradition is gone also. Only then do we come to the much simpler questions: How God's omnipotence and goodness are compatible with the evil in the world; why the religions of other peoples are not just as good as our own; why there are not still miracles, and those very palpable ones; how God can be angry; why the servants of God are so malicious and vindictive, and so on. When ecclesiastical tradition has at length lost the special credit which it claims, and when the Bible is regarded with the same eyes as any other book, we can hardly conceive any degree of intelligence so low as not to see clearly that three times one cannot make one, that a virgin cannot bear a child, and that a man cannot, body and all, soar up into the blue sky. If now some little scientific knowledge is added, such as is current in every primary school, there is no end to the absurdity over which a scoffer can make merry, without in any degree possessing any special intelligence or any thorough education. If now, withal, men of keen understanding and solid education still hold fast to religion, because they have led from childhood up a rich emotional life, and cling to the old, familiar soil with a thousand roots of imagination, of the heart, and of recollection of beautiful and consecrated hours, we have then before us a contrast that shows us plainly enough where are the sources from which flows the stream of religious life.

So long, of course, as religion is cultivated in close ecclesiastical communities by priests who present themselves before the people as privileged dispensers of the divine mysteries, so long the standpoint of the ideal in religion will never be able to assert itself clearly. And indeed, ideology only too easily becomes the prey of the poison of letter worship, the symbol involuntarily and gradually becomes a rigid dogma, as the image of the saint becomes an idol, and the natural contradictions between poetry and reason easily degenerates in the religious sphere into antipathy to the absolutely True, Useful, and Practical, which in our age seem to limit on every side the space in which a free soul may use its wings. We know the mischief that has been wrought in many a nobly disposed mind by the transition from crude ideology to romantic perversity, and finally into angry pessimism. No one can take it ill of the friends of truth and progress, if they feel distrust of everything that opposes itself to the ruling tendency of the age towards prose, especially if a tincture of clericalism is visible. For if in the age of the Liberation Wars Romanticism seemed to fulfil its higher purpose, it is obvious, on the other hand, that the tendency of the age towards inventions, discoveries, political and social improvements, has now to perform enormous tasks which may perchance decide the future of humanity and it cannot be doubted that the utmost sobriety of serious labour, the full unadulterated feeling for truth of a critical conscience, are needed to accomplish these tasks worthily and successfully. When then the day of harvest comes, the glance of genius will again be there also, which from the atoms creates a whole without knowing how it has been done.

Meanwhile the old forms of religion have by no means entirely outlived themselves, and it will hardly ever come to be with their ideal content as with a squeezed lemon, until new forms of Ethical Idealism appear. Things do not go on so simply and unmixedly in the interchange of earthly opinions and aspirations. The worship of Apollo and Jupiter had not yet lost all significance as Christianity broke in, and Catholicism still held a rich treasure of life and spirit within it when Luther began to strike about him. So even today again a new religious community might, by the power of its ideas and the charm of its social principles, conquer a world by storm, while still many a stock of the old planting remains in full vitality and bears its fruit; but mere negation recoils where ends the province of the obsolete and dead, that has become its prey. Whether even out of the old confessions such a stream of new life might proceed, or whether conversely a religionless community could kindle a fire of such devouring force, we do not know. One thing, however, is certain; if the New is to come into existence and the Old is to disappear, two great things must combine – a world-kindling ethical idea and a social influence which is powerful enough to lift the depressed masses a great step forward. Sober reason, artificial systems, cannot do this. The victory over disintegrating egoism and the deadly chilliness of the heart will only be won by a great ideal, which appears amidst the wondering peoples as a "stranger from another world," and by demanding the impossible unhinges the reality.

So long as this victory is not won, so long as no new social bond makes the poor and miserable feel that he is a man among men, we must not be so precipitate in combating belief, lest haply child and bath be poured away together. Let knowledge be spread, let truth be proclaimed in every street and in every tongue, let come of it what may; but let the battle for emancipation, deliberate and mortal battle, be directed against the points where the menacing of liberty, the hindering of truth and justice have their roots – against the secular and civil institutions by which ecclesiastical societies secure a corrupting influence, and against the enslaving power of a perfidious hierarchy that systematically undermines the freedom of the peoples. If these institutions are removed, if the terrorism of the hierarchy is broken, then the extremist opinions may move side by side without fanatical encroachments, and without the steady progress of insight being hindered. It is true that this progress will destroy superstitious fears, a work which is indeed in great part already accomplished even amongst the lowest classes of the people. If religion falls together with the superstitious fears, so let it fall; if it does not fall, then its ideal content will have maintained itself, and it may then continue to be maintained in this form until time produces something new. It is not then matter of any regret if the content of religion is regarded by most believers, and even by a part of the clergy, as literally true; for, that utterly dead and meaningless belief in the letter, whose effect is even more pernicious, is hardly possible any longer where all compulsion disappears.

If the clergyman, as a result of the associations of ideas which dominate him, *cannot* represent the ideal element of life which he represents otherwise than in attributing to it vulgar reality and in taking everything as historical that should only be regarded as symbolical, this must be conceded to him without hesitation, supposing that he does his duty in the more important regard. If the hierarchy is entirely deprived of all worldly power, not excepting even the rights of a civil corporation, and if the formation of a state within a state is resisted in every form, the most dangerous weapon of spiritual tyranny is broken. Moreover, there must be maintained, not merely unconditional freedom of teaching for strict science as well as for its popularisation, but also free scope for public criticism of all wrongs and abuses. That it is the right and duty of the State, so far as it continues to support existing religious communities with its power and resources, to require from their clergy a certain standard of scientific culture is obvious; and we must guard against neglecting these duties, and losing ourselves in the labyrinth of a so-called separation of Church and State. There is only a clear and good sense in the separation of state and faith. Every ecclesiastical organisation of a community of believers is already a state within the state, and may at any moment easily encroach upon the secular province. There may be circumstances in the conditions of civilisation by which such a power may be justified, and may, in fact, be destined to shatter a rotten and outlived form of government; as a rule, however, and especially in our present age, which is more and more assigning to the State the civilising functions that were formerly left to the Church, the political organisation of the latter must simply be to the State a matter of distrust and the most serious anxiety. Only with the dissolution of the political Church is an unconditional freedom of creed possible. At the same time, so long as the Church, with all its ambitious aspirations, still represents also Ethical Idealism among the people, it cannot be the function of the State to aim at the dissolution of its dogmatic system. Fichte, indeed, demanded that the spiritual teacher to whom it falls to mediate between the people and the men of scientific culture, should actually form his religious system in the school of the philosopher. Theology he proposed, unless she solemnly renounced her 'pretension to be a mystery,' to banish entirely from the universities; but if she renounced it, then the practical part of theology must be separated from the scientific part, and the latter be completely resolved into general scientific education.[4] This in itself justifiable requirement is at present still less practicable than when Fichte expressed it. The task of mediation between the people and the better educated, even when it is attempted with all earnestness, is only to be performed by observing the psychological conditions, and that means only gradually and in long periods. But even the imparting of a sufficiently deep philosophical culture to the clergy cannot be effected by a mere organisation of studies. Meanwhile the cultivation of the ideal amongst the people must not be interrupted. It is, of course, to be wished that every clergyman should at least be enlightened as to the limits of the validity of the ideal; but if, because of narrowness of mind and lack of suitable means of instruction, this cannot be without weakening the force which is destined to spread ideas, then it is, on the whole, better for the present to sacrifice enlightenment rather than force.

The case of the Materialistic man of science, on the other side, is entirely analogous. Without doubt, the success of his beneficent and self-sacrificing researches essentially depends upon his devotion to the branch of human activity which he has chosen. There cannot be the slightest doubt that only methodically strict empiricism leads him to the goal, that keen and unprejudiced contemplation of the sensible world and unhesitating consistency in his conclusions are indispensable to him; finally, that Materialistic hypotheses always offer him the greatest prospect of fresh discoveries. If his mind is deep and comprehensive enough to combine with this ordered activity the recognition of the ideal, without introducing confusion, obscurity, or sterile timidity into the sphere of his researches, he then assuredly reaches a higher standard of genuine and complete humanity. But if this cannot be hoped for, it is in most cases far better in these departments to have crass Materialists than phantasts and muddled weaklings. As much of the ideal as is indispensably necessary – and more than the great mass of men ever attain – is already involved in the mere devotion to a great principle and to an important subject. Those Materialists who really accomplish something in their science will, for the most part, have little inclination to play the missionary of negation; and even if they do, they do less harm to mankind than the apostles of confusion.

If, however, both extremes, even in their one-sidedness, are really justifiable, then, too, it must be possible for them to live together in society at least tolerably, if not comfortably, so soon as the last traces of fanaticism are eradicated from our legislation. Whether, of course, this will ever come to pass, is quite another question. It is with the religious revolution just as it is with the social revolution which is before us. It would be very desirable to live through the period of transition in peace, but it is more probable that it will be stormy.

Thus the Materialistic controversy of our days stands before us as a serious sign of the time. Today again, as in the period before Kant and before the French Revolution, there underlies the spread of Materialism a general enfeeblement of philosophical effort, a retrogression of ideas. In such times the perishable material to which our forefathers gave the stamp of the sublime and divine, as they could comprehend them, is devoured by the flames of criticism, like the organic body, which, when the vital spark dies out, becomes subject to the more general action of chemical forces, and has its earlier form destroyed. But, as in the circuit of nature from the decay of lower materials new life struggles into being and higher phenomena appear where the old have disappeared, so we may expect that a new impulse of ideas will advance humanity another stage.

Meanwhile the dissolving forces act only as they must. They obey the inexorable categorical imperative of thought, the conscience of the understanding, which is awakened so soon as in the creation of the transcendental the Letter becomes conspicuous because the Spirit leaves it in search of newer forms. But one thing only can finally bring humanity to an ever-during peace – the recognition of the imperishable nature of all poesy in Art, Religion, and Philosophy, and the permanent reconciliation, on the basis of this recognition, of the controversy between investigation and imagination. Then, also, will be found a changeful harmony of the True, the Good, and the Beautiful, instead of that dead unity to which our Free Congregations are at present clinging, when they make empirical truth their only basis. Whether the future will again build lofty cathedrals or will content itself with light and cheerful halls, whether organ-peal and the sound of bells will with fresh force thunder through the land, or whether gymnastic and music in the Greek sense will be elevated to the center of the training of a new epoch – in no case will the past be entirely lost, and in no case will the obsolete reappear unaltered. In a certain sense the ideas of religion, too, are imperishable. Who will refute a Mass of Palestrina, or who will convict Raphael's Madonna of error? The 'Gloria in Excelsis' remains a universal power, and will ring through the centuries so long as our nerves can quiver under the awe of the sublime. And those simple fundamental ideas of the redemption of the individual man by the surrendering of his own will to the will that guides the whole; those images of death and resurrection which express the highest and most thrilling emotions that stir the human breast, when no prose is capable of uttering in cold words the fullness of the heart; those doctrines finally, which bid us to share our bread with the hungry and to announce the glad tidings to the poor – they will not for ever disappear, in order to make way for a society which has attained its goal when it owes a better police system to its understanding, and to its ingenuity the satisfaction of ever fresh wants by ever fresh inventions. Often already has an epoch of Materialism been but the stillness before the storm, which was to burst forth from unknown gulfs and to give a new shape to the world. We lay aside the pen of criticism at a moment when the Social Question stirs all Europe, a question on whose wide domain all the revolutionary elements of science, of religion, and of politics seem to have found the battlefield for a great and decisive contest. Whether this battle remains a bloodless conflict of minds, or whether, like an earthquake, it throws down the ruins of a past epoch with thunder into the dust and buries millions beneath the wreck, certain it is that the new epoch will not conquer unless it be under the banner of a great idea, which sweeps away egoism and sets human perfection in human fellowship as a new aim in the place of restless toil, which looks only to the personal gain. It would indeed mitigate the impending conflict if insight into the nature of human development and historical processes were more generally to take possession of the leading minds; and we must not resign the hope that in a distant future the greatest transformations will be accomplished without humanity being stained by fire and blood. It were indeed the fairest guerdon of exhausted intellectual labour if it might even now contribute, while averting fearful sacrifices, to prepare a smooth path for the inevitable, and to save the treasures of culture uninjured for the new epoch; but the prospect of this is slight, and we cannot hide from ourselves that the blind passion of parties is on the increase, and that the reckless struggle of interests is becoming less and less amenable to the influences of theoretical inquiries. Yet our efforts will never be wholly in vain. The truth, though late, yet comes soon enough; for mankind will not die just yet. Fortunate natures hit the right moment; but never has the thoughtful observer the right to be silent because he knows that for the present there are but few who will listen to him.

Notes

1   This chapter is taken from Lange's *The History of Materialism* [*Geschichte des Materialismus*], trans. Ernest Chester Thomas. London: Routledge & Kegan Paul, 1950, pp. 513–534. This translation is of the second edition of 1873 (1st ed. 1866). – Ed.

2   That to the principle A = A strictly understood reality nowhere corresponds, A. Spir has recently energetically insisted on and made it the basis of a philosophical system of his own. All the difficulties involved in this fact may, however, be much more easily disposed of in another way. The principle A = A is indeed the basis of all knowledge, yet is not itself knowledge, but an act of the mind, an act of primitive synthesis by which there is posited as the necessary starting-point of all thinking an equality or a persistence which are found in nature only relatively and approximately, but never absolutely and completely. The principle A = A accordingly indicates on the very threshold of logic the relativity and ideality of all our knowledge.

3   (J. G. Fichte's) *Beitrag zur Berichtigung der Urtheile des Publikums über die französische Revolution*, 1793, Book I, I. Kap.

4   *Deducirter Plan einer zu errichtenden höhern Lehranstalt, zu Berlin geschrieben im J*. 1807: Stuttgart and Tübingen 1817, pp. 59 ff.

Introduction

Rudolf Hermann Lotze (1817–1881)

LOTZE WAS BORN IN BAUTZEN IN SAXONY IN 1817, but the family soon moved to Zittau, where young Lotze attended school. In his youth he reports having been strongly influenced by the idealists and Romantics and was inclined towards writing poetry and novels. In 1834, at the early age of 17, he enrolled in the University of Leipzig, where he studied philosophy and natural science, and later medicine. He was heavily influenced by the speculative *Naturphilosophie* of Gustav Theodor Fechner, who under the pseudonym "Dr. Mises" also published writings on mystical experience and occult phenomena. In 1838, Lotze took his doctorate in medicine and returned to Zittau in the same year to practice medicine. In 1840, he moved back to Leipzig to work on his Habilitation in philosophy. He published his first major philosophical work in 1841, his *Metaphysik*, which lays the grounds for much of his later philosophy, though he continued publishing in the field of medicine (he authored, at this time, also a *General Pathology*). It is in this period that he also publishes the first edition of his *Logic* (1843), from which the present selection (a later addition) is taken. He stayed in Leipzig as an unsalaried *Privatdozent* until 1844, when he accepted – at age 27 – a professorship in Göttingen, one of Germany's most prestigious universities. He would remain in Göttingen from 1844 until 1880, the place in which Frege resided as of 1871. Lotze's influence on the latter has been noted early on. It was in Göttingen that Lotze quickly rose to fame and published widely in theoretical philosophy, practical philosophy, as well as aesthetics and physiology. He continued to expand his *Metaphysik* and *Logik*. In the 1850s, Lotze became embroiled in the *Materialismusstreit*, the Materialism Controversy, where he was criticized for being a "spiritualist." The result of this controversy was his three-volume work *Mikrokosmus*, which was intended, according to its subtitle, as a "*Versuch einer Anthropologie,*" an attempt at an anthropology, which significantly broadened his readership. As Beiser notes, *Mikrokosmus* "became Lotze's most successful book, one of the most widely read philosophical works in the second half of the nineteenth century. It went through several editions and was translated into many languages".[1] It is partly translated into English as *Microcosmus: An Essay Concerning Man and His Relation to the World* (1885). Feeling lonely and depressed after the deaths of his wife and one of his sons, Lotze accepted a position at the University of Berlin in 1880, where he taught to great acclaim but died in 1881 from a lung infection.

To group Lotze among the Neo-Kantian movement is a bit risky. His philosophical position cannot easily be summed up. He was influenced by Herbart but, as he admitted, mostly by Leibniz. Rejecting a materialistic "vitalism" in his physiological writings, he called his position a "teleological idealism." His work characteristically finds a middle ground between seemingly irreconcilable positions, and it was criticized for that. His most important contribution, judging from its reception, is his distinction between three realms of being – reality, truth, and value – emphasizing the validity (*Geltung*) of the latter. Although hardly read today, he was arguably the most famous *Kathederphilosoph* of the nineteenth century, a term that is not without negative connotations, as it contrasts the official philosophy of the *Katheder* [lectern] with the more popular philosophy of mavericks such as Schopenhauer, Marx, Feuerbach, or Nietzsche. Given his popularity and influence at the time, the editor has decided to include a selection of his writings in this Reader. The text selected, viz., Lotze's interpretation of Plato's theory of the forms, is undoubtedly his most famous piece of writing and had a decisive influence over the debate of the nature and status of values and the rise of psychologism in late nineteenth- and early twentieth-century philosophy. He was influential for the "core" Neo-Kantians, especially the Southwest School, as well as for Dilthey and the Phenomenological Movement, but also for philosophers in England and the United States, where his influence seems to have outlasted that in his home country. Especially through newer research into this period (notably by Gabriel and Beiser), attention to Lotze seems to have begun to be reawakened.

The World of Ideas (1874)

The passage below is from Lotze's work *Logik*, which was first published in 1843 (the "Lesser Logic") but later expanded into a three-part work, ambitiously called "System of Philosophy". Of these, Lotze only managed to finish two. Part I, the earlier *Logik*, was expanded in the 1874 edition to comprise three books: "On Thinking" (Book I), "On Investigating" (Book II), and "On Cognizing" (Book III). It is from Book III that the present selection is taken. Part Two contained three Books as well: Ontology, Cosmology, Psychology.

As scholars such as Gabriel have pointed out[2], this book's discussion and interpretation of Plato's theory of the forms was a decisive influence on the anti-psychologistic tendency that arose with the Marburg School and continued in Frege and later Husserl. With his Platonizing interpretation of the third realm of "values," Lotze also became influential for the Southwest School. In interpreting the ontological status of ideas as *geltend* [valid], Lotze is in effect retroactively "transcendentalizing" Plato's theory, such that his position has been called "transcendental Platonism" (Gabriel). Lotze thereby construes cognizing, the topic of logic, as the matter for a theory of cognition, clearly separating it from a psychology of cognition (*Erkenntnistheorie*, not *Erkenntnispsychologie*), a distinction that would also become important for the Marburg School and its *erkenntnislogisch* position. Accordingly, the status of a true proposition is that it is valid, regardless of the fleeting fact that it might be thought or cognized by a thinking agent during a mental episode. To distinguish the act of thinking from its ideal content would also be Husserl's main line of argument against psychologism in his *Prolegomena* of 1900. This content might take on the form of a linguistic judgment, but cannot be reduced to it; to overlook this distinction means effectively to commit the error of psychologism. Plato thought that these "eternal ideas" were expressible in the form of concepts, but they are more aptly formulated, Lotze argues, in laws. While Kant interpreted ideas as individual concepts arranged in a formal table, Plato's conception of ideas comes closer to expressing the realm of "*ontos on*" (true reality), though he, too, falls short of achieving this, "leading the mind as it does away from the full concrete reality which is the true aim of its enquiries to a barren playing with empty ideas which have become separated from their natural foundations."

Natorp's interpretation of natural laws as Platonic ideas is equally indebted to this reading of Plato, and Heidegger's later rejection of truth as propositional is likewise a reaction against Lotze's interpretation.

Notes

1   Beiser, *Late German Idealism*, p. 250.
2   Cf. Gabriel 1989, pp. ix–xii.

Further Reading

Beiser, Frederick, *Late German Idealism. Trendelenburg & Lotze.* Oxford: Oxford University Press, 2013, pp. 125–312.
Gabriel, Gottfried, "Einleitung," in: Rudolf Hermann Lotze, *Logik. Drittes Buch. Vom Erkennen.* Hamburg: Meiner, 1989, pp. ix–xxvii.
——, "Frege, Lotze, and the continental roots of early analytic philosophy." In: Erich H. Reck (ed.): *From Frege to Wittgenstein: Perspectives on Early Analytic Philosophy.* Oxford/New York: Oxford University Press, 2002, pp. 39–51.
Sullivan, David, "Hermann Lotze," in *Stanford Encyclopedia of Philosophy.*
Willey, Thomas E. *Back to Kant: The Revival of Kantianism in German Social and Historical Thought, 1860–1914.* Detroit: Wayne State UP, 1978.

Chapter 6

"The World of Ideas" from *Logic* (1874)[1]

313. The problem which we have set before us is one which ancient philosophy long ago declared again and again to be insoluble. That all is in flux was the familiar doctrine of Heraclitus, a doctrine however of which it is difficult to determine the precise significance. That it was understood in the half pathetic sense of a lamentation over the rapidity of change appears in the heightened form subsequently given to his saying that it is impossible to cross the same river twice – 'it is impossible,' it was added, 'even once.' But against the testimony of observation to the transitoriness of things the most ordinary experience might have set counter examples of duration through incalculable periods of time; philosophical reflection could only have universalised the former set of experiences into the doctrine cited by establishing in opposition to superficial appearances, that the latter also do but veil a slow process of change to which in fact they are always subject. We do not know how far this actually took place and whether these speculations passed over without notice the circumstance that the differences in the speed of one set of changes and another at once introduce into the play of phenomena a contrast between the relatively fixed and the more transitory which might be turned to fruitful account. Once more, that nothing can wholly withstand agencies of change operating from without, that everything therefore must be *susceptible* of change, is a conviction too easily derived from the experience of every-day life to have needed a philosophy to discover it. But it remains doubtful how far Heraclitus passed beyond this, and taught that there are changes in all things springing from causes in their own nature and not merely occasioned by outside influences, and whether he taught this simply as a fact of experience, or whether he held continual movement to be the condition of the possibility of all natural existence, and that stable equilibrium and permanence were impossible.

There is much to lend probability to a view which should credit him with this more advanced conception, but the question can as little be certainly decided as the more important one what precisely is to be understood by the 'all' to which he ascribed this ceaseless mutability. The expression included beyond question the things of sense; in fact the very starting-point of the doctrine could have been found nowhere else but in the changing combinations of sensible qualities and relations. But did it include at the same time the content of the ideas by means of which we think this world of sense? Was it intended that not only all that is real but all that can be thought as well is subject to this eternal flux? I doubt if Heraclitus held this latter opinion; the universal instability of all determinations of thought would of course render all enquiry and all affirmation impossible. We may however assume from the lively picture which Plato draws in the Theaetetus of the later activity of the school, that they at all events had no hesitation in giving this extension to their master's doctrine.

At this point it is taken up by the Sophists. I do not mean that section which under the leadership of Protagoras acknowledged only the subjective validity of every perception for the person who experiences it, I mean those who, disciplined in Eleatic dialectic, set themselves to demonstrate that every conception signifies at once what it does mean and what it does not mean. This contention was met, principally in the field of Ethics, where it produced its most pernicious effects, by the sound instinct and sense of truth of Socrates, who called attention to the fact that the conception of good and bad, just and unjust, are fixed and unchanging, and cannot be determined now one way and now another at the pleasure of individuals, but that they have to be accepted as permanent and self-identical conceptions to which everyone has simply to subordinate his own ideas on these subjects. Plato followed, at one with these aims of his master, but impelled by more many-sided motives, and expanded the convictions received from Socrates into his own doctrine of Ideas, a first and most characteristic attempt to turn to account the truth which belongs to the world of our ideas in itself, without regard to its agreement with an assumed reality of things outside its borders. The philosophical efforts of antiquity have the attraction of exhibiting in full detail the movements, the struggles, and the errors of thought, into which every individual still falls in the course of his development, and which notwithstanding the culture of our own day has no longer the patience to follow up and investigate. I shall permit myself to enter therefore into a review of this doctrine of Plato, approaching it at various points which seem pertinent to our present enquiry.

314. The Platonic expression Idea[2] is usually rendered Universal conception[3], and the rendering is so far correct that there are Ideas, according to Plato, of everything which can be thought in a universal form, apart from the particular perceptions in which it is presented. At the same time it is only for the purposes of a later set of conceptions which we shall meet with presently, that it becomes important to be able to think of the ideally apprehended content[4] as something common to many individual contents, that is as a universal. What is essential here at the outset, is not so much that it can be separated from different particular instances which contain it, as that it has been distinguished as a content with a meaning of its own which we *present to* ourselves, from a mere affection which we *experience*. In the latter sense it might have been involved by the Heraclitic or pseudo-Heraclitic doctrine in its ceaseless flux of events, of which each one only is in the moment in which it occurs, and no one has an abiding habitation or significance in the world, because there is no reason why having once occurred it need ever recur again in identically the same form. The former conception on the contrary turns the mere affection of our sensibility into an independent objective[5] content whose significance once is its significance once for all, and whose relation to other contents has an eternal and self-identical validity even if neither it nor they should ever be repeated in actual perception.

I have had occasion to explain my meaning here in an earlier part of this work (§ 3). Perception shows us the things of sense undergoing changes in their qualities. But while black becomes white and sweet sour, it is not blackness itself which passes into whiteness, nor does sweetness become sourness; what happens is that these several qualities, each remaining eternally identical with itself, succeed each other in the thing, and the conceptions through which we think the things have themselves no part in the mutability which we attribute on account of their changes to the things of which the qualities are the predicates – and even he who attempted to deny this would be affirming it against his will, for he could not represent sweetness as passing into sourness, without separating the one property from the other, and determining the first for his own thought in an idea which will always mean something different from the second into which it is supposed to have changed. It is a very simple and unpretending, but yet a very important thought to which Plato here gives expression for the first time. The continual change which goes on in the external world may affect us like a restless whirling eddy, bewildering our intelligence, yet it is not without a pervading truth. Whatever mutability the things may display, that which they are at each moment they are by a transient participation in conceptions which are not transient but for ever identical and constant, and which taken together constitute an unchangeable system of thought, and form the first adequate and solid beginnings of a permanent knowledge.

For it was one of the conclusions at which we arrived before[6], that to the making of this earliest immediate stock of knowledge there contribute not merely the separate unity of each conception in itself, nor again simply the fact of a mere uniform contrast between this and all other conceptions, but also those graduated relations of resemblance and affinity in which different conceptions stand to each other. If the white becomes black and the sweet sour, they do not merely become different in the abstract, but pass over from the domain of the one conception in which they participated before into that of another which is separated from the first by a fixed and determinate degree of contrast, a contrast stronger for example than that which obtains between white and yellow, and altogether incommensurable with that absolute gulf of separation which exists between white and sour.

315. I refer to these simple examples once more in order to make it clear how a knowledge may be possible, the truth of which is wholly independent of the question of Scepticism as to its agreement with a world of things outside it. If the current of the outer world had brought before us only once in a transient appearance the perception of two colours or two sounds, our thought would immediately separate them from the moment of time at which they appeared, and fix them and their affinities and their contrasts as an abiding object of inner contemplation, no matter whether they were ever presented to us again in actual experience or not. Again supposing we could never learn how these ideas are able to appear as predicates in things, and in what that which we have called the participation of things in them exactly consists, a question would indeed be left unanswered which might in the course of our reflections prove important, but still the certain knowledge would remain to us undisturbed that the series of colours and the scale of musical tones themselves are each a connected whole with fixed laws, and that in regard to the relation of the members to each other, eternally valid true propositions are vitally opposed to eternally invalid false ones. And finally the question whether after all colours in themselves and tones in themselves are not different from what they appear to us, is one which no one will care to raise again. Or rather we do meet with it again in the confused notion that sounds are in fact merely vibrations of the air, colours merely quiverings of the ether, and it is only to us that they appear in the form of the subjective feelings which we know. It is unnecessary to enlarge over again on the consideration that these feelings do not cease to be real, and are not got rid of and banished out of existence as intruders, because we have discovered certain external causes not resembling them, which are the occasions of their making their appearance to us. Even if these vibrations of external media appeared to differently constituted beings in the form of modes of sensation entirely unknown to us, still the colouring and tones which we see and hear, would constitute for us, when once we have experienced them, a secure treasure of knowledge with a validity and an orderly connection of its own. The feelings of such other beings would remain unknown to us and ours to them, but this would only mean that we have not *all* truths for our portion, but that what we do possess we possess *as* truths in virtue of the identity of every such content of perception with itself, and of the constancy

of identical relations which obtain between different contents. Thus we readily understand the significance of Plato's endeavour to bind together the predicates which are found in the things of the eternal world in continual change, into a determinate and articulated whole, and how he saw in this world of Ideas the true beginnings of certain knowledge; for the external relations which subsist between different Ideas, and through which some are capable of association with each other and others exclude each other, form at all events the limits within which what is to be *possible* in experience falls; the further question what is real in it, and how things manage to have Ideas for *their* predicates, appeared to Plato not to be the primary question, and was for the time reserved.

316. There is one wide-reaching difficulty connected with the first-named aspect of this question. How precisely are we to conceive colours when they are not seen, or tones and their differences when the former are not heard and the latter not apprehended by comparison? Are we to say that they are nothing or that they do not exist, or are we still to attribute to them some predicate which we can hardly define, some kind of being or reality? We shall not be disposed at first to consider them to be nothing at all; for as long as we fix them in our thoughts, as at present in searching for an answer to this very question, every tone and every colour is a determinate content distinguishable from every other, and so a something and not a nothing. Still this decision becomes doubtful when we consider the answer which we feel ourselves compelled to give to the second part of the question. In regard to things we do imagine ourselves, dimly enough, to know wherein their being consists even when they are objects for no intelligence, but exist purely for themselves; but what is meant by a tone when it is heard by no ear and when even the silent idea of its sound is not called up by any mind, we can no more say than what a pain is when no one is hurt by it. But how can that which is not either in itself or in our consciousness, be any longer anything at all or be distinguished from anything else? Still this conclusion again we hesitate to affirm. There is clearly in our first conclusion, speaking quite generally, a certain element of affirmation, which is not entirely to be cancelled by the denial contained in the second. Perhaps it may appear to us a way out of the difficulty to turn the categorical form of our judgment into a hypothetical; two sounds which are neither heard nor imagined are not indeed actually anything, and stand in no actual relations, but they *will* always be something and the one will be different from the other, and stand in a definite relation of contrast to it, *if* they are heard or imagined. Yet even this does not at once satisfy us, for in order even to imagine how the notes a and b can be subject to this varied fortune of being presented to imagination at one time and not so presented at another, and then how it happens that when they are presented in experience the relation Z is necessarily thought along with them, whereas whenever certain other sounds are presented, they are no less necessarily accompanied by a different relation Z' – in order to imagine this we are constrained to ascribe to them existence and definite existence, at a time when according to this view they did not in fact exist at all; for so alone can we explain their subsequent existence and the definite form which their relations then assumed.

I will not pursue these refinements further, but will conclude with the following remarks. We have undoubtedly a conception of affirmation or 'position' in an extremely general sense, which meets us in various fields of enquiry, and for which languages, dealing as they do in their early stages with highly complex and concrete notions, and not with the simplest elements of thought, have commonly no abstract term which expresses it with the requisite purity. But it would not be wise to invent a technical term to represent it, the meaning of which would always be doubtful, because it could never come naturally to the lips or to the thoughts of any one; the very term 'position' which is frequently used for it suggests by its etymological form the entirely alien sense of an act, or operation of establishing[7], to the execution of which that state of affirmation which we wish to express then seems to owe its being. It is best, however, to keep to ordinary speech, and select a word which can be shown to express in common usage, approximately at all events and unmistakeably, the thought with which we are concerned. We may express it in our own language by the term Reality[8]. For[9] we call a thing Real[10] which is, in contradistinction to another which is not; an event Real which occurs or has occurred, in contradistinction to that which does not occur; a relation Real which obtains, as opposed to one which does not obtain; lastly we call a proposition Really true which holds or is valid as opposed to one of which the validity is still doubtful. This use of language is intelligible; it shows that when we call anything Real, we mean always to *affirm* it, though in different senses according to the different forms which it assumes, but one or other of which it must necessarily assume, and of which no one is reducible to or contained in the other. For we never can get an Event out of simple Being, the reality which belongs to Things, namely Being or Existence, never belongs to Events – they do not exist but *occur;* again a Proposition neither exists like things nor occurs like events; that its meaning even obtains like a relation, can only be said if the things *exist* of which it predicates a relation; in itself, apart from all applications which may be made of it, the reality of a proposition means that it holds or is valid and that its opposite does not hold.

Now misunderstandings must always arise, when under the persuasion that the object which we are considering must have some sort of reality or affirmation proper to it, we endeavour to attribute to it, not that kind of reality which is appropriate to it, but a different kind which is alien to it. Then arises the conflict just noticed between the conviction on the one hand that we are right in ascribing to it some sort of reality, and on the other that the particular form of reality to which our misconception has brought us is inadmissible.

Now Ideas, in so far as they are present in our minds, possess reality in the sense of an Event – they *occur* in us: for as utterances of an activity of presentation they are never a Being at rest but a continual Becoming; their content on the other hand, so far as we regard it in abstraction from the mental activity which we direct to it, can no longer be said to occur, though neither again does it exist as things exist; we can only say that it possesses Validity.

And finally we must not ask what in its turn is meant by Validity, with any idea that the meaning which the word conveys clearly to us can be deduced from some different conception; as if, for example, it were possible to find certain conditions by the operation of which either the Being which belongs to things could be so modified and attenuated, or the momentary act of Becoming or occurring, in which the transient reality of ideas regarded as excitations of our consciousness consists, could receive such fixity and independent existence, as that both the one and the other in different ways might pass into this conception of Validity, which at once excludes the substance of the valid assertion from the reality of actual being and implies its independence of human thought. As little as we can say how it happens that anything *is* or *occurs,* so little can we explain how it comes about that a truth has Validity; the latter conception has to be regarded as much as the former as ultimate and underivable, a conception of which everyone may know what he means by it, but which cannot be constructed out of any constituent elements which do not already contain it.

317. From this point of view some light I think is thrown on a surprising statement which is handed down to us in the history of Philosophy. Plato, we are told, ascribed to the Ideas of which he had achieved the conception an existence apart from things, and yet, as these same critics tell us, of like kind with the existence of things. It is strange how peacefully the traditional admiration of the profundity of Plato acquiesces in the ascription to him of so absurd an opinion; we should have to abandon our admiration of him if this really was the doctrine that he taught, and not rather a serious misunderstanding to which in a quite intelligible and pardonable way it has laid itself open. The expression of philosophical ideas is dependent upon the capabilities of each language, and it is hardly possible, in giving utterance

to our meaning, to avoid using words which language has coined to express a merely cognate thought which is not our real meaning at all. And this is pre-eminently the case when a new field is being opened out, and the necessity of distinguishing the precise meaning intended from the ordinary meaning of the word is as yet little felt. This is I think the explanation of the misunderstanding in question. The truth which Plato intended to teach is no other than that which we have just been expounding, that is to say, the validity of truths as such, apart from the question whether they can be established in relation to any object in the external world, as its mode of being, or not; the eternally self-identical significance of Ideas, which always are what they are, no matter whether or not there are things which by participation in them make them manifest in this external world, or whether there are spirits which by thinking them, give them the reality of a mental event. But the Greek language then as afterwards, was wanting in an expression for this conception of Validity as a form of Reality not including Being or Existence; and this very expression Being came, often indeed quite harmlessly, but in this instance with momentous consequences, to fill the place.

Every possible content of thought, regarded as an individual unity, distinct and separate from others, all that class of things for which the language of the School philosophy in later times invented the not inappropriate name of *Res rationis*[11] was to the Greek a Being (*on* or *ousia*); and if the distinction between a really valid truth and a pretended truth came in question the former was distinguished as *ontos on*[12]. The language of ancient Greece never found any term to express the reality of simple Validity as distinguished from the reality of Being, and this constant confusion has prejudiced the clearness of the Platonic phraseology.

318. We may easily see that everything Plato says of the Ideas presents itself when understood in the manner so explained as natural and necessary, and that the various devices to which he resorts in setting forth their nature have this purpose and no other, to exhaust the conception for which no adequate term could be found, by the help of a variety of expressions limiting and supplementing each other. Eternal, without beginning, and imperishable (*aidia, agenneta, anolethra*) the Ideas could not but be named in the presence of the flux of Heraclitus, which seemed in danger of sweeping them away along with the sense-world in its stream. The reality of Being indeed they have or have not, according as transient things of sense are clothed with them or not; but that reality which consists in Validity, which is a reality all their own, remains untouched by all this change. Their independence of time, when brought into comparison with that which comes and goes in time, would hardly be otherwise expressed than by this predicate of eternity which at once partakes of time and denies its power, just in the same way as we should most easily recognise that which has no validity and could have no validity in itself by the fact of its never occurring at any moment of time.

Again, we understand the ideas being called separable or separate from things (*choris ton onton*), first because the image (*eidos*) of their content can be still called up to memory after the things which originally occasioned its appearance in us have vanished from real existence, and next, because the content is taken to include what can be apprehended in a universal form, and remains the same in different external manifestations, so as to be independent of the mode in which it is realised to sense in any particular instance.

But it was not Plato's intention to represent the ideas as independent merely of things while still depending for their special mode of reality upon the mind which thinks them. Reality of Existence it is true they enjoy only in the moment in which they become, in the character of objects or creations of an act of presentation now actually occurring, members of this changing world of Being and Becoming; but on the other hand we all feel certain in the moment in which we think any truth, that we have not created it for the first time but merely recognised it; it was valid before we thought about it and will continue so without regard to any existence of whatever kind, of things or of us, whether or not it ever finds manifestation in the reality of Existence, or a place as an object of knowledge in the reality of a Thought. This is what we all believe with regard to truth when we set out to search for it, and it may be lament over its inaccessibility at least to any form of human knowledge; the truth which is never apprehended by us is valid no whit less than that small fraction of it which finds its way into our intelligence.

The independent validity of the Ideas Plato emphasises again in a somewhat different form, in answer to the doctrine of Protagoras, rescuing them in their character of being in themselves that which they are (*auta kath' auta onta*) from the relativity in which the famous dictum of that Sophist was in danger of involving them. Even granting that his doctrine has its truth so long as it is confined to the impressions of sense, and that viewed in this relation Plato's opposition to it rests upon a misunderstanding, granting that is to say that my sensation is as true for me as yours which differs from it is for you, Plato would still be right in insisting that for neither of us could the sensation be possible at all, unless that which we felt in the sensation whatever it be, red or blue, sweet or bitter, had a definite and constant significance of its own, as a member of a world of Ideas. This world of Ideas is the permanent and inexhaustible treasure-house from which the things of the external world draw all the diverse and shifting attributes they wear, and the mind the varying series of its experiences; and a sensation or idea whose content has no fixed and determinate place, no fixed relations of affinity or difference in the universal world of thought, but stands in complete isolation, bare of all relations to anything in that world, the possession of a single individual mind alone, is in fact an impossibility.

While Plato by thus describing the Ideas, takes security for their independent validity, he has at the same time abundantly provided against the confusion of the validity thus implied with that wholly distinct reality of Existence which could only be ascribed to a durable thing. When he places the home of the Ideas in a super-celestial world, a world of pure intelligence (*noetos huperouranios topos*), when again more than this he expressly describes them as having no local habitation, such language makes it abundantly clear to anyone who understands the mind of Greek Antiquity, that they do *not* belong to what we call the real world. To the Greek that which is not in Space is not at all, and when Plato relegates the Ideas to a home which is not in space, he is not trying to hypostasize that which we call their mere validity into any kind of real existence, but on the contrary he is plainly seeking to guard altogether against any such attempt being made. Nor is it any objection that the Ideas are called unities (*henades, monades*), for there is no occasion to interpret these titles from an atomistic standpoint, whether in the sense of material indivisibility or of a self-identity resembling that of a self-conscious subject. For in fact what constitutes the *meaning* of an Idea, and of a complex no less than of a simple Idea, is that it manifests itself as a unity, unifying the elements which cohere in it and rejecting that which is alien to it. Nevertheless although these various expressions point one and all to the fact that Plato never asserted the existence of the Ideas but only their eternal validity, he had still no better answer to make to the question, what then are they, than to bring them again under the general denomination of *ousia*. Then the door was opened to the misunderstanding which has since widely spread, though no one has ever been able to say what the nature of that existence, into which he is accused of having hypostasized his ideas, precisely is.

319. There are two objections which may be taken to the view here maintained. First, the use which Plato makes of the Ideas to explain the course of the world, in which they assert their influence not merely as valid truths but as operating forces – this is a point to which I shall come later; and in the second place, the attitude of Aristotle. For it is really the very definite language of Aristotle which has established the doctrine of the reality of the Ideas as a dogma of Plato, whereas Plato's own statements are in no way inconsistent with the other interpretation which we have preferred. It seems incredible that the most acute of Plato's disciples, informed by personal intercourse with the master, should have

misunderstood him in a point of such serious moment as this. At the same time we are justified by the nature of his polemic not against particular statements of Plato but against the doctrine of Ideas altogether, as well as by many details in his criticisms, in assuming that his attack is in part directed against certain misunderstandings of the Platonic doctrine which had gained hold in the Academy at an early period. For he could not well have challenged Plato himself to show *where* the Ideas are, when Plato had said in plain terms that they were nowhere. He could not have directed against Plato the criticism that there must logically be Ideas of products of art, for one passage at least is to be found in the Republic which is entirely in agreement with that criticism, and how far Plato was from having overlooked the difficulty there involved, is evidenced by the opening of the Parmenides. Finally as to Aristotle's objections to the Ideas that they are superfluous, being mere copies of individual objects, and the assumption from which his elaborate analysis frequently starts, that there are as many examples of every Idea as there are instances of its application in reality, these are criticisms which do not really apply to the doctrines of Plato himself. That every Idea is what it is once for all, that what we are to understand by it is not an individual thing but a universal comprehending many things, and that all its manifestations are only copies of this one essential reality, is the doctrine which he never abandons, whatever obscurity may still attach to that operation on the part of the individual things, described as imitation or participation, by which they provide the one Idea with a countless number of realisations in the world of actual existence.

The discussion therefore which fills the XIIth (XIIIth) book of Aristotle's Metaphysics and of which the purport is to exhibit the absurdity of attributing to the Idea a reality identical with the reality of actually existing things, I cannot regard as a refutation of the pure Platonic doctrine, and the less so inasmuch as at the end Aristotle himself equally fails to find a decisive and unambiguous expression for that more appropriate form of reality which he desires, in contradistinction to this, to ascribe to them. To him the only genuine *ousia* is the individual thing, and there we must certainly agree with him; to the individual thing alone belongs the reality of Existence; still for Aristotle as much as for Plato the object of knowledge is always the universal; not only in the sense that we are incapable of exhausting the meaning of the individual thing, but that so far as we investigate it in its nature and its workings with any prospect of a result, we invariably proceed according to universal principles. But Aristotle is entirely at one with his predecessors, that that which is not, or has no reality in any sense, cannot be an object of knowledge either, and so in regard to the universal we cannot say that it simply is not, but that in a sense it is and in a sense it is not.

I do not propose to enter into Aristotle's further treatment of this question in detail. I must however remark that by placing the universal and the Idea within the Individual things and not outside them he does not explain the possibility of knowledge; for the mere fact of the presence of the Idea in one individual does not entitle us to transfer all the consequences which flow from it to a second individual in which it happens also to be found; it can only justify us in concluding from the doings of one real thing to those of another, if it includes within itself a number of characteristics so related that the appearance of any one necessarily implies the presence of the rest. Such considerations would at once conduct Aristotle back to the admission that the Idea is certainly in a sense *choris ton onton*[13]; but in what sense it is so was impossible for him to define, since he no more possessed than his master did a technical equivalent for our term validity; and thus eventually the universal conception or Idea came to be for him also an *ousia*, not indeed a true or *prote ousia* but still a *deutera ousia*[14].

320. It may appear to us a strange spectacle to see two of the greatest philosophers of antiquity struggling with imperfect success to arrive at clearness upon so simple a distinction as that which we have been considering. But such a view would do both of them injustice. The apprehension of the simplest relations of thought is not the simplest act of the faculty of

thought, and the whole long history of philosophy teaches how ready we all are at any moment to be guilty of a degree of obscurity in the application of ideas which if reduced to its simplest terms would appear to us incredible. Whenever men have believed themselves to have discovered a principle which appears to represent the universal element in the constitution and development of the real world, they invariably go on to exalt it into the position of an independent reality and to represent it as a pure form of being, in comparison with which the individual things retire into a position of subordinate and even unreal existence. I need not even refer to the latest phase of German philosophy which aspired to set on the throne of the Platonic Ideas the one absolute Idea, for the same tendency is apparent enough in spheres of thought outside the circle of philosophy. How often do we hear in our own day of eternal and unchangeable laws of nature to which all phenomena and their changes are subjected; laws which would indeed cease to manifest themselves if there were no longer any things for them to control, but which would even then themselves continue in their eternal validity and would revive with their old effective power the moment a new object presented itself from any quarter for them to apply to; nay there is not even wanting on occasion, the enthronement of these laws above all existing realities in that very super-celestial habitation which with Plato is the home of the Ideas. Nevertheless those who hold this language would indignantly repel the imputation of ascribing to those laws an existence whether as things or as persons outside the things which are governed by them, and Plato may resist with equal justice a similar misinterpretation of his doctrines.

Finally it must be added that we ourselves, in drawing a distinction between the reality which belongs to the Ideas and laws and that which belongs to things, and calling the one Being or Existence[15] and the other Validity[16], have so far merely discovered, thanks to the resources of our language, a convenient expression which may keep us on our guard against interchanging the two notions. The fact which the term validity expresses has lost none of that strangeness which has led to its being confounded, as we have seen, with existence. It is merely that we have been so long accustomed to it; we use our thought as we do any other natural faculty without troubling ourselves about it, and take it as a matter of course that the content of manifold perceptions and phenomena does invariably adapt itself to general conceptions and can be read by us in the light of general laws, in such wise that the consequences which those laws lead us to predict are found to coincide with the actual phenomenal order which supervenes. But that this should be the case, that there should be universal laws, which have not themselves existence like things and which nevertheless rule the operation of things, – remains for a mind which realises its meaning, a profoundly mysterious fact which might well inspire rapture and wonder in its discoverer; and that he should have made the discovery will always remain a great philosophical achievement of Plato, whatever the problems it may have left still unsolved.

321. One of these problems is that of the exact nature of the relation of things to the ideas which Plato describes by the terms participation or imitation. I do not propose at present to discuss this question at large; but there is one defect in the doctrine of the Ideas which a criticism of Aristotle's – in itself not well-founded – may suggest to us. Among the reasons which led him to regard the Ideas as both superfluous and useless, he especially emphasises the fact that they supply no beginning of motion. However true this objection may be in itself, the fact that they do not perform this task proves little against the doctrine of the Ideas; the real objection is that they do not, as we shall see, adequately perform the task for which Plato intended them. As concerns Aristotle's criticism let us turn to the sciences of our own day. What shall we say of our Laws of Nature? Do they contain in themselves a beginning of motion? On the contrary, they all presuppose a series of data which they cannot themselves establish, but from which, *once given*, the necessary connection one with another of the phenomena which ensue is deducible. No natural law ordains that

the different bodies in our planetary system should move, or that their course should be directed towards one and not another quarter of the heavens, or that the acceleration which they impose on each other by the force of attraction should have the particular amount which it has and not a different one. But is the whole system of mechanical truths useless and mere empty babble (*kenologein*) because it leaves these first beginnings of motion to be explained from some other source, and starting from the fact of motion as it actually finds it, is satisfied with explaining its different phases in their necessary connection with each other? There may be obscurity enough – though after all not more than in our own mode of representing the matter – in Plato's relegation of the primary motive impulses upon which the succession of phenomena depends, to that dim world of *hyle*, which represents to him the material which is given for the Ideas to be applied to. But for all that to see in the world of Ideas the patterns to which all that is, *if* anything is, must conform, was a thought of which the importance is unfairly ignored by Aristotle. For he was himself on a later occasion to have recourse to that very same thought, for the explanation of individual phenomena: he too found himself unable to allow the cause of motion which communicates the actualising impulse also to control its issue; this had been decided from all eternity by those universal laws, which in their turn take no part in the communication of the impulse.

On the other hand it must undoubtedly be admitted to be a deficiency in the Platonic doctrine that this, which was its actual undertaking, it only half accomplishes. An account of the necessary connection of two contents of thought must always assume the logical form of a judgment; it cannot be expressed in the form of a mere notion which does not in itself contain a proposition at all. Thus we have always employed laws, that is to say propositions, which express a relation between different elements, as examples to explain the meaning of Validity in contradistinction to Existence. The term cannot be transferred to single concepts without some degree of obscurity: we can only say of concepts that they *mean* something, and they mean something because certain propositions are valid *of* them, as for example the proposition that the content of any given concept is identical with itself and stands in unchangeable relations of affinity or contrast to others. Now Plato apprehended the elements of the world of thought which he discovered almost exclusively under the form of the isolated concept or the Idea. We need not look beyond the general impression which his Dialogues leave with us to be aware how rarely by comparison we meet with general propositions; they are by no means entirely absent, on the contrary they are made on occasions the subject of important disquisitions, but that it is propositions as such and nothing else which must necessarily form the most essential constituents of the ideal world, is a truth which never forced itself upon Plato's mind. His peculiar point of view is not without modern parallels. Kant himself in his search for the *a priori* forms which were to give the unity of an inner coherence to the empirical content of our perceptions, made the mistake at starting of developing them in the form of single concepts, the Categories, and that in spite of the fact that he derived them from the forms of the judgment itself. And now having got them, as he thought, in his Categories, it became the more evident that there was nothing to be made of them, and thereupon followed the attempt to derive judgments out of them again, and so he arrived at the 'Principles of the Understanding' which it was now possible to apply as major premises to the minor premises furnished by experience. It seems therefore that this disposition to bring into the inadequate form of a single concept truths which can only be adequately expressed through the proposition, is natural to the imagination at all times, and is not peculiar to the plastic mind of ancient Greece. It may however be remarked in passing how dangerous a tendency it is, leading the mind as it does away from the full concrete reality which is the true aim of its enquiries to a barren playing with empty ideas which have become separated from their natural foundations.

Thus we find our present requirements hardly at all satisfied in Plato, and even the need of satisfying them not clearly or adequately recognised. It is true the abstract thought that the Ideas are not only a multitude of individuals but that they make up all together an organic and articulated whole – this thought is the soul of all his teaching, and he describes with enthusiasm the delight which he finds in the dialectical exercise of resolving the complex structure of the Ideal world into its elements, following the natural joinings, and then putting them together again; even the different degrees of agreement or of contrast between individual ideas and the possible modes of combining them are mentioned as subjects worthy of investigation. But in the examples which he gives of the application of his method, the art of Dialectic ends almost invariably in a mere classification of Ideas, by which we are shown the place which belongs to any one Idea in a system of division in virtue of the elements which it combines, but which furnishes us with no single proposition, adds no jot to our knowledge concerning the nature of any one of the Ideas which could not have been arrived at equally without this circuitous route of classification. If we want to know what can be said or cannot be said of any Idea we have still to learn it, after the classification as much as before, from other sources. The joinings and articulations of truth which Plato's sole aim was not to mutilate he ought to have investigated with a firmer hand; instead of making a systematic collection of the flora of the Ideas, he ought to have turned his thoughts to the general physiological conditions which in each single plant bind limb to limb according to a law of growth. Or, dropping the figure, the existence of a world of Ideas possessing a definite meaning and an unchangeable validity being once clearly and emphatically established, the next task was to investigate the universal laws which govern its structure, through which alone, in an Ideal world as elsewhere, the individual elements can be bound together into a whole. Thus the question to be dealt with at this point was what are those *first principles* of our knowledge under which the manifold world of Ideas has itself to be arranged. This is the more precisely defined form which the systematic enquiry into Truth and the source of Truth now assumes for us.

Notes

1. From *Logik* of 1874. Translation by Bernard Bosanquet. New York: Garland, 1980, Book 3, Chp. II, pp. 201–222. – Ed.
2. *Idee*. Where the term 'Idea' represents '*Idee*' and not '*Vorstellung*' it is printed with a capital 'I.' – Trans.
3. *Allgemeinbegriff*
4. *Inhalt*
5. v. § 3.
6. Cf. §§ 13–16.
7. *Setzung*
8. *Wirklichkeit*
9. Cf. 'Metaphysic,' p. I, and for '*Objectivität*' contrasted with different forms of '*Wirklichkeit*' see above, § 3.
10. *Wirklich*
11. *Gedankending*
12. 'true being'
13. *Separated from the entities*
14. *First essence and second essence*
15. *Sein*
16. *Geltung*

PART 2

The Marburg School

Hermann Cohen, Paul Natorp, Ernst Cassirer

Introduction: Hermann Cohen (1842–1918)

HERMANN COHEN WAS BORN IN COSWIG (Anhalt) in 1842 into an orthodox Jewish family. In many ways, his life is reflective of Jews in Germany at the time. His father, Gerson Cohen, was the cantor of the Coswig Jewish community, and taught at the Jewish school. Much of the family's income, however, derived from the hat shop of his mother, Friederike. Hermann left Gymnasium to study at the Rabbinical Seminary in Breslau (then part of the German empire, now in Polish territory), the town where Hannah Arendt was born in 1906. Such was the orthodox milieu in which Cohen grew up, and from which he distanced himself for a while before moving closer to it again in 1880, when he publicly opposed the anti-Semitic tirades of the politician Heinrich von Treitschke. In 1861, he matriculated in philosophy and classics in Berlin, where one of his teachers was the Aristotelian Friedrich Adolph von Trendelenburg.

It was at the University of Halle, however, that Cohen defended his dissertation in 1865, having submitted it once already in 1863 in Berlin (the work was awarded a prize there, but he would not be promoted to Doctor of Philosophy due to anti-Semitic sentiments in the university). After that, three attempts at receiving his Habilitation in Berlin were thwarted, further indicating the anti-Semitic tenor in German academia at the time. Although his dissertation was on the topic of psychology in Plato and Aristotle, Cohen's first publications were in the journal founded by Moritz Lazarus and Heymann Steinthal, *Zeitschrift für Völkerpsychologie* (a journal for "an anthropological investigation of the origins of cultural products such as art and literature," as Scott Edgar puts it), where Cohen took a psychological stance on the question of the future development of philosophy—a position he would come later to vigorously oppose. By intervening in the dispute between Trendelenburg and Kuno Fischer on the nature of Kant's doctrine of space in 1871, he achieved some recognition amongst contemporaries, while at the same time coming to doubt his earlier psychologistic position. In the same year, Cohen published the first volume of his commentaries on Kant's three Critiques, *Kants Theorie der Erfahrung* (*Kant's Theory of Experience*), which went through three editions in Cohen's lifetime and which counts, to this day, as a foundational work of Kant interpretation. (*Kants Begründung der Ethik* [*Kant's Grounding of Ethics*] appeared in 1877 and *Kants Begründung der Aesthetik* [*Kant's Grounding of Aesthetics*] appeared in 1889). Lange, who had been in

Marburg since 1872, took notice of the young scholar and enabled his Habilitation there in 1873. Cohen was named *Professor Extraordinarius* in 1875 and became Lange's successor in 1876. Natorp's move to Marburg in 1881, facilitated by Cohen, cemented the foundations of the "Marburg School". Natorp was referred to by Cohen as the "minister of the interior," while Cohen, who despised the provincial atmosphere of the university town, preferred to leave Marburg as much as possible and called himself, in turn, the "minister of the exterior."

The Marburg School bloomed between 1890 and 1910. It was, besides the Southwest School of Neo-Kantianism, the strongest and most "compact" (in the judgment of Helmut Holzhey) philosophical grouping in the German-speaking countries. After 1900, Cohen set out to write his own "System of Philosophy," comprising three volumes, which appeared in 1902, 1907, and 1912, respectively: *Logik der reinen Erkenntnis* [*Logic of Pure Cognition*], *Ethik des reinen Willens* [*Ethics of Pure Willing*], *Aesthetik des reinen Gefühl* [*Aesthetics of Pure Feeling*]. The recurring emphasis on "purity" and the "transcendental method" was to become the trademark of the Marburg School: all cultural phenomena, following Kant's canonical threefold distinction, had to be developed *a priori* from the pure "logic of origin" that constructs these fields of culture. The Marburg School in general, and Cohen in particular, are often referred to as "logicistic" or exclusively oriented towards the sciences, in that they equated or reduced philosophy to epistemology or, more precisely, to the theory of cognition (interpreting *Erkenntnistheorie* as *Erkenntniskritik*). However, it must be emphasized that the overall goal of the Marburg School, as stated by Cohen from the very start, was to be a *philosophy of culture*.

Cohen's time in Marburg was marred by his frequent infighting with colleagues and the university administration (as well as the Ministry of Education) over his requests to further the development of the school. Although Cohen had, by all accounts, an abrasive personality, he doubtless received more unfair treatment than a "real" German would have. Disgusted with university politics—for instance, he was unsuccessful in placing Ernst Cassirer, by all lights a rising star at the time, as his successor—he retired in 1912 and moved to Berlin to teach at the *Hochschule für die Wissenschaft des Judentums* [Academy for the Science of Judaism], where he had a profound influence on many students, including Franz Rosenzweig and Martin Buber. He died in 1918 while working on a fourth part of his philosophical system, devoted to a "psychology as unity of cultural consciousness," and his pupils Rosenzweig and Buber edited his last finished work, the 1919 *Religion der Vernunft aus den Quellen des Judentums* [*Religion of Reason out of the Sources of Judaism*], from which a selection is taken here as well.

Cohen's hope for mutual tolerance between Christians and Jews based on their philosophical affinities was posthumously and tragically disappointed. In 1942, his wife Martha Cohen was murdered by the Nazis, at the age of 82, in the concentration camp at Theresienstadt. His syncretism came to be seen by many twentieth century scholars as, at best, naïve (Myers, 2001). Today, a meandering footpath in Marburg, leading from the old town to the *Philosophische Fakultät*, commemorates Hermann Cohen.

Further Reading

Edgar, Scott, "Hermann Cohen," *The Stanford Encyclopedia of Philosophy* (Winter 2012 Edition), Edward N. Zalta (ed.), available online at http://plato.stanford.edu/archives/win2012/entries/cohen/ (accessed 16 March 2015).

Holzhey, Helmut (2005), "Cohen and the Marburg School in Context," in Munk (ed.), pp. 3–37.

Munk, Reinier, ed. (2005), *Hermann Cohen's Critical Idealism*. Dordrecht: Springer, 2005. [This is, so far, the only English-language essay collection encompassing Cohen's entire *oeuvre*.]

Myers, David N. (2001), "Hermann Cohen and the Quest for Protestant Judaism," in: *Leo Baeck Institute Year Book* 46 (2001), 195–214.

Patton, Lydia (2005), "The Critical Philosophy Renewed: The Bridge between Hermann Cohen's Early Work on Kant and Later Philosophy of Science," in: *Angelaki: Journal of the Theoretical Humanities,* 10(1), pp. 109–118.

Renz, Ursula, ed. (2011), "Hermann Cohens Philosophie," in: *Deutsche Zeitschrift für Philosophie* (59/2), pp. 221–322. [This is a theme volume on the philosophy of Cohen with articles by Renz, Andrea Esser, Reinier Munk, Pierfrancesco Fiorato and Hartwig Wiedebach, with a conversation on Cohen's timeliness between Renz, Bienenstock, Helmut Holzhey and Esser.]

Sieg, Ulrich (1994), *Aufstieg und Niedergang des Marburger Neukantianismus. Die Geschichte einer philosophischen Schulgemeinschaft.* Würzburg: K&N.

"Introduction" to *The Principle of the Infinitesimal Method and Its History* by David Hyder

Cohen's 1883 *Principle of the Infinitesimal Method and Its History* appeared shortly before the second edition of *Kant's Theory of Experience* and complements the treatment of extensive and intensive magnitudes of that text (see following selection). Both books argue that there is no distinction between pure and applied mathematics, and the *Principle* unpacks this claim for differential quantities by means of a detailed comparison of Leibniz's "logical" method with Newton's calculus of fluxions, and its connection to Kant's theory of intensive magnitudes.[1] For Cohen, "time is the uniform original measure [*Urmaass*], and thus it becomes the bearer of continuity" (Cohen 1883), §90, p.131; furthermore, since "time is the general expression of that nomologicality whose problem is motion," (§46, 42) space, time and motion are intrinsically connected in a single kinematic science. Leibniz's analytic approach is therefore to be rejected in favor of one that acknowledges the transcendental contribution of intuition. However, by this point, Cohen has already reinterpreted both the terms "experience" and "intuition" methodologically, following his developing program of the "critique of cognition" (*Erkenntniskritik*).

Both terms are to be understood in terms of the foundations of science, and the contribution of our concept of time to the development of the calculi is methodological. Cohen finds a modern ally in the work of Cournot (1841: §85, 122), according to whom the infinitesimal is "*the natural expression of the formation of physical magnitudes,*"[2] and who explicitly rejects contemporary attempts to give such a logical foundation on the grounds that "the abstraction of logical laws should provide the *rudimentary* foundations for all developments of cognitive forms, albeit not all means for this development. We have laid this general logical foundation, which also runs below the roots of intuition, in the *Principle of the continuity of consciousness*. On the condition of this principle, but only on its condition, can one speak of the limit method as a *logical* one" (89–90). However, Cohen's defense of this intuitional residue was ill-timed, since the mathematical community had by this time fully absorbed Weierstraß's work. The question of which approach is preferable – temporal-intuitional or real-analytic – was a starting point for the work of Weierstraß's student, Edmund Husserl, and the earlier approach did not survive the turn of the century.

Further Reading

Cohen, Hermann (1883). *Das Princip der Infinitesmal-Methode und seine Geschichte: ein Kapitel zur Grundlegung der Erkenntnisskritik.* Berlin: F. Dümmler.

Cournot, Antoine-Augustin (1841). *Traité élémentaire de la théorie des fonctions et du calcul infinitésimal.* Paris: L. Hachette.

"The Synthetic Principles" from *Kant's Theory of Experience* (1885) by David Hyder

In his successive editions of *Kant's Theory of Experience*, Cohen articulated the single most influential reading of the *Critique of Pure Reason* – one which, through its impact on the generation of scholars who prepared the canonical editions used in the twentieth century, still sets boundaries on contemporary interpretation. In this chapter of the second edition, Cohen puts several key theses of the Marburg interpretation in their mature form. The first edition of 1871 already contained an extended critique of so-called "physiological" interpretations of Kant's theory of *a priori* principles; however, Cohen had not had time to digest the criticisms raised by Helmholtz against Kant's account of geometry and its relation to kinematics. Defusing these criticisms led to the following adjustments to Cohen's reading. (a) Cohen explicitly prefers the "analytic" method of the *Prolegomena* to that of the *Critique*, meaning that (b) the Principles of Pure Understanding (the "levers of experience") are taken as the data of transcendental analysis. (c) The task of such analysis is not to justify the future validity of mathematical and metaphysical principles, rather it is to explain the "possibility of their aprioricity" in Newtonian science. (d) Not only is the psychologistic approach of the A-edition of the *Critique*, in particular the A-Deduction, rejected in favor of the B-Deduction's account of objective experience, but such experience is identified with the "content" of natural science. (e) Cohen argues that the role of the Transcendental Aesthetic is "negative," and that geometrical propositions make no independent truth-claims. Thus, (f) the distinction between pure and applied mathematics is denied, and geometry is reinterpreted as essentially connected to kinematics. (g) This identification is justified by appealing to the role of the temporal schema of the concept of extensive quantity. Because determinate regions of space are produced in successive synthesis, the metrical element of Riemannian geometry is intrinsically linked to time, and thereby to the science of mechanics. In other words, Kant's theory of geometry was already an instance of what Helmholtz calls "physical geometry."

The last three theses (e–g) can all be seen as implementations of suggestions made by Helmholtz in the conclusion to his 1870/76 "The Origin and Significance of Geometrical Axioms" (reprinted in this volume), where he observes that a "strict Kantian" could save Kant by reinterpreting his theory of geometry as a normative-conceptual stipulation of what is to count as rigid-body motion. Cohen's concluding remarks on physical geometry and the "applicability" of the axioms of geometry directly reflect Helmholtz's use of these terms in the German title to its 1878 sequel (also in this volume) "The Applicability of the Axioms to the Physical World." These ideas were later extended by Poincaré, who was familiar with Cohen's work through the circle around Émile Boutroux, and was in direct contact with Felix Klein.

"The Relationship of Logic to Physics" from the 1914–15 Edition of Lange's *History of Materialism* by Lydia Patton

The *History of Materialism and Critique of its Significance for the Present* is the best known work by the nineteenth-century philosopher Friedrich Albert Lange (1828–1875). Lange began his history of materialism in 1857, as part of a seminar at the Universität Bonn. The timing of Lange's project reflects renewed interest in evaluating theories according to which causality and explanation are based on analysis of the behavior of matter.

Philosophers and scientists who called themselves materialists increased in number over the first half of the nineteenth century. But what was the significance of the materialist tradition, what were its main theses, and what were the significant differences between different materialist approaches? The project of analyzing and defending the materialist position was taken up by, among others, Ludwig Büchner in *Power and Material* [*Kraft und Stoff*] (1855), Jacob Moleschott in *The Circulation of Life* [*Der Kreislauf des Lebens*] (1852), Carl Vogt in *Superstition and Science* [*Köhlerglaube und Wissenschaft*] (1855), and Heinrich Czolbe in *The New Presentation of Sensualism* [*Die Neue Darstellung des Sensualismus*] (1855).

Some materialists attempted to argue that not only particular causal relationships, but also ultimate scientific explanations of the phenomena, could be given via descriptions of the behavior of observable matter. Other materialist philosophers were more cautious. In 1872, Emil Du Bois-Reymond gave a lecture, "On the Boundaries of Knowledge of Nature."[3] Du Bois-Reymond posed seven puzzles, the first of which were the nature of matter and force, and the origin of motion. Du Bois-Reymond regarded these two problems as unsolvable, which led to the well-known nickname of the lecture: the "Ignorabimus" ["we will not know"] lecture.

In later editions of the *History*, Lange distinguishes between materialism about causality and materialism about explanation. He argues that one can be a materialist about causality without sacrificing idealism in explanation. One can argue that no ideal or non-material causes are needed to represent observed relations among the phenomena, but that more is needed to give an ultimate explanation of the phenomena than representing observed relations alone. Lange leaves room for idealist contributions to higher-level explanation, though he rarely defends any particular such explanation.

Lange's attempt to leave room for idealism may have been inspired by a young philosopher with whom he had begun corresponding in the 1860s, Hermann Cohen. Speaking of the 1875 second edition of the *History of Materialism*, "Lange admitted that Cohen's book *Kant's Theory of Experience* (1871; translated in part in this volume) had inspired him to revise his presentation of the Kantian system" (Holzhey p. 3).

Cohen, like Lange, had a keen interest in the history of science and of philosophy, and thought that such history could be a source material for philosophical analysis. Another approach Cohen has in common with Lange is that Cohen considered analysis of his contemporaries to be a kind of "history." Cohen's 1871 essay adjudicating the debate then going on between Adolf Trendelenburg and Kuno Fischer on the nature of Kantian space and time, concludes with a disquisition on the role of the "philosophical historian" in settling contemporary disputed questions. Analyzing the history of a philosophical position, including the motives for building a particular theory or defending a specific belief, can lead the way to discovering which philosopher should win a debate, according to Cohen.

In the *History of Materialism*, Lange did not defend in detail any epistemological position about the source of scientific and philosophical explanations, limiting himself to an account according to which such ideas are a result of poetic or speculative construction in imagination. Cohen, in contrast, argued for a logical and epistemological account of the sources of scientific explanations.[4] These sources included mathematical concepts and methods such as the "infinitesimal method," the subject of Cohen's 1883 monograph.[5]

Cohen's analysis of ideas as sources of scientific theories and explanations is characteristic of the approach of the Marburg school. Cohen's introduction to Lange's *History* is continuous with Lange's project in some ways, but also lays out some features of Cohen's distinct historical and philosophical project.[6] Cohen's approach to the philosophy of science, in particular, involves taking the "facts" of science and of culture as *explananda*, and then of providing explanations that show how the methods of science gave rise to these facts.[7]

Cohen's analysis of the influence of ideas and of scientific methods in history inspired a rich and complex tradition in the history and philosophy of science, which is the subject of renewed recent interest. Cohen was a significant influence on the eminent historian and philosopher of science Ernst Cassirer, an influence that can be seen in the essay translated for this volume.

While Cohen's project has an excitement of its own, in some ways Lange appears the more Kantian. Lange has a keen sense of the limits of knowledge and of scientific and philosophical explanation, akin to Kant's commitment to respecting the limits of metaphysics. Cohen and Lange agree that speculative thought based on ideas makes a contribution to our explanations, but Lange is more skeptical about the possibility of explaining how ideas produce knowledge. The dialogue between Lange and Cohen raises questions about the history of science and of philosophy, about the relationship between the author of a theory and the theory itself, and about the limits of understanding and of explanation.

Further Reading

Büchner, Ludwig (Louis) (1855). *Kraft und Stoff: Empirisch-naturphilosophische Studien.* Frankfurt am Main: Verlag von Weidinger Sohn und Cie.

Czolbe, Heinrich (1855). *Neue Darstellung des Sensualismus.* Leipzig: Hermann Costenoble.

Grier, Michelle (2009). "Kant's Critique of Metaphysics," *The Stanford Encyclopedia of Philosophy (Summer 2009 Edition)*, Edward N. Zalta (ed.), available online at http://plato.stanford.edu/archives/sum2009/entries/kant-metaphysics/ (accessed 16 March 2015).

Holzhey, Helmut (2005). "Cohen and the Marburg School in Context," pp. 3–37 in *Hermann Cohen's Critical Idealism*, edited by Reinier Munk. Dordrecht, The Netherlands: Springer Verlag.

Lange, Friedrich Albert (1866). *Geschichte des Materialismus und Kritik seiner Bedeutung in der Gegenwart.* Iserlohn: J. Baedeker. [Translation following is from the Ninth Edition.]

Moleschott, Jacob (1852). *Der Kreislauf des Lebens: physiologische Antworten auf Liebig's Chemische Briefe.* Mainz: Zabern.

Moynahan, Gregory B. (2003). "Hermann Cohen's *Das Prinzip der Infinitesimalmethode*, Ernst Cassirer, and the Politics of Science in Wilhelmine Germany," in: *Perspectives on Science* Vol. 11 No. 1: 35–75.

Vogt, Carl (1855). *Köhlerglaube und Wissenschaft. Eine Streitschrift gegen Hofrath Rudolph Wagner in Göttingen.* Gießen: Ricker.

"The Discovery of Man as Fellowman," from *Religion of Reason out of the Sources of Judaism* (1918)

The Religion of Reason out of the Sources of Judaism was Cohen's last finished manuscript, but Cohen died, in 1918, before seeing it in print; it appeared in 1919. This work manifests a shift in Cohen's thinking that had been beginning at the latest after his departure from Marburg in 1912, a pivot after Cohen finished his three-volume *System der Philosophie* in that same year. After his retirement, he taught in the Berlin *Hochschule für die Wissenschaft des Judentums* (the Academy for the Study of Judaism). It is noteworthy that the book was edited and published posthumously by his Berlin students Martin Buber and Franz Rosenzweig. This is remarkable since Buber and Rosenzweig indicate Cohen's influence on a wholly different group of students, and they themselves, as is known, were to become renowned thinkers in the Jewish tradition. Some of the themes of the late Cohen can be identified in Buber's and Rosenzweig's work. Although the fate of Judaism, especially in the German diaspora, had been on Cohen's mind for a long time, the move to Berlin also signaled a shift in his philosophical attentions, although Cohen had intended to complete his "System of Philosophy" with a fourth volume on the "unity of cultural consciousness." (Presumably, the work did not get beyond planning stages, though Holzhey describes its purpose as follows: "With the expression 'cultural consciousness' Cohen joined two aspects of the problem of system: the level of the theory of culture and the level of the theory of consciousness."[8])

In cosmopolitan Berlin, Cohen exerted a great deal of influence not only on his students, but also on the general Jewish population in Germany at the time. As someone who does not consider himself an expert in Cohen's thought, Leo Strauss recalls "[growing] up in an environment in which Cohen was the center of attraction for philosophically minded Jews who were devoted to Judaism; he was the master whom they revered".[9] It is no doubt his writings in the context of Judaism that account for this attraction, not his earlier writings on Kant and the Marburg-style "transcendental method."

In the book, Cohen sought to bring out precisely the Jewish sources of a "religion of reason" that he found lacking or underrepresented in the Christian tradition. As someone whose "truly" belonging to Germany and its intellectual tradition had constantly been challenged because he was a Jew (who made statements about Germany's "ownmost" thinker, Kant), Cohen wanted to present a counterweight to the Christian-Protestant tradition of Germany, the soil from which Kant's moral philosophy grew. Hence, the title and the project that the book pursues are a certain provocation to both Cohen's non-Jewish and Jewish contemporaries. As opposed to a "rational religion from the sources of the New Testament," Cohen wants to furnish a complete religion of reason, including a moral philosophy, from Judaic sources. The book is thus a powerful study not only of the central tenets of Jewish thought, but also of its entire worldview whose vision is, as Cohen wishes to argue, more pervasive than the German Enlightenment tradition culminating in Kant, which fed off Protestant-Lutheran Christianity.

Religion of Reason contains twenty-two chapters that lay out this alternative worldview and are intended to move from "the historical concept of Judaism to the *philosophy of religion*" (p. 5), as Cohen characterizes his endeavor. The central chapters are, in the estimation of Kenneth Seeskin, Chapter VIII on "The Discovery of Man as Fellowman," which has been translated here, and Chapter XI, "Atonement". In Chapter VIII, Cohen seeks to articulate an alternative to "the discovery of the individual I," which one can characterize as the Kantian starting point both in theoretical and practical philosophy. Indeed, the Judaic counter-weight to this emphasis is the discovery of "man as fellowman," which was achieved by the "social prophets" such as Ezekiel. What Cohen talks about is the framing of the individual as Thou, as a fellowman, as the other, a correlation which is firstly discovered in the correlation between God and man. The I, as the "isolated individual," is only a derivative form of individuality, the "seeing individual" as man standing before God. Central thoughts that are later entertained by Cohen's student Buber and by Lévinas, another avowedly Jewish thinker, are prefigured here. This novel assessment of the human being also engenders a new way of relating ethics and morality. For the Jewish prophets, Cohen says, "there cannot be even a temporary difference between theory and practice. Their problem is religion, monotheism, the correlation of man and God." This correlation is what firstly enables the relation between "man and man," which is immediately practical. Cohen is likely describing what he sees as his own calling and task as a human being, when he characterizes the prophet as follows: he "becomes the practical moralist, the politician and jurist, because he intends to end the suffering of the poor. And it is not enough for him to assume these various callings; he has to become a psychologist as well: he must make pity the primeval feeling of man; he must, as it were, discover in pity man as fellowman and as *man* in general."

Notes

1 (Cohen 1883, pp. 86ff.) on Newton's "Tractatus de Quadratura Curvarum" and the Anticipations. See (Friedman 1992, pp. 74f.) for a brief discussion of the same texts.
2 Cohen's emphasis. Original at (Cournot 1841), Book 1, Chapter 4, p. 86.
3 "Über die Grenzen des Naturerkennens."

4   See, e.g., Holzhey 2005, p. 5.
5   This work, *Das Prinzip der Infinitesimalmethode und seine Geschichte*, is partially translated in this volume.
6   As Gregory Moynahan puts it, "For proponents, connecting the Marburg school with the philosophy of science was its greatest triumph and source of legitimacy, at once linking it to the key problems of modernity and reconnecting it with the central problems of Kant's philosophy. As Cohen argued in his 1914 introduction to the ninth edition of Friedrich Albert Lange's *History of Materialism*, his reading of the centrality of the Infinitesimalmethode as a philosophical turning point in modern thought was consistent with the thought of Hertz, Planck, and Einstein (245ff.). Indeed, Cohen noted, Planck's *Das Prinzip der Erhaltung der Energie* (1887) had described its own theoretical foundation through the use of the term 'infinitesimal-theorie' in a manner Cohen found similar to his own" (Moynahan 36–37).
7   For a detailed explanation of this method, see the translation of Cassirer's article "Hermann Cohen and the Renewal of Kantian Philosophy" in this volume.
8   Holzhey, "Cohen and the Marburg School in Context," op. cit., p. 31.
9   From Strauss' "Introductory Essay" to the 1995 English translation of *Religion of Reason*, p. xxiii.

Further Reading

Cassirer, Ernst, "The Philosophy of Hermann Cohen and his Conception of Jewish Religion," in: E. C., *Nachgelassene Manuskripte und Texte*, vol. 17, ed. by J. Bohr & K. C. Köhnke. Hamburg: Meiner, 2014, pp. 141–157.

Myers, David N., "Hermann Cohen and the Quest for Protestant Judaism," in: *Leo Baeck Institute Year Book* XLVI (2001), 2001, pp. 195–214.

Seeskin, Kenneth, "How to Read *Religion of Reason*," in: H. Cohen, *Religion of Reason*, 1995, pp. 21–42.

Strauss, Leo, "Introductory Essay," in: H. Cohen, *Religion of Reason*, 1995, pp. xxiii–xxxviii.

Wiehl, Reiner, "The Multiplicity of Virtues and the Problem of Unity in Hermann Cohen's Ethics and Philosophy of Religion," in: R. A. Makkreel/S. Luft, eds., *Neo-Kantianism in Contemporary Philosophy*, Bloomington/Indianapolis: Indiana University Press, 2010, pp. 272–292 (see also the bibliography at the end of this chapter).

Chapter 7

"Introduction" to *The Principle of the Infinitesimal Method and its History* (1883)[1]

TRANSLATED BY DAVID HYDER AND LYDIA PATTON

The grounding of the concept of the infinitesimal as a problem of philosophy

The grounding of the concept of the infinitesimal is a concern of philosophy in *two* respects. First, the conscience of traditional *logic* cannot be set at ease until it has, as far as its means reach, described this basic concept of mathematical science and explained it according to its own norms. Still further, however, an avoidable gap remains in the table of the foundations and *principles of knowledge* so long as this fundamental tool is not recognized and distinguished as a *presupposition* of mathematical cognition and consequently of the cognition of nature.

Both these considerations support one another. For so long as we seek the foundation of the concept of the infinitesimal solely in logic, the lack of such a foundation will remain pressing – despite the innumerable efforts that have been undertaken, since the discovery of the calculus, to give it a logical justification on new grounds. Hence the concept of an infinitesimal quantity can count as a penetrating example of the necessity to *complete logic* with another related, but distinct, area of research.

The presuppositions contained in the limit method

The grounding of the concept of the infinitesimal is also attempted using self-sufficient methods internal to mathematics. In the process, allegedly logical *presuppositions* are made that fall outside the domain of logic. Since D'Alembert, mathematicians are accustomed to grounding the infinitesimal calculus in the *method of limits*. But this method consists in the idea that the elementary concept of *equality* must be completed through the exact concept of a *limit*. Thus the concept of equality is presupposed *first*. But equality does not lie within logic. What corresponds logically to equality is called *identity*. Equality describes a relation of *quantities*. Carnot had already pointed to this distinction, in that he distinguished between "égalité" as "rapport" from "identité" as "relation."[2] Consequently the limit method presupposes, *second*, the concept of *quantity*. And this concept also lies outside of logic.

Moreover, the presupposed concept of quantity simultaneously makes a *presupposition of limit quantities*. The equality defined in the elementary theory of quantity does not consider these limit quantities. Quantities count as equal if, and yet despite [the fact] that, their difference consists in a limit quantity.[3] Hence – this is the thought behind the limit method – the elementary concept of equality must not so much be *completed* as *corrected* by the exact concept of a limit. Equality is to be regarded as a *preliminary stage* of the limit-relation. Without this validity of the correction, the concept of limit would be introduced precariously. Consequently the limit method presupposes, *third*, that concept through which calculation should be *grounded*. Since the concept is *defined*, this presupposition is not a surreptitious move. However, its introduction and definition lie outside logic. And since mathematics neither can nor should carry out a grounding of its concepts that goes beyond definitions and axioms, *the grounding of the basic concept, also presupposed in the limit method*, falls to an area of enquiry that must be distinguished from logic.

The border conflict between intuition and thought lies outside of logic

Equality and quantity presuppose *intuition*. However, not even the *distinction* between thought and intuition belongs to *logic* anymore; the latter distinction should have been judged in the same context as was the border conflict between thought and intuition. Thus the definition of the concept of the infinitesimal is conditioned by drawing borders between intuition and thought, or, more precisely, by determining the *methods* designated by intuition and thought, their principal parts. [For] intuitions, like thoughts, are *abbreviations* for scientific methods, and indeed for those that are so independent of the particular contents of research that they form *general presuppositions of all scientific research*.

The Distinction between Logic and Theory of Cognition[4]

A correction of the boundaries of such general methods, or rather, the conditions of any sort of scientific methods, must be expressly removed from logic; for logic should investigate only those *relations of thought* that are separate from intuition. All help that logic can give cognition is thus limited strictly and exclusively to *securing cognition from the side of those of its foundations that lie in thought*. Such securing is indispensable; it teaches how to avoid errors that may be encountered when operating with the forms of thought, and it promotes *determinacy* in the construction of such forms. Thus the touching attachment[5] to logic is comprehensible as an attachment to an *independent* discipline. On the other hand, the securing is only negative. Hence the thoughtless accusation that logic is a *formal* science; as if what had the task of securing the *entire* content of cognition, however diverse this may be in itself, *from the side of the cognitive means*, simultaneously had to contain *all those other means of consciousness*, which generate and guarantee cognition with its objective content.

Intuition, which is foreign to logic, yet which connects itself with the means of thought in cognition, belongs to these other means of consciousness. All of these narrower, yet more positive presuppositions of the cognition at work in connecting intuition and thought form a specific field of research, which in recent times has acquired the generally accepted title, *theory of cognition*[6].

The Connection of Science and Theory of Cognition

This name is well suited to distinguish the tasks it includes from logic, which is encumbered by the idea and the presumption[s] of an *organon*, in that it points to the *difference between thought and cognition*. The tasks of cognition require still further means and equipment aside from the laws of thought. But it would be completely mistaken to ascribe an awareness of these supplementary requisites only to the recent past, in which the term has become popular; rather, these further requisites were sensed long ago. Descartes and Leibniz, especially, worked and wrestled with these requirements. But it is indeed Leibniz who usually suffered from overestimating logic, which for him counted as the model and the sole instance of ***a priori*** *reason*. Thus he strains the capacity of logic, but he does not discharge it of any of the tasks that motivate his universal research. He makes the mistake of extending the laws of logic, immediately and *as such*, to the problems of mathematics. Nonetheless, he thereby points out and emphasizes *the connection of logic and science* as the problem of his, as of all philosophy. Clearly his method of solving this problem is inadequate; and it is against just this method of discovering a priori truths of thought that the new, narrower type of logic positions itself. Now this new method of research must be grasped in such a way that what Leibniz strove to achieve may be provided – but not with the both historically and materially regrettable result that what this powerful genius introduced into science, and its foundations in metaphysics, is hindered and ignored.

The Distinction between Theory of Cognition and Psychology

Thus those who speak of a theory of cognition in contrast to Leibniz, or in general of a *Lockeian* theory of cognition, confuse matters by [using] this term. Leibniz is rather thoroughly in the right versus Locke, [with respect to] the thinker who comprehends the broad requirements of knowledge at its roots. Locke, by contrast, analyzed the psychic apparatus of cognition and, to the extent that we put trust in his art, he did uncover real and important methods and powers. However, even the best psychology is not a cure for the presumptions of logic, and sensualism is in general only psychology. Theory of cognition *cannot* be meant *as psychology*. For psychology itself presupposes this theory of cognition, in the concept of *consciousness* as in that of *matter*, and, correspondingly, in *sensation* and *stimulus*.

Considerations against the name "Theory of Cognition"

Therefore I must object to the name "theory of cognition"[7]: for it evokes the idea that cognition *as a mental process* forms the object of this investigation, which may be rounded out as a theory by a psychological analysis of the apparatus of cognition. This view is fundamentally wrong, for one cannot, by the path of psychological analysis, arrive at the certainty which is required by the questions treated in this domain. Psychology outlines a *description of consciousness* from its elements. These elements must therefore be hypothetical – and remain so, all while that with which consciousness really begins, and in which it develops, can be unearthed and confirmed by no one operating with consciousness. In contrast, if I take cognition not as a kind and manner of consciousness, but as a *fact*, which came about in *science* and continues to complete itself *on given foundations*, then the investigation no longer refers to a still subjective fact, but to an objectively given state of affairs, however much these may multiply, [that is] *grounded in principles*; not on the process and apparatus of cognition, but on the yield of this, science. The question is immediately and unambiguously suggested: from *which presuppositions* of this scientific state of affairs does its certainty derive? For it must be acknowledged from the outset that such presuppositions must govern, even if a clear consciousness of these principles need not be involved. The *axioms* of mathematics were indeed only culled from the content of mathematical research once the latter had already expanded substantially. But without such latent foundations, mathematics would not have been able to develop. It is the same with all cognition. Science runs ahead of logic and its completion. The investigation of cognition is directed at the acquired facts of science, at proofing their validity and the sources of their laws.

Critique of cognition[8]

Thus I wish to put the less easily misunderstood term "critique of cognition" in place of "theory of cognition," and will use it from now on. This title reminds one more explicitly of *Kant's original* (according to all historical accounts) *discovery*, while the expression "theory of cognition" recalls the expression "theory of science"[9], which Kant rejected. "Since each systematically undertaken doctrine is a science, even the name (*Wissenschaftslehre*) evokes little hope of gain, because it suggests a science of science, and so on in an infinite regress."[10] While Kant himself still battles with psychological ideas and presumptions, we *objectify* – in his sense, in the spirit and letter of the critical system – *reason in science*. *Critique of reason* is *critique of cognition* or of science. The critique discovers what is *pure* in reason insofar as it discovers the *conditions of certainty* on which *cognition as science* rests.

Critique of cognition [is] scientific idealism

The critique of cognition thereby distinguishes Kantian from all other *idealism*, and determines and clarifies the content of the *transcendental*. Idealism in general dissolves things in *appearances* and *ideas*. In contrast, the critique of cognition resolves science into the *presuppositions* and *foundations* assumed in and for its propositions. Cognitive-critical idealism takes as its objects not so much things and events, nor even consciousness as such, but *scientific facts*. Now if the latter are, in general, the only legitimate problems[11] of investigations that are directed towards the legislative grounds of consciousness, then cognitive-critical idealism is *the scientific form of idealism*, [a form] which is attained by the concept of the *transcendental*. For *transcendental* refers to the *possibility* of a cognition that receives the value of *a priori* or *scientific* validity[12]. Hence *cognitive-critical idealism* is synonymous with *transcendental logic*, for its task is to discover the fundamental synthetic propositions, or the *grounding*[13] of cognition on which science builds itself, and on whose validity the latter depends. The presupposition of such a foundation is in no way dogmatic; in fact, to the extent that a suspicion of dogmatism is directed at this assumption, it is itself a symptom of dogmatism. Assumptions and presuppositions must form the grounds of science, for no theoretical structure[14] can be erected without such a latent basis. All development of propositions presupposes foundational principles. Hence the plan of the transcendental, or cognitive critique[15] is *natural* and *methodical*: what science makes into science, which conditions of its certainty it presupposes, from which fundamental principles (*according to their supposed worth*) its realization as science is made possible – this is the natural question of all philosophy; this is the problem of that philosophy which matured in Kant's work.

The historical precondition of the critique of cognition

This philosophical maturity came with the ripening of science that began with Galileo and ended with Newton. Since Newton, there has existed a science built on *principles*, conscious of its foundations and presuppositions, and which proceeds according to the mathematical method. So now the object was given, at which *the transcendental question concerning the possibility of a priori cognition* could be directed. Leibniz himself still collaborated on bringing about this science. He had the ideal of such a science fixed in view, but he did not succeed in realizing it *within self-drawn limits of mathematical natural philosophy*[16]. Newton may have thought of Leibniz as Galileo once did of Kepler: "I have the highest regard for Kepler, due above all to his free and profound spirit, but his way of philosophizing is not mine."[17] We know at least about Leibniz, how he rejected the basic concepts of Newtonian mechanics and hence could not systematize mathematical natural science. We understand this failure in terms of his larger desire: he wanted to force mathematics and all natural philosophy under the codes[18] of logic; but these grew from their own ground, from principles that were not logical. Thus the problem of the critique of cognition had to pass him by; for, to him, cognition only existed in a general and *undetermined* sense, not in the restricted, but *precise* one.

The grounding of the concept of the infinitesimal as a problem of the critique of cognition

Nonetheless, even though Leibniz did not *systematically* validate cognition in the concept of mathematical natural science, nor critique of cognition in the transcendental sense, still, he did bring about that cognition through his discoveries, and primarily through the *concept of an infinitesimal*. The grounding of this concept, which cannot be carried out logically, must devolve onto critical cognition; that is to say, it must be treated as a part and as an *example* of the problem that Kant had established in his *new concept of experience or of mathematical science of nature*. Just as [in the case of] a basic concept, or one of the conditions for the possibility of experience, this powerful instrument of the latter must be carefully expounded, even if its concept must be grounded differently.

Since the concept of the infinitesimal will be given a foundation through the critique of cognition, a doubt could arise that it is thereby removed from its home ground, and that its justification is made to depend on an investigation that pursues the sought-for legitimation with foreign concepts and norms. But this is not the case. Neither is the concept of the infinitesimal divorced from its connection to mathematical problems, in as much as it should be grounded cognitive-critically, nor does this grounding presuppose that the *entire system* of the critique of cognition be set out for this purpose. The first point is disposed of through the concept of the critique of cognition. The concept of the infinitesimal must be examined in its connection to the conditions and general problems[19] of mathematical cognition if it is to be grounded cognitive-critically. The second point, on the other hand, requires more detailed consideration.

Notes

1   Hermann Cohen, *Das Prinzip der Infinitesimalmethode und seine Geschichte*, Berlin: Dümmlers, 1883. pp.1ff. Translated for the first time into English by Lydia Patton and David Hyder.
2   *Réflexions sur la métaphysique du calcul infinitésimal*, §42.

3   Cohen is referring to *aporiae* considered by Euler, Carnot and others, such as that, if differentials are "arithmetically" null, the expression a = a + dx would appear both to assert and deny the equality of the *relata*. – Trans.

4   "*Erkenntnis*" is translated "cognition," as is now standard for Kant, following the Pluhar and Guyer-Wood translations of Kant's first *Critique*. Readers of the Marburg texts should be sensitive to the argumentative context in which "*Erkenntnis*," "*Wissen*" (knowledge), "*Wissenschaft*" (science), and the like occur. Encountering these terms in the text should provoke reflection on how they are used by each author and in the tradition. English translations now use "cognition" for "*Erkenntnis*" partly to distinguish "*Erkenntnis*" from "*Wissen*" in Kant (see Andrew Chignell's 2007 review of Dicker's *Kant's Theory of Knowledge*, *Philosophical Review* 116.2: 307–9). This distinction should be understood in its argumentative context in German and for each philosopher, and not in terms of the connotations of the words in English.

In the years leading up to and following the flourishing of the Marburg School, there were debates about whether to read Kant's *a priori* as a set of psychological faculties or mental processes, or as a set of epistemic conditions for knowledge, or as some combination of these. These debates are ongoing. Despite the fact that the English term "cognition" is associated with psychological processes (see, for instance, the Oxford English Dictionary's entries for "cognition"), a reader ought not read "cognition" as implying substantive reference to mental or psychological processes without independent evidence from the text that the author is speaking about such processes. – L.P.

5   *rührende Anklammerung*
6   *Erkenntnistheorie*
7   *Erkenntnistheorie*
8   *Erkenntniskritik*. The Marburg School, starting with Cohen, wanted to displace the vague term "theory of cognition" (*Erkenntnistheorie*) with the more precise "critique of cognition" (*Erkenntniskritik*), as a critique of existing scientific cognition. – Ed.
9   *Wissenschaftslehre*
10 Letter to Tieftrunk of 1798, 12.241.
11 *Vorwürfe*. Cohen's *Vor-wurf* is a loan-translation equivocating across three classical terms, *pro-blem*, *ob-ject*, and *pro-ject*. – Trans.
12 *Geltung*
13 *Grundlegung*
14 *Lehrgebäude*
15 *Erkenntniskritik*
16 *Naturerkenntnis*
17 E.F. Apelt, *Epochen der Geschichte der Menschheit*, vol. 1, p. 257.
18 *die Paragraphos*
19 *Vorwürfe*

Chapter 8

"The Synthetic Principles" from *Kant's Theory of Experience* (1885)[1]

TRANSLATED BY DAVID HYDER

The synthetic principles are the levers of experience. One could therefore begin the reconstruction of the latter with them; for they alone condition the possibility of experience as a final authority. And if science had not achieved some sort of formulation of them, the specification Kant gave them would not be historically comprehensible: only a Newtonian could have arisen as Kant.

Nonetheless, no consensus concerning the kind, number and formulation of such principles was achieved by Newton, nor by his rivals and disciples, although they all strove for this. That achievement fell to the philosophical genius, whose task was therefore superficially split, although it was actually unified in its duality: In order to aim for the transcendental deduction, he had first of all to pursue the metaphysical one, even if his gaze remained fixed on the former.

On the long road of his development into a philosophical genius such as the world had not experienced since Plato, space and time had initially been singled out as the foundations of cognition.[2] But it remains questionable whether the characteristic of these sensible basic concepts as forms of intuition would have led him to the transcendental discovery; at the very least, we do see these thoughts pursued without this conclusion in the piece from 1770 [*The Inaugural Dissertation*]. It is only in the treatment of the categories that the transcendental perspective occurred to him.[3] Space and time were indeed also means of "imposing" on things, on which the possibility of knowing something about them *a priori* depends transcendentally.[4] But they only ever give things *sicuti apparent* [as they appear]; whereas concepts would give them *sicuti sunt* [as they are].[5] That, by contrast, concepts combine with intuitions so as to determine the appearances of intuition as appearance-objects; that they therefore constitute the objects of experience only *sicuti apparent* – this insight will first be disclosed to him through the discovery of the categories. This was admittedly the transcendental discovery of their principle; but it presupposed that orientation towards the forms of judgment in which the metaphysical deduction consists. And so, first, the category led to the principle and to the recognition of the latter's primary, central value.

The goal of all transcendental investigation is accordingly the explanation of the possibility of synthetic propositions *a priori* from the aprioricity of the synthetic principles. The content of experience given in mathematical science, which could be held up against

Hume as an *a priori* property[6], was to be explained according to its possibility. Thus the elements in which this presumed apriority consisted had to be sought in the content in question. The characteristic values of the *a priori* are necessity and generality. The ground of this cognitive value cannot lie simply in the objects. So the task was to find the concepts in whose parts the *a priori* – that which characterizes the necessity and generality of the content of experience – must be hidden. In this way we came to the categories, as forms of judging, of thinking.

Now, since Kant turned to judgments in order to discover the categories, the luck of genius guided him here more than anywhere. For we saw already that he had not achieved full historical clarity on the fact that Aristotelian logic itself, metaphysical as it was, was guided by the objective[7] interest of cognition; how all logic, the more it was rendered purely formal, had developed along the thread of this innermost means of cognition, which the logical forms are to represent. But Kant turned, driven by the truth of his cause, to address judgments. Their objective[8] unity with the principles, which he sought as his actual purpose, illuminated him, even though he was not able to clearly present this unity factually and historically. Thus a straight road led him from the principles, from which he departed, to the categories, which he was able to order, with the eye of the genius and the thoroughness of a great investigator, as active in the former [principles], and in judgments as the cognitive unities which comprised the actual content[9] of a judgment.

Thus we, who have surveyed his route reflectively and, in particular, with historically augmented expertise, may say that the road did not lead him from the categories to the principles, but from the principles to the categories.[10] [11]

To recall what is well known, we do not proceed from the category of causality in order to establish the second analogy of experience; rather, the question aims at the possibility of the latter. It is indeed the synthetic principle which is prejacent, which must be explained and, along with it, its peers as well. This route is clearly marked in the *Prolegomena*, but also in the *Critique*.

Insofar as Kant departed from the Humean problem and proceeded to the thought that the necessity of this controversial principle could only be cognized in a pure concept of the understanding, in other words in a basic form of scientific thinking, he had thereby himself appealed to the forms of judgment. Insofar as synthetic propositions *a priori* can be pronounced in judgments that form the content of given experience, as well as the ways of connecting our cognitions, there must be in them "connecting concepts," connecting unities, synthetic elements, thus the sought-for *a priori*. Now some of these deductions[12] could be seen as artificial or indeed unsuccessful; however, if one keeps the meaning of the deduction in view, one cannot be systematically put off by such incidentals. And even if the synthetic unity of causality itself could not be derived from hypothetical judgment, the possibility of the second analogy of experience, "all changes occur according to the law of connection of cause and effect," must be explained. According to the first, methodological condition of the *a priori*, this necessity can lie only in a pure concept of the understanding, only in something that we "impose on the things." So one should seek a more fitting synthetic unity than that which offers itself in the form of hypothetical judgment. The Kantian system would not fall even with the rejection of this deduction. It does not stand on the metaphysical, but on the transcendental deduction of the categories. We can now also express this thought as follows:

The system of experience depends on the deduction of the principles.

Although Lange in some ways grasps the apriority of space more sharply, he shares the error of others regarding the categories, namely that Kant believed himself to have discovered these *a priori*. This would be his original sin, that of the metaphysician. But Lange acknowledges: "If we were certain that we knew the actual and permanent basic forms of judgment, then it would not be at all unmethodological to derive from these the proper fundamental concepts, since it must indeed be suspected that the same properties of our organism that determine our whole experience also give their type[13] to the various directions of the activity of our understanding. But here Kant made the awful mistake of assuming the original forms of judgment to be known or proven, whereas we are just here standing before one of the most difficult problems of the future."[14] Lange's error is expressed in the words "or proven." Kant wanted to explain the possibility of that experience which is given, with the character of necessity and generality, in mathematical science. Thus he tested the kinds of judgment for their underlying connecting unities. He did not take them "as permanent" but only as "actual." But they are not actual as "properties of our organism," but rather as forms of given experience, with whose elimination the "possibility of experience," and "possible experience" would be eliminated. This is where the source of Lange's error lies, in that he places aprioricity in the "psycho-physiological organisation of the human,"[15] and does not acknowledge the possibility of experience as the point of departure for transcendental investigation. On our conception, according to which space, time and the categories are formal conditions of experience, it is only according to the synthetic manner of presentation of the *Critique* that the principles lie behind the concepts; for the analytic one, by contrast, which is followed in the *Prolegomena*, [they lie] before the latter; and the concepts, which are the synthetic unities of judgments, as the various ways of uniting representations into cognition, are only *a priori* because they contain the synthetic unities for the basic forms of the synthetic propositions, which have their template in the logical forms of judgment.[16]

The transcendental aprioricity of the forms of thought, as the formal conditions of our scientific experience, accordingly rests on the aprioricity of the synthetic principles, insofar as these are the basic forms of synthetic judgments *a priori*. Kant noted this restriction himself, that he understood under the principles only those "which relate to categories" (B150). For [while] space and time are not in themselves mere "delusions"[17], they cannot independently generate any principles of experience at all. The axioms do indeed rest on them, and their aprioricity would have no sense if they could not demonstrate[18] the same [aprioricity] of these axioms, at whose root they lie. But these principles of mathematics are not the ones sought here. And just this point provides insight into the concept of Kant's principles: The principles are neither propositions of mere sensibility, nor of pure understanding, but are instead basic forms of thinking, which connect the manifold of intuition by means of the synthetic unities.

Accordingly one must say of the principles of mathematics that (1) they partially presuppose and involve the categories; but that (2) as principles of mathematics, and not of mathematical natural science as such, they do not yet have the validity[19] of the synthetic principles. According to these determinations, which have been proposed for the sake of better orientation, Kant's remarks between "second" and "drawn" (*gezogen sind;* B188–89) are to be made more precise or, for that matter, corrected by the following sentence: "Mathematics has such [principles], but their application to experience, thus their objective validity, indeed the possibility of such synthetic cognition *a priori* (its deduction) still always rests on the pure understanding." (B199)[20]

Above all one must explain the "artificial" division. Schopenhauer calls it the fruit of Kant's love of symmetry: everything is drawn on the "Procrustean bed of the categories." We, on the other hand, do not maintain that this division arose from the so-called nature of the matter, for all logical division involves conceptual art. But we know that this division was also not made after the categories and forms of judgment, but rather, following the main idea, the other way round, they after it. The principles were inquired into first. The number and formulation of them was, however, not known, only their aprioricity was so determined, that they could only lie in concepts, and thus basic concepts were next assumed. If now, by contrast, an exhaustive survey of the first should be achieved, then one would have to be produced for the latter. Thus it came to a parallelisation of the table of judgments, the basic concepts, and the principles. But since judgments and concepts were divided and ordered with regard to the principles, we will have to lay out the formulation of the former [concepts and judgments], and first their organisation[21], in accordance with the latter [principles].

We had first of all divided judgments and categories with regard to quantity. But this does not in any way mean [numerical] quantity[22], but only the scope of the judgment. But as concerns categories, we have identified and named these individually as they function in judgments. Thus it is a fatal error if one thinks that because of judgments of quantity, there is also a category of quantity. We do not know *one* category in this regard, but three. The summation of the latter under one heading is a matter of classification. There is, in consequence, not yet a category of quantity, rather we will see in detail that there is no such thing at all; for it is only in a principle, more accurately in two principles, that the concept of a quantity arrives at completion.

Attention to this idea, that quantity is a principle, not a category, leads us immediately to an important insight into the meaning and purpose of the principles. Principle and category clearly have in common that they designate what is general in the object, which is why the category could be explained as a "concept of an object in general." The principle also does not designate an individual object, but only legitimates its objectivity, in that it grasps it as a case of its law. Nonetheless, the principle is not only valid as a "concept of the object itself," so that its [the object's] objectivity is only determined by it [the principle] from the side of thinking. Rather just as it encloses intuition, so it reaches the object already with its full outfit, anchored in sensibility and thought.

The principle accordingly has a direct relation to the object of experience: it describes and determines the latter. As many kinds of principles must be distinguished as there are kinds of objects. For every principle is a perspective from which all objects of mathematical science can be ordered in a group and their objectivity determined, as opposed to merely being made surveyable. Thus the principle is not "the concept of an object in general," but the cognition of the object in general, or the law of each determinate object as determinate. It is the last restriction that distinguishes the principle from a natural law. Natural laws determine the object as a particular case of a law, whereas a principle determines the object as one determined by law *at all*. It makes its nomological determination possible, and it expresses this [determinability].

If then all principles originate in the highest principle, and this [principle] is that of the unity of consciousness as well as the unity of experience, and if the unity of experience is also the unity of the objects of experience, then we may also call this highest principle that of the unity of the object. For the object is grounded only in its unity, that is to say that of consciousness. We can accordingly consider the principles as unities of objects. And we must divide the highest principle into as many unity-considerations[23] as we regard in constituting the object. We had divided judgments and categories with regard to these considerations of the unity of the object. So we may now proceed to an analogous development of the principles.

Principle of the Axioms of Intuition

We said above that the concept of the synthetic principles could be made clear in their difference from the mathematical principles. The axioms of intuition, which are synthetic propositions *a priori*, are beyond philosophy proper. They are intuitive, not discursive principles. They are evident because they proceed from intuition. But although they, as mathematical propositions, require no proof, because they are capable of none other than that of formal intuition, nonetheless the principle of their transcendental possibility must be proven. This principle is the one listed under the first heading. It is not itself an axiom, for philosophy has no axioms, "but served only to provide the principle of the possibility of the axioms in general, and was itself only a principle from concepts." (A733|B761) And this is the characteristic of the principles which immediately becomes discernible here: pure propositions of the understanding underlie the mathematical principles as well, to the extent that these claim the value of cognition, i.e., that their transcendental possibility is considered. In every actual cognition, both roots are intertwined. This is Kant's fundamental thought, by means of which he could avoid both errors, the "sensibilising" as well as the "intellectualising" of appearances.

What is called a principle[24] in the second edition is termed a fundamental proposition[25] in the first, so that the distinction just raised does not clearly present itself. It could as a result seem as if the axioms, even as axioms, still had fundamental propositions above them. This is only mentioned in order to caution the careful reader, who is interested in a thorough understanding of Kant, always to reflect carefully whenever he notices an even apparently small change in the second edition. One often finds the principle of the axioms designated as an axiom itself. For instance Erdmann, "the proposition that all quantities are extensive quantities is called an axiom of intuition."[26] Similarly K. Fischer:[27] "The Axiom of Intuition." "Therefore Kant calls this first principle[28]: 'Axiom of intuition.'" The principle[29] was also called a "Principle of Pure Understanding" in the first edition.

This first principle must be a principle of quantity; for that is the very first point of view from which we determine appearances as objects. Quantities are mathematical individuals, and mathematical formation[30] was the first requirement of transcendental objectification. Thus we began with time and space, because mathematics begins to produce experience as mathematical natural science out of these basic means of consciousness. If we now wish to obtain a principle of mathematical quantity, then the category must be schematised.

If unity, plurality and totality should be sketched[31] on the "pure image" of everything multiple, which is represented by time, then this means "that I generate time itself in the intuition of the manifold." (B182) For time is indeed for us the form of multitude[32] as it produces itself as such (compare above p. 223f).[33] Thus plurality is a multitude of unities which are comparable, which belong together, in which the unity of consciousness can prevail in its entirety. And so, by means of this connection of unities in plurality and totality, there results a new and extremely important concept, that of the "homogeneous," which does not mean what is identical for analytical consciousness. If the successive addition of one to one is allowed, the homogeneous is thereby justified. And this concept constitutes the schema of homogeneous unities, the schema of number.

The first kind of unity of the object, which we are seeking as the first synthetic principle, is therefore that of numerical quantity[34]. Objects must above all be comparable as objects; this homogeneity is validated in number[35]. As one determines the numeration of its units, one concomitantly determines its object-unit[36]. So one will have to look to this first principle as the justification for valorising[37] the laws and images of inner space and inner time – which would be "mere delusions" in themselves – in objects of experience, and thereby fulfilling their objective validity. The first principle of quantity must therefore appear to us as a bridge between mathematics and mathematical natural science.

Galileo says: "Philosophy is written in the book of nature with mathematical characters." And Pythagoras already made number the substance of things. So the objects of experience, the objects of nature, must above all be quantities, and indeed numerical quantities. "Now consciousness of the multiply homogeneous in intuition in general, insofar as the representation of an object first becomes possible through it, is the concept of a quantity (*quanti*)." [B204] So it stands in the proof of the principle. The homogeneous makes the manifold into a quantity. But it must be observed that the sensible foundation of this manifold is time, from which the numerical schema arises, and not space.

This yields an important difference between number and quantity. Number arises in and with time, with the form of the multitude that is forming. Whereas quantity inscribes itself, once arisen as numerical unity, in the collocation of the multitude, in space. So quantity determines appearances as intuitions in space and time, thus as extended, as "extensive" quantities. Accordingly, the fundamental proposition[38], or better the "principle"[39] of the Axioms of Intuition says:

"All intuitions are extensive quantities."

This is the wording of the second edition, which we must prefer to the first here as well. Because what should be proven is the core, that intuition is only possible through the synthesis of understanding. The result of the transcendental aesthetic is not required to this end, but only the basic doctrine of the latter, that time and space are the necessary forms of our intuition. These forms are nothing finished; rather, they demand a synthesis. But the latter, the composition of the manifold, which [manifold] becomes something homogeneous through consciousness of synthetic unity, plurality and totality, thereby generates the concept of a quantity. And through this, the concept of an object is possible, as one knows well enough concerning the connection between category and object in general from the transcendental deduction. Thus cognition of the object of intuition is conditioned by consciousness of the concept of quantity, or, more precisely, of the principle of quantity. And only now may one say, with the first edition, that the "appearances" themselves are "extensive quantities according to their intuition." For appearances are objects of intuition that are first determined through the concept of the homogeneous.

This objectifying meaning of the principle therefore does not give priority to a psychological insight into the necessary connection between intuition and synthesis. At the same time, it assigns the space-problem to its systematic location in our principle. And the exclusive reference to the aesthetic doctrine of space in the discussion of the principle is thus a clear symptom of the external and insufficient critique to which Kant is constantly exposed from this side.

For here in the synthetic principle it is explicitly stated that "the representation of a determinate space" is first made possible by synthesising the homogeneous (which means synthesising the manifold into the homogeneous), so that the form of space only signifies the negative law of the manifold. But in all mathematical questions it is only a matter of the positive laws of this unity of this manifold. The principle grounds these. Thus the "mathematics of extension (geometry) with its axioms" is by no means grounded only on the pure form of space, but rather on "the successive synthesis of the productive imagination in the production of shapes." But then the most serious criticisms against the Kantian doctrine of space become irrelevant.

1) space cannot be something subjective if it produces the object by means of extensive quantity.
2) space cannot contain the completing condition for geometry itself if geometry deals with determinate spaces, whereas these presuppose quantity.

Let us consider the second point first. In recent geometry, the metrical element is distinguished from that of position. Measure is the principle of extensive quantity. Determinations of quantity in propositions such as axioms can therefore rest only on the principle. But the geometry of position itself is also determined by the principle. For "I cannot represent a line to myself, however small it may be, without drawing it in thought, that is to say by generating all the parts from one point, one upon the other, and thereby sketching this intuition in the first place." (B203) Thus even the simplest relations of extension relate to "sets" of successive parts, to "aggregates." And this is the meaning of extensive quantity: "in which the representation of the parts makes possible the representation of the whole." Insofar as these parts yield a whole, they are "homogeneous," and as such homogeneous parts they compose the whole as extensive quantity.

Now does Kant say in this unrestricted sense that space is an intuition, only an intuition and in no way a concept? The case with respect to determinate space is rather that the concept alone does not suffice to determine space; that the concept of unity schematised in number, as unity of the plurality in the principle of extensive quantity, constitutes the object as a determinate space.

Thus if someone says that Kant did not show how, from the pure intuition of the form of space, the individual spaces are determined, let him attack our principle and show that the concept of an extensive quantity is indefensible or unfruitful. We saw above (p. 223f.) that the concept of a manifold and of quantity advanced by recent mathematicians must be traced back to a distinct type of conditions; in particular, that the concept of a quantity must first be rendered more precise by means of the numerical schema, as that of an extensive quantity. Extension presupposes space and time, but quantity [presupposes] the unity of consciousness of the manifold in the concept of unity, which produces homogeneous plurality and totality in successive synthesis. Thus a determinate space also lies in synthesis, which constitutes the extensive quantity-space in the homogeneous parts.

But extensive quantity is by no means dissipated[40] or subjectivised in the synthesis of the homogeneous, rather it is the most preferable and unavoidably primary means of objectifying. We thus turn to the first worry. How was it at all possible that Kant could be accused of subjectivism regarding space, given that he divides and determines the form of space extensively in the synthesis of the homogeneous? If appearances, extended in space and time, become quantities by means of the numerical units schematised in the homogeneous, then they are thereby truly objectivised; for the objects of nature rest first of all on number and measure.

One thereby betrays in this accusation that one is mired in popular realism, as if the quantities were there in themselves and not as means to cognition. If extensive quantity presupposes the parts that make the whole possible, then not only is the whole not given in itself, but neither are the parts. The parts are rather only divisions of a manifold, which in the final analysis is the content of inner sense. Insofar as these divisions order this manifold of inner sense as something homogeneous, they objectify the whole in homogeneous parts as quantity, as a principle which does not merely constitute mathematical quantities, but instead represents[41] and confirms[42] these latter as objects of experience at the same time.

Thus Kant regards the equivalence of applied and pure mathematics with respect to idealistic worries as the actual transcendental yield of this principle. It lies at the basis of the axioms of pure mathematics, but at the same time it permits the application to objects of natural scientific experience, which one surely wants to ground with all mathematics. Quantity, thought as a synthetic principle, consists in a synthesis which, for its part, is the necessary and final condition of the unity of experience. Synthesis is that which "makes possible every external experience, thus also all cognition of objects of the latter, and what mathematics proves in its pure application also holds necessarily of these. All objections against this are merely the chicanery of a falsely instructed reason, which erroneously thinks to free the objects of the senses from the formal conditions of sensibility, and represents them as objects in themselves, given to the understanding, although they are merely appearances."[43] (B207) But in this case the transcendental beginning would be cut off; for synthesis presupposes the manifold on which it can produce its unity. Otherwise the unities of numbers would not strictly speaking be "possible," the units would be mere unschematised thought-unities. Thus, through such dissociation, pure mathematics would also not be explained according to its possibility. If, on the other hand, the latter [possibility] is accepted on the basis of the transcendental aesthetic, then its application to the objects of experience is not only shown in itself as justified, but as necessary. This coincidence is expressed in synthesis, which indeed presupposes synthetic unity on the one hand, but on the other also presupposes the manifold of sensibility, which is to be connected into something homogeneous.

The importance of this sentence can be brought forth more determinately. Kant himself mentions Euclid's twelfth axiom: two straight lines do not enclose a space. One can say that he also has in mind the ninth: the whole is greater than its part.[44] For he places all these axioms under the principle in question and defines extensive quantity according to the latter axioms. By means of this explicit and repeated emphasis on the necessity of producing space in successive synthesis, the dialectical opposition between applied and pure mathematics is now, from a transcendental point of view, dissolved.

The distinction between pure and applied mathematics either concerns something quite popular, for instance the distinction between mathematics and architecture or engineering, or it results from the metaphysical prejudice of dogmatic realism. If I recognise the transcendental significance of mathematics, I thereby recognise it in its indivorcible connection with pure natural science, and thus I am permeated by the insight that, as Apelt says,[45] the ellipse is the means of objectifying the path of a planet. And since applicability is internal to space as it is regular, so application may never be held up against the latter as distinct. This is the "chicanery of a falsely instructed reason," which is thwarted by our principle, because the distinction between pure and applied logic was also quite differently formulated and applied, since pure logic, as transcendental, furthers and prepares the application to objects. Through this meaning of the principle, the much-discussed aprioricity of mathematics is restricted in a fashion worthy of reflection. If Kant, as one says, had been able to think that mathematics itself might not be permitted to advance the claim of *a priori* certainty, then he would not have stuck with his claim concerning the aprioricity of space. Here we see it stated most explicitly how the axioms of intuition, on which geometry builds, are given a principle whose validity[46] rests not only on intuition but also on the categories. Emphasising this thought, that the principle of quantity is a constitutive element of every empirical intuition of an object, is the ground and content of the proof added in the second edition.

But if we have arrived at this point, then there is no escaping from the machinery of the transcendental proofs. The circle drawn by the concept of possible experience encloses apodictic mathematics no less, and this principle is accordingly the actual ground of the aprioricity of mathematics, not simply the formal condition of space. And the pure determinations in space resulting from this principle seem to be the only anticipations that we can carry out *a priori* for appearances.

Thus one may speak of a physical geometry only with this restriction to the principle of an extensive quantity, as that in which pure [geometry] achieves confirmation. Not as though physical application had to decide the regularity of spatial shapes, but only insofar as one distinguishes geometry from mechanics. Here extensive quantity, which the geometry of position need not concern itself with, comes to be applied from the [geometry] of measure. And this view of Newton concerning the internal connection of geometry with mechanics is expressed in the principle of extensive quantity. All intuitions with respect to content, not all intuition[47] as pure activity, all determinate objects in intuition are extensive quantities, forming a homogeneous whole out of parts. Such wholes are the line and the path[48], which helps to designate the mechanical quantity.

Notes

1. Excerpted from Cohen, Hermann, *Kants Theorie der Erfahrung*. 2 ed. Berlin: Dümmlers, 1885, Chapter 12, "Die synthetischen Grundsätze," pp. 406–22.
2. "Erkenntnis" is translated "cognition," as is now standard for Kant, following the Pluhar and Guyer-Wood translations of Kant's first *Critique*. –Trans.
3. Laas has recently agreed to this hypothesis *Idealismus und Positivismus III Theil* 1885, p. 434.
4. *Mittel des "Hineinlegens" in die Dinge.* Cf. Kant, *Inaugural Dissertation* §15E, 2.395; *Prolegomena* §38; *CpR* B9. – Trans.
5. Compare Kant's self-criticism in the letter to M. Herz from 1772. Vol XIa p. 26 and *Critique of Pure Reason*, B304.
6. *Besitz*
7. *sachlich*
8. *sachlich*
9. *Aussage*
10. So we have stated this idea in the first edition p. 206 and similarly, but more definitely, p. 208, which was here retained because of the debate with Lange. A. Stadler is to be thanked (*Die Grundsätze der reinen Erkenntnistheorie in der Kantischen Philosophie*) for its thematic execution.
11. The second reference is to the following passage, which is retained in this text. "For our conception, according to which space, time and category are the formal conditions of experience, the principles only come after the concepts according to the synthetic method. For the analytic one, by contrast, which is followed in the *Prolegomena*, they come before; and the concepts, that is, the synthetic unity of judgments as the different ways of bringing representations to concepts, are only *a priori* because they contain the synthetic unities for the basic forms of synthetic propositions, which have their template in the logical forms of judgments." (Cohen 1871), p. 208. – Trans.
12. *Ableitungen*
13. *Gepräge*
14. Geschichte des Materialismus, 1st ed. pp. 269 f.
15. Ibid. p. 249
16. Compare Lange's contrary remark in his second edition II, pp. 131f. and my reply in *Kants Begründung der Ethik*, pp. 25f. This polemic led to the connection I was granted with this friend of truth.
17. *Hirngespinste*
18. *erweisen*
19. *Geltungswerth*
20. Cf. B189f., where Kant emphasizes that "the correctness and apodictic certainty" of mathematical principles rests on intuition only, and not on the categories. While at B199, Kant is discussing not the apodictic character of mathematical propositions (that their contraries are impossible, *cf.* 16.256, 18.290), but rather their *objective validity*, that is, how they are binding on empirical data (cf. B44, B52, B121–22), thereby developing the central problem of the Transcendental Deduction (B118 ff). – Trans.
21. *Anordnung*
22. *die Größe*
23. *Einheits-Rücksichten*
24. *Princip*
25. *Grundsatz*
26. Geschichte der neurn Philosophie, 1848, I p. 91. Compare also Johann Schulze, Erläuterungen über des Herrn Professor Kant [*sic.*] Kritik der reinen Vernunft, 1784, p. 39. By contrast the in many ways excellent Mellin'sches Wörterbuch is also correct on this point.
27. Geschichte der neurn Philosophie, 2. ed. Vol III, p. 392. Unaltered 3. ed., p. 382f.
28. *Grundsatz*
29. *Grundsatz*
30. *Gestaltung*
31. *verzeichnet*

32 *Mehrheit*
33 KTE 1885 p. 223f. "But what does this manifold mean to us? Nothing other than the datum [*Gegebenheit*] of a multitude of elements. If I think this multitude as given in the manner it must indeed first of all be given – namely as the elements of the latter arise in consciousness, thus following one upon another – then the manifold is determined as time. If, on the other hand, I ignore that the multitude must arise in the succession of elements, then I take them instead as a multitude in their amount [*Bestande*], so the datum determines itself as a collocation of elements [*als Beisammen der Elemente*], as space." – Trans.
34 *Zahlgröße*
35 *diese Gleichartigkeit gewährt die Zahl*
36 *Gegenstandseinheit*
37 *zur Verwerthung zu bringen*
38 *Grundsatz*
39 *Princip*
40 *verflüchtigt*
41 *darstellt*
42 *beglaubigt*
43 See note 20 above. The subject of this sentence from B206–207 is "The synthesis of spaces and times as the essential forms of intuition is what makes possible every external experience…." – Trans.
44 Cf. B17. – Trans.
45 Of importance in philosophical respect as well are, along with the *Theory of Induction* and *Metaphysics*, also the *Epochs of the History of Mankind* and the *Reformation of Astronomy*.
46 *Beweiskraft*
47 *alles Anschauen*
48 *Strecke*

Chapter 9

The Relationship of Logic to Physics from the Introduction, with Critical Remarks, to the Ninth Edition of Lange's *History of Materialism* (1914)[1]

TRANSLATED BY LYDIA PATTON

If we appeal to the critical method of Kant for our perspective, we will feel free of dogmatic dependence. We understand this orientation in the way that *Schiller* formulated it in the letter to *Goethe*: as long as there has been humanity and as long as there has been reason, people have tacitly recognized the Kantian philosophy and, in general, have acted according to it. To us, Kant means nothing other than a peak of a mountain range, which begins with *Plato* and leads to *Descartes* and *Leibniz* among the more recent. The history of philosophy should not limit itself to these peaks; several smaller elevations are not only points along the way to these, but achieve a freer perspective themselves. The only standard that should determine their height is that according to which the critical philosophy, the philosophy of Kant is defined. The appeal to history should establish the characteristic identification of this philosophy: Critical philosophy is that which is obviously related, not only to science, and not just to natural science, but in the first instance to mathematics, and is only related to natural science by means of, and guided by, mathematics.

Mathematics is thus a *method of natural science*, and indeed the one with which natural science in the proper sense first becomes a science: any other starting point for natural science without it thus can be known to be without method, even though centuries may have to make do with these and must be content with them. In this tradition of philosophy with mathematics, as the basic method of natural science, *Plato*, *Descartes*, and *Leibniz* are the leaders of philosophy; *Kant* also is affiliated with it and is to be counted within it. From this perspective, Kant's position appears narrower and more limited; the suspicion of an orthodoxy becomes ever less valid.

One could be tempted as well to see the achievements of these three ancestors as not only more fundamental, but also more rich in content. When *Plato* asked the fundamental question: *What is science?*, there he thought already of mathematics as science, and most of all, that part of the part of it that the Greeks primarily refined, geometry; and *he discovered* the decisive method of geometry, *the analytic*. The *analytic method* first made possible the progress of that method of geometry in which the ancients were masters, and remained so until our century. The analytic method of Plato prepared the way for the synthetic geometry of the Greeks, and strengthened its roots.

Representation in intuition thus was made into an inevitable method of proof; the operation of proof must take place in sensible intuition; but *pure thought*, to which Plato appealed overall, and in the last instance, was certainly, although latently, elevated to an instance of proof. For the relationship between the conditions for the solution of a task and the solution itself was not given in intuition, and could not be established through intuition alone; to do so it needed calculation and inference, thus those operations which, as the concurrence of the ancient words makes clear, are thought or rest on thought. The methodologists of intuition thus remain, as they always were, methodologists of thought.

The *collision* between *intuition* and *thought* develops through the common history of science and of philosophy. Often the collision became conflict, and for the epigones the conflict became in the meantime a technical debated term, which was scrimmaged over in the plans for *pedagogy* reform.[2] But one cannot assess the profound meaning of the question, debated in antiquity, in this way; rather, the real direction of these practical plans is first shown in its true light when the meaning of the distinction between thought and intuition is brought to clear, thorough and fruitful development by rigorous, purely scientific methodology, by research into the methodological foundations of science.

Modern philosophy begins with *Descartes*; in him the reform first achieves its mature expression. Even he struggled with the distinction between thought and intuition. And even he said of pure thought: it is to open new paths for the purposes of intuition. *He discovered analytical geometry*, which rests on the thought that intuition is not superior, rather, that *pure calculating thought can produce and determine images*[3] *in regions of space itself*. Thus *Descartes* freed scientific thought from the common prejudice that *sensibility* first receives the contents and the objects of thought and, on this basis, transfers them to the mind. And although sensualism, with its wisdom, emerges again in the tradition immediately following Descartes, within this historical succession lies nothing less than an inner causal nexus of world history, in its sources in guiding thoughts; but also, such a succession, as often as it repeats itself, proves only the single fact, *that there are at least two types of philosophy*: not only the one true one, which springs from the source of science and grows only on the soil that nourishes this root, but also another for household undertakings, as *Kant* would say, which strives to reason, or at least to create, without working with the sources of science.

Descartes, who preached pure thought, not only enriched science by giving intuition new content, but also deepened it through a new domain of sources. On the other hand, as diverse as was *Locke's* knowledge in the realms of natural science, he was so distant from the methods of natural science that his friend *Newton* made him an extract from the *Principia*, on Locke's request, which did not include mathematical foundations. But even in the new resource of mathematics that Newton had discovered, there was sharp opposition to the pretension of sensibility and intuition to be the true and single resource of the mind. For, even more than Descartes's, this new mathematics was a spawn of the purest, most audacious thought, conscious of its own powers. It was the *fluxion calculus*, the other expression of the simultaneous discovery of the infinitesimal calculus.

The other discoverer described this same principle of calculation with the infinitely small as *infinitesimal analysis*. And as Descartes, the discoverer of analytical geometry became, beyond that, the ambassador of the cogito, *Leibniz*, the discoverer of infinite analysis, became the source of the *intellectus ipse*, which cannot rest in the senses, not in sensible experience, and not in so-called immediate intuition, because it [the *intellectus ipse*], for its part, has to show the senses, experience, and intuition the way along which they must follow it, insofar as they can. Thus, Leibniz also is an advocate and ambassador of *pure* thought, even when newly founding the science of experience.

Analytical geometry and infinitesimal calculus: these are the two instrumental methods of modern science, in whose power the character of the new science consists, with which no discovery, however universal, can compete in terms of principled, methodological value. That these two basic powers of science were discovered by men who began at the same time with programs for the new foundation of *philosophy* cannot be a mere biographical proof of the intimate kind of relation between philosophy and science; it is the double-signpost of both: where its sources begin, and where its goals lead.

The way that scientific reason advances through its leading minds is not so simple and unambiguous. The triumph won by thought in mathematics for natural science was celebrated afterwards almost too gladly in other arenas, in which thought has nothing more than the name in common with the pure thought of science, which generated the creative methods and in these, science itself. The two types of philosophy rest on this ambiguity, and are connected in each philosophizing person. For the misuse of scientific or insufficiently methodical reason is not the only thing that leads to a widening or blunting, through which the concept of thought becomes ambiguous. Here the other problems of the intellect and mind still are present, which move the consciousness of humans along with those of science, and stimulate the solution of their puzzles. Descartes and Leibniz did not want to, and could not, restrict their concern to the mathematics of nature, but cared just as intensively for the skills of human existence; thus, thought for them had to remain, or become, a methodological resource for the questions of *morality* and *religion*.

Although Newton did not found a school tradition of philosophy with particular texts, as his predecessors and rivals did, did he make this question a focus of his reflections any less energetically and less ambiguously? In fact, Newton wandered even further beyond independent philosophy and took refuge in mysticism, which inserted itself into literary feuds with the ruling parties and forced its spokespeople into the churches by means of accommodations and leniencies, indeed always maintained a free space for philosophy and thus the jurisdiction of thought. Newton thus does not have the advantage over Descartes and Leibniz, that he advocated thought in a more rigorous sense, while they used it for questions of God and the soul; for nothing growing in the soil of mathematical natural science prevents the disease of the mind, into which any moral issue can degenerate.

Indirectly, Newton could incur the reproach that he did not develop a theory and terminology of science in fundamental scientific works as Descartes and Leibniz did, that he did not determine the capabilities of thought as a critic of cognition, and thus overreaching is inevitable.[4] Newton could work more confidently with intuition. He could even more confidently use the advantages of the synthetic proof style, the geometry of the ancients, as secured by analytical geometry, and through this latter itself, in the *fluxion*, the decisive instrument for the geometry of motions, for mechanics, was refined. His mission was broader than Leibniz's, but broader only within the narrow range of mathematical natural science. Here Newton received the more modest reward, towards which Leibniz strove, although in the broader philosophical sense: Newton became the creator of the *system* of natural science. While Leibniz is usually preferentially named as the creator of a system, for which he characteristically had different names, Newton became the systematizer of natural science, insofar as he gave natural philosophy principles, which he described as "mathematical."

Within these limits Newton is the master. He determined the mathematical principles of natural science: but are these the only ones? There was already debate about this among his contemporaries. And this debate is not settled even in the present day. Newton borrowed the principles of natural science from mathematics, and called natural science "natural philosophy". In this baptism, which remains predominant in English usage, the problem is struck dead. Insofar as philosophy is said to be identical to science, it is, in fact, cut short. Philosophy is annulled, when it is not recognized as a method, and when it therefore becomes a most comprehensive result. *It belongs next to mathematics as the method*, which completes the method of mathematics, when natural science results from the connection of the two.

Newton's significance in the positive and in the negative sense lies in his double position with respect to the basic questions. He fought for intuition and *experience*, as he secured and deepened the basis of *thought*. So he became a guard, albeit intermittently, against the overextension of, and the obscurities of, philosophical terminology. He worked toward, and achieved, the highest goal of the philosophical enterprise within the narrow realm of science: the system. But the foundation of principles, on which he built it, is defined inadequately; moreover, the error reaches the basic laws. He committed not only a subreption, but also a confusion of principles; he confused one part of the principles with the fact that is derived from it.[5] Mathematics alone contains the principles of natural science; the naturalness of philosophy flowers in its own blossoms, as method and principle.

This methodological weakness of Newton's became significant even in natural science itself, its hypotheses and its basic concepts: for instance, it caused his opposition to the *undulation theory*, and his confusions about the concept of *heavy matter*. Afterward, [he] went back to *Huygens* in the fundamental hypothetical concepts. His rigid opposition to the concept of hypothesis in general, which *Kepler*, the Platonist, already understood so much more profoundly, is explained thus; also the fact that Newton himself only conceived and formulated the concept of system, but could not develop and ground it; his timidity was exploited by the Cartesians. But these gradually became Leibnizians. And among these arose a new relationship between philosophy and science.

The text, in which this new relationship is developed, is revealed as in opposition to Newton's title, although it was composed at the end of the path that first began with Newton. The *Philosophiae naturalis principia mathematica* conflicts with the *Metaphysical Foundations of Natural Science*. By foundations is meant no more and no less than the principles, but now *metaphysics* as such appears, *for* natural science, which to this extent is separated from natural philosophy. Kant arises from this double relationship of Newton's to the desiderata of philosophy for science; in fact, he was trained more as a Newtonian than as a Leibnizian.

This part of Kant's background remained decisive for the construction of his system, although that was carried out only in later years. Above all, in the selection of basic questions with which the *Critique* begins, in the *separation* of the question of the apriority of mathematics from that of the apriority of natural science: as if mathematics meant anything to Kant outside its methodological relationship to natural science. The dependence on Newton had an effect on this opposition. Even mathematics should not be recognized exclusively as a method for natural science. So it happened that mathematics was not evaluated as a method, but as an independent science, as a self-sufficient synthesis *a priori*.

But a worse effect is the fact that philosophy, as complementary method of natural science, is not proven valid solely in pure *thought*, rather, mere mathematics is brought to a separate analysis in the forms of *pure intuition*. Newton's preference for the synthetic method of the ancients had significant effect for the entire system, in thus elevating intuition above thought. Already the foreign terminology came into difficulties, with the collision of the concept of *intuition* with that of *sensation*, from which it should have been distinguished *toto caelo*, as pure intuition. But if this distinction could be taken seriously, then it is not easy to understand why intuition still must be distinguished so rigorously from thought. And already the new geometers, like *Helmholtz*, appear in these points more Platonist and Leibnizian than Kant, insofar as, for them, the achievements of geometry remain connected to pure thought.

Kant's original treatment of the concept of *sensation* is even more significant. From the beginning it appeared as if sensation were merely empirical, and as if it must be treated thus, which is to say, unphilosophically and unscientifically, as only a question mark about the scientifically expressible moment which is totally and in principle eliminated from the foundations of science and remains so; for it, the worth of the *a priori* is impenetrable.[6]

Incidentally, this is not to say that the *question mark*, which sensation poses, can be eliminated completely as such: only that the appropriate pure concepts must be in readiness for it first.

Already, the distinction Kant used in introducing sensation can raise opposition and objections: it is the old scholastic distinction between *matter* and *form*. Certainly, he took it in the classical usage, as was usual since the renaissance for all rationalists and idealists: that *form* means the *being*, the essence, the intrinsic content, while, at best, *material* can only set it as a problem to show all that belongs to this as content. And Kant made this definition of form, typical of the entire modern philosophical tradition, more precise and profound with his own new concepts, in the following way: that the form of power means, to determine any matter according to what is solid and real in it, to generate it, thus first to realize it itself.

Despite this new direction of the new transcendental *a priori*, matter was not brought to disappear completely, rather, it could have a continued frightening, ghostlike existence under different disguises. One such shadow is the expression: *the given in intuition*; although naturally there is no lack of textual citations, in which the proper expression breaks through, that any given can and could only mean *pure* givenness.

One such remnant, not quite dispensed with, is the description of *sensation as matter*; although the Transcendental Aesthetic already thought to eliminate it, and discovered the concept of *pure* intuition, or, more correctly, rediscovered it from the history of the development of classical idealism. The Transcendental Logic made a new attempt to root out this antediluvian concept, insofar as it appended the *Principle of the Anticipations* to the *Principle of the Axioms*. Now it must appear clear to the most unperceptive eye that thought, alone and exclusively, can satisfy the demands of sensation; for the real, which is defined as the *object* of sensation, was recognized as a category, in which he grounded reality. It must follow immediately, that sensation is nothing but an expression for what thought is to determine, to correct, to exhaust in order to refer to as substantial; that, thus, the so-called matter of sensation matures in the contents of pure thought in the proper objects of science.

However, the power of this remnant against *intellectualist* idealism did the most damage when it received the expression of *thing in itself*; for Kant was not guilty of coining the term, which belongs to the most ancient inventory of philosophical usage. Here *Fichte*, despite his real philosophical talent, is a crackpot on Kant[7], and Fichte was encouraged in his blindness by the belief that he was called to improve on Kant. However, without connection to mathematical natural science the concept of the transcendental becomes nonsense; and here Fichte carried out other literary studies and other subjects near to his heart – for instance, to apriorize matter, as "light and wind" in the rigorous sense of working science, so it is only too easy to understand why his attempt to chase off the phantom of the thing in itself should fail entirely. But the chatter about the thing in itself, which has not been hushed up to this day, is pathetic and unforgivable. One can remark upon the total misunderstanding of what Kant taught and wished, the complete lack of an internal relationship between our contemporaries and Kant, as much as they spring from him, and some will falsely allege about Kant that Kant helped himself to the thing in itself, or that he did not, and nowhere do they compromise themselves as obviously and sheerly insufferably as in the most learned discussion. As if Kant had busied himself with natural science from his youth to old age without discovering in it the eternal foundation of cognition, but rather indulged in the obstinacy of skepticism, according to which everything that people devise from the real objects of experience as reason, as truth, as science is merely a vain delusion.

But certainly, they pit Kant against *Hume*, instead of against *Newton*, which would be more correct, and at the same time would prove a more instructive test. But they also investigate lengthily whether *Plato* has reached adequate comprehensive revelation and certainty about the *relationship of things to the Ideas*. Kant accused the project of so-called higher idealism of "intentional misinterpretation". Supposedly, according to Fichte, Kant was free of the suspicion of an inadequately formulated idealism, from which Kant rescued himself subsequently by taking on an independent thing in itself, as Fichte explains, with his weak intellect, by way of giving a sign of Fichte's intentional benevolence, of the solidity of his heart and stalwart charity. Notwithstanding all this, it must be admitted, that Kant did not express it determinately, completely and unmistakably clearly: *the thing in itself means to Kant only a step, and nothing but this, in the progress of his terminology from the categories to the ideas, from the synthetic principles to the regulative principles of ends.* We recognize the manifold transmitted influence of Newton's concept of matter in the lack of such an expression.

When *Leibniz* opposed *Descartes's* concept of substance to the concept of *force*, it could appear that Kant returns to Descartes, insofar as he prefaced the category of substance with that of causality, while he had found already the correct conception for the new foundation of the concept of force in the category of reality. However, through the description of the *category of being* or of actuality there arose a new impetus for pure and clear development of the Leibnizian idea, which became the real basic idea of critique: that matter should be grounded in thought, *substance in force*. Those following thus returned to Leibniz's concept of force, to develop from his *principle of vis viva* the concept of *energy*, and with and through this basic concept to exhaust the concept of matter, and first of all the concept of substance.

Here we have arrived at the problem that our *Lange* himself has discussed already illuminatingly, to which he has brought understanding with his idealistic spirit, which since his death has served at least for greater clarity, but in the very last years, indeed we can say also: for principled clarification. Theoretical idealism, which was displayed as the driving force in the mathematical science of nature, had already begun to rock the theoretical materialism of wider circles of natural scientists, and it can only require a short time in these basic questions to bring the mystery to cultivated truth:[8] that all true science always and forever was and is nothing other than as idealism.

Now, if we wish to regard the effects of idealism in the new physics in a short summary, we must concern ourselves with the old opposition between the *atomistic* and the *dynamic* conceptions of nature. Originally, and indeed with the first conception of the atom through *Democritus*, it was the pure thought of the *Eleatics* that proved fruitful in these concepts. Whoever does not see this right away in the concept of the atom itself must see it in its correlative concept, that of the *empty*. In both a pure, rigorous thought-element, as opposed to sensible intuition, is made the ground of being, the ground of the real. According to the unfriendly report of *Aristotle*, *opposition* to sensibly *perceptible* bodies is itself the principle motivating the concept of the atom.

However, this opposition to sensibility, and positively, this constitutive sovereignty of *thought* in antiquity never itself came to a comprehensive expression in the debates. With *Epicurus* the atom, instead, is the basis of materialism. And since atomism has been exhumed more recently, it was a favorite of the materialist viewpoint as well. Hence the enthusiasm for reviving Epicurus, which promotes the restoration. In the meantime, another concept came to the fore in the middle point between theoretical speculation and work: the concept of *force* threatened that of the atom.

The force concept arose from the *Eleatic* school; admittedly, however, there it was woven from mythical representations. The *static* concept of force was determined first through *Archimedes'* discovery of the *center of gravity*, and indeed in connection with the thus-refined concept of the *body*, which, for a center of gravity, demands a *central point* and thus a concentrated *unity* freed of all accidents of sensible aspect. However, only the *dynamic* concept of force could complete what was only pre-formed in the static one. And so the new viewpoint on force dates from the time of the discoveries of *Galileo*.

From this perspective, which must lead the way in our account here, what is decisive in these discoveries?

What is most profoundly decisive, among all the many intervening contributing moments, lies solely and adequately in those concepts whose deferred effect, at the same time, is the richest example of the internal common grasp of the moments, in the mining of which progress in the intellectual world takes place. *What is new in Galileo's concept of force consists* not so much in the concepts of velocity, but in those of *acceleration*.

Galileo could not perceive or even conceive of this type of force in fish, not in the realm of the animal, nor, in general, in any sensible occurrence of force. The notions of impetus, which were connected to it still, were in error, and did not find the thread that succeeding interpretations attached to Galileo. What is new with Galileo is the assumption, the *anticipation* of this concept, which later would come to be discovered: the *differential concept* is already contained in Galileo's conceptions in creative efficacy. *Pure thought* thus achieved the highest triumph, not only in bringing the images of geometrical imagination to the most audacious connection with the operations on unbounded numerical structures, but also in conceiving the concept of the *infinitely small* in direct and incremental uses for analysis of natural processes. *Even before its definition*, the concept had a latent, but not yet freely realized productivity. The deeper progress in science takes place overall in distinguishing and in establishing those hypotheses which, without explicit recognition, have already contributed to prior research.

Now after the differential concept was uncovered as the motivating force in Galileo's case, the interests of atomism could no longer remain in the foreground, prior to those of dynamics. *Mechanics*, newly grounded in the doctrine of motion, became the *fundamental theory of natural science*. At the same time, *nature* was no longer thought as a *being*,[9] namely not as something to presuppose under this concept for scientific research, but rather as an *embodiment of motions*. And in general the *origin* of motion is force. As there can be no foundation of physics on these grounds, through mechanics, then all theoretical conceptions of nature must be *dynamic*. Insofar as natural science becomes physics, *atomism* must yield to *dynamics*.

At the same time, when it appeared that the new dynamics had won unlimited dominance with the triumphs of Newtonian science over the fossilized remains of the Cartesian school, modern physics gave rise to a science that steered research into matter into new paths, even though it did not rest immediately on the concept of motion. With the new *chemistry* interest in the *atom* revived, and it was only in question, not whether one would push the other out, but how they could be connected – whether chemistry could be allowed and recognized in theoretical natural research, even if only as a precursor. This pact, this reconciliation of apparently conflicting methods, was undertaken in the last century, and, more than any other theoretical achievement, was the *signature of the time*.

Drawing on chemistry for the principal problems of natural science, and resolving special chemical problems through the general principles of physics, this great achievement, which intended to find a direction of orientation for modern physics, had its mature origin in *Faraday*.

It is a wonderful turn of phrase, that the return to problems of chemical substance must lead to a fundamental defeat of the materialistic view of matter. As *Thales* achieved the first abstraction of *substance*,[10] connected – the tradition does not tell us the possible connections – to speculations over the *electron*, so the *theory of electricity* was decided, the greatest transmutation of the conception of matter, and so, through the metamorphosis of matter into force and energy, the triumph of idealism was accomplished. *Faraday's* resistance to *atomism* grew from these physicalist interests in the problem of force. It was not his way, though, to develop principles in mathematical-mechanical or even in merely logical opposition; the scattered beginnings, which are found in manifold ways in the work and essays of the latter, allow at least for the knowledge that overall the sure impetus of genius not only guided his research, but also prescribed his systematic work. Just as *Galileo*, rigorously educated and creatively talented, certainly in philosophy as well as in mathematics, anticipated the decisive concept of mathematical natural science, Faraday is the true thread-finder of the new natural-scientific era, owing to his connection of chemistry to physics in the theory of electricity, and owing to his overcoming of the problem of sensible substance through the problem of force.

We will consider here a fruit, which has matured in our country since *Lange's* entry in this type of physics, along with the most important consequences it has brought forth in recent years, and will consider the basic idea of *Lange's* life's work, that idealism is the latent principle in all research into matter, in order to bring it to new illumination.

Along with the positions of contemporary philosophical production in the guilds, not yet shaken off outside of narrow school circles and reawakened to fruitful methodological work, and along with the behavior, careless of principles, of the average academic teacher of research into nature in philosophy, there is also the glorious example, to which we will refer here, a true consolation from the perspective that it is one of the ways for the German national future yet again to become satisfactory. I mean the philosophical disposition from which the achievements of *Heinrich Hertz* emerge.

It is a disposition, from which the methodological tendency of these great works arises; and it is of great worth, that Hertz did not disdain to make it known wholeheartedly that this was his disposition. In the introductory "Overview," which he appended to the collected edition of his *Inquiries into the Propagation of Electrical Force*, he himself evaluated the philosophical character of his inquiries. "All of these well-supported experiments deliver a proof for the temporal propagation of a so-called *action at a distance*.[11] This fact is the *philosophical*, and at the same time the most *important* result of the experiments, in a certain sense."[12] This judgment is simply an expression of the precise and clear insight that the fundamental hypothesis of the *Faraday-Maxwell theory* rests on those philosophical grounds. According to this fundamental philosophical insight, the measure of *electrical forces* is associated with that *of ponderable matter*, and further, the measure of forces is connected to *space*, to the nature of space itself, and concurrently to *time*, thus, to the most significant basic concepts of mechanics.

Likewise, Hertz says in the preface to his mechanics, which appeared after his so early death: "What, as I hope, is new, and *on which I put especial value*, is the ordering and compilation of the whole, thus the *logical, or if you will, the philosophical* side of the matter. My work has achieved or fallen short of its goal, insofar as it has done something in this direction, or not."[13] One sees that Hertz takes a few shy considerations of the mistrust of his colleagues for philosophy in this *distinction of the philosophical side from the logical*; we are even more thankful to discover the philosophical orientation, in what a high degree Hertz achieves the goal he sets for *progress in philosophical cognition*. To appreciate this victory, one must survey the methodological preparations that Hertz devised with the clarity of a discoverer, and in this connection the inheritance of his *Mechanics* is of enduringly instructive value. In his foundations is revealed his truly critical, truly transcendental, truly Kantian spirit, and we could say this, even if he himself had not been aware of it: "The subject matter of this first book is entirely separate from *experience*. All the following statements are *a priori judgments in Kant's sense*."[14] It is the transcendental method, the critical preparation of the problem of the relationship of things to cognition, which makes this entire method of research one carried out in Kant's spirit.

Hertz recognized this critical basic relationship of things to cognition on the first page of his introduction to the *Mechanics* with a general idealist expression. Namely, he begins by describing the most significant task of the cognition of nature as the capacity: that we can "make inner depictions, or symbols, of the appearance of external objects". The guarantee that these depictions are capable of reaching out to the objects, lies in the additional subtle determination: "the form we give them is such that the necessary consequents of the symbols in thought are always the depictions of the necessary consequents in nature of the things pictured."[15] Here the hypothesized correspondence between the simulacrum and the object is extended and made more precise through the required correlation between *a consequence necessary in thought* and *a consequence necessary in nature*, the one in the *depiction*, the other in the *object*. Thus more is put into the *apparent depiction* than what a depiction commonly means or can mean, be that depiction ever so true and reliable, namely *necessity in thought*. Necessity in nature rests on it, but is also reduced to it.

One could conceive the construction of depictions as a means of sensibility determined by nature; but thought points to a more scrupulous methodology. Our author developed this train of thought: "So that this requirement can be fulfilled in general, certain agreements must exist between nature and our mind." That is the general idealist expression of the Copernican correlation between object and subject, matter and consciousness, experience and *a priori* cognition, nature and mind. The mind stands here for methodological, inquiring, proving thought in contrast to the alleged natural demands of sensible intuition. Certainly, the ambiguous expression of *representation* is not avoided. "The depictions, about which we are speaking, are our representations of things; they have a *substantial agreement* with things."[16] No other *agreement* between depiction, representation, and object is required, and we have "also no means to experience," whether there is another agreement. The determinacy of depictions must be developed in another way.

The unequivocalness[17] of depictions is determined through *three* criteria: first through that of *permissibility*: "that all our depictions be logically permissible or, briefly, that they shall be permissible." This permissibility rests on the validity of the "laws of our thought" or: "What enters into the depictions, in order that they may be permissible, is given by the nature of our mind." To mention the works in which we ourselves have clarified Kant's terminology, one can see that Hertz does not distinguish consciously between the metaphysical and the transcendental *a priori*; but, at any rate, his further criteria are sufficient to construct boundaries against the ill effects of this confusion.

The second criterion is that of *correctness*. The requirements for this are "contained in the *facts of experience*, from which the depictions have been built up." Correctness is, then, not within the power of the *a priori*. One the other hand, the *third* criterion leads back to it again. He describes it as that of *fitness to the purpose*. It expresses the number of "*essential* relations" that are "reflected" in the depiction. Fitness to the purpose is manifest, then, as "clearness" and as "simplicity," as the latter, insofar as a "smaller number of superfluous or empty relations" are contained in the depiction.

What, then, are the criteria for these moments of fitness to the purpose? "What can be added to the depictions to contribute to their fitness to the purpose is contained in the descriptions, definitions, abbreviations, in short in that which we can add or remove through arbitrary choice."[18] Therefore, the assessment of the so-called materiality of the objective relationships lies with the arbitrariness of the descriptions. And thus this fitness to the purpose is formal, but, properly understood and employed, also transcendental.

Permissibility can be "distinguished unequivocally using yes and no, and indeed this decision has validity for all time," *correctness* "only according to the state of our current experience"; for fitness to the purpose, however, there is in general "no unequivocal decision". The distinction of the properties of depictions according to these three conditions is the task of scientific explanation. And "the value of physical theories" and their presentation must be judged according to these points of view.

From this presentation of mechanics, Hertz now proceeds to the determination of *the concept of a principle of mechanics*. The ambiguity of this expression bespeaks a deficiency in the constitution of this fundamental science. Hertz determines the principle through the condition, that from it, "without further appeal to experience, the whole of mechanics can be derived purely deductively". A "selection" of the propositions set at the foundation [of mechanics] could satisfy this condition, and thus different presentations can be given of the principles of mechanics, or different depictions "of the things of the sensible world and the processes that occur in it." Hertz delineates and tests *three* such depictions.

The *first* depiction is that of the usual presentation of mechanics in almost all textbooks and lectures. It appeals mainly to *Newton*, insofar as *four* basic concepts appear first and connected to each other, namely *space, time, force*, and *mass*. "Thus, force is introduced as the constant cause of motion, before and independent of motion". This concept of force is consistent with the first two Newtonian laws; but in the third a *new* concept of force is presupposed. Force arises, as a *counterforce*, from motion. *Inertia* yet again is presupposed in *momentum*, and thus put in the calculations twice, "namely, first as mass, and second as force". This is an unclarity that not only touches the concept of force, as Hertz observes, but at the same time, though only indirectly, the concept of mass. "I think Newton himself must have discovered this confusion when he did some violence to *mass* by defining it as the product of volume and density. I think that *Thomson* and *Tait* must have re-discovered the confusion, when they remarked that this is really more a definition of *density* than mass, but, at the same time, contented themselves with this as the only definition of mass. Even *Lagrange*, I think, must have felt this embarrassment and the wish to move forward at any price, when he referred briefly to the definition that a force is a cause, which imparts motion 'or tends to impart it,' [though it is] certainly not without logical rigor to discover such an overdetermination."[19] Thus, not only is an ambiguity of the concept of *force* common, but even the basic concept of *mass* remains undetermined.

Hertz modestly described himself as only speaking of "a logical confusion," which makes "the form of presentation equivocal," and the contradictions only reach the "unimportant traits" of a depiction; his judgment on scientific presentation itself is even sharper: it has "still never penetrated to scientific completion". However, in the logical characteristic towards which Hertz is moving, there is an important concept with which he operates in most cases: that of the *laws of thought*.

Taken in its proper sense, *permissibility* consists only in failures of impermissibility. This, however, consists in conflict with "the laws of our thought". The indeterminacy of this idea and expression is revealed already in the possessive pronoun. Logicians of mechanical principles content themselves here with the comfortable facts of "our" laws of thought. And thus one can yet again see in this famous example, how deeply rooted is the notion of a merely negative meaning of the laws of thought, when one makes use of it in a positive sense. For what more positive value could be imagined, than that according to which the concepts of force and of mass explain each other? However, this insertion leads beyond the first depiction; we will have to take it up again with the other depictions.

Hertz touches further on the positive significance of the laws of thought with the *second* question, with which he investigates the *correctness* of the first depiction. The correctness is a complete one, "according to the entire range of our *experience* up to now." "We limit our perspective to the content of experience up to now."[20] And if such a caution seems absurd, Hertz instructs that "that which originates in experience can again be annulled by experience."[21] But he explains, at the same time, that empiricism can maintain and can develop the confidence that it instills: "That all too common definition of the basic laws can evidently only arise because in it the elements of experience are somewhat *concealed* and are mixed with the unchangeable elements *necessary in thought*."[22] If such a mixture of logical elements with those of experience is possible, this demonstrates a connection to thought-elements whose intimacy is not captured adequately by the expression "concealed." If the latency is revealed, the effective, positive character of this connection must emerge. At first it can seem as if the limitation of the correctness of the mechanical laws to experience *up until now* can have the consequence, at most, of a surplus of the meaning of that experience: "Not all motions, which the basic laws admit of, and which mechanics treats as mathematical tasks for calculation, occur in nature." But a deficit comes along with this surplus: "we can say more of the natural motions, forces, stable connections than what the assumed basic laws allow."[23] This deficit in the principles leads from the question of correctness to that of *fitness to the purpose*, and shows how closely these two points of view are related to each other.

This question, which really deals with the *transcendental method*, namely with the *attempt to understand* concepts in the things to be constructed using them, is dealt with by Hertz in turn in the concepts of force. "The weight of a stone, the force of an arm appear equally actual, equally accessible to immediate perception, as the motions generated through them. But we only need to shift our focus to the motion of the stars, already to have other relationships. Here forces have never been the object of immediate experience... only with the derivation of future experiences from prior ones do gravitational forces appear temporarily as auxiliary quantities, only to disappear again on consideration. Quite generally, it is the same with molecular forces, with chemical and many electrical and magnetic effects. And if we return, after more mature experience, to the simple forces, of whose existence we are in no doubt, then we are instructed that these forces, perceived by us with convincing certainty, are at any event not actual."[24] Thus, the criteria of correctness and of fitness to the purpose come together. Where forces are missing, others will be substituted, which should not be there. "Some properties of natural motions are not accounted for in mechanics; many relationships considered in mechanics are apparently missing in nature."[25] And it unfolds, that all methodological shortcomings of mechanics rest on the *first* mistake in the expression of the concept of force: that before motion, *force* was taken *as cause* of motion.

The *second* depiction that Hertz sketches of mechanics rests on the standpoint of the basic law that has ruled physics since the middle of the century. While the ultimate goal of physics until then was to reduce natural events to *actions at a distance* between the atoms of matter, the ultimate aim of modern physics is to reduce appearances to the *laws of the exchange of energy*. The concept of force is replaced by the concept of energy. The basic concepts on which this depiction of mechanics is based are *space*, *time*, *mass*, and *energy*. But initially, the logical character of energy is not distinguished substantially from that of force. Hertz expresses this disposition of his ideas in the distinction: "Two of them have a mathematical character: space and time; the other two, mass and energy, are introduced as physical entities, in their given quantity present, indestructible, and imperceptible."[26] His critique is established with these concepts of physical entity, but it conceals this point of attack, in order to present graphically the advantages that accrue thereby. The "real" reason, "why physics at the present time prefers to express itself in terms of the energy theory," is that it is most familiar with a representation of *atoms* that is in no way suited "to serve as a known and secure foundation for mathematical theories." Insofar as energy cuts off the concept of the atom, it appears not only to deal with the concept of force, but at the same time to supplant that of mass. But the disadvantages of the energy-based depiction begin with the conflicts about this concept.

We restrict ourselves to the account of those disadvantages that have to do with logical permissibility. "At the present time many distinguished physicists tend so much to attribute to energy the properties of a substance as to assume that every smallest portion of it is associated at every instant with a given place in space, and that through all the changes of place and all the transfers of energy into new forms it retains its identity."[27] In the conflict of the concept of energy with that of *substance* is concealed the conflict with the concept of *mass*.

And this conflict increases, when the true penchant of the energy concept comes into consideration, in the *distinction between types of energy*. "Also, a particular difficulty must prepare the way from the outset, that energy, supposedly akin to a substance, appears in two so entirely distinguishable forms, as those of the *kinetic* and the *potential* form. Kinetic energy requires basically, in itself, no new fundamental determination, for it can be derived from the concepts of velocity and of mass; potential energy, in contrast, which requires an independent establishment, resists at the same time any definition, which attributes to it the properties of a substance... Finally the amount of any substance contained in a physical system can depend only on the state of the system itself; the amount of potential energy contained in given matter depends, though, on the presence of *distant* masses, which perhaps never have any influence on the system."[28] Thus, it is at least an "open question," whether this depiction can be developed "in a logically unexceptionable form."

Now, here Hertz makes important methodological remarks, which demonstrate the power and clarity of his philosophical thought, and at the same time manifest its fruitfulness for the work of this fortunate physicist. He connects these considerations, which appear as commitments and cautions, to *metaphysical* considerations against the *Hamiltonian principle*.[29] The answer, which "contemporary physicists" hold ready to give to such attacks, is: "that physics has renounced, and no longer considers it as a duty, to meet the requirements of metaphysics... A doubt which makes an impression on our mind cannot be removed by calling it metaphysical; every thoughtful mind as such has needs which scientific researchers are accustomed to denote as metaphysical... It is true that we cannot *a priori* demand from nature *simplicity*, nor what we judge what in her opinion is simple. But with regard to images of our own creation we can lay down requirements... The same conviction finds expression in the desire we feel to penetrate from the external acquaintance with such a law to the deeper and real meaning which we are convinced it possesses."[30] It is this desire which leads him to the delineation of a *third depiction*.

Let us remember, in the consideration of this third depiction, that endowing energy with "the character of substance" was the circumstance behind the true logical difficulties with the second depiction, while the rejection of the concept of atom was the most important condition for this second depiction. But what is the *concept of atom* other than a version of the concept of substance? We remain in the conflicts involved with the philosophical basic problem, the basic concept of existence in this second depiction. The *third depiction* will give up this fusion of energy and substance. Which path will it then take? If it gives up energy, then there is a danger of falling back into the concept of force in the first depiction, which takes force as a cause and thus makes it material. On the other hand, if the third depiction gives up mass, then it is threatened with the fate of the second depiction: to have to illicitly substitute mass-substance for energy.

Another possible question could be: whether, perhaps, the concept of mass, like that of energy, could be replaced with a simpler concept, to finally resolve the conflicts between force and mass. Hertz does not discuss or mention this possibility. He chooses it, though, and supports it by employing it himself.

The *third depiction*, of his own mechanics, is based on only "three independent fundamental conceptions:" *space*, *time* and *mass*. These three basic concepts are "objects of experience." "A fourth idea, such as the idea of force or energy...as an independent fundamental conception, is here avoided." Certainly, it cannot remain "completely without a substitute." He attempts to bridge this remaining gap through a *hypothesis*: "the manifold of the actual universe must be greater than the manifold of the universe which is revealed *immediately to our senses*." "If we wish to obtain a depiction of the universe which shall be well-rounded, complete, and conformable to law, we have to presuppose, *behind* the things which we see, other, *invisible* things – to imagine *concealed confederates* behind the limits of our senses."[31] In the first two depictions the concepts of force and of energy were "entities of a special and particular kind." The third depiction wants to do away with these "entities." "We may admit that there is a *hidden something* at work, and yet deny that this something belongs to a special *category*."[32] Hertz makes use here of category, a term of the Kantian system, but entirely without the intention of terminological accuracy.

Kant describes neither mass nor force as categories: why did Kant not describe these most significant concepts of mechanics as categories, although the entire theory of categories revolves around them? Force could appear already to be sufficiently recognized in the category of causality; why, though, is mass not considered? Or should it be recognized in the category of substance? For Hertz, crediting energy with the character of substance was the objectionable element of the second depiction. Perhaps, too, the description of causality as a category was objectionable to him already, in that it had a tendency to disclaim energy as a basic concept; perhaps he scented behind this the category of substance.

Hertz means no terminological opposition to the Kantian theory of categories with his view that the *hidden*, the *concealed confederate masses* do not make up a "specific category," rather only to contradict the particular "being" of force and energy. "It is freely available to us, that even the *hidden* could be nothing other than motion and mass again, which are not distinguished in themselves from the *visible*, but only in relationship to us and to our usual means of *perception*. This way of putting it is just our hypothesis."[33] Only perception is attributed to "us" here; but could perhaps the perception that operates outside the "usual means" be – thought?

It is important to note, about the logical character of this hypothesis, that the "something" is not called only mass, but mass and motion. *Thus, motion is the determining element in the new concept of mass. Concealed mass leads thereby to a refined concept of motion.* If one overlooks this connection, then for a moment the outrageous suspicion could surface, that here again an enlightened mind is led astray by speculative curiosity into the error of mysticism, vaulting beyond the limits of perception, and making an *unobservable something* into mass. However, if motion and mass, rather, were explicitly to make up a hendiadys, then the new mass can belong only to the physical motion, for which along with motion at the same time *differential equations* are conceived, and not in the first instance to that which we perceive and manipulate.[34] "We assume that it is possible to *conjoin* with the *visible* masses of the universe *other masses obeying the same laws*, and of such a kind that the whole thereby becomes intelligible and conformable to law."[35] However, "the same" laws, which the unobservable masses must also obey, are laws of motion. "What we are accustomed to denote as force and as energy now become nothing more than an action of mass and motion, but not necessarily of mass recognizable by our *coarse senses* and motion demonstrable to our coarse senses."[36] Thus, Hertz can call his theory *dynamic* without paradox, although he eliminates force and energy, and *not* a mechanical one, although he retains mass. Accordingly, he describes as new his evaluation of the hypothesis by *Maxwell*, *Thomson*, and *Helmholtz*: that, while these eliminate the occult forces of mechanics, he prevents their entrance.

This purely dynamic sense of Hertz's concept of mass outlines the contours of the new depiction. It distinguishes the physical content of his depiction from its mathematical form. But since it has to do with the physical content of the association between space and mass, then it deals at least with geometrical determinations, which, since mass is a variational concept of motion, must verge upon determinations of infinitesimal geometry. Thus the concept of the *straightest path* arises for the motion of material systems, and in it the *basic principle* of the new depiction. From this *infinitesimal* account of *new* movement comes the possibility of a new determination for the "mathematical expression" of force, as "the merely thought mediation between two motions."[37] Here a *new concept* comes in with the expression: "merely thought". While elsewhere the new thing is only negatively described as "not perceptible," here it is positively described as "thought." What, however, is the positive force of its being thought? This question is not posed.

Now, it is characteristic that, in the discussion of the mathematical form that Hertz gives to the physical content, he discusses principally a logical problem. "The most significant characteristic of the terminology used consists in the fact that, already from the beginning, it presents entire *systems* of points and their consideration, and does not begin from the single points each time." This concept of *system* is also described as *origin* of the concept of *path*, thus also of that of the *path elements*, whose *quantity* and *direction* are analytically and synthetically definable characteristics. Thus, the concept of system appears as *presupposition* for the most fundamental concepts of analysis.

And Hertz is aware of the fact that he introduces a fundamental presupposition here. To the objection that his so hotly pursued simplicity is artificial, which is to say unnatural, he replies: "there may be some justification for regarding the consideration of whole systems as being more natural and obvious than the consideration of single points. For, in reality, the material particle is simply an abstraction, whereas the material system is presented directly to us; all actual experience is obtained directly from systems; and it is only by processes of reasoning that we deduce conclusions as to possible experiences with single points."[38] It is a consequence that the concept of *mass* for Hertz is the concept of a *system in motion*, and that its mass, its *basic concept of existence*, is connected not to the point-atom, but to the motion of points and the posited connection of these points.

Hertz strives for such a mathematical formulation, grounded in pure thought, and to do so he abolishes the usual teleologicization, asserted for metaphysics, from which he frees the *Gaussian* principle of least action to make its expression "more straightforward and true." This *rejection of false teleology* is even more important since it allows for the *real* version, insofar as it delimits the limits of mechanics for the questions of *biology* with conceptual determinacy, although even greater clarity about the resurfacing Neo-Vitalism would be desirable.

The discussion of the logical *permissibility* of this depiction is related to this concept of systems of points as well. "I put the greatest importance on this advantage of the presentation, indeed unique importance," namely that it can satisfy "rigid requirements." Among the possible objections, he only wants to discuss the *petitio principii* that physicists could find in his concept of *rigid* connections: that thereby already forces "are introduced in a way which is secret, and therefore not permissible."[39] He answers: "Your assertion is correct for the mode of thought of ordinary mechanics, but it is not correct independently of this mode of thought." And what is the final sense of the new method of thought? "Suppose we find in any way that the distance between two material particles remains *constant* at all times and under all circumstances. We can express this fact without making use of any other concepts than those of space; and the value of the fact stated, as a fact, for the purpose of foreseeing future experience and for all other purposes, will be independent of any explanation of it which we may or may not possess." The understanding of this matter of fact will not be improved through the addition of *force*.

But how do we find the matter of fact of such an equivalence? Immediately, in so-called sensible perceptive experience? Or, rather, do we find it first, once we have formulated and established it in thought? "In seeking the actual rigid connections we shall perhaps have to descend to the world of atoms. But such considerations are out of place here; they do not affect the question whether it is logically permissible to treat of fixed connections as independent of forces and precedent to them."[40] The demonstrated logical permissibility is demonstrated in the posited concept of a *system*, and indeed against the unnaturalness of the concept of point. Logical permissibility is not only the so-called *freedom from contradiction*; rather, it is demonstrated and consists in the positive force of a scientific basic concept. Hertz did not distinguish this positive meaning, which he actually added to his methodological concept of logical permissibility, from the so-called formal, deductive sense, and while he used this distinction, he did not define it. This omission has the consequence that the reasons for the separation of the concepts of force and energy, and for the description of the concept of mass, were not sufficiently clarified.

And indeed, overall, this positive meaning of thought is not only alluded to, but placed at the center of the entire system. One can recognize this especially clearly in the discussion of the *correctness* of the depiction. Here it is to do with a determinate mathematical limitation of the possible relations in nature. "It seems to me that the reason for our conviction should more properly be stated as follows. All connections of a system which are not embraced within the limits of our mechanics, indicate in one sense or another a discontinuous succession of its possible motions. But as a matter of fact it is *an experience of the most general kind that nature exhibits continuity in infinitesimals everywhere and in every sense*: an experience which has crystallized into firm conviction in the old proposition – Natura non facit saltus.[41] In the text I have therefore laid stress upon this: that the permissible connections are defined solely by their continuity."[42] Thus the law of continuity, which is the *law of the infinitely small*, appears here expressly as an "experience of the most general kind." But that this most general kind of experience, which indeed according to Hertz's own basic ideas cannot be that of sensible matter, is developed in pure thought, this is not accentuated, and thus the general character of the new empirical concept of mass is not brought to clear and simple, nor to sufficiently logical determination.

In the previous remarks we might have pointed out, that there are *two* expressions, to which even the most profound scientific formulation is connected: the first is the *sensible*, the other *thought*. As old as these contradictions are, and as immutable as they seem, modern speculation is certainly bound up with them. The *sensible should be* combated and *replaced*; for it is not the appropriate expression for the usual representations of mass, of motion and of the forces of nature. "It must also be admitted that the co-operation of *concealed* masses…is the commonest case in the problems which occur in daily life and in the arts."[43] The unchallenged sovereignty of sensibility does not disorient only in the concept of mass alone, but also in that of force, and not least in that of energy, the investiture of which with a substantial existence can be unmasked as a relic of materialism. Owing to this shipwreck of the energy theory, the *third depiction* returns to the concept of mass, but not to that of *sensible* mass.

Expressions, which at times creep in, at times are emphasized with insistence, already could show the terminological deficiencies of these determinations. "Recognizable to coarse senses" it reads; could the new mass then be recognizable to fine senses? And what *characteristic* distinguishes fine from coarse in the class concepts of sensibility, which, thus, appear to need to be retained? And further, the expressions "*concealed* masses" and "concealed motion" are supposed to be, through Helmholtz, "up-to-date as technical expressions in German."[44] But here is not a negative determination invested with an entirely excessive authority? Is the concealed only the not-observable, or also the not-thinkable? However, if only the first is the case, and with respect to the method of thought should the thinkable not only be logically permissible, but rather is what *must* be thought, not only what can be thought – does it not follow, then, that the other expression, which the new way of thinking does not eliminate, should be grounded more profoundly in its great positive meaning, and that the course of its achievements should be newly illuminated?

Or could it be the correct opinion, that mass should be determined only negatively, as the daunting appearance could have it, as if the concepts of force and energy could be dismissed, because and insofar as a "kind of substance" is connected to them, but not only because they are thought of as "entities" of a particular kind? Then those who maintain the energy theory would be right. But it would then be entirely inexplicable, how Hertz maintains the concept of mass, into which substance is squeezed in its entirety. The problem[45], which is contained in substance, can lead us to the right path. Perhaps *too much* is already anticipated in the concept of substance; perhaps the concept of ponderable matter could already be thought with the concept of substance. Perhaps it is to be required, to begin with a concept which is more elementary than substance, and which can serve as a grounding even for the definitions of mass, force, and energy.

It can be questionable, how one should describe this most basic initial concept, or whether one should borrow, recoin and develop the concepts of the Greeks, the classical masters of scientific truth; *but it cannot be in doubt, which concept effective in science must be part of this logical illumination*. It must be that basic concept of the new mathematics, which at the same time is the basic concept of the new mechanics. This state of affairs, that the basic concept of analysis is at the same time, in its logical value, the basic concept of mechanics, has not yet come to logical comprehension and recognition. People argue over the basic concepts of mechanics, whether one should choose mass or force or energy, but they forget that with all three the same *mathematical* basic concept is presupposed alongside, without which the new considerations cannot be engaged at all; just as it was itself first brought to a concrete definition as a mechanical basic concept.

The difficulties the concepts of mechanics encounter are connected to the difficulties with which the concept of the *differential* is beset. And if, the problem of the mechanical basic concept should have to do in the first case with *logical* permissibility, then it is more precise to describe as the *primary and basic problem of logic: that it clarify the central methodological significance of the concept of the differential.*

Here I can mention the attempts that I myself have published in the course of the last years, to improve on the weaknesses of the presentations of *idealism* to date, even that of Kant himself, and to satisfy the claims of *realism* through a new grounding of the most fundamental and instrumentally important concept of mathematical natural science, with a radical attack on the materialist view. These are the texts *The Principle of the Infinitesimal Method and Its History. A Chapter in the Foundations of the Critique of Cognition* (1883) and *Kant's Theory of Experience*, second edition (1885).

Here, I can only describe the development of these works in connection with the problems raised here. In so doing, I must strive even more for concision, since the further development of these viewpoints pursued in the meantime has also caused changes to the methodological sense of the other basic concepts of the system. The revision concerns even the concept of space, which already, with Faraday, plays a heavy role in the problem of actions at a distance. In the meantime, my deliberations were brought to a conclusion in the book that appeared at the same time as the publication of the second edition of this *Introduction*: *System of Philosophy. First Part: Logic of Pure Cognition* (First Edition, 1902).

I singled out the basic concept of *reality* for the logical legitimation of the differential concept. I refer to the text of *Dimitri Gawronsky: The Judgment of Reality* (1910). Reality is the problem which, in the concepts of mass, force, and energy, anticipates the difficulties that the infinitesimal method will encounter. The overcoming of the difficulties succeeds, as it can only succeed in general, on the basis of mathematics. The final remedy, the utmost instrument of power there is the *definition*. The axioms, the principles and whatever else one still can call the final privileges of an inquiring reason, all return in the final instance to definition. Definition is the immediate, the indisputable evidence and product of sovereign thought. It is thought that describes the claim of, and through that description grounds, that which one calls concealed mass, motion, and force. The naïves, which *aprix cheroin*, as Plato puts it, wish to understand being, are not yet quite dead.[46] All the negative expressions will not suffice to supplant those who sought the *me on*[47], the non-existent in matter. Only the self-consciousness of thought can help and suffice here: that it alone should be responsible to determine being and authenticate as being. Of the many expressions, with which being alone is named already in the field of logic, that of *reality* is distinguished in that it strives for the independence of being, while *substance* just as much as *actuality* not only includes a connection to another concept, but has its specific force and meaning in that determination of relation. Reality, on the other hand, describes and wishes to describe that which in and for itself, without consideration of classification and structure will be thought with and through others as existing and only as existing.

Such an independence of the existing will be legitimized only through the concept of *origin*. If any concept requires a logical characteristic, and challenges it, it is that of origin. For how could identity interest me with a product of thought, if its origin were not already discovered by me and if its pure derivation from the origin were not established? It is not now the case for logicians, that they can challenge the recognition of this problem, rather, they must recognize this recognition as their inevitable and most fundamental task, if logic wants to be a science. Since the seventeenth century, science has been rooted in those same concepts, which, in mathematical language, tackle the same problem and define the same idea. Or if it were another: where, then, in the formulations of modern logic do we find a discussion of the basic concept of the differential with another alleged meaning?

All further features and tasks, which are mixed up with the problem of reality, are derived from the concept of origin. That which is to be achieved for force and mass from the side of substantiality must be able to spring from the original concept of reality. One can suspect there neither a "kind of substance," nor an "entity of a particular kind," nor does it require another derivation of substance, through which the concept of reality is reduced only to a relational concept of variation. This is the weakness, with which K. Lasswitz in his excellent works *The History of Atomism*, in two volumes (1890) has detracted from the agreement, with which he supports my theory. Ungrounded being will be obliterated and uprooted. The concealed will be revealed and established. Reality is the real in mass, force, and energy: the reality of the infinitely small.

Or is there another way only to describe the real, refraining from grounding it, whether for the Newtonians in mass and force, or for the energeticists, or finally for the dynamicists with electrical mass? Is there another way than the differential? In the infinitesimal there is not only the origin of quantity, but also that of the existing itself, that of the real: for in order to comprehend this, it takes quantity in the last instance as origin. As mass is developed from motion, the real, in the last instance, shall be developed from quantity.

It is instructive, orienting, and corroborative, that in a book that connects the systematic critique of the mechanical basic concepts to research into its historical development, the foundations of modern physics is described with the same name from mathematical methodology. *Max Planck* describes in his prize essay *The Principle of Conservation of Energy* (1887) the principal question, to which all others must lead back: whether the intervening medium should be assigned as the complete intermediary of action at a distance. And what name does he choose for the theory expressing this problem? "Lacking a short appropriate name for this theory, I will allow myself in the following to describe it as *infinitesimal theory*" (244). "If the infinitesimal theory is thus confirmed, then at the same time a general new natural law is proven, namely, the law, that all alterations that occur in and on some material element, are completely determined through instantaneous processes within and on the boundaries of the element. It is understood, that this proposition reaches deep into the being and the modes of action of all natural forces" (244). But Planck recognizes indirectly the origin of the infinitesimal theory from thought. "And indeed it is explicitly and above all of the greatest importance, to divide the existence of this theory entirely from all hypotheses, with which one helps observation, which, however, have nothing to do with the theory in and for itself. The difficulties, which our means of representation could plant here, do not come into consideration at all" (245ff.). The infinitesimal theory is here recognized as the principle and foundation of the new theoretical physics from the theory of one of its own researchers.

Meanwhile, *A. Einstein* has brought idealist thought to sharper development, insofar as he made mass in general independent of the content of energy, further, sought to reduce heavy mass to inertia, insofar as he puts the two in the same quantitative relationship, and, finally, interprets the Fizeau experiment so that, while Lorentz took the ether as at rest, Einstein took the ether as a kind of matter in general. This is the great achievement of Einstein, that secures his established place in the history of idealism, and is indeed a watershed. Further research is to be expected on his characterization of space and time, before a logical judgment can be made; but through the abolishing of the ether the most difficult barrier to the problem of matter was removed. The fact that matter in its final sources is not observable now is insufficient: with unobservability, existence itself must be given up. What remains, then, as the final ground of existence? Thus, today perhaps Boltzmann would question Einstein in the same way that he questioned the energeticists.

Einstein appears not to have looked at these speculations himself independently as yet; in these questions, he refers to Planck. With Planck it is characteristic that he poses questions only about "the unchangeable building blocks, from which the physical world is put together." If substance were in fact nothing other than the unchangeable, then thus nothing would be proven but that substance cannot be the last link in the chain of the questions about the final ground of existence. We would then have to reach back further than substance, to reality.

Planck's answer goes the same way as his problem: "The unchangeable elements of the system of physics based on the relativity principle are the so-called *universal constants*, above all the velocity of light in a vacuum" and so on. As the question does, the answer ignores the problem of those elements that define the *first* pure ground of being. It cannot be replaced with unchangeability. Unchangeability can be appealed to only under the unavoidable prerequisite, that there can be no doubt over its fundamental purity. So we see here substance put in the first place, while only the second is proper – the first must be accorded solely and exclusively to infinitesimal reality, which, for mechanics, matures as intensive reality. But the history of theoretical physics must be penetrated by the rigorous formation of mechanical principles securely on the condition of these that is laid down in analysis, and thus the realizing force of idealism established in the final instance.

The path of research leads securely and sanely to idealism; materialism is obliterated at the root of physical concepts, and it is mathematics that brings about the liberation and establishes it as permanent. The old Platonic connection between philosophy and mathematics stands the test of time in its eternal power; the mathematical ideas prove themselves yet again as the paradigm of ideas and offer themselves as solution to the basic question of philosophy, the question: What is science?

Notes

1 From reprint, 1928. *Hermann Cohens Schriften zur Philosophie und Zeitgeschichte*, Albert Görland and Ernst Cassirer, eds. Berlin: Akademie Verlag, pp. 231–267.
2 In 1865, Otto Liebmann published a very influential book, *Kant und die Epigonen* (*Kant and the Epigones*, of which chapter 1 is reprinted here as 2.1). The "epigones" were Fichte, Schelling, Hegel, Herbart, Fries, and Schopenhauer. "Epigone" implied that these followers of Kant had distorted his teachings. The original for "debated term" here is "*Schulstreitwort*". – Trans.
3 *Gebilde*
4 "Erkenntnis" is translated "cognition," as is now standard for Kant, following the Pluhar and Guyer-Wood translations of Kant's first *Critique*. Readers of the Marburg texts should be

sensitive to the argumentative context in which "Erkenntnis," "Wissen," "Wissenschaft" (science), and the like occur. Encountering these terms in the text should provoke reflection on how they are used by each author and in the tradition. English translations now use "cognition" for "Erkenntnis" partly to distinguish "Erkenntnis" from "Wissen" in Kant (see Andrew Chignell's 2007 review of Dicker's *Kant's Theory of Knowledge*, *Philosophical Review* 116.2: 307–9). This distinction should be understood in its argumentative context in German and for each philosopher, and not in terms of the connotations of the words in English. Especial care should be taken not to understand "cognition" as involving mental or psychological processes, unless there is independent evidence in the text that supports such a reading. While consistency with the philosophical tradition motivates the translation of "Erkenntnis" as "cognition," "knowledge" is a straightforward translation of "Erkenntnis" into English. Thanks are due to Scott Edgar, David Hyder, Sebastian Luft, Samantha Matherne, and Alan Richardson for extensive discussion of this issue from all sides, though of course they are not responsible for my remarks above or for any infelicities of translation. – Trans.

5   Kant uses the word "*Erschleichung*," subreption, to describe "the surreptitious substitution of different *kinds* of terms and concepts. Kant usually uses the term to refer to the error of confusing or substituting concepts and principles meant for use in experience (those which properly apply to appearances) with principles of 'pure reason'" (Michelle Grier, 2009). The word is a legal term still in use, meaning fraudulent misrepresentation of the facts. – Trans.

6   In the Anticipations of Perception in the first *Critique*, for instance, Kant gives examples of "moments" as sensations of gravity, of heat, and of weight. – Trans.

7   *ist an Kant irre*
8   *Bildungswahrheit*
9   *Seiendes*
10 *Stoff*
11 "*Fernkraft*"
12 Hertz 1894, *Gesammelte Werke*, Vol. 2. Leipzig, p. 20.
13 Hertz 1894, *Gesammelte Werke*, Vol. 3, 27. Also in Hertz (1956 [1894]), *The Principles of Mechanics*, trans. Jones and Walley, New York: Dover, preface.
14 Hertz 1894, *Gesammelte Werke*, Vol. 3, 53. Also in Hertz (1956 [1894]), 45.
15 Hertz (1956 [1894]), 1, translation revised.
16 Hertz 1956 [1894], 1, translation amended. Interestingly, in the Jones and Walley translation, "*Vorstellungen*" is rendered as "conceptions," not "representations."
17 *Eindeutigkeit*
18 Hertz 1956 [1894], 2–3, translation amended.
19 Hertz 1956 [1894]), 7, translation amended.
20 Hertz 1956 [1894], 9, translation amended.
21 *Ibid*.
22 *Ibid*.
23 Hertz 1956 [1894], 10, translation amended.
24 Hertz 1956 [1894], 12, translation amended.
25 Hertz 1956 [1894], 13, translation amended.
26 Hertz 1956 [1894], 15, translation amended.
27 Hertz 1956 [1894], 21.
28 Hertz 1956 [1894], 22, translation amended.
29 Hertz and Cohen are discussing Hamilton's *principle*, which is a minimizing principle of variational mechanics. Hamilton's *principle* is not the same thing as the much more familiar Hamiltonian *equation*, which is an integral equation summing potential and kinetic energy within a system. The two are related, of course, but they are not the same. – Trans.
30 Hertz 1956 [1894], 23–24, translation amended slightly.
31 Hertz 1956 [1894], 25, translation amended.
32 *Ibid*.
33 *Ibid*.
34 A hendiadys is a rhetorical device in which a phrase that would usually be a noun modified by an adjective becomes a noun and an adjective used substantivally, joined by "and." English

expressions such as "nice and warm" instead of "nicely warm" are examples of this rhetorical device, also used frequently by Goethe and Schiller. In this case, Cohen is saying "motion and mass" is a hendiadys for "moving mass" – that is, "motion" or "moving" is adjectival and "mass" substantival. Cohen uses the original Greek: *hen dia duoin*. – Trans.

35 Hertz 1956 [1894], 25–26, emphasis added.
36 Hertz 1956 [1894], 26, translation revised.
37 The original German is "*das nur gedachte Mittelglied zwischen zwei Bewegungen.*" Jones and Walley do not preserve the sense of Cohen's reading here, rendering this phrase as "a middle term conceived only between two motions," but the original German makes it clear that Cohen's reading is the more natural: "*nur gedacht*" modifies "*Mittelglied*." For Jones and Walley to be correct, the phrase would have to read "*das Mittelglied nur gedacht zwischen zwei Bewegungen*". This is not to agree with Cohen's interpretation, only to observe that Jones and Walley obscure an important textual nuance. Hertz 1956 [1894], 28. Z– Trans.
38 Hertz 1956 [1894], 31.
39 Hertz 1956 [1894], 34.
40 *Ibid*.
41 Nature does not make jumps – Ed.
42 Hertz 1956 [1894], 37, emphasis added by Cohen.
43 Hertz 1956 [1894], 39–40, emphasis added by Cohen.
44 Hertz 1956 [1894], 26.
45 *Anstoß*
46 This is a reference to line 155e in the *Theatetus*, in which Socrates says "The uninitiated are those who think nothing is except what they can grasp firmly with their hands (*aprix toin cheroin labesthai*), and who do not admit that actions and generation and all that is invisible are a part of being." – Trans.
47 Greek for "non-being." This expression is found in the *Gorgias*, where there is an extended discussion of the non-existent, and in the *Republic*, e.g. at 478d2. – Trans.

Chapter 10

"The Discovery of Man as Fellowman," from *Religion of Reason out of the Sources of Judaism* (1919)[1]

1. Up to now we have come to know man only as holy spirit, only as a being of moral reason. In this concept man is only an abstraction of religion based on its share in reason, in morality. Considered as this abstract moral creature, man has as yet no relation to historical experience, let alone to the knowledge of nature, except insofar as historical experience presupposes the relation to morality. But morality itself denotes up to now only a problem that originates in the correlation between God and man, and which is to be solved through holiness. Therefore man himself is only a problem.

2. Experience, natural as well as historical, shows man in new problematic shapes, and these branch off into two main groups. One of these groups is formed by man as *individual;* the other by man as *plurality*[2]. Plurality, in turn, raises the problem of *totality*[3]. In the first instance these groups are distinguished only from the point of view of singularity and plurality.

One cannot stop with singularity, for, properly speaking, it belongs to plurality, in which it forms just one link. But plurality, as a logical class, forms a unity, and as such it needs and is able to form a new class, that of totality; in the same way singularity too poses the problem of unity, by virtue of which it is able to join totality, which it also needs. Whenever abstractions such as classes and ranks are in question, unity becomes a problem.

3. We shall not consider yet the unity of singularity, but first the unity of plurality, and we shall do this without at first taking in consideration how it flows into and joins with totality. The unity, which makes plurality into the concept of a class, extends its power over every individual member of the plurality. Thus, man arises as plurality, which in itself forms the unity of a group. At the same time man as such, as one member of this group, also poses in himself the problem of unity. Thus a concept arises that grasps man, not yet indeed as an individual with the full weight of the concept but as a unit in a series: one man next to other men, just *the next man*[4]. And this experience – for this conception of the next man is taken from experience – poses for ethics and also for religion, in accordance with the latter's share in reason, the problem of the *fellowman*[5].

Popular thinking finds it strange that the fellowman is a problem for ethics as well as for religion. To be sure, the next man is simply perceived, but is he not already a fellowman? The assumption of such an identity of the next man and the fellowman is the prejudice of popular thinking in which ethics, as the teaching about the pure man, cannot exist, from which it cannot arise. And insofar as it could arise, it would have constantly to fight the prejudice that this next man of the natural and historical experience is the whole man and that he represents the whole problem of man. The next man is in no way already the fellowman. Experience itself contests and refutes this identity.

It is therefore necessary that there be a conceptual knowledge that expedites the development of the next man into the fellowman. Only conceptual knowledge, only ethics on the basis of logic can achieve this; and by virtue of the share of religion in reason, this task has also to be allotted to religion. For what value would the share of religion in reason have, if this difference between the next man and the fellowman did not become a problem for religion also? If, however, the correlation between God and man is the fundamental equation of religion, then *man* in this correlation must first of all be thought of as fellowman.

4. The concept of the fellowman conceals a correlation of its own, namely, that of man and man, but in this narrower correlation there is merely an initial unfolding of the meaning and the content of the more universal one. For the correlation of man and God cannot be actualized if the correlation of man and man is not first included. The correlation of man and God is in the first place that of man, as fellowman, to God. And religion proves its own significance first of all in this correlation of the fellowman to God, in which, indeed, man as fellowman becomes a problem, and is engendered through this problem.

The share of religion in reason is the share of religion in morality, and no problem of morality takes precedence over this problem of the fellowman. The possibility of ethics is tied to this problem. If the fellowman is leveled down to the next man, it would still be questionable whether sociology could arise; but there is no question that in that case ethics would be impossible. And since the share of religion in reason consists in its share in morality, if ethics is impossible religion also becomes untenable; for then the correlation disintegrates: man then is no longer fellowman, the link in the correlation with God, and no other concept of man but the moral concept of the fellowman can be established in this correlation. Hence ethics and religion depend, with regard to the concept of man, on the concept of the fellowman.

5. The sources of monotheism flow within the historical and literary experience of the Jewish people and the Jewish community. The antinomies, which we found in the development of monotheism in regard to its determination by a national literature, will recur in the human part of the correlation. The experiences of man as the next man contradict the demands on the fellowman that the correlation of man and God makes.

The national consciousness calls first upon the Israelites. This, however, contains an ambiguity, insofar as the Israelite is a son of Adam and a son of Abraham. We shall see how this opposition is reconciled in an unifying concept.

The concept of the Israelite also contains a further ambiguity, insofar as it signifies not only a difference of religion but also a political distinction. For Israel became a state, and in the concept of a *citizen* of a state an opposition arises between the native and the foreigner. We shall also see that this opposition is reconciled and overcome through a unifying concept, which eradicates not only hostility but also indifference to the foreigner.

6. Finally there is another opposition in man, as fellowman, which emerges from the meaning of plurality. The fellowman is a member of a *people*, in the first place of the people of Israel. But Israel is surrounded by other peoples and it makes wars and concludes peace treaties with them. Opposition with regard to the state is repeated on the level of the people, but it is not the same. For the concept of the people was altered through the national goal of monotheism. Unavoidably, uniqueness is attached to one's own people. This uniqueness is demanded by monotheism, the fulfillment of which is dependent on national opposition to other peoples.

With regard to other peoples, therefore, Israel is not simply a people among a plurality of peoples. Because of its calling to profess the unique God and also to accomplish the historical work of the universal recognition of the unique God, Israel itself is distinguished as a unique people. The other peoples are enemies of the unique God and therefore enemies of the unique people. If this opposition were to exhaust the relationship between the people of Israel and the peoples of the world, the concept of monotheism would fail. At the same time, that member of the correlation that is constituted by fellowman in the plurality of the peoples would drop out of the concept of monotheism. We shall see how this conflict, upon which the destiny of monotheism hinges, is resolved through a unifying concept. The significance of this concept becomes all the more important, as through it the plurality in the concept of fellowman is transformed and elevated into totality.

7. Let us first consider the antinomy between the Israelites and the foreigner (נכרי). It is resolved through the concept of the stranger (גר).

The stranger is not a new concept first discovered by monotheism and put in opposition to the foreigner. The natural communication of men and peoples, even in war, brought it about. Wandering and traveling were always in use among men and peoples; through this the immigrant became both guest and friend, a *guest-friend*[6].

The humanism of the Greek teaching about the gods is shown by the fact that the highest god, Zeus, is made to be the god of hospitality, of guest-friendship (*Zeus xenios*). And to the guest-friend one must be faithful, in war and in peace. When Diomedes and Glaucus recognize each other as guest-friends in the midst of the fighting, they do not, it is true, cease to fight one another, but a knightly feeling of guest-friendship induces them to exchange their weapons. To be sure, the knightly feeling of guest-friendship does not prevent them from cheating. This paradigm of classical sentimentality unmasks the moral indifference that still afflicts the concept of guest-friendship. The guest-friend is still far from being the stranger in that positive sense of the idea which monotheism develops.

8. The moral powers that are released by the various representations of the concept of the fellowman can only be depicted in collaboration with their opposing motives and their conciliatory concepts. But it is from the point of view of monotheism, and the creation and revelation corresponding to it, and, on the other hand, also from the point of view of man, as the holy spirit, that we must first of all inspect the biblical sources of this opposition. There we at first encounter Noah, who is no longer Adam but not yet Abraham. Conceptually, therefore, the wonderful concept formation of the *Noachide, the son of Noah* (בן נח) is, as a conciliatory concept, much loftier than that of the stranger; but the latter originates in the first beginnings of biblical monotheism, whereas the former is devised only later by rabbinical thought as a significant consequence of monotheism.

The significance of the Noachide for monotheism is already contained in the biblical reinterpretation of the Babylonian Flood saga. Noah becomes the symbol of the human race, whose preservation God sets himself as a task. He makes a covenant with Noah that no flood will recur to destroy all living things. God makes, therefore, a covenant with living creatures in general and in particular with the human soul. And nature becomes, as it were, the witness for this covenant in the form of the rainbow which appears on the vault of heaven. Thus God places himself into an unceasing, a conceptual, correlation with nature and with the human race within nature, with man as fellowman.

The account, to be sure, begins with the verse; "And God said unto Noah: the end of all flesh is come before Me; for the earth is filled with violence through them; and, behold, I will destroy them with the earth" (Gen. 6:13), or as is said later: "And I, behold, I do bring the flood of waters upon the earth, to destroy all flesh, wherein is the breath of life, from under heaven: every thing that is in the earth shall perish" (Gen. 6:17). Nevertheless this verse immediately follows: "But I will establish My covenant with thee; and thou shalt come into the ark, thou, and thy sons, and thy wife, and thy sons' wives with thee." Thus through this exemption of Noah and his family, God's announced intent is immediately thwarted. The revision of the whole saga is initiated and expressed in the self-correction of this intent. Nor is an expressed motivation lacking: "For thee I have seen righteous before Me in this generation" (Gen. 7:1). Thus righteousness has not entirely vanished among men, and it must be preserved in man. The human race, therefore, cannot be destroyed.

9. The expression in which God announces his renunciation of the flood seems to be unique: "And the Eternal said in his heart: 'I will not again curse the ground any more for man's sake; for the imagination of man's heart (imagination[7] does not mean impulse, but the product of it) is evil from his youth; neither will I again smite anymore everything living'" (Gen. 8:21). And thus God blesses Noah and his children and at the same time prohibits the eating of meat with blood in it, connecting with it the warning: "And surely your blood of your lives will I require; at the hand of every beast will I require it; and at the hand of man, even at the hand of every man's brother, will I require the soul (life) of man. Whoso sheddeth man's blood, by man shall his blood be shed; for in the image of God made He man" (Gen. 9:5,6). It seems that in order to prevent murder, the eating of meat with blood in it was prohibited. Only man, the image of God, is mentioned here, and one man is called the brother of the other. Consequently, according to the covenant with Noah, every man is already the brother of every other.

10. It is in this connection that the covenant which God establishes with Noah is to be understood: "Neither shall all flesh be cut off any more by the waters of the flood; neither shall there anymore be a flood to destroy the earth" (Gen. 9:11). And thus the rainbow is set up as a sign of the covenant between God and the earth, between God and every living soul in all flesh, and, to be sure, as an "everlasting covenant" for "perpetual generations" (Gen. 9:12,16). As a natural consequence of this covenant between God and man, which comes into being through the mediation of Noah, the Talmud creates the wonderful concept of the son of Noah.

In the prehistory of monotheism, Noah is followed by Abraham. God makes an "eternal covenant" with him also, for his descendants and their possession of Canaan. It is already significant that the angels, who announce the son to Sarah, are directed, after having completed their mission, not to hide from Abraham the destruction of Sodom: "Shall I hide from Abraham that which I am doing; seeing that Abraham shall surely become a great and mighty nation, and all the nations of the earth shall be blessed in him" (Gen. 18:18). The reasons for the blessing of the descendants of Abraham are not missing: "They may keep the way of the Eternal, to do righteousness and justice" (Gen. 18:19).

And now comes the episode of Sodom, which is introduced by Abraham's dialogue with God. The angels had already left, when Abraham drew near before God and said: "Wilt Thou indeed sweep away the righteous with the wicked?" (Gen. 18:23). "That be far from Thee to do after this manner, to slay the righteous with the wicked, that so the righteous should be as the wicked; that be far from Thee; shall not the Judge of all earth do justly" (Gen. 18:25). Already here God again comes into relation with the entire earth, and indeed not only as its preserver, as in the case of Noah, but as its *judge*. And as such He will show forbearance for the whole city if there be found fifty, or forty-five, or thirty, or twenty, or finally only ten righteous men in the city.

Thus the blessing that Abraham shall bring "to all the nations of the earth" is based on law and justice. And the promise made to the great people whose father shall be Abraham, is connected to the blessing for "all the families of the earth" (families!). This promise at the very origin of the people of Israel connects this people with the peoples of the world and thus paves the way for the idea of the "fellowman."

11. Therefore the dispute between Rabbi Akiba and Ben Azai about the very verse that introduces the love of one's neighbor is not idle. Akiba says: "Thou shalt love your other[8], he is as you. This is a great embodiment of the Torah," Ben Azai says: "This is the book of the generations of man (Gen. 5:1). This is a greater embodiment than the other" (Talm. Jeras. Ned. p. 9). We should consider the conclusion that follows: "In the day that God created man, in the likeness of God made He him." Which foundation is the superior? Perhaps the first, which stresses the equality between man and man, which makes man into "the other," and therefore into the fellowman? Or the one that makes man, as God's creature, the image of God? Evidently Ben Azai is right.

We can understand how the acknowledgment of the other as the fellow countrymen only arose from a biased misinterpretation. Not to speak of the fact that it is senseless to say, love your fellow countryman as yourself, if the love of man in general has as yet not even been discovered – either the national feeling is already so strong that I feel in my fellow countryman my blood and my image, in which case the commandment is superfluous; or the national feeling still has to be taught, in which case, however, the intensification "as yourself" or even "he is as you" is only intelligible if the notion of the fellow countryman has already been permeated by the concept of man in general. The equality of the fellow countryman is clearly based on the equality of man; otherwise my fellow countryman is my neighbor, with whom I quarrel, or the poor man, who hates the rich who oppress him. The moral concept of the fellow countryman has as its indispensable supposition the general concept of man.

It is this general supposition to which Ben Azai refers. And therefore it makes no sense to think one perceives the fellow countrymen in Rabbi Akiba's sentence. The whole Torah, starting with the creation of man, refutes this vexatious opinion. The love of the neighbor is dependent upon God's creation of man, and not upon the subjective feeling with which I love myself or somebody else. "This is the book of the generation of man ... in the likeness of God made He him." Upon this principle rests the history of mankind. In monotheism lies the origin of the history of man. And monotheism itself prevents any inner partition between believers in monotheism and all nonbelievers. The Israelite is a son of Noah before he is a son of Abraham. And even as the son of Abraham, his blessing is dependent on the blessing of all the peoples of the earth. But before he is a son of Abraham and a son of Noah, the Israelite is, just as every man is, God's creature and is created in his image.

12. We turn now to the political antinomy between Israel and the *foreigner*. We have already encountered the necessity that the mission of monotheism imposed on humanity, namely, that this mission required the destruction of polytheism, which destruction in turn entailed the destruction of idolatrous peoples. This anomaly can be resolved only on the basis of historical considerations. The share of religion in reason retreats in this case before the logic of facts, a logic that cannot hold its own before pure ethics. Can one, however, ask why God did not arrange it, did not command it, differently? Theodicy becomes absurdity in the case of this question. We therefore have to disregard this anomaly and, despite its contradictory character, attempt a conciliation.

Although the worshippers of idols have to be fought no less in one's own people than in the alien peoples, it nevertheless says: "Thou shalt not abhor an Edomite, for he is thy brother." This is one of the golden sentences in support of neighborly love: the Edomite, this enemy of Israel, is called "brother." Consequently not only is the Israelite a brother, but even the hostile worshiper of idols is called the same. Then it is no wonder that this prohibition is also extended to the Egyptian: "Thou shalt not abhor an Egyptian" (לח כעחח מצִיך). And the four hundred years of slavery are not recalled there; rather, there this thought is emphasized: "because thou wast a stranger in his land" (Deut. 23:8). The stranger is not thought of as a slave, but as a guest-friend, who requires the piety of guest-friendship. Humanity is already so rooted in the stranger that the slave, as stranger, can be admonished to the bond of gratitude.

13. Thus the concept of the stranger is extended to include the whole problem of the foreigner[9]. At this point we shall not go into the exceptions, which can be explained by the state law as well as by the religious ritual. We are concerned only with the formation and distinctiveness of the basic concept of the fellowman. In this respect, however, Solomon's speech at the dedication of his Temple is significant: "Moreover concerning the foreigner[10] when he shall come out of a far country...and prays toward this house, hear Thou in heaven" (1 Kings, 8:41–43). It is not far from this to the sentence in which Messianism reaches its peak: "For mine house shall be called a house of prayer for all peoples" (Isa. 56:7). Thus the foreigner becomes fellowman through the community of prayer, but this development presupposes the collaboration of Messianism. It would seem, therefore, that monotheism must be fully developed if the foreigner is to be recognized as fellowman.

14. The meaning of monotheism penetrated deeper into the concept of man, so that monotheism could discover this concept even without actualizing its own concept in the messianic concept of man. In this way monotheism was best able to correct its own teaching with respect to the strict commandment to destroy idol worship and idolatrous peoples. Thus, man is also recognized in the *non-Israelite*, and this recognition is also confirmed by a political acknowledgment of him. The blemish of idol worship is thus separated, if not from the concept, at least from the representation of man. Man need not be an Israelite in order not to have to be a worshipper of idols.

Of course, the worship of idols is ineradicably blemished. The worship of idols signifies in ancient Jewish consciousness in no way a religious notion exclusively, but at the same time chiefly a purely moral one. It is a profound saying of the Talmud that the Israelites would not have submitted so constantly to idol worship if sensual pleasure were not connected with it. And the prohibition of idol worship also affects the sexual licentiousness, which was particularly connected with the worship of Astarte. The more striking, therefore, is the purely moral share of reason in monotheism, as seen in the literary fact that monotheism made the foreigner into fellowman, even without his joining the monotheistic religion. And this consideration is the more important as it is actualized in the realm of politics.

15. Out of the foreigner and stranger comes to be a new concept of the *"stranger-sojourner"* (גֵּר תּוֹשָׁב).

The legislation with regard to this member of the state, as which he was received, is first of all characterized by the complete equality under the law that was granted to the *ger* [stranger]: "One Torah shall be to him that is homeborn, and unto the stranger that sojourneth among you" (Exod. 12:49). Thus the distinction from the homeborn is invalidated in favor of the sojourner. The law has to be uniform for all who live in the country and do not merely pass through it. And the sojourner does not need a patron in order to conduct a case in court, as he did in Greece and in Rome, for "the judgment is God's" (Deut. 1:17). Law does not have its origin in human statutes but comes from God. Therefore God gives also to the stranger his share in the law of the land, although he does not profess the one God.

This is a great step, with which humanitarianism begins, namely, in the law and in the state, even though this state is based on the unique God, and even though the sojourner does not recognize him! Thus it is understandable that this first step is consequently followed by others.

16. It is exactly in this steady progress in the development of monotheism in all its human relations that the basic concepts of its later period are uniformly connected with the primitive beginnings. The stranger-sojourner became, in talmudic times, the *son of Noah*. We still need elucidation exactly at what point in the talmudic sources the one concept changes into the other. In the codification of Maimonides, however, which takes into consideration

a third concept that is instrumental for the concept of the fellowman, it is perhaps possible to detect, in the difference between the new concept and the other two, the respective difference between the first two.

This third concept denotes "the pious of the peoples of the world" (חסידי אומא העולם). This concept relates to the peoples outside of Israel, and therefore abstracts from Israel's religion and still acknowledges piety in these people.

Hence, this wondrous concept is unequivocally a borderline concept between religion and morality, a concept that delineates, and frees, morality from religion.

Through this concept Maimonides completes the distinction between the "sojourner" and the "Noachide." He is in need of such a distinction because he codifies the entire law, including the law of the state. For the law itself in its own development it is not necessary to make this distinction. The law can consider both concepts as two terms for the same legal idea. The stranger is in the first place a son of Noah, and this is his protection against the deficiency that he is not the son of Abraham. But as a Noachide he is not bound to the law of Moses, but only to the seven precepts, "the seven commandments of the sons of Noah" (כשבע מצות בני נח). And these seven precepts have a strictly moral character.

Only *one* religious tie seems to be contained in them, namely, the abstinence from blaspheming God and from worshiping idols. Here, the difference between the ethical concept of the Noachide and that of the political sojourner contains an admonition. If the law already goes so far as to permit nonbelievers in the unique God to settle in the land, then provision must be made that the land should not be desecrated through idol worship and its inhabitants not be induced to it. Otherwise, however, there are only moral precepts to which the Noachide is obligated, and the precept of the "juridical institutes"[11] (דינים), to which the Noachide must submit, deserves particular attention. We recall the "statutes and ordinances" which Deuteronomy emphasized with great vigor as the meaning and value of the Torah. In the acceptance of the law the Noachide acknowledges morality, while the acknowledgment of religion is not imputed to him.

The concept of the Noachide is the foundation for natural law not only as an expression of the objective law but also as a determination of the subject of law. Noah has received no other revelation yet but that of man as a living creature. Man is, to begin with, life and soul. But already upon this foundation he becomes fellowman. The Noachide embodies this thought, and it is important evidence for the inner coherence in the history of monotheism, for the homogeneous continuation of the biblical spirit by tradition, that the Noachide as an institution of state law belongs to the oldest reports of the Mishnah.

The seven obligations of the Noachide consist of six prohibitions and one precept. The prohibitions, except for the blasphemy of God and idol worship, are the following: incest, murder, robbery, eating of a limb of a living creature. And the precept is concerned with the establishment of courts of justice. Consequently, with the exception of the concern for the preservation of monotheism in the land against the seductions of idol worship and blasphemy, the precepts required of the Noachide are moral precepts. The belief in the Jewish God is not required.

One is not permitted to force even a slave to this belief. Further, whoever turns to Judaism together with his children is not permitted to accomplish the conversion for his immature children; until they are able to decide themselves, they remain Noachides (Tr. Ketuboth, 11a).

The Noachide is therefore not a believer, and yet is a citizen of the state, insofar as he becomes stranger-sojourner. The Noachide is *the forerunner of natural law* for the state and also for freedom of conscience.

The Noachide thus is evidence for the true meaning of the theocratic constitution: that it is not built on the unity of state and religion, but on the unity of state and morality. The

Noachide, who is not a believer in God, may still join the state, because he is recognized as a moral person by his acceptance of the seven precepts. This consequence also follows from the further development of the notion of the Noachide in the Talmud into the "virtuous or pious among the peoples of the world." And these virtuous people have a share in bliss, in eternal life, which is the religious expression of morality (Tosefta Sanhedrin 13 and the formulation of Maimonides, with his own addition, which undoubtedly follows as a deduction from Sanhedrin 105a).

17. Through the legislation of the Talmud we therefore recognize the decisive equation: Stranger = Noachide = Pious of the [gentile] Peoples of the World. Johann Seiden in *De jure naturali et gentium juxta disciplinam Ebraeorum* [*Natural Law and the Gentile Peoples of the World According to the Hebrew Teaching*] (London, 1640) already knows this equation. And he explains the title of his book by the fact that the significance of the Hebrews for the law of the world *(pro jure mundi)* is a result of their laws. But Christian writers "nowhere explicated" this (p. 158). Professor Andreas Georg Waehner of Göttingen also expressly recognizes the connection of the Noachides with the "Virtuous of the Peoples of the World" in a book of the year 1743, *Antiquitates Ebraeorum* (I, 601). Hugo Grotius also praises the institution of the Noachide.

The connection of these three concepts is understandable. As for the two latter concepts, they are already explicable from the basic tendency of Deuteronomy: to make understandable to this great people the Torah as a document of reason and "insight." This reason therefore reaches beyond the border of the people itself, and the Torah on Sinai receives its preparation, so to speak, in accordance with the "statutes and ordinances" upon the justice of which the entire Torah is finally based.

The Noachidic obligations therefore form an original Torah of their own, which is the foundation for law and state. The harmony between religion, on the one hand, and law and state, on the other, becomes a principle of *theocracy*. The Noachide, indeed, grew out of the stranger-sojourner.

Monotheism created a spirituality of God and thereby also a spirituality of man's soul. This idea is developed in Deuteronomy. In this way the principle of spirituality could and had to become the principle of morality, and therefore, in connection with the law and politics, mature to the principle of freedom of *conscience*. The Noachide, with his offshoot the "Virtuous of the Peoples of the World," is the first and perhaps the most genuine representative of the freedom of conscience and of tolerance.

18. These developments prove unambiguously the true meaning of the commandment of so-called *neighborly love*. If the neighbor originally had had the basic meaning of fellow countryman, then the concept of the Noachide, not to mention the purely theoretical concept of the "Virtuous of the Peoples of the World," could not have developed out of the stranger. But even the stranger is not the ultimate source of this development, which is to be seen rather in monotheism itself. Out of the unique God, the creator of man, originated also the stranger as fellowman.

In spite of all these connecting thoughts, one has to emphasize mainly the *political* and legislative execution of the basic concept of the stranger. Johann David Michaelis, in his *Mosaic Law*, already recognized the connection between the stranger and the neighbor: "Moses commands, as far as a lawgiver can do it, the love of strangers, and explicitly subsumes them under the name of neighbor, whom one has to love as oneself" (3rd. ed., 1793, part 2, p. 445). It is, alas, understandable that not only denominational bias fails to acknowledge this climax of the Jewish spirit in its prehistory. Does not even the world today still struggle with these conflicting concepts, and this not only in the necessity of war, which moreover, in no way excuses this confusion and brutalization? Only pure monotheism explains and only its strict acknowledgment can solve this riddle.

19. Let us now review the main determinations of this *legislation for strangers*. The principle is: "As for the congregation there shall be *one* statute both for you and for the stranger that sojourneth with you, a statute forever throughout your generations; as ye are, so shall the stranger be before the Eternal" (Num. 15:15,16). "Ye shall have one manner of law, as well for the stranger as for the homeborn; for I am the Eternal your God" (Lev. 24:22). This reasoning is quite instructive: it deduces the law pertaining to the stranger from monotheism. And it is particularly instructive that monotheism is expressed here through an appeal to "your God." Because the Eternal is your God, you must make one law for the stranger as well as for yourselves. This is also applicable to the slave, according to the preceding ordinances, which will be considered later.

The first chapter of Deuteronomy begins with the account: "And I charged your judges at that time, saying: 'Hear the causes between your brethren, and judge righteously between a man and his brother and the stranger that is with him'" (Deut. 1:16). The admonition does not stop with the brethren, but with the stranger, since for each one "the stranger is with him" is added to it. "Thou shalt not pervert the justice due to the stranger, or to the fatherless; nor take the widow's raiment to pledge. But thou shalt remember that thou wast a bondman in Egypt" (Deut. 24:17,18). Here, as everywhere else, the stranger is put together with the orphan and the widow, and in the national memory Egypt is to remain the country in which the Israelites, though they were bondmen or slaves, yet were strangers.

20. Also in the money traffic the equality of law is extended to the stranger, at least in principle: "And if thy brother be waxen poor, and his means fail with thee; then thou shalt uphold him; as a stranger and sojourner shall he live with thee. Take thou no interest of him or increase; but fear thy God; that thy brother may live with thee" (Lev. 25:35ff.). In the following verses there is again a reference to the exodus of the Israelites from Egypt. But here the most remarkable thing happens: the *stranger-sojourner* too is called *brother;* and it is commanded that his life be preserved. Almost more important than the prohibition of taking interest from the stranger is this recognition of him as brother.

Unfortunately Kautzsch made a senseless and deplorable mistake in his translation of this verse: "And if thy brother waxes poor...thou shalt uphold him as a stranger and sojourner, so that he shall have his sustenance next to you." If then the brother becomes poor he is to be made into a stranger and sojourner! So far, indeed, equality under the law did not go as to put the poor Israelite on a par with the stranger. And to "live with thee," means more in the biblical language than to "have sustenance next to you." These errors of translation could hardly find another explanation than in a basic error about the original meaning of monotheism.

In the sentences on Mount Ebal in which the curses are expressed it says: "Cursed be he that perverteth the justice due to the stranger, fatherless, and widow" (Deut. 27:19). Legislation concerning aliens is here put under the protection of the basic principles of public and private morality.

21. A monstrous defamation of the Israelitic law is the slogan *an eye for an eye*. We consider it here only insofar as it concerns the stranger. "And if a man smite the eye of his bondman, or the eye of his bondwoman, and destroy it, he shall let him go free for his eye's sake. And if he smite out his bondman's tooth, or his bondwoman's tooth, he shall let him go free for his tooth's sake" (Exod. 21:26,27). Thus is revealed the meaning of the above legislative abbreviation: that a slave is immediately set free through injury of an eye, or even only of a tooth. How much more must this meaning prove true for the free Israelite. That the law relates also to the stranger follows from the fact that Israelite may be sold to a stranger to whom he is indebted (Lev. 25:47). The principle of equality before the law goes even so far as to draw the consequence that the Israelite may become a slave to a stranger.

22. From these concepts of the civil law, we may explain why the *cities of refuge* were also open to the stranger. "For the children of Israel, and for the stranger and for the sojourner among them, shall these six cities be for refuge, that everyone that killeth any person through error may flee thither" (Num. 35:15). Thus, the unintentional sin of killing, the *shegagah*, is to be extended to the stranger also. Hence, it is only a modest consequence that Ezekiel draws that at the division of the inherited land, the stranger should be allotted an equal share with the Israelite (Ezek. 47:22). Hence the equality of Israelite and stranger is carried through down to the basic rights of the soil.

23. To this political equality corresponds the religious equality, which is carried out under the guidance of tolerance. The stranger is not subject to circumcision and just as little to the prohibition of eating dead animals (Deut. 14:21). It is therefore characteristic that the prohibition of eating blood is also extended to the stranger. "For the life of the flesh is in the blood" (Lev. 17:11, ff.). And life is, linguistically, at the same time the soul. And the soul should attain reconciliation. Therefore the blood is only consecrated upon the altar for atonement.

Even without this relation, however, an immediate connection is recognizable between blood and bloodshed, so that the inclusion of this prohibition into the moral code of the stranger is not a liberation for him. On the contrary, it is an amazing superficiality, met with far and wide in exegetical literature, to proclaim that the exception which permits the stranger to eat dead animals constitutes a proof of discriminating legislation for the stranger.

As Solomon in his dedication of the Temple prays also for the stranger, so also is the stranger free to sacrifice (Num. 15:14–16; 1 Kings 8:41–43). Hence, it is a consequence of this that the Talmud ordered sacrifices for the seventy peoples.

24. Finally, out of these basic determinations of the law the general commandment of the love of the stranger becomes intelligible. Verses 17 and 18 in chapter 19 of Leviticus, which reveal the so-called love for the neighbor, are elucidated by verses 33 and 34 of the same chapter, which are as follows: "And if a stranger sojourn with thee in your land, ye shall not do him wrong. The stranger that sojourneth with you shall be unto you as the homeborn among you, and thou shalt love him as thyself; for ye were strangers in the land of Egypt; I am the Eternal your God." Here, too, through the concluding sentence "I am the Eternal your God," one is enjoined to recognize the distinctiveness of this commandment. "And a stranger shalt thou not wrong, neither shalt thou oppress him; for ye were strangers in the land of Egypt" (Exod. 22:20).

Finally this *love* is based on the highest motive; God loves the stranger. In the wonderful speech reported in Deuteronomy it says of God: "He doth execute justice for the fatherless and widow, and loveth the stranger, in giving him food and raiment. Love ye therefore the stranger, for ye were strangers in the land of Egypt" (Deut. 10:18,19). And about this God it is said: "He is thy glory and He is thy God" (Deut. 10:21). Here, too, national history is understood as a support for the love of the stranger, which, psychologically as well as objectively, is the foundation for the love of the fellowman.

25. The proper historical understanding of monotheism must be based on the correct understanding of the Israelitic *theocracy*. Religion develops in connection with the development of the state. This connection can result in unavoidable disadvantages; in the observation of the primitive development of these ancient relationships, however, it is better to begin with the resulting advantages, which in turn diminish the disadvantages. The prophets fight the priests. But if the priests are servants of the state and therefore also rulers of the state, so also are the prophets politicians, and they are unable to develop religion in any other way than by participating in the conflicts within the state and society. If, therefore, their religion must affirm and realize its share of reason in morality, it must be inextricably linked with politics and its view of the social question. Therefore the stranger as such cannot

be the exclusive origin of the idea of the fellowman, but the legal and political conditions of the native, the native born, brought about the intervention of the prophets in behalf of the stranger.

The social differentiation between poor and rich poses the most difficult question for the concept of man, for the unity and equality of men. The "next man"[12] becomes unavoidably the "opposing man"[13], for the social differentiation does not appear to be organized according to rank and order of coexistence, but according to subordination and subjugation. It is in opposition to this that the problem of the fellowman has to arise. Even more than the question of the stranger, the question of rich and poor is asked in one's native land and among one's own people; this human question is asked with regard to every man, with regard to every fellowman.

God, the Unique One, as the unique creator of all men – how can he be responsible for this deep inequality of men? This question certainly originated very early, but the difficulty of the economic problem always pushed it aside. Already in Deuteronomy two sentences stand side by side: one sets up the negative demand, while the other represents the inherited experience against utopianism. The one says: "There shall be no needy among you" (15:4). The other, however: "For the poor shall never cease out of the land," (15:11). The demand in its rigor is not softened by the presumed experience. For if the latter were right, still the admonition that there should be no needy would be correctly stated. This correction of society and its history is the demand of the unique God.

26. How can God allow this gaping difference between men? This question is answered by religious consciousness, and the gradations in the shades of the answers it provides correspond to the steps of its own development.

The difference between poor and rich is not the only one among men. Neither are the distinctions represented by the mental and aesthetic appearances of man the most conspicuous, nor are these the ones that arouse the most shocking doubts about God's justice. For man is as gladly appreciative as he is skeptical. When he sees disadvantages in himself, he rejoices in the advantages of others, whom he is always willing to honor as masters and demigods. A mean between the intellectual and the aesthetic is bodily strength and heroic courage, which men need more immediately than intellectual advantages, and whose aid gives to men's existence a more positive value than the aesthetic gleam emanating from them. The primitive man, being a nomad and hunter, lives in the magic of war; therefore, heroism is his first ideal of man. And hence he surmounts the offense the awakening religious consciousness ought to take at the unequal distribution of the vital powers in man.

This awakening, however, also stirs up the recognition of the other difference in man. Cain kills his brother. The Bible does not fail to supply a reason for Cain: God turned his favor to Abel's sacrifice and not to his. Was it unjustified envy, or did the feeling originate in a justified accusation against God? It is as if the Bible wanted to teach in this, properly speaking, the first sin, that no apparently justified pretext whatever should be an inducement to envy. The pretext aims at God; the envy, however, aims at man, rather upon two men: upon the other as much as upon oneself. And hence in this simple example the paradigm of every moral conflict originates. Questions are raised against providence and God's government from all sides, so that the relation of man to God remains everywhere obscure. But this obscurity can never govern the relation of man to man. Murder does not accord in any way with the preferential treatment that God allows. Indeed, the whole history of mankind is such that God seems to favor some over others. However, men should not govern their relation to other men according to this appearance.

In spite of this, man acts this way even if he does not take God's injustice as a pretext. Disordered relations and wrongdoing do arise among men. The moral difference between good and bad arises. This difference arises out of the primeval moral problems that primitive social relations bring forth, even before religious motives play their part. The violation of legal norms, which are already set up in primitive forms of society, makes moral distinctions necessary: the legal becomes the moral. For already in the archaic forms of society the ideal human relations, such as those of the generations and the family, intertwine with the material-legal relations of tribe and property. Thus the difference of good and bad arises as a purely human distinction.

27. Soon, however, gods enter the horizon of primitive man, and the spheres of man are touched by them. In monotheism it is significant that the first human sin is fratricide; the murdered man is the brother, and the murderer is the brother. The ties of blood are already known, but not acknowledged. All men are brothers, yet murder is transmitted among them. The bond of blood is an unreliable tie among men. Moreover, vengeance, which man is able to exercise, is also afflicted with defectiveness and injustice. Therefore the Bible intercedes for the murderer: "Whosoever slayeth Cain, punishment shall be taken on him sevenfold" (Gen. 4:15). Human justice always remains imperfect. In God alone can justice be found.

28. Thus arises the difference between good and bad in the light of the unique God. In polytheism, therefore, the religious and hence absolute difference between good and bad cannot arise. The gods favor men in accordance with their own discretion, even in accordance with their caprice. Because of this Homer is the Bible of freethinkers. The gods cannot be united in their government, for then they could not be different individuals. Monotheism is based on a uniform comprehension of the distinction of good and bad, and thus on a uniform attitude of God to man, as well as of man to God. The correlation between God and man is defined as that between religion and morality.

Polytheism is deprived of any norm for the correction of religion by morality. If Hippolytus remains chaste toward Phaedra, then he transgresses against the worship of Aphrodite. Every divinity has his own code of morality. Monotheism creates with the one divinity also the one morality as well. The unique God, therefore, also unifies the concept of man, and every breach of this unity of man is a violation of morality. The distinction between good and bad is more and more removed from the obscurity of the divine, and is independently expressed in human relations.

Gradually, however, specifically religious conceptions also unfold, and in monotheism especially they must be interwoven with purely moral ones. There the question may already arise, how can God vindicate the distinction of good and bad in man, how could it come about in his creation? The serpent seduced Eve, and Eve, Adam; God, however, does not sanction this excuse, and he punishes the transgression of his prohibition.

This first *sin* of the human couple was committed only against God, but Cain's sin was the first sin against man. And for this sin Cain is taken under God's protection. This difference in *retribution* already shows the relation that God assumes with regard to man's transgressions: the transgressors against man are punished and at the same time protected, whereas the transgression against God is the origin of culture insofar as its consequence is the establishment of labor. Thus from the very outset God's sovereignty is established with regard to all human sins.

29. Does this sovereignty prevail with regard to *social* differences? Good and bad are under God's grace, as this sovereignty is called later. The primitive religious conscience does not ask about the reason for and the justice of the differences in the bodies and minds of man; for this purpose it is still too much engrossed in mythical beginnings. But the social differences become offensive not only in themselves, but especially since they are felt as a hindrance to the mental, and even perhaps to the moral, development of man. Therefore it must become a religious question how the difference between poor and rich is compatible with the unity of God.

30. The question soon becomes more intense when the simple religious consciousness takes cognizance of social processes. A comparison between social and moral differences emerges, and the question is raised whether there is any correspondence between these differences. On the contrary, the insight is unavoidable that there is no such harmony between them, that instead a strict opposition seems to be the rule. Thus the statement: "The righteous, he fares badly; the bad one, he fares well!"

Language does not yet know how to overcome this dissonance, it does not yet distinguish between good and well-being, between bad and ill. But the question in which "the bad one" is called the villain (עשׁו) and "the good one" is called the righteous (קדיצ) shows that the feeling for the difference is already manifest. The question could not have arisen, except on the basis of this difference.

And how does the religious consciousness find an answer to this primeval question? Should perhaps the answer suffice that in God's knowledge the thing is correct, and that only in our knowledge does it appear incorrect? This answer might perhaps suffice in the case of a villain who is well off, because the more profound consciousness may be able to ignore this well-being, and because his villainy itself is, properly speaking, a riddle in every sense, so that the knowledge of it and the judgment about it can be only subjective and illusory. On the other hand, in the case of the righteous one who fares badly, the question cannot be left in suspense. Should one perhaps lose confidence in his righteousness and with this be in danger of losing confidence in God's justice in general? This danger, however, would be unavoidable; for how could the misfortune of the righteous be reconciled with God's justice?

31. Should one perhaps find a way out of this by declaring that misfortune is irrelevant? Should the religious consciousness perhaps adopt the wisdom of *Stoicism*? The religious consciousness was protected against this ambiguity by its natural connection with the political and purely moral. Even if the individual were able and were permitted to train himself successfully and with good reason to disregard his own well-being and woe, he is not permitted to disregard the woe of the other fellow. He might perhaps even disregard the well-being of the evil one, but he is not permitted to disregard the woe of the good one.

Precisely in this lies the sound value of the connection between religious consciousness and morals, and of the grounding of the moral on the social and political. Thereby, the feeling of *indifference* with regard to well-being and woe cannot arise and assert itself. For well-being and woe do not have the vague meaning of a subjective well- or ill-feeling, although this subjectivity is more or less attached to all variable and passing states of the body. But when well-being and ill are actualized objectively in the social differences of poor and rich, then the indifference toward them becomes insincerity, frivolity, cruelty. No man may doubt that these differences are not indifferent to men. From the social point of view, Stoicism is either hypocrisy or unforgivable ignorance.

32. Monotheism completes its development in the prophetic teaching; from the social-moral point of view, one may even say it develops toward the prophets. For the *peculiar* characteristic of the prophetic teaching consists in the connection of the alleged independence of evil with the alleged independence of morals. The prophet does not know this isolation. He knows only the correlation of God and man, of man and God. He is therefore as much interested in *politics* as in the divine rule of the world. And politics for him certainly includes foreign, international politics, but is, in the first place, social politics.

The relations between man and man form the lower or rather the inner correlation within the correlation of God and man. Therefore the questions of the prophet cannot be isolated either from the distinction of good and bad, or from the meaning of good and bad in the absolute relationship of man to God; rather, his question about the distinction of good and bad must objectify itself by turning to the social differences of poor and rich. The moral excellence of the prophets consists in their refusal to measure and weigh the difference between well-being and ill according to subjective differences, to which disease and death itself belong. Instead, they measure them according to the objective social contradictions that upset the balance of society.

The prophet rises above the level of primitive belief, which blindly assumes a correspondence between goodness and well-being and between evil and woe. This correspondence would do well if well-being and woe were only subjectively distinguished. The social differences, however, must be recognized as objective; otherwise, the concept of the essential moral and cultural tasks of man is in danger of being destroyed. The concept of man grows in the reciprocal correlation between men, and accordingly the content of the correlation of God and man also grows.

The social complexity of men grows into this correlation and cannot be isolated from it. This is the meaning of the prophetic teaching. The prophet does not close his eyes to moral corruption, to the moral doom that lies in social differences. The prophet's truthfulness does not allow the slightest trace of a solution in which well-being is considered as the *reward* and ill-fatedness as the punishment for the moral, for the religious behavior of man. Man's relation to God may remain a mystery; his conduct to other men is not permitted to be considered such. With regard to man, one has to judge and to decide. For the decision about good and bad is connected with this decision. The distinction between good and bad comes to nothing if it coincides with the distinction of well-being and ill.

If this were the case, then the concept of man with regard to the creation of the concept of man as fellowman would be defeated. The concept of the fellowman cannot come to my consciousness if his well-being and woe are indifferent to me. Even without any consideration of a more or less intimate knowledge of the man's physical well-being and woe, this indifference simply blocks the formation of the notion of man as fellowman. This is even more so if the indifference stands firm with regard to moral behavior also. This connection of moral with physical behavior contains implicitly the distinction between the religious and the moral. The behavior of man to God, which may be a mystery, can, however, in some way be controlled by the behavior of man to man. The distinction of good and bad originates in this behavior, not in the behavior of man toward God. The prophetic teaching brings forth the sobriety and clearness, and its originality consists in the elucidation of these concepts.

It is therefore not any concern for *eudaemonism* that caused the prophets to enter into the question of the correspondence that exists between the moral and the physical – in this respect they truly do not fall short of Stoicism – but rather the fact that the fundamental question about God and man, about religion and morality, is at stake in this relationship. So far as I am concerned, my own well-being or woe might remain indifferent to me, but this cannot be the case with regard to the next man. But this need not be especially the case with regard to the complication that arises out of the question whether well-being and woe coincide with good and bad. And with regard to this complication there need be no demand for indifference, perhaps there ought to be none, even with regard to myself.

33. This fundamental point should be considered once more. With regard to well-being and woe the point is that they are not indifferent physical, even bodily goods. Life and health themselves might become indifferent in the face of fate and death. For *death* is a metaphysical evil, and mystics may brood about its cause or possible abolition. This is no theme for moralists, and therefore also not for true religiosity. It is different with *sickness*, for it is a chapter of the social question. And it is the social well-being or woe that comes into relation with moral distinctions. As little as moral distinctions could be indifferent, so little is it permissible that social well-being or ill should simply be indifferent.

The great achievement of the prophetic teaching, and that which also shows its inner connection with true morality, consists in this; prophetic thought does not indulge in speculations about the meaning of life in the presence of the riddle of death; it puts aside the question of death and therefore also of *afterlife*, despite the fact that their moral significance is not hidden from it. Nonetheless prophetic thought puts aside these questions of life and afterlife in the face of the life whose meaning is in question because of the evil which is represented by *poverty*. *Poverty becomes the main representation of human misfortune.* Thereby physical ill in general becomes moral ill; but in that sense that the question of morality is directed to God, and it has to be divorced entirely from the question of man's guilt, if it is not to become ambiguous.

34. Another form of woe also, which is no less ambiguous, namely, *suffering*, is settled and surmounted by social objectivization and by the isolation and precision of the problem. In suffering, physical ill changes into the psychic ill, and with this transition ambiguities are unavoidable. The psychic is as much physical as spiritual, as much material as moral. Which meaning predominates in suffering as the woe of man? And to what extent is this meaning in harmony or disharmony with moral behavior? The metaphysics of suffering, which considers suffering as the fate of mankind, or even more ambiguously, as the fate of all living creatures, does not belong to an earnest religion; its earnestness has nothing to do with the play of poetry and art. Suffering only reaches ethical precision as social suffering. Whoever explains *poverty* as the suffering of mankind, he creates ethics, or, if not philosophical ethics, yet still religion with its share of reason. Only the religion of reason is moral religion, and only moral religion is truthful and true religion.

35. The prophets, as well as the psalms, have the social insight that poverty represents the great suffering of mankind, and they therefore have the religious insight that poverty is the great question mark against divine *providence;* they realize that the true riddle of human life is not death, but poverty, and that it is the true riddle because its solution requires truthfulness and is conceivable only by truthfulness, while death is a riddle only the mystic can solve. The mystic, however, would dispense with truthfulness, even if it contained truth.

For truthfulness can only be brought about in one of two ways: either in the way of scientific method or in the way of religion's analogy to reason. Religion, however, which in accordance with its share in reason, has to strive to be analogous to ethics, must and can undoubtedly prevail in the social conception of man, in the social conception of the relation of man to man. The correlation of God and man is built only upon the basis of this social relationship.

36. Ill, as represented objectively in poverty, led us to consider suffering. And we considered the ambiguity in the psychic meaning of suffering. The depression that the consciousness undergoes in suffering may also be the consequence of physical effects. Exaltation also, which marks the feeling of happiness, is connected with the body. And as with happiness, so every kind of feeling of unhappiness remains undetermined and ambiguous not only morally but even psycho-spiritually. But we are not interested in the development of this idea for the sake of uncovering the feeling of well-being in the bad man. We are concerned not so much with the denial of this elated feeling but rather with the pressing question, which we have to put to God, of how his idea is compatible with this psychic success, which is not merely physical, that evil has in man.

Likewise the unhappy feeling must also not be leveled down to subjectivity and made psychically illusory. Suffering is an actual feeling, which is not only mirrored in a social reality, namely, poverty, but also has to be conceived and understood as a prevailing reality of consciousness; it fills the entire human consciousness and helps to determine all its other proceedings and activities. Therefore its objectivization should not be permitted to be erased; the suffering of poverty must always remain the problem: the religious problem, but not the metaphysical one.

37. If we have previously said that in the problem of poverty the woe of man has to be recognized by the true religion, we can now say with the same firmness that in poverty the

woe becomes the *suffering of the human race*, as far as we can trace it in human history up to now. Woe and ill are not only physical concepts; suffering has elevated them to the psychic and thereby to the whole complexity of the soul, which comprises the spiritual and the moral.

A new factor of consciousness has thus been revealed; the suffering of the human soul, of the human spirit. This suffering, as everything psychic, is not entirely separated from the physical; suffering is also *pain*. But the suffering of the spirit is not the pain of the animal; for the animal is not social. It is questionable whether the physical pain of another animal, if it is not its own young, arouses its sympathy in it; in no case can this reaction be caused by a spiritual suffering not present in the herd. *Only social suffering is spiritual suffering.* All the complexity of consciousness, including knowledge, is affected by it and brought to take part in it. This is the profound meaning of social suffering: that the entire consciousness of culture is implicated in it.

Stoic apathy is therefore entirely inadmissible; it excludes ethics and at the same time includes the renunciation of culture. I cannot be indifferent to poverty, because it is the sign of the distress of culture, and because it calls into question true morality. Poverty cannot be compared to physical suffering, because the latter is individual and subjective, whereas social suffering is not only the suffering of the majority but also the qualitative evidence of the low level of the culture.

38. This situation brings about a new tragic motive of its own. However, in tragedy only the hero, only the individual suffers; in social suffering the entire culture assumes a tragic role. And culture here is not an abstraction, but the most vivid actuality, the majority of the human race in every people and in every epoch. Thus the poor man typifies man in general. Thus the next man becomes fellowman. For even if I had no heart in my body, my education alone would have brought me to the insight that the great majority of men cannot be isolated from me, and that I myself am nothing if I do not make myself a part of them. In these unavoidable connections between myself and the majority, a relationship arises that means more than merely coordination or even subordination, but which produces a community. And this community produces the fellowman.

39. The community is *reciprocal action*. In reciprocal action community comes to be and is achieved. How will the reciprocal effect between the suffering that in my consciousness becomes an object of my insight and knowledge, and the other parts and activities of my consciousness manifest itself? Until now the community, the fellowman, remained merely the problem posed by suffering as a social problem, a problem not yet solved, however. The solution depends on the way in which the reaction to suffering is voiced.

40. According to the mythological point of view which everywhere is the original form of religion, the solution is the same as that indicated by tragedy, which itself arises from the myth: the *guilt* of man, of the hero himself, is the ground of his suffering. This ground is probably also the cause, at least the only intelligible subjective ground. Upon this mythical ground tragedy builds its own aesthetic microcosm of man and its world of the spectator. Religion, however, goes its own way, and it cannot rest satisfied with myth. The goal of its way is, however, always God. Through the correlation of man and God it seeks man and finds God; it seeks God and finds man. However, how is this correlation to teach one to find a way out of this great conflict of suffering, a way that brings a solution?

41. The book of guilt must be destroyed; social insight destroys it. For, disregarding the antinomy between individual and society in the question of guilt, the latter cannot be considered in this connection because thereby the discovery of the fellowman would be missed. I am to change the next man into the fellowman. For this purpose the idea that the suffering of the majority of men is an attribute of the majority because of its guilt is of no help. Already in the tragedy the hero cannot be a scamp, for then I would not be able to be

morally interested in him. Much less can the idea of guilt be useful for the discovery of the fellowman out of the suffering of the majority.

If suffering is to be taken as the result of the history of the world, how can I reconcile God's justice with it? If I can neither understand the justice and meaning of providence in the world, on the one hand, nor, on the other, consider social suffering as the consequence of guilt, does not the correlation between God and man become disordered?

42. The prophets here take the straight road upon which monotheism methodologically parts from polytheism. The latter everywhere proceeds from the gods. Mythical consciousness takes this as its starting point and stops at that. From the gods the mythical fantasy turns to the cosmos and only gradually to men, whom, however, it at first knows only as heroes, and this means as demigods. Religion, on the contrary, is concerned more with man than with God. God's justice will somehow be accomplished, but law and order among men are not to remain the great question. This question affects the heart. From the heart must come the reaction, the counteraction which we seek so that the community may be formed, so that the fellowman may arise. The counteraction must become a counter feeling to suffering: it must not remain simply knowledge but must become a powerful feeling.

Therefore suffering, to the exclusion of any other feeling, must fill out the consciousness, if it is to be understood correctly and evoke a correct reaction. Therefore any trace of an interest in a subjective or in an individual ground for suffering has to be eliminated. As much as such an interest may be justified for the individual from another point of view, at this point it would disturb and hinder the insight to be gained. Suffering is a social suffering; therefore, an understanding of it cannot be furthered by any kind of insight that concerns only the individual.

Guilt is and remains the attribute of the individual. And the plurality is also only a plurality of individuals. The plurality itself cannot have any guilt. And about the individual in general I do not want to know at this point. The suffering is not an individual suffering but the social state of distress of the human race. Poverty is an economic concept, not a moral one. Guilt, from the point of view of religion, is written on an entirely different page. If religion intends to discover the fellowman through social suffering, and if this discovery is tied up with the reaction to the knowledge and feeling of suffering, then religion has to disregard its other interests and obligations and ascertain this reaction exclusively in the psychic nature of man's consciousness. Hence *pity* is disclosed as a psychic factor.

43. Since the time of the Stoics pity has been suspect, although in ancient tragedy it was valid as the natural tragic lever; even though it was still connected with fear, it was elevated above this selfish motivation, elevated to a more universal motive and acknowledged as a tragic factor. The Greek word means "to be moved to pity," which shows itself in lamentation (*eleos*). This natural power of antiquity also withered away in the age of the Stoics, and humanitarian abstraction replaced the immediate naturalness of human feeling. Pathos is replaced by ethos. *Apathy* becomes the goal of morality.

The Stoics, it is true, in no way lack the precision of morals and humanity which respects the slave, extends the law to foreigners and allies; in a word, they are not lacking in the objectification of morality in law and state. But all this objectification bears the stamp of the Roman character; it lacks the free subjectivity of Hellas, which even Hellenism cannot transmit. Tragedy becomes comedy, insofar as it achieves significance at all. The image of divinity becomes a portrait, as the ideal of art. The natural feeling for suffering has slackened long ago and almost died away. In the Saturnalia the Roman finds consolation for his bad conscience about his slave economy.

Men, to be sure, remain men, but when pity moves the Stoic, it becomes like a faded tale of moral abstraction; there are many such tales, more or less valid only for utopia. In this atmosphere of dying antiquity the thought of Epicurus is more natural than stoicism, which is only a paradox, as is also their key word about the ideal of apathy, the virtue of the *wise*.

44. To what extent Stoic morality is only an abstraction is most clearly seen in the repudiation of pity. This repudiation is motivated by the point of view of the individual, who is represented by the wise. And a slave also may be wise. Therefore the slave does not represent social misery. Man consists of his spirit. Everything else about him is accidental. Therefore only the spirit is connected with him. Man, that is to say the wise man, therefore does not suffer, he has no feeling: how would I with my feeling encounter his? He does not suffer: how could therefore my pity affect him, or even discover him for me?

It is very consistent that in Stoicism pity becomes an *affect*, and indeed in the indeterminate way which here surrounds the idea and concept of affect. Pity is nothing other than an *elemental common feeling*, like hunger and ease, like pleasure and aversion and pain, like pride and envy, in short, like *passion* in general. The passions, however, are pinpricks of the lower body, as are the elemental common feelings also; they are the bodily, the nervous lower strata of the psychic. They do not belong to the clear transparent upper regions of the psychic, of the consciousness. Therefore they cannot be the levers, much less the regulators of moral consciousness.

Therefore, also, pity cannot be marked out and distinguished as a social affect. Hence it is considered as an ambiguous factor of consciousness, determinable by no criterion, guided by no spiritual norm. I have pity in the same way as I yawn, too, when somebody else yawns. It is an echo of the reflex movement – then, to be sure, animals too should unmistakably show it. Nevertheless human reflex action might perhaps have a hidden drawer in its reflex mechanism. This ignorance notwithstanding, the fact remains that pity is seemingly unmasked as a mere bodily function. Where the social idea does not become a fundamental problem, there pity is not honored.

45. Spinoza has found much approval with his theory of affects. In it, however, he follows the path of Stoicism. Pity, according to him, stems from the same source as envy. This one sentence passes judgment on the validity of his view, and at the same time illuminates the ground of it. Envy, as I think, originates only out of a presumed insight into a surplus by which another exceeds me. If transferred to society, the ground of envy would therefore be only the opinion of a plus on the one side, not of a minus on the opposite side. Envy could therefore originate only with the poor man, who discovers the surplus, the plus of the rich. Envy would thus be the opposite of pity.

Spinoza, however, in no way wants to interpret pity as such an opposite motive. He wants to teach the wisdom that one should not trust pity, because its source is as subjective as the source of envy. Just this, however, shows the abyss in his thinking; he does not see the chasm that exists between pity and envy. This comparison is only possible when one does not think about social suffering. And as the Stoic which he ultimately is, Spinoza indeed fails to think about the social suffering of the human race.

According to him, the "many" are, in any case, wholly incapable of real morality, which rests on true knowledge. How could the many, who always reveal only the preliminary stage of human dignity, be worthy of true pity? As there is no social suffering, so there can and need not be social pity. This is the reason for Spinoza's disdain and rejection of pity.

46. And what is the reason behind pity according to Schopenhauer? With him, too, the reason in the first place lies in his metaphysics, in the predominance of knowledge which constitutes his metaphysics, though the latter sets the so-called *will* above the intellect. For this will is anything else but will. Therefore it is understandable that pity also is deprived of its immediate power of feeling and unmasked as a kind of metaphysical clairvoyance. Pity should only reveal to me that the other is rather myself. Therefore if I have pity for him, I have it rather for myself. Pity raises the veil of Maya and unveils the mystery of the

individual, the *principium individuationis:* I am always only myself, and as many men as I seem to see, yet they are all always only myself.

Knowledge, of course, would never have brought me to this truth if it had not dawned on me in the thing-in-itself of the will, if pity, the organ of the will, had not put this truth into focus. Thus pity is more than knowledge, which represents merely the phenomena. Pity is the messenger of the will, therefore of the thing-in-itself. And this thing-in-itself means the identity of all that appears as man.

47. Pity, as understood by Schopenhauer, becomes a mediating concept for the metaphysical knowledge of man. But exactly at this point the difference between metaphysics and ethics becomes clear, and no less also the difference between metaphysics and religion. This characterization of pity is also unable to help me to discover the fellow-man. For the latter becomes in this view an illusion. For the majority of people knows man not as fellowman but only as the next man, and even he is only an appearance which, according to this metaphysics, is no different from an illusion.

The thing-in-itself, however, as unity, is not even the unity of men, but that of the universe. The will is certainly not differently present in man and in the stone, which falls according to the force of gravity. And Schopenhauer is entirely in agreement with Spinoza, according to whom the stone too would ascribe freedom of the will to itself, if it were to have consciousness. According to Schopenhauer also, the will can mean the world in itself only by being removed from any knowledge and therefore also from the knowledge of morality. Wherever morality does not present a special problem which is to be distinguished from the logical roots of the principle of sufficient reason, there the fellowman cannot become a problem, even within the thing-in-itself of the world. Neither can pity there become a factor of the moral will.

48. And this exactly is what is of importance: pity must be stripped of the passivity of a reaction and must be acknowledged as a whole and full activity in itself. The moral, the pure will, is determined by the factor of the affect. The affect therefore must be *pure*, it must be freed from the bodily duality and ambiguity. Pure activity is never a reaction, if the latter merely represents a terminating process. But reaction, as a reciprocal effect, aims toward a goal. This goal is the community, in which the fellowman originates. This kind of counter effect, which is a reciprocal effect, is achieved by pity. And pity turns out to be a factor of the pure will, as a lever of moral consciousness. It is the fundamental power of the moral universe, which unlocks the fellowman. Pity constitutes the key to the fellowman.

49. Morality and religion have here a common border. This border is not a limit. The share of reason in religion draws this border, which cannot be a limit for it. Ethics does not despise the affect, which, though not a factor, is yet *a motor* of the pure will. We have determined the distinction in this way in our *Ethics of Pure Will*. And if I am to make the distinction between affect and the appearance of an indifferent agility more exactly recognizable, the affect of pity, as an original power of the pure will, will best serve this purpose.

Every metaphysical and ethical misunderstanding of pity originates in the erroneous view that pity is only reflexive and is only incited in and by myself. We, on the contrary, recognize the connection of pity with the problem of the fellowman. Consequently, pity is so little reflexive from the other man back to the self that, rather, the other man, who supposedly merely drives me back to myself, and who until now counts only as the next man and does not yet exist as the fellowman, is to be created through pity as the fellowman. How could, therefore, pity mean the reflection from him back to myself?

50. It is even a question, as yet not asked, whether I myself already do exist before the fellowman is discovered. Consequently the end point of the reflex motion is not yet given, let alone the starting point. Also from the point of view of the I, it therefore turns out to be

a misinterpretation that pity is a mere passive reflex action upon myself. Even from the point of view of this alleged end point of the I, we can now discern that the whole conception is wrong and that the error consists in this; the fellowman is thought of merely as the next man and not as a new problem, as a new concept of man. However pity, as a concept for the discovery of the fellowman, is no longer suspect and loses all the appearance of an ambiguous passivity; it is recognized as an ethical factor, although only as a motor of the pure will.

51. What, however, can religion initiate through pity, if it has to disregard the guilt of the one who is to be discovered as fellowman? This question is answered satisfactorily only by the social point of view. In the face of poverty it no longer makes sense to ask about guilt. No age in which poverty becomes a problem is so primitive as to connect guilt with this turbulent problem. By the early epoch of culture it is possible to trace the separation of morality from religion in the treatment of this problem.

Morality in law, in politics, and also in the beginning of ethics traces only the basic relation of these two concepts, the poor and the fellowman, not, however, their later interpenetration. Even with Socrates it is to be noted that he has no sense for the problem of poverty. He lets Solon worry about that. But Solon also rests satisfied with a temporary measure, such as the remission of debts, the *seisachtheia*. The state would have to intervene in the law, change its foundations, if it wished to assist organizationally in this case.

Socrates' teaching is preserved through his assertion of the preeminence of the intellect. This assertion is his contribution to ethics. Virtue is knowledge. But the poor man too can have knowledge. Can he actually? Socrates does not ask this question, for his world-historical spirit is directed to the creation of pure ethics. He does not let himself be diverted from his theory by premature questions about matters of practice and application. This disadvantage is connected with the advantage which the new theory establishes for the future.

52. The prophets, on the contrary, are not theoretical moralists. Therefore for them there cannot be even a temporary difference between theory and practice. Their problem is religion, monotheism, the correlation of man and God. And this correlation is intertwined with the correlation between man and man. The first, between God and man, may seem to be merely theoretical; the other, however, between man and man is immediately practical. And the fellowman belongs to this second correlation. Therefore the prophet cannot allow any doubt to divert him from the problem: how the fellowman is to originate out of pity for the poor man.

Poverty is the universal suffering of the human race. Pity must meet poverty if man is finally to arise as an I. Before this social fact of human suffering the primeval human feeling of pity has to flame up; otherwise one would have to despair about human feeling in general Should the prophet have curbed human feeling because the religious idea of guilt restrained him? The prophet would not beget religion if he remained suspended in this dilemma.

53. The distinction between religion and mythology, between monotheism and polytheism, again clearly asserts itself here. Polytheism has its center of gravity in the myth. The spell of myth fills the spirit of primitive man much more strongly than his heart can be stirred by suffering and therefore be moved to pity. Tragedy, too, which grows out of myth, is and basically remains a product of polytheism.

Perhaps the absence of tragedy in Israel's mind can be explained through the onesidedness of its monotheism. Suffering is to be resolved in reality and not merely in the illusory feeling of the spectator. The prophet becomes the practical moralist, the politician and jurist, because he intends to end the suffering of the poor. And it is not enough for him to assume these various callings; he has to become a psychologist as well; he must make pity the primeval feeling of man; he must, as it were, discover in pity man as fellowman and *man* in general.

Notes

1 *Religion of Reason out of the Sources of Judaism*, trans. Simon Kaplan, Atlanta: Scholars Press, 1995, Ch. 8, pp. 113–143.
2 *Mehrheit*
3 *Allheit*
4 *Nebenmensch*
5 *Mitmensch*
6 *Gast-freund*
7 *jezer*
8 *rea*
9 *nokri*
10 *nokri*
11 *Gerichtsverfassung*
12 *Nebenmensch*
13 *Gegenmensch*

Introduction

Paul Natorp (1854–1924)

PAUL NATORP WAS BORN IN 1854 IN DÜSSELDORF. The son of a Protestant minister, he studied mathematics and music in Berlin and Bonn. Throughout his lifetime, Natorp continued to compose romantic *Lieder* and ambitious musical scores and toyed with the idea of becoming a professional musician. In 1875, he sent some of his compositions to Johannes Brahms, whom he admired. Brahms' rather damning response caused Natorp's career plans to shift radically and led him to dedicate his life to philosophy. He went on to study philosophy and classics in Strassburg, where he was, however, dissatisfied with the positivistic philosophy of Ernst Laas, under whom he nonetheless wrote his dissertation. At the time, he had already studied Cohen's writings enthusiastically and had been impressed by his "criticism." Upon making contact with Cohen, he moved to Marburg in 1880, first occupying the position of a librarian in the University Library. In 1881, he submitted his Habilitation thesis, which revealed Cohen's influence already in the title: "Descartes' Epistemology. An Investigation in the History of Criticism." He occupied various positions within the university, but it was not until 1893 that he received a professorship in Marburg, with concentration in philosophy and pedagogy. Cohen and Natorp collaborated closely beginning in the 1880s, and by the 1890s there was talk of the "Marburg School," which was a term that neither had coined, but that they proudly utilized and promoted. Around 1900, the Marburg School of Neo-Kantianism, centered around their "twin stars" Cohen and Natorp, was the most recognized philosophical school in the German-speaking countries and also exerted influence abroad. The students of this school included, among others, Boris Pasternak, Karl Barth, Ernst Cassirer and, later, Hans-Georg Gadamer, who wrote his dissertation under Natorp.

Along with Cohen, Natorp's philosophical quest was to turn philosophy into a science, in close conjunction with the natural sciences of their day. In this respect, Natorp was more closely aligned than Cohen with modern developments in the sciences, including Einstein's revolution in physics. But Natorp's *oeuvre* was vast (and his output astonishing). He published widely in the history of philosophy, especially ancient philosophy (most notably Plato), but also in the philosophy of science and, due to his dual appointment of his professorship, in pedagogy, especially on the reform pedagogue Pestalozzi. An offshoot of his pedagogical interests were his writings in social pedagogy (*Sozialpädagogik* of 1899, which was reprinted six times during Natorp's life), which resulted in his being a sought-out expert on new pedagogical ideas for the Ministry of Education. He wrote, for instance, several op-ed articles in support of the concept of the *Gesamtschule* to replace the traditional three-tier system in secondary education. Another rather lamentable aspect of his work, which may not be passed over in silence, are his "War Books" celebrating the "German Vocation for the World" (*Deutscher Weltberuf*) around the time of the Great War. These books no doubt were partly responsible for the school's decline of popularity after 1918.

Natorp's main philosophical writings are his influential interpretation of Plato (*Platos Ideenlehre*, 1902), his sketch of a psychology "from the critical standpoint" in 1912, and his philosophy of science. In general, Natorp's writings were considered more lucid and accessible than Cohen's, such that the former's treatment of Cohen's themes were often the preferred reading for understanding the main goals of the Marburg School (cf. his text, below, on "Kant and the Marburg School"). Natorp is also the only author of what can be called a Neo-Kantian "manifesto," the slender volume *Philosophie. Ihr Problem und Ihre Probleme* [*Philosophy. Its Problem and its Problems*] (1911). After Cohen's departure from Marburg in 1912, Natorp was the only real extant and active member of the school. In his late years, his work underwent a "mystical" turn that removed him significantly from the standard stance of the Marburg School. His last works, the *Vorlesungen zur praktischen Philosophie* of 1925 and the posthumously published *Philosophische Systematik* (finished in 1923, but not published until 1954!) moved, allegedly, out of the Neo-Kantian (Marburg) rank into a celebration of "the pure 'there is' of Being." It was with the young Martin Heidegger, who came to Marburg in 1923 under Natorp's influence, that Natorp discussed his most recent ideas. There can be no doubt that there is a certain, yet to be determined, influence of Natorp on Heidegger's *Seinsfrage*. There is some speculation that Heidegger advised against publishing Natorp's last work at the time of his death in 1924. The phenomenologist Heidegger became the successor to Natorp's chair in philosophy in 1924, effectively sealing the fate of the "Marburg School of Neo-Kantianism."

Further Reading

Jegelka, Norbert. *Paul Natorp. Philosophie – Pädagogik – Politik*. Würzburg: Königshausen & Neumann, 1992.

Kim, Alan, "Paul Natorp," *The Stanford Encyclopedia of Philosophy* (Fall 2008 Edition), Edward N. Zalta (ed.), available online at http://plato.stanford.edu/archives/fall2008/entries/natorp/ (accessed 16 March 2015).

Natorp, Paul, "Selbstdarstellung," in: R. Schmidt, ed., *Die Philosophie der Gegenwart in Selbstdarstellungen*, vol. I. Leipzig: Meiner, 1921, pp. 150–176.

"On the Objective and Subjective Grounding of Knowledge" (1887)

In this short article, published alongside his short book *Einleitung in die Psychologie nach kritischer Methode* [*Introduction to Psychology According to the Critical Method*] (1888), Natorp lays out the ground of the possibility of a psychological "grounding" (*Begründung*) of knowledge or cognition (*Erkenntnis*). The possibility of a psychology "according to the critical method" – according to the epistemology of the Marburg School, in other words – was an interest of Natorp's beginning at this early stage and reaching into his late phase. Indeed, a "second edition" of the *Einleitung*, which was more than three times the size of the earlier book, was published in 1912 under the new title *Allgemeine Psychologie nach kritischer Methode* [*General Introduction to Psychology According to the Critical Method*]. The interest in such a "psychology" or a subjective grounding of knowledge was, thus, a continuous interest on the part of Natorp in the shadow of Cohen. What was the nature of this interest?

Cohen's version of transcendental philosophy as criticism was in clarifying the conditions of cognition, that is, of existing cognition in the sciences. For this reason, he preferred the term "*Erkenntniskritik*" (critique of cognition) over the traditional term "*Erkenntnistheorie*," standardly translated as epistemology. His interest was in the logic governing the achievement of cognition, hence – in Natorp's rendering – an *objective* grounding of cognition; a cognition, that is, directed at the *object* of cognition. Any investigation into a subjective origin of cognition was branded by Cohen as a fallback into psychologism.

It is at this point that Natorp begins his investigation. Would an inquiry into the subjective conditions of cognition necessarily lead to a psychologism? Natorp goes back to

Kant to motivate this direction of inquiry. Kant himself does not speak of a subjective grounding of cognition, but he does grant the possibility of an investigation into the subjective "side" of cognition (especially in the A-edition of the Transcendental Deduction). In Natorp's words, Is not knowledge a content (an "episode") in the subject?; Is not every content of cognition, in order to *be* cognized, related to the subject? In broaching the issue of the content of cognition, Natorp happens upon nothing other than what phenomenologists later would call the intentionality of consciousness, its necessary relatedness to "a content." If one frames the problem in this way, namely that a subjective "grounding" is not about grounding knowledge in the contingent subject (leading, inadvertently, to a psychologism), but simply in acknowledging the necessary relation of every content to a subject, then one poses the question of such a "subjective account" in an entirely novel manner. Moreover, the objective grounding turns out to be merely the "positive" direction of the "negative" or "inverse" question compared to the subjective direction, towards the "*phainesthai*," the "immediate relation to the subject."

When one gains a higher-perspective view of both "directions" of "grounding," then one takes a higher vantage point on the problem of knowledge as it had been posed already by Plato: that of the relation of the universal (objective) to the individual (subjective). If both stand in a necessary relation, one gains access to the most basic law, namely the law of lawfulness as the "relationality" (the essential relatedness) of objective and subjective. To the constructive direction of the objective grounding of knowledge stands the opposite, reconstructive direction of the relation to the subject. In this manner, Natorp achieves a meta-epistemological standpoint that makes possible, from the critical perspective, a "psychology" that does not succumb to the threat of psychologism. This is perhaps the most original systematic contribution Natorp makes to the epistemology of the Marburg School. It was also his most influential work, having a significant impact on the Phenomenological Movement and especially on Husserl. Husserl's construal of phenomenology as transcendental and his later genetic, "reconstructive" method bear clear marks of Natorp's influence. It is worth mentioning, in conclusion, that Natorp himself later abandons his own psychology in favor of a speculative "panmethodism" that unites both the objective (constructive) and subjective (reconstructive) methods into a "method of unity."

Further Reading

Gadamer, Hans-Georg, *Philosophical Apprenticeships*. Cambridge, Mass.: MIT Press, 1985.
Luft, Sebastian, "Einleitung des Herausgebers," in: Paul Natorp, *Allgemeine Psychologie nach kritischer Methode*. Darmstadt: Wissenschaftliche Buchgesellschaft, 2013, pp. xi–xxxviii.

"Kant and the Marburg School" (1912)

This text – based on a lecture Natorp was invited to give before the Kant Society of Halle – is perhaps the most comprehensive, while concise, account of the Marburg interpretation of Kant and by extension of the philosophy of the Marburg School. Natorp begins by invoking some general tenets of the Marburg School, for instance that members of the latter are interested in reviving "the spirit, not the letter" of Kant's philosophy. Thereby, Natorp emphasizes that it was always the Marburg intention to revive the "key act" of Kant's thought, to go back to his "inalienable insight." To the Marburgers, starting from Cohen, this basic insight is the "transcendental method." This essay, thus, is as much an interpretation of Kant from the Marburg vantage point, as well as of Cohen's transformation of Kant. The transcendental method, as interpreted by the Marburg School, as being (allegedly) Kant's main insight, is thus the key method of a Kantianism that is freed of Kant's limitations and his rigidity. What does it consist in, then?

Kant's purpose, in the first Critique, was to provide a transcendental justification, a *deduction iuris,* for the "verifiable facts of science"; it is thus a regressive questioning-back into the conditions of the possibility of the *facta* of the sciences, in which the *factum* of reason becomes manifest. The Marburgers mean by "science" (*Wissenschaft*) more than just natural science; indeed, each cultural formation is treated by a science (natural science, as much as art or history), and hence philosophy begins with the "truths" established in the former scientific (or "scholarly") disciplines. Philosophy, thus, is to spell out the respective logics of cultural creations in order to show the "unity of *logos* or reason in all constructive acts of culture." The transcendental method, thus, provides the philosophical justification of all human deeds, all of which result in the creation of culture. This interpretation certainly goes beyond Kant's concept of a transcendental deduction, though Natorp (and Cohen) are right to point out that Kant's concept of "deduction" has in no way the purpose to "deduce" something from a highest principle (an interpretation that was further demonstrated by Dieter Henrich's well-known research into Kant's understanding of "deduction" from the contemporary legal genre of "*Deduktionsschriften*").

Despite Natorp's express alliance with Cohen in the interpretation of what is the central tenet of Kant's philosophy, Natorp nonetheless points out how the transcendental method allows at the same time for a "return to the immediate, concrete 'life' of consciousness," which is, as we know from the previous text, Natorp's own project. Hence, the concept of "experience," as reinterpreted by Cohen to mean the experience of the scientist in her acts of achieving insight into nature, is given a "subjective" reinterpretation in Natorp's insistence on the processual, dynamic character of the life of the subject in achieving cognition. The objective and subjective paths are, thus, two paths of one and the same method. Or, as Natorp puts it, combining Cohen's and his own efforts, the "*factum* [what has been made] is a *fieri* [something being made]." Since this making of culture is seen as a ubiquitous deed of the human being in every aspect of culture, making comprehensible reality around us as the world of our own, this spells out the deeply humanistic aspect of the Marburg School. This humanistic reading also makes clear that the Marburg form of transcendental philosophy, critical idealism, is not a rigid formalism, but is deeply rooted in culture and its material achievements; transcendental idealism, in the Marburg reading, "turns out to be the true empiricism," as Natorp says provocatively. In this sense, as accounting for the totality of what *is,* Natorp does not hesitate to call this stance "absolute idealism," while distinguishing it from that of Hegel. Natorp closes with some interesting reflections on the difference between Hegel and the transcendental idealism of the Southwest School (esp. Rickert). Natorp characterizes transcendental idealism, in the Marburg School, as an "idealism not just for the head but also for the heart," and in this sense its members are the "true disciples of Kant."

"The Problem of a Logic of the Exact Sciences" (1921)

Judging from the general perception of the Marburg School as providing a justification for the exact sciences, Natorp's *Die logischen Grundlagen der exakten Wissenschaften* [*The Logical Foundations of the Exact Sciences*] (first edition in 1910; second unaltered reprint in 1921) is arguably his *magnum opus*. It is also, apart from Cohen's pronouncements that transcendental philosophy should provide such a justification, the only actual and detailed *execution* of this program within the Marburg School. Natorp shows himself to be extremely well-read in the discussions regarding theories of science and the logical foundations of the exact sciences of his day (both from scientists as well as theoreticians). It is noteworthy, in terms of the Marburg School's avowed close ties to the scientific work *du jour*, that Natorp adds in the foreword to the second edition:

"The strong transformations which the exact sciences themselves and the philosophical assessment[1] of their logical foundations have experienced since the first appearance of this book, would have necessitated a thorough reworking of the latter. Only because currently, due to other more pressing tasks, the possibility to do so is lacking for me, I have agreed to an anastatic [i.e., unchanged] reprint of the old book, in the hopes that it, in its current shape, will yet offer enough questions and suggestions that may serve for further clarification. I hope to present the 'system of the logical basic functions'[2] soon in a mature form. What otherwise would have required a substantial change is what I have remarked upon the principle of relativity. Here I can refer, as an *Ersatz*, to the book of Ernst Cassirer, 'On Einstein's Theory of Relativity' (Berlin 1921), which moves in a direction close to mine and contains a lot of what would have had to be said from my perspective on the matter" (p. VII of the Foreword).

That is to say, Natorp recognizes the need to provide logical foundations for the new scientific paradigm inaugurated by Einstein's revolution in physics, a task he himself saw as necessary but unable to carry out himself. But it is in the good tradition of the Marburg School that *somebody* had to carry on this task, thus continuing the program of the school while passing the baton on to the new generation (a selection of Cassirer's book on Einstein is published as Chapter 15, below). In speaking of his plan to present a "system of logical basic functions," Natorp presumably has in mind his last work, the *Philosophische Systematik*, which was based on a lecture course in the summer of 1923 and reworked in 1924 for publication, though Natorp died before its completion. Natorp's systematic work was not published until 1954 (edited by his son, Hans Natorp).

The following excerpt is Chapter One of the book, in which Natorp explains the general *problem* of the logic of the exact sciences, and as such it is "preparatory work" that is necessary to ground the exact sciences. Exact sciences are those – following Kant – that are mathematical in character; but since Natorp declares the nature of mathematics to be logical (which proves its *a priori* character), what is needed are the logical foundations of mathematics itself. The discussion of the logical character of mathematics and the implied formalism of logic (Natorp here is in conversation with Frege, Russell, Couturat, Hilbert, and others) will be of special interest for historians of mathematics.

The other articles lay out, once again, the main tenets of the Marburg School epistemology (understood as epistemo-critique). They can be listed here, without renewed explanation, as the emphasis on the *factum* of the sciences (and the concomitant understanding of experience as that of the scientist), the dynamic nature of cognition, and cognition as an infinite progress (the givenness of cognition, the *Gabe*, as an *Aufgabe*, a task, as Natorp says with a play on the cognate *Gabe*). What is perhaps new is Natorp's discussion of the Marburg interpretation of the notion of the thing-in-itself. The Marburgers interpret the thing-in-itself as the idea of fulfilled and finished cognition, which, as an idea, lies in infinity, since the process of cognition is an infinite and ongoing progression. The object thus is the "general notion" of the problem of cognition as such. Furthermore, Natorp also discusses Cohen's notion of origin (*Ursprung*) as the "fundamental principle of the logical," which turns out to be the "exact correlate" of the object thusly construed. A closer look at Natorp's presentation shows that he is really presenting his own notion of unity as fundamental correlation between the subjective and objective methods (as discussed in the previous text), rather than Cohen's concept of origin, which Cohen develops in his *Logik der reinen Erkenntnis* (1902). A detailed discussion of the differences between the concepts lies beyond the scope of this introduction. With these basic notions in place, Natorp can proceed to develop the system of the logical basic functions modeled on the four generic groups of Kant's categories (quantity, quality, relation, modality) and, in conclusion, the mathematical principles of natural science. The relation of logic to the individual sciences is defined, thus, such that "logic ... is the study of logos, but not of all that is logical, since that extends ultimately to all of science."

Notes

1   *Durcharbeitung*
2   *logische Grundfunktionen*

Further Reading

Lembeck, Karl-Heinz, "Einleitung des Herausgebers," in: Paul Natorp, *Philosophie. Ihr Problem und ihre Probleme*. Göttingen: Edition Ruprecht, 2008, pp. 7–21.

Chapter 11

"On the Objective and Subjective Grounding of Knowledge" (1887)[1]

1.

Each separate science or theory seeks laws for a limited and determined range of appearances. Science, theoretical knowledge[2] considered as a whole and as a unity, seeks to unfold a unified network of laws, into which all particular laws for given appearances must fit. Logic, the theory of knowledge, aims at displaying how knowledge forms an inner unity through a process of composition according to laws.

This unity of knowledge is not ensured by the simple lack of inner contradiction and by the consistent connection of thoughts which is called, in a limited sense, the "form" of true knowledge (what Kant called the negative criterion of knowledge). The inner unity of knowledge must concern the object[3] or, to be more exact, the universal relation of knowledge to the object.[4]

Gradual consensus on this might be attained among scholars. We are taking a position basically not far from that of Kant; indeed we accentuate the essence of his view if we deny that an exclusively "formal" logic can serve as an adequate theory of knowledge and not merely as a technique. According to Kant, there are no laws of purely formal truth which do not have their roots in laws of objective truth. There is therefore no formal logic which is not grounded in "transcendental" logic. If both are related in the same way as the lawgiving found in the analytic and synthetic functions, and if all analysis presupposes synthesis (because the understanding cannot analyze anything which it has not first synthesized) then everything which formal logic can teach must be able to be grounded transcendentally.

We hold that it was settled a long time ago just how it is possible to have a theory of objective truth, a legislation of the laws of knowledge, through which the relation of truth and knowledge to the object is originally determined with universal validity. We do not need to settle this matter for the first time here.

If we regard knowledge as a task similar to an equation to be solved, then the object is the sought-for, not yet determined X which can only be determined through the data. This X, however, is not totally unknown; just as the X in the equation is itself determined in its significance[5] by its expressed relation to the known quantities.[6] Even before solving the equation of knowledge the significance of the object must be determined by its determinate relation to the data for knowledge. Otherwise, the task of knowing the object would be not only unsolvable but incomprehensible. Thus it is necessary that knowledge have an original relation to the object if even the question concerning the object and the demand for knowledge to agree with the object are to have a specifiable meaning. And indeed, as the universal meaning[7] of the X is predetermined by the form of the equation, in the same way the universal meaning of the object will be predetermined by that which we call the "form" of knowledge. From this it is already clear that the real form of knowledge must refer to its relationship to the object and not be sought in abstraction from all objects and all relations to them. Even Kant, whose authority it is popular to claim in favor of a merely "formal" logic (in the latter sense), demanded for "pure" logic abstraction not from all relation to the object, but only from specific relation to particular objects. Clearly the first abstraction would be unworkable if we are still to speak of knowledge at all. We may indicate this second claim, too, as one on which all competent scholars concur.

Finally, we are not seeking the general nature of the relationship between the sought-for object and the data of knowledge. This has already been decided, since what is being sought is the object, the "being"[8] which is the ground that corresponds to the "appearance". Anyone who has asked about an object will have known what the question seeks.

The data of knowledge are "phenomena" in the most general sense: those appearances which are to be explained[9] by science, that is, are to be traced back to the truth[10] which appears in them. The object should be the object for the appearance; the appearance should be proven to be the appearance of the object. Here there is already expressed an original relation of the object to what is given in knowledge which is analogous to the relation of the X to the known quantities of the equation. The meaning of this relation must be discoverable through analyzing what the questioner about the object intends, seeks, and since he seeks, presupposes. If every science inquires after the objective foundation underlying each appearance of its truth, then every science must have some concept of this foundation and of the grounding relationship of the object to the appearance.

All scientific knowledge aims at the law. The relation of the appearance to the law (the relation of the "manifold" of the appearance to the "unity" of the law) must therefore explain the original relation to the object in all knowledge. The interpretation of the appearance in accordance with laws is taken as the objectively true interpretation. We may take as impartially established this universal correlation between law and object, ancient as it is in the history of philosophy and the sciences. It has been established not through the whim or the passion for system of this or that philosopher, but rather through the action of science that everywhere constitutes the object in law.

Given these fundamentals we can confidently take a stand on the pending problems of logic. Whoever cannot agree with us on this common basis will probably find most of the following said in vain. And yet these conclusions are merely preliminary. Only beyond them do the really difficult questions of logic arise, the first and most vital of which will be discussed here: the question *of logical method*, which may be formulated for the present as follows: must that foundation which logic is to give knowledge be achieved by *objective* or *subjective* methods?

2

The expressions "objective" and "subjective" of course refer to the object and the subject of knowledge. The law of the objectivity of knowledge must be sought, and sought in knowledge itself. Knowledge, however, shows itself from the start as two-sided: as "content" (as what is known or to be known) and as "activity"[11] or experience[12] of the subject (as knowing). To be sure, in every knowing both relations are present together and closely connected; there can no more be a known without a knower than there can be a knower without a known. But in the abstract both must be differentiated, and clearly a theory which grounds knowledge in its own laws can only refer *immediately* to one of the two relations. Consequently, we must ask which of the two should be regarded as first, underlying, and determining in the grounding of knowledge. Must the law of objectivity lie exclusively in the contents of knowledge which are to be related to the object? Must the law be proved from these without taking any account of the relation to the subject? Or is it perhaps in precisely this relationship to the subject that the foundation of the laws of objectivity must be originally sought? In this case it would be only secondary, in as far as the content of knowledge is somehow affected, that the ground could be recognized in the content.

We must confess that at first the latter interpretation appears convincing. It can easily appear as if one were explaining the same by the same when one grounds the objectivity of knowledge by a relationship already originally present in the content of knowledge; it appears to be a far more basic explanation which turns to the subject which after all pronounces itself as the underlying ground by its very name.[13] Thus many take as established that the true grounding of knowledge is to be sought in relationship to the subject, in subjective "consciousness".

We will not here examine the historical reasons why this view has become rooted so deeply in contemporary philosophy. Clearly it has been the influence of Kant which had the main impact on this stream of thought, at least in Germany. Kant appears to seek at least the most fundamental laws and conditions for the objective truth of knowledge in the laws of our subjectivity – the laws of our senses and our understanding. To what extent this interpretation of Kant is correct can remain undecided for now; it is more important to know what considerations of content serve as apparent supports for the subjective viewpoint.

Knowledge is in every case an occurrence in the context of subjective experience, an event in consciousness, a psychic encounter. As such, it is naturally grasped and treated scientifically in the context of the whole subjective life of consciousness. Lawfulness in knowledge thus appears to be a necessary result of laws for psychic life. If "objective" validity is to be ascribed to knowledge at all, then since this validity is an attribute of knowledge it must somehow be grounded in the subjectivity of knowledge. It must have its roots in the activity or the subjective experience of knowing. The "act" of knowing seems as if it must be first, while knowledge, regarded as content, seems the dependent result or product. The product must be called objective; the manufacture is subjective. To be sure, according to this view, logic becomes unavoidably dependent on psychology, which conclusion at least the most consistent advocates of the subjective viewpoint have not shied away from. Kant, of course, from whom they come historically, took the opposite stand with unequivocal firmness on precisely this point; but even some of his first otherwise faithful disciples, such as Fries, believed it necessary to correct him here and to trace transcendental philosophy back to its true psychological foundation.

On the other hand it is easy to see that our preliminary conclusions point much more to the opposing position.

In order to ascertain the general relation of knowledge and its object we regarded knowledge as an equation to be solved; that is, we considered it purely in terms of its objective content. We believed that we could answer in advance the question of the meaning and ground of objectivity using only that content which knowledge supposes when it confronts the object as that which is to be known. In this connection there was no mention of knowledge as activity or experience, or of the knower as subject. To be sure, we readily conceded that there could be no "known" without a "knower," that knowledge is only given in the experience of a subject, in the consciousness of the knower. But as this relation to the subject is not the point in question, it is not necessary for us to turn to this in answering the question. Each appeal to the subject of knowledge and the way in which consciousness participates in knowledge must on the contrary appear to us from the start as a category mistake (*metabasis eis allo genos*).

We can easily remove the appearance of explaining the same by the same in seeking the ground of objectivity purely on the objective side of knowledge. What grounds something not only must not, it *cannot* belong to another genus than what is grounded. It is usually said that the mere reduction to law does not really explain a phenomenon, since after all it simply repeats the given state of affairs in a universal expression. Whoever says this must be understanding something very obscure by explanation. The universal expression leading a particular incident back to a universal pattern of occurrences contains just what has always been understood by explanation. The synthetic connection of the unlimited manifold of appearances in the unity of law, the bringing into unity (*syllabein eis hen*), as Plato says (Theaetetus 147D), is what makes the phenomenon understandable and so explains it. The essential point on which all depends is that the explaining ground can never be in any other relationship to that which is explained by it than that of universal to particular, of law and recognized instance of the law. The central force which helps to determine the movement of the planets is explained by gravity because it is shown to be an instance of the latter and connected by the same law with known instances. This is the common pattern. Accordingly, the ground of the law of the objective relation can only be sought in the nexus (literally: connection together)[14] of what is related as content to objects, i.e., in the universal features of this relation. It is impossible to find the ground in the quite other, more or less opposed relation of knowledge to the knower. However, every objective relation which occurs can also be expressed in a subjective relation. Through an expression which subjectifies the objective, the appearance may arise (as it did in Kant's case) that subjectivity actually contains the ground of the objective relation.

All this gives a positive and direct solution to our question. Perhaps for those who have already thought through the relationship of the objective and subjective aspects of knowledge it needs no further comment. Yet this relationship, clear in itself, has become so confused by the dispute over Kant's legacy and the ensuing dissipation of this inheritance, that a more probing discussion does not seem unnecessary. On principle, we will not take into account the dispute over what Kant really taught and what position should be taken in regard to his doctrine. This has by now become unedifying; we will make some remarks on Kant's position on the question only after we have decided the matter on the basis of its content and aside from any historical considerations.

3

One consideration above all renders the subjectivist point of view unacceptable: if, as this point of view demands, one makes logic in principle dependent on a particular science, namely psychology, one negates the whole meaning of logic as a universal theory grounding the truth of knowledge. However much contention may exist about the precise limits and methods of a universal science of knowledge, this much at least should be agreed on by all who believe in the possibility of such a science; it must be a science of a more fundamental validity[15] than any other. A science which according to its name and claim treats knowledge in general and its laws may not be dependent for its own grounding upon any particular scientific knowledge (which of course can only be called valid according to logic's laws). The science of knowledge must be the ground of all particular sciences. If logic treats the criterion of truth, if it treats that which determines the truth of an act of knowledge according to laws and so universally, then the validity of this criterion cannot be dependent on an act of knowledge which can only be asserted as true according to this criterion. Thus there is either no logic at all, or it must be able to make the claim of building entirely on its own ground without borrowing its foundation from any other science.

But it is possible that this claim cannot be upheld. At least, anyone who without hesitation makes logic a branch of psychology obviously sees things differently. For him, psychology is the basic science and logic is at best its application.

The possibility of this objection forces us to go yet a step further. We claim that not only the meaning of logic, but the meaning of all objective science is mistaken and almost turned into its opposite if one makes the objective truth of knowledge dependent on subjective experience. One not only destroys logic, as the independent theory of the objective validity of knowledge, one also cancels out objective validity itself and changes it into purely subjective validity if one attempts to support it on subjective grounds and to deduce it from subjective factors. Because of this we believe we stand not only for the rights of logic, according to its hitherto accepted concept, but also for the claim of all science to objective validity for its truths, when we maintain that objective validity must be founded objectively.

In fact, all science which makes a claim to objectivity starts from the presupposition that with regard to the validity of its truth-claims it must not be dependent on any other laws than those which can be made certain within the science, in that inner connection[16] to be developed in logical form, independent of any further assumptions which might be dragged in. Knowledge is only to be grounded through other knowledge, namely by logical mediation in a network[17] thought as a unity and determined by the one lawful system of Science or Knowledge. In particular, any appeal to the subject and its powers is in itself completely alien to subjective science. The objectivity to which science makes claim unquestionably means a validity which truly overcomes the subjectivity of consciousness and not merely appears to. In the object, in the matter[18] which is asserted as true, should lie that which makes up the truth of knowledge, completely independent of the givenness of a suitable representation[19] as a subjective experience of this or that consciousness. Of course, the consciousness of truth in sciences such as mathematics and the mathematical natural sciences (to remain with those which pride themselves on the strongest grounding of their propositions) is completely independent of the understanding of forces or functions through which this truth in its subjective possibility becomes a comprehensible possession of the psyche. We become certain of the truth within the proper internal network of the science, developed from primary objective content assumptions as they are formulated in the basic concepts and propositions of that science. Thus science not only makes its claim, it also justifies in action its claim to a thoroughly autonomous validity and grounding, since it lays bare its objective foundation in the form of basic concepts and principles. The mathematician or physicist who truly grasps the nature of his science will find it superfluous to seek the grounds for the laws of truth for his knowledge in psychology. He will in principle deny such a search; he recognizes only the laws of his own science, not an alien science, as the judge of truth.

The theory of truth will also have to stand opposed to psychology in just the same way, independent in the same sense as the truth of scientific knowledge itself. For the theory of truth aims at nothing other than comprehending and making certain within the unified network of Science just that autonomous legislation of objective truth which the sciences, each in their limited field, claim as the basis of their authority. Thus each science must proceed from basic concepts and principles, not subjective acts. We thus insist that the autonomous, purely objective grounding of truth which we demand is necessary to give fully serious meaning to logic, to truth, and to the objective validity of scientific knowledge.

However, our argument, even in this expanded and intensified formulation, still seems to support itself on a mere claim or postulate (although now of all objective science and not only logic). Perhaps there is one firm defender of the subjectivist view who will take it upon himself to dispute the correctness of this claim to objectivity, not only of logic but of all science which calls itself objective. We could perhaps claim it as a victory to see our enemy forced into this extreme position. And yet, we do not want to have merely argued *ad hominem*. Therefore we will attempt to delve deeper into the core of the problem and show how the desired purely objective grounding of knowledge can be carried out according to its law, and at which point the attempted subjective grounding fails (and perhaps failed long ago). Thus we now have to confront the two standpoints in more detail, in order to decide through experiment the feasibility of the one and the unfeasibility of the other.

4

Objective validity signifies a validity independent of the subjectivity of knowledge – this is well established. What is to be objectively valid, is to be valid apart from the givenness of its representation in this or that consciousness. The question is what this non-subjective validity, so far merely defined negatively, signifies positively, and how it can be grounded.

It appears that only one of two answers is possible. Objects in themselves are there, outside and independent of all subjectivity, without any original relation to it. Of course, they are represented only through subjective representation, but the representation only stands for (represents or signifies) the object, it is not the object itself. Thus objectivity is not negated by subjectivity. That is the first answer.

Perhaps this actually means something correct, but at least as it is presented, it is not really an answer to the question. The being-in-itself of the object is itself an enigma[20] and thus cannot serve as a solution to our present enigma. If we understood what it meant to say the object in itself is there independent of all subjectivity and then is appropriated in our subjectivity by knowledge there would be no problem in the knowing of objects or in the objectivity of knowledge.

Thus one is naturally led to seek the solution in the opposite direction. Rather than starting from the object and proceeding to make subjective knowing understandable in relation to the object, which after all is not given but is in question, one must first take the standpoint of knowledge and ask how knowledge itself understands objectivity, how knowledge goes about confronting the object as independent of the subjectivity of knowing, and what objectivity signifies for knowledge. Obviously this way promises to lead more quickly to our goal. No object is given to us in any other way than in knowledge. Thus the meaning and ground of objectivity are not available for comprehension in any other way. To begin with, "object" signifies that which knowledge stands over against. The meaning and ground of this confrontation can best be communicated by knowledge itself. For it is precisely knowledge's business to proceed with consciousness, to know what it does and why. To question this consciousness of knowledge about its own activity was the direction indicated by our first considerations; this was the opinion of Kant when, after many promising attempts by his predecessors, he made the demand to prove the conditions and laws of objectivity out of consciousness, that is, out of the consciousness of science.

But by this, objectivity seems more threatened than ever, in that the object seems to be determined only from the viewpoint of knowledge and thus of *subjectivity*. Knowledge itself confronts the object almost on its own authority, obeying only its own laws; it demands, in Kant's curt description, that the object should conform to knowledge, and not vice versa. Knowledge – isn't that subjectivity? However, it has been said that knowledge confronts the object as *independent* of the subjectivity of knowing. Obviously the pivotal point of the problem is how to understand and ground this independence.

It will be clear from the outset that it can only be understood by means of an abstraction. Objects are really only given to us in the knowledge which we have of them. Yet if even in this knowledge the object is regarded as independent of the subjectivity of knowing, this cannot be understood unless one abstracts from subjectivity, from the relation of the represented to the representer, and from the content of his subjective experience. That this abstraction in itself is possible needs no proof. It is actually carried out in all sciences, in that they claim to know "the object"; and it is carried out in a naive way in common representation which seeks to encounter "things" and believes that it does. Perhaps this abstraction which is carried out naturally also explains that first attempt at an answer which we rejected in its initial form; the in-itself-ness of the object can only mean the abstraction from subjectivity, an abstraction whose authority and necessity are regarded just as quite self-evident and in no need of grounding. In fact, this abstraction is carried out without any reflection whatsoever; thus the object appears to be present and given from the outset, and not first reached through abstraction. If one thinks back on its relationship to knowledge, the illusion arises that the object, present[21] and given from the beginning, subsequently comes to our subjectivity in a new relation alien to itself – to be known. Actually the object is not first there with subjectivity coming later. It is only that in natural consciousness reflection on the object is thoroughly primary and immediate; reflection on subjectivity, if it happens at all, is secondary.

However, the mere possibility of the abstraction from subjectivity, proved by its actual performance, cannot also ground its authority and necessity. The possibility explains the significance of the claim to objective validity but has not yet proven this claim to possess any legitimacy. The question thus advances to a new stage: what are the grounds which determine why the abstraction from subjectivity which gives us the knowledge we call objective is not only possible but necessary?

In order to clarify the content of this question, one must recall the meaning of any *valid abstraction*. I believe when one understands abstraction as merely negative, one's explanation is, if not completely off the mark, at least starting badly and doomed to failure. To consider abstraction negatively is to consider it logically as the removal of a characteristic, psychologically as disregard, turning away from or removing the mental view from a particular aspect actually contained in the representation. This explanation is insufficient as long as it fails to mention the positive aspects for whose sake and advantage one must disregard other aspects as not pertinent. For the positive is the determining point, the other merely its consequence. When I focus my attention on one particular thing, I automatically exclude from the present examination whatever has no part in the unity of this view[22]. Characterized psychologically, what is primary is the concentration of the mental eye, logically, the unity of determination; the other is merely the reverse side of the matter, not the matter itself. Thus geometric concepts (point, straight line, etc.) abstract from deviations and non-uniform aspects in the perception of the senses when they fix the mind's eye on what is uniform, unified, and unchangeably determined.

If we apply this to our case, our question is immediately made more precise. As long as the abstraction from subjectivity demanded in the concept of the object is seen merely in its negative meaning, it is understandable that the overcoming of subjectivity seems an empty fiction which can scarcely be maintained in actual life. It seemed thus to the modern sensualists, who so far were not entirely wrong. If one strips everything from the object which is merely given in subjective representation – and that seems to be the meaning of the demanded abstraction as long as one understands it only negatively – then of course nothing whatever remains except that unnameable something, that "something, I know not what" which has haunted sensualist philosophy for a long time. Abstraction from subjectivity, understood only negatively, can certainly ground no being[23]; at most, it could only ground the fiction of being. But because of this more effort should have been made to go beyond sterile negation and investigate whether the desired abstraction did not perhaps have some positive content in reserve. The positive character, of which the disregard for subjectivity is merely the result, could ground a type of being which is not merely a fiction.

What the object signifies positively has already been stated, at least in general terms. Taken positively, the object signifies the *law;* it signifies the lasting unity in which the changing manifold of appearance is unified and determined in thought. This significance of the object, of "being" differentiated from "appearing," has been won for philosophy since Plato, or perhaps since the Eleatics. This meaning of objectivity is the whole rationalist direction in philosophy which, I would say, stands secure because of the concept of reason (*ratio*) since reason ultimately means law, and nothing else. But science too strives at least since Galileo to make this sense of "object" true. The objectification of appearance is carried out in the reduction to law; there is no other way. In this, the autonomy which science claims is guaranteed. When the appearance is reduced to law then the appearance is reduced to the object appearing in it. The appearance of the daily movement of the sun around the earth signifies objectively the daily movement of the earth on its axis, since according to this representation of the object which is the ground of the appearance, the given appearance is explained by its connection[24] with other known laws. On the other hand, that representation which accepts the object according to direct sensual appearance frustrates the reduction to law and thus cannot have objective validity. Also, whoever seeks what is objectively good and just as distinguished from what passes for such with any particular subject, whoever in addition, like Adeimantos in Plato's *Republic*, searches for that which does not merely appear, but is, such a person also believes in and seeks a law of the good, of the just. He seeks the harmonious view of these unique "objects" in which all change and contradiction of subjective opinion is overcome. He seeks the "steady pole in the flood of appearances" and strives "to make fast with lasting thought that which floats in varying appearance".

Thus, if it is in general the law which gives the concept of the object its positive significance, then the solution to our problem must be sought by asking how *the concept of law* makes abstraction from subjectivity not only possible but necessary.

5

The answer to this will be found in the most direct way if we first succeed in understanding the meaning of that *subjectivity* which must be overcome in the representation of the object.

Subjectivity signifies the relationship of the represented to the representer, in so far as it is represented by him, that is, in so far as it forms the content of his subjective experience. Subjectivity signifies *the immediate relationship to the ego*. What is given in immediate relationship to the ego is finally nothing other than what in relationship to the object is called the appearance. Multiform and constantly changing, presenting itself now this way now that, this appearance is to be related back to the unified basic form of the object appearing in it. The appearance is multiform and changing precisely for the multiple and changing states of subjects. The ultimate immediate appearance, however, the *phenomenon of ultimate authority*, is nothing other than what is given on each occasion to a determined subject in a determined situation. It is this which we must name as what is *ultimately subjective;* there is absolutely nothing else by which the concept of subjectivity could be positively determined, aside from *the appearing, the phainesthai itself*, which, as Hobbes had already stated, is both the most noteworthy and the most original of all "phenomena".

If this is established, then it is immediately clear how far subjectivity is overcome in the concept of the law. The function of law in knowledge is just this: confronting the appearance which from the outset presents itself not in an identical, unified, determined manner but rather varying according to the subject and its situation, the law is to ground that representation of the object which is unanimously valid for all subjects in all circumstances. However, just as the lawful interpretation of the object represents that which is objectively valid, even so the appearance, before the reduction to law and thus to the object, is the most concrete expression of subjectivity. Appearance is the representation which is not yet objectified in law and consequently is still subjective, just as an objective representation is one which has been raised to law and brought to the standpoint of universal validity and to unity.

That this concept of subjectivity is the only tenable one should be proven in more detail in another place. Yet it should be immediately evident that for judging the relationship of subjective and objective absolutely nothing else is given to us except knowledge, in which we differentiate the subjective and objective sides, the appearing as such (or the direct givenness of the appearance in the experience of consciousness) and the reduction to law (the objectification of appearance).

Yet it may be useful to make a distinction here without which this relationship of subjective and objective, though clear in itself, may easily become confused.

We distinguish two types or stages of objectification. A certain objectification is already present in the simple differentiation of the "content" of a representation from representing as an "activity" (or better, "experience") of the subject. The content abstracted from the activity already signifies not merely that which is represented and thought by someone or other at this time, but also that which is representable or thinkable in the same way by anyone at any time. Raising what has been represented one single time to what is to be universally so represented already signifies a rise to the standpoint of the universal, namely universal *validity* and thus objectivity. Just as at this first level the opposition of subjective and objective rests on a relationship of particular and universal, this same relationship also controls every further objectification.

What the sciences call a "phenomenon," the appearance which is to be explained, i.e., reduced to law, is in general *not* what is ultimately subjective, what we called "the phenomenon of ultimate authority". Instead it is always already somehow raised to objective significance. It is not regarded as being represented merely once by one individual, but rather as something to be so represented universally by every individual. Thus it has already undergone the first objectification, the raising of the single represented to universal validity. The scientific phenomenon itself must for the most part be first established by scientific means before it can serve as the basis for other more general proofs. To establish[25] a fact means to prove it something to be universally recognized, verifiable by everyone at all times. A fact is "established"[26] when it is *unambiguously* determined in confrontation with the multiformity and thus the indetermination of the original and direct appearance. One can also easily see that such determination is always possible only from the universal standpoint and according to universal measures. Thus it is through an objectifying act that science arrives at the particular "fact" which as "phenomenon" grounds science. If it was said earlier that the data of knowledge, in the most general understanding, were "phenomena," then we must add the reminder that what we usually call phenomena are not the first data. The first data would be what is given in the absolutely particular act of consciousness.

Yet what is already somewhat objectified in the way just described has the same relationship to each representation of a particular subject (the universal to the particular) as that universal which we call the law has to the particular state of affairs or phenomenon which has already been established as universally valid. It is the same function of knowledge by which the single represented is raised to something which is to be universally represented and by which the single universally valid state of affairs is raised to the universality of law. These are merely two internally connected stages of one and the same process of objectification, which can be expressed by a two-fold relationship of particular and universal.

With them the relationship of subjective and objective in knowledge can be explained *completely* by the relationship of the *particular* and the *universal*.

With this reduction we seem to be led more than ever into the darkest abyss of metaphysics. The significance of the universal and particular in knowledge has certainly been the key point in metaphysical disputes since antiquity. Yet we believe that today the ancient question can be answered simply and precisely, and it will be seen that its answer will with one stroke reveal the solution to our problem.

6

The dispute over the primacy of the particular or the universal lies at the root of the opposition between Platonic and Aristotelian philosophy. This dispute renewed itself in the medieval debate between realism and nominalism and has exerted a deep influence on recent and contemporary philosophy. If we see philosophy today divided into two enemy camps by the opposition between positivism and idealism, we can easily perceive that the ultimate basis of the division lies in the question of the primacy of the particular or the universal. This is not to say that philosophy has made no essential progress in all this time. On the contrary, when one compares today's prevailing opposed principles with those of Aristotle a double difference and progression appears.

First of all, with Aristotle and even with the medieval scholastics, it was essentially a question of the particular thing, or individual, and the universal of the thing, or species. More recent philosophy, in as far as the vast reform of the sciences since the start of modern times has not left it unaffected, knows the universal essentially and originally under the form of law. The thing is no longer the primary given, but rather first an unknown. As Kant concisely summed up the basic result of modern science since Galileo, things have dissolved into mere "relationships," although among these there are some which are "independent and constant" and which from now on must represent things for us. From now on it is primarily and essentially a matter of the universality of *relation* (which gives the concept of law).

As important and revolutionary as is this alteration of the problem, a second change is still more important for our present investigation. Today the question of the particular and the universal no longer concerns merely the relationship of the particular thing, particular occurrence, or particular instance of a relation to the universal of this thing, this occurrence, or this relation. It concerns at bottom the relationship of the final, absolutely particular subjective representation or appearance to that which has somehow already been raised to universal and so objective significance. Thus it is correct, as we established, that the ultimate particular is the absolutely particular appearance in consciousness, and that our question should be directed there. Hence the easily understood opinion of today's so-called "Positivist," that what is "here and now given" each time, that ultimately concrete, absolute particular which we called the "phenomenon of ultimate authority" must form the foundation of all knowledge, if, as has been handed down, the universal only borrows its significance from the particular and by itself signifies nothing. Every other particular which has already been thought objectively in some way, whether it be a thing or occurrence or instance of a relation is already a universal in comparison with that ultimate concrete entity, i.e., it has been already raised to universal validity, even though it is a particular thing in relationship to the higher universality of the species or the law. It already supposes and includes the first objectification.

Positivism is only the consistent fulfillment of nominalism in so far as it keeps in view the ultimate particular and only grants original and indissoluble truth to this its "positive fact," while only awarding reality or truth to that which has already been generalized (thus also to the particular, in so far as it has already been raised to that which is to be universally so represented) in as far as what is generalized represents that ultimate "positive fact".

Idealism, on the contrary, seeks the root and ground of truth and reality, even of the particular, in universal or "ideals". For idealism the law is plainly what is determining, primary, basic. Through it and according to its standards alone the particular receives the validity and significance of truth, reality.

For the Positivists, the universal has significance in knowledge only in as far as it signifies the particular whose universal it is; it borrows all the validity which it can claim in knowledge from the particular. In itself it has no original claim to validity.

For the Idealists, on the contrary, the particular has significance in knowledge because of the universal whose particular it is; it borrows all the validity which it can claim in knowledge from the universal. In itself it has no original claim to validity.

Measured against this sharpest formulation of the opposition, the position which Aristotle took shows itself a weak compromise. It is no less noteworthy that in spite of this the large majority of recent philosophers were still first inclined to accept Aristotle's attempted compromise. According to Aristotle the universal surely has its unimpeachable significance in knowledge. Objectively, however, only the particular is designated as real; the universal is only real as representative of the particular, that is, as representing many similar entities. The universal is not an object for itself apart from the particular objects, but just the same it is the only grounding element in knowledge, the first and the determining factor in validity.

Why this compromise in untenable hardly needs discussion. Knowledge should after all correspond to its object. If the very thing valid for knowledge should not be valid for its object this would signify that knowledge would neither correspond to its object nor need to.

Certainly the species "human" is never present[27] as a thing (much less as a particular thing) in addition to or apart from the individuals of the species. Certainly the species of occurrences (to borrow Helmholz' term for the laws of nature) never represent a (single) occurrence apart from or in addition to the particular instances of such occurrences. Similarly, universal relations such as those expressed in the statement 1+1=2 do not exist or occur apart from the particular instances of such relations. If Aristotle proved these conclusions, then he proved something which has never been disputed by a thinking being. Probably even Plato did not need to be taught that the universal is not "real" in this sense, that is, does not represent a thing or event or actual process beyond being the representative of the particular, in the particular, namely in all particulars that fall under this universal.

On the other hand Plato knew that the particular could only be valid as something actual, or being (whether thing, occurrence or relationship) by virtue of the universal, as a particular instance of the universal, or to put it in modern terms, as an instance of the law. And that is the meaning of all "Idealism," at least the meaning of the Idealism which we intend to uphold.

What is the particular, if it is not the particular instance of the universal? The particular is no more for itself, apart from and in addition to the universal (*choris para ta katholou*) than the universal is for itself, in addition to and apart from the particular (*choris para ta kath' hekasta*).

One could be tempted to say that Aristotle, fighting a supposed Platonic hypostasis of the universal as existing on its own, fell into a no less untenable, incomprehensible hypostasis of the particular. In much the same way as in Aristotle's opinion Plato made universality a property *of things*, Aristotle made particularity a property of things. Apart from the consideration[28] to which things are subject *in knowledge* particularity is as thoroughly inexplicable and meaningless as is universality.

The thing is particular, to be sure, in as far as it is taken as particular in (objective) consideration, but neither apart from this nor for itself. And what is valid for the particular thing is also valid for the particular occurrence and the particular instance of a relation.

Therefore not only universality but particularity too – or more correctly and concisely, the *relation* of the particular and the universal – takes place in knowledge. *Consequently* that relation has its place in the object in as far as the object exists for knowledge, for we cannot know or speak of any object, so not of any (objective) meaning of universal or particular other than that which exists for knowledge. The particular thing "in itself" suffers from exactly the same absurdities as the supposedly Platonic universal thing "in itself". The Platonic *kath'hauto* rightly signifies the unity in which the law is thought, the Aristotelian *kath' hekaston* the particularity in which the instance of the law is thought – in knowledge.

The particular entity can always be characterized only by universal determinations, through classification in the universal, all-inclusive frameworks of space and time and in the all-inclusive network of causal connection through which each particular is fixed in its place in space and time, i.e., determined with universal validity. Thus the particular proves itself in fact an instance of the universal, as conversely the universal is the essence[29] of the particular.

But finally it is the fundamental law of *knowledge* which prescribes the opposition and mutual relation of particular and universal, which is unremovable in knowledge and *therefore* valid for the object (as object of knowledge).

7

Now we have only to apply this result to that ultimate concrete, the absolute particularity, the "here and now given" of the Positivist, in order to reach a sure resolution of the question we raised.

It is an error to believe that that ultimate concrete "here and now given" or representation could be the ground of knowledge as the primary and sole positive factor which includes everything in advance. Not only can this opinion not be supported, not only does it lead to unacceptable consequences, but it also shows itself on closer inspection to be an almost incomprehensible illusion. How do we grasp this ultimate concrete here and now appearing? It is to be grasped, if at all, only when it is determined in concepts; but every such determination occurs from the standpoint of the universal. Every answer which can ever be given to the question what is the here and now appearing is only possible in universal expressions, universal determinations of quality and quantity, universally expressed relations to other already known objects. If I say "it is here, it is this, it is now," all these determinations aim at denoting the particular as particular, but they denote it only through determinations of universal applicability. They classify the particular in the universal order of space and time, an already presupposed order of things. Thus all the expressions with which the Positivist attempts to characterize his "positive fact" before any universal conceptual determination – particularity and concreteness, identity of place and of time, givenness (as content of consciousness, so subjectivity) and, finally, positiveness itself (incontestable position[30]) – all these contain nothing but conceptual determinations, indeed of the highest universality and abstractness. Even the "positive fact" can obviously not be grasped other than through such means, and yet the goal set was to overcome the emptiness of mere abstraction.

Naturally the Positivist will seek to justify himself. He will say that while universal abstract concepts are surely necessary to describe and arrange what is immediately experienced, the immediate experience is in itself absolutely particular and concrete.

This seems to me to be a rather exact repetition of Aristotle's error. Aristotle believed that the thing itself was in itself concrete and particular, even though, as he could not deny, knowledge could only describe and interpret it with the help of universal abstract concepts. What then is the thing itself, or as the Positivist would say, the appearance itself? What does it mean that it has in itself the absolute particularity and determinacy which we demand? If it is not determinate *for us*, then it cannot be the origin of knowledge for us, but it is only determinate for us in so far as we have determined it, and this can only happen through universal concepts.

However, the Positivist will say that that which is universally determined in the concept must after all be concretely given in the particular appearance; otherwise the determination would not apply to the given appearance, as we too required.

But what does "given" mean here? Known? Perceived? That would again include the determination which one must admit is only possible through concepts. The concreteness of the appearance is only "given" in the act as a *determinable X which is now to be determined*, like an Aristotelian potential being. It is given only in the sense of an appointed task, not as a datum of knowledge through which other unknowns could be determined.

Thus it becomes more and more clear that the "positive fact," the supposed primary given, is much more that which is sought. One might even say it is the ultimate goal. It is in the concept of this goal that the utmost is demanded which could be achieved by knowledge in its final completion. And this last has been made first, the sought-for has been taken for a *datum*, so the task of knowledge has been turned upside-down. The "positive fact" is spoken of as having been already determined, while determination is always first the achievement of knowledge.

Yet Positivism rests on a correct insight. Even if all determination is first the achievement of knowledge, one cannot dismiss the reflection that something must be "given" before this achievement, something subjectively original and immediate which is to be determined and so first brought to objectivity. In fact there is something given before the *achievement* of knowledge, namely the *task*.

One might also say: the object is given, namely as an *X*, something which is yet to be determined, not as a known quantity.

Thus positivism does not fail by seeking the ultimate given, the subjectively original "phenomenon of ultimate authority" and seeing in it the immediacy of (subjective) consciousness. What is false is the opinion that this sought-after (actually, postulated) immediate and original content of subjective consciousness can be made the basis of *knowledge* as an immediate original *datum*. Rather the question is now whether it can be at all arrived at by the means of knowledge? Subjectivity as such will not allow itself to be grasped in its immediate aspect. It can only be grasped, in as far as this is possible at all, in concepts, because there is absolutely no other organon of knowledge. Yet when it is grasped in concepts it is no longer absolutely immediate and subjective, but has always already been objectified. The level *of pure* subjectivity would be identical with the level of absolute indeterminacy. One may reason back to this, as to the original chaos, but one cannot lay hold of it in itself. The *constructive* objectifying achievement of knowledge always comes first; from it we *reconstruct* as far as possible the level of original subjectivity which could never be reached by knowledge apart from this reconstruction which proceeds from the already completed objective construction. In this reconstruction we, so to speak, objectify subjectivity as such. This objectification of subjectivity deserves to be called a constructed fiction much more than does that construction on which "objects" rest, which grounds reality and overcomes all fiction. Our task at first seemed to be to show how subjectivity could be overcome in a non-fictitious concept of the object. Now objectivity shows itself so impossible to overcome that it appears much more difficult to salvage a proper non-fictitious significance for subjectivity.

Subjectivity is primary, in so far as the task of knowledge is posed before it is solved, but it cannot be called a given in the sense of being a datum of knowledge. The real beginnings and grounds of knowledge are instead always ultimate *objective unities*. Thus mathematics is not founded on phenomena which are given before any abstraction. On the contrary, it rests on fundamental abstractions, expressions of the *unity of determination* of possible phenomena such as the point, line, straightness, equality, etc. These together comprise and express in determinate ways the basic function of objectification: *unification*[31], the Kantian (also Platonic) "unity of the manifold". Only thus are the *unequivocally determinate* "Phenomena" of the sciences (particularly the natural sciences) possible; only the phenomenon which is *determined* in this way can be called a datum of knowledge and serve as a basis for further determinations. Whoever seeks the object in appearance seeks such unequivocal determinations. Even common representation seeks them; in its naming, in the unified meaning of words, it has at least an analogy to those unities which ground the sciences. These basic scientific unities attempt to fulfill in a more developed and durable way the same tasks which language fulfills sufficiently for the immediate purposes of practical life. Even the Positivist intends his positive facts to mean something unequivocally determinate, as all his expressions betray. But one asks in vain how this determinacy, this positiveness would be possible without the determining and thus "positing" function[32] whose original rights we have asserted.

This should have sufficiently proven the independence and priority of the objective grounding of knowledge as opposed to the subjective. Science not only may not, it cannot proceed from anything other than objective unities; there is just no other possible beginning for knowledge. It is completely impossible to grasp the ultimate subjectivity in itself; it can only be determined by objective unities in concepts. Something which cannot be grasped for itself in a way appropriate to knowledge cannot be used to support knowledge. So we have justified the autonomy of objective knowledge and its claim to be allowed to seek its grounding only in its own internal connections[33]. In that network of connections every more concrete objectification first presupposes highly conceptual determinations which make it possible. Science therefore correctly takes these highest unities as its foundation, its secure beginning on an already objectivized basis. Thus what we believed necessary to assume from the outset has held good: that the grounding of the objective validity of knowledge can and must itself be thoroughly objective. Questions about the subjective origins of knowledge do have legitimacy and significance, but both their legitimacy and significance are derived and, so to speak, borrowed. The true and original legitimacy lies on the side of objective unities, as we had hoped.

We might designate the law of *lawfulness itself as* the basic objective law of knowledge. This is the law that the view of things according to laws[34] is the true and objective view. All specific laws of knowledge are only the specific concrete forms of this basic law. The two beloved propositions of formal logic, non-contradiction and sufficient reason, are only very abstract *analytical* versions of this basic law whose concrete, i.e., synthetic, form it was Kant's great undertaking to discover.

We must call the grounding of knowledge reached in such a way absolutely objective, not subjective. The demand for the autonomy of knowledge has been fulfilled, for grounding occurs through knowledge's own law. This grounding belongs to a different genus, moves in the opposite direction than that reconstruction or original subjectivity in which we saw the most acceptable sense of the demand for a psychological grounding of knowledge. Nor does the objective presuppose the psychological, but rather forms the indispensable prerequisite for the psychological view. To authenticate the laws of knowledge we must move in the *constructive* direction of knowledge, in the direction of *objectification*, for it is the ultimate *objective* unities we seek.

With this our main task is accomplished. Some supplementary observations which would be useful for further explanation of the relationship between objective and subjective grounding may be left untouched for the present. To begin with, one could comment on the positive significance and methods of subjective grounding (especially considering the relationship between logic and psychology), to which could properly be appended the contemplated elucidation of Kant's position on our question. Secondly, on the basis of our findings, the type of lawfulness which belongs to the objective laws of knowledge could be more exactly determined. This is a point over which a certain lack of clarity reigns among logicians. Thirdly, it might seem appropriate to at least point out the next steps which logic should take beyond the fundamental determinations which we have reached. These three points may be kept in reserve for another essay.[35]

Notes

1. Original "Über objective und subjective Begründung der Erkenntniss," was published in *Philosophische Monatshefte* xxiii (1887), pp. 257–286, trans. by Lois Phillips and David Kolb. Natorp's *Einleitung in die Psychologie* (Freiburg i. B.,: Mohr), published in 1888, section 14 bears the same title and covers similar arguments. – Ed.
2. *Erkenntnis*
3. *Gegenstand*
4. Throughout the essay Natorp uses "*Objekt*" and "*Gegenstand*" and their derivatives interchangeably. I have translated both by "object". – Trans.
5. *Bedeutung*
6. Natorp uses "Sinn" and "Bedeutung" and their derivatives in a somewhat confusing fashion. I have preserved the difference by translating "Sinn" as "meaning" and "Bedeutung" as "significance" throughout. – Trans.
7. *Sinn*
8. *Sein*
9. *erklären*
10. *Wahre*
11. *Tätigkeit*
12. *Erlebnis*
13. I.e. *sub-ject, hypo-keimenon*, that which underlies. – Trans.
14. *Zusammenhang*
15. *Geltung*
16. *Zusammenhang*
17. *Zusammenhang*
18. *Sache*
19. *Vorstellung*
20. *Rätsel*
21. *vorhanden*
22. *Betrachtung*
23. *Sein*
24. *Zusammenhang*
25. *constatieren*
26. *festgestellt*
27. *vorhanden*
28. *Betrachtung*
29. *Innbegriff*
30. *Setzung*
31. *Einsetzung*
32. "*setzende*" *Funktion*

33 *Zusammenhang*
34 *gesetzmäßige Ansicht*
35 No single essay of Natorp's fulfills the promissory note with which this essay ends, but the topics are treated in his larger systematic writings, the *Logische Grundlagen* and the *Allgemeine Psychologie*, and in such essays as "Quantität und Qualität in Begriff, Urteil und gegenständlicher Erkenntnis," *Philosophische Monatshefte* xxvii (1890) pp. 1 ff. and pp. 129 ff. and "Zur Frage der logischen Methode. Mit Beziehung auf E. Husserls *Logische Untersuchungen*". *Kantstudien* vi (1901), pp. 270 ff. – Trans.

Chapter 12

"Kant and the Marburg School" (1912)

TRANSLATED BY FRANCES BOTTENBERG[1]

The Society[2] to which I have the honor of addressing myself today is well-respected and flourishing – clear evidence that the philosophy of Kant, so often labeled passé, survives and is well among us. Anyone wishing to advance in philosophy today considers it his first duty to come to terms with Kantian philosophy. This duty is recognized to a special degree, though, by a philosophical school whose original intention it was to examine Kant's theories in their immutable historical form, to understand them from within their own principle, and not to judge them through some externally derived means.

That said, it was never anyone's wish nor intent to cling to Kant's doctrines in an absolute way. Talk of an orthodox Kantianism within the Marburg School was never justified, and it has lost every shred of supposed justification as this school has continued to develop. Hermann Cohen, in his three basic texts dedicated to the interpretation of Kant, constantly drove this point home, and rightly so: one must clarify the literal senses of Kantian tenets and their inherent, documented core concepts before venturing beyond Kant. Cohen was not denying (as it is in fact not deniable) that there is more than one tendency at work in Kant, and that no straightforward equilibrium between the various motifs has been established. This very insight invites the following questions: What was Kant's key act? Where is his thought the most forceful, thematically speaking? Closely related but not identical questions include: What was the crucial historical effect of his thought? Which of his teachings were destined to fade, and which to survive and develop further, fueled by an inner vitality? An historian of philosophy who is himself a philosopher would not hesitate to pose such questions. They in turn suggest that a return to Kant is desirable per se to revisit the inalienable insight which he supplied to philosophy, and to continue to explore its consequences for the enrichment of philosophy's eternal questions. According to the classical meaning of the term, philosophy is the eternal striving for fundamental truth, not the aspiring to possess it. Kant in particular, grasping philosophy as critique and as method, wanted to teach philosophizing rather than "a" philosophy. He who thinks otherwise is a poor student of Kant!

Cohen suggested that the *transcendental method* is the core notion to which everything else in Kant relates, from whose vantage point everything is to be conceived and evaluated. For this reason, it played a key role in his presentations; individual treatises were of importance only relative to their being a pure expression of this method. Cohen's three books on Kant's theory of experience, his ethics, and his aesthetics[3] aim with a strict purpose and conscious focus on this alone: to expose the method as that which moves things forward and pushes on, as the creative power fueling Kant's conceptions. It is precisely because [Kant's] individual treatises are not really pure and complete expressions of the method that Cohen subjected them to ever deeper and more incisive critique. The method is indeed everywhere at work in them, yet serious curtailment and modification is frequently required if they are to conform to it.

The philosophy of Kant, as it is, as a whole, as a system, cannot ultimately be viewed as a codex of laws that fell from the sky. Taken in its entirety, Kant's philosophy is without doubt a brilliant accomplishment on a par with any other in the history of human thought, and it flows within the great stream of progress in philosophy, science and humanistic culture. It belongs to a remarkable intellectual heritage that reaches back at least to Plato and Parmenides and that in modern times extends to Descartes and Leibniz, but also to Galileo, Huygens, Newton, Euler, as well as nearly all of the philosophically oriented scientists. Cohen was aware of this from the very beginning. On the one hand, his scholarly work on Plato reaches further back than even his work on Kant. On the other hand, his special study on the principle of the infinitesimal directly reveals how deeply he was absorbed in the philosophical aspect of the history of exact science. My studies of Galileo, Descartes, and so on, Cassirer's book on Leibniz, and all of his work on the problem of knowledge from Nicolas of Cusa to Kant, are all the fruit of Cohen's suggestions, as is so much else in the history and critique of the sciences that has come from our school since then. What we have researched and presented these past three decades on the philosophy of Plato, Aristotle, Democritus, skepticism, and so on, all lies along this trajectory. Little wonder, then, that Cohen's completely updated "theory of experience" of 1885[4], as contrasted with that of 1871, reveals the beginnings of a very independent future terrain for theoretical philosophy. His writings on ethics and aesthetics drew on Kant's doctrines perhaps even more freely. Cohen's creation of his own system, the three most powerful pillars of which already exist, removed any last vestige of a rigid Kantianism within the Marburg School. It would not have been possible for me, nor the flock of younger researchers who enrich our school, to have entered into consortium with our honored leader, had this thematically open attitude not won out against the attitude of sticking to the letter of Kantian law and to Cohen's reading of that law; it is what justifies talk of a school in the first place. In a certain sense, I was of course never a student of Cohen. Yet even those who were, were never students in the narrow sense, as if there were "a" philosophy valid there. Instead, one became familiar with and propagated a method of philosophizing. This was consistent with Cohen's principles and the whole style of his teaching. That said, we were all well aware of having learned the method from him. Thus it can be guaranteed that all of our work, even in its utter independence or indeed even because of it, will invariably fit together in a useful manner and will possess a consistent character, to a degree rarely seen in the history of philosophy.

As a result of this, that which was not searched for has presented itself: in the *necessary corrections of Kant's teachings* endeavored among us, a great thematic unity prevails despite some particular differences of formulation. To give account of this is the challenge I have set myself for this talk, and I request your friendly attention as I attempt to meet it.

Our fixed point of departure, the steadfast leading idea of our entire philosophizing is, as noted, the "transcendental method." We distinguish it, notably with reference to Kant's multi-faceted use of the term "transcendental," from the psychological as well as the metaphysical, and also from a mere logical method in the old Aristotelian and perhaps Wolffian sense. Modern "logistics," despite having made very important progress in exceptional cases, strays little from the latter in its basic trajectory, beginning as it does with ultimate, irreducible terms or unprovable, axiomatic statements, and proceeding with pure judgments of identity ("analytic" judgments in the Kantian sense). The duty to seek a foundation ought to be taken seriously, and we also think this foundation should be sought in a purely objective way. Nevertheless, it remains totally manifest that the old way of Aristotelian apodicticity cannot amount to much in the study of the principles of human cognition. Kant rightfully declined to give "proofs" in the Aristotelian apodictic sense for his foundational principles.

What, then, do we mean when we demand, with Kant and even more strictly than he, a "transcendental" foundation or justification, a *deductio iuris* (as Kant says) for every philosophical statement? The transcendental method comprises two essential parts. The first is the secure reference back to current, historically verifiable facts of science, morals, art and religion, given that philosophy does not wish to breathe in the "airless space"[5] of pure thought, in which simple understanding seeks to alight on the wings of ideas. Recalling Kant's evocative words, philosophy eschews the "high towers" of the metaphysical master-builders, around which there is "commonly much wind"; it searches out the "fruitful bathos, the bottom-land" of experience in the broadest sense of the word, i.e., it strives to root itself firmly in the total creative work of culture.[6] This includes "spelling out appearances" scientifically,[7] practical forms of social order and the life of human dignity for the individual living within these, artistic creation and the aesthetic sculpting of life, and even the most intimate forms of religious life. For, "In the beginning was the deed," it is the generative act which creates all manner of objects. Only humankind builds its own human essence and, by objectivating itself therein, imprints in the deepest and most completely unified manner the character of its spirit onto its world. There is indeed a whole world of such worlds, all of which humankind can call its own.

The creative foundation for all such acts of object formation remains the *law*, however, which is ultimately that primordial law described quite aptly as the *logos*, *ratio*, and *reason*. And now for the second, key requirement of the transcendental method: verifying the basis of the "possibility" of the fact and therewith its "warrant," i.e., to show that law's foundation, to show the unity of logos or reason [*Ratio*] in all constructive acts of culture, and to uncover its pure form. For when the act of formation itself occurs first, its own purity, i.e., the strict, unwavering lawfulness of configuration is not necessarily guaranteed. Thus, in that the method of philosophy always remains strictly and exclusively directed at the constructive act of object formation of all kinds, but only recognizes that act in its purely lawful basis and secures it in this cognition, so from a certain perspective philosophy naturally rises above the act, "transcends" it in this purely methodological sense. Yet this methodological ascendance to a higher plane of observation, implied by the word "transcendental," in no way conflicts with the immanence of the real experiential standpoint, but instead coincides precisely with it. This is because the method does not force laws on the experiential act from the outside, nor prematurely lay down the tracks which it must follow. Rather, it seeks to uncover in its purity that law which makes experience "possible in the first place," even as a task. Once securely conscious of this law, the method's own law is also prepared for future development and protected from distraction. This is how the transcendental method becomes a "critical" one: critical of metaphysical encroachments, but also critical of a lawless, law-eluding empiricism. It makes the autonomy of experience count against both the heteronomy of any metaphysicalism that seeks to master it and the anomy of an empiricism devoid of or even quite hostile to laws.

This being said, such an immanent method cannot locate the law of objective formation anywhere else but in that objective formation itself, in the creation of human cultural life that is always at work and never concluded. For this reason, it simultaneously preserves a strict *objective* character, hence distinguishing itself sharply from any "*psychologism.*" Even though Kant, and also Cohen in his first writings, fearfully avoided the language of psychology, the deep difference between the transcendental perspective and that of psychology was nonetheless often apparent, even to the point that there remains not terribly much left to learn in this respect, not even from Husserl's fine expositions (in the first volume of the *Logical Investigations*), which we gladly welcomed. Not that it was our desire to shut psychology out of philosophy entirely, to unconditionally hand it over to empiricism – psychology simply cannot serve as a basis for philosophy. To lend logos to psyche, language to the soul, is not the first, but rather exactly the last job of philosophy. The immediate within spiritual-intellectual experience does not reach us immediately, it only reaches us retrospectively through its objectivations. These must therefore be secured ahead of time in their purely objective founding.

One justified motive is nevertheless entailed by the return to the immediate, concrete "life" of consciousness in the face of all mere abstractions, whether these appear in science or in philosophy. That motive is the well-justified intention to safe-guard the unendingly fluid life of consciousness against absolutistic philosophy's pretence towards mastery, towards real violation, towards stilling the eternally coursing stream of that life by means of pure logic and a set sum of conceptual elements. The transcendental method, as an immanent method, poses no such danger; it is itself *forward moving* and has arisen out of *infinite* development. The transcendental method is not inflexible, trapped in the stasis of the Eleatic world, nor does it circle a simple fixed point or run along fixed tracks in an eternally balanced cycle, as did the stellar world of ancient astronomy. This is precisely what philosophy as "method" tells us: all fixed "being" must fall into a "gait," a *movement* of thought. Only in this way can the Eleatic, and in general the idealistic equating of being with thinking lose its seemingly bleak tautology, which grounds being in thinking only by means of freezing thinking into a new thing-like being. True idealism is certainly not that of Eleatic "being," nor of the rigid "Ideas" (still Eleatic) of Plato's early period. Instead, it is that of "movement," of the "transformation" of concepts, the "limiting of the unlimited" of Plato's *Sophist*, the eternal "becoming towards being" of the *Philebus*. These notions are echoed in Kant, when he describes thinking as spontaneity, i.e., as production[8] from an infinite foundation[9], and hence as action and function. They also surface in the conclusion to the transcendental analytic, when understanding in respect to "form" qua lawful function is posited as the originator, not just the translator of nature (i.e., the Nature of natural science). These notions are shown especially lucidly and poignantly in the dissolution of the antinomy, which liberates "experience," as unending task, from every dogmatic barrier. Precisely in view of the infinite progression of experience, the antinomy's dissolution also frees the "thing in itself" from the fixed place it initially seemed to inhabit, and transforms it into a purely liminal concept, which constrains experience in nothing but its own creative law, just as the mathematicians' "infinitely distant point" expresses the unwavering directional unity of the infinite line. This directional unity originates with the line rather than being assigned to it from the outside. For, to be sure, the "gait" of experience cannot be considered directionless, even in its infinity. The word "method," *metienai*, does not only imply a "going"[10], a moving oneself forward, nor, as Hegel thinks, a mere going along with or alongside; rather it means a going towards a goal, or in any case going in a secure direction: a "going after"[11]. Philosophy, too, is not interested in just any arbitrary method, a strategy which could produce a new method for every new task. It instead asks about "the" method, about the conclusive unity of method, in which "the" cognition, the conclusive unity of cognition, and therewith the creative act of culture, are grounded. Cohen clearly and powerfully captured the unity of this inexhaustible source of lawful formation with his principle of "origination": nothing can be taken as "given" without any tracing-back[12], without at least a possible traceability[13] back to the ultimate ground of the unity of productive cognition[14]. A "givenness" cannot mean more than the character of the yet to be solved task – the task of giving evidence for origination[15] from the ground of the unity of cognition. This task may be infinite; in the final analysis it always is. Yet precisely for this reason it always persists as a task. There is no such thing, there could be no such thing, as a "given" in the sense of something completed, resolved, something which draws away from the ever pervading work of cognition. Along the same lines, the *procedural* character of cognition is worth emphasizing: its character as *fieri*[16], rather than as rigid, resolved fact; in other words, its "becoming," in Plato's sense of becoming being, as the movement towards a being, rather than the coming to a halt in resting being. The demand for a conclusive unity of method, and also for its unending continuation, lies in the demand for the method itself. If one does not think these contained therein, then it immediately becomes doubtful whether philosophy persists even as a task; philosophy's continued existence becomes dubious for all those who remain uncommitted to this strict demand for unity.

This basic idea of philosophy as method, then, has led us to believe that we have grasped the core, unassailable basic content of the "transcendental method," and hence also the unassailable basic content of Kant's philosophy. Their core lies in the method of idealism, as the method of infinite, creative development. We believe ourselves to be the first to have carried out these ideas faithfully. That said, this basic motive is indeed at work, is even ultimate throughout Kant's writing. It makes the lawfulness of nature and of morals a self-governance of reason, and artistic production and even religion into a never-ending, singular act of the human spirit. It makes the world our own, just as the words of Schiller, the Kantian among the poets, state: "It is not *outside*, the fool looks for it there, It is *inside* you, *out of you it ever arises*".[17] Kant's doctrine, available to us in its historically contingent nature, nonetheless does stray from this core consideration neither infrequently nor non-trivially. It is thus in need of correction, following the inexorable demand of its own deepest and most ultimate principle.

Right at the entry into the *Critique* we run into the old problem: "intuition"[18], a different and special mode of givenness from the side of the affecting[19] object and of receptivity from the side of the affected[20] subject, is contrasted with *thinking*, which is the only unique function of cognition and is pure spontaneity. If the core idea of the transcendental method is to be taken seriously, it is simply not possible to leave this dualism of cognitive factors unresolved.

As a result, the givenness of *sensation*[21] must be posited as the "material" of cognition alongside subjective receptivity and objective affectivity. One ought no longer to speak of given "manifolds" which the understanding, bound further to the given forms of intuition, must simply line up, link together and – retrospectively – re-cognize. This signals, though, that the whole sense of "synthesis" or "apperception," in short, almost everything in Kant's formulations, must change.

How can the affective effect[22] of an object correspond to a certain receptive mode on the part of the subject – that is the initial, well-established question. Put differently: how can a subject and an object, existing prior to cognition and within a given (affecting) and receiving (affected) causal relationship, be assumed at all, let alone placed at the very start, so that they underlie all that follows? This precisely suggests the desire to build cognition from the outside, letting it emerge from a causal relationship of an obviously transcendent nature, despite the fact that an extra-cognitive standpoint is unthinkable. Such a fall back into metaphysicalism is absolutely incompatible with the transcendental method; it is moreover wholly dissolved by Kant's radical conclusion, upon which all the significance and justice of the critical method is founded: All relations to the object, all concepts of the object as well as of the subject arise in cognition alone, following its law. The thing must orient itself to cognition, rather than cognition to the thing, if a lawful relation between them is to be at all conceivable.

At the same time, Kant's distinctions between intuition and thinking, form and matter, possess a profound fact-bound rationale[23]. For Kant, the first of these distinctions expresses a great, indeed a crucial accomplishment, namely that time and space, as forms of intuition, must be sharply distinguished from concepts of pure thinking, yet they are still not sensuous givens. He perceives this, with good reason, to be a very important step beyond Plato and Leibniz towards idealism, believing to have discovered an *a priori* even of sensibility. Purely factually however, as a "fact" of science, the distinction between space and time as individual, singular constructions and a conceptual "genericum," as Euler (1748) aptly put it, undeniably existed. But are space and time, as plainly individual, singular constructions – given – to us? Certainly, world-time and Newton's cosmic space[24] were such singular constructions, such fixed hierarchies, and could not themselves change their station. It was hence necessary, by virtue of their concept and whole function in cognition, to *think* of them as plainly unique, unshakeable and absolute. Indeed, the possibility of a "fact" pure and simple and even its mere concept *demands* this, for, without fixed temporal and spatial reference, the fact would lack the definite determinacy that its very concept entails. But that such constructions are no less *given* in the absolute that is so necessary for thought is already made clear enough by Newton himself, and Kant champions the idea with forceful argumentation. They must be given, or at least could be given, whenever an object of experience, a "fact" per se, is given, i.e., is to be conclusively determined. For such determinacy undoubtedly includes determinacy in respect to time and place, and the latter would have no meaning as a condition, were the points in space and time themselves not fixedly determinate, in other words: thought of as given. Consequently, natural science can confidently assert this premise, take it as foundational, for it would not get anywhere without it, indeed not even get started – for what would occupy it if there were no "facts"? This point aside, the stability and absoluteness of the spatio-temporal order is not given, and could never be given. Instead, that which the scientific fact secures is only an *intention* directed at that stability. This intention lies compulsively in all empirical method, in its very conception. Givenness *means* unique determination, thus of a spatio-temporal nature, in respect to a unique time and a unique place. But this "givenness" itself is not *given, but rather demanded* by thought. For thought means determining; nothing is determined for cognition, which it has not itself determined. At the same time, determination per se is demanded to an unlimited extent. It is a determination to leave *nothing indeterminate*. This determination of the object (as "fact") as demanded by thought is thus also achieved by thought – the only way it can ultimately be achieved. It is achieved by means of the *venture of the hypothesis*[25], which is entirely unavoidable if the process of experience is to be put into gear at all and to be kept running. Just as my foot must take its stand[26] if it is to walk, holding a stance[27] is necessary, but so is continually leaving that stance. This is the only way to understand "assessment"[28], for it is only in this manner that assessment fixes the transitive points[29] of time and space. Their very stability is mere hypothesis and can never get beyond hypothetical validity, as continually demonstrated by the modern, radical relativization of the concepts of time and space. In respect to the "fact of science," especially as it has shaped itself since Kant, Kant himself would surely have fully understood (for in many respects he was ready for this) that in the basic determinations of time and space, thinking takes shape in a downright typical fashion *as a "function,"* rather than as an "intuition" that retains something of the character of mere receptivity. "Givenness" itself becomes a problem – the problem of thinking. I submit that Kant himself prepares this turn in many ways. In the *Transcendental Aesthetic*, the unity of time and space was not simply (as he said) "counted as sensibility," but in fact formed the distinct character of sensible intuition. In the "*Transcendental Deduction*" (second edition) it is quite obvious that this unity initially rests on an achievement of thinking, in which "the understanding determines the sensibility" such that space and time "can first be given as intuitions"[30]. The systematic place for this achievement of "reason," however, would of course be *modality*, the modal category of reality, which, being a category, expresses not a conclusion of cognition, but rather only a "condition of *possible* experience" (emphasis added).

In the end, "intuition" no longer remains a cognitive factor which stands across from or is opposed to thinking. It *is* thinking, just not thinking in terms of laws[31], but thinking in terms of full objects[32]. In its implementation, in its exercise, intuition is to conceptual thought[33] as function is to the law of function. This requires that every one of its stages be strictly and unambiguously determined, but they must be determined in respect to the lawful functions of thinking itself: particularity, quantity, quality and causal reciprocality must be determined according to their respective laws. The result is something which *is* "given" for the first time, but which seemed to *be* given as a fixed sum. This makes quite transparent the following oddly illuminating sentence (which appears in the section concerning the highest principle of synthetic judgments): "To give an object, if this is not again meant only mediately, but it is rather to be exhibited immediately in intuition, is nothing other than to relate its representation to experience (whether this be actual or still possible)"[34]. Kant is only now in a position to prove the "possibility" of experience within a system of grounding principles. Givenness has transformed itself into a *postulate* of reality; it adopts purely modal meaning.

This is pure idealism and nothing else. To neither consider nor straightforwardly carry out this radical correction, which at its core is a self-correction already contained in Kant, would entail giving up the most profound dimension of the critique of reason, only for the sake of saving, at any cost, the long-disproven, stale provisions of the *Transcendental Aesthetic* contained in the inaugural dissertation of 1770 (an at least partially if not wholly dogmatic account).

Entirely the same thing must be said regarding the givenness of the "material"[35] of cognition, which represents "*sensation*" in the same preliminary provisions of the *Transcendental Aesthetic* that set up the concept of "intuition." This givenness, too, has to take on the modal category of reality, and only that category. Sensation itself becomes the plain expression of the *problem* of experiential determinateness and the *intentional* claim to reality of a particular quantity, quality and relation. Already in the *Transcendental Deduction*, sensation essentially becomes the setting of the particular in "apprehension," just as perception does in the process of "reproduction," which in truth is more like the production of a picture of reality. While the concept of sensation expresses the ultimate determinacy of the empirical-real, it is only fulfilled in the determining acts of "re-cognition"[36]. This cannot be the "recognition"[37] of a prior given identity, but must simply be the original positing of an identity – even if, according to the clear conclusion of the transcendental method, thinking cannot be anything that it has not itself determined.

The distinctive character of "intuition" and "sensation" is not irreplaceably lost. It merely ceases to imply a second, totally independent cognitive element that ultimately contrasts with and controls thinking, something that is alien to thought, which thinking must completely join itself to. Determining is thinking; experiential determinateness hence must be the full determinateness of thought, in contrast to the abstract determinateness of the general laws, which simply points to determinacy and possibilities for determination, rather than being real determinacy itself. "Spontaneity" is both law on the one hand, and real fulfillment of spontaneous determination on the other, which receives nothing from the outside, as in accordance with the law. Kant helpfully describes this as the "exercise of spontaneity" at one point.[38]

Some have wondered whether our claim concerning the pure spontaneity of cognition causes a particular difficulty for *experiment*. How could one ever deny, though, that the statement that formulates the result of an experiment is composed *of* determinations of thought, not *as* determinations of thought? This touches upon identity and difference, as these exist within a continuum, and upon numerical and most of all relational determinations: If A, then B; if not A, then not B, etc. All of this would be completely meaningless outside of thought, except as a determination of thought.

It is the distinction just mentioned that regularly creates the semblance of a falling out of thought: the venture towards full determination, which of course "mere" thinking (in the sense of thinking in terms of laws) could not justify on its own. The meaning of and justification for this venture has already been noted. That it is a *venture* and of *thought*, however, becomes evident every time a fresh experiment corrects the supposedly fixed result of an earlier one, exposes indeterminacies in places where full determinacy was assumed reached, and supplants these with more refined and careful limiting determinations[39]. Certainly, such determination is neither voluntarily nor straightforwardly in our hands; but this simply supports the assumption that causal relationships preside across the entirety of nature's expanse – which is precisely the assumption of thinking. For surely causality, despite Hume, is not "given," but is rather first posited in a special way by thinking, and, when cognized, is only hypothetically cognized, meaning that it is certain within thinking. Such a cognition is obviously an achievement of thought, an attempt to construct unity, and nothing else. Critical idealism is not making an extravagant claim here, since it holds that all experience only contains hypothetical positings. It is empiricism that talks of absolute data which exist yet which even the most probing research cannot verify, but only continually reveal as deception. Thus, while empiricism, at odds with idealism, always turns out to be a false absolutism, transcendental idealism, by not recognizing an experiential absolute, turns out to be the true empiricism.

One scolds idealism for being "absolute" insofar as it excludes from thought every element that is alien to thought, in an absolute way, and allows for no instance of cognition outside of cognition. But how could it admit something alien to thought within thinking, even something only minimally alien; how could it admit the irrational into reason[40] itself? Nothing irrational, nothing utterly unthought is negated in claiming that what stands outside of reason is indistinguishable, and that what cannot even be thought, can certainly not be cognized. Instead, something truly irrational is cognized precisely when cognition – let's say theoretical cognition – executes the unending, never completing or completable process of thinking, i.e., the determining of the indeterminate that occurs when the supposed "given" of experience becomes an *X*, something to be determined but never simply determinable. That is to say, there is no "absolute" that thinking comes up to like a bare wall and must halt before. If that were so, one could rightly complain: "Into nature no created spirit can enter – joyful is he who merely sees its outer shell!"[41] Kant, as well as Goethe (with his "Oh thou Philistine!"),[42] have protected themselves from this absolute outer shell. "Observation and analysis of the appearances," Kant responds to the "philistine," "penetrate into what is inner in nature, and one cannot know how far this will go in time".[43] To be sure, one cannot know; one could at most claim to know that this process reaches infinity, but never the conclusive absolute, which one had falsely and emptily thought of in connection with this "inner" of nature. This would force cognition to a halt; yet cognition is not inertia, but an eternal progression. We naturally deny, then, an absolute irrational element, in other words a negative absolute, something that is absolutely *not* cognizable, and yet is still given. We deny such an irrational element, but we do not deny the irrational as the *me on*[44] of *Ratio*, as reason's non-being in the sense of its correlative opposite term – as that *X*, which forever eludes our attempts to cognize and to rationalize it. This must naturally be so, and eternally; it will never be exhausted by means of any rationalization.

This very insight also secures transcendental idealism from all danger of returning to any kind of *subjectivism*. The presumption of a subject existing beyond, before or outside of cognition is as unacceptable to us as the notion of an object existing beyond, before or outside it. This is because from the start we only permit talk of the contents of the positings of thought. What appeared as subjectivism in Kant has now been wholly dissolved as a result of the above considerations. What remains of it is only the character of the conditionality[45] of object cognition, which is itself founded on the endless gradation[46] of thinking as it is directed at the object. At each respectively attained cognitive stage, the object is an object once and for all, rather than being a "not yet" for every higher stage, and a "not anymore" for every lower one. This should not cast doubt on the objective character of cognition, however. Objectivation remains de-subjectivation, a filtering out of the subjective. Subjectivation is only a subsequent, not an antecedent problem, hence the problem of *psychology*. Object relations of all kinds are foundational to all subject relations. While recent philosophers enjoy working with the distinction of "content" and "object," this is surely justified for the purpose of contrasting opposite approaches[47], but not an absolute distinction. There are no absolute subjective contents, as little as there is an absolute trans-subjective object. Instead, what is on one level "contents," was on a lower one "object"; what on one level is an object that is only now cognizable, is, as now cognized, "content" in a higher one, which in turn refers to a more distant "object" = X that has yet to be cognized. The contrast between subjective and objective relativizes itself, but in such a way that the direction[48] of objectivation is prior to subjectivity. Subjectivity is only retrogressively definable in relation to the lower levels of objectivation. Malebranche grasped this insight peculiarly clearly. It is there in Kant, too, but not followed through on. This idea helps shed light on even the difficult phrase "objective self-consciousness," without any hint of psychologizing or even of objective cognition itself. The unconditional rejection of subjectivism is incidentally expressed often enough by Kant himself (most strongly in the *Prolegomena* and the second account of the "Paralogism"), just as he very clearly distinguishes transcendental idealism from every subjective idealism.

Having said all of this, if the transcendental method is to reach its full import, *one* substantial challenge remains to be addressed. In Kant, the pure functions of thought appear alongside the forms of intuition, taking the shape of a seemingly only historically derived table of judgments and categories, which operate as fixed givens, albeit of thought. To be sure, Kant thought to have determined the "system" of categories "according to a principle," expressly seeking exhaustiveness. Yet as everyone today accepts, in so doing he relies all too uncritically on the "finished work" of logicians, considering it necessary to correct only minor deficiencies. The wholly new role which he assigns the categories, however, demands a radical new beginning, instead of mere mending activities. If this thinking, which is to be understood as method and as method of unity,[49] is not capable of proving its own strict inner unity, then the notion that being is grounded in thinking remains merely an opaque catchphrase. Here "unity" is meant not in the sense of the fixed singularity of a principle or of a system that is subdivided yet set in its subdivision – in other words, as it appears in Kant; but rather in the sense of correlation, which does not exclude the possibility of development, even infinite development. For this reason, there is no straightforwardly descending rational grounding[50] to be sought here, and thus no deduction in the Aristotelian sense (as already mentioned at the beginning). Instead, a compelling relation of mutual implication is revealed, which actually precludes antecedent/consequent relations. This relation is made up of cognitive posts[51] leaning into one another, which hold each other and the entire construction up. Thus, in Cohen, the construction of the pure functions of thought is concentric, and it is very clear that the center would mean as little without its relation to the expanding periphery, as the periphery would without relation to the center. Cohen seeks the proof for the adequacy of his construction not just in the fact that these exact presumptions, in this relation to one another, are necessary and sufficient for the methods and lawfulnesses of the concrete sciences. That is a mere *a posteriori* proof that cannot offer more than provisional security, since the "fact of science" is an eternal *Fieri*. Instead, he seeks to show that these functions of thought all mutually require one another and could not persist without one another, such that from each individual securely arrived at function all others can be reached. I attempted a still simpler rational grounding in *Logische Grundlagen*[52] that stems directly from the requirements for "synthetic unity," i.e., the thoroughgoing reciprocality that makes up the entire being of thinking.

All of these explorations ought still be taken further, and our most intense efforts are now needed. We might seem to be following entirely in the tracks of Fichte and Hegel, who, as it is well-known, began at this precise point. We have been seeking to overcome the dualism of intuition and thinking, and of form and matter, just as they did. We must part ways with them, though, in their attempts to meet the demands which the basic idea of the transcendental method originally posed and which Kant himself did not completely meet in an obvious way. Hegel apparently formulated the three-step[53] of the "dialectical method" from indications left by Kant (especially regarding the three once-and-for-all categories of each class, which contrasts with the yes or no dichotomy supposed necessarily to hold for logical divisions). Incidentally, the core of the dialectical idea is already evident in *The Sophist*, when Plato juxtaposes the "one" with the "other," as *its* other, its *me on*[54], and then goes on to grasp this contrast as a correlation, as a continuity, indeed an interpenetration, whereby all thinking dissolves itself into movement and process (*kinesis*). The motif of the "being of non-being," i.e., relative non-being, gave rise to Cohen's concept of origin, and its manifold creative significance is emphasized in N. Hartmann's book on Plato. Thus, it is the gesture towards an infinite development, present in Plato already, the gesture towards thinking as the "limiting of the limitless" and as an infinity itself, i.e., a positively inexhaustible self-development, that first makes Kant's "idea" as infinite task transparent and compelling. It is precisely in this continuous infinitude that the unity of thought is both secured and clarified. In the process, this unity of thought casts off any appearance of the "principle" being a fixed singularity, and for the first time becomes a unity of "the manifold" in the full sense, i.e., a unity through correlation, a unity of simultaneously infinite and continuous development.

No doubt we have somewhat approached the great idealists in all of this, notably Hegel. But in the end there is nothing particularly Hegelian about our analysis, since Hegel's work was itself the germination of seeds already present in Kant and even Plato. These Hegelian features could just as well be called Platonic. We link Plato with Kant, as Hegel did, and this creates significant and deep similarities between our accounts, even down to the particulars; various accounts have pointed this out in recent times, von Aster's Munich papers being perhaps the most accurate.

Deep differences remain, however. Hegel presumes to have brought the lawfulness of thinking to an absolute conclusion, which he invariably describes as circular and which is expected to produce the entire contents of thought. It is for this reason that his philosophy could adopt the outrageous pretense of itself being the conclusion of philosophy, in the form of absolute philosophy, which is at the same time absolute science. Transcendental idealism, as we view it, is legions away from such pretense; in an entirely non-Hegelian manner, it presents philosophy with the modest task of critique, or, positively applied, of method. This method is thought to be immanent to research and quite generally to cultural achievement, but also to be open to infinite further development. Consequently, this method, as absolute as it is in its unifying conditions[55], cannot in any sense be conclusively settled by means of a stipulated stage, even after its progression into particularity[56]. Such a commitment would after all constrain research and the creative deed of cultural production more generally. This is exactly what the transcendental method must fundamentally and absolutely reject. It does so by referring the task of philosophy strictly to the *factum*, rather than the eternal *Fieri* of cultural production.

Of course, as Hegel did, we view the X to be cognized only in relation to the functions of cognition itself. Following a close analogy, it is for us the X in a cognitive equation[57], whose whole meaning as that very X (i.e., that which is to be determined) only becomes comprehensible in relation to the equation and the data of the equation, i.e., the lawful modes of the determination of thought. But we have admitted that this "equation" in our cognition is of such a character that it leads to an infinite calculation and that X is therefore never conclusively determinable via an A, B, C, etc. Not to mention the fact that the A, B, C, etc. series would also have to be thought of as non-conclusive and capable of continuous expansion. In contrast, Hegel lets the irrational be wholly resolvable into the rational, and so all becomes thought, and thought becomes all for him. For us, too, all is thought and thought is all, but in an entirely different sense. As it has been said of the genuinely Hegelian ossification[58] of socialism into Marxism: the path is all, the goal, nothing. Despite having not reached his goal, Hegel certainly intended to logically master the path in its entirety, which comes out to the same thing. In the end he was and remains an absolutist. The logical "method" is to him the "absolutely infinite force to which no object ... could offer resistance ... and could not be penetrated by".[59] As an absolute power, it literally cannot lead to an infinite progression.[60] Instead, thanks to it, "the science presents itself as a circle that winds around itself".[61] It simply references itself,[62] the thinking of thought (*noesis noeseōs*, cf. *Encyclopaedia of the Philosophical Sciences* § 236); "as true infinite, bent back upon itself ... *closed* and *wholly present*, without *beginning* and *end*";[63] *fulfilled being*: "being as the *concrete* and ... *intensive* totality" ... ;[64] absolutely certain of itself and internally at rest.[65] "As Spirit that knows what it is, it does not exist before, and nowhere at all, till after the completion of its work"; "it appears in Time just so long as it has not grasped its pure Notion, i.e., has not annulled Time," sublating the difference between objectivity[66] and content.[67] Therefore, following the dictum that has become famous, what is rational is actual, and what is actual is rational; what is eternal is present, what is present is eternal.[68] And so Hegel discards any mere ought-to-be,[69] scoffs at Kant's infinite approximation — "as something 'neither cold nor hot,' it 'spews out of its mouth'".[70] The absolute idea naturally only appears as "the thought of the world ... when actuality has gone through its formative process and attained its completed state".[71] "When philosophy paints its grey in grey, a shape of life has grown old, and it cannot be rejuvenated, but only recognized, by the grey in grey of philosophy; the owl of Minerva begins its flight only with the onset of dusk".[72] Our philosophy lies far from such twilight of the gods' sentiment. Entirely following Kant's lead, it takes the process of world creation, in theory and in practice, as unending, as the consequence of the ever reached and reachable effects of the "equation" of experience, as the "asymptotic approximation" to a goal that is merely ideally posited in the mind's eye. In a good many other respects, Hegel sides with us — one could almost say that he is committed to all of the essential aspects of "critical idealism" that we have described and developed further, except for one: his absolutism. But that is akin to stating that Tycho Brahe was all of one mind with Copernicus, except for the small matter of denying Earth's movement. This particular comparison is fitting in another way, too: notwithstanding the fact that Hegel seeks to ground thought in "process" and in the movement of concepts, his absolutism in reality brings thought to rest. Its world cycle[73] is completed and finished in those four well-known stages; this is what we will never agree to.

Moving away from our conception of the transcendental method, Rickert's newer transcendental idealism takes things in an entirely opposite direction. In contrast to the omnipotence which logic possesses in Hegel, Rickert attempts to severely restrict logic's reign. He does so by questioning our right to conceive number, not to mention time and space, as a purely logical formation. A brief consideration of this view seems in order, since

Rickert's investigation concerning "*Das Eine, die Einheit und die Eins*" (1911) evidently refers to statements I made in *Logische Grundlagen*.[74] In addition, the recent book of Frischeisen-Köhler, *Wissenschaft und Wirklichkeit*[75], assumes that our school's entire conception of the logical has been refuted by the Rickertian inquiry.

I do not think this critique is accurate. Rickert initially agrees with me on the key points of the matter, despite differences of expression. He conceives neither of quality nor — and this is most significant — of quantity in an essentially different manner than I. With great subtlety, he lends the same meanings to distinctions which I accept and which I trace back to Plato. He shows in particular that quantity is neither quality nor a derivative thereof, much less the other way around. But when he concludes that quantity cannot therefore be as logical as quality, he provides scant reason for this claim, save that he prefers to view all thought as qualitative thought. According to my thesis, quantity is certainly not quality, nor quality quantity, yet both stand to one another in such compelling correlation that the one necessarily calls forth the other, the one conditions the other, and both stand and fall together. This conclusion seems to me to follow from Rickert's own assumptions. The genus is founded in quality, which with him is also supposed to represent a "synthesis" of the "manifold." "Homogeneity," which according to Rickert himself is the definitive condition for quantity, is, however, supplied with the genus, insofar as the latter contains the manifold of kinds (at least of those two). Yet how can one possibly speak of a manifold, in other words, a plurality of kind[76], i.e., a plurality of kinds[77], as belonging to one category, and hence to a superordinate category, without the foundation for number being laid down at the same time? After all, just like Plato's *Sophist* and Kant's concept of synthesis, Rickert wants not mere tautology, but heterology. This being the case, he must recognize both of them, along with their bond[78] and indelible correlation; in other words, he must recognize that the same (referentially speaking) can be identical and different, while the concept of identity of course cannot be equated with difference, nor difference with identity. Under these irrefutable assumptions it is not feasible to consider quantity as less logical than quality; indeed, there can be no *logos* — no concept, no judgment, no conclusion — without both being taken together. In my view, it seems plausible that quality is central and quantity peripheral, since, on the one hand, such an arrangement clarifies their necessary interrelation: a center only exists for a periphery, just as a periphery only exists for a center. Conceptually, both are indeed sufficiently distinctive; the central aspect[79] stands to the peripheral like the plus- to the minus-sign. Moreover, in that quantity lies in the peripheral direction of cognition, as it were, it is understandable how quantity could appear alogical in the eyes of someone who narrowly associates "logical" with the central aspect, though it would seem to him the prime alogical aspect, i.e., the alogical aspect that seems closest to the logical. Thus, with Rickert, for instance, quantity is distinct of the spatio-temporally determinate — the intuitive according to Kant — as it is entirely distinct from all empirical givenness, and it seems to straddle the logical and the alogical; even in an *a priori*, rational sense. But this is just what *we* call "logical"; *Ratio* is the translation of *logos*. This strange and ambiguous position, I maintain, is made somewhat comprehensible by the fact that quantity expresses the peripheral direction of the logical, as quality expresses the central one. This is not to say that these aspects are directed at something wholly outside of thinking. Rather, the contrast between inner and outer is absorbed into the contrast within thinking itself of the relation between center and periphery, where thinking is grasped as process. For the periphery of thinking is, as we know, not fixed, but fluid; the cycle of cognition is not to be thought of as having a fixed radius, but a motile one, which extends toward the infinite. The peripheral aspect is thus not thought's relation out toward something wholly alien to it. What, indeed, could such a thing be? Likely that famous "inner nature," which remains forever external, a "shell" to us. But we have had quite enough of *that*.

I ought not further dwell on these comments at this time, for they all have solely to do with theoretical philosophy. The *relation of ethics and aesthetics to theory* in the Marburg School stands in contrast to Hegel's views and must be more closely examined, if only briefly, in particular since colleagues have recently commented on it quite a bit. That there is a profound difference between us and Hegel has been noted by, for instance, von Aster. Yet this difference is not simply that with us, moral values and artistic imagination stand alongside scientific thought as "equal functions, in which consciousness encompasses an objective sphere".[80] Such a view entails that history must either be replaced by natural science – just as psychology is being absorbed into natural science – or, insofar as it is viewed from an ethical standpoint, that history falls outside the bounds of a thoughtful, scientific worldview. If this were our view, the hierarchy of the sciences would apex in mathematical natural science.

Nearly every word in these sentences is in need of revision. Simply placing logic, ethics and aesthetics on par represents our view just as little as Kant's. In this matter, too, we move along a trajectory from Plato to Kant and from Kant to a pure and thorough methodological idealism. The relation of ethics to theory – to pause here for a minute – seems to us, as it did to those thinkers, to be defined by the relation of the *Anhypotheton*[81] to hypothesis, by the relation between that which is unconditioned, i.e., unconditioned lawfulness, and that which is conditioned and conditioned lawfulness. But at work is the *same logos, the same "reason"* that in theory operates at the borders of spatio-temporal and causal contingency[82], and unfolds free of this contingency within ethics. Thus, "logic," in the original broad sense of the doctrine of reason[83], holds a high place with us. It comprises not only theory, in respect to the logic of "possible experience," but ethics, too, in respect to the logic of volition[84], and even aesthetics, in respect to the logic of pure artistic creation. It is the basis for vastly expanding scientific terrains: social science (as the study of economics, justice and education), as well as history, art history, even the study of religion – i.e., the so-called human sciences[85], and not just the natural sciences or mathematics. And these are organized into a particular hierarchy, strictly following the Kantian primacy of practical reason. Nothing has hence less warrant than the accusation made by Windelband against Cohen concerning a purported naturalization of ethics, whose counterpoint is found in von Aster's accusation against myself concerning a purported naturalization (irrationalization, de-scientification) of history. How one could glean such a conception from our writings is mysterious. "Nature" is not a final absolute for us, the apex of the hierarchy of the sciences, as von Aster states. For us, it is only a hypothesis, crudely put, the fiction of a completion, not a completion actually attained or ever attainable. For this reason, only contingent "being" ever emerges from it – "transcendentally," as Cohen avers (in the sense of the Platonic *epekeina*). This is the unconditioned normative ought[86], which brings with it the domain of ethics, problematic in an entirely different manner. This domain is not, however, distinct of logic, thought and reason. It represents their development as unconstrained by spatio-temporal and causal contingency, and as not conditioned by an abandonment of reason, but by an extension of its domain beyond the border which, with good reason, necessarily limits pure theory. What ought complete this limiting, if not reason itself? The earlier "critique" was simply the expression of reason's self-recognition. Again, what else could move beyond the self-imposed limit of theory into a new form of cognition? If placing ethics above theory does not destroy the unity of reason, the two must clearly differ from one another in the deepest way possible within the domain of reason: namely, that barely conceivable difference (Plato's *mogis hapton*) between that which is unconditionally posited and that which is conditionally posited. Beyond this final contrast we of course can know nothing, there is no "higher" reason, for instance, but just simply bare irrationality, which commands the will, though only the impure will, feeling, though only impure feeling, and imagination, though only impure imagination. Of course we cannot be made to be interested in such things. If we were, Plato and Kant, along with all true philosophy, would have withered more than two and a half millennia ago.

One speaks of a "world of values." If that is but another expression of what ought to be, then the basis of this ought must be demonstrated and, if possible, one must explain why it is not in the places we are studying in Kant and Plato: namely, in the reference of all conditioned rational positing back to the ultimate, unconditioned unity of consciousness in which reason was first grounded, wherein (according to Spinoza) truest "being" of this ought persists – indeed, not just persists (that is a false perspective of mere theory), but ascends ever higher and is self-encapsulating. This might be called life-value[87], but it is the value of a life whose conception emerges in reason's positing of the unconditioned and no earlier. This has not really revealed the "world of values" to us. However, we are worried that this phrase bars us from the path to the infinite, which the ethics of an unconditional law places us on, and that it guides us to a safe haven away from the shoreless ocean of infinite tasks that we have dared to embrace. For we do not wish to be saved: *navigare necesse est*! The ethics of infinite responsibility places us right in the midst of daring to become[88]. It also prohibits us from plainly conserving our "being," and demands of us unwearying progress, an unceasing augmentation of ourselves. It is this which first grounds actual pure willing, and raises ethics above every shadow of naturalism. To be sure, the cognition of nature is an infinite task; but it only occurs "in negative understanding," since it seeks to be conclusive in regards to temporally-constrained being, but by its very nature is incapable of conclusion. In natural law, a conclusion is reached when that natural law counts absolutely, as in the fiction of the Laplacian demon who, by means of his formulas, can calculate every event in the world forwards and backwards in time to infinite reaches, or as in the absolutistically expressed preservation of the world's energy in an unchanging quantum. This quantum, in preserving itself, would naturally need to be thought of as finite, and then only as sufficient for a finite and ever-repeating series of identical events at best locked in a tiresome cycle. In the case of the infinite striving of the will, things are different. Despite the fact that the realization of all that is willed remains dependent on natural law, for reality is a category or a hypothesis for "possible experience," the will recognizes no such limitation, and thus is surely not "determined" by particular, unalterable terms. In this sense, we have steadfastly preserved Kant's doctrine of freedom and have at least begun to construct the philosophical foundations for economics, jurisprudence, education, history and all of the natural sciences. We readily admit that most of this work remains to be accomplished (see note at end of text).

If one tells us that the *philosophy of culture* poses an important new challenge, we can but answer that, from the start, we have viewed and described the philosophy of Kant – not to mention the philosophy of the transcendental method – as philosophy of culture, which we, embracing Kant's initiative, wish to work through in a more strict and consistent manner. We do not consider this philosophy of culture to be in opposition to philosophy of nature or natural science. If anything, we think that nature as an object for philosophy, the nature precisely of natural science, provides an essential basis for humane culture. Rather than asserting culture to be a problem for natural science, we on the contrary take natural science to be only one factor of humane culture from the perspective of philosophy, albeit an essential one.

For us, transcendental idealism is vital force[89]. With this in mind, we seek to enrich Kant through Plato, whose work was thoroughly suffused with the notion that philosophy is not a luxury of the scholar's study or of a refined education, but rather the most indispensable nourishment for a life that is truly worth living; philosophy would otherwise be a poor aim (*eis skopos*) and actually cease to be a life. Furthermore, we remain as true to the spirit of Kant as to Plato – to convince us otherwise would prove difficult. Just as our forebears Schiller, Wilhelm von Humboldt and all the others saw Kantianism not just as a matter for the head but also for the heart, so we see the matter as well. And it seems that our time in particular calls out for nothing so much as a philosophically saturated life, and thus for an infusion of philosophy itself with the warm life-blood of the most heralded growth of culture. We feel the pulse of such life in the supposedly marble-cold thoughts of the great critic of reason. Because this vital energy courses through him, he will live on for as long as there are human hearts and minds still working on this earth. Naturally it is said: that which thou sowest is not quickened, except it die (Corinthians 15:36). Not even the most vital force in human life can evade this "*Stirb und Werde*"[90]. We consequently do not shy away from burying the living body of this philosophy so that its spirit may live. We consider ourselves in this respect to be true disciples of Kant, and to remain as such.

Note. In this context it is worth mentioning another interesting comment of von Aster concerning my treatment of the concept of *time*. One of my supposedly assailable theses concerns the irreversibility of time, an idea that much occupies philosophers these days. On its own, it offers no proof against its origin in pure thought, nor against the claim that time can be grounded purely mathematically. For there are not only numbers of measurement[91], but also ordinal numbers[92], which are mathematically more fundamental and also irreversible. Time is based on the latter, insofar as it is number, in the same sense that space is based on numbers of measurement. It is true that the time of pure mechanics is not time in a simple sense, but rather is sequence as translated into simultaneity. But it is not mathematics itself which urges this; mathematics per se leads to an infinite, irreversible progression. Irreversibility in the laws of pure mechanics, in contrast to general natural law, results from the special task which just this science (which is actually still mathematics and not yet natural science) is accorded and must be accorded due to its uniqueness: namely, "to derive temporally occurring events and the temporally dependent properties of material systems from their *temporally independent* properties," as Heinrich Hertz states. Such a calculative derivation is of course only thinkable within the hypothesis of a closed system, since without controlled variables this whole calculation would not be possible. Yet this only confirms, following Plato and Kant's remarks, that like all merely theoretical cognition, this is an hypothesis, external to which the deeper logos raises the demand for an *Anhypotheton*. From the viewpoint of such a hypothesis, time might nonetheless appear as reversible and perhaps as the fourth dimension of space. However, in itself, and indeed following its purely logical derivation, I assert, it remains characterized by eternal irreversible consequence.

The relation of time to *space* as I posited it gave my critics further pause. I ultimately had to place time before space in a logic of the exact sciences. Time per se just is the more radical condition as compared with space, like the ordinal number as compared with the number of measurement in mathematics. Time has to represent the character of natural science and more narrowly of pure mathematical science. However, it in fact only acts as their final parameter, just as the dimensions of space do; thus the proper perspective must clearly be that of measurement[93] rather than of ordination[94]. We find this problem in Kant's doctrine of the antinomies. Recalling the antinomies makes it immediately clear that we are working entirely within Kantian territory. It is the absolutism of the thesis which threatens to rupture the indestructible character of time's unceasing and irreversible progression. The antithesis, as the antinomy's resolution, is taken as, i.e., corrected as *pure empiricism*, and fully does justice to the unique character of time. This "pure empiricism" is at the same time the only assumption which can clearly unify ethics with theory and which makes possible the general concept of history as developing event. This in turn exposes the error in thinking that the Marburg School's "logical idealism" takes mathematical physics to be the apex of scientific method, and that it thereby overrides every development, every developing causality, indeed even time itself (as an irreversible order) in favor of a spatial juxtaposition that is only mathematically graspable. Such a view could not be formed by anyone who has studied my

Logische Grundlagen, which expressly deals with natural science rather than with all branches of knowledge, alongside, for instance, my writings on social pedagogy[95].

Notes

1. Original: "Kant und die Marburger Schule," *Kant-Studien* 17 (1912): pp. 193–221. Translated for the first time. – Ed.
2. This talk was presented at a meeting of the Kant Society in Halle, on April 27, 1912. – Ed.
3. *Kants Theorie der Erfahrung* [*Kant's Theory of Experience*] (1st ed. 1871), *Kants Begründung der Ethik* [*Kant's Grounding of Ethics*] (1877), *Kant's Begründung der Aesthetik* [*Kant's Grounding of Aesthetics*] (1889). – Ed.
4. 2nd edition of *Kant's Theorie der Erfahrung* (from which the selection in Chapter 8 is taken). – Ed.
5. CPR A5/B9.
6. Kant, *Prolegomena to Any Future Metaphysics*, P. Guyer & A. Wood, trans., Cambridge/New York: Cambridge University Press, 2001, p. 106.
7. CPR, A314/B371.
8. *Erzeugung*
9. *Unendlichkeitsgrunde*
10. *Gehen*
11. *Nachgehen*
12. *Rückführung*
13. *Rückführbarkeit*
14. *schaffender Erkenntnis*
15. *Ursprungnachweis*
16. Natorp likes to emphasize the dynamic character of the *factum* as the result of being-made (lat. *fieri* is passive infinitive of *facere*, to make). – Ed.
17. "Es ist nicht *draussen*, da sucht es der Tor, Es ist *in dir, du bringst es ewig hervor.*" (from Schiller's poem of 1797, *Worte des Wahns*). – Ed.
18. "*Anschauung*"
19. *affizierend*
20. *affizierend*
21. *Empfindung*
22. *affizierenden Einwirkung*
23. *sachlicher Begründung*
24. *Weltraum*
25. *die Wagnis der Hypothese*
26. *einen Stand nehmen*
27. *Standnehmen*
28. *Feststellung*
29. *Wegpunkte*
30. CPR, B161.
31. *Gesetzesdenken*
32. *volles Gegenstandsdenken*
33. *Denken des Begriffs*
34. CPR, B195/A156.
35. "*Materie*"
36. *Rekognition*
37. *Wiedererkenntnis*
38. CPR, B 152.
39. *Grenzbestimmungen*
40. *Ratio*
41. "*Ins Innre der Natur dringt kein erschaffner Geist – Glückselig, wem sie nur die äussre Schale weist!*" (Albrecht von Haller). – Trans.

196 CHAPTER 12

42 From Goethe's polemical reply (in his poem "*Dem Physiker*" ["To The Physicist"]) to Haller's poem.
43 CPR, B 334.
44 Greek for "non-being"
45 *Bedingtheit*
46 *Stufengang*
47 *Richtungsgegensatz*
48 *Richtung*
49 *Einheitsmethode*
50 *gradlinig absteigende Begründung*
51 *Pfeiler*
52 *Die logischen Grundlagen der exakten Wissenschaften* (1921), from which Chapter 9 (this volume) is taken. – Ed (5.3).
53 *Dreischritt*
54 Greek for "non-being"
55 *Einheitsgründe*
56 *Entwicklung ins Besondere*
57 *das X der Gleichung der Erkenntnis*
58 *Verhärtung*
59 Hegel, *The Science of Logic*. G. di Giovanni (trans., ed.), Cambridge: Cambridge University Press, 2010, p. 737; 12.238.
60 Ibid., p. 749; 12.250.
61 Ibid., p. 751; 12.252.
62 Ibid., p. 747; 12.248.
63 Ibid., p. 119; 21.136.
64 Ibid., p. 752; 12.252.
65 Ibid., p. 753; 12.253.
66 *Gegenständlichkeit*
67 Hegel, *Phenomenology of Spirit* (trans. A.V. Miller), Oxford: Oxford University Press, 1977, pp. 486–7; § 800, 801.
68 Hegel, *Elements of the Philosophy of Right* (ed. A.W. Wood, trans. H.B. Nisbet), Cambridge: Cambridge University Press, 1991, p. 20.
69 *Science of Logic*, op. cit., pp. 103 ff.
70 *Elements of the Philosophy of Right*, op. cit., p. 22.
71 Ibid., p. 23.
72 Ibid.; cf. *Encyclopaedia* § 237: philosophy as old man.
73 *Weltgang*
74 "Oneness, Unity and the Number One," in: *Logos* 2 (1), pp. 26–78.
75 *Science and Reality*, 1912.
76 *Mehrheit der Art nach*
77 *Mehrheit der Arten*
78 *Koinonie*
79 *Zentralbezug*
80 Presumably a quotation from Ernst von Aster's *Neukantianismus und Hegelianismus: eine philosophische Parallele* of 1911. – Ed.
81 The Greek term indicates a principle that is not to be taken as a hypothesis, but is absolutely justified. The term is used by Plato to describe the principle that is reached through dialectical reasoning. – Ed.
82 *Bedingtheit*
83 *Vernunftslehre*
84 *Willensgestaltung*
85 *Geisteswissenschaften*
86 *unbedingtes Sollen*
87 *Lebenswert*
88 *Wagnis des Werdens*

89 *Lebensmacht*
90 "Die and become," a reference to Goethe's poem "Selige Sehnsucht" from the *West-östlicher Diwan*. –Ed.
91 *Masszahl*
92 *Ordnungszahl*
93 *Masscharacter*
94 *Ordnungscharakter*
95 Cf. Natorp's *Gesammelte Abhandlungen zur Sozialpädagogik* (3 vols.) of 1907. – Ed.

Chapter 13

"The Problem of a Logic of the Exact Sciences" from *The Logical Foundations of the Exact Sciences* (1921)

TRANSLATED BY FRANCES BOTTENBERG[1]

§ 1. (Mathematics and logic.) This chapter will introduce and bring to a head the problem of establishing a logical foundation for exact science; it will not offer a concrete solution. This preparatory work is necessary because the project itself, as here understood, is generally not viewed to be a worthwhile one.

Mathematics and every exact science, in other words, every science possessing a mathematical character, strives to proceed logically to the extent that it has that character, i.e., to only make use of strictly defined concepts and to only prove that which it is capable of proving. Yet this alone cannot make it into an eminently logical science or ensure that logic is its sole foundation. Indeed, every branch of study seeks to work logically in this general sense, taking into account the different degrees of logical rigor which each can achieve; but this does not mean that all branches of study are eminently logical or possess essentially logical foundations. The distinction rides on this: whether the core concepts of a branch of study are dictated by logic, whether they are themselves logical concepts, and whether their first principles are contained in the laws of logic or are derivable thereof, or are they merely logical in a loose, general sense, i.e., consistent and coherent. The logical character of mathematics, along with that which is mathematical in all other branches of study, is captured by this more precise meaning, while the character of non-mathematical branches of study is not, at least not in an equally strict sense.

This view of the mathematical as essentially logical was held by Plato among the ancients and those who followed him. Descartes and Leibniz are philosophers of more recent times who believed it especially strongly. Kant seems to deviate from the trend by introducing a non-logical factor into "pure intuition," which is involved in the founding of mathematics. But "pure" intuition in the end seems closely related to the logical and is bound to the logical in close unity. Indeed, at the level of the Kantian system, intuition seems to entirely dissolve into the logical, when "synthesis," initially meant to express the unique character of "intuition," becomes one of the original functions[2] of thought. Subsequent philosophy inspired by Kant, including today's nothing less than "orthodox" neo-Kantian line, has increasingly objected to the dualism of pure intuition and pure thought and has now decisively parted ways with it. Perhaps even too decisively: a non-trivial problem lay hidden in Kant's concept of intuition, as we shall soon see. Nevertheless, it was initially the very principle of Kantian transcendental philosophy which required that Kant's two factors — pure intuition and pure thought — be reconciled in a strict unity and grasped as one single factor, which one may quite harmlessly call "pure thought."

Roughly since Kant, one can find the same division of opinion among mathematicians. There is an older view, clearly influenced by him, which seems to have but few adherents left and which holds that intuition plays a special role in the founding of mathematics, alongside pure thought. The avant-garde, however, at whose forefront stand Frege, Dedekind, Cantor (and Grassmann earlier on), as well as Russell and Couturat (to name only the youngest and most ambitious international researchers) rejects this dualism entirely and energetically seeks to construct mathematics on a purely logical basis. Both sides agree on the pure *a priori* character of mathematics; the empirical-psychological and nominalist position, as still represented in, for instance, Helmholtz (1887)[3] and Kronecker's (1887) essays in honour of Zeller, has been refuted by means of impressive arguments (Frege deserves special credit). A purely logical grounding of mathematics unproblematically affirms its *a priori* character; to try to found pure thought in experience reveals a plain confusion in respect to the core concern.

The present volume also seeks to found mathematics purely logically and thereby prove its *a priori* character, though in a manner different than the aforementioned. It starts with the final assumptions of Kant's epistemology, but does not cling in the same way to the distinction between pure intuition and pure thought. This single deviation, however, ushers in drastic changes to the core epistemological concepts. A concern should be raised at this juncture that makes clear how the logical founding of mathematics is being understood here. This concern directly addresses the idea of the purely logical origin and character of mathematics, and its exposition will therefore cast us into the midst of the problem at hand.

§ 2. (The error of formalism.) If mathematics is to be built on logical foundations, its method must be entirely logical; does any division or technical difference remain, then, between logic and mathematics? Is mathematics to *be* logic, and logic mathematics?

One extreme approach, chiefly represented by Russell and Couturat, replies affirmatively to this question, and almost without reservation. All "pure" mathematics works with the tools and methods of pure thought; the term "applied" designates that which is no longer pure mathematics. Along with Frege, these researchers seek outright to build arithmetic exclusively on classical, if vastly expanded and revised formal logic. Hilbert (1908: 266) rightly finds that since formal logic assumes quite a bit of arithmetic, such an approach begs the question. But much more can be said: classical formal logic has generally been transformed into a branch of mathematics, taking the form of symbolic logic or logistics, which is assumed to continuously filter into the remaining mathematical disciplines (cf. especially Whitehead 1898, Natorp's review of the same 1901: 177ff and 372ff; and Russell 1903). Has mathematics become not *one* form of logic, but *the* logic, a logic entirely in the fashion and general sense of classical formal logic, but with much greater scope? And has logic as a result fully become mathematics, not just one form of it, but the entire field? Couturat (1908: 230), who perhaps most sees things this way, nonetheless expresses himself carefully. On the one hand, he sees mathematics as part of logic: its form is entirely logical, even though its content captures only part of logic's scope; on the other hand, he seeks to construct logic in a purely calculative manner, thus definitely making it into a branch of mathematics. Would it not then be consistent to deny any difference between logic and mathematics? For if A is entirely contained in B, and B in A, then according to the well-known axiom of calculative logic, both are necessarily identical.

The decisive assumption that led to this perhaps neither sought nor desired conclusion is the following: that logic is itself a deductive science. Since, on this view, mathematics is not merely a deductive science, but all pure deduction is mathematical, it inescapably follows that logic as a whole becomes mathematics, and mathematics as a whole becomes logic.

Herein are exposed, in our view, the error of this approach and the reason for the error. Logic is to be a deductive science; yet one of its tasks is without a doubt to establish the laws of the deductive process itself and to perform the requisite founding of their general validity. But can the establishment and founding of a logical process be provided by that process itself? Such an idea is nonsensical, since the deductive process would already need to be assumed as established and founded in order to validly provide the establishment and founding called for. The circular reasoning is obvious; were logic, as the deductive science of deduction, to expose circular reasoning as a breach of logic, it would in the process pass sentence on itself.

The impossibility of the matter becomes even more apparent when one further explores how the deductive process itself is set up. At the start are definitions that designate only conventional agreements concerning the use of certain symbols, thus not necessarily true or false propositions. Principles are then formulated keeping these symbols in view, i.e., one creates prescriptions concerning the acceptability of particular combinations of these symbols as they shift in various ways. These prescriptions are also not necessarily true or false judgments, since they refer only to the combination of symbols of undefined meaning. For these combinations, too, no further meaning is posited or looked for; their one constraint is that they may not cancel themselves out. From then on one calculates, i.e., moves these symbols around according to set prescriptions. Understanding the process as a whole is not in the least encouraged, it is not even desirable and might have a disruptive effect. The calculation proceeds exactly according to plan and remains just as compelling if all one understands is the need to follow the rules. One might imagine fixed core concepts being replaced by calculational symbols that are inserted into an automaton in an order pre-determined by the basic rules, only to be spewed out by that automaton as a result, in other words, as the same calculational symbols or only some of these, arranged in a different order. In this manner, one could literally "draw" conclusions.

Whether this be science or play, instructive or merely entertaining, or both or neither, for us the example suffices to demonstrate what we do *not* take the task of logic to be. Logic, in our view, begins and ends with meaning, with understanding[4], though we admit frankly and freely that we understand very little, in fact nothing at all of the enterprise as a whole. The fact that the process unfolds according to pre-given rules does not give us a sense of the whole enterprise; neither does the fact that the conclusion sometimes (but not always) coincides with something we thought to have understood elsewhere. Must the enterprise make sense at all?

§ 3. (Reason for the error. Synthetic and analytic directions of thought[5].) The philosophers mentioned began with a reasonable, perhaps even correct aim, so it is worth pausing to reflect on the reasons for their going astray. The main reason was most likely their dogmatic adherence to the traditional scheme of classical, i.e., Aristotelian, logic, where one is expected to define and to prove; one must define until certain ultimate concepts and principles are reached which cannot be further defined. How do we come to be certain of their ultimacy? Aristotle evidently finds himself in a quandary. For him, ultimate concepts and principles are self-evident, or given by means of a capacity of pure reason, and their functions are established in and sufficiently guaranteed by the most general form of experience. There is perhaps a hint of hidden and overlooked truth in this (see Natorp 1903: 373 on Plato's theory of ideas). These two ways of grounding concepts are evidently quite unsatisfying, though, and a third was not clearly ascertained; in the end it was deemed necessary to cease looking for any further evidence or proof of the ultimate starting points, any further guarantee of their epistemic value. It was thought sufficient to simply posit these final concepts and principles, i.e., symbols and the rules for their combination, but to do so in such a way that, in executing a hopefully unfailing mechanism, the very results emerge for which these final concepts were established in the first place. Only basic concepts and principles are expressly supposed (according to Couturat 1908: 39) to function in this way (i.e., as undefinable and unprovable), and they always function relative to a particular system of definitions and a particular argumentative series, never as such. One can, and indeed "from the formal perspective" one ought to view basic concepts as pure symbols "whose meaning is undefined and indifferent, and which are bound only to the condition of being adequate for the basic principles"; in other words they can be combined only according to set prescriptions. This is precisely what we cannot agree to. For us, "logic" is the meaning of what is said[6]. Symbols of indefinite and indifferent meaning are for us anything but logical, whatever other value they may possess.

The reason for the mistake hence lies, as mentioned, in the Aristotelian assumption, which, if consequences are sought and circular justification shunned, must lead to a formalism devoid of meaning. Yet this assumption is closely related to the basic error of naïve realism: that over the course of perception, things are presented as a kind of reflection in our imagination, and the entire achievement of cognition consists in the analytical processing of its pre-given thingly content in respect of its essential constitution. This is how the analytical process became a process for dealing with things, as represented by equally thinglike symbols. The instrument of Aristotelian syllogistic logic did provide the proper resources for this, as do the more comprehensive and, no one will deny, more rigorous machinations of modern logic. But as a result, nothing is understood, and the entire mechanism could play out just the same without an ounce of understanding.

To be sure, the analytic function of thought with which these logicians seem exclusively to be concerned has its own logical warrant and technical meaning. Nonetheless, we firmly hold to the sensible statement made by Kant: "where the understanding has not previously combined anything, neither can it dissolve anything".[7] He concludes, in other words, that synthesis must of necessity come first in the logical understanding of cognition, and that the analysis of meaning enters only as the pure reverse of synthesis. Pre-given things, insofar as it makes any sense to speak of these, are instead simple pre-constituted things, which at a glance are not always pure and hence not always properly constituted syntheses of a primitive understanding. The rules for analysis are useful for testing and correcting these primitive syntheses; yet the latter's original formation is bound to respective laws of synthesis, which also underlie the laws of analysis and ultimately form logical sense. This is why the path of analysis yields correct results. In contrast, every attempt to understand and justify those results from within must certainly fail, and thus is born the strange assumption of a mechanistic process that has nothing to do with understanding or justification – an assumption which no logician or mathematician would ever adopt were he not pressed to do so.

The attempt to justify analysis through analysis itself is doomed to failure. By contrast, the attempt to understand and support synthesis by means of itself is not irrational. One must follow the course of cognition from the beginning in order to recognize this directly; trying to begin at the end – with analysis – reveals nothing unless the entire course, i.e., the course of synthesis, has not already been described from beginning to conceived end.

At the same time, in one sense it remains true that logic does not place one directly at the start of cognition. Instead, one must return to this start by means of analysis, to become clear on the lawful course of synthesis itself. "In the beginning was the deed": this goes just as well for the epistemic act known as science. Lawful, synthetic thought must have been at work and have reached some advantageous results, well before the question concerning the laws of synthetic thought, which make science possible in the first place, can arise. Only in the already present "fact" of science can logic reveal the laws of science, for only by means of the fact can it observe the effectiveness of the laws of which it speaks and can it found their reality, i.e., in a technical sense, their efficiency in action, as it were. Such analysis serves us well and we welcome its tools, as abstruse as they may seem; that said, it is suited to no other task but uncovering underlying syntheses. Indeed, thought (in the sciences) is generated according to the secure laws of synthesis, but to a great extent it is not aware of these laws. The epistemic content brought in by virtue of the laws' power is its intrinsic interest, rather than the laws themselves. Thought is always directed at its special object; to ask not about a particular object, but instead about the laws by which it and indeed any object of science first form themselves into objects, is really an entirely novel stage of reflection. This novel reflective mode is what we call logic, which ensures that there is no more danger of logic fusing entirely with science (e.g., mathematics) that is directly engaged with its object; nevertheless, all the work of science, of all science, is ultimately defined logically, i.e., through none other than the laws of logic.

This description of the task of scientific logic and its relation to science itself, especially to mathematics, is, however, still not nearly radical enough. We made use of the contrast between synthesis and analysis as they are commonly used in philosophical discourse, and as they are described by Kant in a quite straightforward way. But this contrast is in need of further clarification. The great weight of the problem at hand has as yet hardly been exposed, and in no sense has it been conclusively formulated, not to mention solved.

§ 4. (The genetic view of cognition. Fact and justificatory basis. The process; the method; logos itself.) What, then, is synthesis? Initially, it is only a defensive term applied against a simply analytical account of cognitive foundation. The flaw of analysis is that, in the best case, it transforms cognition into a tautology. Synthesis, then, must mean heterology: not "A is A," but "A is B." For any sort of progress to be made, precisely that which is different must be posited as identical, and that which is identical as different. Cognition is progress, not coming to a stop or even reversing course; these last have meaning only insofar as they refer back to the continuity of progress, and they only serve to bring that progress to a clear awareness of itself and the securing of its laws. Here indeed lies the core of the problem: the *genetic* view of cognition must replace the *ontic* one (cf. Natorp 1903: 366 ff regarding the following exposition). This is the real import of the position supporting the originally synthetic, rather than analytic foundation of cognition. But this genetic sense of cognition is also in need of explication.

The *fact* must be assumed and its *justificatory basis* inquired into – this was Kant's central idea within his treatment of "transcendental" logic. It nevertheless invites doubt. What is the fact of science? Is it supposed to be complete, its work "done" to a certain extent, perhaps even concluded? A science can be complete only once its principles are proven; in other words, only once every principle that could be accepted as correct, has been. Why would it need another, external justification? This is counter-intuitive.

Closely related and perhaps more transparent is Plato's view concerning the relation of logic to science. According to him, a science that directly focuses on an object, such as mathematics, makes certain *assumptions* (hypotheses) that the science does not further justify, yet which experimentally underlie the science, as it were. These assumptions, along with its reliable method, allow conclusions to be drawn, which prove its principles, in the particular sense that these conclusions correspond to the original assumptions and thus are correct insofar as they just are those assumptions. The justification of the assumptions themselves falls to another, more fundamental science; Plato calls it dialectic, and from it logic emerges.

This approach in a certain way explains science's reliance on the fact. It is factually certain and free of further doubt that, given these particular assumptions, these particular consequences must follow. In this manner, science retains autonomy within its own domain. At the same time, though, that domain is strictly limited. The validity of ultimate assumptions is not questioned at all within the scope of the science that directly focuses on its object. All of its principles are meant only conditionally. As a result, the justification of its ultimate assumptions is a peculiar project left for another science to handle, a science of a totally different nature or level.

And yet, if this is the case, the positing of the fact and the demand for justification do not refer to the same thing precisely. In Kant, the relation between the two is not thought of this way: the same thing given as a fact in science forms a problem seen from the higher perspective of philosophy (here of logic); "experience" as *science* is the fact whose "possibility" is investigated in the transcendental logic.

One of Plato's conclusions shows this approach to be accurate. His point, however, has only matured into full significance in the face of the newly modern formation of the exact sciences; it also played a decisive role in Kant's transformation of classical logic into a transcendental one.

It was Plato's most profound discovery: scientific cognition persists within an *infinite process* of "limiting the unlimited"; there are no absolute beginning and end points in science; all that can be sought and surely found (as it is once keenly stated in *Parmenides*) beyond every (relative) beginning is an earlier and more central beginning, beyond every (relative) ending a later ending, and even within every fixed centre of an idea, there is a further centre. There can hence be no further talk of a "fact," in the sense of finished knowledge; furthermore, every cognition that fills a prior gap in knowledge will call forth newer and bigger problems; indeed, following Spencer's analogy, it is like a sphere whose radius grows infinitely according to the growing circumference of knowledge gained (represented by the growth of content within the sphere) and the growing circumference of the questions still to be solved (represented by the sphere's external border, i.e., the surface area of the sphere). Henceforward, "to understand" no longer means to come to a halt with one's thoughts, but rather the opposite: to resolve every apparent standstill into movement. "I am stunned"[8] is a popular idiom to express one's inability to understand – even it implies that comprehension equals movement, standstill non-comprehension. Progress, *method*, is everything; the Latin word is *process*.[9] Thus, the "fact" of science can only be understood as a *Fieri*.[10] What matters is not what has been done, but what is being done. Only the *Fieri* is the *factum*: all being that science seeks to "establish"[11] must dissolve into the stream of becoming. Of this becoming, in the end *only* of this becoming, can it be said that it *is*.

These considerations explore from a different angle and in a deeper way the kind of arguing from presuppositions, which Plato considers to be an intrinsic part of the always conditional character of object-directed science. At stake are not arbitrary, random assumptions, but precisely those assumptions required to sequentially determine the X of experience – the indeterminate, to be determined object – within an unending process that is never simply conclusive. In order to gain some hold on this unending task of object determination in experience, to generally acquire some limit within the unlimited, one must of necessity "posit" an initial beginning point and proceed from there, as far as one can securely go given that particular beginning, proceeding with the intention to go back behind this beginning as soon as there is occasion and possibility to do so. For this reason, though, one must also move on from every seeming conclusion at which thought would otherwise halt. For every radical beginning leads to further and deeper developments. There can consequently be an infinite regression within the sciences from assumptions to more fundamental assumptions of equally conditional validity. Plato's prescription of looking down from above, from what is conditional to what is conditioning, from what is merely valid for the time being to ever more fundamental assumptions, remains called for. Ultimately, one thereby reaches something that is not merely temporarily valid, the Platonic *Anhypotheton*. What else could this ahypothetical be than the law behind the entire process, the law that predetermines the *trajectory of the entire course* of cognition into infinity, in Plato's manner of speech the law of "logos" itself, the original law of "the logical," or the law of pure thought? This law is the same as the law of method, which Plato, by adding the modifier "dialectical," characterizes clearly enough as process. For the dialectic of Plato is simply the Socratic art of interlocution profoundly realized, i.e., the development of an idea out of a question that leads not to a conclusive answer, but to always more radical questions; the unbarring of the path of questioning, towards an unlimited deepening of the *problem*. It thus becomes understandable how that which is sure fact in science – not the individual position, but rather its entire course – becomes a problem from logic's higher vantage point, incidentally without forfeiting any of the security it possessed within the inner domain of science.

§ 5. (The object as infinite task. Connectedness[12].) Even at its most coherent, dogmatism has always bristled at the "genetic" view of cognition. Aristotle often expresses without inhibition: that if something is to count as founded for us, its foundation cannot extend into the infinite; there must be some final element which needs no further foundation. – Entirely true: given our finite powers of understanding, *we* can only realize a finite path. But does it follow that the path itself necessarily must be finite? The notion that the path of cognition, if infinite, must be closed off to our finite cognition is inaccurate. Rather, there can be and there really is a way of knowing the law of infinite cognitive process, of the infinity of its task and of its one and only developmental track into infinity. That this infinite task could ever be absolutely resolved, or the infinite course ever measured, this alone is and remains impossible.

Of course, this absolutism, articulated so naively by Aristotle, lies deep in the heart of men. One wants after all to know that which "is." This being transforms the genetic view of cognition into eternal becoming. Becoming, one might think, is merely subjective: becoming is for us; in itself it just is. But were it so, being in itself would help us, but not our knowledge; we would not have it, could never have it, it would remain ever sought after. And so, just as before, only progress into infinity would count as valid for us. One need not, however, be deterred by this subjectivistic or subjectivistic-seeming perspective. Rather, becoming *is*, the course *persists*, development into infinity takes place, as objectively as anything else. On the contrary, what are subjective and valid only for us are all of the arbitrary conclusions that give the illusion of halt, but are in reality part of the eternal progression. As an objective science, mathematics is certainly as free of the caprice of merely subjective suppositions as any other science; its object is that which always exists[13], according to Plato. And yet it continues to unfold – or there continues to unfold – an endless and eternal object. The infinite, as the suprafinite[14], is infinite unto itself, is "infinite to the power of infinity" and the entire progression, is itself infinite, through the series of the infinite. This all *persists* in virtue of the securely founded concepts of mathematics, which are just the concepts of pure method, of the lawful course of thinking itself, which attempt to bring the infinite course to its highest possible clarity. The course is not temporal, and therefore certainly not psychological or merely historical. Time itself is only one of its expressions, and not the most fundamental. The development, process or course of pure thought must instead be grasped in the sense that the number one is foundational to the number two, which in turn emerges from out of the number one; as the infinite develops on through the series of the finite and into the suprafinite. This is quite plausible: the number one can stand on its own just as little as the numbers two, three, and so on to infinity can. It is the beginning, but it would not be the beginning if there were not also something which begins from it: the series; just as, in its very concept, the finite as end-positing[15], refers to that which it ends: the infinite. It is for this reason that there is precedence[16] and succession[17], and that it is necessary to posit both a beginning and something which follows it. The series can only be thought of as a progression from earlier to later; the infinite can only be thought of as development through (comparatively final) finite stages, not only in the psychological sense of the single cognizer, nor only in the historical, i.e., group-psychological sense of the sequence of human generations, over the course of which human science has become ever more sophisticated; but also in terms of the logical content of science. The progression persists even if one thinks of that content as complete, and in this way in a literal sense it always remains correct that the object is not, but becomes.

There ought thus be no more talk of "given" objects, nor of cognition as the mere analysis of the given. It is precisely the object which poses the *task*, the infinite *problem*. And cognition, as directed at the object, must therefore consist of synthesis in Kant's sense, i.e., as expansion and ongoing progression. The claim that scientific cognition, and mathematical cognition foremost, is made up of simple analysis, expresses the absurdity that one never learns anything new in mathematics, but only carves up what is already known ever more carefully. This objection might seem merely psychological or historical, but it would mean that mathematics, and hence every science, consists of a closed set of finished truths, which could one day be fully known. Of course, one never intended to say this; an expansion of knowledge, indeed its infinite expansion was surely held dear (by Frege very clearly so). What was meant, rather, was that analysis could be ampliative (Couturat's words). But this is an unnecessary, technically unfounded alteration of logical language. In any case, this is not the analysis of which Kant speaks and with which he contrasts synthesis. It is also not the Aristotelian sense of analytic, which assumes a self-contained cognition exhausted by means of limited argument, nor the Wolffian sense, against which Kant first postulated synthetic cognition. On this point one ought to read M. Mendelssohn's wonderfully clear tract, presented in debate with Kant in 1763 and esteemed to have won the debate by the judges of the day (but not by those of history). According to Mendelssohn's treatise, following the principle of non-contradiction, the effect of analysis is analogous to that of a magnifying lens, which only puts further distance between the parts of an observed object, without bringing forth anything new in it. In sum: the object is given, and cognition's work consists in making this given "clear." This is the entire accomplishment of the analytical thought process in general, also according to Aristotle. Whoever takes thought to be ampliative, ampliative even to an infinite degree, has much more in mind what Kant means by synthesis rather than what he means by analysis.

Analytical cognition is, according to Kant, that which rests solely on the "principle of non-contradiction." Contradiction cannot, however, be a principle of progress, but rather at most a principle of exclusion, which disables irrational progressions that are attempted. There would be no need of it, if progression occurred strictly according to its law. Contradiction, in other words, produces nothing, and also contains nothing produced. It does not dismantle that which has been logically produced, but only uncovers the false appearance of logical construction, where really there was none; such an appearance often accompanies logical construction, and inserts itself rather cunningly. The principle of non-contradiction is thus at most, as Kant proposed, a principle of clarification, not, however, an expansion of knowledge. Its whole sense and content generally depend not on itself, but ultimately on the law of original synthesis, whose fundamental expression is likely to be identity. In that law, too, tautology seems present; but only until one grasps that B, posited after A, is nothing new, but more of the same. But A and B (or if one prefers, A_1 and A_2), identically placed, are posited by thought in a somewhat different manner. Identity must first be recognized. Identity between differents, however, is without a doubt a "unity of the manifold," i.e., synthetic unity. Kant thus proposed "recognition" (of the same as the same, i.e., the positing of identity) literally as the most fundamental function of *synthesis*. This Kantian act of "recognition" recalls, oddly enough, Plato's anamnesis. Both carry the aura of appearance, as if that which is to be recognized must have been known in advance in some basic way (why not, then, also cognized?), and yet both also seek to express an original recognition prior to which that which is posited "is" not at all. Kant articulates this by declaring recognition to be the original act of synthesis, which is in turn the original act of object-forming cognition. Indeed, logical identity is first posited in thought, is first created for it, since it must establish and declare in thought and as thought the identity of that which is simultaneously distinguishable, precisely in respect to and in contrast with difference.

By the same token, difference is not given to thought in advance, but must initially be posited in strict correlation with identity, as the content of thought, as thinking – for thinking means differentiating as much as identifying. Differentiation of a certain kind is difference, and in that respect it is again identity; A and B are mutually distinct in respect to one and the same thing, yet must equally, i.e., identically, refer to, or rather must take up this reference, in order to distinguish themselves. The underlying one and the same thing must be grasped as the basis of all difference, differentiation, or opposition that is at the same time a for-one-another[18]. This reveals the basis for the difference and also the strict correlation of the analytic and synthetic tendencies in the unity of the course of thought; affirmation and negation oppose each other and belong together, just as identity and difference in general do. It follows accordingly that the primordial[19] is *neither* affirmation *nor* negation, neither identity nor difference (nor contradiction), neither synthesis nor analysis, but rather *connectedness*; connectedness not by virtue of subsequent conciliation and agreement, but rather by virtue of a deep-rooted unity, an original unity[20]. This idea certainly underlies Kant's synthesis; synthesis should get at the origin of cognition. Yet it also follows that "synthesis" is not the most adequate term here, since it implies a contrast with analysis; a contrast which cannot be ultimate, because it implies a still more original unity as its source. It is worth mentioning here that Kant distinguishes "synthetic unity" (the unity of synthesis, i.e., that which *gives* synthesis unity) from a polymorphous synthesis that is more original and indeed *the* origin. Synthetic unity actually represents for him a "function," an "act"[21], and hence expresses the ultimately determining and creative aspects of thought. With this, he comes quite close to the notion of the fundamental principle of the logical, for which H. Cohen coined the term "origin"[22].

§ 6. (The principle of origin.) It is now plausible to champion this original unity, to make it the basis for the entire construction of logic. What else could one posit as the basis of or, as Kant prefers to say, "at the base"[23] of cognition, than the base[24] itself, in the deeper sense of origin?

There is no denying that one *makes* the latter the foundation insofar as it *just is* that. Nonetheless, we were not given it in complete form to begin with, we first had to locate it; in other words, we first earnestly had to posit it as foundational. Logic can only ask about it *retrospectively*, since it is supposed to serve as basis for all of logic. One can and must certainly set it at the start of logic, but only as question, as universal task of logic, and not as a principle of solution given right away. The question of logic is the question of origin; but we cannot create from this source, waiting for our cup to be filled (for the source flows eternally). Faced not with the *factum*, but the *Fieri* of cognition, we do not find ourselves at the origin, but must first ask about the way to it. What one can confidently assert at this initial point is only that the strong current of cognition must also have a source from which it flows, and it must be possible to ascend to this source.

Yet we cannot end there. To draw on the analogy of a source presents another difficulty: by what right do we demand only *one* source? Does a stream not pull its waters from a thousand sources, from a region of sources, much more wide in scope than what it itself draws in? The search for "the" principle has caused such confusion in philosophy – a singular principle that is supposed to give rise to the universe of things, or at least of all things cognized! In essence, a metaphysician searching for this principle proceeds no more wisely than the boy who holds his hand over one source of the Danube river and thinks: now the whole Danube will run dry. Therefore, we cannot grasp the origin as a single place where the universe gapes wide to tell us its secret. It is the very demand for the singularity of the principle that shallows the origin into a mere beginning, a beginning arbitrarily assumed, starting wherever one wants: in virtue of the original connectedness of all creative aspects of thought one could immediately and continuously transition from one true contact to all others. Yet for this very reason, one beginning is as little the sole and complete origin as any other. The unity of the cognitive foundation should not possess the shallow sense of the logical number one, from which and by means of which further counting occurs. Instead, this unity can only be one of comprehensive *connectedness*, in which every salient cognitive element compels all others forward and seems to posit them by its own power. This makes all the more obvious why one cannot begin with this unity as given; one can only begin with it in the sense that the entirety of the logical task is thereby antecedently described. This is not insignificant, though, since the formulation of the task continues to direct the whole construction of the logical system. But the idea, the demand of the system, its pertinent question is not itself the system, nor its first member, but rather lies entirely beyond it; hence, it really does not itself belong in the system.

A more definite description of this task is also not without its difficulty. It is nearly impossible to say something specific of it, without assuming not only something of the task, but ultimately everything that logic as a whole must develop. Thus, the word "system" pitches the "coherence" of its factors as quite perfect, and yet this is exactly the last task, indeed it cannot be reached conclusively, because it is an infinite task. With this in mind, it would be better to speak of "systasis"[25]: nothing remains isolated, everything fuses into unity and connectedness with everything else, "comes together" in cognition, and a complete reciprocality unfolds in the return to the common origin. It is obviously here, however, that one would have to presume and connect everything that logic has yet to develop, as it were, as soon as the condition of meaningful connectedness is to be more closely determined; we reached the condition of origin in the same way, starting with identity and difference. In thinking of the totality of the task or of the course of thought's movement, one assumes at a minimum the bi-directionality[26] of the epistemic route, a notion we earlier evoked by contrasting peripheral and central trajectories, unification and diversification, synthesis and analysis, and also the mutual relation of cognition and object, the A and X of the cognitive equation. In the latter, the relations, which Kant calls "modal," lie just below the surface. It would be easy to show, however, that in this bi-directionality, "relation" and determinations of "quantity" and "quality" are in turn assumed; in short, it appears that all that is logical is already hidden within the origin thus conceived and can therefore subsequently be recovered.

In Cohen's efforts to root logic securely in the concept, or rather the judgment, of origin, this difficulty plays out in an instructive way. One can assume nothing, because there is simply nothing to be assumed before it is produced in thought. But nothing begets nothing. So, this "so-called" nothing must in fact be a something – the original something. But strictly speaking, this seems to once again rescind the condition that one not posit something as foundational if it must first be founded. This difficulty can be expressed in another way: if the origin permits something to emerge out of it – *the* something or whatever else in the particular – that something must have been in it beforehand. Yet, this seems to undermine what the origin was designed to express, namely the pure production of thought content. We interpret this as the same difficulty that surfaces in Plato's anamnesis and Kant's recognition. The nothing that seems to assume the pure production of cognitive content, is in fact, according to Cohen as well, only a "relative nothing"; it refers to the other and indeed more radical element that stands across from every posited or to be posited particular. The origin can be entirely reduced to the possibility of transition, logical progression and also regression[27], and thus to the total continuity of connectedness, as foundational connectedness. In the end, cognitive continuity reveals itself to be the most relevant sense of Cohenian origin. It is described as "that which conditions origin" (Cohen 1902: 76). What is most likely to be ultimately foundational is the connectedness and bi-directionality of thought, where what is distinct is at once unified, and the unified is differentiated, with unity still maintained in that difference. It is properly speaking only another expression of that original law of thought, which was earlier (in the introduction to Cohen's *Logik der reinen Erkenntnis*, 1902: 52) defined as "merging together[28] within singling out[29], and singling out within merging together." This supports our general caution against setting up a singular principle. Nothing at all could be inferred of the origin, the primal source of the logical, without forward reference to that which is supposed to flow or emerge from it; nothing could be inferred of the foundation or principle without reference to that which is supposed to be founded on it and in it. Everything is assumed transparently enough in singling out, merging together and their mutual preservation: identity and negation, unity and plurality, quantity and quality; relation, too, stability and change, movement, all modality (as mentioned above), even the idea as infinite task; in short, whatever one wishes.

§ 7. (The correlation of the basic moments of logic.) But it is precisely the *unity* of all these, unity through *correlation*, that is at stake. In fact, this unity ought be thought of as the principle of principles, in a particular superordinate relation to the entire series of individual basic moments of the logical, which are correlative; as was naturally to be expected, there is no possibility of isolating these moments, save to the degree that they must be conceptually kept apart despite their correlativity.

This relation, i.e., correlation, is the accepted true meaning of Kant's "synthetic unity." This conceptual relation, this mutual relation is what brings together what otherwise remains separated in thought, and in so doing also keeps these distinct, since without a one[30] and an other[31] there would be no coming together[32]. Cognition is hence again only "possible," i.e., comprehensible, as expansion, as infinite progression rather than stasis; it is a going forth beyond everything that is given, that is, what has been posited (in a limiting manner) in thought. Analysis and abstraction then entail an extraction from the correlative context, which is not thereby destroyed, but rather placed to the side for the purpose of detailed observation of individual moments, which ultimately permits new connections to come to light within every individual member, even of those which are for now ignored. This supports the view of analysis as ampliative. Mendelssohn's analogy could be similarly interpreted: the microscope magnifies and presents new things to cognize. So everything is in truth connectedness, and hence synthesis, and while analysis retains its authority, it does so only as a moment of synthesis itself, analysis being in reality wholly encompassed by synthesis. Context ensures the preservation of the special logical authority of each individual position within the binding process of higher logical entities, and vice versa. Merging together and singling out are strictly correlative to one another; singling out, however, points back to the unity that is the origin. The origin of diversification is glimpsed in this unity; the origin is nothing but the required final unity, namely the unity of connectedness[33]. Thus the task of analysis is what we assigned it from the start: to uncover the underlying synthesis, to "describe" it in an extended sense, as one says: "to describe a circle"[34], i.e., to present the logical constituents individually, in order to build up, to *construct* the entire formation out of their unification.

Here we have aimed to fully justify the central placement of the principle of origin. This position was represented in my earlier essays on logic (Natorp 1890; 1900; 1904) by the simple Kantian term "synthetic unity." That the full import of Cohenian origin is contained therein has been demonstrated. But for this reason one may not speak of an original "judgment," as one of the basic logical judgments, even only apparently coordinated with eleven others, since judgment would then have to be supposed. Judgment, however, according to the view represented here, is only completed via the merging of all fundamental constituents of the logical, and these are not each a judgment unto their own right, but rather only one component of a judgment. It is true that every one of these can also be expressed in the form of a judgment, but only retrospectively so; they are the factors, or better yet (as Kant says) the functions (individual accomplishments) of judgment. But this is not what is most difficult about the "judgment of origin." If the origin represents the original correlation of all elements of thought, then it also represents the coming together of all constituents not to *one*, but to *the* judgment; in other words, the origin is actually the judgment of judgment. We are not essentially concerned with its coordination with the other basic logical judgments, for such coordination is for Cohen indeed merely artificial; the order he assigns to the basic elements of thought is better grasped as "concentric," where the central position serves as the starting place of the original judgment. Even put in these terms, though, there seems to be a kind of hierarchical segregation at work, which I see no reason to adopt. It is only the relation to the centre, rather than the centre point itself, which matters, the mutual relation between centre and periphery, or to put it more precisely: the mutual relation of the central and peripheral trajectories of cognition. This mutual relation already contains, however, the totality of the laws of the circle, which expresses the very essence of the logical. We are no longer dealing with *one*, but *the* constituent. I wish to point out or revise, or – to put it in as neutral a manner as possible – to draw on Cohen's basic notion, but this naturally entails leaving aside some of his account, for this principle can no longer stand amongst a series of arbitrary constituents. At the core it matters little whether we speak of method, of process, of the logical itself as the presuppositionless assumption, or – what ultimately surfaces in every one of these approaches – of the necessary correlation of basic logical moments; this multiply-named one thus does not, as the first of the series, sit above all logical constituents, but rather must precede the whole series, as the total and requisite unity of the logical.

§ 8. (Overview. The object as general expression of the problem of knowledge.) We now look back over the path taken thus far, so that we may see clearly how we arrived at our positions, which are actually all supposed to be the requirements, or the various expressions of, *the* requirement of the logical.

Among others, the following notions have come to light here, and have been provisionally accepted, with the caveat of the need for more precise description and support: the requirement of a central unity, which at once contains the foundation and the source for infinite peripheral extension and differentiation; the opposition of hypothesis and *anhypotheton*, ideas and the idea of idea; the infinite progressive series of knowledge formation and its necessary unity of direction; continuity and correlation. In one sense, induction has led us to all of these, induction not based on the fact, but rather on the *Fieri* of the sciences; induction which has not been carefully described here, but which, according to general consensus, is indeed at work in the development of the sciences. This induction cannot found anything itself, and moreover it can never be completed, because in truth it is itself in need of founding, no less than all those other assumptions, and presumably its founding will depend on all of them. In another sense, particular assumptions led us to the above-mentioned notions, which are historically and thus factually available logical theorems. For these particular assumptions, the only justification I can offer is that they have passed the test of researchers who have been intensely occupied with such problems for a long time; of course this cannot serve as absolute support. The inexactitude and inadequacy of such a justification ought to be made clear. Yet it cannot be avoided at the beginning, and it need not worry us at the point in the logical examination when the logical problem is first uncovered, before any single thing is presented as definitively valid. Anyone ignorant or uncritical of the relevant and momentous work in science and philosophy of ancient and newer times will grasp the problem to be less lofty and general, less central and radical than it in fact is. This must be made clear: no other justification can be required upon arriving at the ultimate origin of cognition, than that it reveals the well-suitedness of the lawfulness of the structure of cognition; this, however, will only become clear over the course of the inquiry.

The difficulty of final justification cannot be avoided in any way, no matter how one looks at the problem. If one seeks to draw on evidence, nothing unfortunately seems as little evident as ultimate principles, for nothing is as controversial. If one seeks to form a deductive proof, every attempt will lead to an unavoidable circle, as shown earlier. An inductive proof, though, will not only fall prey to this same logical error of assuming the ultimate principles it seeks to prove; given the extent to which it relies on the whole prior course of research, such a proof would additionally never be safe from being disproven by further research.

One might attempt an apagogical proof, to show that every attempt to logically determine certain assumptions as either true or false, on the basis of more fundamental assumptions, entails assuming the truth of the first assumptions; these assumptions could hence not be evaded in any way. Even still, one might accede to the pressure to recognize it, but still vainly strive against that pressure in private, were these same assumptions not continually sustained and proven fruitful for factual use in thought; a kind of proof that is certain only to the extent that it always seems adequate, yet still contributes to the certainty attainable in domain-specific scientific statements.

Proceeding in such a manner always seems artificial and indirect, however. One can arrive at the same conclusion more directly by beginning with the concept of the *question* or the *problem*, and searching from there for secure access to the certainty of foundational knowledge. This was, for example, the essence of Descartes' beginning from doubt. One cannot meaningfully doubt that which must already be presupposed, if the doubting and also the question are to make any sense at all. One cannot inquire further beyond that which is assumed in every meaningful questioning. One cannot meaningfully ask: Why is there a why at all? Why a question at all? or: What meaning is meaningful at all?

This consideration is utterly sound; yet it is a mistake to think that it enables escape from having to assume what is to be founded. The question ultimately already contains everything in itself. It casts us into the midst of the cognitive process. The question persists in every respective stage of that process. It contains a retrospective knowing, without which even the assumptions required for the question would be missing; a prospective not-knowing; in the midst [of both] a knowing of not-knowing, in which the demand for and thus the presumption of knowledge is particularly obvious and which indeed forms the very uniqueness of the questioning. This last stage represents nothing other than the logical connection that is missed, called for, and as a result assumed in itself and in general; indeed, not just in general, but also in relation to the particular question posed. It seals the precise gap that its absence makes us aware of.

This peculiar basic phenomenon – that the question *is*, and even more strangely, that it always anticipates the answer – is better known under another expression, an expression that relates more closely to the question of cognition, but in reality simply expresses the self-determined question of cognition: it is that of the *object*[35], a term which we have continually made reference to. Even the word "object"[36], literally a "return throw"[37] or in more liberal rendition: to "confront"[38], is quite a close translation of the Greek "*problema*." That the object seems to lie outside of cognition, but is supposed to be appropriated by the latter, can be explained in terms of anticipation. The object cannot be *its* problem, if it is to be an object for cognition, it cannot be searched for outside of cognition's domain. The well-known objections of the sceptics are thus refuted; if the object is to be the X in the cognitive equation, as it were, it must be completely determined in terms of the equation, despite being that which is sought. The X, Y and so on of an equation only possess meaning for and within the equation, only on the basis of the meaning of the equation itself and always in relation to known quantities, i.e., constants in the sense of variables, which are the "roots" of the equation (values, which "fulfil" it). Just so and only in this way can the profound X of cognition, the object, be made comprehensible. One cannot ask about the object at all, except from the vantage point of cognition itself, following the original relations that make knowledge "possible" to begin with: the object as undetermined but to-be-determined; as something that lies within the scope of general determinate possibility, even if it is not further fixed within that scope; indeed, it is never to be fixed absolutely, but in the final analysis remains forever variable, since the cognitive progression is never broken off. If the object, as the X of cognition, is contained in the question, in the problem, then everything is contained therein. The basic modes of relation, which make cognition possible at all, are taken for granted therein, are already prefigured in the "confrontation"[39] of cognition, are "projected"[40]. The object of cognition becomes the project, the return throw a confrontation[41]. The process or course of cognition as a whole is assumed, in terms of direction: this is method. And because the process, as direction, necessarily persists into infinity, so the object, too, can never be exhaustively known, or be thought of as completely determined. Instead, regardless of the extent of its present determination, the object always remains further determinable and to be determined. The object as the task of cognition, which is eternal progression rather than stasis, becomes the never-ending task; every finite determination of the object is a mere notch in the continuum of progression. But this never-ending task is a never-ending *projection*[42].

The object thus reveals itself to be the exact correlate of the "origin." What the latter formulates in terms of a requirement of cognition, the former expresses not as the mere possibility, but as the sure fulfilment of that requirement, in the only way this fulfilment can be grasped: as eternal progress, rather than final completion. Both expressions reveal the same radicality of logic, just from two different lines of thought, which run parallel to each other. The root (*radix*) is the origin, and the root of the cognitive equation is the object. The move from science to logic can be expressed in the same way from either direction: starting with objects, one must ask about the object; starting with principles, each of which might solve a particular question or an exemplar of questions, one must ask about the principle, indeed the principle of principles – that is the origin. This very move from particular cognitions to cognition itself, from many positings to thought in general, conveys the task of logic: it is the study of logos, but not of all that is logical, since that extends ultimately to all of science.

Notes

1   Originally published as: "Das Problem einer Logik der exakten Wissenschaften," in: *Die Logischen Grundlagen der exakten Wissenschaften* (Leipzig/Berlin: Teubner, 1st ed., 1910, 2nd ed. 1921), pp. 1–34. Translated for the first time by Frances Bottenberg.
2   *Urfunktionen*. *Ur-* is translated as "original" throughout. – Trans.
3   Natorp references the works he cites by mentioning their dates of publication. A list of cited works is to be found at the end of this chapter. – Ed.
4   *Verstehen*
5   *Denkrichtungen*. As in Chapter 11 (and later in his *Allgemeine Psychologie nach kritischer Methode*), Natorp distinguishes between two opposing directions of thought (subjectivating, objectivating), which he also describes as moving into the plus or minus direction on a vector. What he talks about in this paragraph as the difference between the analytic and synthetic direction of thought is roughly the same distinction. For this reason, I have kept the literal, though somewhat off-sounding metaphorical term "direction." – Trans.

6 *den Sinn des Ausgesagten*
7 CPR, B 130.
8 *Da steht mir der Verstand still*: literally, "here my understanding comes to a standstill." – Ed.
9 That the process character of cognition is the true sense of "synthetic a priori" seems to be the actual motive for Poincaré's (1905: 12ff) view, when he locates the expression of the synthetic a priori especially in "reasoning by recurrence." (This is why both analytical and empirical arguments fail in the face of the infinite.)
10 This play with the latin *facere* and its cognates is explained in the previous text. – Ed.
11 *Feststellen*: literally, "to bring to a standstill." – Ed.
12 *Zusammenhang*
13 *das Immerseiende*
14 *das Überendliche*
15 *Ende-setzen*
16 *Vorausgehen*
17 *Folgen*
18 *Füreinander*
19 *das Ursprüngliche*
20 *Ursprungseinheit*. The unity of synthesis and analysis in a primary unity, which is nothing but "connectedness" or "relation" marks the final stage of Natorp's thought, which is articulated in his *Philosophische Systematik*. – Ed.
21 *Handlung*
22 *Ursprung*. Cohen calls his concept of logic in his *Logik der reinen Erkenntnis* an "*Ursprungslogik*" (logic of origin). – Ed.
23 *zum Grunde*
24 *Grund*
25 "*Systase*"
26 *Doppelrichtung*
27 *Rückgang*
28 *Vereinigung*
29 *Sonderung*
30 *Eines*
31 *Anderes*
32 *Zueinander*
33 *Zusammenhangs-Einheit*
34 *einen Kreis beschreiben*
35 *Gegenstand*, literally "something that stands against" as derived from the latin *ob-iecere*, passive participle *ob-iectum*, "something that is thrown against." Here and in the following Natorp plays on the term "*werfen*" (to throw). – Ed.
36 *Objekt*
37 *Gegenwurf*
38 *Vorwurf*
39 "*Vorwurf*"
40 *entworfen*
41 *der Gegenwurf Vorwurf*
42 *Projektion*

References

Cohen, H., *Logik der reinen Erkenntnis*. Hildesheim: G. Olms, 1902.
Couturat, L., *Die philosophischen Prinzipien der Mathematik*, C. Siegel (German trans.), *Philosophisch-soziologische Bücherei* 7. Leipzig: W. Klinkhardt, 1908.
Helmholtz, H., "Zählen und Messen," in: *Philosophische Aufsätze. Eduard Zeller zu seinem fünfzigjährigen Doctorjubiläum gewidmet*, E. Zeller (ed.). Leipzig: Fues, 1887, pp. 76ff.

Hilbert, D., *Grundlagen der Geometrie*, 3rd ed. Leipzig: B. G. Teubner, 1908.
Kant, I., *Critique of Pure Reason*, P. Guyer and A. W. Wood (trans.). Cambridge/New York: Cambridge University Press, 1998.
Kronecker, L,. "Über den Zahlbegriff," in: *Philosophische Aufsätze*. Leipzig: Fues, 1887, pp. 97ff.
Natorp, P., "Quantität und Qualität in Begriff, Urteil und gegenständlicher Erkenntnis," in: *Philosophische Monatshefte* 27: 1–32; 129–160, 1890.
———. "Nombre, temps et espace dans leurs rapports avec les fonctions primitives de la pensée," in: *Bibliothèque du Congrès international de Philosophie* I. Paris: Colin, 1900.
———. "Zu den logischen Grundlagen der neueren Mathematik," in: *Archiv für systematische Philosophie* 7: 177–209, 1901.
———. *Platos Ideenlehre. Eine Einführung in den Idealismus*. Leipzig: F. Meiner, 1903.
———. "Logik," in: *Leitsätzen zu akademischen Vorlesungen*. Marburg: N. G. Elwert, 1904.
Poincaré, H. *Science and Hypothesis*, W. J. Greenstreet (trans.). London: Walter Scott Publishing, 1905.
Russell, B., *The Principles of Mathematics*, vol. 1, London/New York: Cambridge University Press, 1903.
Whitehead, A., *A Treatise on Universal Algebra*, Cambridge, MA: Harvard University Press, 1898.

Introduction

Ernst Cassirer (1874–1945)

ERNST CASSIRER IS CONSIDERED THE "poster boy" of the Marburg School and is by all accounts the most famous and most influential philosopher to emerge from the Neo-Kantian movement in general. His adherence to central Neo-Kantian tenets (whatever they may be) and to those of the Marburg School in particular have, however, been disputed. Indeed, although Cohen claimed Cassirer as his pupil, and although Cassirer, in turn, always recognized Cohen and Natorp as his intellectual fathers, Cassirer's philosophical proximity to these is, at the very least, not easily answered. Nor was his alliance with "Marburg" in any way close, preferring, as he did, urban life over the small town atmosphere that Marburg has to this day. In the estimation of Michael Friedman, Cassirer plays a pivotal role for philosophy in the twentieth century, being the only philosopher who saw the gulf between the "two cultures" in academia and attempted to bridge it with his encompassing philosophical vision.

Ernst Cassirer was born into a well-to-do Jewish family in Breslau with extended family members across Germany. He studied, thoroughly and without haste, several subjects (jurisprudence, philosophy, classical and modern philologies) in Berlin, Leipzig, and Heidelberg. Although he considered himself a secular Jew, he nonetheless suffered anti-Semitic recriminations. Being independently wealthy, however, he never aspired to become a professor and preferred his existence as a *Privatgelehrter*, working quietly in libraries. He first heard of Cohen in Georg Simmel's lectures on Kant in Berlin and subsequently began reading Cohen's works and took up contact with him. It was in Berlin, however, that Cassirer wrote his dissertation and Habilitation thesis, the latter of which first experienced resistance within the faculty, but was eventually passed upon the intervention of the old Dilthey, who recognized and admired Cassirer's work in the history of Renaissance philosophy. Between 1906 and 1919, Cassirer remained an unsalaried *Privatdozent* until receiving a professorship at the newly founded university in Hamburg. Cassirer stayed in Hamburg from 1919 until 1933 and was the first Jew to ascend to the presidency of the university in 1930/31 (there were altogether only four Jews who served as presidents of German universities). It was at this time that Cassirer's star began to rise. While publishing his first systematic work, *Substance and Function* (*Substanzbegriff und Funktionsbegriff*) in 1910, Cassirer worked out his philosophical system, culminating in the three-volume *Philosophy of Symbolic Forms*, published in 1923 (*Language*), 1925 (*Myth*) and 1929 (*Phenomenology of Knowledge*). It was also in the latter year that

Cassirer had the famous debate with Heidegger in Davos, which some consider the greatest philosophical event of the twentieth century (a transcript is reproduced here as Chapter 33).

Cassirer and a large part of his extended family left Germany in 1933, seeing clearly the disaster on the horizon. From then on, Cassirer was on the move, finding temporary positions first in England, then in Sweden, and finally, as the Nazis invaded Sweden, in the United States. His work remained, astonishingly, continuous, with the same steady stream of output. In his later years, he dealt with problems in epistemology, philosophy of science, and myth, published studies on central figures of European thought and wrote an introduction to his philosophy in the United States, *An Essay on Man*, in 1944. His last work, *The Myth of the State*, published posthumously, contains a penetrating critique of modern fascism. Cassirer left behind a significant amount of unpublished material that did not begin to be published until the 1990s. His collected works comprise 26 volumes of published work, and the edition of his unpublished lectures, writings, and letters is projected to encompass 18 volumes. There can be no doubt that Cassirer is the Neo-Kantian with the broadest range of knowledge and themes. His knowledge has been described as "encyclopedic," making him, arguably, the "Leibniz of the twentieth century." After a first wave of rediscovery in continental Europe in the 1990s, his significance is slowly being recognized and his works studied in North America.

Further Reading

Friedman, Michael, "Ernst Cassirer," in: *Stanford Encyclopedia of Philosophy*. Available online at http://plato.stanford.edu/entries/cassirer/ (accessed 16 March 2015).
Cf. also the biographical material by friends and students in: P. A. Schilpp, ed., *The Philosophy of Ernst Cassirer*. LaSalle: Open Court, 1973 (Library of Living Philosophers), pp. 1–72. (The articles on Cassirer's thought from this volume published originally in 1949 are for the most part obsolete.)

"Hermann Cohen and the Renewal of Kantian Philosophy" (1912)

Published in the main Neo-Kantian outlet, *Kant Studien*, Cassirer's 1912 essay commemorates Cohen's time in Marburg and his departure for Berlin. Comparable to Natorp's essay on "Kant and the Marburg School" (in this volume), Cassirer's essay can be considered as much an introduction to the Marburg School in general as to Cohen's thinking in particular, at least prior to the latter's "religious turn," which Cassirer does not tire to emphasize in later essays on his revered teacher and mentor. What is remarkable in Cassirer's presentation is the proximity he emphasizes – as opposed to Natorp's focus on the Marburg School as promoting a philosophy of culture – between philosophy and science, both philosophy *as a science* and as a philosophy *of the sciences*. In this sense, Cassirer's piece is also a splendid and highly informative exercise in the history of science of the nineteenth century, which recounts the developments (some of which are reprinted here in Part I) that led to Cohen's own philosophizing. In this method of presenting Cohen's achievement, Cassirer can be seen as talking about himself, when he characterizes Cohen's work such that "there is no division, no partitioning wall between the historian and the systematic philosopher."

Interesting highlights of the work – both for Cassirer's view of the Marburg School and his own self-situating with respect to it – include the following: Cassirer's focus on the transcendental method as the central philosophical achievement of Cohen's thought (alongside Bolzano's and Husserl's work in refuting psychologism), especially since the parallels between the Marburg School and the Phenomenological Movement are typically not recognized to be substantial (but it is also a significant truncation of Husserl's achievements to view him as merely refuting psychologism, yet this was the "standard" Marburg view of Husserl, also promoted by Natorp); Cassirer's presentation of Cohen's form of transcendental idealism as not merely limited to theoretical cognition, but also relative to practical activity and aesthetical contemplation, orienting itself to a "given" in each case. This is perhaps an anticipation of Cassirer's own system of symbolic forms, which starts out from a given *factum* in each cultural region, while "relaxing" the rigid requirements of Cohen's transcendental method (but being thereby still within the boundaries of the Marburg School); Cassirer's presentation of Cohen's concept of the historical *a priori* – the *a priori* not as a timeless "necessary and universal" truth, but as developing in the form of scientific progress itself. This is perhaps Cohen's most original idea and a crucial pointer to how Cassirer sees his own work as furthering this notion of *a priori* philosophy (philosophy as transcendental philosophy of culture); Cassirer's in-depth treatment of Cohen's ethics, given the dearth of attention given to it otherwise, and Cassirer already hints at the importance moral thought has for Cohen in the context of religion, pointing to the connection between moral philosophy and religion in the late Cohen (cf. Chapter 10, above), sidestepping, as he does, the most neglected (and arguably, weakest) part of Cohen's work, his work on aesthetics. Written, as it was, in 1912, this essay comes a year after Cassirer's own system began taking shape, in his *Substance and Function*. It is as if Cassirer was looking back for one last moment before looking ahead at his own system of philosophy in his *Philosophy of Symbolic Forms*, the first volume of which appeared in 1923.

"Euclidean and Non-Euclidean Geometry" from *Einstein's Theory of Relativity* (1921) by Lydia Patton

In *Einstein's Theory of Relativity*, which first appeared in 1921, Ernst Cassirer reads the Einsteinian theory of general relativity as providing an occasion for reflection on the role of geometry in physics, and for broader analysis of the relationship between physical theories and claims of objectivity. Cassirer argues that "the result of the general principle of relativity" was "that by it 'the last remainder of physical objectivity' was to be taken from space". The goal of *Einstein's Theory* was to show how the objectivity that "has lost all meaning" in the case of space can nonetheless be ascribed to "the physically real object." In Einstein's theory, Cassirer notes, "Only the various relations of measurement within the physical manifold, within that inseparable correlation of space, time, and the physically real object, which the theory of relativity takes as ultimate, are pointed out".

Ryckman (2003) points out that Cassirer's notion of physical objectivity was influenced by Max Planck's 1908 lecture "The Unity of the Physical World-Picture." Cassirer was influenced as well by Hermann von Helmholtz's rejection of the "copy theory": "one must guard against taking the 'preëstablished harmony between pure mathematics and physics,' that is revealed to us in increasing fullness and depth in the progress of scientific knowledge, as a naïve copy theory." Rather, Cassirer argues, "if we conceive the geometrical axioms, not as copies of a given reality, but as purely ideal and constructive structures, then they are subjected to no other law than is given them by the *system* of thought and knowledge." Cassirer mentions Henri Poincaré as a source of his view that the structures of geometry can be "purely ideal and constructive" (see Folina 1994). As Heis (2013) notes, Cassirer did not adopt Poincaré's more fully fledged conventionalism.

Cassirer's reading put him at odds with Moritz Schlick, with whom he engaged in a debate over the interpretation of the theory of relativity. Cassirer's view was more consistent with the interpretation of his student in Berlin, Hans Reichenbach (see Heis 2013). On Cassirer's account of the *a priori* more generally, see Friedman 2009 and Ryckman 2003.

Einstein's Theory of Relativity provides a concrete example for Cassirer's contention that certain moments in science stimulate reflection on the basic concepts and interpretation of scientific theories. Moreover, here Cassirer argues for his influential claim that the *a priori* structures of scientific theories develop over time in the history of science, as successive, and "genetically" related, attempts to characterize and to constitute the object of knowledge, a view given significant attention in the work of Michael Friedman. Finally, Cassirer argues here against Aristotelianism and empiricism in geometry, which would become a key issue in his debate with Schlick.

Further Reading

Folina, J., "Poincaré on Mathematics, Intuition and the Foundations of Science," 1994, pp. 217–226 in *PSA* Vol.
Friedman, M., "Einstein, Kant, and the Relativized *A priori*," 2009, pp. 253–267, in: *Constituting Objectivity*. Springer.
Heis, J., "Ernst Cassirer, Kurt Lewin, and Hans Reichenbach," 2013, pp. 67–94, in: *The Berlin Group and the Philosophy of Logical Empiricism*, BSPHS Vol. 273. Springer, Heidelberg.
Ryckman, T., "Two Roads from Kant," in: Parrini, Salmon & Salmon, eds. *Logical Empiricism*. University of Pittsburgh Press, 2003.

"The Place of Language and Myth in the Pattern of Human Culture" from *Language and Myth* (1925)

The booklet *Language and Myth*, originally dedicated to his father-in-law's eightieth birthday, was the first book by Cassirer translated into English (if one does not count the *Essay on Man* and *Myth of the State* that had been written in English by Cassirer but redacted by Karl Hempel). It was translated by Cassirer's American student Susanne K. Langer, who later became famous through her Cassirer-inspired *Philosophy in a New Key* (1941). Langer's translation appeared in 1946 and can be seen as an introduction "from below" to Cassirer's system of symbolic formation, if an introduction "from the top" can be seen to be presented in the *Essay on Man*. To understand this claim, one needs to say a few words about Cassirer's system of symbolic formation, which had been presented in preliminary form in the three volumes *Language* (1923), *Myth* (1925), and *Phenomenology of Knowledge* (1929). As written originally in 1925, the present essay can be seen as a highly condensed summary of the first two volumes, at least with regard to their research program.

Beginning in his first systematic work, *Substance and Function*, Cassirer's paradigm for explaining the creation of meaning in the world around us – culture – is functionalism. Things stand in a functional relation of meaning to one another. They do not exist in themselves (as mind-independent substances) and then receive a "baptism" of meaning. Rather, this meaning is created by the human mind. The functional nexus is a nexus of meaningful relationships, which function, however, according to different spheres of meaning as expressions of the human mind. The human being as the *animal symbolicum* creates different contexts of symbolic meaning, which Cassirer calls symbolic forms.

Language and myth present two such forms, which are also the most fundamental ones for the way the culture-creating being we are relates to the world. The overall project Cassirer also calls, invoking Kant, a shift from the critique of reason to the critique of culture. If this is the case, critical philosophy does not deal firstly nor foremost with the clarification of knowledge – thus, theory of knowledge, or theory of cognition (Cohen) – but with the symbolic construction of reality as culture. Transcendental Idealism thus becomes, in Cassirer's hands, Symbolic

Idealism. In the last chapter of *Einstein's Theory of Relativity* (reproduced here as Chapter 15), Cassirer describes his overall task as follows: "It is the task of systematic philosophy, which extends far beyond the theory of knowledge, to free the idea of the world from this one-sidedness. It has to grasp the *whole system* of symbolic forms, the application of which produces for us the concept of an ordered reality, and by virtue of which subject and object, ego and world are separated and opposed to each other in definite form, and it must refer each individual in this totality to its fixed place."[1]

Thus, language and myth are parts of the task this systematic philosophy has to elucidate. With respect to these allegedly "lower" forms of relating to the world – "lower" may not be meant in any pejorative sense vis-à-vis theoretical cognition – Langer characterizes Cassirer's "great thesis" as the claim that "*philosophy of mind involves much more than a theory of knowledge; it involves a theory of prelogical conception and expression, and their final culmination in reason and factual knowledge*".[2] In the following first introductory essay of what is originally a study in six chapters, Cassirer explains where language and myth have their systematic locus, insofar as the philosophy of the symbolic forms of language and myth are precisely such a theory of prelogical conception and expression.

Starting from the rather depreciatory interpretation of myth in antiquity, Cassirer emphasizes, following contemporary research in ethnology and anthropology, that myth has a logic of its own which is far from "primitive." Instead, the functional logic of myth assumes an "intimate relation" between names and essences, such that the named object *is* the demon or godhead summoned thereby. This connection, in turn, suggests equally such an intimate connection between language and myth. Contra the mythologist Max Müller, Cassirer argues that myth and mythical consciousness are not some lesser form of consciousness, "a world of illusion," but a consciousness *sui generis* with its own rules and logic. Just as artistic production is no mere imitation of reality, myth, too, is not passive and a distortion of reality "out there" (the result of a naïve realism), but a creative force with its own *sui generis* "grasp" and thereby creation of reality. Thus, myth, like all other mental formation, is not a symbolism that mediates our access to reality, in contrast to direct (perceptual) access to reality that we also have. Instead, we never have anything but a symbolic, mediated relation to reality (myth being just one form of such a mediated relation). Reality correlates to our way of intuiting it. The only way to understand these forms of consciousness correctly is by accepting "in all seriousness" Kant's Copernican Revolution, but in a ubiquitous sense. These forms of expression, such as myth, language, art, are not "copies of reality," but the condition of the possibility of having a reality. "We must see in each of these spiritual forms a spontaneous law of generation; an original way and tendency of expression. ... From this point of view, myth, art, language, and science" – the main symbolic forms Cassirer analyzes – "appear as symbols ... in the sense of forces each of which produces and posits a world of its own." As such, the symbolic forms, as forms of intuition in a wide sense, are "*organs* of reality." For the study of myth and language, this means that they each must be described in their own internal logic, which is irreducible to any other form and incommensurate with all others. Regarding language, Cassirer sees himself in the tradition of Wilhelm von Humboldt: language is its own light which illuminates reality in its own way, it has, like myth, "its particular and proper source of light" that can only be explained by immersing oneself in these forms, rather than by explaining them through something else, from a standpoint outside of them. Thus, language as well as myth are their own original "ways of world-making" that deserve to be studied *from within*. In the study of myth and language, Cassirer also lays out in which way philosophy and the study of myth as well as philology can fruitfully interact; the latter "can fill in the outline and draw with firm, clear strokes what philosophical speculation could only suggestively sketch." This is a further indication of the Marburg-style view of the interaction between philosophy and the sciences; just as the relation between systematic and historical philosophizing is one of mutual support, the sciences and philosophy are divisible only artificially. Likewise the problems of linguistic and intellectual history are in equal measure those of logic and epistemology and their difference only one of degree.

Further Reading

Cassirer, Ernst, *Philosophy of Symbolic Forms*, Vol. I: *Language*; vol. II: *Myth*.
Schultz, William, *Cassirer and Langer on Myth. An Introduction*. London: Routledge, 2000.

"The Problem of the Symbol and Its Place in the System of Philosophy" (1927)

The present text was originally presented as a paper at the third conference for general aesthetics (*Ästhetik und allgemeine Kunstwissenschaft*) in Halle in 1927. This is noteworthy, since its audience was not that of the typical philosophy conference but consisted mainly of art historians; nor did Cassirer have any qualms about presenting his central ideas regarding a philosophy of the symbolic before a for the most part non-expert audience. The discussants in the question-and-answer session (not reproduced here) included, according to the official transcript, the philosopher and philologist Willy Moog and the Austrian philosopher and pedagogue Walther Schmied-Kowarzik. This text presents a non-technical and succinct summary of Cassirer's overall philosophical project, not only in explaining the crucial role and importance of the symbol and symbolic formation, but also explicating it in the symbolic forms of myth, language, science, and – as is fitting for this occasion – art.

The text presents a lucid explanation of the problem of the symbol and the symbolic, in good Marburg fashion by giving an account of the history of the *scholarship* of the problem, here Vischer's research into the central problem of symbolism in aesthetics, philosophy of language as well as philosophy of religion. Precisely because it is such a ubiquitous problem, this justifies Cassirer's treating it as a "systematic focal point towards which all the basic disciplines of philosophy are directed," indicating once again that a circumspect treatment of the problem can only arise from a collaboration between all of these disciplines, including philosophy. Indeed, the symbol, the way Cassirer understands it, is ubiquitous, in that we are surrounded by symbols. Things, in other words, which are real things "out there" in the world are yet endowed with meaning, as belonging to a larger sphere of spirit (as Hegel might call it, and Cassirer is increasingly less shy in invoking this term). Thus, we are confronted with symbols in the spheres of religion, art, even in problems of logic, if we survey the history of newer logical developments starting from Leibniz and going into the nineteenth century (Hilbert, Helmholtz). Taken in this general and pervasive manner, this is a reversal of the normal (substantial) conception of things in favor of that after the Copernican Turn: things are what they are based on the way we intuit them. Indeed, it is further proven that the same "real" (physical) thing can have an entirely different meaning depending on the symbolic gaze we direct at it. It is here where Cassirer recounts – in greater detail than elsewhere – the example that recurs several times in different contexts in his writings, namely that of the meandering line. Depending on the gaze I direct at it, it literally is the curve of a function to the mathematician, an ornament to the aesthetic gaze, a magically enchanted carrier of a mythic-religious meaning, or a curve indicating a periodic oscillation of a monitor to a physicist. For the philosopher, this leads to the general conclusion: "Philosophy is not permitted to settle for establishing one of these points of view no matter how comprehensive it may nonetheless appear to be. Instead, it must attempt to encompass them all in a higher synopsis and understand each of them in its constitutive principle, for it is precisely the totality of these principles which constitutes the objective unity and totality of mind."

In the rest of the text, Cassirer indicates how the different worlds of form in their "directionality" achieve their respective symbolic forms and what the general philosophical problem consists in. Cassirer sees a general mapping of the symbolic function in the triad of expressive, representative, and signifying functions, which are not enacted equally in each form. On the contrary, each form "has a different relationship to the three basic poles that we have tried to distinguish here." (This theme is later treated in greater detail in his late text on "base phenomena.") In the general manner of describing faithfully each symbolic form, Cassirer also makes explicit reference to the phenomenological method (in the contemporary, not Hegelian, sense). These symbolic functions Cassirer sketches briefly in the areas of linguistics, modern physics, and ends with a brief discussion of the nature of aesthetic form. Cassirer ends by spelling out the idealistic upshot of his philosophy of the symbolic. If every symbolic form has its own internal logic of functioning, each of them lays claim to truth, a "kind of truth" that is relative to this form, but which does not end up in a relativism of truths. Rather, by spelling out the "architectonic connection" in every sphere of objectivity we bring into view the "meaningful order of the construction" of each respective form, carried out by an "original formative principle." To carry this through with respect to each symbolic form is nothing other than being true to the spirit of Kant's Copernican Revolution.

Notes

1 *Einstein's Theory of Relativity*, p. 447.
2 *Language and Myth*, p. x.

Further Reading

Krois, John Michael, *Symbolic Forms and History*, New Haven/London: Yale University Press, 1987.

"Hermann Cohen and the Renewal of Kantian Philosophy" (1912)[1]

I

The three works dedicated to securing the foundation of Kantian doctrine are linked inextricably to Hermann Cohen's philosophical life's work.[2] For as much as Cohen distanced himself from Kant's conclusions on individual points in building his own system, the methodological consciousness that inspired all of Cohen's individual achievements certainly first achieved clarity and maturity in his scientific, comprehensive analysis of Kant's fundamental works. So in this case there is no division, no partitioning wall between the historian and the systematic philosopher. The impact that Cohen's books on Kant have had rests above all on this inner cohesion. The particular power of these books, and certainly, at the same time, their peculiar difficulty, consists in the fact that here the understanding of Kant is not considered as a matter for a detached historical professionalism, rather, it presupposes throughout a particular systematic position on the fundamental problems. The thinker positions himself in the great context of the history of philosophy and of science: "philosophizing on one's own steam," in which each individual tries to find the solution to the problem of being solely in a personal, contingent reaction, should be brought to an end. But, at the same time, a historical perspective opens up here that cannot be achieved by any pragmatic description of a mere succession of "systems." Each thought, each authentic fundamental theme for philosophizing, is situated in an ideal community with all the others: initially, this community of ideas lends sense and life to historical consideration as well. Cohen situates his works within this view of the task of history, outside the sphere of all mere "Kant-philology." Kantian doctrine is not taken here as a dead and indifferent subject matter to be dissolved, as it were, into its individual isolated elements by a disinterested manipulation of concepts, and then put back together again in clever and erudite permutations. Rather, from the outset a highly unified point of view is present here, according to which the details of the system should be surveyed and grasped as a true whole. For Cohen, Kant's system answers the truly fateful question of philosophy in general: the question of the relation between philosophy and science. The reconstruction of this system from its original driving forces takes us into the midst of the historical debate over the continuation of philosophy itself. The value of Kant's doctrine is that the sharpest, most concise expression of this debate is found in his work: it is the quintessential revelation of his thought, the seminal significance of which is attached to no single time and no single school.

To feel the true weight of this way of looking at the problem, one must place oneself back in the era in which Cohen's studies of Kant began.[3] At the time the fundamental questions of philosophy appeared to be solved, because, insofar as these questions were shared with the disciplines of the natural sciences, they seemed to be absorbed by the sciences. Any independent methodological awareness of the fundamental presuppositions of cognition[4] was regarded now as a relapse into dialectic, and the now mature discipline [of philosophy] believed itself to be free, finally, of the demands of dialectic. The meaning and content of cognition should be determined by specific empirical methods and by the empirical results of particular sciences, rather than by the abstract generalities of speculative reflection. So according to the fundamental view of the time, all that the consideration of nature and history can deliver in terms of positive data takes the place of any system that tries to encompass the whole of actuality.[5] Cohen's position on this fundamental view is characteristic, in its positive aspects as well as in the negative ones. He takes the fact of science as a foundation unrestrictedly; but, with Kant, he transforms this fact in turn into a problem. Now, with this simple methodological change, it appears that the sense of the leading model of cognition undergoes a radical conversion. Even when it was most prevalent, "naturalism" as a *metaphysical* view never achieved unlimited dominance. In the circles of speculative philosophy, Schopenhauer's idealist doctrine was opposed to it, and in research circles, most notably, Helmholtz's epistemological research (which was, again, linked deliberately to Kant) was opposed to it. But one can see the power exercised by the methodology of naturalism even in these conflicts, even where one thought the real content of its worldview had been surmounted. True, from his metaphysical heights Schopenhauer looked down genteelly on the "men of the crucible and of the alembic,"[6] but nonetheless in his epistemology[7] he used, utterly naively and without critical scrutiny, the *language* that natural science, and in particular physiology, had constructed. In fact, *Helmholtz* made this language incomparably sharper and more precise; but even he used it far beyond the limits within which it is valid in a strict sense, and within which alone it possesses a real meaning beyond the metaphorical. The entire doctrine of the *a priori* appears from now on as a mere extension of a certain individual result of natural science: it becomes a continuation of and a correlative to *Johannes Müller*'s doctrine of specific nerve energies.[8] The power of the generally naturalistic method of reasoning is demonstrated most persuasively by the fact that this method immediately casts a spell even over Kantian epistemology, which is invoked against it. As much as *Friedrich Albert Lange* attempts to overcome the dogmatism of naturalism, "psychophysical organization," which surely describes the puzzle of cognition rather than solves it, remains the last word to him nonetheless.[9] Even *Otto Liebmann*'s early writings, despite all their freedom of thought, move unquestionably in this direction. Liebmann's 1869 text "On the objective perspective" attempts to pursue Schopenhauer's and Helmholtz's insights further, and even Liebmann's discussion in *Analysis of Actuality* finds definite confirmation of Kant's doctrine that space is phenomenal in modern physiological theories and results.[10] Thus, all these efforts effectively take on the color of the very systems they are fighting. They search in vain to analyze the whole critically, meanwhile taking one element of the cognition of nature as fixed. The *a priori* truths, understood in terms of "type classification,"[11] become a particular class of psychophysical "actualities," and thus inevitably are classified under, and subordinated to, the conditions for cognition of actuality, rather than being able to ground them and analyze them independently. Likewise, whether phenomenal actuality is interpreted as "a product of the brain" or, in seemingly refined usage, as "a product of representation,"[12] the mere concept of a "product" still begs the entire question from the standpoint of epistemology.

Cohen's interpretation and critique of Kant introduces an original twist on this point. It comes about through simple reference to those ideas that Kant himself places constantly at the center of his doctrine. The "revolution of thought" developed in the critique of reason is rooted in the transcendental problem; however, "transcendental," for Kant, means an approach that begins not from the objects but from our *kind of cognition* of objects in general. The fundamental error[13] of the "naturalistic" offshoots emerges clearly right away, in the light of this definition of the concept: for these offshoots must always presuppose a particular domain of objects, and a particular form of interaction between them, to describe the process of cognition. As long as the question of what kind of cognition of the object justifies knowledge[14] of the object remains unanswered, the question of the being of the object in the transcendental sense remains undetermined and inexplicable. Accordingly, the true object of *philosophy* is not the "organization" of nature, nor that of the "psyche," rather, above all it must determine and bring to light only the "organization" of the *cognition of nature*. This start sets the course of all the following inquiries accurately. In fact, from now on there are no more unsuspected or paradoxical twists: the new starting point determines further progress unambiguously and necessarily. From now on, the "facts" of natural science are valid only insofar as they can be justified by secure and exact *judgments*. Now we can achieve such security in that way only where particular natural judgments are anchored effectively in general fundamental judgments of mathematics. The order of *certainty* goes from mathematics to physics, not vice versa. So the transcendental question should be directed at *mathematical natural science* first. Of course, it is not at all accurate when it is said that Cohen's cognition-critique addresses itself one-sidedly to mathematical theories of nature alone. The origin of this fundamental idea already rules out such a view, for this view requires us to overlook Cohen's critique of *physiology*, no less than that of *physics*, within the general context of the problem that Cohen encountered. But the most general, fundamental meaning of the concept of object itself, which even physiology presupposes, cannot be determined rigorously and securely except in the language of mathematical physics. The concept of sensation leads to that of "stimulus," which leads back to the general concept of motion. "Nature" must be conceived as a system of mechanical processes[15] that stand in a lawful relationship to each other before we can count on it for cognition, as we would count on a fixed and well-founded datum. While dogmatic materialism attempts to derive thought as a special case of mechanics, this way of seeing it only needs to be developed, and thought through to a conclusion, to lead quickly to a peculiar about-face. For when the concept of mechanics is taken not in its unclear sense as a popular catchphrase but in its precise scientific meaning, mechanics itself leads back to mathematical, that is, to *ideal* fundamental elements. What motion "is" cannot be expressed except in concepts of quantity; understanding these presupposes a fundamental system of a pure doctrine of quantity.[16] Consequently, the principles and axioms of mathematics become the specific foundation that must be taken as fixed in order to give content and sense to any statement of natural science about actuality.

In so doing, we achieve an immediate consequence, strictly continuous with the same idea. The analysis of cognition does not concern itself with the sphere of discussion of any kind of existing actualities and their causal interactions; rather, it develops a general ideal interrelation between truths and their reciprocal dependency relations, regardless of all such assumptions about the actuality of things. It is enough to secure the pure meaning of these truth relations before making any application to existing things. So already, in its very ideality, cognition-critique takes a strictly *objective* turn: it does not deal with representations and processes in the thinking individual, but with the validity relation[17] between principles and "propositions,"[18] which as such must be established independently of any consideration of the subjective-psychological event of thinking.[19] This fundamental idea of "transcendental" method has proven particularly effective and fruitful in the development of nineteenth-century philosophy. All of contemporary logic appears to be guided and pervaded by it. The idea [*of "transcendental" method*], which initially must have appeared paradoxical next to the leading naturalism and psychologism of the 1870s, begins to be more and more of a scientific common ground. From its disparate starting points, philosophical development drew ever nearer to it: the "pure logic," whose challenge *Husserl* took up following *Bolzano*, as well as the new "object-theoretical"[20] research that branched off bit by bit from psychology, are directed toward the ideal that *Cohen*'s texts on Kant first worked out in its full precision and forcefulness.

The energy with which science is referred to as the true and indispensable correlative to the transcendental method explains the need to preserve the "objective" sense of Kantian idealism. Where this connection is relaxed, theoretical idealism loses its sure guide. For then, despite all efforts toward interpersonal content, theoretical idealism approaches the problematic sphere of psychological representational idealism. For Cohen, on the other hand, the "unity of consciousness" is only another expression for the unity of the synthetic principles on whose validity rests the possibility of experience and, thus, the possibility of objectivity in general. The organization of the "mind"[21] that idealism seeks can be deciphered nowhere else but in the structural relationships of natural science, ethics and aesthetics.

> So initially critique is the warning not to equate philosophy with mathematics or natural science or to put them only on the same terms. Philosophy does not have to create things, or, as the seductive and notorious phrase looted from mathematics has it, to "construct" them, but instead simply to understand and to re-examine how the objects and laws of mathematical experience are constructed. But with this warning, critique brings the insight, and at the same time the consolation, that mathematical natural science does not rest on mathematics and experience alone, but is itself an element of philosophy. Critique teaches how to recognize this element, and thus when the philosopher re-examines the object of his critique, he sees a mind from his own mind.[22]

Certainly, following Kant's words, we can know nothing of things *a priori* besides what "we ourselves" put into them: but the self that is at issue here will not be grasped in speculative musings about science, but solely in the continuity and lawfulness of the subject's activity. This lawfulness is the first hypothesis of transcendental research, which, insofar as that research itself makes progress, is transformed more and more into assertoric certainty. And the same relationship is repeated in the remaining areas of philosophy. Even ethicists cannot create the content of the moral law, but instead establish the "formula" for this content.

> And even for aesthetics, the final element of the system, critique says something positive as well as negative: namely, what the philosopher is entitled to for the discovery of the aesthetic law. He does not need to give the rule and law – as if he were the genius – but instead to learn from art works, and from the relationship between special aesthetic interests and the innocence of nature, on which rests the devotion to the lovely allure of "purposefulness without a purpose," as well as our means of understanding it in general and situating it conceptually. The law of the beautiful cannot be discovered philosophically, rather, it is to be composed out of that on the basis of which such a law can exist and does exist.[23]

Thus, even this doctrine recognizes throughout a "given" to which philosophical consideration is to orient itself; but it is almost a given of a higher level, which consists in the logical structure of principles and ideas, rather than in the material determinateness of things.[24]

At the same time, this transformation brings about a completely modified account of the oppositions on whose basis the problem of cognition had been considered and described until now. Above all, this involves the opposition between "subjective" and "objective" itself, which from now on must withdraw, for it cannot count any longer as any kind of a clear expression of the connection that the "transcendental" approach establishes between cognition and science. It is undeniable that Kant's *language* still supports this distinction wholeheartedly; but the *fundamental idea*[25] of critique has grown beyond him on principle. For the transcendental-"subjective" is that which is demonstrated as a necessary and generally valid factor in cognition of any kind; but the highest "objective" view we can attain accounts for just that. So before taking any further steps, it is enough to see that "subjective" and "objective" are no longer to be seen as elements of a proper disjunction *after* the "Copernican revolution in thought" has once been completed. Just as transcendental cognition never begins as cognition of the object as such, but of the kind of cognition of objects in general, as far as this can be possible *a priori*: likewise, the value of the *a priori* can never be identified as belonging directly to any class of objects as a predicate, but in every case can be meant only as a characterization of a certain kind of cognition. "That the two concepts are complements that belong together elevates the *a priori* above the realm of oppositions: actual–possible; object–concept; thing–idea[26]; objective–subjective"[27]. The idea is the basis of "thingness"[28], but certainly only as the objectivity[29] and necessity of a judgment; the concept becomes the "ground" of the "object"[30], but where objecthood[31] is understood as nothing but the expression of a necessary theoretical relation, of belonging together. The principal concept that contains all these disparate points of view, and gives them their unity and their relative meaning, is the "possibility of experience." "Things"[32], then, are given to us only as contents of a possible experience; however, experience itself is never exhausted by the matter of particular perceptions, but necessarily contains a relation to specific formal principles of connection. This insight overturns even the opposition of "empiricism" and "rationalism"; for that "reason" of which theoretical idealism speaks must be exhibited in the *system of experience itself*. Thus, insofar as experience must be conceived as a unity, the moment of the logical is within experience, while, in contrast, the necessary relation to the problem of giving form to the empirical is brought forward in the logical functions, and thus an indissoluble relation between both elements is forged. Without cognition of this correlation, experience itself remains only an unclear catchphrase; and the problem with historical "empiricism" consists in the fact that it has "considered and put forward this most imprecise and indeterminate word, about which one can allow oneself to think all the right things as well as all the most perverse, as the final solution to all questions about the foundations and, not least, about the value of cognition."

The reciprocal connection of the logical and the empirical moment of cognition emerges most clearly in the further treatment that Cohen has given Kant's principle of the "Anticipations of Perception." Here lies the path that, in its continuation, has led on to Cohen's own systematic formation of the *Logic of Pure Cognition*.[33] The thought-structure that begins here forms the final and fateful step in the overall direction of Cohen's approach to the renewal of the Kantian doctrine. The natural-scientific "realities" should no longer count as the self-evident and unquestionable *beginning* of cognition-critique. They reveal themselves to a progressive analysis as *ideal* structures:[34] as contents whose determinacy rests on the logical content[35] they contain. In this way, matter and motion, force and mass are conceived as instruments of cognition. However, the high point of this development will be reached only when we return to the fundamental mathematical motive,[36] which comes before all specific conceptual formation in the natural sciences. This motive lies before us in the theoretical method of the "infinitesimal." Without it, it would be impossible to describe rigorously the concept of motion as mathematical natural science presupposes it, let alone to have a conceptual command of the lawfulness of motions. Thus, the circle of critical research closes here. For there can be no further doubt that the concept of the infinitely small describes not a sensibly graspable "existence"[37] but a specific kind, and fundamental orientation, of thought: but in this fundamental orientation the concept of the infinitely small proves itself to be, henceforth, the necessary presupposition for the object of natural science.

Certainly an objection can be raised against this narrow dependence of logic on the fundamental forms of mathematical natural science. Philosophy appears to be robbed of its self-sufficiency by this dependence, and to be linked inextricably to the contingent particularities of a specific science. Will not philosophy be entrapped in the fate of this science as well, in its temporal rise and fall? If it is true that, as Cohen formulated it explicitly, "only a Newtonian could come forward as Kant," then any revision to Newton's mechanics threatens the system of "synthetic principles" to its essential core. However, Cohen's own development has refuted this account of his doctrine. For, with the same energy that Cohen devotes to placing the Newtonian system at the focus of attention, he has followed the transformations that Newton's system has experienced in the physics of the nineteenth century with resolute interest and impartial appreciation. Not only was he one of the first to point out the *philosophical* significance of *Faraday*, he delved into the principles of *Heinrich Hertz's* mechanics, to understand and to justify their content for the critique of cognition.[38] So, for Cohen, the orientation to science does not imply any commitment to its temporal, contingent form. The "givenness" that the philosopher recognizes in the mathematical science of nature ultimately means the givenness of the *problem*. In its actual form the philosopher seeks and recognizes an ideal form, which he singles out, to confront it with the changing historical configuration as a standard for measurement.[39] If this is an apparent circle, it is an unavoidable circle, for it arises from that reciprocal interaction between idea and experience through which – according to the words of Goethe – the ethical and scientific world is governed.

On another front, Cohen's own system not only allows for but directly requires an advance over the boundaries of the problems of mathematical natural science. The problem of the organism, the problem of life can never be completely absorbed in the forms of motion of pure mechanics. Insofar as the ideality of these forms of motion is known, it is understood at the same time that the true *forms of life*, the individuals of biology, are indeed categorically subordinate to mechanics, but simultaneously, that the full content of the individuals of biology could never be exhausted by mechanics. The point-masses that underlie the motions of pure mechanics as subjects are only the first abstract *approach* to the problem. The classification of chemical substances already poses a new problem for science, and the more we expand our consideration of the embodiment of *natural history*, the farther and more unfathomably it stretches before us. It will not be gratuitous to present "systematic unities," which any descriptive natural science presupposes, next to the synthetic unities of the mathematical-dynamical principles; "for the system of nature, like experience, must include any natural science that does not proceed mathematically, whether it is constrained to do so or whether it does so willingly."

> Even assuming that the ideal of mathematical natural science were entirely realized, and that we were able to express all natural forms in static mechanical equations, mechanics still would not have exhausted the interest of the description of nature. For we want to classify natural forms, not merely as relations of equilibrium under mechanical processes, but instead according to the quality of their structure. It is not enough to fix the sun as the center of gravity, the sun should also be described according to the kind of substances that burn in it. Now when the plant and animal bodies sustained by the sun come into the question, it becomes evident that the

structures and objectivizations[40] that are at issue certainly go beyond the mechanical abstractions of points in motion, but can in no way be absorbed into them with nothing left over. At best, it can appear that the ideal of research, to measure all nature by the system of points in motion, is realized in the case of chemical reactions. But if, even in chemistry itself, ordering and distinguishing elements as such necessitates another principle besides that of material points, then the urgent need for such a principle is unmistakable in the case of organisms that certainly tend to be investigated, after all, as mechanical–chemical aggregates, but which, for all that, form unities that are distinguished from those point-unities of mechanics by the problem and interests of research.[41]

Nonetheless this extension of the *range* of the concept of nature does not invalidate its *content* as it has been defined until now. For the idea of an *end*,[42] which steps in now as the fundamental principle of what is peculiar to living phenomena,[43] does not oppose the causal explanation, but rather shows the way to the continuous employment of this kind of explanation. As an "idea,"[44] the concept of an end aims for the systematic completion of the causal account, and for its unlimited realization. On these points Cohen follows closely the view realized in the *Critique of Judgment*. The purposefulness[45] of organisms represents a "boundary" but not a "barrier" to mechanical causality: for it sets forth a problem that as such, in and for itself, is certainly unfinishable, but whose completion must be progressively *sought after* by means of the causal explanation itself. Thus, purposefulness describes a new and specific direction of research; it is a regulative [idea] of *cognition*, but not an objectively[46] absolute power that underlies phenomenal causation. So the "turn,"[47] toward which Cohen's entire critical *oeuvre* is directed, was brought a step further into the center of work in natural science at the time. At the moment, it appears yet again that wherever, in the popular view, one has only to do with things and their effective forces, philosophical analysis is led to concepts and methods of cognition instead, determines their intrinsic validity, and distinguishes them from one another. However, insofar as the problem of *being* is directed back to the problem of *actuality* in this way, a new and broader problem arises. That problem is to determine the meaning of the concept of actuality within a comprehensive *system of validity*[48] and, since until now the single directions of theoretical consciousness were isolated from each other, to determine the whole, the fundamental orientation of theoretical reason in general, by confronting it with the kind of validity of ethical and aesthetic consciousness.

II

The foundation of theoretical philosophy carried out in the transcendental case has achieved an entirely new standpoint on the justification of ethics. Every worldview that begins with the "things"[49] and their real interaction and that calculates with them as if with established, absolute data sees itself landed in a particular difficulty with regard to the problem of ethics. For as much as one wants to describe and analyze this thing-world[50] as well: the phenomenon of the "ought"[51] has no location in it and cannot be teased out of it by any analysis, however astute. So when seen from this standpoint, this phenomenon remains a stranger to philosophy. Thus, skepticism must always be rehearsed over and over about whether the ethical problem in general deals with a meaningful, factually necessary question or, rather, with an illusion peculiar to representation. In the most favorable case, the ethical appears as a peculiar and paradoxical side-effect of the world of the existing and actual: as an epiphenomenon that materializes as a particular individual step of "being," which stands in a relationship with being itself, but not in an internal and necessary one.

In contrast, from the beginning the critical reduction of being to the validity of first principles reorients even the determination of ethics[52]. Now the "maxims" and "rules" don't make up anything plainly new, for which a logical state of affairs would be tracked down first: rather, they are the particular material of any philosophical consideration in general, which is established already by the foundation of theoretical science. The question of the lawfulness of cognition immediately stands aside for the question of the lawfulness of the will. In both cases, however, the law is not considered as a specific actual natural agent, which would be demonstrated somehow in the organization of the particular individual. The ethical norm cannot be represented as a kind of natural-scientific *average*, which is to be abstracted from consideration of actual human actions. In full agreement with Kant, any *anthropological* turn here will be rejected even more sharply than in the area of pure cognition. Such a turn does not solve the problem, but rather defeats its purpose, insofar as it misjudges the particular meaning and orientation of the problem. The "actual" from experience in human history should not be made the standard of the ethically "possible," because, on the contrary, all productivity of ethical thought consists in just that: to seek out and to establish a "possible," which itself demands a new "actuality" beyond anything given until now. The anthropological "rule" is never inherent in such a revolutionary stance with respect to the factual, for it must content itself with describing this factual itself according to its general historical type. Covering up this relationship with profound metaphysical formulas that claim to represent and to discover the "being" of the ethical cannot alter it. "A metaphysical wisdom, which can betray the psychological artifice of treating the in-itself of the world as so-called ethical drives, does not wish to designate ethics as a particular philosophical discipline, despite any revelation of its worth".[53]

In these matters, a distinction comes into play that Cohen had already made within the theoretical sphere, but which now demands a more rigorous definition. The questions of the lawful structure of theoretical and ethical "fact-of-being-conscious"[54] should not be confused with the question of why, of the metaphysical origin of consciousness. It is a question about consciousness when one demands to know how it occurs that representations are joined in us in spatial and temporal orders, that thought follows the determinate forms of substance, of causality and so on – instead of contenting oneself with what each of these forms means as a part of the logical whole of cognition, and with what ideal value is to be ascribed to them as a result. But only the latter problem allows for a real and precise answer, while the first threatens to lead us once more beyond the language of science into that of myth.

> The question of consciousness is the question of old metaphysics, not of cognition-critique. It has to do with the possibility of the qualitative determinations of consciousness: how it comes about that we have sensations, representations, feelings and desires, how it comes about that we sense blue, that we think of causality, that pleasure and pain stir in us. The old metaphysical schools gave their answers to this question as spiritualism or as materialism, with their nuances. These questions of consciousness as such become antiquated with cognition-critique.[55]

This insight, when applied to ethics, means that we do not need to look for the "law" of the will in itself, in the sense of asking: from which obscure source of the constitution of the world does the fact of the ethical will itself come forth? For while a decision about this may result, it certainly has nothing to do with the meaning of the ethical norm itself and can neither add to nor subtract from its validity.

> It is all the same, whether the men in [our] experience can love each other because it is blown into their souls by a creator, or indeed because they hate each other, but

love such a creator just because it exists, and thus love even its mirror images... We may marvel at the profundity of such decipherings of the code of the person, or we may appraise them as cheap half-truths of a one-sided anthropology; it can be acknowledged, though, that such analyses of our ethical representations and events have their uses for the explanation of moral judgments, and even, in a limited way, for the conception of political history. Nonetheless, we call such considerations and research *psychology* or *anthropology*, but not – ethics.[56]

For ethics does not look for the causal unity of the final cause of the determination of the will, but for the teleological unity in the content itself of these determinations. Ethics does not seek to establish where the determinations originate, but which form and quality they must have insofar as they are to be incorporated into a true unity, into a *system* of determinations of ends. Thus, the question is exactly analogous to that of pure cognition-critique: while the latter calls into question the possibility of their logical form and the conditions of this possibility, barring all assumptions about the origin of representations, here it suffices to establish those conditions to which the maxim of the individual act of will must conform, insofar as that maxim needs to have universal validity beyond the contingent particularity of the specific thing willed.

This connection between ethics and the doctrine of experience sheds new light on the main features of the general methodology. The comprehensive expression of the "law" henceforth will be the central point of the system: so much so that *Kant's Grounding of Ethics*[57] could venture the formulation that the law itself is the "thing in itself."[58] Appearances must stand under laws, must be expressed as single cases of laws to achieve the status of objective reality and objective validity. They constitute the fulfillment of the content of the synthetic principles, and play a part in "being"[59] to the extent that they do so. However, if one inquires further into the "being" of these principles themselves, it is important to avoid confusion of this being with any manifestly given, "palpable" actuality. As soon as such a confusion is made, any approach to the mere question of *ethics* is certainly out of the question; but, fundamentally, *logic* too is given its sense in this way.

> It is still the same old [argument about the] impulse of the stone.[60] As the ideas should eke out a kind of existence in an intelligible realm, in order to signify an innate true being, so the lawful realities[61] still have an individual existence as well, so they can lend that existence to appearances. However, existence means not only to be in the form of our spatial intuition, but also to be demonstrable in *sensation*. Further, the laws of appearances call for, and indicate, a unification of our forms of intuition with still other particularities and conditions of our knowledge. This unification, residing again in the form of spatial intuition and also completely, demonstrably, represented in sensation, is what the ancients called the third man.[62] It is nothing but the sheer, indestructible confusion between *intuitive* representation and *conceptual* thought, which the word leads to even here. The law is the reality – that is to say, reality is to be conceived as a *conceptual* thought, not as intuitive, intuitable representation; *as a sign*[63] *of the validity of cognition* and as nothing else. The appearance is any half-baked object that we confront ourselves with by means of intuition.[64]

This affiliation of being with a "sign" provides the "ought" as well with a secure and unassailable persistence in the whole system: the highest persistence, of which only the "idea" is capable. Once one overcomes the hereditary defect of materialism, "to think of all objectivity as material, in the unexplained forms of space and time," one can appreciate that

that which is true, is real, is valid, does not need to appear as such in sensible materiality: thus, in principle, nothing more stands in the way of the recognition of the specific ethical "*a priori.*" Cohen never made an attempt to reduce "being" to the "ought"; rather, he held the moments strictly separate according to their specific individuality, while, admittedly, they are posited and combined again, in connection with one another, under the general main concept of "validity."[65] Cohen's Kant books have determined decisively the direction of modern research on these points as well. The category of "validity," which for *Lotze*[66] accompanies a specific metaphysics, first achieves full methodological clarity and independence here with Cohen, while at the same time the single types of validity, not reducible to each other, preserve their full individuality and remain recognized for it.

Cohen's account of the *concept of freedom*, and his presentation of the Kantian doctrine of freedom, supports a clearer determination of his fundamental insight in ethics. Here his method is presented with a difficult problem: for this part of the Kantian system is the most closely interwoven with metaphysical motives. Personality reveals itself in "intelligible character" as the autonomous core and the true "in itself" of actuality. In fact, any purely historical reproduction of the Kantian system would have to recognize that even Kant himself did not reach a sharp and clear distinction between the purely *methodological* and the *ontological* questions quite yet. In particular, the treatment of the concept of freedom in the *Critique of Pure Reason* presents both interests next to each other and still almost undistinguishable from each other, and the original *critical* meaning of the concept is defined precisely only with the new completion of content that the concept achieves in the *Groundwork for a Metaphysics of Morals* and in the *Critique of Practical Reason*. Thus, Cohen's analyses are not so much simple reproduction as they are a conscious sharpening and development of the Kantian fundamental idea. As Cohen emphasizes himself,

> Here is one of the most outstanding features with which to approach the method that will be put into practice in these books, which are dedicated to the reconstruction of the Kantian system as a method that is historically fruitful as much as systematically: not to introduce and to announce the appropriate path on the basis an awareness of improvements one has made oneself, let alone on the basis of a cheaply inflated opposition; but to establish independently the foundation of the transcendental method, rediscovered and laid anew in the spirit of its creator, and, not less, to complete the structure according to the plan of the system, with free choice of each single building block, with no limits on the investigation into the adequacy of each one of them, and with the undisputed right to include some missing concepts and to exclude false ones.[67]

But the Kantian doctrine of freedom is allowed to achieve a clearer and sharper sense under this assumption, if we maintain that freedom, according to the new meaning that it attains with Kant, is no concept of cause but purely and exclusively a *concept of end*.[68] Understood in this sense, the concept of freedom does not describe the mysterious cause from which our ethical behavior originates, but the content of the determination of the goal on which it converges. This relationship can be expressed, perhaps, as follows: as ethical subjects, we act not from freedom, but towards freedom.[69] Thus, for Cohen, the idea of "autonomy" becomes the idea of "autotely":[70] the only act that is ethically autonomous and worthy is directed to the realization of a community,[71] in which each individual that belongs to it is [treated] "always at the same time as an end, and never as a mere means." The idea of such a community is an indispensable and unwavering *regulative*[72] of our action: but we mustn't sensualize it as a *corpus mysticum* of existing "intelligible essences." Here is the front of Cohen's battle against such accounts of the Kantian doctrine of freedom as became popular with *Schopenhauer*. If we understand freedom as if it is taken from the empirical I and brought forward from an intelligible I, as if it has given a certain form to the will in an autonomous act located beyond all temporality – then while one may consider its theoretical truth or falsity, in any case the problem and the orientation of ethics are frustrated through this mystical explanation. For this "freedom," which remains suspended in the mere indifference of an originally timeless determination of choice, still has no *positive* sense and content, in itself, at all. From the standpoint of the empirical individual, it is indifferent whether we relinquish the conditions of nature or an unknown mythical power that confronts the individual extrinsically: his "personality" in the ethical sense is annulled in the former as in the latter case. Thus, it does not help anything to take the responsibility for the phenomenal subject and to saddle him with an "Adam from a transcendental rib"; that way, the problem is only pushed back into an impenetrable obscurity, but is in no way solved or even formulated. "Freedom" is a truly "intelligible" concept only insofar as it is not broken down into any kind of givenness, but rather strictly retains the character of a *problem*.[73] Thus, the thought of the ideal "community of ends" gives the criteria for an individual: according to this idea, the individual becomes "free" insofar as he dissociates himself from contingent empirical ties. Thus, freedom is not understood as a "noumenon" already available in actual existence; rather, freedom itself, as the correlative concept of the ethical law, makes up the *content* of the noumenon, for it proposes a requirement that goes beyond all determinate, particular empirical ends. The idea preserves its pure validity and meaning only where one has learned to dispense with the need to support it with, and to ground it in, some purported existence. The whole fundamental orientation of the view makes it clear that the *application* of the idea of freedom to the empirical actuality of human history will not wither away as a result; for as the theoretical *a priori* promotes a constant reference back to "experience" and its possibility, so the idea of a "kingdom of ends" is the maxim to which the phenomenal order of nature conforms – in fact, according to which that order itself should be constructed from the active subject from within temporality. In contrast, from an apparently lofty perspective, spiritualism abstracts away from even all these truly "practical" goals.

> And so truly there is no lack of examples from any time of enthusiastic idealism ossified into a base, contemptible realism, which endows its creations of reason with sublime attributes – but people indulge them as if they pleased God; since it would make it easy for them if it did please God. The physical man[74] climbs onto any step of the ladder of spiritualism, which arrogates to itself the name of idealism and holds itself to be in mystical readiness – this ladder lies outside all experience, in the miraculous. And so, with the opportunity to climb down, the possibility to climb up is also lacking. The idea, which acquires the status of a sensible existence, loses the value of cognition that is secure in the maxim.[75]

Here, as with the doctrine of experience, we can go into only a few of the details of Cohen's view of Kantian ethics: only the continuous kinship of the structure of the *principles* of both doctrines must be discussed here, for each clarifies the other in turn. And this analogy between the fundamental themes anticipates, already, that new connection that both sets of problems encounter within *aesthetics*. The foundation of aesthetics is, like that of ethics, interwoven systematically with the problem of "actuality." As long as the theoretical sense of this problem remains unilluminated, the conceptual status of any "being" alive in and specific to the art work will remain unidentified. The question arises always as to whether the world of aesthetic imagination[76] is a mere "imitation"[77] of nature or stems from a particular structural principle, which causes, autonomously, a new objective world to emerge from it. With this view of the question, the problem of being steps out of any abstract isolation which it seems to suffer while staying within pure epistemological[78] considerations. For in the eighteenth century, aesthetic culture itself was led back to these fundamental questions purely as a result of its own needs. Thus, the circle of cultural interests closed here: art became the *formation*[79] of that relationship between "idea" and "actuality" that theoretical critique formulated and grounded in general. Cohen's presentation of Kantian aesthetics pursued this connection in detail, in its manifold ramifications, [272] and, to an extent, had grasped again the intellectual principle from which its historical effectiveness developed. The general standpoint of the reconstruction that Cohen had put at the forefront proves its worth at just this point.

> The historical existence of a person coincides in no way with his personal action and will. Thus, historical understanding obtains by fraud the principle that any individual belongs in a powerful sense to an historical order, even if he may see it that way himself. Then we understand an event historically only when we conceive of it in that connection, which must remain hidden from it itself.[80]

Even if one refrains from considering *Schiller's* relationship to Kant, nonetheless those "secret-yet-fully-open" relationships remain, between *Kant* and *Winckelmann* or between *Kant* and *Goethe* or *Beethoven*. Even the *theoretical* picture of Kantian aesthetics will be completed only when one includes these relationships in the whole picture, even if that picture is only "intelligible." At the same time, in this completion of the system the transcendental fundamental idea of method comes to the fore yet again, with full acuity. From now on, full "homogeneity" exists between the two fundamental orientations of consciousness: like the world of art, the world of empirical, spatio-temporal existence, and likewise the world of ethical values, is not "encountered" immediately, but rests on principles of formation[81] that critical reflection discovers, and whose validity critical reflection demonstrates. Thus, art is no longer isolated among the kinds of consciousness; rather, art is that which presents the "principle" of these kinds and their relationship in a new sense. The transcendental system does not present so much a cohesive relationship between cognitions as it does a relationship between the kinds of development[82] of consciousness, of which each brings forth a content specific to it. "These contents must be related to each other, because the kinds of development of all contents are related as kinds of development of consciousness, and consequently they form a systematic unity." The various subspecies of the comprehensive idea of *validity* are enumerated within this unity. Pre-critical idealism failed to realize this double turn, for from its perspective the world melted into a uniform unit of validity.[83]

> It wanted to derive all kinds of reality from consciousness; but it did not claim the right to determine a distinction between the values of cognition. Not only was the distinction between nature and ethics not determined clearly, even in the matter of the cultural spheres, but even such an important, encompassing, wide and universal sphere of culture as that which art presents had no place in the system of philosophy, and remained without a systematic validation, without the demonstration that consciousness, as the principle of all spheres of culture, is the source and condition for its value and end, and the foundation for its kind of development. Thus, the principle of consciousness was determined inadequately as long as it was unable to explain art.[84]

A fully resolved general ideal arises with these claims, toward which Cohen's systematic main works are directed throughout. In fact, there is the closest kind of interdependence between these works and the writings dedicated to the interpretation of the Kantian doctrine.

The tight interrelation between all the elements of Cohen's historical work is realized only with the rigor of his own systematic research, and only with the fully objective commitment to Kant's works could his own system determine its ideal, universal-historical position.

Notes

1. Translated by Lydia Patton. Originally published as "Hermann Cohen und die Erneuerung der Kantischen Philosophie," *Kantstudien* 17 (1912), pp. 252–73. In general, in what follows, I give the original words for many technical philosophical terms in footnotes. In cases where I think confusion might arise from the use of similar words (for instance, *Sache* and *Ding* used for "object" and "thing" in close proximity), I give the original in square brackets in the translated text. My own footnotes appear in square brackets followed by my initials; references to original German terms appear on their own – Trans.
2. *Kants Theorie der Erfahrung* (first ed. Hildesheim: Ferdinand Dümmler, 1871), hereafter KTE. *Kants Begründung der Ethik* (first ed., Berlin: Harwitz und Grossman, 1877), hereafter KBE. *Kants Begründung der Ästhetik* (first ed., Berlin, Ferdinand Dümmler, 1889), hereafter KBA – Trans.
3. Cohen began his studies for a doctorate in philosophy at the Humboldt University in Berlin, in 1864 – Trans.
4. *Erkenntnis*. In the following, I translate *Erkenntnis* as "cognition" in every case. As far as I know, Werner Pluhar (Immanuel Kant, *Critique of Pure Reason*, trans. Werner S. Pluhar (Indianapolis: Hackett, 1996)) originated this translation, pointing out that *Erkenntnis* does not actually correspond to the English word "knowledge." Related terms are translated in the same way: for instance, Cohen's term *Erkenntniskritik* becomes "cognition-critique." However, this translation is for purely linguistic reasons, and I do not intend it to indicate a philosophical stance – Trans.
5. In his work on Kant, Cohen distinguishes carefully between *Realität* [reality] and *Wirklichkeit* [actuality]. – Trans.
6. *Herren vom Tiegel und von der Retorte*. That is, empirical researchers – here, chemists. An alembic (*die Retorte*) is a device for distilling chemicals. – Trans.
7. *Erkenntnistheorie*. At the time, the term *Erkenntnistheorie* had a specialized meaning. For a discussion of this meaning, see Klaus Christian Köhnke, *The Rise of Neo-Kantianism: German Academic Philosophy between Idealism and Positivism*, trans. R.J. Hollingdale (Cambridge: Cambridge UP, 1991), pp. 36 f. – Trans.
8. *Lehre von spezifischen Sinnesenergien*. Helmholtz's mentor Johannes Müller had observed in research that the same stimulus could produce different responses in each sense organ. Instead, Müller observed, each sense organ has its own mechanism, distinct from the others, that determines the quality of sensations. Müller explained this by arguing that there is a "specific nerve-energy" for each nerve in the body (see, for example, Hermann Helmholtz, "Über das Ziel und die Fortschritte der Naturwissenschaft" in *Das Denken in der Naturwissenschaft* [1869] (Darmstadt: Wissenschaftliche Buchgesellschaft, 1968), p. 56) – Trans.
9. While the two clashed over Kant-interpretation, Lange was Cohen's strong supporter and mentor until he died, whereupon Cohen was chosen as Lange's natural successor for his professorship at Marburg. See especially Ulrich Sieg, "Die frühe Hermann Cohen und die Völkerpsychologie," *Ashkenas* 13.2 (2003), pp. 461–83 – Trans.
10. "Über den objektiven Anblick," 1869, and *Analysis der Wirklichkeit*, first ed. 1876.
11. "*Gattungsorganisation*." A technical term found in Lange and many early neo-Kantians. – Trans.
12. "Product of the brain" is *Gehirnprodukt*, "product of representation" is *Vorstellungsprodukt*. – Trans.
13. *proton pseudos*
14. *Wissen*
15. *Bewegungsvorgänge*.
16. *Grössenlehre*.
17. *Geltungszusammenhang*.

18 "*Sätzen*," which could also be translated as "theorems." Quotation marks in the original. – Trans.
19 *Subjektiv-psychologischen Denkgeschehens.*
20 *Gegenstandstheoretisch.* Cf. Husserl's *Logical Investigations*, esp. Vol. I, ch. 11, "The Idea of a Pure Logic." With an object-directed research, Cassirer presumably means Alexius von Meinong's "Gegenstandstheorie" [Object Theory], cf. his *Über Annahmen*, 1st ed. 1902, 2nd 1910. – Ed.
21 "*Geist*."
22 *Geist von seinem Geiste.* KTE 578.
23 KTE 578.
24 *Dinge*
25 *Grundgedanke*
26 *DingeSache*
27 KTE, p. 135.
28 *Sachheit*
29 *Sachlichkeit*
30 *Gegenstand*
31 *Gegenständlichkeit*
32 *Dinge*
33 *Logik der reinen Erkenntnis.*
34 *Gebilde*
35 *als Inhalte, deren Bestimmtheit auf dem logischen Gehalt beruht*
36 *Das mathematische Grundmotiv*
37 In the whole of the text, I have translated "*Dasein*" as "existence" to distinguish it from *Sein*, which I have translated as "being." – Trans.
38 Both of these analyses can be found in Cohen, *Einleitung, mit kritischem Nachtrag, zur neunten Auflage von Langes Geschichte des Materialismus* in *Hermann Cohens Schriften zur Philosophie und Zeitgeschichte* (in this volume). – Ed.
39 *Maßstab*
40 *Objektivierungen*
41 KTE, pp. 508 f.
42 *Zweck*
43 *Lebenserscheinungen*
44 That is, as a "regulative idea" in Kant's sense. – Trans.
45 *Zweckmäßigkeit*
46 *Dingliche*
47 "*Umwendung*"
48 *System der Geltungswerte*
49 "*Dinge*"; quotation marks in the original.
50 *Dingwelt*
51 "*Das Sollen*"
52 *Sittlichkeit.*
53 KBE 2nd ed., p. 7.
54 "*Bewußtheit*" – A neologism coined by Natorp. – Ed.
55 KTE, pp. 207 f.
56 KBE 2nd ed., pp. 144 f.
57 *Kants Begründung der Ethik*
58 *Kants Begründung der Ethik*, p. 36.
59 *Sein*
60 This refers to Galileo's argument against Aristotle in the *Dialogue Concerning the Two Chief World Systems*. The *Dialogue* is Galileo's discussion of the relative merits of the Copernican heliocentric system and the Ptolemaic geocentric system. Galileo insists that his defense of the Copernican model is not absolute, but rather is directed against specific Peripatetics who had argued that the earth does not move. Within five months of publication of the *Dialogue* in 1632, Galileo was charged with heresy, and he was condemned in 1633. – Trans.
61 *Gesetzrealitäten*

62 *tritos anthropos*
63 *Wertzeichen*
64 KBE, pp. 28 f.
65 "*Geltungswert*"
66 Cf. the text reprinted in this volume as Chapter 6. – Ed.
67 KBE, 2nd ed., pp. 245 f.
68 *Zweckbegriff*
69 *Wir handeln [...] als ethische Subjekte nicht von der Freiheit aus, sondern auf die Freiheit hin.*
70 "*Autonomie*" and "*autotelie.*" That is to say freedom of "norms" is changed to freedom of "telos," or in Kant's sense, the freedom to set one's own ends – Trans.
71 *Gemeinschaft*
72 "*Regulativ*," i.e., again, a regulative idea in Kant's sense. – Trans.
73 *Aufgabe*
74 *Sinnenmensch*, perhaps as opposed to *Geistesmensch*, or spiritual man – Trans.
75 KBE 2nd ed., p. 301.
76 *Phantasie*
77 "*Nachahmung*"
78 *Erkenntnistheoretisch*
79 *Gestaltung*
80 Cassirer does not give the reference to this quotation from Cohen, but it seems to be from KBA. – Trans.
81 *Prinzipien der Gestaltung*
82 *Erzeugungsweisen*
83 *Eine unterschiedslose Geltungseinheit*
84 KBA, p. 96.

Chapter 15

"Euclidean and non-Euclidean Geometry" from *Einstein's Theory of Relativity* (1921)[1]

In the preceding considerations, however, we have taken up only incidentally an achievement of the general theory of relativity, which, above all others, seems to involve a "revolution of thought." In the working out of the theory, it is seen that the previous Euclidean measurements are not sufficient; the development of the theory can only take place by our going from the Euclidean continuum, which was still taken as a basis by the special theory of relativity, to a non-Euclidean four-dimensional space-time continuum and seeking to express all relations of phenomena in it. Thus a question seems answered physically which had concerned the epistemology of the last decades most vitally and which had been answered most diversely within it. Physics now proves not only the possibility, but the reality of non-Euclidean geometry; it shows that we can only understand and represent theoretically the relations, which hold in "real" space, by reproducing them in the *language* of a four-dimensional non-Euclidean manifold.

The solution of this problem from the side of physics was, on the one hand, for a long time hoped for as keenly, as, on the other hand, its possibility was vigorously denied. Even the first founders and representatives of the doctrine of non-Euclidean geometry sought to adduce experiment and concrete measurement in confirmation of their view. If we can establish, they inferred, by exact terrestrial or astronomical measurements, that in triangles with sides of very great length the sum of the angles differs from two right angles, then empirical proof would be gained that in "our" empirical space the propositions not of Euclidean geometry, but of one of the others were valid. Thus, e.g., Lobachevskii, as is known, used a triangle $E_1 E_2 S$, whose base $E_1 E_2$ was formed by the diameter of the orbit of the earth and whose apex S was formed by Sirius and believed that he could, in this way, prove empirically a possible constant curvature of our space.[2] The fallacy in method of any such attempt must be obvious, however, to any sharper epistemological analysis of the problem, and it has been pointed out from the side of the mathematicians with special emphasis by H. Poincaré. No measurement, as Poincaré objects with justice, is concerned with space itself but always only with the empirically given and physical objects in space. No experiment therefore can teach us anything about the *ideal* structures, about the straight line and the circle, that pure geometry takes as a basis; what it gives us is always only knowledge of the relations of material things and processes. The propositions of geometry are therefore neither to be confirmed nor refuted by experience. No experiment will ever come into conflict with the postulates of Euclid; but, on the other hand, no experiment will ever contradict the postulates of Lobachevskii. For granted that some experiment could show us a variation in the sums of the angles of certain very great triangles, then the conceptual representation of this fact would never need to consist in, and methodologically could not consist in, changing the axioms of geometry, but rather in changing certain hypotheses concerning physical things. What we would have *experienced*, in fact, would not be another structure of space, but a *new law of optics*, which would teach us that the propagation of light does not take place in strictly rectilinear fashion. "However, we turn and twist," Poincaré therefore concludes, "it is impossible to attach a rational meaning to empiricism in geometry."[3] If this decision holds and if it can be proved, on the other hand, that among all possible self-consistent geometries the Euclidean possesses a certain advantage of "simplicity" since it defines the minimum of those conditions under which experience is possible in general, there would then be established for it an exceptional position from the standpoint of the critique of knowledge. It would be seen that the different geometries, which are equivalent to each other from a purely, formal standpoint, as regards their logical conceivability, are yet distinguished in their fruitfulness in the founding of empirical science. "The geometries are distinguished from each other in principle," one can conclude, "only by reference to their epistemological relation to the concept of experience; for this relation is positive only in the case of the Euclidean geometry."[4]

In connection, however, with the new development of physics in the general theory of relativity, this epistemological answer seems to become definitely untenable. Again and again the fact has been appealed to in the controversy concerning the epistemological justification of the different geometries that what determines value must not be sought in formal but in transcendental logic; that the compatibility of a geometry with experience is not involved but rather its "positive fruitfulness," i.e., the "founding of experience," that it can give. And this latter was thought to be found in Euclidean geometry. The latter appeared as the real and unique "foundation of possibility of knowledge of reality," the others, on the contrary, always as only the foundations of the possible. But with regard to the extraordinary rôle that the concepts and propositions of Riemannian geometry played in the grounding and construction of Einstein's theory of gravitation, this judgment cannot be supported. Supported by the same logical criterion of value, one now seems forced rather to the opposite conclusion: non-Euclidean space is alone "real," while Euclidean space represents a mere abstract possibility. In any event, the logic of the exact sciences now finds itself placed before a new problem. The fact of the fruitfulness of non-Euclidean geometry for physics can no longer be contested, since it has been verified, not only in particular applications, but in the structure of a complete new system of physics; what is in question is the explanation to be given to this fact. And here we are first forced to a negative decision, which is demanded by the first principles of the theory of relativity. Whatever meaning we may ascribe to the idea of non-Euclidean geometry for physics, for purely empirical thought, the assertion has lost all meaning for us that any space, whether Euclidean or non-Euclidean, is the "real" space. Precisely this was the result of the general principle of relativity, that by it "the last remainder of physical objectivity" was to be taken from space. Only the various relations of measurement within the physical manifold, within that inseparable correlation of space, time, and the physically real object, which the theory of relativity takes as ultimate, are pointed out; and it is affirmed that these relations of measurement find their simplest exact mathematical expression in the language of non-Euclidean geometry. This language, however, is and remains purely ideal and symbolic, precisely as, rightly understood, the language of Euclidean geometry could alone be. The reality which alone it can express is not that of things, but that of laws and relations. And now we can ask, epistemologically, only one question: whether there can be established an exact relation and coördination between the symbols of non-Euclidean geometry and the empirical manifold of spatio-temporal "events." If physics answers this question affirmatively, then epistemology has no ground for answering it negatively. For the "*a priori*" of space that it affirms as the condition of every physical theory involves, as has been seen, no assertion concerning any definite particular structure of space in itself, but is concerned only with that function of "spatiality" in general, that is expressed even in the general concept of the linear element *ds* as such, quite without regard to its character in detail.

If it is seen thus, that the determination of this element as is done in Euclidean geometry, does not suffice for the mastery of certain problems of knowledge of nature then nothing can prevent us, from a methodological standpoint, from replacing it by another measure, in so far as the latter proves to be necessary and fruitful physically. But in either case one must guard against taking the "preëstablished harmony between pure mathematics and physics," that is revealed to us in increasing fullness and depth in the progress of scientific knowledge, as a naïve copy theory. The structures of geometry, whether Euclidean or non-Euclidean, possess no immediate correlate in the world of *existence*. They exist as little physically in things as they do psychically in our "presentations" but all their "being," i.e., their validity and truth, consists in their ideal *meaning*. The existence, that belongs to them by virtue of their definition, by virtue of a pure logical act of assumption is, in principle, not to be interchanged with any sort of empirical "reality." Thus also the applicability, which we grant to any propositions of pure geometry, can never rest on any direct coinciding between the elements of the ideal geometrical manifold and those of the empirical manifold. In place of such a sensuous congruence we must substitute a more complex and more thoroughly mediate relational system. There can be no copy or correlate in the world of sensation and presentation for what the points, the straight lines and the planes of pure geometry signify. Indeed, we cannot in strictness speak of any degree of similarity, of greater or less difference of the "empirical" from the ideal, for the two belong to fundamentally different species. The theoretical relation, which science nevertheless establishes between the two, consists merely in the fact, that it, while granting and holding fast to the difference in content of the two series, seeks to establish a more exact and perfect correlation between them. All verification, which the propositions of geometry can find in physics, is possible only in this way. The particular geometrical truths or particular axioms, such as the principle of parallels, can never be compared with particular experiences, but we can always only compare with the whole of physical experience the whole of a definite system of axioms. What Kant says of the concepts of the understanding in general, that they only serve "to make letters out of phenomena so that we can read them as experiences" holds in particular of the concepts of space. They are only the letters, which we must make into words and propositions, if we would use them as expressions of the laws of experience. If the goal of harmony is not reached in this indirect way, if it appears that the physical laws to which observation and measurement lead us cannot be represented and expressed with sufficient exactitude and simplicity by a given system of axioms, then we are free to determine which of the two factors we shall subject to a transformation to reestablish the lost harmony between them. Before thought advances to a change of one of its "simple" geometrical laws it will first make the complex physical conditions that enter into the measurement responsible for the lack of agreement; it will change the "physical" factors before the "geometrical." If this does not lead to the goal and if it is seen on the other hand, that surprising unity and systematic completeness can be reached in the formulation of the "laws of nature" by accepting an altered conception of geometrical methods, then in principle there is nothing to prevent such a change. For if we conceive the geometrical axioms, not as copies of a given reality, but as purely ideal and constructive structures, then they are subjected to no other law than is given them by the *system* of thought and knowledge. If the latter proves to be realizable in a purer and more perfect form by our advancing from a relatively simpler geometrical system to a relatively more complex, then the criticism of knowledge can raise no objection from its standpoint. It will be obliged to affirm only this: that here too "no intelligible meaning can be gained" for empiricism in geometry. For here, too, experience does not *ground* the geometrical axioms, but it only selects from among them, as various logically possible systems, of which each one is derived strictly rationally, certain ones with regard to their concrete use in the interpretation of phenomena.[5] Here, too, Platonically speaking, phenomena are measured by Ideas, by the foundations of geometry, and these latter are not directly read out of the sensuous phenomena.

But when one grants to non-Euclidean geometry in this sense meaning and fruitfulness for physical experience, the general methodic difference can and must be urged, that still remains between it and Euclidean geometry. This difference can no longer be taken from their relation to experience, but it must be recognized as based on certain "inner" moments, i.e., on general considerations of the *theory of relations*. A special and exceptional logical position, a fundamental simplicity of ideal structure, can be recognized in Euclidean geometry even if it must abandon its previous sovereignty within physics. And here it is precisely the fundamental doctrine of the general theory of relativity, that, translated back into the language of logic and general methodology, can establish and render intelligible this special position. Euclidean geometry rests on a definite axiom of relativity, which is peculiar to it. As the geometry of space of a constant curvature 0, it is characterized by the thoroughgoing relativity of all places and magnitudes. Its formal determinations are in principle independent of any absolute determinations of magnitude. While, e.g., in the geometry of Lobachevskii, the sum of the angles of a rectilinear triangle is different from 180° and indeed the more so the more the surface area of the triangle increases, the absolute magnitude of the lines enters into none of the propositions of Euclidean geometry. Here, for every given figure, a "similar" can be constructed; the particular structures are grasped in their pure "quality," without any definite "quantum," any absolute value of number and magnitude, coming into consideration in their definition. This indifference of Euclidean structures to all absolute determinations of magnitude and the freedom resulting here of the particular points in Euclidean space from all determinations and properties, form a logically positive characteristic of the latter. For the proposition, *omnis determinatio est negatio*, holds here too. The assumption of the indeterminate serves as the foundation for the more complex assumptions and determinations which can be joined to it. In this sense, Euclidean geometry is and remains the "simplest," not in any practical, but in a strictly logical meaning; Euclidean space is, as Poincaré expresses it, "simpler not merely in consequence of our mental habits or in consequence of any direct intuition, which we possess of it, but it is in itself simpler, just as a polynomial of the first degree is simpler than a polynomial of the second degree."[6] This logical simplicity belonging to Euclidean space in the system of our intellectual meanings wholly independently of its relations to experience, is shown, e.g., in the fact that we can make any "given" space, that possesses any definite curvature, into Euclidean by regarding sufficiently small fields of it from which the difference conditioned by the curvature disappears. Euclidean geometry shows itself herein as the real geometry of infinitely small areas, and thus as the expression of certain elementary relations, which we take as a basis in thought, although we advance from them in certain cases to more complex forms.

The development of the general theory of relativity leaves this methodic advantage of Euclidean geometry unaffected. For Euclidean measurements do not indeed hold in it absolutely but they hold for certain "elementary" areas, which are distinguished by a certain simplicity of physical conditions. The Euclidean expression of the linear element shows itself to be unsatisfactory for the working out of the fundamental thought of the general theory of relativity, since it does not fulfill the fundamental demand of retaining its form in every arbitrary alteration of the system of reference. It must be replaced by the *general* linear element

$$ds^2 = \sum_1^4 g_{\mu\nu}\, dx_\mu\, dx_\nu,$$

which satisfies this demand. If, however, we consider infinitely small four-dimensional fields, it is expressly demanded that the presuppositions of the special theory of relativity, and thus its Euclidean measurements shall remain adequate for them. The form of the universal linear element here passes over into the Euclidean element of the special theory when the ten magnitudes g, which occur in this as functions of the coordinates of particular points assume definite constant values. The physical explanation of this relation, however, consists in that the magnitudes $g_{\mu\nu}$ are recognized as those which describe the gravitational field with reference to the chosen system of reference. The condition, under which we can pass from the presuppositions of the general theory of relativity to the special theory, can accordingly be expressed in the form that we only consider regions within which abstraction can be made from the effects of fields of gravitation. This is always possible for an infinitely small field and it holds further for finite fields in which, with appropriate choice of the system of reference, the body considered undergoes no noticeable acceleration. As we see, the variability of the magnitudes $g_{\mu\nu}$ which expresses the variation from the homogeneous Euclidean form of space, is recognized as based on a definite *physical* circumstance. If we consider fields in which this circumstance is absent or if we cancel it in thought, we again stand within the Euclidean world. Thus the assertion of Poincaré that all physical theory and physical measurement can prove absolutely nothing about the Euclidean or non-Euclidean character of space, since it is never concerned with the latter but only with the properties of *physical reality in space* remains entirely in force. The abstraction (or, better expressed, the pure function) of homogeneous Euclidean space is not destroyed by the theory of relativity, but is only known as such through it more sharply than before.

In fact, the pure meaning of geometrical concepts is not limited by what this theory teaches us about the conditions of measurement. These concepts are indeed, as is seen now anew, neither an empirical datum nor an empirical *dabile*, but their ideal certainty and meaning is not in the least affected thereby. It is shown that in fields where we have to reckon with gravitational effects of a definite magnitude, the preconditions of the ordinary methods of measurement fall short, that here we can no longer use "rigid bodies" as measures of length, nor ordinary "clocks" as measures of time. But this change of relations of measurement does not affect the calculation of space, but the calculation of the physical relation between the measuring rods and rays of light determined by the field of gravitation.[7] The truths of Euclidean geometry would only be also affected if one supposed that these propositions themselves are nothing but generalizations of empirical observation, which we have established in connection with fixed bodies. Such a supposition, however, epistemologically regarded, would amount to a *petitio principii*. Even Helmholtz, who greatly emphasizes the empirical origin of the geometrical axioms occasionally refers to another view, which might save their purely ideal and "transcendental" character. The Euclidean concept of the straight line might be conceived not as a generalization from certain physical observations, but as a purely ideal concept, to be confirmed or refuted by no experience, since we would have to decide by it whether any bodies of nature were to be regarded as fixed bodies. But, as he objects, the geometrical axioms would then cease to be synthetical propositions in Kant's sense, as they would only affirm something that would follow analytically from the concepts of the fixed geometrical structures necessary to measurement.[8]

It is, however, overlooked by this objection that there are *fundamentally synthetic forms of unity* besides the form of analytic identity, which Helmholtz has here in mind and which he contrasts with the empirical concept as if the form of analytic identity were unique, and that the axioms of geometry belong precisely to the former. Assumptions of this sort refer to the object in so far as in their totality they "constitute" the object and render possible knowledge of it; but none of them, taken for itself, can be understood as an assertion concerning things or relations of things. Whether they fulfill their task as moments of empirical knowledge can be decided always only in the indicated indirect way: by using them as building-stones in a theoretical and constructive system, and then comparing the consequences, which follow from the latter, with the results of observation and measurement. That the elements, to which we must ascribe, methodologically, a certain "simplicity," must be adequate for the interpretation of the laws of nature, cannot be demanded *a priori*. But even so, thought does not simply give itself over passively to the mere *material* of experience, but it develops out of itself new and more complex *forms* to satisfy the demands of the empirical manifold.

If we retain this general view, then one of the strangest and, at first appearance, most objectionable results of the general theory of relativity receives a new light. It is a necessary consequence of this theory that in it one can no longer speak of an immutably given geometry of measurement, which holds once for all for the whole world. Since the relations of measurement of space are determined by the gravitational potential and since this is to be regarded as in general changeable from place to place, we cannot avoid the conclusion that there is in general no unitary "geometry" for the totality of space and reality, but that, according to the specific properties of the field of gravitation at different places, there must be found different forms of geometrical structure. This seems, in fact, the greatest conceivable departure from the idealistic and Platonic conception of geometry, according to which it is the "science of the eternally existent," knowledge of what always "is in the same state" (*aei kata tauta hosautos echon*). Relativism seems here to pass over directly into the field of logic; the relativity of places involves that of geometrical truth. And yet this view is, on the other hand, only the sharpest expression of the fact that the problem of space has lost all ontological meaning in the theory of relativity. The purely methodological question has been substituted for the question of being. We are no longer concerned with what space "is" and with whether any definite character, whether Euclidean, Lobachevskiian or Riemannian, is to be ascribed to it, but rather with what use is to be made of the different systems of geometrical presuppositions in the interpretation of the phenomena of nature and their dependencies according to law. If we call any such system a particular "space," then indeed we can no longer attempt to grasp all of these spaces as intuitive parts to be united into an intuitive whole. But this impossibility rests fundamentally on the fact that we have here to do with a problem, which as such stands outside the limits of intuitive representation in general. The space of pure intuition is always only *ideal*, being only the space constructed according to the laws of this intuition, while here we are not concerned with such ideal syntheses and their unity, but with the relations of measurement of the empirical and the physical. These relations of measurement can only be gained on the basis of natural laws, i.e., by proceeding from the dynamic dependency of phenomena upon each other, and by permitting phenomena to determine their positions reciprocally in the space-time manifold by virtue of this dependency. Kant too decisively urged that this form of dynamic determination did not belong to intuition as such, but that it is the "rules of the understanding" which alone give the existence of phenomena synthetic unity and enable them to be collected into a definite concept of experience.[9] The step beyond him, that we have now to make on the basis of the results of the general theory of relativity, consists in the insight that geometrical axioms and laws of other than Euclidean form can enter into this determination of the understanding, in which the empirical and physical world arises for us, and that the admission of such axioms not only does not destroy the unity of the world, i.e., the unity of our experiential concept of a total order of phenomena, but first truly grounds it from a new angle, since in this way the particular laws of nature, with which we have to calculate in space-time determination, are ultimately brought to the unity of a supreme principle, – that of the universal postulate of relativity. The renunciation of intuitive simplicity in the picture of the world thus contains the guarantee of its greater intellectual and systematic completeness. This advance, however, cannot surprise us from the epistemological point of view; for it expresses only a general law of scientific and in particular of physical thought. Instead of speaking ontologically of the being or indeed of the coexistence of diversely constituted "spaces," which results in a tangible contradiction, the theory of relativity speaks purely methodologically of the possibility or necessity of applying different measurements, i.e., different geometrical conceptual languages in the interpretation of certain physical manifolds. This possible application tells us nothing concerning the "existence" of space, but merely indicates that by an appropriate choice of geometrical presuppositions certain physical relations, such as the field of gravitation or the electromagnetic field, can be described.

The connection between the purely conceptual thought, involved in the working out of the general doctrine of the manifold and order, and physical empiricism[10] here receives a surprising confirmation. A doctrine, which originally grew up merely in the immanent progress of pure mathematical speculation, in the ideal transformation of the hypotheses that lie at the basis of geometry, now serves directly as the form into which the laws of nature are poured. The same functions, that were previously established as expressing the metrical properties of non-Euclidean space, give the equations of the field of gravitation. These equations thus do not need for their establishment the introduction of new unknown forces acting at a distance, but are derived from the determination and specialization of the general presuppositions of measurement. Instead of a new complex of things, the theory is satisfied here by the consideration of a new general complex of conditions. Riemann, in setting up his theory, referred to its future physical meaning in prophetic words of which one is often reminded in the discussion of the general theory of relativity. In the "question as to the inner ground of the relations of measurement of space," he urges, "the remark can be applied that in a discrete manifold the principle of measurement is already contained in the concept of this manifold, but in the case of a continuous manifold it must come from elsewhere. Either the real lying at the basis of space must be a discrete manifold or the basis of measurement must be sought outside it in binding forces working upon it. The answer to this question can only be found by proceeding from the conception of phenomena, founded by Newton and hitherto verified by experience and gradually reshaping this by facts that cannot be explained from it; investigations, which, like the one made here, proceed from universal concepts, can only serve to the effect that these works are not hindered by limitations of concepts and the progress in knowledge of the connection of things not hindered by traditional prejudices."[11] What is here demanded is thus full freedom for the construction of geometrical concepts and hypotheses because only thereby can physical thought also attain full effectiveness, and face all future problems resulting from experience with an assured and systematically perfected instrument. But this connection is expressed, in the case of Riemann, in the language of Herbartian *realism*. At the basis of the pure form of geometrical space a real is to be found in which is to be sought the ultimate cause for the inner relations of measurement of this space. If we carry out, however, with reference to this formulation of the problem, the critical, "Copernican," revolution and thus conceive the question so that a real does not appear as a ground of space but so that space appears as an ideal ground in the construction and progress of knowledge of reality, there results for us at once a characteristic transformation. Instead of regarding "space" as a self-existent real, which must be explained and deduced from "binding forces" like other realities, we ask now rather whether the *a priori* function, the universal ideal relation, that we call "space" involves possible formulations and among them such as are proper to offer an exact and exhaustive account of certain physical relations, of certain "fields of force." The development of the general theory of relativity has answered this question in the affirmative; it has shown what appeared to Riemann as a geometrical hypothesis, as a mere possibility of thought, to be an organ for the knowledge of reality. The Newtonian dynamics is here resolved into pure kinematics and this kinematics ultimately into geometry. The content of the latter must indeed by broadened and the "simple" Euclidean type of geometrical axioms must be replaced by a more complex type; but in compensation we advance a step further into the realm of being, i.e., into the realm of empirical knowledge, without leaving the sphere of geometrical consideration. By abandoning the form of Euclidean space as an undivided whole and breaking it up analytically and by investigating the place of the particular axioms and their reciprocal dependence or independence, we are led to a system of pure *a priori* manifolds, whose laws thought lays down constructively, and in this construction we possess also the fundamental means for representing the relation of the real structures of the empirical manifold.

The realistic view that the relations of measurement of space must be grounded on certain physical determinations, on "binding forces" of matter, expresses this peculiar double relation one-sidedly and thus, epistemologically regarded, inexactly and unsatisfactorily. For this *metaphysical* use of the category of ground would destroy the *methodological* unity, which should be brought out. What relativistic physics, which has developed strictly and consistently from a theory of space and time measurement, offers us is in fact only the combination, the reciprocal determination, of the metrical and physical elements. In this, however, there is found no one-sided relation of ground and consequent, but rather a purely reciprocal relation, a correlation of the "ideal" and "real" moments, of "matter" and "form," of the geometrical and the physical. In so far as we assume any division at all in this reciprocal relation and take one element as "prior" and fundamental, the other as "later" and derivative, this distinction can be meant only in a logical, not in a real sense. In this sense, we must conceive the pure space-time manifold as the logical *prius*; not as if it existed and were given in some sense outside of and before the empirical and physical, but because it constitutes a principle and a fundamental condition of all knowledge of empirical and physical relations. The physicist as such need not reflect on this state of affairs; for in all the concrete measurements, which he makes, the spatio-temporal and the empirical manifold is given always only in the unitary operation of measurement itself, not in the abstract isolation of its particular conceptual elements and conditions.

From these considerations the relation between Euclidean and non-Euclidean geometry appears in a new light. The real superiority of Euclidean geometry seems at first glance to consist in its concrete and intuitive determinateness in the face of which all "pseudo-geometries" fade into logical "possibilities." These possibilities exist only for thought, not for "*being*"; they seem analytic plays with concepts, which can be left unconsidered when we are concerned with experience and with "nature," with the synthetic unity of objective knowledge. When we look back over our earlier considerations, this view must undergo a peculiar and paradoxical reversal. Pure Euclidean space stands, as is now seen, not closer to the demands of empirical and physical knowledge than the non-Euclidean manifolds but rather more removed. For precisely because it represents the logically simplest form of spatial construction it is not wholly adequate to the complexity of content and the material determinateness of the empirical. Its fundamental property of homogeneity, its axiom of the equivalence in principle of all points, now marks it as an abstract space; for, in the concrete and empirical manifold, there never is such uniformity, but rather thorough-going differentiation reigns in it. If we would create a conceptual expression for this fact of differentiation in the sphere of geometrical relations themselves, then nothing remains but to develop further the geometrical conceptual language with reference to the problem of the "heterogeneous." We find this development in the construction of metageometry. When the concept of the special three-dimensional manifold with a curvature 0 is broadened here to the thought of a system of manifolds with different constant or variable curvatures, a new ideal means is discovered for the mastery of complex manifolds; new conceptual symbols are created, not as expressions of things, but of possible relations according to law. Whether these relations are realized within phenomena at any place only experience can decide. But it is not experience that grounds the content of the geometrical concepts; rather these concepts foreshadow it as methodological anticipations, just as the form of the ellipse was anticipated as a conic section long before it attained concrete application and significance in the courses of the planets. When they first appeared, the systems of non-Euclidean geometry seemed lacking in all empirical meaning, but there was expressed in them the intellectual preparation for problems and tasks, to which experience was to lead later. Since the "absolute differential calculus," which was grounded on purely mathematical considerations by Gauss, Riemann, and Christoffel, gains a surprising application in Einstein's theory of gravitation, the possibility of such an application must be held open for all, even the most remote constructions of pure mathematics and especially of non-Euclidean geometry. For it has always been shown in the history of mathematics that its complete freedom contains the guarantee and condition of its fruitfulness. Thought does not advance in the field of the concrete by dealing with the particular phenomena like pictures to be united into a single mosaic, but by sharpening and refining its own means of determination while guided by reference to the empirical and by the postulate of its determinateness according to law. If a proof were needed for this logical state of affairs, the development of the theory of relativity would furnish it. It has been said of the special theory of relativity that it "substituted mathematical constructions for the apparently most tangible reality and resolved the latter into the former."[12] The advance to the general theory of relativity has brought this constructive feature more distinctly to light; but, at the same time, it has shown how precisely this resolution of the "tangible" realities has verified and established the connection of theory and experience in an entirely new way. The further physical thought advances and the higher universality of conception it reaches the more does it seem to lose sight of the immediate data, to which the naïve view of the world clings, so that finally there seems no return to these data. And yet the physicist abandons himself to these last and highest abstractions in the certainty and confidence of finding in them reality, *his* reality in a new and richer sense. In the progress of knowledge the deep words of Heraclitus hold that the way upward and the way downward are one and the same: *hodos ano kato mie*. Here, too, ascent and descent necessarily belong together: the direction of thought to the universal principles and grounds of knowledge finally proves not only compatible with its direction to the particularity of phenomena and facts, but the correlate and condition of the latter.

Notes

1 "Euclidean and non-Euclidean Geometry" is chapter VI of *Einstein's Theory of Relativity* (in original *Zur Einsteinschen Relativitätstheorie*) of 1921. English trans. by William Curtis Swabey and Marie Collins Swabey. Chicago: Dover, 1943, pp. 430–444.
2 Cf. N. Lobachevskii, *Zwei geometrische Abhandlungen*, trans. Fr. Engel, Leipzig 1898.
3 H. Poincaré, *La Science et la hypothèse*, Paris 1902, pp. 92 ff.
4 Cf. R. Hönigswald, "Über den Unterschied und die Beziehungen der logischen und der erkenntnistheoretischen Elemente in der kritischen Philosophie der Biologie" (Heidelberg 1908); on the following cf. B. Bauch, *Studien zur Philosophie der exakten Wissenschaften* (Heidelberg 1911), pp. 126 ff.

5   On this relation of the problem of metageometry to the problem of "experience," cf. esp. Albert Görland (*Aristoteles und Kant bezüglich der Idee der theoretischen Erkenntnis untersucht*, Gießen 1909), pp. 324 ff.).
6   *La Science et la hypothèse*, p. 67.
7   Cf. H. Weyl, *Raum. Zeit. Materie. Vorlesungen über allgemeine Relativitätstheorie*, 3rd. ed., Berlin 1920), pp. 85 ff.
8   Cf. H. Helmholtz, "Über den Ursprung und die Bedeutung der geometrischen Axiome" (1870), in: *Vorträge und Reden*, Braunschweig 1896 (4th. ed.), vol. II, p. 30. [The reworked version of 1876 is published as Chapter 2 in this volume – Ed.]
9   Cf. above p. 79 [of *Substance and Function*].
10 *Empirie*
11 B. Riemann, *Über die Hypothesen, welche der Geometrie zugrunde liegen* (1854).
12 A. Kneser, *Mathematik und Natur* (Breslau 1911), p. 13.

"The Place of Language and Myth in the Pattern of Human Culture" from *Language and Myth* (1925)[1]

The opening passage of the Platonic dialogue *Phaedrus* describes how Socrates lets Phaedrus, whom he encounters, lure him beyond the gates of the city to the banks of Ilissus. Plato has pictured the setting of this scene in nicest detail, and there lies over it a glamour and fragrance well-nigh unequaled in classical descriptions of nature. In the shade of a tall plane tree, at the brink of a cool spring, Socrates and Phaedrus lie down; the summer breeze is mild and sweet and full of the cicada's song. In the midst of this landscape Phaedrus raises the question whether this be not the place where, according to a myth, Boreas carried off the fair Orithyia; for the water is clear and translucent here, fitting for maidens to sport in and bathe. Socrates, when pressed with questions as to whether he believes this tale, this "*mythologemen*," replies that, although he cannot be said to believe it, yet he is not at a loss as to its significance. "For," he says, "then I could proceed as do the learned, and say by way of clever interpretation, that Orithyia, while playing with her companion Pharmacia, had been borne over yonder cliffs by Boreas the Northwind, and because of this manner of her death she was said to have been carried off by the god Boreas.... But I," he adds, "for my part, Phaedrus, I find that sort of thing pretty enough, yet consider such interpretations rather an artificial and tedious business, and do not envy him who indulges in it. For he will necessarily have to account for centaurs and the chimaera, too, and will find himself overwhelmed by a very multitude of such creatures, gorgons and pegasuses and countless other strange monsters. And whoever discredits all these wonderful beings and tackles them with the intention of reducing them each to some probability, will have to devote a great deal of time to this bootless sort of wisdom. But I have no leisure at all for such pastimes, and the reason, my dear friend, is that as yet I cannot, as the Delphic precept has it, know myself. So it seems absurd to me that, as long as I am in ignorance of myself, I should concern myself about extraneous matters. Therefore I let all such things be as they may, and think not of them, but of myself – whether I be, indeed, a creature more complex and monstrous than Typhon, or whether perchance I be a gentler and simpler animal, whose nature contains a divine and noble essence."[2]

This sort of myth interpretation, which the Sophists and Rhetoricians of the time held in high repute as the flower of polite learning and the height of the urbane spirit, seemed to Plato the very opposite of this spirit; but although he denounced it as such, calling it a rustic science (*agroikos sophia*), his judgment did not prevent the learned from indulging in this sort of wisdom for centuries to come. As the Sophists and Rhetoricians vied with each other at this intellectual sport in Plato's day, so the Stoics and Neoplatonists did in the Hellenistic period. And it was ever and always the science of language, of etymology, that served as a vehicle for such research. Here in the realm of spooks and daemons, as well as in the higher reaches of mythology, the Faustian word seemed ever to hold good: here it was always assumed that the essence of each mythical figure could be directly learned from its name. The notion that name and essence bear a necessary and internal relation to each other, that the name does not merely denote but actually *is* the essence of its object, that the potency of the real thing is contained in the name – that is one of the fundamental assumptions of the mythmaking consciousness itself. Philosophical and scientific *mythology*, too, seemed to accept this assumption. What in the spirit of myth itself functions as a living and immediate conviction becomes a postulate of reflective procedure for the science of mythology; the doctrine of the intimate relation between names and essences, and of their latent identity, is here set up as a methodological principle.

Among the philosophers it was especially Herbert Spencer who tried to prove the thesis that the mythico-religious veneration of natural phenomena, as, for instance, the sun and the moon, has its ultimate origin in nothing more than a misinterpretation of the names which men have applied to these objects. Among the philologists, Max Müller has taken the method of philological analysis not only as a means to reveal the nature of certain mythical beings, especially in the context of Vedic religion, but also as a point of departure for his general theory of the connection between language and myth. For him, myth is neither a transformation of history into fabulous legend nor is it fable accepted as history; and just as certainly it does not spring directly from the contemplation of the great forms and powers of nature. What we call myth is, for him, something conditioned and negotiated by the agency of language; it is, in fact, the product of a basic shortcoming, an inherent weakness of language. All linguistic denotation is essentially ambiguous – and in this ambiguity, this "*paronymia*" of words lies the source of all myths. The examples by which Max Müller supports this theory are characteristic of his approach. He cites, as one instance, the legend of Deucalion and Pyrrha, who, after Zeus had rescued them from the great flood which destroyed mankind, became the ancestors of a new race by taking up *stones* and casting them over their shoulders, whereupon the stones became men. This origin of human beings from stones is simply absurd and seems to defy all interpretation – but is it not immediately clarified as we recall the fact that in Greek men and stones are denoted by identical or at least similar sounding names, that the words *laoi* and *laas* are assonant? Or take the myth of Daphne, who is saved from Apollo's embraces by the fact that her mother, the Earth, transforms her into a laurel tree. Again it is only the history of language that can make this myth "comprehensible," and give it any sort of sense. Who was Daphne? In order to answer this question we must resort to etymology, that is to say, we must investigate the history of the word. "Daphne" can be traced back to the Sanskrit *Ahanâ*, and *Ahanâ* means in Sanskrit the redness of dawn. As soon as we know this, the whole matter becomes clear. The story of Phoebus and Daphne is nothing but a description of what one may observe every day: first, the appearance of the dawnlight in the eastern sky, then the rising of the sun-god who hastens after his bride, then the gradual fading of the red dawn at the touch of the fiery rays, and finally its death or disappearance in the bosom of Mother Earth. So the decisive condition for the development of the myth was not the natural phenomenon itself, but rather the circumstance that the Greek word for the laurel (*daphne*) and the Sanskrit word for the dawn are related; this entails with a sort of logical necessity the identification of the beings they denote. This, therefore, is his conclusion:

"Mythology is inevitable, it is natural, it is an inherent necessity of language, if we recognize in language the outward form and manifestation of thought it is in fact the dark shadow which language throws upon thought; and which can never disappear till language becomes entirely commensurate with thought, which it never will. Mythology, no doubt, breaks out more fiercely during the early periods of the history of human thought, but it never disappears altogether. Depend upon it, there is mythology now as there was in the time of Homer, only we do not perceive it, because we ourselves live in the very shadow of it, and because we all shrink from the full meridian light of truth... Mythology, in the highest sense, is the power exercised by language on thought in every possible sphere of mental activity."[3]

It might seem an idle pursuit to hark back to such points of view, which have long been abandoned by the etymology and comparative mythological research of today, were it not for the fact that this standpoint represents a typical attitude which is ever recurrent in all related fields, in mythology as in linguistic studies, in theory of art as well as in theory of knowledge. For Max Müller the mythical world is essentially a world of illusion – but an illusion that finds its explanation whenever the original, necessary self-deception of the mind from which the error arises, is discovered. This self-deception is rooted in language, which is forever making game of the human mind, ever ensnaring it in that iridescent play of meanings that is its own heritage. And this notion that myth does not rest upon a positive *power* of formulation and creation, but rather upon a mental *defect* – that we find in it a "pathological" influence of speech – this notion has its proponents even in modern ethnological literature.[4]

But when we reduce it to its philosophical lowest terms, this attitude turns out to be simply the logical result of that naive realism which regards the reality of objects as something directly and unequivocally given, literally something tangible – *aprix taiu chetoin*, as Plato says. If reality is conceived in this manner, then of course everything which has not this solid sort of reality dissolves into mere fraud and illusion. This illusion may be ever so finely wrought, and flit about us in the gayest and loveliest colors; the fact remains that this image has no independent content, no intrinsic meaning. It does indeed reflect a reality – but a reality to which it can never measure up, and which it can never adequately portray. From this point of view all artistic creation becomes a mere imitation, which must always fall short of the original. Not only simple imitation of a sensibly presented model, but also what is known as idealization, manner, or style, must finally succumb to this verdict; for measured by the naked "truth" of the object to be depicted, idealization itself is nothing but subjective misconception and falsification. And it seems that all other processes of mental gestation involve the same sort of outrageous distortion, the same departure from objective reality and the immediate data of experience.

For all mental processes fail to grasp reality itself, and in order to represent it, to hold it at all, they are driven to the use of symbols. But all symbolism harbors the curse of mediacy; it is bound to obscure what it seeks to reveal. Thus the sound of speech strives to "express" subjective and objective happening, the "inner" and the "outer" world; but what of this it can retain is not the life and individual fullness of existence, but only a dead abbreviation of it. All that "denotation" to which the spoken word lays claim is really nothing more than mere suggestion; a "suggestion" which, in face of the concrete variegation and totality of actual experience, must always appear a poor and empty shell. That is true of the external as well as the inner world: "When *speaks* the soul, alas, the *soul* no longer speaks!"[5]

From this point it is but a single step to the conclusion which the modern skeptical critics of language have drawn: the complete dissolution of any alleged truth content of language, and the realization that this content is nothing but a sort of phantasmagoria of the spirit. Moreover, from this standpoint, not only myth, art, and language, but even theoretical knowledge itself becomes a phantasmagoria; for even knowledge can never reproduce the true nature of things as they are, but must frame their essence in "concepts." But what are concepts save formulations and creations of thought, which, instead of giving us the true forms of objects, show us rather the forms of thought itself? Consequently all schemata which science evolves in order to classify, organize, and summarize the phenomena of the real world turn out to be nothing but arbitrary schemes – airy fabrics of the mind, which express not the nature of things, but the nature of mind. So knowledge, as well as myth, language, and art, has been reduced to a kind of fiction – to a fiction that recommends itself by its usefulness, but must not be measured by any strict standard of truth, if it is not to melt away into nothingness.

Against this self-dissolution of the spirit there is only one remedy: to accept in all seriousness what Kant calls his "Copernican revolution." Instead of measuring the content, meaning, and truth of intellectual forms by something extraneous which is supposed to be reproduced in them, we must find in these forms themselves the measure and criterion for their truth and intrinsic meaning. Instead of taking them as mere copies of something else, we must see in each of these spiritual forms a spontaneous law of generation; an original way and tendency of expression which is more than a mere record of something initially given in fixed categories of real existence. From this point of view, myth, art, language and science appear as symbols; not in the sense of mere figures which refer to some given reality by means of suggestion and allegorical renderings, but in the sense of forces each of which produces and posits a world of its own. In these realms the spirit exhibits itself in that inwardly determined dialectic by virtue of which alone there is any reality, any organized and definite Being at all. Thus the special symbolic forms are not imitations, but organs of reality, since it is solely by their agency that anything real becomes an object for intellectual apprehension, and as such is made visible to us. The question as to what reality is apart from these forms, and what are its independent attributes, becomes irrelevant here. For the mind, only that can be visible which has some definite form; but every form of existence has its source in some peculiar way of seeing, some intellectual formulation and intuition of meaning. Once language, myth, art and science are recognized as such ideational forms, the basic philosophical question is no longer that of their relation to an absolute reality which forms, so to speak, their solid and substantial substratum; the central problem now is that of their mutual limitation and supplementation. Though they all function organically together in the construction of spiritual reality, yet each of these organs has its individual assignment.

From this angle, the relation between language and myth also appears in a new light. It is no longer a matter of simply deriving one of these phenomena from the other, of "explaining" it in terms of the other – for that would be to level them both, to rob them of their characteristic features. If myth be really, as Max Müller's theory has it, nothing but the darkening shadow which language throws upon thought, it is mystifying indeed that this shadow should appear ever as in an aura of its own light, should evolve a positive vitality and activity of its own, which tends to eclipse what we commonly call the immediate reality of *things*, so that even the wealth of empirical, sensuous experience pales before it. As Wilhelm von Humboldt has said in connection with the language problem: "Man lives with his objects chiefly – in fact, since his feeling and acting depends on his perceptions, one may say exclusively – as language presents them to him. By the same process whereby he spins language out of his own being, he ensnares himself in it; and each language draws a magic circle round the people to which it belongs, a circle from which there is no escape save by stepping out of it into another."[6]

This holds, perhaps, even more for the basic mythical conceptions of mankind than for language. Such conceptions are not culled from a ready-made world of Being, they are not mere products of fantasy which vapor off from fixed, empirical, realistic existence, to float above the actual world like a bright mist; to primitive consciousness they present the *totality* of Being. The mythical form of conception is not something superadded to certain definite elements of empirical existence; instead, the primary "experience" itself is steeped in the imagery of myth and saturated with its atmosphere. Man lives with *objects* only in so far as he lives with these *forms;* he reveals reality to himself, and himself to reality, in that he lets himself and the environment enter into this plastic medium, in which the two do not merely make contact, but fuse with each other.

Consequently all those theories which propose to find the roots of myth by exploring the realm of experience, of *objects*, which are supposed to have given rise to it, and from which it then allegedly grew and spread, must always remain one-sided and inadequate. There are, as is well known, a multitude of such explanations – a great variety of doctrines about the ultimate origin and real kernel of mythmaking, hardly less motley than the world of objects itself. Now it is found in certain psychical conditions and experiences, especially the phenomenon of dreaming, now in the contemplation of natural events, and among the latter it is further limited to the observation of natural objects such as the sun, the moon, the stars, or else to that of great occurrences such as storms, lightning and thunder, etc. Thus the attempt is made again and again to make soul mythology or nature mythology, sun or moon or thunder mythology the basis of mythology as such.

But even if one of these attempts should prove successful, this would not solve the real problem which mythology presents to philosophy, but at best would push it back one step. For mythical formulation as such cannot be understood and appreciated simply by determining the *object* on which it is immediately and originally centered. It is, and remains, the same miracle of the spirit and the same mystery, no matter whether it covers this or that realistic matter, whether it deals with the interpretation and articulation of psychical processes or physical things, and in the latter case, just what particular things these may be. Even though it were possible to resolve all mythology to a basic astral mythology – what the mythical consciousness derives from contemplation of the stars, what it sees in them directly, would still be something radically different from the view they present to empirical observation or the way they figure in theoretical speculation and scientific "explanations" of natural phenomena. Descartes said that theoretical science remains the same in its essence no matter what object it deals with – just as the sun's light is the same no matter what wealth and variety of things it may illuminate. The same may be said of any symbolic form, of language, art, or myth, in that each of these is a particular way of seeing, and carries within itself its particular and proper source of light. The function of envisagement, the dawn of a conceptual enlightenment can never be realistically derived from things themselves or understood through the nature of its objective contents. For it is not a question of what we see in a certain perspective, but of the perspective itself. If we conceive the problem in this way, it is certainly clear that a reduction of all myth to one subject matter brings us no nearer to the solution, in fact it removes us further than ever from any hope of a real answer. For now we see in language, art and mythology so many archetypal phenomena of human mentality which can be indicated as such, but are not capable of any further "explanation" in terms of something else. The realists always assume, as their solid basis for all such explanations, the so-called "given," which is thought to have some definite form, some inherent structure of its own. They accept this reality as an integrated whole of causes and effects, things and attributes, states and processes, of objects at rest and of motions, and the only question for them is which of these elements a particular mental product such as myth, language or art originally embodied. If, for instance, the phenomenon in question is language, their natural line of inquiry must be whether names for things preceded names for conditions or actions, or vice versa – whether, in other words, nouns or verbs were the first "roots" of speech. But this problem itself appears spurious as soon as we realize that the distinctions which here are taken for granted, the analysis of reality in terms of things and processes, permanent and transitory aspects, objects and actions, do not precede language as a substratum of given fact, but that language itself is what initiates such articulations, and develops them in its own sphere. Then it turns out that language could not begin with any phase of "noun concepts" or "verb concepts," but is the very agency that produces the distinction between these forms, that introduces the great spiritual "crisis" in which the permanent is opposed to the transient, and Being is made the contrary of Becoming. So the linguistic fundamental concepts must be realized as something prior to these distinctions, forms which lie between the sphere of noun conception and that of verb conception, between thinghood and eventuality, in a state of indifference, a peculiar balance of feeling.

A similar ambiguity seems to characterize the earliest phases to which we can trace back the development of mythical and religious thought. It seems only natural to us that the world should present itself to our inspection and observation as a pattern of definite forms, each with its own perfectly determinate spatial limits that give it its specific individuality. If we see it as a whole, this whole nevertheless consists of clearly distinguishable units, which do not melt into each other, but preserve their identity that sets them definitely apart from the identity of all the others. But for the mythmaking consciousness these separate elements are not thus separately given, but have to be originally and gradually derived from the whole; the process of culling and sorting out individual forms has yet to be gone through. For this reason the mythic state of mind has been called the "complex" state, to distinguish it from our abstract analytic attitude. Preuss, who coined this expression, points out, for instance, that in the mythology of the Cora Indians, which he has studied exhaustively, the conception of the nocturnal heaven and the diurnal heaven must have preceded that of the sun, the moon, and the separate constellations. The first mythical impulse, he claims, was not toward making a sun-god or a lunar deity, but a community of stars. "The sun-god does indeed hold first rank in the hierarchy of the gods, but...the various astral deities can stand proxy for him. They precede him in time, he is created by them, by somebody's jumping into a fire or being thrown into it; his power is influenced by theirs, and he is artificially kept alive by feeding on the hearts of sacrificed victims, i.e., the stars. The starry night sky is the necessary condition for the existence of the sun; that is the central idea in the whole religious ideation of the Coras and of the ancient Mexicans, and must be regarded as a principal factor in the further development of their religion."[7]

The same function here attributed to the nocturnal heavens seems to be imputed by the Indo-Germanic races to the daylit sky. Their religions show many traces of the fact that the worship of light as an undifferentiated, total experience preceded that of the individual heavenly bodies, which figure only as its media, its particular manifestations. In the Avesta, for instance, Mithra is not a sun-god, as he is for later ages; he is the spirit of heavenly light. He appears on the mountaintops *before* the sun rises, to mount his chariot which, drawn by four white horses, runs the course of heaven during the day; when night comes, he the unsleeping still lights the face of earth with a vague glimmering light. We are explicitly told that he is neither the sun, nor the moon, nor any or all of the stars, but through them, his thousand ears and ten thousand eyes, he perceives everything and keeps watch over the world.[8]

Here we see in a concrete instance how mythic conception originally grasps only the great, fundamental, qualitative contrast of light and darkness, and how it treats them as *one* essence, one complex whole, out of which definite characters only gradually emerge. Like the spirit of language, the mythmaking genius "has" separate and individualized forms only in so far as it "posits" them, as it carves them out of the undifferentiated whole of its pristine vision.

This insight into the determining and discriminating function, which myth as well as language performs in the mental construction of our world of "things," seems to be all that a "philosophy of symbolic forms" can teach us. Philosophy as such can go no further; it cannot presume to present to us, *in concreto*, the great process of emergence, and to distinguish its phases for us. But if pure philosophy is necessarily restricted to a general, theoretical picture of such an evolution, it may be that philology and comparative mythology can fill in the outline and draw with firm, clear strokes what philosophical speculation could only suggestively sketch. An initial and portentous step in this direction has been taken by Usener in his work on divine names. "An Essay toward a Science of Religious Conception," is the subtitle he has given to his book, which brings it definitely into the realm of philosophical problems and systematic treatment. To trace the history of the divinities, their successive appearance and development among the several tribes of man, he tells us, is not an attainable goal; only a history of mythic ideas can be reconstructed. Such ideas, no matter how manifold, how varied, how heterogeneous they may appear at first sight, have their own inner lawfulness; they do not arise from a boundless caprice of the imagination, but move in definite avenues of feeling and creative thought. This intrinsic law is what mythology seeks to establish. Mythology is the science (*logos*) of myth, or the science of the forms of religious conception.[9]

His findings in this field may certainly give pause to philosophers, who tend to regard the human mind as endowed *ab initio* with logical categories. "There have been long periods in mental evolution," he observes, "when the human mind was slowly laboring toward thought and conception and was following quite different laws of ideation and speech. Our epistemology will not have any real foundation until philology and mythology have revealed the processes of involuntary and unconscious conception. The chasm between specific perception and general concepts is far greater than our academic notions, and a language which does our thinking for us, lead us to suppose. It is so great that I cannot imagine how it could have been bridged, had not language itself, without man's conscious awareness, prepared and induced the process. It is language that causes the multitude of casual, individual expressions to yield up one which extends its denotation over more and more special cases, until it comes to denote them all, and assumes the power of expressing a class concept."[10]

Here, then, it is the philologist, the student of language and religion, who confronts philosophy with a new question, which emerges from his own investigations. And Usener has not merely indicated a new approach; he has resolutely followed it up, employing to this end all the clues which the history of language, the precise analysis of words, and especially that of divine names provided. The question naturally arises whether philosophy, not commanding any such materials, can handle this problem which the humanistic sciences have presented to it, and what intellectual resources it can tap to meet such a challenge. Is there any other line than the actual history of language and of religion that could lead us closer to the origin of primary linguistic and religious concepts? Or is it, at this point, one and the same thing to know the genesis of such ideas and to know their ultimate meanings and functions? This is the issue I propose to decide in the following pages. I shall take up Usener's problem in exactly the form in which he has cast it; but I shall attempt to tackle it on other grounds than linguistic and philological considerations. Usener himself has indicated the propriety, in fact the necessity of such an approach, in that he formulated the main issue as not merely a matter of linguistic and intellectual history, but also of logic and epistemology. This presupposes that the latter disciplines, too, can handle the problem of semantic and mythic conception from their own standpoint, and treat it by their own methodological principles and procedures. Through this expansion, this apparent overstepping of the usual boundaries of logical inquiry, the science of logic really comes into its own, and the realm of pure theoretical reason becomes actually defined and distinguished from other spheres of intellectual being and development.

Notes

1. In *Language and Myth* (New York: Dover, 1953, pp. 1–16), trans. Susanne K. Langer.
2. *Phaedrus*, 229D ff.
3. Max Müller, "The Philosophy of Mythology," appended to *Introduction to the Science of Religion* (London, 1873), pp. 353–355.
4. E.g., B. Brinton, *Religions of Primitive Peoples* (New York and London, 1907), pp. 115 ff.
5. After Schiller's poem *Sprache* (Warum kann der lebendige Geist dem Geist nicht erscheinen? // Spricht die Seele, so spricht, ach!, schon die *Seele* nicht mehr.). – Ed.
6. W. von Humboldt, *Einleitung zum Kawi-Werk*, S.W. (Coll. ed.), VII, p. 60.
7. Preuss, *Die Nayarit-Expedition I: Die Religion der Cora Indianer*, Leipzig, 1912. Cf. further, Preuss, *Die geistige Kultur der Naturvölker*, pp. 9 ff.
8. Yasht X, 145; Yasna I, ii (35); cf. Cumont, *Textes et monuments figurés relatifs aux mystères de Mithra* (Brussels, 1899), I, p. 225.
9. H. Usener, *Götternamen. Versuch einer Lehre von der religiösen Begriffsbildung* (Bonn, 1896), p. 330; cf. esp. pp. v ff.
10. Ibid., p. 321.

Chapter 17

"The Problem of the Symbol and Its Place in the System of Philosophy" (1927)[1]

About forty years ago, in philosophical essays written for the occasion of Eduard Zellers' fiftieth doctoral anniversary, Friedrich Theodor Vischer focused attention again on the concept of the symbol, which he had previously treated extensively in his aesthetics.[2] On that occasion he characterized this concept as a changing *Proteus* that is difficult to come to grips with and confine. In fact there is probably no other concept in aesthetics that has proven to be so rich, so fruitful, and to have so many applications as this one. But there is also hardly another one that is so difficult to contain within the limits of a fixed definition or to unequivocally restrict in its use and meaning. This difficulty increases and intensifies if one takes the problem of symbolism so broadly that it does not belong exclusively to any single province of thought but, as will be done in this paper, as a systematic focal point towards which all the basic disciplines of philosophy are directed – logic no less than aesthetics and the philosophy of language as well as the philosophy of religion.

It is not difficult to show the importance of the concept and problem of the symbol for the internal conceptual development of these fields. We need only to turn to the historical advance of their basic problems to see it stand out clearly and distinctly. But every new area seems, along with the enrichment of the problem, to repeatedly bring a shift of problems – an actual *metabasis eis allo genos*. When we look from the philosophy of religion to the philosophy of art and from there to logic and the philosophy of science we find the problem of the symbol as an important concern in all of them. Yet the universality of this importance must unmistakably be paid for with a constant change of meaning. The symbol differs depending upon each new context of thought in which it stands.

In the religious sphere where the concept of the symbolic is originally rooted, it appears above all to be taken in a purely thinglike and thoroughly "objective" sense. Here the symbol bears nothing of the merely mediated comparison, metaphor, or emblem; it stands as an immediate reality before us because it is immediately efficacious. In the first epoch of the Christian faith, according to Harnack, symbolism was not considered the opposite of the objective or real but was rather the mysterious and sacred – the *Mysterium* to which the natural, clear, and profane was opposed.[3]

However, symbolism falls in another light as soon as we leave the sphere of religious meaning and look at aesthetic meaning. Here its actuality and reality as a thing now seems more and more to fade while a new aspect that is genuinely ideal appears all the more distinctly. In the whole of speculative aesthetics from Plotinus to Hegel the notion and problem of the symbol arises exactly at that point where the relationship between the world of the senses and the intelligible world, i.e., between appearance and reality, is to be determined. The beautiful is essentially and necessarily a symbol because, to an extent, it is cleft within itself. It is always both a unity and double. The internal division of the beautiful between adherence to and transcendence of the sensory, not only expresses the tension which pervades the world of our consciousness but also expresses the original and fundamental polarity of being itself – the dialectic that maintains between the finite and the infinite or between the absolute idea and its representation and embodiment within the world of particular beings.

Another situation confronts us again within the area of purely logical problems. Here too the order and development of these problems shows that the coherence of the logical world of form cannot be adequately grasped or exactly represented unless we use certain concrete material signs for this representation. Through them as representatives of logical meaning, its inner structure is truly opened up to us for the first time. In modern philosophy it was most of all Leibniz who first realized this fundamental relationship and pursued it in every direction. It is well known how this, his basic view, like his demand for a "universal characteristic" that should always accompany logic, proved itself in his work and showed its productive capacity in the creation of the algorithm of the infinitesimal calculus. However, it has been effective far beyond these quarters. In fact it is not saying too much to maintain that the entire scientific development of logic and mathematics as it was carried out in the nineteenth century stood under its influence. The continuing development of Leibniz' leading idea has led, on the one hand, to Hermann Grassman's calculus of extension just as, on the other hand, the effort to found symbolic logic with Boole, Peano, and Russell has depended on it. And today the *princeps mathematicorum*, a thinker like Hilbert, sees the sole salvation of mathematics along these lines. His only hope for securing its foundations and a consistent proof of the absence of contradictions is from a general "formalization" of mathematics that is carried out to full completion.

This trend is so strong and dominant that under its influence a complete transformation in the understanding of the object of mathematics has begun to assert itself. Now the actual object of mathematics is no longer numbers or quantities but rather the perceived sensory signs themselves. "Because I assume this attitude," Hilbert emphasizes, "the objects of the theory of numbers for me, in direct opposition to Frege and Dedekind, are the signs themselves ... Herein lies the firm philosophical attitude which I hold to be requisite to the foundation of pure mathematics as well as to all scientific thinking, understanding, and communication; in the beginning – we must say – was the sign."[4]

Certainly we may not overlook or ignore the fact that this radical conclusion is still quite contested today. A dangerous opponent to Hilbert's attempt at a reduction of all mathematics to a "theory of signs" has arisen in the "intuitionist mathematics" represented by Brouwer and Weyl. But the attempt itself to fit the entire contents of mathematics into a "theory of signs" in his way is characteristic of a typical and fundamental direction of modern mathematical thought. We need only to indicate briefly how much this way of thinking has influenced the understanding of scientific concepts and their epistemological foundations.

As early as with Helmholtz the concept of the sign becomes central to the epistemology of science. It is responsible for the unique form of his entire theory of perception and his presentation of physiological optics. In addition, Heinrich Hertz has pursued this direction of thought further and given it precise and explicit formulation in his *Principles of Mechanics*. According to Hertz all scientific thinking and all concept and theory formation in physics consists in a fundamental symbolic activity. "We form for ourselves images or symbols of external objects; and the form which we give them is such that the necessary consequents of the images are always the images of the necessary consequents in nature of the things pictured."[5]

Now we must ask ourselves, however, if the very abundance of applications to which the concept of the symbol has proven to lend itself has not progressively eroded and destroyed its clear and definite content. Do we really still have a unified systematic problem to deal with here, which extends to all areas of knowledge and all provinces of culture? Or do we not, on the contrary, have a question possessing merely an apparent unity that dissolves into a mere word as soon as we try to grasp and define it more closely? Does the term "symbol" as it is used today in the philosophy of religion, aesthetics, logic, and the philosophy of science conceal some kind of unified content? Does it refer to an all-embracing function of thought that remains the same in its basic characteristics even though it takes on a new and unique form in each of its outgrowths? But if this is so, where do we find the unifying bond that connects the profusion and variety of meanings which the concept of the symbol has gradually assumed in its immanent development?

In the closely measured time that is available to me here I cannot think of answering this question with real exactitude and precision, let alone attempt to give a truly systematic foundation for the answer that I have in mind. I can only try to present a few guidelines that should serve more to suggest the course for inquiry than provide you with any positive findings. In accordance with this let me begin with a simple example that should place us in the center of the question. We start with a particular perceptual experience, with a line drawing that we see before us and which we take in some way as an optical structure and as a connected whole. Here we can direct ourselves to the purely sensory "impression" of this drawing and take it perhaps as a simple drawn line which differs and stands out from others through certain visible qualities and basic characteristics of its spatial form. We do not need to concern ourselves for the time being with whether spatial form is thereby already included and imparted in this simple sensory impression or if this organization itself only results through the cooperation of higher mental functions. Nor need it concern us now if perhaps what we usually refer to as the immediate "perception" of space already embraces definite intellectual processes such as "unconscious inferences." The experience of perception itself as a purely phenomenal actuality in any case exhibits no such division. It is only subsequently introduced through epistemological or psychological analysis.

But while devoting myself to this simple experience of perception, while I follow the individual lines of the drawing in their visible proportion, in their lightness and darkness, in their contrast against the background, and their upward and downward design, the drawn line suddenly begins, as it were, to animate itself from within as a whole. The spatial image becomes an aesthetic image. In it I see the character of a particular ornament that combines for me a certain artistic meaning with a particular artistic significance. I can be engrossed in the pure contemplation of this ornament. I can represent it to myself, so to speak, as something timeless. Or, instead, I see in it something else; it presents itself to me as an excerpt and expression of an artistic language in which I recognize the language of a certain time and the style of an historical epoch. This style and the entire artistic aim of the time stands all at once pregnant and alive before me in the concrete experience of the line drawing.

And once again the form of consideration can change so that what at first presented itself to me as a pure ornament discloses itself as the carrier of a mythic-religious meaning. As soon as I do not merely grasp this meaning outwardly with reflection but am rather seized inwardly by it so that I live in it and am consumed by it, then the shape which I see before me is as though saturated and impregnated with a new meaning. It is surrounded by a tinge of magical enchantment. It no longer acts as a mere aesthetic form but is like a primeval revelation from another world, from the world of the "sacred." Here, in the middle of sensory phenomena, it overwhelms whoever is open to it with mystery and awe.

Finally, we can deliberately draw a sharp contrast between this form of interpretation and inner assimilation and another one which is diametrically opposed to it. Where the aesthetic observer and connoisseur devotes himself to the perception of pure form and where the form reveals a mystical meaning to the religious person, the form which is visible to the eye can also offer itself to thought as an example of a purely logical conceptual structure. As Plato said, the constellations themselves mean nothing to the calculating astronomer but serve him only as "paradigms" through which he becomes conscious of the purely mathematical nature of their movement and the timeless ideal essences of "faster" and "slower." Thus for the mathematical mind the line drawing becomes nothing but a visible graphic representation of a certain functional development. He perceives something in its immediately given form that is completely beyond perception as such. He sees in it the illustration of a law, a form of ideal relation, which is the last foundation of all mathematical thought.

And here too it is the whole of the presented form, not merely a part or fragment of it, that appears from this point of view and is accordingly imbued with a certain content of meaning. Where the attitude of aesthetic contemplation perhaps sees a beautiful line in the style of Hogarth, the mathematician's view sees the illustration of a certain trigonometrical function such as the illustration of a sine curve, while the mathematical physicist perhaps recognizes in just this same curve the law of a certain natural process such as the law of periodic oscillation.

We attempt to express this systematic relationship by considering the fundamental sensory experience with which we are dealing in this case as received into, determined, and given form by various "symbolic forms."[6] However, this way of speaking should not and may not be understood as though we were dealing here with a case of the separation or temporal succession of "form" and "matter." If we may distinguish these in the manner of Husserl's terminology, between the sensory material and animating acts, between the sensual *hyle* and intentional *morphe*, then this abstract separation can never mean that these may be separated in the phenomenon or that in itself formless matter were something given that is gradually taken up into various modes of interpretation and subsequently given shape by them. Whoever in this way converts the Kantian "dualism" of form and matter, which is a difference of meaning and transcendental "validity," into a separation of things actually existing next to and apart from each other has thereby already missed the decisive point of view needed for the profound understanding of this difference.

For us, in any case, it is certain that phenomenologically sensation and meaning are only given as in indivisible unity. We can never completely separate the sensory as such, as some naked "raw material" of sensation, from the whole complex of meaning relationships. Yet we can indicate the different ways it appears and how it signifies and refers, according to the perspective of meaning under which it comes.

Philosophy is not permitted to settle for establishing one of these points of view no matter how comprehensive it may nonetheless appear to be. Instead, it must attempt to encompass them all in a higher synopsis and understand each of them in its constitutive principle, for it is precisely the totality of these principles which constitutes the objective unity and totality of mind. A strictly "critical" philosophy cannot direct its attention towards schematically simplifying the wealth and profusion that is offered here in the fundamental attitudes of cultural consciousness by trying to force them together into a general form. We must rather try to grasp *in concreto* the particular manner in which the sensory becomes the carrier of meaning within each of these areas. And we must show what the fundamental laws are under which all these various processes stand.

In all of these particular worlds of form, no matter how they differ in principle and structure, there is nonetheless a certain directionality in their order and a certain manner in which they develop from elementary to more complex forms. By trying briefly and therefore, of course, only in an abstract and schematic way to indicate the guidelines of this development we can introduce a very broad relational system of thought according to which we want to describe and ascertain the "orientation" of each symbolic form.

Just as we can completely render the shape of a spatial curve by introducing three vertical axes one after another and measuring the distance of every point of the curve from these axes, so it is permissible to distinguish three various dimensions of symbolic formation from each other. The simplest and in a sense the most original and primitive type of this relation is found wherever a sensory experience of some sort confronts us, possessing a certain content of meaning such that a kind of expressive value adheres to it with which it seems to be saturated. Even here we are in a fundamental way beyond the abstraction of a "mere" sensation as dogmatic sensationalism understands it. This is because the sensory content stands before us, as Spinoza says, not like a mute picture on a tablet but rather immediately manifests an inner life as something that appears through its objective nature. This transparency of the sensory is inherent in every aesthetic perception but it is by no means restricted to the area of the aesthetic. It can be recognized nonetheless in every instance of spoken language and in every elementary form of myth.

Our inquiry here is not directed to the possibility of this state of affairs, nor are we trying to recognize the fundamental psychological or metaphysical characteristic that gives something external and sensory the power to express something mental in this way and immediately reveal it to us. The answers that have been proposed to this question either misinterpret the problem that we are dealing with here by substituting another situation for it, such as the logical content of an analogical inference, or, at best, they merely create another name for the phenomenon by speaking of a symbolic empathy of the internal into the external. Yet the more problematic that all theories of the primary phenomenon of expression prove themselves to be the deeper we examine them, expression still remains clearly and definitely before us as a phenomenon.

On the other hand, however, a look at language and especially the linguistic sentence, which can more rightly be termed the actual elementary linguistic structure than can the word, shows that language does not remain in this first sphere, the sphere of expression. Instead, it must necessarily transcend it in order to fulfill its actual task. For in every sentence there is always a certain positing which aims at an objective state of affairs that language seeks to contain and describe in some way. Here we do not just have to do with the mere communication of states of the speaker. Rather, a relationship in being is asserted which is supposed to maintain "in itself" and is conceived to be accessible and essentially understandable in the same way to every sensitive, perceiving, and thinking subject. The "is" of the copula is the purest and most pregnant mark of this new dimension of language. It can be signified with the term that Bühler[7] introduced with reference to Husserl as the representative function[8]. But beyond this function of representation yet another and third sphere appears which we want to term of pure significance[9]. It is distinguished from the sphere of representation by the fact that it has separated itself from the basis of observational configurations in which representation is rooted and out of which it continuously draws its strength. It is suspended, so to speak, in the free ether of pure thought. The sign in the sense of pure signification serves to be neither expressive nor representative. It is a sign in the sense of an abstract coordination. It presents a reciprocal relationship and correspondence that is grasped as a general law. But we must refrain from thinking of the elements which enter into this relationship as independent entities and contents that can exist and have meaning outside of this relation.

This relationship is perhaps most clearly seen in the modern foundations of geometry introduced by Pasch and brought to completion by Hilbert. In the system of Pasch and Hilbert points, lines, and planes, which we are accustomed to view in terms of the older interpretations as perceptual structures, have now lost all of their representative meaning. Now they only function as signs for a certain purely significant content – for that mathematical content of meaning that is formulated in the axioms of geometry. Whatever fulfills these axioms can be chosen as representative of this content. The important thing in every genuine geometric proposition is the constitutive law of this content, not the perceptual character of the elements.

Thus the points and straight lines in this abstract geometry can be replaced in a certain manner by structures of a completely different perceptual nature. The variety of perceptual interpretations does not change anything of the character of the logical content of the particular geometry in question because this is based solely upon the pure form of the axioms themselves, that is, on general principles of coordination and not on particular forms and structures.

If we take this general differentiation of the expressive, representative, and significative functions as our basis, which I can, of course, no more than sketch for you, then we have a general plan of ideal orientation within which we can now indicate to a certain extent the position of each symbolic form. Of course this position cannot be indicated in the sense of something fixed for all time so that it could be referred to within this basic plan by a stationary point. On the contrary, it is characteristic for each form that in the various stages of its development and formation in thought it has a different relationship to the three basic poles that we have tried to distinguish here. It shifts positions in this development and in virtue of this movement is able to attain its own area of being and meaning. Thereby it reaches its completion and internal limits.

Let us try to make this clear once more with the example of language. There can be no doubt how very much language is founded on the purely expressive and how strongly it is rooted in it from its most primitive forms to its highest stages. As one-sided and insufficient as it is to attempt to understand language, merely as expressive movement, as did Wundt, and to attempt to determine its essential intellectual character from that perspective, there can still be no doubt that a certain expressive or "physiognomic" character still adheres in highly developed language. The modern psychology of expression has called attention to these features of language. Heinz Werner has recently undertaken experiments in the Hamburg psychological laboratory to try to shed light on this physiognomic side of linguistic experiences. On the other hand, however, there is no question that only a single stage or dimension of linguistic expression is thereby of concern and that language as a whole is truly constituted and perfected only when it goes beyond this stage.

In order to make the nature and continuity of this process clear to us one needs only to observe the procedure that is usually employed in language to coin the first designations for spatial relationships. Language has a new task wherever such relationships are signified linguistically, where "here" is distinguished from "there," where the location of the speaker is distinguished from the one spoken to, or where greater nearness or distance is rendered by various indicative particles. Here the merely subjective sensation and stimulus is transformed into an objective perception and sounds that express feeling become sounds with representational meaning.

The continuity of development that is manifested here consists in the fact that the new form to which language is now elevated still uses the older material means. The old characteristically expressive components are not discarded. Rather these are preserved while at the same time they are given a new meaning and, as it were, a new life. This two-sided relationship or bipolar character is clearly recognizable in the basic indicative words, the demonstrative pronouns of primitive languages. They come from a purely "physiognomic" determination, shading, and coloration of the vowel. But in this sensory tone coloration they contain certain basic distinctions of the objective world view. The sharper vowel, for instance, signifies nearness to the speaker, the duller, greater distance. And in a similar manner the direction from the ego to the other, that is, the centrifugal direction, is distinguished from the opposite centripetal direction. Temporal directions can also be differentiated in this way solely by sound. In the Somali languages, for example, the vowel "a" serves as a suffix to a noun in order to signify it as present temporally while the vowel "o" indicates the temporally absent past or future. Thus language proceeds from expressive meaning to pure representative meaning and from this it is constantly directed towards the third realm of pure significance.

Language is not confined to the sphere of the observable and tangible but attempts to grasp what is ultimate and highest in the realm of thought. But of course the limits of language become visible in this attempt. For even where language is elevated to the expression of pure relations, sensory coloration still adheres to it. The attempt has been repeatedly made to contain the expression of purely logical distinctions and relations in language using images taken from the sphere of immediate observation. This is perhaps most clearly seen in the most universal expression of relation, the copula of the predicative sentence. The pure "is" of the predicative statement is signified in the majority of languages, including highly developed and refined ones, in such a way that a secondary perceptual connotation adheres to it so that logical "being" is replaced by the spatial being of "here" or "there." Thereby the holding of a relation is replaced by a statement about existence, a proposition about a certain entity and its nature. A basic characteristic of language shows itself in this kind of substitution, which it cannot abandon without forfeiting its own nature.

Thinkers in the tradition of philosophical sensationalism frequently liked to refer to this fact in order to conclude from language's inability to break through the sensory perceptual sphere that the same inability holds for thought as a whole. Locke makes use of the theory of language in order to utilize it as one of the foremost pieces of evidence for his theory of knowledge. But the most essential aspect is thereby overlooked because although pure cognition can in no way dispense with language as a genuine *Organon* of thought, it changes this instrument in this very employment. It is not bound by the limits of spoken natural language. Instead, thought extends this beyond its original nature by making it serviceable for its own ends. Now, that universal language or *Lingua universalis* is developing, as already foreseen by Descartes and Leibniz, as a necessary organ for the progress of scientific thought. Only today in modern mathematics and symbolic logic, which serves as its foundation, has it reached its true cultivation and consummation. With this, language has completely left the area in which it is originally rooted. It has resolutely cast aside everything that is merely expressive. Nothing adheres to the signs of the symbolic language of mathematics and logic that in any way includes a relationship to the "subject" or to the individual world of feeling and sensation. They serve exclusively to represent the most general, objective, and necessary states of affairs.

But also the world of observation to which the representative function of language is always directed now begins more and more to recede. It finally disappears completely in the new world that comes into view here. As our awareness of this world grows it impresses its unique characteristics upon us more and more. Russell has given a well-known humorous definition of pure mathematics, which says that it is an area in which one never knows what one is talking about or if that which one says is true. Naturally this definition seeks in no way to deny the specific significance of pure mathematics or, what is synonymous with it for Russell, pure logic. But it does deny that this significance still requires any observational basis or object. Here the final radical step has been taken; the realm of pure relations and meanings has become independent and absolved itself from every bond to observational existence. The specific nature and tendency of this separation is particularly prominent where it is not confined to the sphere of pure mathematics as a theory of abstract formal relations but extends to the cognition of reality and defines it in accordance with this new ideal.

It can be said that it is precisely this new methodological approach and revision in the basic view of the meaning and means at the disposal of the cognition of nature that is responsible for the crisis in modern mathematical physics. What principally differentiates the world of classical mechanics from the world view of the general theory of relativity is the different roles and importance which they assign to observation in the construction and constitution of the scientific object, the object of experience. Of course the classical Newtonian system is also based upon concepts that are principally of a non-observational nature. Newton's absolute space and time, which flows evenly according to its own nature separately from all relations to an outer object, are not observational concepts. However, when one considers their structure more closely it turns out that they refer throughout to the field of observational being and that they are derived from it by a continual process of progressive idealization. They merely follow to the end the path which perception points out. They subjugate physical being to a fixed geometric observational scheme within which all natural processes are to be ordered. Space and time appear here at least as analogies of empirical perceivable entities. Even in their absoluteness they are still understood as thing-like concrete structures.

The concept of mass in Newtonian physics also has this concrete substantial character. A piece of matter can be fixed as a self-identical thing and recognized in various locations in space as being one and the same. It can to an extent be followed by our gaze in all phases of its movement. The infinite number of positions which it can occupy in space at different times form nonetheless a surveyable totality insofar as they steadily emerge from each other and are all bound to the same observational substratum. But precisely this substantiality of space, time, and mass has been progressively abandoned by modern physics. Already Maxwell's theory of light and electricity forms here an important and methodologically essential beginning. The mechanical theory of light had to attempt to explain optical phenomena by thinking of them in the image of a certain movement modeled on that of rigid bodies. Even after it had progressed from the theory of undulation, the light waves were still considered as something concrete, as a movement of particles, which propagated themselves in the medium of ether in the same manner that a wave spreads out in water or the vibration of an elastic string spreads through the air. Maxwell's theory, on the other hand, breaks through this manner of explanation. In place of this kind of description of physical processes, which is like a transcription into known observational circumstances, there is a purely mathematical definition. Every single position of the ether is associated with a certain state of affairs. The periodic change of these states as it is expressed by certain equations replaces the metaphorical figurative expression of the "light wave." The character of the ether is restricted to the fact that for every one of its points two directed quantities are given, the magnetic and electrical vector. It is well-known how modern theory has progressed in this direction and has become the pure physics of fields. But it could only complete this transformation by freeing itself more and more from the restrictive demands of observability upon which older theory was based.

I do not need to enter any further into all of these matters; here they should only serve as a confirmation of how the "symbols" in which the modern physicist describes the process of nature have in fact taken the last decisive step and left the area of observation and representation for the province of pure signification. The newer mathematics and physics have not gone this way by chance. They have been led to it by the peculiar character of their methods and their objects. Of this there can be no serious doubt. But the kind of intellectual symbolic formation that is effected here now stands out all the more sharply from the basic attitudes of other areas of thought.

In this regard and before this audience I do not need to enter into the particularity of aesthetic form. One thing is immediately clear. The aesthetic object is rooted in the world of perception and its conditions in a wholly other and far deeper sense than is the case with the empirical physical object. No matter how far or how high aesthetic representation reaches beyond the sensory givenness of appearances or how much it strives towards the ideal – the area of *noeton kallos* – it remains restricted to perceptual being and must closely cling to it.

It appears to have become more difficult for aesthetic theory to understand the relationships which maintain within aesthetic apprehension and formation, between the world of pure expression and the world of pure representation. Not infrequently the attempt has been made to relate the aesthetic exclusively or at least chiefly to one of these two poles and thereby to give it a foundation. There are aesthetic systems that try so much to restrict art to the emotional and have it so fully absorbed by purely expressive experiences that, as a result, that which is characteristic of the aesthetic object is almost lost. On the other hand, there are others that try to separate the aesthetic in the strict and actual sense from its roots in subjective "feeling" so that to them it becomes nothing but a certain basic form of understanding and knowing objects which as such stands on the same level as the theoretical knowledge of nature.

But the specific form of the aesthetic is unmistakably negated rather than recognized through this isolation and abstract opposition of the "subjective" and the "objective." What is unique about the basic character of the aesthetic form of meaning is that in it these two motifs, which prove to be separable and relatively independent of each other in other forms of meaning, no longer are separated and stand instead in a purely correlative kind of relationship. Here we can no longer ask which of these two aspects, the aspect of expression or the aspect of representation, is the *proteron te physei*, the earliest or the later according to nature. For the nature of the aesthetic itself excludes every such anterior and posterior relationship of dependence of the one on the other. It is the merger of the one in the other, the ideal balance which presents itself between them that constitutes the aesthetic stance as well as the aesthetic object. Here I would like to appeal to what Herr Prinzhorn presented yesterday on the problem of rhythm.[10] The gist of his characterization of rhythm was precisely that it is the equalization of the tension between the poles of expression and representation. Glancing once more at language, the language of poetry is distinguished from that of ordinary life and from that of science by the fact that for it there is no opposition and no separation of representative meaning. It aims at pure representation in the power of pure expression and vice-versa. Every perfected poem by Goethe, for instance, presents us with both in an indissoluble unity and totality. It is completely submerged in a particular mood and saturated with it in every tone and in its entire rhythmical movement. But precisely in this melodic-rhythmic expressive content a new shape of the world is constructed for us which then stands before us objectively. The various art forms, poetry, music, and spatial arts, including painting and sculpture, may attain this unity in various ways and by different means but it is absent in none of them because it belongs to the essence of artistic formation as such.

I cannot enter more closely into the host of interesting specific questions which a treatment of the topic that has been given to me demands. I have only attempted here to sketch a general outline. I just wanted to create a framework for a treatment of the problem of the symbol, realizing that I cannot fill it out in any fashion. Filling out this framework must be left to the individual lectures, each of which will illuminate the problem from a particular angle.

By way of conclusion I may at least say a few words about a very general basic question that arises with the analysis of every symbolic form. One cannot even use the term "symbol" without raising the general question which we may call the question of truth. A symbol would not be a symbol if it did not lay claim to a kind of truth. A mere sign that is detached from every relationship to something that is to be signified or to a meaning that it seeks to contain and bring to expression would thereby no longer be a sign. It would be reduced to a mere presence in which the characteristic sign function was extinguished. The difference, therefore, between our idealistic interpretation of symbolic forms and a realistic view does not lie in any denial of the objective nature of these forms. On the contrary, the attempt here is to establish this objective nature and to understand it by means of a general principle.

Kant saw the basic character of Platonic idealism in the fact that Plato did not stop with the "copy view of the physical world order"[11] but elevates himself instead to a view of its "architectonic connection." In this sense the standpoint of the mere "copy view" must be exchanged for that of "architectonic connection" in every sphere of objectivity, no matter what kind or type it is. Such a sphere cannot, by the simple imitation and rendering of some given being, evidence the truth and objectivity which characteristically belongs to it, but accomplishes this rather in the meaningful order of the construction that it carries out by virtue of an original formative principle.

It is well known how this basic thought has proven itself in the "Copernican revolution" that Kant executed in his attempt to lay the foundations of cognition. Nature, the object of knowledge, stands under the pure concepts of the understanding because it is these alone which allow us to spell out appearances so that we can read them as experiences – that is, so that we can unite them to objective wholes. But we also have to realize that besides in purely theoretical cognition the respective form of synthesis, the synopsis, does not imitate the object that is seen in this synthesis, but constitutes it. To be sure, aesthetics like the critique of knowledge has also taken centuries until it learned to understand and define the concept of "natural truth" in this sense. Again and again it was forgotten that nature as "beautiful" nature is not given nor set before the sculptor or painter as the goal of imitation. Instead it is the character and course of artistic creativity out of which the modes of viewing nature typical of the individual arts originally come. The stylistic law and hence the immanent law of truth cannot be taken from some fixed "nature of things." It is rather the independent originality and autonomy of this law which itself determines this truth. The agreement with this inner norm, which is a norm of productive activity, gives the work its basis. In this sense the aesthetic of the eighteenth century, the aesthetics of Mendelssohn and Lessing, already pronounced this thought by asserting that we must begin with the kind of signs that each art uses in order to reach a certain demarcation of its area and possibilities.[12] The definition of an art lies in what it is capable of by virtue of its specific signs, not in what other arts are just as much or more capable of accomplishing. In the end, this principle of Lessing's informs us that it is none other than the style of each art that is decisive in determining its immanent truth and its objects – not the other way around.

If we conceive this basic thought in general terms then we are thereby required, as in the case of the individual arts, to inquire after the law of formation in all areas of thought and through this law to understand the objective structures that become visible in them. Let us recall once again our example of the line drawing that could be first taken as an aesthetic ornament, then as a magic-mythic insignia, and then again as a mathematical curve which served to indicate a functional development. This drawing had a completely different character as an object in each instance. In this way it now becomes clear how that which we call the object is not to be understood in the manner of a fixed and rigid *forma substantialis* but rather as a functional form. At the same time it can be seen how the richness of being originally unfolds out of the richness of meaning and how the manifold character of the meanings of being do not stand in contradiction to the demand for the unity of being. It is this manifoldness that actually fulfills the demand for this unity.

Notes

1 Originally published in *Zeitschrift fur Aesthetik und allgemeine Kunstwissenschaft* 21 (1927), pp. 295–322, reprinted in *Schriften zur Philosophie der symbolischen Formen* (Hamburg: Meiner, 2009). Translated by John M. Krois.
2 Friedrich Theodore Vischer, "Das Symbol" in *Philosophische Aufsätze: Eduard Zeiler zu seinem fünfzigjährigen Doktor-Jubiläum gewidmet* (Leipzig: Fues's Verlag, 1887), pp. 153–193.
3 Adolph von Harnack, *Lehrbuch der Dogmengeschichte*, 2nd ed. (Freiburg: J. C. B. Mohr, 1894), I, p. 198.
4 David Hilbert, "Neubegründung der Mathematik," *Abhandlungen aus dem Mathematischen Seminar der Hamburgerschen Universität*, 1 (1922), p. 163.
5 Heinrich Hertz, *The Principles of Mechanics Presented in a New Form*, trans. D. E. Jones and J.-T. Walley (New York: Dover Publications, 1956), p. 1.
6 Cassirer first uses the term "symbolic form" in print in 1921 in the German edition of *Einstein's Theory of Relativity*, p. 447. – Trans. – This passage is to be found in Chapter 15. – Ed.
7 The reference is to Karl Bühler (1879–1963), a representative of the so-called Würzburg School of *Denkpsychologie* (psychology of thought), which has a certain proximity to *Gestalt* psychology. – Ed.
8 *Darstellungsfunktion*
9 *reine Bedeutung*
10 Hans Prinzhorn, "Rhythmus im Tanz," *Zeitschrift für Aesthetik und allgemeine Kunst-wissenschaft*, 21 (1927), pp. 276–87, esp. pp. 286–287. – Trans.
11 *Critique of Pure Reason*, B 370.
12 For a related discussion see Ernst Cassirer, *The Philosophy of the Enlightenment*, trans. F. C. A. Koeller and J. P. Pettegrove (Princeton: Princeton University Press, 1951), Chapter 7. – Trans.

Part 3

The Southwest School

Introduction: Wilhelm Windelband (1848–1915)

WILHELM WINDELBAND WAS BORN 1848 IN POTSDAM as a son of a Prussian civil servant. He studied first medicine and natural sciences, then history of philosophy at the Universities of Jena, Berlin, and Göttingen. His philosophical teachers were Kuno Fischer and Rudolf Hermann Lotze. In 1870, Windelband defended his dissertation under the guidance of Lotze on "The Doctrines of Chance" [*Die Lehren vom Zufall*]. In 1873, he finished his Habilitation thesis on "The Certainty of Cognition." He received his first professorship at the University of Zurich in 1876, and in 1877 he was recruited to Freiburg. In 1882, he switched to the (then-German) University of Strasbourg, where he became successor to Otto Liebmann. He stayed there for twenty years, marking the most productive period of his life. The main result of his research there was the *Lehrbuch der Geschichte der Philosophie* [*A History of Philosophy*], which he revised and re-edited until his death and which was translated into many languages. In 1903, he was recruited to the University of Heidelberg to take over the chair of Kuno Fischer, where he stayed until the end of his life. He became elected a member of the Heidelberg Academy of Sciences in 1910. At the time of his death, Windelband was one of the most respected figures in German philosophy.

Together with his pupil Heinrich Rickert, he founded what was called the "Southwest or Baden School" of Neo-Kantianism. Since Rickert taught in Freiburg and in Heidelberg after Windelband's death, the school received this vague geographic title. Both cities were then in the State of Baden (after World War II, it was enlarged to the State of Baden-Württemberg). Due to their orientation towards the problem of values and norms, the school has also been called the "*werttheoretische Schule*" or "value-theoretical school" of Neo-Kantianism, in contrast to the Marburg school with its putative focus on logical cognition. Although united under the umbrella of "Neo-Kantianism," competition between the two schools was fierce.

Because of his meticulous historical scholarship, which is one defining feature of the Neo-Kantian movement (following Windelband's model), Windelband is mostly seen as an historian of philosophy, which is a very limited view of his work (and also underestimates his sophisticated method of writing the history of philosophy; on this, see Chapter 20, below). From early on, the question of the normative function of thinking and the connection between empirical (human) thinking and universally valid norms (or as he prefers to say, values) was of primal interest for him. In this, he rejected any psychologistic conception of knowledge (alongside others, such as Frege and Husserl), something he thought was left not fully clarified in Kant. But the relation of empirical thought to universally valid values also has an eminently ethical component for Windelband. Ethics should be the ultimate interest of philosophy. Hence, for Windelband, "logic is the ethics of thinking".[1] This informed his reading of Kant's critical philosophy, which should be, when fully developed, concerned with universally valid norms in the realms of the theoretical, practical and aesthetic, together making up the whole of culture. This reading of Kant enlarged the latter's transcendental philosophy into a philosophy of culture and stands in marked difference to the conception of the Marburg School.

Windelband's most popular book, besides his many works in the history of philosophy, is the essay collection "*Praeludien,*" which he conceived as an "introduction to philosophy" via different themes not only in theoretical philosophy, but also in aesthetics, religious and literary studies. The first edition appeared in 1883, and four more editions were issued during Windelband's lifetime and one more after his death (the fifth edition was published in 1914, and there was one further printing in 1924). This collection contains what is undoubtedly Windelband's most known contribution to systematic philosophy, namely his presidential address from Strasbourg, "History and Natural Science" (reprinted here as Chapter 19) of 1894. In it, he introduces his famous distinction between nomothetical and idiographic sciences, which became very influential for the development of the *Geisteswissenschaften*, the human or cultural sciences, and their theory, while also being the target of heavy critique on the part of Dilthey, Husserl and Heidegger, and others.

His systematic *magnum opus*, published in 1914, a year before his passing, is modestly and misleadingly called *An Introduction to Philosophy*.

Another project that Windelband pursued is noteworthy in terms of the context of global university politics and place of the Neo-Kantian movement in it: the project of an "encyclopedia of philosophical sciences" that Windelband conceived and that was to be carried out across the major countries of the world in a collaborative effort. The project's members included Windelband and his student Arnold Ruge in Germany, Louis Couturat in France, Josiah Royce in the US, Benedetto Croce and Federigo Enriques in Italy, and Nicolai Losskii in Russia. The idea was to come up with such an encyclopedia with the input of a combined effort on the part of researchers in the developed nations of the world. Of this project, which was to comprise a volume, respectively, on Logic, Ethics, Aesthetics, the Philosophy of History, and the Philosophy of Religion, only vol. I (Logic) was realized in 1913. It was first published in German and translated into every language from which the contributors stemmed. The project came to an end with the onset of the Great War and was never taken up again, in part because the initiator Windelband had died. It was paired with a multi-national philosophical journal, *Logos*, the "international journal for the philosophy of culture," co-edited (in Germany) by Georg Simmel, Heinrich Rickert, and younger members of the Neo-Kantian movement. The express purpose of both outlets was to contribute to the understanding between peoples on a scholarly level to avoid a further "crisis of civilization." The journal, too, was to branch out to outlets in these other countries, although this plan never materialized for the same reason as in the case of the *Encyclopedia*.

Further Reading

Windelband, Wilhelm, *An Introduction to Philosophy*. Trans. Joseph McCabe. London: T. Fisher Unwin Ltd., 1921.

Ruge, Arnold, Wilhelm Windelband, Josiah Royce, Louis Couturat, Benedetto Croce, Federigo Enriques, Nicolai Losskii, *Encyclopedia of the Philosophical Sciences*, Vol. I, Logic. Trans. Meyer, B. Ethel, London: MacMillan & Co., Ltd., 1913.

Beiser, Frederick, C. *The German Historicist Tradition.* Oxford/New York: Oxford Univer
    2011, ch. 9, "Wilhelm Windelband and the Forces of History," pp. 365–392.
Chang, Tsun-Hwa, *Wert und Kultur. Wilhelm Windelbands Kulturphilosophie.* Würz
    2012.
Krijnen, Christian & Ernst Wolfgang Ort, eds., *Sinn, Geltung, Wert. Neukantianische Motive in d*
    modernen Kulturphilosophie. Würzburg: K & N, 1999.

There is almost no literature in English that deals with Wilhelm Windelband, except for the masterful essay by Beiser (see above). A short outline of his life and works can be found in Ollig's *Der Neukantianismus* (pp. 53–58). Some background can be found in Andrea Staiti's entry on Heinrich Rickert in the *Stanford Encyclopedia of Philosophy.* Most of his work is out of print in German as well. New projects on him are underway, but so far, he is the most neglected of the "major" Neo-Kantians.

"Critical or Genetic Method?" (1883)

In this article, Windelband contrasts two methods of explaining the acquisition of cognition. By the "critical method," he means Kant's transcendental method, at least according to Windelband's modified understanding. By the "genetic" method, Windelband has in mind explanations in terms of evolutionary theory that explain "genetically" the development of cognition through the human species' development. Essentially, what Windelband is arguing against is a form of psychologism in the theory of knowledge which might be contrasted with Husserl's and Frege's refutations of psychologism, and which might also be of interest for contemporary arguments regarding the development of the "mind-brain" in cognitive psychology. In terms of the history of the Neo-Kantian movement, this text comes at a pivotal point, as around this time, Hermann Cohen on the Marburg side began doubting any accounts of knowledge according to "folk psychology" [*Völkerpsychologie*]. The refutation of any psychologistic or subjectivist reading of cognition can be seen as one of the dominant themes on the part of philosophers in the latter third of the nineteenth century.

As regards the "critical" method that Windelband sees prefigured in Kant – although Kant, too, was not always clear on the "subjective" and "critical" elements in his account of cognition – Windelband takes this to interpret knowledge as *a priori* cognition, which is necessary and universal. But he goes beyond Kant when he claims that these *a priori* cognitions rest on axioms that are to be taken as absolute and not further provable and which obtain in all regions of knowledge, theoretical, practical, and aesthetic (as well). Hence, Windelband defines the "*problem of philosophy* [as concerned with] *the validity of axioms.*" "Validity" [*Wert*] is, thus, the general term applying to axioms in all spheres of cognition, not just in ethics. In turn, validity cannot rest on an empirical or factual validity, but must have a "teleological necessity that has to be accepted as immediate, if otherwise certain ends are to be fulfilled." For the critical method, then, these axioms are "norms that should be valid under the precondition that thought would achieve the end of being true, willing – the end of being good, feeling – the end of perceiving beauty, in a way that is to be universally accepted and recognized." This critical method, thus, is based on the "belief in universally valid ends and their capacity to be known in empirical consciousness," which is able to understand everywhere the principle of the teleological nexus. Windelband applauds Fichte for having understood this teleological character of the critical method and rejects Hegel's "artificial" dialectical method. Nonetheless, from Hegel we can learn the historical dimension of the progress of knowledge and therefore the necessity to derive the values of reason from the "critical illumination of history" vis-à-vis an historicism to which Dilthey's project of a "critique of historical reason" would lead. The latter theme will be further dealt with in the next text.

"History and Natural Science" (Presidential Address, Strasbourg, 1894)

As already mentioned, this is undoubtedly Windelband's most famous piece of writing, though given the scope of Windelband's scholarly output, this is both unfair and surprising.[2] Yet, its popularity may be explained by the weight given at the time to discussions regarding the character of those sciences that are not natural sciences, namely (depending on one's understanding of them) the human, cultural, or spiritual sciences (in German, *Geisteswissenschaften*).[3] Given the overall preponderance of positivism in the natural sciences, Windelband's reflections are certainly meant to counteract this positivistic tendency and to give a justification for these "other" sciences and also for their status as "science," which translates the German *Wissenschaft*. The German term has a much broader meaning than the English word "science," as can be seen both in Kant, who spoke of philosophy as being able to "come forth as science," and in the great systems of German idealism that utilize this term, as in Fichte's *Wissenschaftslehre* and Hegel's *Wissenschaft der Logik*. To Windelband, too, all types of knowledge, not just that of the physical laws of nature, are to be captured under the umbrella term "science."

In the Presidential Address at Strasbourg, Windelband attempts to account for *two different types* or *directions* of science: *nomothetic* science that posits laws and *idiographic* science that narrates the particular. This distinction cuts across the one Dilthey made between explanatory [*erklärende*] sciences and understanding or interpretive [*verstehende*] sciences. Dilthey designated the former as natural sciences, the latter as human or spiritual sciences [*Geisteswissenschaften*], thereby in effect presupposing, Windelband alleges, an *ontological* distinction between a realm of nature and a realm of culture[4] Windelband takes issue with this distinction, which he considers naïve and pre-transcendental. Instead, Windelband wants to use an epistemological criterion, following Kant's transcendental turn, such that what we cognize depends on the type of gaze we turn upon the world, on what we read into the world with a particular type of gaze. Windelband believes it to be true to the Kantian spirit, but to go beyond Kant's characterization of the lawful character of (our cognition of) nature, when he introduces the other type of gaze: namely, that which wants to understand and describe the individual. The goal of the former is "the general, apodictic judgment," and the goal of the latter is "the singular, assertoric proposition." Based on these two opposed cognitive interests, the "same" object may be the basis for nomothetic or idiographic insights. These two types of cognition are nothing but the two opposed directions of our human interest in the world, that towards abstraction on the one hand, and towards intuition on the other. Both are equally valid in their opposed cognitive interest and can be applied to any object; the law and the lived-experience as the two opposed poles of our mind "remain as the ultimate, incommensurable entities of our worldview." This expansion into the idiographic is thus, according to Windelband, the fulfillment of Kant's Copernican turn. This is perhaps one of the most original and ingenious ways of interpreting Kant's transcendental turn, though it has been rejected wholesale by contemporary readers, such as Dilthey, Husserl, and others (cf. Chapter 32.).

Further Reading

Dilthey, Wilhelm, *The Formation of the Historical World in the Human Sciences*, ed., with an introduction, by Makkreel, R. A. & F. Rodi. Princeton: Princeton University Press, 2002.

Makkreel, Rudolf A., "Wilhelm Dilthey and the Neo-Kantians: On the conceptual distinction between *Geisteswissenschaften* and *Kulturwissenschaften*", in: Makkreel, R. A. & S. Luft, *Neo-Kantianism in Contemporary Philosophy*. Bloomington/Indianapolis: Indiana University Press, 2010, pp. 253–271.

——, "*Naturwissenschaften* versus *Geisteswissenschaften*", in: *Encyclopedia of Philosophy and the Social Sciences*, ed. B. Kaldis, London 2013, pp. 649–653.

"Introduction" to *A History of Philosophy With Special Reference to the Formation and Development of Its Problems and Conceptions* (1900)

Windelband's works in the history of philosophy are an exercise in the history of problems [*Problemgeschichte*]. This way of writing the history of philosophy is typically taken to be a trivial and simplistic procedure. However, in the history of philosophical historiography this method is actually novel to the nineteenth century and fully developed and perfected by Windelband (and later, in Cassirer's *The Problem of Knowledge*).[5] It is quite sophisticated, as it comes together with sound "philologico-historical" work and rests on these solid foundations. Indeed, writing the history of philosophy in a *philosophical* manner involves more than just a correct presentation of chronology, history, and personality of the philosophers (or those that we call philosophers in hindsight). Instead, if done correctly and consciously, it is to be itself a "*critico-philosophical science*" that is "to *estimate* what value for the total result of the history of philosophy belongs to theories thus established and explained as regards their origin." All other methods of writing the history of philosophy, such as history of ideas [*Ideengeschichte*], history of a philosophy's or a philosopher's reception [*Rezeptionsgeschichte*], or others, are indebted to, or critiques of, the Neo-Kantian paradigm of *Problemgeschichte*. Also, Gadamer's concept of history of effects or effective history [*Wirkungsgeschichte*] can be seen as a nod, however critical, to this conception.

Windelband once again takes lessons from Hegel, in that the history of philosophy is itself a historical development and a constant progress of civilization's self-consciousness, but rejects any ascent to an absolute standpoint. Nonetheless, this means that the history of philosophy is an indispensable part of *doing* philosophy. Thus, any strict separation between the historian of philosophy and the systematic philosopher would be artificial, for Windelband. Despite its philosophical ambition, the introduction reproduced here brings to the fore the meticulous work that Windelband, among all great Neo-Kantians, did with respect to the philological side of the history of philosophy. Indeed, this work comes at the same time when classical philology became a rigorous science focused heavily on historical-critical editions, and when the neo-Kantians themselves began rigorous historical-philological work on Kant himself. But as becomes clear through this text, this historical-philological appreciation is always, and has to be, bolstered through a philosophical *justification* of the importance and necessity of looking at the history of philosophy with a philosophical eye, which, in turn, can only be itself clear-sighted when being able to look at the sources in the best possible presentation.

Philosophy of Culture and Transcendental Idealism (1910)

In this piece, originally published in the journal *Logos* and based on a talk given in 1909 in Munich, Windelband lays out the character and task of a philosophy of culture. As the title indicates, this philosophy of culture needs to be brought forth in the form of transcendental idealism, thereby fulfilling the Kantian promise of a completely worked-out transcendental idealism in all areas of culture. In this short sketch, then, Windelband brings together motifs from his earlier thought as presented in "Critical or Genetic Method?" and "History and Natural Science," insofar as a *philosophy* of culture cannot rely on "genetic" or psychological explanations of what culture is. Moreover, it needs to be conceived as a full execution of transcendental philosophy, insofar as it pertains to all regions of culture. This sketch also illustrates a general difference in the Southwest School from the Marburg conception of a philosophy of culture that must start out, in each region of culture, with the given, more precisely with a given science (Windelband makes clear at the very outset the difference between his own conception and the Marburg School's). Specifically, for Windelband, it is the task of a philosophy of culture to extract the rational elements in each cultural formation (the distillation of which, to the Marburgers, would be the task of a particular science of that cultural region, not that of philosophy proper).

Windelband's idea of a transcendental philosophy of culture consciously charts a course between a Scylla of an aloof philosophy of culture and the Charybdis of a merely empirical study of historically appearing and disappearing cultural formations. While he sides with the Marburg conception of culture as what has been created by the synthetic power of human consciousness and its deeds, he does insist on the limits of such a *philosophical* account of culture. In this sense, he proposes a two-tiered account of culture: a *philosophical* one, which extracts the "absolute *a priori*" that is valid in itself across all cultural formations according to "all-encompassing necessities of reason," and a less rigorous general account that determines the "specification upon which depends the determination of empirical consciousness." The latter can only discover common generalities in an ascent of cognition from the specific to the general level of "world reason," which "enters into our finite consciousness." This distinction can be applied in all regions of reason's reign: theory, practice, aesthetics, and, finally, religion as that which postulates the "totality of all values of reason in an absolute unity," however inexperienceable. Acknowledging the differentiation of cultures in today's scattered world, Windelband ends on a somber note, in that he asserts that an all-encompassing rational view of culture will be forever impossible; instead, we should strive to work out the rational elements of those cultural formations that we see around us, forfeiting any grand ambitions, and also rejecting any praise of the individual in creating cultural values. Instead, in our "little worlds of knowledge, willing, and formation," we are only cogs in the great overarching cultural machine, but thereby we should be strengthened in the belief that we live in "contexts of reason that mean more than ourselves." Such a sketch of a philosophy of culture is also singular within the Southwest School.

Notes

1. Ollig, *Der Neukantianismus,* p. 54.
2. Indeed, Windelband himself expresses surprise at this fact in the preface to the third edition of the *Praeludien* of 1907.
3. The Marburg Neo-Kantians preferred the term *Kulturwissenschaften,* and also Windelband seems to prefer this term (cf. also Chapter 19), but the term that has survived in contemporary German is *Geisteswissenschaften,* which refers to those disciplines that might simply be called "humanities" or "liberal arts."
4. On this dispute, cf. Makkreel 2010. Cf. also Section IV of the chapter on Windelband in Beiser's book (Beiser 2011).
5. The four-volume study, of which only the last part is translated as *The Problem of Knowledge: Philosophy, Science, and History Since Hegel,* was originally entitled *Das Erkenntnisproblem in der Philosophie und Wissenschaft der neueren Zeit* [The Problem of Knowledge in the Philosophy and Science of Modernity].

Chapter 18

"Critical or Genetic Method?" (1883)[1]

TRANSLATED BY ALAN DUNCAN

In the *Critique of Pure Reason*, which was, of course, less intended as a system of philosophy than as a "tractate on method," Kant posed a new conception of philosophy's task and mode of knowledge against the psychologism of his contemporaries; since then, the question of the essence of its method has not disappeared from philosophy's agenda. This is all the more understandable because the decision of this question at the same time decides the position one is to assume within or vis-à-vis philosophy.

Also, in the interest of this decision it is to be lamented that Kant's own doctrine, with all the difficulty of its problems, with the great elasticity of its portrayals, with the extremely complicated treatment of multifarious, in part antagonistic trains of thought, with the uncertainty of its yet nascent terminology, did not appear so unambiguously and finely determined that the concept of critical method that he intended to create would be protected with self-evident clarity against every misunderstanding, and might be posited indubitably as historical fact. The new that he brought was wrapped up in the old; it was not precluded that one might read the old empiricism on the one hand, and the old rationalism on the other into his doctrine, and thus his new principle fell between two stools.

Nevertheless, the historical efficacy of this principle is obvious. For the Kantian treatment of the problems directly or indirectly influenced the whole of nineteenth century philosophy in such a way that the latter can only be understood from out of the former. All post-Kantian philosophy is either the development and more or less comprehensive cultivation of the Kantian principle, or the struggle of the older schools against his. Principally, nothing new has been created since. Here and there the metaphysical, or psychologistic tendencies of the eighteenth century have been renewed, but never without being more or less strongly modified by the influence of Kantian philosophy. The great metaphysical systems of German philosophy differ from the earlier ones mainly in their adoption of the Kantian elements; that wherein contemporary positivism diverges from that of the Encyclopedists – aside from the physiological and psychological manner of expression – rests solely on the influence of Kantian thought and on the consideration of critical problems, as it appears in the French and English writers of this school unconsciously and unrecognized, and consciously recognized in the only original German positivist, Carl Göring. Psychologism, as e.g. Fries and Beneke[2] represent it, or rather as it was redeveloped in ethno-psychological research[3], finally owes the great superiority that it doubtlessly has over the earlier corresponding theories alone to the connection to critical philosophy. This is the greatness of Kantianism: that it has ennobled all its opponents.

Yet the opposition of critical philosophy to the various schools of thought it encountered was not always uttered with equal poignancy. Against the metaphysical tendencies, the new doctrine was so energetically polemic that there was no danger of being confused directly with them. Furthermore, a series of historical influences shifted this opposition of the critical to the metaphysical method to the center of interest, and sharpened it to the utmost. For a long time the Transcendental Dialectic, with the whole contrivance that it piled up as evidence of the impossibility of any knowledge of the thing-in-itself, was considered the actual core of Kantian doctrine! Yet on the other side the danger of a misunderstanding of the critical method is much greater and more widespread. For the nature of the matter led to some extent to Kant's investigation necessarily going hand in hand with the usual research on the "origin" of ideas, and his own habit of regarding problems in the manner of his contemporaries made it difficult for him to hold fast to and clearly define the fundamental difference that he himself posited between "origin" and "grounding,"[4] that Schleiermacher could already level the accusation, oftentimes repeated since, that the fundamental distinction between analytic and synthetic judgments proved fluid and indefensible when subjected to psychological insight. Kant himself was guilty of allowing the new concept of apriority to be quickly reduced to the old notion of psychological apriority, such that the most valuable of his creations was misunderstood.

It is all the more necessary to make that fundamental difference as clear and distinct as possible in which insight into the possibility of a critical conception of philosophy is rooted. And the best way to do this is to reflect on a chief methodological difference of the remaining sciences and the ultimate significance of this difference: how these relations have been considered by hitherto existing logic, under the predominant consideration with respect to the epistemic goals of natural scientific research.

If one follows all distinctions that are to be made with respect to the *procedure of scientific proof and inference*, they can finally be reduced to the deductive and inductive method, and this pair of opposites is rooted in the fundamental relation upon which all our thought is based: that between the general and the particular. The coherent tendency that dominates all our reflection can be summed up in the fact that we want to understand the dependency upon the general in which the particular finds itself. For this reason, this is the absolutely fundamental relation of scientific thought [in general]. On this point the scientific and aesthetic function diverge, in that the view of the artist lovingly perceives only the particular in its entire configuration, whereas the knowing mind, just as that of the practical agent, begins to subsume the object under a more general form of conception, to eliminate that which is unsuited to this end, and to retain only the "essential." Therein consists also the comprehensive power that Aristotle exercised upon the development of the human sciences, that he made this fundamental relation of the general and the particular the pivotal point to both his metaphysics and his logic. Nor does it change anything concerning this fundamental relation or its general validity that the general and essential have another meaning in historical research than in natural science; that it means there a value-connection[5] of facts, here their lawfulness[6].[7]

Thus, all human knowledge moves between two poles: on the one side stand the individual sensations, on the other the universal propositions that express definite rules about the possible relations or connections of the former. All scientific thought is aimed at subsuming those sensations under these universal propositions via forms of logical connection. For this very reason the relation of the individual to the general, the dependency of the former upon the latter, inheres in all logical forms. All our knowledge consists in interweaving the universal together with the most particular through the intermediary links[8] produced by our thinking.

The certitude and truth of all these intermediary links is thus rooted in the final instance in the certitude and truth of the two elements that are woven together in them through logical operations: of the sensations and the universal propositions. Everything that lies between the two is proven by inferring it from through the application of the laws of logic. Hence, it follows on its own that these starting points, as the indispensable preconditions of all proof, cannot themselves be proven. All certitude that rests on proof is mediate: it stands and falls with the certitude of the proof's presuppositions. But as our proving activity cannot regress *ad infinitum*, it must have an absolute beginning, and this must be sought in such notions[9] as cannot themselves be proven. Everything provable is mediately certain; the last preconditions of all proof are immediately certain. So this immediate certitude pertains to those two diametrically opposed starting points: the sensations and the general propositions according to which the relations of what is intuited are to be conceived. If the latter are called axioms, as is usually the case, then one may say: all human knowledge has the mediate certainty that can be gained from the logical subordination of sensations to axioms. All propositions that the individual sciences state and prove are logically generated intermediary links between axioms and sensations: vis-à-vis the axioms they are the more or less particular, vis-à-vis the sensations they are the more or less general.

Therefore, it is, as Lotze rightly emphasized, a "happy fact"[10] that the mass of our sensations is indeed suited to subsumption under our axiomatic presuppositions – a fact that is not necessary in the sense that one could not cancel it out in thought, but only necessary in the sense that it is an absolute *prerequisite* for thought to be at all possible for us. Our conviction that we must be able to deal with all our perceptions by thinking is identical to the presupposition that relations of all our sensations can be subordinated to our axioms, which in this respect can also be called postulates. If the two types of immediate certainty that we have were entirely incomparable, or if they were even only so different that our logical consciousness could not relate them to one another, then there would be no connecting-inferential thought[11] for us.

But from the formal essence of thought it also follows, although we cannot go into detail on this here, that those intermediary links, in whose configuration[12] the activity of any and all science consists, can only be proven through common utilization of both starting points: nothing ever follows from axioms alone without the aid of the particular. In order to infer anything from a universal proposition, one must have something particular, according to the principle of the syllogism, something that is subsumed under the subject of the universal proposition; in order to pass over from a general proposition to particular ones, one must know a relation of subordination or division, a relation that can be gained purely analytically, and not from any concept, but that must be given somehow by some other kind of insight. But it is no less possible from mere sensations only with the formal operations of inferential thought to generate universal propositions valid for the sensations' interconnection: one always presupposes not only that such a connection obtains at all, but also a special presupposition about this connection's type as expressed by some category, and only if one presupposes these as the final major premise of inference, will the treatment of the facts be a real, valid and compelling proof. Neither mere axioms nor mere sensations suffice to prove anything else. Who only has the most universal, will not find in it the material to weave out the specific; who stands only before the mass of the specific will find no way to smuggle in a universal.

One therefore misdetermines the contraposition of deductive and inductive method, if one thinks the former would prove only from axioms, the latter only from sensations. Both are false. In mathematics, as well, the individual propositions follow from the axioms only in that the latter are applied to certain intuitively accessible combinations whose idea was not contained in the axioms, and could not be inferred from them alone. The plane triangle theorems follow from the axioms of geometry only with the help of the very idea of the triangle, and no merely logical-analytical necessity can deduce the concept of the triangle from those axioms. On the other hand, though, every inductive proof that one avers for an individual natural law has its final ground in the presupposition of a universal lawful nexus of natural phenomena that reveals itself in their constant succession; without resorting to this axiom, every reinterpretation of the hitherto observed order of events as a "law" and every expectation of its repetition is ungrounded and moot.

Subordination of the specific to the general is hence in all cases the essence of proof. The principles of induction, according to this formal orientation, are also to be sought in the syllogism, and on the other hand, every syllogism requires a minor premise in addition to its major premise. The antithesis between deductive and inductive proof must therefore be sought within this their common, fundamental character. It consists essentially in that the deduction subsumes a special idea content, however gained, under a universal premise, in order hence to infer something for this specific case; and that contrarily the induction subsumes a group of facts under a general proposition, in order thence to infer a proposition standing in between those facts and this general proposition with respect to universality. Only in this quite modified and restricted sense can it be rightly said that the deductive method proceeds from the universal to the particular, and the inductive from the particular to the *more* general. The former presupposes the particular, the latter the universal. The particular, of which every deduction has need in order to progress away from the universal, is either a random and spontaneous intuition, as in mathematics, or, as e.g. in jurisprudence, an assumption of possibilities based on experience, or, as in history, a complex of facts that are supposed to be bound to a whole by a value relation common to them, or, as in the deductive parts of theoretical natural sciences, the special cases of the more general laws given by experience. The universal, on the other hand, without which no deduction is possible, consists always in entirely universal presuppositions about cohesion or value relations of the intuited contents, in the fundamental laws self-evident to all normal thought. This is why, in the execution of the inductive method, one does not first address these self-evident axioms at every juncture of relevancy; it would be pedantic and boring to mention the principle of causality in every inductive step, although it is yet its indispensable major premise. But from this easily springs the danger of overlooking this final premise and thinking that the premises of the inductive proof were exhausted with the facts that are realized. This led to the unfortunate view that a science was a mere pile of facts that could be swept together as with a broom.

In any case, it is undeniable that all activity of knowing in the individual sciences, both in an inductive and a deductive process, is based on the recognition of axioms, whose sense consists in that through them alone can anything be proven, i.e., solidified as truth, about facts and from out of facts. To portray the system of these axioms and to develop their relation to knowing activity – nothing else than this can be the task of theoretical philosophy, of logic. But just as much axiomatic validity, validity conditioning and grounding all special functions, belongs to universal ends in the realm of ethics, and to an extent even the realm of history, ends whose recognition and acceptance are demanded of everyone, and according to which all special end-oriented activity is judged – in the realm of aesthetics the rules of the effects of emotions, with which the general communicability of certain emotions can be grounded. With an expansion of the customary parlance, one can thus also speak of ethical and aesthetic axioms, and the task of all philosophical investigations can then also be formulated thus: *the problem of philosophy is the validity of axioms.*

It belongs to the concept of axioms, as has been demonstrated, that they are not provable, because they themselves constitute the ground of all deduction, and because this proof would then have to resort to yet more general, less mediate, thus even higher axioms. Even less can they be proven inductively, for every induction in the realm in which it is undertaken already presupposes the axioms' validity. From this follows, hence, that philosophy can make use neither of the deductive nor of the inductive method, as is customary in the other sciences. The validity of axioms can neither be inferred from anything else nor proven from the mass of individual cases in which their validity is shown. Thus, philosophy must approach its problem in another way.

Kant called those axioms whose validity is addressed in his critique by the name of synthetic *a priori* judgments, and his three chief works pursue them in the three areas mentioned above. If one is to portray his concept in an unmistakable way, without the terminology that has since become so ambiguous, having been completely tilted by the psychologistic interpretation, then one might say: philosophy is concerned with the validity of those intuitive connections[13] which, being themselves unprovable, are the foundation of all proof with immediate evidence.

Therefore, for philosophy, everything depends upon how this immediate evidence of axioms is to be shown. There is no *logical* necessity with which the axioms' validity could be proven. Hence, only two possibilities remain: either one shows the *factual* validity, one seeks to demonstrate that in the actual process of human imagining, willing and feeling, these axioms are actually recognized as valid, that they are principles accepted and recognized as valid in the empirical reality of psychic life[14] – or one shows that another sort of necessity inheres in them, namely the *teleological necessity* that their validity must be recognized as unconditioned, if certain ends are to be achieved.

This is the point at which the genetic and the critical conception of philosophy part ways. For the genetic method, the axioms are actual modes of conception that have formed and asserted themselves as valid in the development of human ideas, feelings and willful decisions; for the critical method these axioms are norms – entirely regardless of how far their actual acceptance extends – norms that should be valid under the precondition that thought would achieve the end of being true, willing – the end of being good, feeling – the end of perceiving beauty, in a way that is to be universally accepted and recognized.

If the teleological viewpoint is claimed in this way for critical philosophy, then it is without any metaphysical hypostasizing of the concept of the end, and so it is therein that the fundamental difference appears in which philosophy finds itself to the rest of the sciences. The concept of the end has no place among the principles of the explanatory sciences, or at most a quite humble one; the judgment on the degree to which a thing or an activity suffices to any end is no theoretical judgment, nor any insight through which the reality of the thing or the activity is conceived. Teleology is not genetic knowledge. In explanatory science, ends are only spoken of within the restricted region of psychology, sociology and history, where conscious intention must be taken into account as one of the causally and lawfully effective factors of individual or common life: besides that, however, the insight into the purposiveness of this or that state of affairs constitutes no causal knowledge of the same.[15] Teleological necessity does not explain reality. And so it is not to be feared that the way in which the teleological viewpoint is here claimed for the philosophical method should come into any contradiction with the presuppositions of the remaining sciences: by foregoing any interference in the business of the explanatory sciences, philosophy gains the courage to own up to the idea of teleological connection on its very own terrain, claiming it as its own principle.

In a certain sense, then, what Schiller said of a specific doctrine of Kantian philosophy is true of all critical philosophy: what it cannot prove, it shoves "into one's conscience." Theoretical philosophy cannot prove its axioms; neither formal logic's so-called laws of thinking, nor the principles of any and all world views developed from the categories, can in any way be grounded in experience; but logic can speak to anyone and everyone: You want truth; bethink, you must accept and recognize the validity of these norms, if this wish is ever to be fulfilled. Practical philosophy can gain moral maxims neither through an all-round induction nor infer it from any theoretical knowledge stemming from metaphysics, from psychology or from empirical sociology; but ethics can address everyone with this argumentation: You are convinced that there is an absolute standard according to which it shall be decided what is good and evil; very well, as soon as you reflect on it, you will find that this is only possible if the validity of certain norms is accepted as indispensable. Aesthetic philosophy cannot prove the rules of beauty by way of theoretical world cognition, nor by asking around among all, or even many feeling individuals; but it can compel us to consider that, if beauty is to be anything else than individual pleasantness, we must recognize a universally valid norm for it. The validity of axioms is everywhere conditioned by an end that must be presupposed as an ideal for our thought, willing and feeling.

Whoever would be disturbed by the indispensability of such a fundamental prerequisite to the critical method ought to at first be reminded that the genetic method must make yet many more presuppositions, and much more specific ones, without even then yielding a satisfactory result. Included are pre-eminently all those axioms without which there is no explanatory theory, all those through which alone the establishment of facts and the interpretation of their connection can be grounded. The entire content of a system of epistemology must be presupposed in order to found any "theory" in the philosophical sense; and this is also true of the actual proof and the genetic observation of axioms. So it is not only the laws of so-called formal logic whose validity must be granted from the beginning, but the very same principles of epistemology (such as, e.g., that of causality) whose investigation is at issue. Naturally, for the axioms of formal logic, for the rules of judgment and inference, it is a matter of course that their validity for every investigation, hence for that concerning themselves as well, must also be admitted from the beginning. If one starts to think at all, even if about thought itself, then one must already apply the rules of correct thinking, even where one would prove their validity; if one communicates at all, one must make use of the norms that apply, even if one is only about to investigate how one communicates. To undertake logical investigations without thinking in a logically correct way would truly be "learning to swim before one enters the water." All intelligent logicians have recognized this, and no rebuke may be made toward any logical mode of treatment, for this is true of all standpoints without exception. But the prerequisites of the genetic method are also far from exhausted with these formal determinations: as was demonstrated above, every establishment of facts and every theory that is based upon it or refers to it, always rests upon the universal "prejudices" under which we subsume our perceptions, specific or in their entirety, and just these are the axioms of epistemology, whose validity is supposed to be demonstrated. And it is entirely evident, and requires no further substantiation that this is especially true of any attempts that, under the pressure of the presently empiricist tendency, would make philosophy into a sort of natural science, an "inductive" discipline.

To every such "theory," though, belongs also yet another great, voluminous material, either of psychological knowledge, or of both psychological and historical knowledge. If one would show that the axioms are really valid, and make it comprehensible how they came to bear on the process of human psychic life as it is governed by natural, physical laws, then it is only possible on the basis partially of psychology, and partially of cultural history (in the broadest sense of the word). For the genetic method, psychology and cultural history are therefore the actual heart of philosophical investigation. The data of these empirical sciences are for this method the decisive material of knowledge; for it, philosophy is nothing other than a psychological-cultural-historical reflection directed at axioms. It is the "hopeless attempt" to found by way of an empirical theory that which is itself the presupposition of any and every theory.

But even if the entire mass and peculiarity of all these prerequisites are conceded, it is still not to be foreseen what is to be accomplished for the philosophical task by such a restriction to the empirical-genetic treatment of the axioms. The highest thing that could be achieved in such a way could consist only in the determining that the axioms are in fact valid and making this conceivable from out of the laws of psychic life. But it would seem to stand just as unfavorably with this proof and this explanation alone as with the factual validity itself. If "validity" is taken in the sense of the factual state that something is accepted and recognized, then the axioms are in fact "valid" for individuals and from time to time, but by no means for all, nor always. And this applies to the genus as well as to the individual. For all the objections can be quite rightly voiced against the factual validity of axioms that Locke raised against the so-called innate ideas; and one need not first go to the Botocudos and other interesting peoples in order to find that something factually universally valid in the broad reaches of human psychic activity cannot be encountered; – excepting perhaps that urge toward happiness that can be found realized everywhere and always as a purely formal concept of striving toward satisfaction of each wish, whichever wishes they may be, as lofty and as base as you please. It is consequentially also the only thing that the empirical method of the psychologists has determined as universally valid, with which they then naturally tend to have their greatest success with the mob, to whom this all reveals nothing new. But from no universally valid statement, neither from a law of cognition in formal logic, nor from an epistemological axiom, neither from a moral maxim nor from an aesthetic rule, can a factual universal acceptance and recognition be determined. Children and idiots can be presented as negative instances everywhere, and even if one should forego this, the full-grown specimens of the species *homo sapiens* offer so many varieties that nothing may count as universally valid among them all. Neither through inductive comparison of all individuals and peoples nor through deductive inference from a concept of the universal human "essence" can the universally valid[16] be found.

So if anyone in this respect really wanted in all earnest to insist on the standpoint of "pure experience," he would have to declare it a matter of pure whim that there is any talk at all of universal validity in the strict sense: at most, one might attribute an approximative universality to the actual validity. The necessary process of psychic life in nature[17] yields certain general modes of apprehension in individuals just as in individual peoples. These are the constant forms and standards of apperception, which, after they have formed themselves according to the laws of association and reproduction, determine the further course of psychic movement and connect themselves to a feeling of subjective certainty – "*belief*" as Hume calls it, Jacobi translates it rather unhappily as "*Glaube*,"[18] Schleiermacher christens it "*Überzeugungsgefühl*"[19] – which portrays itself in each individual so sophisticatedly as though all others must think, will, and feel thus as well. Before the psychological treatment, though, all these apperceptions are equally necessary, and from this treatment it is absolutely unpredictable how it should ever be decided that one is more right than the other. Both the genetic explanation and the factual determination apply to all equally. For them there is hence no absolute standard, it must recognize an equal claim in all these convictions, because they are all to be recognized as equally necessary in terms of nature[20]. For them, all these universal propositions and the judgments based upon them only have relative value, partially from the standpoint of the individual, partially from the entire psychic life of a historically conditioned society.

Thus is relativism the necessary consequence of the purely empirical conception of the cardinal question of philosophy. As all forms of worldview are developed in sharply honed form with typical simplicity and grandiosity in the clear course of Hellenic intellectual life, so this consequence too emerges quite plausibly with the Sophists, and all later manifestations of relativism, such as the doctrine of the Encyclopedists, or modern Positivism and

Pragmatism, are only newly dressed up and fashionably adapted imitations of that Protagorean: *panton chrematon metron anthropos*.[21]

However, it is not as severe with this relativism as it may seem to fearful souls. Where it appears as a scientific theory, it is a monstrous self-deception. For precisely in wanting to be a theory it tacitly recognizes all those presuppositions upon whose basis a theory is possible in the first place, and upon whose basis a theory can even be founded. If it would prove its proposition, it presumes it possible to determine facts in a universally valid way, and that it is just as possible to access what all ought to recognize through them. It testifies itself to that which it opposes, to the validity of epistemological principles and logical norms. If it does not, then for it remains only, as for many prating Greek sophists, to explain that one actually must refrain from asserting anything, which is then the wisest end of their wisdom. In the theoretical region, at least, every theory, even nihilistic and relativistic theories recognize the validity of axioms, the presence of an all-binding norm. The more the relativist piles up his proofs, the more ridiculous he becomes: for he refutes all the more what he would prove. In truth there is therefore no seriously scientific theory of relativism: rather, this opinion that for everyone only that is valid which presently appears to him, is really present only as a little enviable sort of conception of life. Relativism is the "philosophy" of the blasé, who believe in nothing any more, or of the metropolitan gamin, who shrugs his shoulders and pokes his impertinent fun at everything, finding it quite appropriate to speak one way today and another tomorrow.

Therefore, in one way or another even the advocates of the genetic method always seek to preserve the concept of the normal and universally valid, and two ways are available to them for this that connect from time to time. If actual universal validity must be abandoned, then the normal appears to be determinable partially by quantitative relations, and partially by the historical process. If there be nothing on which all men at all times agree, then on the one hand an opinion of the great mass is yet present each time, on the other a decisive step forward with which axioms and norms have gradually come to "factual validity" in human history, at least with the majority, or with the "upper crust." This factual validity is to be sought either with the majority or to be asserted through progress of history.

The appeal to the masses has the advantage of especial plausibility: the superstitious belief in the majority belongs to the specialties of our time. Through our perspective bound to the laws of natural lawfulness we have come so far that we define madness, which is just as natural a development as "normal" thought, as nothing more than a movement of ideas that diverges from the customary – that we see in the criminal only the unfortunate one who, just as all of us according to natural necessity, just happens to will and act in another way than is approved of by the great majority. What was once called the abnormal is all but the merely unusual for us. On the broad ground of natural necessity, though, the unusual is just as justified as the usual: there is no right at all, but only power, existence, and what the majority does with the individual who diverges from its customs, which rests only on the brutal "right" of the more powerful one. If one has no other point of view than that of the factual determination and the genetic explanation, then it is in every way impossible to ascertain the value of individual phenomena in relation to one another: what the majority accepts – be the majority ever so great – need nevertheless not be right. Science must protest if the process of contemporary politics is to be introduced into it. The quantity of actual approval is never a proof of normality. The majority can err just as easily as the individual, and which of these be the more probable is a very real question. And who would seriously advocate the opinion that the norm consisted in the belief of the majority, one must only ask him whether the majority had never erred or been mistaken. The submission to the judgment of the masses would be a morose ending to all of philosophy's efforts.

A similar acquiescence to the brutal fact is also present if, from the mere standpoint of the genetic explanation, one seeks the proof criterion for axioms' "validity" in the motion of human history, and if one thinks that the normal might be grounded in that which has come to ever deeper, more stable, widespread acceptance through the progress of history. One also presupposes, in all of this, that in the course of history reason breaks through of its own accord through its own naturally necessary development, and one constitutes, as it seems, the conception of the normal through reflection on the progress of history. Even if this presupposition, which is far from beyond any doubt, were first conceded, it would yet remain to be determined what ought to be called progress in historical motion, i.e., improvement, approximation to the normal and rational. It is to be hoped that everyone will most likely concede that what comes later is not always *eo ipso* better. Change is not progress. This sounds quite trivial and self-evident. But to state this triviality explicitly is perhaps to insert a finger into an open wound of our times. For, the more standard the purely genetic view becomes, the more easily the deception arises, that in the development of human culture whatever is new is always better, more worthy of acceptance. For the standpoint of explanatory theory there is only earlier and later, only flux: whether the change be progress cannot be decided with the genetic investigation alone; at the very least, a standard is necessary, the idea of an end according to which the value of the change might be determined. Hence, whoever speaks of "progress" in history at all, always assumes, however consciously or unconsciously, some ideal, an end, a norm as a standard, by judging the genetic process to be explained, in order to call these changes progress, the others stagnation or regress, with an eye to this end. The purely naturalistic view knows only necessary changes, and nothing of their value. If one also expects evidence of progress from the historical investigation, then it must also have a presupposition about the end according to which the progress is to be measured; critical history, in the sense of a history that makes judgments[22], is only possible with a teleological mindset[23]. Hence, who would infer axioms' validity from historical progress must already have a principle according to which he determines in this respect what is to be called progress; so he must either presuppose the consciousness of the axioms as a standard for the critical evaluation of historical decisions, or he must recognize whatever happens to enjoy some sort of general acceptance or approval as a "valid" axiom for every moment in history. In the latter case a historical relativism would result as has never seriously been asserted; in the former case the developmental historical view thus covertly presupposes precisely an absolute validity according to which it judges the historical process. Once one has first determined or assumed the axioms, then one can also very well demonstrate how they have come to the factual recognition in humanity's historical development and how the progress of this history consists precisely therein. In order to demonstrate reason in history one must know not only history, but also reason.

A "critique of historical reason"[24] is thus a quite praiseworthy enterprise: yet it must still be a *critique*, and for this it needs a standard. If one regards the course of history "entirely unprejudicially," one finds that now this, and now that, has been believed and accepted; one can discover the linguistic processes and historical movements of thought that occasioned these beliefs; one can also finally determine which axioms are accepted currently in the privileged circles of humanity that call themselves cultivated peoples: but for all that one does not pass beyond this simple fact, and the circumstance that the causally determined process of human generic life led to the consciousness of certain propositions provides not the slightest proof of their absolute validity or their justification: it could just as well be that, for instance by virtue of originally unfortunate direction and constant accumulation of mental associations under the influence of everyday needs, this entire development might have led to nothing but deception and foolishness that we would now hold for truth, only because we had become inescapably enclosed within it. Therefore, if the genetic method in the so-called ethno-psychological[25] treatment, which is its most significant and noblest manifestation, presents the Indo-Germanic race's gradual genesis of axiomatic consciousness in terms of linguistics and cultural history, it thus accomplishes a great historical task, but does not solve the philosophical problem: for the "validity" of axioms cannot possibly exhaust itself in that it has come to acceptance among certain groups of humans through historical necessity; and progress that is thus to be demonstrated to be in history may be called such only because one presupposes the axioms' validity from the very beginning, and regards everything that has led to the consciousness and acceptance of these as progress.

Thus, it is clear that the genetic method can never reveal anything else for the axioms than a certain scope of their empirical validity, and yet precisely in this revelation it refers back to their normative significance. The quantitative and the temporal relations do not suffice to guarantee these axioms any higher position[26] than what every other product of the psychic mechanism enjoys, and all evolutionary investigations presuppose, just as all empirical research, the entire system of normal consciousness. In contrast to this, aside from the agreement to the formal rules of thought, without which, as stated above, it is also unable to think, the critical method needs but a single general presupposition: namely, that there be such a thing as a normal consciousness whose principles must be recognized, insofar as anything at all is to have universal validity. The universal validity addressed here must not be understood in the sense of merely being factually recognized and accepted, but only in the sense that it ought to be recognized and accepted[27]. Regardless of how far the factical recognition extends, the critical method builds upon the conviction: there are universal values, and in order that these be arrived at, the empirical process of imagining, willing and feeling must move in those norms without which the very accomplishment of the end is unthinkable; these universal values are the truth in thought, the goodness in willing and acting, the beauty in feeling, and all three of these ideals represent each in its own realm only the demand for that which is *worthy* of universal recognition and acceptance. Naturally, this worthiness cannot be inferred from the factical processes of recognition and acceptance; it rather possesses an immediate evidence with which, once it has come to awareness of any random empirical content, it brings itself to actual validity in the individual consciousness.

Thus the critical method's presupposition is the belief in universally valid ends and in their ability to be known in empirical consciousness. Who has no such belief, or who would require that it first be "proven", who convinces himself artificially – for we all have such a belief naturally – that there be nothing universally valid – he may stay at home: critical philosophy has no dealings with him. The logician does not address one who denies that there be any compulsion in normal thought; ethics has nothing to do with one who accepts absolutely no mandate of right will, and aesthetics is preposterous for anyone who disputes the general communicability upon which the essence of the aesthetic impression is based. A philosophical investigation is only possible among those who are convinced that a norm of the universally valid stands above their individual activities, and that it is possible to find this norm.

With this presupposition, the critical method finds itself in a circle from the very outset. Who would employ it must presuppose that both he himself and the one he addresses with his investigation possess normal consciousness at least to a certain degree. Nowhere else can aesthetics find the principles of good taste than with those with whom it surmises it in the first place. Where in the whole world shall ethics seek the principles of morality, if not in the common consciousness of those of whom it is presumed that they judge and act rightly? Thus, logic too can only seek the rules of true mental representation in those whom it deems capable thereof in the first place. All three thus have an ideal of the normal human being that they presuppose in order to bring it to representation. Here, too, the old adage of Lotze's applies, that, since this circle is already unavoidable anyway, one ought to execute it well.[28]

In order to do this, it is first necessary to refute the gravest accusation leveled against the critical method, which arises at precisely this juncture. For all those who would orient themselves toward normal consciousness, and to this end must presuppose it in themselves and others, are themselves, after all, empirically determined individuals, and it is a matter of psychological necessity that what has been produced in them as axiomatic consciousness through the historical process appears to have that highest evidence of normal consciousness immediately, so that they hence mistake what is for them factically valid for something universally valid. The critical method appears to make the most severe mistake by raising the standpoint of the philosophizing individual to an absolute norm, and if this were the case, it would be easily refuted.

This serious danger does in fact exist, and it has shown itself to be in grave error often enough, most often in ethics and aesthetics. The absolutizing of historically determined modes of conception, brought about by special social, or even individual, circumstances is precisely what is mostly cited against the critical method and in favor of the genetic. And this danger appears unavoidable indeed, as long as the matter is conceived as though one only had simply to bethink that which is supposed to be generally recognized and accepted, and as though the feeling of evidence would suffice to assure the individual that he were not confronted with a mere individual opinion, or one present in several individuals. The deceptibility of subjective evidence is the well-known fact on which this procedure must inevitably fail. Philosophical reflection must not settle for simple and immediate evidence alone; rather, the critical method requires an evidence mediated by way of certain systematic standard rules; an evidence, hence, that is in itself corrected and thereby alone justified.

And it is here that the principle of the teleological connection first introduced to critical philosophy by Fichte, if it is correctly understood, clears away the difficulties. If the main issue is obviously to exclude what is empirical in origin from what the individual must hold for normal and axiomatic by virtue of the historical determination of his mental life, then this is impossible, considering everything that has been discussed here, by way of comparative induction or genetic observation, and all that remains is hence to *seek out* the normal by considering it from a teleological point of view. From its only presupposition, that there ought to be ideas, voluntary decisions and emotions that may be accepted as universally valid, the critical method has to bring all those patterns of movement in psychic life to consciousness that can be demonstrated to be indispensable conditions for the realization of that task, and in this demonstration it must not take recourse to any sort of special, given, individual determinations of actual psychic life as premises. Only this can be meant, when it is demanded that the proof of *a priori* valid axioms and norms must not itself be empirical in character.

The system of logic is thus the epitome of all those principles to be developed teleologically, without which there could be no universally valid thought; the norms of ethics are developed as the means to the achievement of a will and action that deserves universal approval; the rules of aesthetics are the conditions under which alone a universally communicable emotion is possible. All axioms, all norms, prove – independent of any special content and any historical determination – to be means to the end of universal validity. There is no logic, unless, regardless of what the content of the ideas be in each individual case, certain modes of connection and order apply as laws of thought – no ethics, unless, regardless of the empirical determination of our motives, certain norms exist that pertain to their affairs and relations – no aesthetics, unless, whatever the content of the individual perception and the emotions aroused through them, certain rules govern the way they work together.

In this consists the undying greatness and at once the historical impact of *Fichte*, that he recognized this teleological character of the critical method clearly, and directed philosophy's task toward erecting a system of (in the teleological sense) necessary actions of reason. Therefore he developed everything that Kant had called intuitions, concepts, principles, ideas, maxims, rules, etc., in a sequence, to conceive each of these normal functions as one of the links in a system of the solution of a conglomerate task of consciousness: he deduced norm-consciousness as a teleological system. The main reason why up until the present day only very few have understood this thought lies, apart from all manner of whimsicality in his presentation, mainly in the metaphysical tendency that he gave his construction, and the fact that its implications turned the usual opinions upside down, sufficed to make him unpopular among the masses.

But the deeper error of the "*Wissenschaftslehre*" consists in that it supposes itself able from the determination of the end alone (it formulated the end as the task of the empirical I to become the universal I!) to *deduce* all the means to its realization. This is why, in order to teleologically construct the progress from one "action of reason" to the other, it had to lay down contradictions from one step to the next, whose dissolution was supposed to propel it onward,[29] and so the critical method became the *dialectical* method. But this can no more retrieve the manifold of the specific out of its principle than any other form of deduction. The teleological construction, too, requires not only a determination of an end, but also a sufficient consideration of the material in which the end is to be realized.

Admittedly, it never needs it – and this is to be emphasized quite explicitly, contrary to the character of the genetic method's preconditions – it never needs it to ground the teleological demonstration of axioms and norms; but it needs it all the more to find the axioms and norms, and to bring them to consciousness. Just as the norms in the first place can come to consciousness only through mediation of the individual experiential activities both in the individual mind and in that of the genus of the norms, so can philosophy also only solve its task of searching for norms *with the aid* of experience, by considering, vis-à-vis the individual activities that it finds, what requirements they must fulfill in order that one might accept them as universally valid. One need not know the individual content, but one must very well know the universal character of the material in order to become aware of the tasks to be solved through it.[30]

Thus, after the most universal view of the mechanism of the imagination, logic can already establish that there would be no common thought, and in this no universally valid result, if there were no formal necessity of thought[31]. Its essence can be roughly stated as the "*axiom of consequence*," that, once any ideas have been recognized as true, all those relations and connections must also be accepted as true that follow from them according to the logical norms yet to be sought. The proposition that whoever has conceded the presupposition must also admit its logically developed consequences is such a self-evident expansion of the old rule: "with the premise the conclusion is also given," that it can just as well count as the principle of proof, but at the same time expresses the universal character of necessity of thought. Likewise, from the end of universal validity through reflection on the psychologically familiar functions of approval and disapproval, one can easily, teleologically, render the prohibition plausible that what is affirmed must not be denied, and will have to formulate it as the principle of non-contradiction. Finally, for the suspension of judgment lying between affirmation and negation, one will be able to consider the principle that one's bearing vis-à-vis all judgments for which sufficient reasons neither for affirmation nor for negation are present must be problematic, and this can then be formulated as the principle of sufficient reason.

May these propositions ever so self-evidently assert themselves with teleological consequence in the subsumption of the mechanism of imagination under the end of universally valid thought, different empirically familiar relations of the imaginative process must nevertheless *occasion* the reflection on these norms or axioms. Admittedly, the reason for their validity is not in those occasions; but they somehow build the framework we need to work on the construction of normal consciousness. And now as logic advances further, seeking out the individual norms of thought, it must always attach its critical reflection of their correct configuration to the forms of concatenation of ideas[32], as described in empirical psychology, albeit only in the roughest way. Only in smaller, closer groups does a connection, itself partially logical, partially teleological, show itself among the logical norms, the former e.g. in the relation of some inferences to the conclusions, the latter in the connection of the categories, when the problem of substantiality, for instance, proves only solvable with the concept of causality, and so forth.

In this way, even in the most thoroughly structured and systematically developed philosophical discipline, logic, the fact comes to light that the in itself coherent system of norms coheres only here and there in our consciousness, that we are rather generally reliant upon reorienting ourselves toward the individual norms in light of the empirical occasions that lie in the factual motions of individual and of social life of the mind, and, with respect to the end of universal validity, bringing their teleological significance to our awareness.

Hence arises the methodological significance that the material facts[33] stemming from psychology and intellectual history have for philosophy and its critical treatment of the axioms. Having hitherto decisively emphasized that the proof for the normative validity must never be sought in all these facts, and so not in the psychologically or historically demonstrable empirical validity either, we must now turn our attention to the positive relation in which these same facts make possible an ordered discovery of norms and a coherent reflection on the rightfulness of their validity. The critical method must never accept the facts of psychology and history as reasons for the norms' validity[34], but it needs them as objects with which it executes its philosophical test and reflection. This test itself will always amount to an examination of the teleological connection and the teleological necessity in the sense elaborated above: but its prerequisite and its object form the very *claims to validity*, which are asserted partially with the natural necessity of the general psychic essence of the human being, partially with the historical necessity of the progressing development of culture. The genetic facts are never the grounds for a proof in philosophy, but they are the objects of critique: psychology and history must have elaborated the material for cognition out of its pre-scientific vagueness to such an extent that the problems of philosophy can be developed out of it in a conceptually determined and orderly way.

It is according to this that the relation of philosophy to empirical psychology is determined. As there is no possibility to deduce merely from out of the end of universal validity all the special conditions for its fulfillment – in other words, because we know normal consciousness not in itself, but only in its relation to empirical consciousness, philosophy needs the *guiding clue* of empirical psychology in order to consider the individual axioms and norms in an orderly fashion. Yet the general ideas of the psychic functions that are thus taken out of empirical knowledge are still far from being able to support the norms and the universal propositions that are gained from them in a teleological fashion. The grounding of axioms and norms lies solely in themselves, in the teleological significance that they possess as means to the end of universal validity. Where they can be demonstrated as such, however, there is no longer the mere factuality of validity, but there is the *immanent necessity of the teleological nexus*.

Thus, the philosophical consideration of empirical psychology takes over, e.g., the tripartite division of the psychic functions that finds itself repeated in the triad of philosophical disciplines, this classification being for it quite clearly no ground for knowledge at all, but providing only a guideline, which it needs, for lack of a deductive procedure, to seek after norms. The specific distinctions with which empirical psychology classifies its objects play the same role, then, within the individual regions of philosophy. If all these psychological classifications were done away with, then would the classification of philosophy perhaps also fall, but not the certainty of norms and axioms, which does not rest upon these empirical psychological concepts, but only came to awareness with their help.

Still, the help that the critical method can expect from psychology is restricted essentially to this determination of the formal order: in substance,[35] it is very limited. For in the general, naturally determined essence of the human being, toward a scientific theory of which psychology strives, and can only strive, is ultimately never anything given but the formal possibility for the substantive development of rational values and thus of normative determinations that are at issue in philosophy. This development itself, however, is the matter and the actual meaning of the historical process. Therefore, history is much more the *organon* of critical philosophy than is psychology, critical philosophy having to make the formation in which the norms are given historically as factually valid principles of cultural life into the object of its teleological investigation, and thus the empirical occasion for its critical reflection. And the flux and the multifariousness of these historical formations protect critical thought from historicism, i.e., from historical relativism, which would settle, e.g., for the temporal validity of each of these formations, to be conceived as historically necessary, and dispense with the conception of any absolute validity independent of this. All historically determined thought will of course have to have the modesty of being convinced of the limitations of its own capabilities: warned by the flux of opinions through history, it will always be reminded that it can never be absolutely certain, even with the most perfect evidence and its teleological mediation, that it has come to completely unshakable results. But this pertains only to the individual, historically conditioned and limited capability of philosophers: juxtaposed with this persist unwaveringly the task of philosophy, the constant work on its solution, and the conviction that a solution has indeed already been solved in a number of points.

It was therefore with a profound wisdom that *Hegel* undertook to elaborate the systematic content of philosophy from out of the motions of rational consciousness[36] in history. But in his execution of this idea, the critical conceptual work is in a way, and for reasons that cannot be treated in more detail at this juncture, so peculiarly bound up with historicism that they can hardly be separated from one another anymore, and allow for one interpretation just as well as another. For in the intention to save for each form that the principles of reason have received in the course of historic life the form's relative share in the right of validity[37] of the whole, Hegel resorted to dialectic as an artificial means to unite them all, despite their differences, and even contradictions, to an internally structured whole. Therefore, before this positive, harmonizing feature of historical optimism, the energy of criticism, the dividing and eliminating measurement of the individual against the ideal of absolute validity – although it is certainly not missing from Hegel – had to recede and be blurred, at least in its presentation, often unto unrecognizability.

Through the same peculiarities of his method Hegel also came to attribute systematic significance to the historical sequence in which the rational contents arose: precisely in this consists the peculiar characteristic of his dialectic, for which the temporal mediations became therefore negligible. For the critical method, the course of historical development, in its essentially empirical determinedness, which is contingent vis-à-vis the "idea," cannot have this systematic significance. Yet it is not insignificant for it either, for the historical process in itself yields an immanent critique. In order to understand it as such, one must not understand, admittedly, the temporal sequence *eo ipso* as "progress," nor regard the subsequent as the "truer," and finally stand still at the latest as that which is valid for the time being; rather, the constant view to those ends of normality is necessary; ends that constitute the universal guiding clue for the critical method. Hence, this historical critique is far from binding itself to success as its authoritative criterion; it is in every respect independent of factual acceptance.

In this way arises for philosophy the knowledge of all substantial rational values out of the critical illumination of history. In the historical development of the sciences and their axiomatic presuppositions, in the great concentrations of moral, political, and social life, and in the characteristic manifestations of the institutions and organizations, in the formations of artistic creative power that lay hold of and conquer the present and the future[38] – in this much intertwined historical development of cultural values, logic, ethics and aesthetics find the mutually complementary and corrective materials for their application of the critical method.

A valuable result that at last philosophy owes to such historical orientation is the delineation of absolute values. Precisely the historical reflection shows the points at which the determination of the "*a priori*" – of that which is absolutely and indispensably valid in the teleological structure – ceases, the points at which therefore the criteria of factual acceptance and of historical guarantee must eventuate through an apparently and indubitably onward going process of fixation and elimination. At such junctures the critical method leads in part to the negative result of determining the regions in which the claim to normative universal validity that is the object of its investigation cannot be justified, or at least not yet. Philosophy's different disciplines show a very different yield in this respect. The greatest extension of the universally valid that we may assert with complete critical certainty lies doubtlessly in logic: it is considerably less in ethics, and it is the least in aesthetics.

Notes

1 "Kritische oder genetische Methode?" in: *Präludien. Aufsätze und Reden zur Philosophie und ihrer Geschichte*, Mohr/Siebeck: Tübingen, 1921, Vol. II pp. 99–135. Trans into English for the first time by Alan Duncan. – Ed.
2 Carl Göring (1841–1879); Friedrich Eduard Beneke (1798–1854); Jakob Friedrich Fries (1773–1843). – Ed.
3 *völkerpsychologische Richtung*
4 *"Ursprung" und "Begründung"*
5 *Wertzusammenhang*
6 *Gesetzmäßigkeit*
7 On this, cf. H. Rickert, *Die Grenzen der naturwissenschaftlichen Begriffsbildung* [*The Limits of Concept-Formation in Natural Science*] (Tübingen 1902), esp. pp. 305 ff.
8 *Zwischenglieder*
9 *Vorstellungen*
10 "*Glückliche Tatsache*" – a famous and often quoted phrase from Lotze's *Logik*. – Ed.
11 *verknüpfendes Denken*
12 *Aufstellung*
13 *Vorstellungsverbindungen*
14 *Seelenleben*
15 In more recent times, one likes to say that the research into developmental history, which takes such an important place in explanatory science, makes the purposiveness of living creatures into a principle of explanation and is for that reason essentially also of teleological character. Here, however, there is an enormous confusion due to the equivocal nature of the word "purposive." The purposiveness that the explanation along developmental history has in mind, is not, say, normality, conformity with an ideal, but simply the capacity to live [*Lebensfähigkeit*]. "Purposive," from this standpoint, is everything that is capable of living, may it otherwise be what it may, and when one finally comes to the insight that in the struggle for existence only that which is purposive is preserved, then this is not a great new wisdom, but rather a tautology or simply the analytic judgment: what is capable of living, continues living.
16 *das Allgemeingiltige*
17 *naturnotwendige Prozess des Seelenlebens*
18 (religious) belief – Ed.
19 feeling of conviction – Ed.
20 *naturnotwendig*

21 "Man is the measure of all things."
22 *beurteilende Geschichte*
23 *zweckbestimmtes Bewusstsein*
24 Allusion to Dilthey. – Ed.
25 *völkerpsychologisch*
26 *Recht*
27 *nicht im Sinne des tatsächlichen Anerkanntwerdens, sondern nur des Anerkanntwerdensollens*
28 Another often quoted phrase from Lotze's *Logik*. – Ed.
29 Cf. on this, in greater detail, the author's *Geschichte der neueren Philosophie*, Vol. II., 5th ed., Leipzig 1911, pp. 214 ff.
30 Lotze has demonstrated this very nicely with respect to the questions pertaining to logic in the Introduction to his *Logic* (1874).
31 *Denknotwendigkeit*
32 *Vorstellungsverknüpfung*
33 *das Tatsachenmaterial*
34 *Geltungsgründe für die Normen*
35 *sachlich*
36 *Vernunftbewusstsein*
37 *Geltungsrecht*
38 *die Mitwelt und Nachwelt*

Chapter 19

"History and Natural Science" (Presidential Address, Strasbourg), 1894[1]

On the commemoration day of the university, it is a valuable privilege of the rector to be able to ask the guests and members of the university to focus upon a problem which lies within the province of his own scholarly discipline. But the obligation which corresponds to this privilege creates difficulties for the philosopher which are altogether singular. It is, of course, relatively easy for the philosopher to select a theme that will certainly be able to hold a general interest. However this advantage is significantly outweighed by the difficulties that are entailed by the peculiarities of the philosophical mode of investigation. All scientific and scholarly work has the purpose of putting its special problems into a wider framework and resolving specific questions from the standpoint of more general perspectives. In this respect, there is no difference between philosophy and the other disciplines. It is permissible for the other sciences to regard these more general perspectives and principles as given and established. This assumption is sufficiently reliable for the purposes of specialized research within the discipline in question. The essential feature of philosophy, however, is the following: its real object of investigation is actually these principles themselves. It follows that the solutions to philosophical problems cannot be deduced from more general propositions. On the contrary, every philosophical inquiry is obliged to establish the most general premises. Strictly speaking, there are no specialized investigations in philosophy. Each of the specialized problems of the discipline extends to the most abstract and ultimate philosophical questions. Whoever proposes to discuss philosophical matters philosophically must, above all, have the courage to take a general position. He must also possess a kind of fortitude that is even more difficult to maintain: the boldness to steer his audience onto the high seas of the most abstract reflections, where the solid earth threatens to vanish from the eye and disappear beneath the feet.

In view of these considerations, the philosopher might well be tempted to provide nothing more than an historical sketch of some aspect of his discipline. Or he might take refuge in the specialized empirical science which the existing academic customs and dispositions still persist in assigning to him: psychology. Psychology poses a profusion of problems that concern each of us. The analysis of these problems promises more certain results if the methodological and substantive perspectives that have come to light in the lively development of this discipline during the last few decades become more diverse and manifold. I shall not employ either of these routes of escape. I do not propose to lend credence to the view that philosophy no longer exists, but only its history. Nor do I want to lend support to the view that philosophy, as it was newly founded by Kant, could ever again be reduced to the confines of a specialized science: that specialized science the cognitive value of which Kant himself judged to be the most modest of all the theoretical disciplines. Precisely to the contrary. Indeed, it seems to me to be a duty, on an occasion like the present, to bear witness to the following position. Even philosophy in its contemporary form – divested of all its metaphysical pretensions – is capable of grappling with the great issues to which it owes the significant aspects of its history as well as its value for literature and its place in the academic curriculum. In other words, the hazards of the enterprise have enticed me to provide you with an illustration of the motive force of philosophical inquiry in virtue of which every specialized problem leads to the ultimate riddles of our cosmology and philosophy of life. This account will demonstrate the necessity with which each attempt to understand completely matters that seem to be clear and simple swiftly and inescapably presses us to the most extreme limits of our cognitive capacities, limits that are enveloped in obscure mysteries.

For this purpose, I shall choose a theme from logic; specifically from methodology, the theory of scientific investigation; for in the discussion of such a theme, the intimate interrelationship between philosophical inquiry and research in the other sciences and scholarly disciplines should appear in an especially clear and perspicuous fashion. Philosophy, both in the present and in the past, does not exist in its own imaginary world, a universe that is alien to other forms of knowledge. On the contrary, it maintains a rich and fruitful intercourse with all vital forms of knowledge of reality and all the axiological contents of an authentic intellectual life. If the history of philosophy is the history of human error, then the reason for this is the following. Philosophy, acting in good faith, employed the conclusions established by the theories of the specialized sciences as if they were perfectly sound and certain. At best, however, these doctrines could only qualify as probable hypotheses. This intimate and vital interconnection between philosophy and the other disciplines is exhibited most clearly in the development of logic. Logic has never been anything more than critical reflection upon the existing forms of knowledge that are actually employed in practice. A productive method has never been established on the basis of abstract constructions or the purely formal reflections of logicians. The task of the logician is simply to define the general form of specific methods which have proven to be successful and, following this, to determine the significance, the cognitive value, and the limits of the use of these methods. Suppose we employ the preeminent illustration of the point which is at stake here. Consider the most fully developed conception of the nature of induction which we find in modern logic, but not in its Greek mother. What is the source of this conception? It does not lie in the programmatic recommendations of Bacon, who provided a scholastic description of induction and advocated its use. On the contrary, it lies in reflection on the energetic application of this mode of thought. Since the era of Kepler and Galileo, this methodology has proven itself in specialized research in the natural sciences. In progressing from one specialized problem to another, it has become increasingly refined and sophisticated.

It is obvious that the problems peculiar to the more recent logic rest on the same considerations: the attempt to establish conceptually determinate lines to delimit the single provinces within the heterogeneous manifold of the fully developed domain of human knowledge. Consider the vicissitudes in the preeminence which philology, mathematics, natural science, psychology, and history have enjoyed in the scientific interests of the recent era. The shifting predominance of these sciences is reflected in the different plans for a "system of the sciences," as such a taxonomy was once called, or a "classification of the sciences," as it is now called. The universalistic methodological tendency of this way of thinking was committed to a serious error: the failure to recognize the autonomy of individual provinces of knowledge. This methodological tendency subjected all phenomena to the constraints of one and the same method. In consequence, the only remaining grounds on which a classification of the sciences could be based were substantive: in other words, metaphysical. Consider the successive claims raised by the mechanistic method, the geometrical method, the psychological method, the dialectical method, and, most recently, the evolutionary-historical method. Transcending the limited domain of phenomena to which their original fruitful application was restricted, these methods have been generalized as much as possible in the attempt to comprehend the entire circumference of human knowledge. As the conflict between these different methodological tendencies appears to grow more pronounced, the crucial task of an autonomous and responsible logical theory becomes all the more pressing. This task is to provide a just evaluation of these conflicting claims and a balanced analysis of the legitimate domain of these various methodologies by means of the general premises of epistemology. At this point, the prospects for the success of this enterprise do not seem to be unfavorable. In the work of Kant, the methodological controversy in which philosophy confronted mathematics – and, in principle, also psychology – was consummated. In the nineteenth century, a certain paralysis of the philosophical impulse set in, an impulse that was excessively stimulated and overstrained at the beginning of the century. At the same time, the nineteenth century experienced an increasingly heterogeneous variety of tendencies and movements in the specialized sciences. In the mastery of numerous novel problems and new kinds of problems, our methodological apparatus has been completely transformed. To an unprecedented extent, it has become both more comprehensive and more sophisticated. In this development, the various methodologies have become ramified and interrelated in many respects. Nevertheless, every single methodology claims a predominant status for itself in our contemporary world view and philosophy of life. This predicament poses new problems for theoretical philosophy. Without intending to present an analysis that is in any sense exhaustive, these are the problems to which I should like to draw your attention.

It is hardly necessary to mention that the taxonomies which I have in mind cannot coincide with the classification of the sciences that is employed in order to distinguish the academic faculties from one another. The academic division of labor within the sciences is a consequence of the practical tasks of the universities and their historical development. In this process, practical requirements have often combined provinces which, from the perspective of pure theory, should be separated. They have also differentiated areas which, theoretically, should be intimately combined. The same practical motive has repeatedly obliterated the distinction between the genuinely scientific disciplines and the practical and technical disciplines. However we should not suppose that this tendency would necessarily prejudice the actual practice of scientific research. Just to the contrary. In this context too, the practical relationships between the sciences have been successful in producing a richer and more vital interaction between the various provinces of scientific research than perhaps would have been the case had they been interrelated on the basis of the more abstract criteria employed in the scientific academies. Consider, nevertheless, the various shifts and dislocations which the various faculty divisions of the German universities have experienced in the last few decades, especially in the old faculty of the arts. These shifts betray a certain tendency to lend more weight and significance to methodological criteria for the classification of the sciences.

Suppose that we examine these criteria from a purely theoretical perspective. Then the following assumption may be presupposed as valid from the outset: philosophy can be juxtaposed to the empirical sciences. Most probably, this same assumption also still holds true for mathematics. Philosophy and mathematics fall under the archaic denomination of "rational" sciences – in very different senses of the word, however, which I shall not undertake to discuss here. At this point, it suffices to identify the common properties of philosophy and mathematics in a negative or privative fashion: their immediate purpose is not knowledge of data given in experience, even though other sciences can and should employ the propositions established in philosophy and mathematics for empirical purposes. From the formal perspective, a logical property common to both philosophy and mathematics corresponds to this substantive factor. Although the actual, psychogenetic occasion for research and discovery in philosophy and mathematics may very well lie in empirical motives, the propositions of philosophy and mathematics are never based on single observations or collections of observations. By empirical sciences, on the other hand, we understand disciplines which undertake to establish knowledge of reality which is somehow given and accessible to observation. The formal criterion of the empirical sciences may be described as follows. The validation of the results of these sciences includes not only the general, axiomatic presuppositions and the norms of valid thinking which are necessary conditions for all forms of knowledge; it also requires the verification of facts on the basis of observation.

At present, a certain classification of the disciplines which attempt to establish knowledge of reality is regularly employed. They are distinguished into natural sciences[2] and sciences of the mind[3]. Stated in this particular form, I regard the dichotomy as unfortunate. Nature and mind is a substantive dichotomy. In the denouement of ancient thought and the beginnings of medieval thought, it acquired a dominant position. In more recent metaphysics, from Descartes and Spinoza to Schelling and Hegel, this dichotomy has been maintained with absolute rigidity. If my evaluation of the disposition of the most recent developments in philosophy and the consequences of epistemological criticism is correct, however, then this dichotomy, which has become fixed in our general modes of thinking and speaking, can no longer be acknowledged as so certain and self-evident that it may serve – just as it stands and without any inquiry into its grounds – as the foundation for a classification of the sciences. In addition, it should be noted that this dichotomy of objects is not equivalent to a dichotomy based on modes of cognition. Locke reduced Cartesian dualism to the following subjective formula: external and internal perception, sensation and reflection. These are the two distinctively different organs or faculties on the basis of which knowledge of the external, corporeal world, or nature, is to be distinguished from knowledge of the inner world, or mind. In turn, recent epistemological critique has shaken this conception in an unprecedented fashion. At the very least, it has provided strong grounds for doubting the justifiability of accepting a form of "inner perception" as a special, autonomous mode of knowledge. In addition, this view holds that there is no sense in which it can be acknowledged that the facts of the so-called sciences of the mind are established exclusively on the basis of inner perception. The incongruity between the substantive principle and the formal principle of classification, however, is most clearly exhibited by the following consideration: an empirical discipline as important as psychology cannot be classified unambiguously either as a natural science or as a science of the mind. From the perspective of its subject matter, psychology can only be a science of the mind. In a certain sense, it may be described as the foundation of all the other sciences of the mind. From the perspective of psychology as an investigation, however, its entire methodological procedure is exclusively the method of the natural sciences. In consequence, it is inevitable that psychology has sometimes been described as the "natural science of inner perception" or even as the "natural science of the mind."

A classification which produces such difficulties has no systematic basis. In order to provide a systematic foundation for this dichotomy, however, perhaps only a few conceptual changes in definition are needed. What is the source of the methodological relationship between psychology and the natural sciences? It evidently lies in the consideration that both psychology and the natural sciences establish, collect, and analyze facts only from the viewpoint and for the purpose of understanding the general nomological relationship to which these facts are subject. Diversity in the objects of scientific investigation, of course, has the following consequence: the specialized methods for identifying and verifying facts, the methods for the inductive use of facts, and the formulae in terms of which established laws can be articulated are also very different. From this perspective, however, the distance between psychology and chemistry is hardly greater than the distance between mechanics and biology. However – and this is what matters here – all of these substantive differences become quite insignificant in comparison with the logical equivalence with which these disciplines are endowed by the formal property of their theoretical purposes. Although the phenomenon in question may be a motion of bodies, a transformation of matter, a development of organic life, or a process of imagination, emotion, and volition, the purpose of these disciplines is invariably the discovery of laws of phenomena.

In contrast to these sciences, the majority of the disciplines that are usually called sciences of the mind have a distinctively different purpose: they provide a complete and exhaustive description of a single, more or less extensive process which is located within a unique, temporally defined domain of reality. Consider the subject matter of these disciplines and the specialized techniques on which the comprehension of their data is based. They are also extremely diverse. The sciences of the mind are concerned with a single event or a coherent sequence of acts or occurrences; the nature and life of an individual person or an entire nation; the definitive properties and the development of a language, a religion, a legal order, an artifact of literature, art, or science. Each of these objects requires a mode of investigation which conforms to its own special properties. The theoretical purpose of the investigation, however, is invariably the same: to reproduce and understand in its full facility an artifact of human life to which a unique ontological status is ascribed. It is clear that, in this sense, the sciences of the mind comprehend the entire domain of the historical disciplines.

At this point, we have before us a purely methodological classification of the empirical sciences that is grounded upon sound logical concepts. The principle of classification is the formal property of the theoretical or cognitive objectives of the science in question. One kind of science is an inquiry into general laws. The other kind of science is an inquiry into specific historical facts. In the language of formal logic, the objective of the first kind of science is the general, apodictic judgment; the objective of the other kind of science is the singular, assertoric proposition. Thus this distinction connects with the most important and crucial relationship in the human understanding, the relationship which Socrates recognized as the fundamental nexus of all scientific thought: the relationship of the general to the particular. From this point on, there is a cleavage in classical metaphysics. Plato sought reality in the immutable generic concepts or forms; Aristotle, in the purposeful development of individual natures. Modern natural science has taught us to define real existence in terms of the constant, necessary connections in phenomena. It has replaced the Platonic idea with the natural law.

In view of the foregoing considerations, we are justified in drawing the following conclusion. In their quest for knowledge of reality, the empirical sciences either seek the general in the form of the law of nature or the particular in the form of the historically defined structure. On the one hand, they are concerned with the form which invariably remains constant. On the other hand, they are concerned with the unique, immanently defined content of the real event. The former disciplines are nomological sciences. The latter disciplines are sciences of process or sciences of the event. The nomological sciences are concerned with what is invariably the case. The sciences of process are concerned with what was once the case. If I may be permitted to introduce some new technical terms, scientific thought is *nomothetic* in the former case and *idiographic* in the latter case. Should we retain the customary expressions, then it can be said that the dichotomy at stake here concerns the distinction between the natural and the historical disciplines. However we must bear in mind that, in the methodological sense of this dichotomy, psychology falls unambiguously within the domain of the natural sciences.

We should also bear in mind that this methodological dichotomy classifies only modes of investigation, not the contents of knowledge itself. It is possible – and it is in fact the case – that the same subjects can be the object of both a nomothetic and an idiographic investigation. This is related to the fact that, in a certain respect, the distinction between the invariable and the unique is relative. Consider an entity which undergoes no immediately perceptible change within a very large span of time. For this reason, its unchangeable forms can be investigated nomothetically. From a more comprehensive perspective, however, the same entity may prove valid for a more limited time-span only, i.e., it may qualify as a unique phenomenon. For example, all of the single instances of the use of a language are governed by its formal laws. These laws remain the same throughout all changes of expression. On the other hand, this same distinctive language as a whole, together with the totality of its special formal laws, is nothing more than a unique and transitory phenomenon in the life of human languages as such. The same sort of point also holds true for the physiology of the body, for geology, and in a certain sense even for astronomy. Thus the historical principle is transposed onto the domain of the natural sciences.

The science of organic nature constitutes the classical example of this phenomenon of transposition. As a taxonomy or a systematic science, it has a nomothetic character, insofar as the invariable types of organisms which have been observed during the last few thousand years may be represented as the nomological form of these organisms. Consider, however, the subject matter of the biological sciences as evolutionary history in which the entire sequence of terrestrial organisms is represented as a gradually formative process of descent or transformation which develops in the course of time. There is neither evidence nor even a likelihood that this same organic process has been repeated on some other planet. In this case, the science of organic nature is an idiographic or historical discipline. Kant himself, in his anticipatory sketch of the modern theory of evolution, called the thinker who would have the audacity to embark upon this "adventure of reason" the future "archeologist of nature."

Suppose we consider the following question: what has logical theory thus far made of this crucial antithesis which distinguishes the specialized sciences? This question identifies precisely the point on which logical theory is most in need of reform, even today. The entire development of logic betrays the most decisive preference for nomothetic forms of thought. This is easily explained. All scientific research and verification assume the form of the concept. Therefore the investigation of the nature, foundation, and use of general concepts invariably remains the most immediate and significant interest of logic. The force of history has also had its influence. Greek philosophy had its origins in the natural sciences, in the question of *physis* or nature: that is, the question of the permanent form of existence which endures throughout the changes of phenomena. A parallel course – causally mediated by the historical tradition in the Renaissance – was followed by modern philosophy. Its autonomy developed in the context of the natural sciences. Therefore it was inevitable that logical reflection above all concerned itself with nomothetic forms of thought, and persistently made its general theories dependent on them. This still holds true today. Our entire traditional theory of concept, proposition, and inference is still tailored to the Aristotelian principle according to which the general proposition is the focal point of logical investigation. One need only leaf through any logic textbook in order to be convinced that the great majority of examples are chosen from mathematics and the natural sciences. Moreover even the logicians who have ample grasp of the peculiarities of historical research still seek the ultimate orientation of their theories in the province of the nomothetic sciences. It would be desirable, though there are few signs of it, if logical reflection devoted the same attention to the immense reality of history – exhibited in historical thought itself – that it has devoted to the detailed understanding of forms of inquiry in natural science.

For the present, suppose that we examine the relationship between nomothetic and idiographic knowledge more carefully. As noted above, natural science and history are both empirical sciences. In other words, the foundations of both sciences – or, from a logical perspective, the premises of their arguments – lie in experience, the data of perception. Both disciplines also agree that what the naive man usually means by experience is not sufficient to satisfy the requirements of either discipline. The foundation of both disciplines rests upon a scientifically refined and critically disciplined form of experience which has been subjected to conceptual analysis. Consider the problems of identifying differences in the structure of intimately related organisms; the correct use of a microscope; the certain interpretation of simultaneity in the amplitude of a pendulum, and the position of a needle on a meter. In each of these cases, the perceptions must be scrupulously educated. For the same reason, the laborious techniques of identifying the characteristic features of a certain handwriting, observing the style of a writer, or comprehending the intellectual horizon and the range of interest of an historical source must also be learned. In both the natural sciences and history, what one acquires by nature is usually nothing more than a very incomplete mastery of these techniques. In both inquiries, the tradition of scientific research has produced a profusion of refined and increasingly sophisticated technical concepts which the apprentice must learn how to employ. On the one hand, every such specialized method of investigation is based upon substantive results which have already been confirmed or are at least hypothetically accepted. On the other hand, these methods are also based upon logical relationships that are often extremely complex. At this point, we should again note that, up to now, logic has been much more interested in the nomothetic sciences than in the idiographic sciences. There are exhaustive logical investigations concerning the methodological significance of precision instruments, the theory of experimentation, the determination of probability on the basis of multiple observations of the same phenomenon, and other similar questions. However, philosophical concern with parallel problems in the methodology of history does not even remotely approximate its interest in the methodological problems of the natural sciences. This has to do with the fact that philosophical endowment and productivity coincide much more frequently with scientific ability than they do with historical gifts. This is in the nature of things and confirmed by history. And yet from the perspective of the theory of knowledge in general, it would be of the greatest interest to discover the logical forms according to which the critique of observations in historical research proceeds; and also to formulate the "maxims of interpolation" that are employed in order to construct hypotheses in history: here too it would be of the greatest interest to determine the role played by facts in the interdependent structure of our knowledge of the world, and the role played by the presuppositions according to which we interpret these facts.

In the final analysis, however, all empirical sciences are based on the same ultimate principle. This principle requires the mutual consistency of all those conceptual elements which refer to the same object. The difference between research in the natural sciences and history appears only when the issue concerns the cognitive or theoretical use of facts. In this context, we may note the following points. Natural science seeks laws; history seeks structural forms. In the natural sciences, thought moves from the confirmation of particulars to the comprehension of general relationships; in the historical sciences, it is devoted to the faithful delineation of the particulars. From the perspective of the natural scientist, the single datum of observation never has any intrinsic scientific value. The datum is scientifically useful only to the extent that the scientist believes he is justified in representing the datum as a type, a special case of a general concept which is developed on the basis of the datum. He is concerned only with the properties of the datum which provide insight into a general nomological regularity. The historian's task, on the other hand, is to breathe new life into some structure of the past in such a way that all of its concrete and distinctive features acquire an ideal actuality or contemporaneity. His task, in relation to what really happened, is similar to the task of the artist, in relation to what exists in his imagination. This is the source of the relationship between historical accomplishment and aesthetic creativity, the kinship between the historical disciplines and *belles lettres*.

It follows that in the natural sciences the bias in favor of abstraction predominates. In history, however, the bias in favor of perceptuality[4] is predominant. This claim will surprise only those who are in the habit of limiting the concept of perception in a materialistic fashion: as restricted to the psychic reception of the perceptual data of the present. This limited view fails to consider that there is a perceptuality – that is, the concrete and individual animation of the ideal present – which may be ascribed to the eye of the mind just as well as to the anatomical eye. Of course this materialistic conception of perception is very widely accepted today. However there are good reasons to doubt the soundness of this view. Suppose that, wherever possible, the stimulation or excitation of ideas is interpreted as a consequence of tactile and visual sensations. As a result of the preponderance which this interpretation ascribes to perception as an act of passive reception, the spontaneous faculty of perception threatens to atrophy as a result of disuse. Anyone who accepts this interpretation should not be astonished if the perceptual fantasy becomes indolent and ineffective whenever it is divorced from physically tactile and visual perception. This same point holds for pedagogy and for art. It holds true especially for the art of drama. In contemporary drama, every effort is made to keep the eye so completely preoccupied that nothing more remains for the inner perception of literary forms.

The comparison of research in the natural sciences and history will establish even more clearly the predominance of abstraction in natural science and of perceptuality in history. Consider the conceptual apparatus which historical criticism requires in order to analyze the historical tradition. These analytical techniques may be extremely refined and sophisticated. Nevertheless, the ultimate aim of history is always to extract and reconstruct from the raw material of history the true shape of the past in robust and vital clarity. History produces images of men and human life in the total wealth and profusion of their uniquely peculiar forms and with their full and vital individuality preserved intact. Past languages and nations, their beliefs and their forms, their struggle for power and freedom, their literature and their thought speak to us through the voice of history – resurrecting what is forgotten into a new form of life. The world which the natural sciences construct is completely different. No matter how perceptually concrete and graphic the starting points of the natural sciences may be, their cognitive goals are theories – in the final analysis, mathematical formulations of laws of motion. Consider the single perceptual datum which appears and disappears. In genuine Platonic fashion, the natural sciences ignore this datum as a negligible and insubstantial appearance. They strive to acquire knowledge of the nomological necessities whose timeless immutability governs all events. From the colorful world of the senses, the natural sciences construct a system of abstract concepts. The purpose of such a conceptual scheme is to comprehend the true nature of things that lies behind the phenomena: a silent and colorless world of atoms in which the earthy aura of perceptual qualities has disappeared completely: the triumph of thought over perception. Utterly indifferent to the past, the natural sciences drop anchor in the sea of being that is eternally the same. They are not concerned with change as such, but rather with the invariable form of change.

If the dichotomy between the two kinds of empirical science is so profound, we can understand why a conflict must break out between natural science and history for the decisive influence upon our general world view and philosophy of life. The question is: from the perspective of our total cognitive purposes, which is more valuable, knowledge of laws or knowledge of events? Is it more important to understand the general, atemporal nature of things or to understand individual, temporal phenomena? From the outset, it is clear that this question can only be resolved on the basis of reflections concerning the ultimate aims of scientific research.

At this point, I shall only touch superficially on the extraneous resolution of this question from the standpoint of utility. From this standpoint, both forms of knowledge are equally justifiable. Knowledge of general laws always has the practical value of making possible both predictions of future states and a purposeful human intervention in the course of events. This point holds true for the processes of the inner world as well as for those of the external, material world. In the external world, knowledge which is grounded on nomological thought makes possible the tools by means of which the mastery of nature by man is enlarged to a constantly increasing extent. All purposeful activity in human social life, however, is no less dependent upon the experience acquired as a result of historical knowledge. To employ a variation upon a classical expression, man is an historical animal. From generation to generation, his cultural life becomes an increasingly dense and substantial historical structure. Anyone who intends to produce a vital effect on this structure must understand its development. Where this thread of historical development has been broken, its fragments must be laboriously gathered and woven together. History itself proves that this is the case. Suppose that as a result of some singular and violent event – an external transformation of the planet or an inner transformation of the human world – our contemporary culture were destroyed. We can be quite certain that later generations will attempt to uncover its traces just as zealously as we search for the cultural remains of classical antiquity. For these reasons alone, the human race is obliged to carry the immense school bag of history. If in the course of time it threatens to become increasingly heavy and burdensome, then the future will not lack means to lighten this burden prudently and without damaging consequences.

However we are not really concerned with utility in this sense. We are more interested in the immanent value of knowledge. We are also not concerned with the personal satisfaction which the scholar gains from knowledge solely for its own sake. For the subjective pleasure of inquiry, discovery, and confirmation can be found in every form of knowledge in the same way. The extent of this pleasure is determined much less by the importance of the object than by the difficulty of the investigation.

There is no doubt that there are also objective and nevertheless purely theoretical differences in the cognitive value of objects of knowledge. But their measure is simply the extent to which they contribute to the totality of knowledge. A single datum, unless it becomes a building stone in a more general cognitive structure, remains nothing more than an object of idle curiosity. Thus, in the scientific sense, "fact" is already a teleological concept. Not every phenomenon of reality qualifies as a fact. A phenomenon qualifies as a fact only if – to state the matter quite briefly – science can learn something from it. The validity of this point is most important for history. There are many events which do not qualify as historical facts. In the year 1780, Goethe had a door bell and an apartment key made. On February 22 of the same year, he had a letter case made. Of this there is documentary proof in a locksmith's bill. Hence it is completely true and certain to have happened. Nevertheless it is not an historical fact, neither a fact of literary history nor of biography. On the other hand, within certain limits it may be impossible to determine *a priori* whether or not the value of a "fact" can be ascribed to a given datum of observation or historical documentation. Science must therefore act like Goethe in his old age: to gather and accumulate everything it can get hold of. Then it can rejoice in the knowledge that it is not neglecting anything that might at some time prove useful. It can have the confidence that the task of future generations, insofar as it has not suffered from the external and arbitrary accidents of historical transmission, may be compared to the work of a large sieve that retains the items that are useful and allows those that are useless to drop through.

Consider this essential objective of the single datum of knowledge: its incorporation into a more extensive whole. There is no sense in which this aim is restricted to the inductive classification of the specific datum under the generic concept or the general proposition. This objective is met equally well in a case in which the individual feature is incorporated as a significant component of a total organic conception. The commitment to the generic is a bias of Greek thought, perpetuated from the Eleatics to Plato, who found not only real being but also real knowledge only in the general. From Plato this view passed to our day. Schopenhauer makes himself a spokesman for this prejudice when he denies history the value of a genuine science because its exclusive concern is always with grasping the specific, never with comprehending the general. It is no doubt correct that there is a great deal that the human understanding can grasp only by comprehending the common content of diffuse and fragmented particulars. But the more we strive for knowledge of the concept and the law, the more we are obliged to pass over, forget, and abandon the singular fact as such. We can see this disposition in the characteristically modern attempt "to make history into a natural science" – the project of the so-called positivist philosophy of history. In the final analysis, what is the product of such an inductive system of laws of the life of a people? A few trivial generalities which can be excused only on the basis of a careful analysis of their numerous exceptions.

In opposition to this standpoint, it is necessary to insist upon the following: every interest and judgment, every ascription of human value is based upon the singular and the unique. Simply consider how swiftly our emotions abate whenever their object is multiplied or becomes nothing more than one case among thousands of others of the same sort. "She is not the first," we read in one of the most terrifying texts of *Faust*. Our sense of values and all of our axiological sentiments are grounded in the uniqueness and incomparability of their object. This is the basis of Spinoza's theory of the transcendence of the emotions by knowledge. For Spinoza, knowledge is the submersion of the particular in the general, of the unique and the ephemeral in the eternal.

Every dynamic and authentic human value judgment is dependent upon the uniqueness of its object. It is, above all, our relationship to personalities that demonstrates this. It is not an unbearable idea that yet another identical exemplar of a beloved or admired person exists? Is it not terrifying and inconceivable that we might have a second exemplar in reality with our own individual peculiarities? This is the source of horror and mystery in the idea of the *Doppelgänger* – no matter how great the temporal distance between the two persons may be. It has always been painful to me that a people as refined and sensitive as the Greeks could tolerate one of the doctrines which persists throughout their entire philosophy. According to this doctrine, the personality itself – with all its actions, afflictions, and passions – will also return in the periodic recurrence of all things. Life is debased when it has already transpired in exactly the same way numerous times in the past and will be repeated again on numerous occasions in the future. Consider the dreadful idea that as the same person I have already lived and suffered, striven and struggled, loved and hated, thought and desired exactly the same things and that when the great cosmic year has elapsed and time returns I shall have to play exactly the same role in the same theater over and over. This point concerning individual human life has even more force when it is applied to the total historical process: this process has value only if it is unique. This is the principle which the Christian philosophy of the Church Fathers successfully maintained against Hellenism. From the outset, the fall of man and the salvation of the human race had the status of unique facts situated at the focal point of the world view of the Church Fathers. This was the first significant and powerful insight into the inalienable metaphysical right of historiography: to maintain the past in its unique and unrepeatable reality for the recollection of mankind.

On the other hand, general propositions are necessary at every stage of inquiry in the idiographic sciences. And these they can borrow only – with perfect legitimacy – from the nomothetic disciplines. Every causal explanation of any historical occurrence presupposes general ideas about the process of things on the whole. When historical proofs are reduced to their purely logical form, the ultimate premises will always include natural laws of events, in particular, laws of mental events or psychological processes. Consider someone who has no idea at all concerning how men in general think, feel, and desire. It would not only be impossible for him to comprehend individual happenings in order to acquire knowledge of events and processes. He would already have failed in the critical determination of historical facts. Under these conditions, of course, it is quite remarkable that the claims which the historical sciences make upon psychology are so undemandingly lenient. The notoriously incomplete formulations which the laws of mental life have been able to achieve thus far have never stood in the way of historians. By means of natural common sense, tact, and genial intuition, they have known quite enough in order to understand the heroes of history and their conduct. This fact provides material for serious reflection and makes it appear doubtful that the most recently projected mathematical-scientific conception of elementary psychological processes will make a significant contribution to our understanding of real human life.

In spite of the shortcomings in the details of the above exposition, it clearly follows that in the total synthesis of knowledge, which is the ultimate aim of all scientific research, these two cognitive moments remain independent and juxtaposed. The general nomological regularity of things defines the space of our cosmic scheme; it transcends all change and expresses the eternal essence of reality. Within this framework, we find the vital development of the structure of all the individual forms which have value for the collective memory of humanity.

These two moments of human knowledge cannot be derived from a common source. Consider the causal explanation of the single phenomenon as the reduction of this phenomenon to general laws. This may indeed give us the idea that, in the final analysis, it must be possible to understand the singular historical form of the real event as a consequence of the general laws of nature. This is what Leibniz means when he claimed that, ultimately, the sufficient grounds or principles of all *vérités de fait* lie in *vérités éternelles*. However Leibniz was only able to postulate this for divine thought; he could not demonstrate it for human thinking.

The foregoing point can be clarified by means of a simple logical scheme. From the perspective of causality, every individual event assumes the form of a syllogism. The major premise is a law of nature, a collection of nomological necessities, for example. The minor premise is a temporally given condition or the totality of a set of such conditions. The conclusion of the syllogism is the individual event itself. In the same way that the conclusion logically presupposes these two premises, so the event presupposes two kinds of cause: on the one hand, the timeless necessity in which the constant nature of things is expressed; on the other hand, the specific condition which appears at a certain moment in time. In one sense – the nomothetic sense of causation – the cause of an explosion lies in the nature of the explosive material itself, expressed as physical and chemical laws. In the other sense – the idiographic sense of causation – it lies in a single event or motion, a spark, shock, or something similar. Only both together cause and explain the event. But neither cause is a consequence of the other. The relationship between these two kinds of causation is not grounded in the causes themselves. In a deductive syllogism, the minor premise is an independent proposition which is not derived from the major premise. Likewise, in the causal explanation of an event, the existing condition which is appended to the general nature of the case is not derived from this general, nomological nature. Rather, since this condition is a temporal event, it is a consequence of another temporal condition, from which it follows with lawlike necessity – and so on, *ad infinitum*. It is logically impossible to identify the first member of this infinite sequence. And even if we attempt to represent it in an imaginary fashion, such an initial state is always something completely novel. It is appended to the general nature of things. Therefore it is not a logical consequence of this general nature. Spinoza articulated this point in his distinction between two forms of causality, infinite and finite. The brilliant simplicity of this distinction eliminates many of the difficulties concerning the "problem of the plurality of causes" which have troubled more recent logicians. In the language of contemporary science, this point could be expressed in the following way. A description of the present state of the universe follows from the general laws of nature only if the immediately preceding state of the universe is presupposed. But this state presupposes the state that immediately precedes it, and so on. Such a description of a particular, determinate state of the arrangement of atoms, however, can never be derived from the general laws of motion alone. The definitive characteristics of a single point in time can never be immediately derived from any "cosmic formula." The derivation of the description of a single temporal point always requires the additional description of the previously existing state which is subordinated to the law.

General laws do not establish an ultimate state from which the specific conditions of the causal chain could ultimately be derived. It follows that all subsumption under general laws is useless in the analysis of the ultimate causes or grounds of the single, temporally given phenomenon. Therefore, in all the data of historical and individual experience a residuum of incomprehensible, brute fact remains, an inexpressible and indefinable phenomenon. Thus the ultimate and most profound nature of personality resists analysis in terms of general categories. From the perspective of our consciousness, this incomprehensible character of the personality emerges as the sense of the indeterminacy of our nature – in other words, individual freedom.

There are many metaphysical concepts and problems which have their source in this point. The concepts may be misleading and unfortunate. And the problems may be mistaken and badly framed. Nevertheless, the ground or motive for both still remains. The totality of temporally given phenomena seems to be independent of the general nomological laws according to which these phenomena occur. The content of the cosmic process cannot be understood as a consequence of its forms. Consider all the attempts to derive the concept of the particular from the general, the "many" from the "one," the "finite" from the "infinite," and "existence" from "essence." This is the point at which all of these attempts miscarry. The great philosophical systems which undertake to explain the cosmos may have been able to conceal this breach, but they have not been able to repair it.

Leibniz perceived this when he ascribed the origin of *vérités éternelles* to the divine understanding and the origin of *vérités de fait* to the divine will. Kant saw the same point. In his view, all the data given in perception fall under the forms of the intellect and can be classified and understood accordingly. In this fortunate but incomprehensible fact, Kant perceived an intimation of a divine teleology which greatly transcends our own theoretical knowledge.

In fact, thought can contribute nothing further to the resolution of these questions. Philosophy can identify the limits of knowledge in each of the individual disciplines. Beyond these limits, however, philosophy itself can no longer establish any substantive conclusions. The law and the event remain as the ultimate, incommensurable entities of our world view. This is one of the boundary conditions where scientific inquiry can only define problems and only pose questions in the clear awareness that it will never be able to solve them.

Notes

1   "History and Natural Science," trans. Guy Oaks, in: *History and Theory*, 19/2, May 1980, pp. 169–185. Original: "Geschichte und Naturwissenschaft," in: *Präludien. Aufsätze und Reden zur Philosophie und ihrer Geschichte*. Tübingen, 1924, Volume II, pp. 136–160. – Ed.
2   *Naturwissenschaften*
3   *Geisteswissenschaften*
4   *Anschaulichkeit*

Chapter 20

"Introduction" to *A History of Philosophy With Special Reference to the Formation and Development of Its Problems and Conceptions* (1900)[1]

§ 1. The Name and Conception of Philosophy

R. Haym, Art. *Philosophie* in Ersch und Grüber's *Encyclopädie*, III. Abth., Bd. 24.
W. Windelband, *Praeludien* (Freiburg i. B., 1884), 1 ff.
[A. Seth, Art. *Philosophy* in *Enc. Brit.*]
[G. T. Ladd, *Introduction to Philosophy*. N.Y. 1891.]

By "philosophy" present usage understands the scientific treatment of the general questions relating to the universe and human life. Individual philosophers, according to the presuppositions with which they have entered upon their work, and the results which they have reached in it, have sought to change this indefinite idea common to all, into more precise definitions,[2] which in part diverge so widely that the common element in the conception of the science may seem lost. But even the more general meaning given above is itself a limitation and transformation of the original significance which the Greeks connected with the name "philosophy" – a limitation and transformation brought about by the whole course of the intellectual and spiritual life of the West, and following along with the same.

1. While in the first appearance in literature[3] of the words *philosophein* and *philosophia* the simple and at the same time indefinite meaning, "striving after wisdom," may still be recognised, the word "philosophy" in the literature after Socrates, particularly in the school of Plato and Aristotle, acquired the fixed significance according to which it denotes exactly the same as the German word "*Wissenschaft*."[4] According to this meaning,[5] philosophy in general is the methodical work of thought, through which we are to know that which "is"; individual "philosophies" are the particular sciences in which individual realms of the existent are to be investigated and known.[6]

With this first *theoretical meaning* of the word "philosophy," a second was very early associated. The development of Greek philosophy came at the time when the naive religious and ethical consciousness was in process of disintegration. This not only made the questions as to man's vocation and tasks more and more important for scientific investigation (cf. below, Part I. ch. 2), but also made instruction in the right conduct of life appear as an essential aim, and finally as the main content of philosophy or science. Thus philosophy in the Hellenistic period received the *practical meaning* of an *art of life, based upon scientific principles* – a meaning for which the way had already been prepared by the Sophists and Socrates.[7]

In consequence of this change, purely theoretical interest passed over to the particular "philosophies," which now in part assumed the names of their special subjects of research, historical or belonging to natural science, while mathematics and medicine kept all the more rigorously that independence which they had possessed from the beginning with relation to science in general.[8] The name of "philosophy," however, remained attached to those scientific efforts which hoped to win from the most general results of human knowledge a conviction for the direction of life, and which finally culminated in the attempt (made by Neo-Platonism) to create from such a philosophy a new religion to replace the old that had been lost.[9]

There was at first little change in these relations, when the remains of ancient science passed over into the culture of the present peoples of Europe as the determining forces of their intellectual life. Content and task of that which the Middle Ages called philosophy coincided with the conception held by later antiquity.[10] And yet the meaning of philosophy underwent an essential change by finding philosophy's task already performed, in a certain sense, by religion. For religion, too, afforded not only a sure conviction as a rule for the guidance of personal life, but also in connection with this, a general theoretical view of all reality, which was the more philosophical in its character, as the dogmas of Christianity had been formulated entirely under the influence of ancient philosophy. Under these circumstances, during the unbroken dominance of Church doctrine there remained for philosophy, for the most part, only the position of a handmaid *to ground, develop, and defend dogma scientifically*. But just by this means philosophy came into a certain opposition to theology as regards method; for what the latter taught on the ground of divine revelation, the former was to win and set forth by means of human knowledge.[11]

But the infallible consequence of this relation was, that the freer individual thinking became in its relation to the Church, the more independently philosophy began the solution of the problem which she had in common with religion; from presentation and defence of doctrine she passed to its criticism, and finally, in complete independence of religious interests, sought to derive her teaching from the sources which she thought she possessed in the "natural light" of human reason and experience.[12] The opposition to theology, as regards methods, grew in this way to an opposition in the subject matter, and modern philosophy as "world-wisdom" set itself over against Church dogma.[13] However manifold the aspects which this relation took on, shading from a clinging attachment to a passionate conflict, the office of "philosophy" remained always that which antiquity had assigned to it, to supply from scientific insight a foundation for a theory of the world and of human life, where religion was no longer able to meet this need, or at least to meet it alone. In the conviction that it was equal to this task, the philosophy of the eighteenth century, like that of the Greeks, considered it its right and duty to enlighten men with regard to the nature of things, and from this position of insight to rule the life of the individual and of society.

From this position of self-security philosophy was shaken by *Kant*, who demonstrated the impossibility of a philosophical (i.e., metaphysical) knowledge of the world beside of or above the individual sciences, and thereby restricted once more the conception and the task of philosophy; for after this claim, the realm of *philosophy, as a particular science*, was narrowed to just that *critical consideration by Reason of itself*, from which *Kant* had won his decisive insight, and which needed only to be extended systematically to activities other than that of knowing. With this function could be united what *Kant*[14] called the universal or cosmic conception of philosophy, its vocation in the practical direction of life.

It is, to be sure, far from true that this new and apparently final conception of philosophy gained universal acceptance at once. It is rather the case that the great variety of philosophical movements of the nineteenth century has left no earlier form of philosophy unrepeated, and that a luxuriant development of the "metaphysical need"[15] even brought back, for a time, the inclination to swallow up all human knowledge in philosophy, and complete this again as an all-embracing science.

2. In view of these mutations through which the meaning of the word "philosophy" has passed in the course of time, it seems impracticable *to pretend to gain a general conception of philosophy from historical comparison*. None of those brought forward for this purpose[16] apply to all those structures of mental activity which lay claim to the name. Even the subordination of philosophy under the more general conception "science" is questionable in the case of those types of teaching which place a one-sided emphasis on the practical significance of their doctrine:[17] still less can we define the subject-matter and form of philosophy considered as a special science, in a way that shall hold good for all cases. For even aside from the primitive or the revived standpoint for which philosophy is a universal science,[18] the attempts to limit it are extremely various. The problems of natural science form at first almost the sole objects of interest for philosophy, then for a long period are included in its scope, and do not separate from it until modern times. History, on the other hand, has remained an object of indifference to most philosophical systems, and has emerged as an object of philosophical investigation relatively late and in isolated cases. Metaphysical doctrines, again, in which the centre of philosophy is usually sought, we see either pushed to one side at important turning points in history or declared to be entirely impossible:[19] and if at times the ability of philosophy to determine the life of the individual or of society is emphasised, a proud standpoint of pure theory has renounced such a menial occupation.[20]

From still another side it has been claimed that philosophy treats the same subjects as the other sciences, but in another sense and by another method; but neither has this specific characteristic of form historical universality. That there is no such acknowledged historical method would of course be no objection if only the endeavour after such a method were a constant characteristic of all philosophies. This is, however, so far from being the case that in fact many philosophers imprint on their science the method of other disciplines, e.g., of mathematics or of investigation of nature,[21] while others will have nothing at all to do with a methodical treatment of their problems, and regard the philosophic activity as analogous to the creations of genius in art.

3. From these circumstances is explained also the fact that there is no fixed *relation of philosophy to the other sciences*, which is capable of a definition valid for all history. Where philosophy presents itself as the universal science, the other sciences appear only as its more or less distinctly separated parts.[22] Where, on the contrary, philosophy is assigned the task of grasping the results of the particular sciences in their general significance, and harmonising them into a comprehensive knowledge of the world, we have as the result peculiarly complex relations: in the first place, a dependence of philosophy upon the existing condition of insight reached in the particular disciplines – a dependence which expresses itself principally in the furtherance of philosophy by the prominent advances made by individual sciences;[23] in the next place, an influence in the opposite direction, when philosophy takes part in the work of the particular sciences. This action is felt as help or as hindrance, according as the philosophical treatment of the questions embraced under the particular disciplines sometimes contributes valuable factors for their solution, by means of its wider range of vision and its tendency toward unity,[24] but at other times presents itself only as a duplication which, if it leads to like results, appears useless, or if it wishes to furnish other results, dangerous.[25]

From what has been said, it is evident farther that the *relations of philosophy to the other activities of civilisation* are no less close than its relation to the individual sciences. For the conceptions arising from the religious and ethical and artistic life, from the life of the state and of society, force their way everywhere, side by side with the results won from scientific investigation, into the idea of the universe which the philosophy of metaphysical tendencies aims to frame; and the reason's valuations[26] and standards of judgment demand their place in that idea the more vigorously, just in proportion as it is to become the basis for the practical significance of philosophy. In this way humanity's convictions and ideals find their expression in philosophy side by side with its intellectual insights; and if these convictions and ideals are regarded, erroneously often, as gaining thereby the form of scientific intelligence, they may receive under certain circumstances valuable clarification and modification by this means. Thus this relation also of philosophy to general culture is not only that of receiving, but also that of giving.

[27]It is not without interest to consider also the mutations in *external position* and *social relations* which philosophy has experienced. It may be assumed that science was from the first, with perhaps a few exceptions (Socrates), pursued in Greece in closed schools.[28] The fact that these, even at a later time, had the form of societies with religious laws[29] would not in itself alone, in view of the religious character of all Greek judicial institutions, prove a religious origin of these schools, but the circumstance that Greek science worked out its contents directly from religious ideas, and that certain connections with religious cults present themselves unmistakably in a number of directions,[30] makes it not improbable that the scientific societies sprang originally from religious unions (the Mysteries) and continued in a certain connection with them. But when the scientific life had developed to complete independence, these connections fell away and purely scientific schools were founded as free unions of men who, under the guidance of persons of importance, shared with each other the work of research, exposition, defence, and polemic,[31] and at the same time had an ethical bond in a common ideal of the conduct of life.

With the advent of the larger relations of life in the Hellenistic and Roman period, these unions naturally became loosened, and we frequently meet writers, especially among the Romans, who are active in the field of philosophy in a purely individual way, neither members of a school nor professional teachers. Such were Cicero, Seneca, and Marcus Aurelius. Not until the latest period of antiquity were the ties of the schools drawn more closely again, as in Neo-Pythagoreanism and Neo-Platonism.

Among the Romanic and Germanic peoples the course of events has been not unlike that in the ancient world. The science of the Middle Ages also appears in the train of the Church civilisation; it has its seats in the cloister-schools, and is stimulated toward independent development primarily by questions of religious interest. In it, too, the oppositions of various religious orders, such as the Dominicans and Franciscans, assert themselves for a time, and even the freer scientific associations out of which the universities gradually developed, had originally a religious background and an ecclesiastical stamp.[32] Hence there was always but a slight degree of independence with reference to Church doctrine in this corporate philosophy of the universities, and this held true on into the eighteenth century for the Protestant universities also, in the foundation and development of which ecclesiastical and religious interests had a foremost place.

On the other hand, it is characteristic of the "world-wisdom" or secular philosophy which was gaining its independence at the beginning of the modern period, that those who bring and support it are not at all men of the schools, but men of the world and of life. An escaped monk, a state-chancellor, a cobbler, a nobleman, a proscribed Jew, a learned diplomat, independent men of letters and journalists – these are the founders of modern philosophy, and in accord with this, their work takes for its outer form not the textbook or the deposit of academic disputations, but the free literary production, the essay.

Not until the second half of the eighteenth century did philosophy again become corporate, and domesticated in the universities. This took place first in Germany, where the most favourable conditions were afforded by the rising independence of the universities, and where a fruitful interchange between teachers and students of the university was beneficial to philosophy also.[33] From Germany this spread to Scotland, England, France, and Italy, and in general it may be said that in the nineteenth century the seat of philosophy is essentially to be sought in the universities.[34]

In conclusion, the *share of the various peoples* in the development of philosophy deserves a brief mention. As with all developments of European culture, so with philosophy – the Greeks created it, and the primitive structure of philosophy due to their creative activity is still to-day an essential basis of the science. What was added in antiquity by the mixed peoples of Hellenism and by the Romans does not, in general, amount to more than a special form and practical adaptation of the Greek philosophy. Only in the religious turn which the last movement took (cf. below, Part II. ch. 2) do we find something essentially new which sprang from the harmonising of national differences in the Roman Empire. The scientific culture of the Middle Ages was also international, as is implied in the universal employment of the Latin language. It is with modern philosophy that the special characters of particular nations first present themselves as of decisive influence. While the traditions of medieval scholasticism maintain themselves most vigorously and independently in Spain and Portugal, the Italians, Germans, English, and French supply the first movements of the new science which reached its highest point in the classical period of German philosophy. Compared with these four nations, the rest stand almost entirely in a receptive attitude; a certain independence is noticeable, if anywhere, in more recent time among the Swedes.

§ 2. The History of Philosophy

The more varied the character assumed by the problems and content of philosophy in the course of time, the more the question arises, what meaning there can be in uniting in historical investigation and exposition products of thought which are not only so manifold, but also so different in kind, and between which there seems to be ultimately nothing in common but the name.

For the anecdotal interest in this checkered diversity of various opinions on various things, which was perhaps formerly the chief motive of a "History of Philosophy," stimulated too by the remarkable and strange nature of many of these views, cannot possibly serve as the permanent centre of a genuine scientific discipline.

1. At all events, however, it is clear that the case stands otherwise with the history of philosophy than with that of any other science. For with all these the field of research remains fixed on the whole at least, however many the variations to which its extent, its separation from a still more general field, and its limitation with reference to neighbouring fields, may be subject in the course of history. In such a case there is no difficulty in tracing the development of knowledge over a field which can be determined in this way, and in eventually making just those variations intelligible as the natural consequences of this development of insight.

Quite otherwise, however, in the case of philosophy, which has no such subject-matter common to all its periods, and whose "history," therefore, sets forth no constant advance or gradual approximation to a knowledge of the subject in question. Rather, it has always been emphasised that while in other sciences, a quiet building up of knowledge is the rule, as soon as they have once gained a sure methodical footing after their rhapsodical beginnings – a rule which is interrupted only from time to time by a sudden new beginning – in philosophy the reverse is true. There it is the exception that successors gratefully develop what has been already achieved, and each of the great systems of philosophy begins to solve its newly formulated problem *ab ovo*, as if the other systems had scarcely existed.

2. If in spite of all of this we are still to be able to speak of a "history of philosophy," the unity of connection, which we find neither in the objects with which philosophers busy themselves, nor in the problems they have set themselves, can be found only in the *common work which they have accomplished* in spite of all the variety in their subject-matter and in the purposes with which they have worked.

But this common product, which constitutes the meaning of the history of philosophy, rests on just the changing relations which the work of philosophers has sustained in the course of history, not only to the maturest results of science in general and of the special sciences in particular, but also to the other activities of European civilisation. For was it that philosophy had in view the project of a general scientific knowledge of the universe, which she would win either in the role of universal science, or as a generalising comprehension of the results of the special sciences, or was it that she sought a view of life which should give a complete expression to the highest values of will and feeling, or was it finally that with a clearly defined limitation of her field she made reason's self-knowledge her goal – the result always was that she was labouring to bring to conscious expression the necessary forms and principles in which the human reason manifests its activity, and to transfer these from their original form of perceptions, feelings, and impulses, into that of *conceptions*. In some direction and in some fashion every philosophy has striven to reach, over a more or less extensive field, a formulation in conception of the material immediately given in the world and in life; and so, as these efforts have passed into history, the constitution of the mental and spiritual life has been step by step disclosed. *The History of Philosophy is the process in which European humanity has embodied in scientific conceptions its views of the world and its judgments of life.*

It is this common fruit of all the intellectual creations which present themselves as "philosophies," which alone gives to the history of philosophy as a genuine science its content, its problem, and its justification. This, too, is the reason why a knowledge of the history of philosophy is a necessary requirement, not only for all scholarly education, but for all culture whatever; for it teaches how the conceptions and forms have been coined, in which we all, in every-day life as well as in the particular sciences, think and judge the world of our experience.

[35]The beginnings of the history of philosophy are to be sought in the historical compositions (for the most part lost) of the great schools of antiquity, especially the Peripatetic School. As we may see in the examples given by Aristotle,[36] these works had the critical purpose of preparing for the development of their own views by a dialectical examination of views previously brought forward. Such collections of historical material were planned for the various fields of science, and doxographies[37] in philosophy arose in this way side by side with histories of particular disciplines, such as mathematics, astronomy, physics, etc. As inclination and power for independent philosophic thought later declined, this literature degenerated into a learned scrap-book work, in which were mingled anecdotes from the lives of the philosophers, individual epigrammatic sayings, and sketches of their doctrines.

Those expositions belonging to the modern period which were based upon the remains of ancient tradition had this same character of collections of curiosities. Such were *Stanley's*[38] reproduction of Diogenes Laertius, and *Brucker's* works.[39] Only with time do we find critical discernment in use of the sources *(Buhle,*[40] *Fülleborn*[41]*)*, a more unprejudiced apprehension of the historical significance of individual doctrines *(Tiedemann*[42]*, Dégerando*[43]*)*, and systematic criticism of these upon the basis of the new standpoint *(Tennemann*[44]*, Fries*[45]*, and Schleiermacher*[46]*)*. It was, however, through *Hegel*[47] that the history of philosophy was first made an independent science, for he discovered the essential point that the history of philosophy can set forth neither a motley collection of opinions of various learned Gentlemen "*de omnibus rebus et de quibusdam aliis,*" nor a constantly widening and perfecting elaboration of the same subject-matter, but rather only the limited process in which the "categories" of reason have successively attained distinct consciousness and reached the form of conceptions.

This valuable insight was, however, obscured and injured in the case of Hegel by an additional assumption, since he was convinced that the chronological order in which the above "categories" have presented themselves in the historical systems of philosophy must necessarily correspond with the logical and systematic order in which these same categories should appear as "elements of truth" in the logical construction of the final system of philosophy (i.e., in Hegel's view, his own). The fundamental thought, right in itself, thus led to the mistake of a construction of the history of philosophy under the control of a philosophical system, and so to a frequent violation of historical fact. This error, which the development of a scientific history of philosophy in the nineteenth century has set aside in favour of historical accuracy and exactness, arose from the wrong idea (though an idea in logical consistence with the principles of Hegel's philosophy) that the historical progress of philosophical thought is due solely, or at least essentially, to an ideal necessity with which one "category" pushes forward another in the dialectical movement. In truth, the picture of the historical movement of philosophy is quite a different one. It depends not solely upon the thinking of "humanity" or even of the "*Weltgeist*," but just as truly upon the reflections, the needs of mind and heart, the presaging thought and sudden flashes of insight, of philosophising individuals.

3. The history of philosophy, considered as such a sum-total, in which the fundamental conceptions of man's views of the world and judgments of life have been embodied, is the product of a great variety of single movements of thought. And as the actual motives of these movements, various factors are to be distinguished, both in the setting of the problems and in the attempts at their logical solution.

The logical, *pragmatic factor* is no doubt sufficiently important. For the problems of philosophy are in the main given, and this is shown by the fact that they are constantly recurring in the historical movement of thought as the "primeval enigma of existence," and are ever anew demanding imperiously the solution which has never completely succeeded. They are given, however, by the inadequacy and internal contradictions of the material which consciousness presents for philosophical consideration.[48] But just for this reason this material contains the real presuppositions and the logical constraining forces for all rational reflection upon it, and because from the nature of the case these are always asserting themselves anew in the same way, it follows that not only the chief problems in the history of philosophy, but also the chief lines along which a solution is attempted, are repeated. Just this constancy in all change, which, regarded from without, makes the impression that philosophy is striving fruitlessly in ever-repeated circles for a goal that is never attained, proves only this – that the problems of philosophy are tasks which the human mind cannot escape.[49] And so we understand how the same logical necessity in repeated instances causes one doctrine to give birth to another. Hence progress in the history of philosophy is, during certain periods, to be understood entirely pragmatically, i.e., through the internal necessity of the thoughts and through the "logic of things."

[50]The mistake of Hegel's mentioned above, consists, then, only in his wishing to make of a factor which is effective within certain limits, the only, or at least the principal, factor. It would be the opposite error to deny absolutely the "reason in history," and to see in the successive doctrines of philosophy only confused chance-thoughts of individuals. It is rather true that the total content of the history of philosophy can be explained only through the fact that the necessities existing in the nature of things assert themselves over and over in the thinking of individuals, however accidental the special conditions of this latter may be. On these relations rest the attempts made to classify all philosophical doctrines under certain types, and to establish a sort of rhythmical repetition in their historical development. On this basis V. Cousin brought forward his theory of the four systems, Idealism, Sensualism,

Scepticism, Mysticism; so too August Comte[51] his of the three stages, the theological, the metaphysical, and the positive. An interesting and in many ways instructive grouping of philosophical doctrines about the particular main problems is afforded by A. Renouvier in his *Esquisse d'une Classification Systématique des Doctrines Philosophiques* (2 vols., Paris, 1885 f.). A school-book which arranges the philosophical doctrines according to problems and schools has been issued by Paul Janet and Séailles; *Histoire de la Philosophie; les problemes et les écoles* (Paris, 1887).

4. But the pragmatic thread very often breaks off in the history of philosophy. The historical order in particular, in which problems have presented themselves, shows almost a complete absence of such an immanent logical necessity. Here, on the contrary, another factor asserts itself which may best be designated as the *factor contributed by the history of civilisation*. For philosophy receives both its problems and the materials for their solution from the ideas of the general consciousness of the time, and from the needs of society. The great conquests and the newly emerging questions of the special sciences, the movements of the religious consciousness, the intuitions of art, the revolutions in social and political life – all these give philosophy new impulses at irregular intervals, and condition the directions of the interest which forces now these, now those, problems into the foreground, and crowd others for the time being aside; and no less do they condition also the changes which questions and answers experience in course of time. Where this dependence shows itself with especial clearness, we have under certain circumstances a philosophical system appearing, that represents exactly the knowledge which a definite age has of itself; or we may have the oppositions in the general culture of the age finding their expression in the strife of philosophical systems. And so besides the constant dependence upon the essential character of the subject-matter – the pragmatic factor – there prevails also a necessity growing out of the history of civilisation, or current state of culture, which warrants a historical right of existence to structures of thought in themselves untenable.

[52]This relation also was first brought to notice in a greater degree than before by *Hegel*, although the "relative truth" which he ascribes to the particular systems has with him at the same time a systematic meaning, owing to his dialectical fundamental thought. On the other hand, the element due to the history of civilisation has been best formulated among his successors by *Kuno Fischer*,[53] who has also availed himself of it in most brilliant manner in his exposition of the subject. He regards philosophy in its historical unfolding as the progressive self-knowledge of the human mind, and makes its development appear as constantly conditioned by the development of the object which in it is attaining self-knowledge. Although this applies to a number of the most important systems, it is yet but one of the factors involved.

The influences from the history of civilisation which condition the statement and solution of philosophic problems, afford an explanation in most cases of an extremely interesting phenomenon which is of great importance for understanding the historical development. For when interest is directed chiefly on certain lines of thought, it is inevitable, according to psychological laws, that associations will be formed between different bodies of thought – associations which are not based on the subject-matter – and so, that questions which in themselves have nothing to do with each other become blended and made to depend upon each other in their solution. An extremely important and very often recurring example of this is the intermingling of ethical and aesthetic interests in the treatment of theoretical problems. The well-known fact of daily life that men's views are determined by their wishes, hopes, fears, and inclinations, that their theoretical are conditioned by their ethical and aesthetic judgments[54] – this fact is repeated on a larger scale in their views of the universe, and has even been able to rise so high in philosophy that what had been previously involuntarily practised, was proclaimed (by Kant) an epistemological postulate.

5. Meanwhile the historical process we are tracing owes all its variety and multiplicity of forms to the circumstance that the development of ideas and the formulation of general beliefs into abstract conceptions are accomplished only through the thinking of individual *personalities*, who, though rooted ever so deeply with their thought in the logical connection and prevalent ideas of a historical period, always add a particular element by their own individuality and conduct of life. This *individual factor* in the development of the history of philosophy deserves so great attention for the reason that those who have borne the leading part in the movement have shown themselves to be marked, independent personalities, whose peculiar nature has been a determining influence, not merely for the selection and combination of problems, but also for working out the conceptions to furnish solutions, both in their own doctrines and in those of their successors. That history is the kingdom of individualities, of details which are not to be repeated and which have value in themselves, is shown also in the history of philosophy: here, too, great personalities have exercised far-reaching and not exclusively beneficial influences.

[55]It is clear that the above-mentioned complication of problems is brought about by the subjective relations in which individual philosophers stand, in a much greater degree than by the occasions presented in the general consciousness of a time, of a people, etc. There is no philosophical system that is free from this influence of the personality of its founder. Hence all philosophical systems are creations of individuality, presenting in this respect a certain resemblance with works of art, and as such are to be understood from the point of view of the personality of their founder. The elements of every philosopher's *Weltanschauung* grow out of the problems of reality which are ever the same, and out of the reason as it is directed to their solution, but besides this out of the views and ideals of his people and his time; the form and arrangement, however, the connection and valuation which they find in the system, are conditioned by his birth and education, his activity and lot in life, his character and his experience. Here, accordingly, the universality which belongs to the other two factors is often wanting. In the case of these purely individual creations, aesthetic charm must take the place of the worth of abiding knowledge, and the impressiveness of many phenomena of the history of philosophy rests, in fact, only upon the magic of their "poetry of ideas"[56].

In addition, then, to the complication of problems and to the ideas determined by fancy and feeling, which are already enough to lead the general consciousness astray, there are in the case of individuals similar, but purely personal, processes to lend to the formation and solution of problems still more the character of artificiality. We cannot fail to recognise that philosophers have often gone about struggling with questions which have no basis in reality, so that all thought expended upon them was in vain, and that, on the other hand even in connection with the solution of real problems, unfortunate attempts in the *a priori* construction of conceptions have slipped in, which have been hindrances rather than helps toward the issue of the matter.

The wonderful feature in the history of philosophy remains just this, that out of such a multitude of individual and general complications there has yet been on the whole laid down that outline of universally valid conceptions for viewing the world and judging life, which presents the scientific significance of this development.

6. *Investigation in the history of philosophy has accordingly the following tasks to accomplish:*

(1) To *establish with precision* what may be derived from the available sources as to the circumstances in life, the mental development, and the doctrines of individual philosophers; (2) from these facts to reconstruct the *genetic* process in such a way that in the case of every philosopher we may understand how his doctrines depend in part upon those of his predecessors, in part upon the general ideas of his time, and in part upon his own nature and the course of his education; (3) from the consideration of the whole to *estimate* what value for

the total result of the history of philosophy belongs to the theories thus established and explained as regards their origin. With reference to the first two points, the history of philosophy is a *philologico-historical*, with reference to the third element it is a *critico-philosophical science*.

⁵⁷*(a)* To establish its facts the history of philosophy must proceed to a careful and comprehensive examination of the *sources*. These sources, however, vary greatly at different times in their transparency and fullness.

The main sources for investigation in the history of philosophy are of course the *works of the philosophers* themselves. For the *modern period* we stand here upon a relatively safe footing. Since the discovery of the art of printing, literary tradition has become so well established and clear that it offers in general no difficulties of any kind. The writings which philosophers have published since the Renaissance are throughout accessible for the research of today. The cases in which questions of genuineness, of the time origination, etc., give rise to controversies are extremely seldom; a philological criticism has here but a narrow field for activity, and where it can enter (as is the case in part in reference to the different editions of Kant's works), it concerns solely subordinate, and in the last instance indifferent, points. Here, too, we are tolerably sure of the completeness of the material; that anything of weight is lost, or still to be expected from later publication, is scarcely to be assumed; if the sharpened philological attentiveness of the last decades has brought us new material for Spinoza, Leibniz, Kant, Maine de Biran, the philosophical outcome has been only vanishing in comparison with the value of what was already known. At most it has concerned the question of supplementing our knowledge, and this must continue to be its province. The importance of occasional expressions in letters has been specially felt here, for these are adapted to shed more light on the individual factor in the historical development of philosophy.

With the sources of the *Medieval Philosophy* the case stands less favourably. These have in part (a small part, to be sure) still only a manuscript existence. *V. Cousin* and his school have rendered valuable service in publishing the texts, and in general we may be convinced that for this period also we possess material which has indeed gaps, but is on the whole adequate for our purpose. On the other hand, our knowledge of the Arabian and Jewish philosophy of the Middle Ages, and so of the influence of those systems on the course of Western Thought, is still very problematical in details; and this is perhaps the gap most sorely felt in our investigation of the sources for the history of philosophy.

Much worse still is the situation as regards the direct sources for *Ancient Philosophy*. Of the original works, we have preserved, to be sure, the most important: the fundamental portion of the works of Plato and Aristotle though even these are often doubtful in form. Besides these we have only the writings of later time, such as those of Cicero, Seneca, Plutarch, the Church Fathers, and the Neo-Platonists. By far the greater part of the philosophical writings of antiquity is lost. In their stead we must content ourselves with the fragments which the accident of an incidental mention in the writings of extant authors has kept for us, here too often in a questionable form.⁵⁸

If, nevertheless, success has been attained in gaining a view of the development of the ancient philosophy, clearer than that of the medieval, presenting a picture whose accuracy extends even to details and is scientifically assured, this is due not only to the unremitting pains of philologists and philosophers in working through their material, but also to the circumstance that beside the remains of the original works of the philosophers there are preserved also as secondary *sources*, remains of historical records made in antiquity. The best, indeed, of these also is lost: namely, the historical works which arose from the learned collection made by the Peripatetic and Stoic schools at the end of the fourth and in the third century BC. These works passed later through many hands before they were preserved for us in the extant compilations prepared in the Roman period, as in the *Placita Philosophorum*,[59] going by the name of Plutarch, in the writings of Sextus Empiricus,[60] in the *Deipnosophistae* of Athenaeus,[61] in the treatise of Diogenes Laertius, *Peri bion dogmaton kai apothegmaton ton en philosophia eudokimesanton*,[62] in the collections of the Church Fathers and in the notes of the Commentators of the latest period such as Alexander Aphrodisias, Themistius, and Simplicius. H. Diels has given an excellent and thorough treatment of these secondary sources of ancient philosophy *Doxographi Graeci* (Berlin, 1879).

Where the condition of the sources is so doubtful as is the case over the entire field of ancient philosophy, critical ascertainment of the facts must go hand in hand with examination of the pragmatic and genetic connection. For where the transmission of the material is itself doubtful we can reach a decision only by taking a view of the connection that shall accord with reason and psychological experience. In these cases it becomes the task of the history of philosophy as of all history, after establishing a base of operations in that which is assured by the sources, to proceed to ascertain its position in those regions with which tradition finds itself no longer directly and surely in touch. The historical study of philosophy in the nineteenth century may boast that it has fulfilled this task, to which it was stimulated by Schleiermacher, by the labours of H. Ritter – whose *Geschichte der Philosophy* (12 vols., Hamburg, 1829–53) is now, to be sure, antiquated – Brandis and Zeller for the ancient philosophy and of J. E. Erdmann and Kuno Fischer for the modern. Among the many complete expositions of the history of philosophy by far the most trustworthy in these respects is J. E. Erdmann's *Grundriss der Geschichte der Philosophie*, 2 vols. (3d ed.), Berlin, 1878; [Erdmann's *Outline of the History of Philosophy*, trans. ed. by W. S. Hough, Lond. and N.Y., 1890].

An excellent bibliography of the entire history of philosophy, assembling the literature in exhaustive completeness and good arrangement is to be found in Ueberweg's *Grundriss der Geschichte der Philosophie*, 4 vols., 8th ed., ed. by M. Heinze (Berlin, 1894–98). [Ueberweg's *Outline of the History of Philosophy*, trans. from the 4th ed. by G. S. Morris (N.Y. 1811), contains additions, but of course does not give the bibliography of recent works.] Under the general literature may also be mentioned, R. Eucken, *Die Lebensanschauungen der grossen Denker* (Leipzig 1890).

(b) Explanation of facts in the history of philosophy is either pragmatic (logical), or based on the history of civilisation, or psychological, corresponding to the three factors which we have set forth above as determining the movement of thought. Which of these three modes of explanation is to be applied in individual cases depends solely upon the state of the facts with regard to the transmission of material. It is then incorrect to make either one the sole principle of treatment. The pragmatic method of explanation is dominant with those who see in the entire history of philosophy the preparation for a definite system of philosophy; so with Hegel and his disciples (see above); so from a Herbartian standpoint with Chr. A. Thilo, *Kurze pragmatische Geschichte der Philosophie* (2 pts.; Coethen, 1876–80). Kuno Fischer and W. Windelband have emphasised in their interpretation of modern philosophy, the importance of considering the history of civilisation and the problems of the individual sciences.

The purely *biographical* treatment which deals only with successive personalities is quite inadequate as a scientific exposition of the history of philosophy. This mode of treatment is represented in recent time by the treatise of G. H. Lewes *The History of Philosophy from Thales to the Present Day* (2 vols., Lond. 1871), a book destitute of all historical apprehension, and at the same time a party composition in the spirit of the Positivism of Comte. The works of the French historians (Damiron, Ferraz) are inclined to take this form of a separate essay-like treatment of individual philosophers, not losing from sight, however, the course of development of the whole.[63]

(c) The most difficult task is to establish the principles according to which the critical philosophical estimate of the individual doctrines must be made up. The history of philosophy, like all history, is a critical science; its duty is not only to record and explain, but also to estimate what is to count as progress and fruit in the historical movement, when we have succeeded in knowing and understanding this. There is no history without this critical point of view, and the evidence of a historian's maturity is that he is clearly conscious of this point of view of criticism; for where this is not the case he proceeds in the selection of his material and in his characterisation of details only instinctively and without a clear standard.[64]

It is understood, of course, that the standard of critical judgment must not be a private theory of the historian, nor even his philosophic conviction; at least the employment of such a standard deprives the criticism exercised in accordance with it of the value of scientific universality. He who is given to the belief that he possesses the sole philosophical truth, or who comes to this field imbued with the customs of the special sciences in which, no doubt, a sure result makes it a very simple[65] matter to estimate the attempts which have led to it, such a one may well be tempted to stretch all forms that pass before him upon the Procrustean bed of his system; but he who contemplates the work of thought in history, with an open historical vision, will be restrained by a respectful reverence from reprimanding the heroes of philosophy for their ignorance of the wisdom of an epigone.[66]

In contrast with this external method of pronouncing sentence, the scientific history of philosophy must place itself upon the standpoint of *immanent criticism*, the principles of which are two: *formal logical consistency* and *intellectual fruitfulness*.

Every philosopher grows into a certain set of ideas, and to these his thinking remains bound, and is subjected in its development to psychological necessity. Critical investigation has to settle how far it has been possible for him to bring the different elements of his thinking into agreement with each other. The contradiction is almost never actually present in so direct a form that the same thing is expressly maintained and also denied, but always in such a way that various positions are put forward which, only by virtue of their logical consequences, lead to direct contradiction and really irreconcilable results. The discovery of these discrepancies is formal criticism; it frequently coincides with pragmatic explanation, for this formal criticism has been performed in history itself by the successors of the philosopher in question, and has thus determined for them their problems.

Yet this point of view alone is not sufficient. As purely formal it applies without exception to all attested views of a philosopher, but it gives no criterion for decision on the question, in what the philosophical significance of a doctrine really consists. For it is often the case that philosophy has done its work just in conceptions which must by no means be regarded as in themselves perfect or free from contradiction; while a multitude of individual convictions which there is no occasion to oppose, must remain unnoticed in a corner, so far as our historical survey is concerned. In the history of philosophy great errors are weightier than small truths.

For before all else the decisive question is: what has yielded a contribution to the development of man's conception of the universe and estimate of life? In the history of philosophy those structures of thought are the objects of study which have maintained themselves permanent and living as forms of apprehension and norms of judgment, and in which the abiding inner structure of the human mind has thus come to clear recognition.

This is then the standard, according to which alone we can decide also which among the doctrines of the philosophers – concerning, as they often do, so many various things – are to be regarded as properly philosophical, and which, on the other hand, are to be excluded from the history of philosophy. Investigation of the sources has of course the duty of gathering carefully and completely all the doctrines of philosophers, and so of affording all the material for explaining their genesis, whether from their logical content, or from the history of civilisation, or from psychological grounds; but the purpose of this laborious work is yet only this, that the philosophically indifferent may be ultimately recognised as such, and the ballast then thrown overboard.

It is especially true that this point of view must essentially determine selection and presentation of material in a *text-book*, which is not to give the investigation itself, but to gather up its results.

§ 3. Division of Philosophy and of its History

It cannot be our purpose here to propose a systematic division of philosophy, for this could in no case possess universal validity historically. The differences which prevail in the course of the historical development, in determining the conception, the task, and the subject-matter of philosophy, involve so necessarily and obviously a change also in the divisions, that this needs no especial illustration. The oldest philosophy knew no division at all. In later antiquity a division of philosophy into logic, physics, and ethics was current. In the Middle Ages, and still more in modern times, the first two of these subjects were often comprised under the title, theoretical philosophy, and set over against practical philosophy. Since Kant a new threefold division into logical, ethical, and aesthetical philosophy is beginning to make its way, yet these various divisions are too much dependent upon the actual course of philosophy itself to make it worth our while to recount them here in detail.

On the other hand, it does commend itself to preface the historical exposition with at least a brief survey of the entire circuit of those problems which have always formed the subject of philosophy, however varied the extent to which they have been studied or the value that has been attached to them – a survey, therefore, for which no claim is made to validity from a systematic point of view, but which is determined only by the purpose of preliminary orientation.

1. *Theoretical problems.* Such we call those which refer, in part to our knowledge of the actual world, in part to an investigation of the knowing process itself. In dealing with the former class, however, the general questions which concern the actual taken as a whole are distinguished from those which deal with single provinces of the actual. The former, *viz.*, the highest principles for explaining the universe, and the general view of the universe based on these principles, form the problem of *metaphysics*, called by Aristotle the first, i.e., fundamental, science, and designated by the name now usual, only on account of the position which it had in the ancient collection of the Aristotelian works – "after physics." On account of his monotheistic view of the world, Aristotle also called this branch of knowledge theology. Later writers have also treated *rational* or *natural theology* as a branch of metaphysics.

The special provinces of the actual are Nature and History. In the former, external and internal nature are to be distinguished. The problems presented to knowledge by external nature are called *cosmological*, or, specially, problems of *natural philosophy*, or perhaps *physical*. The investigation of internal nature, i.e., of consciousness and its states and activities, is the business of *psychology*. The philosophical consideration of history remains within the borders of theoretical philosophy only if it be limited to the investigation of the laws that prevail in the historical life of peoples; since, however, history is the realm of man's purposeful actions, the questions of the *philosophy of history*, so far as this deals with the end of the movement of history viewed as a whole, and with the fulfilment of this end, fall under the head of practical problems.

Investigation directed upon knowledge itself is called logic (in the general sense of the word), and also sometimes *noetic*. If we are occupied with the question how knowledge actually arises, this *psycho-genetic* consideration falls in the province of *psychology*. If, on the other hand, we set up norms or standards according to which our ideas are estimated as regards their worth for truth, we call these *logical* laws, and designate investigation directed upon them as *logic* in the narrower sense. The application of these laws gives rise to *methodology*, which develops the prescriptions for a systematic ordering of scientific activity with reference to the various ends of knowledge. The problems, finally, which arise from the questions concerning the range and limit of man's knowing faculty and its relation to the reality to be known, form the subject-matter of *epistemology* or *theory of knowledge*.

H. Siebeck, *Geschichte der Psychologie*, Vol. I., in two parts (Gotha, 1880–84), incomplete, extending into the scholastic period.

K. Prantl, *Geschichte der Logik im Abendlande*, 4 vols. (Leips. 1855–70), brought down only to the Renaissance. Fr. Harms, *Die Philosophie in ihrer Geschichte*. I. "Psychologie"; II. "Logik" (Berlin, 1877 and 1881).

[R. Adamson, *The History of Psychology* (in prep.).]

2. *Practical* problems are, in general, those which grow out of the investigation of man's activity, so far as it is determined by ends. Here, too, a psycho-genetic treatment is possible, which falls under psychology. That discipline, on the other hand, which considers man's action from the point of view of the ethical norm or standard, is *ethics* or *moral philosophy*. By *morals*[67] in the narrower sense is usually understood the proposal and grounding of ethical precepts. Since, however, all ethical action has reference to the community, there are attached to morals or ethics, in the narrower sense, the *philosophy of society* (for which the unfortunate name *sociology* seems likely to become permanent), and the *philosophy of law or right*. Further, insofar as the ideal of human society constitutes the ultimate meaning of history, the *philosophy of history* appears also in this connection, as already mentioned. To practical problems, in the broadest sense of the word, belong also those which relate to art and religion. To designate philosophical investigation of the nature of the beautiful and of art, the name *aesthetics* has been introduced since the end of last century. If philosophy takes the religious life for its object, not in the sense of itself intending to give a science of the nature of the deity, but in the sense of an investigation with regard to man's religious behaviour, we call this discipline *philosophy of religion*.

Fr. Schleiermacher, *Grundlinien einer Kritik der bisherigen Sittenlehre* (collected works, III., Vol. I., Berlin, 1834). L. v. Henning, *Die Principien der Ethik in historischer Entwicklung* (Berlin, 1825). Fr. *v.* Raumer, *Die geschichtliche Entwicklung der Begriffe von Staat, Recht, und Politik* (Leips., 3d ed., 1861). E. Feuerlein, *Die philos. Sittenlehre in ihren geschichtlichen Haupformen* (2 vols., Tübingen, 1857–59). P. Janet, *Histoire de la philosophie morale et politique* (Paris, 1858). W. Whewell, *History of Moral Science* (Edinburg, 1863). H. Sidgwick, *The Methods of Ethics*, 4th ed. (Lond. and N.Y. 1890). [*Outlines of the History of Ethics*, by same author (Lond. and N.Y., 3d ed., 1892). J. Martineau, *Types of Ethical Theory* (2d ed., Oxford and N.Y. 1886).] Th. Ziegler, *Geschichte der Ethik*, 2 vols. (the third not yet appeared; Strassburg, 1881–86). K Köstlin, *Geschichte der Ethik* (only the beginning, 1 vol., Tübingen, 1887). [J. Bonar, *Philosophy and Economics in their Historical Relations* (Lond. and N.Y. 1893). D. G. Ritchie, *The History of Political Philosophy* (in prep.).]

R. Zimmermann, *Geschichte der Aesthetik* (Vienna, 1858). M. Schasler, *Kritische Geschichte der Aesthetik* (Berlin, 1871). [B. Bosanquet, *The History of Aesthetics* (Lond. and N.Y. 1892). W. Knight, *The Philosophy of the Beautiful* (an outline of the history, Edin. and N.Y. 1891). Gayley and Scott, *A Guide to the Literature of Aesthetics*, Univ. of California, and *Introd. to the Methods and Materials of Literary Criticism* (Bost. 1899) have bibliographies.]

J. Berger, *Geschichte der Religionsphilosophie* (Berlin, 1800). [Pünjer, *History of the Christian Philosophy of Religion* (Vol. 1., Edin. and N.Y. 1887). O. Pfleiderer, *The Philosophy of Religion*, trans. by Menzies (Lond. 1887). Martineau, *Study of Religion* (2 vols., 1888), and *Seat of*

Authority in Religion (1890). J. Caird, *Introd. to the Philos. of Religion* (1880). E. Caird, *Evolution of Religion* (2 vols., Lond. and N.Y. 1893).]

The division of the history of philosophy is usually connected with that current for political history, so as to distinguish three great periods – Ancient, Medieval, and Modern Philosophy. Yet the sections made in this way are not so favourable for the history of philosophy as they perhaps are for political history. Other points of division must be made, equally important as regards the nature of the development; and, on the other hand, the transition between the Middle Ages and modern times demands a shifting of the point of division on either side. In consequence of this, the entire history of philosophy will here be treated according to the following plan of division, in a manner to be more exactly illustrated and justified in detail by the exposition itself:

1) *The Philosophy of the Greeks:* from the beginnings of scientific thought to the death of Aristotle – from about 600 to 322 BC.
2) *Hellenistic-Roman Philosophy:* from the death of Aristotle to the passing away of Neo-Platonism, – from 322 BC to about 500 AD.
3) *Medieval Philosophy:* from Augustine to Nicolaus Cusanus – from the fifth to the fifteenth century.
4) *The Philosophy of the Renaissance:* from the fifteenth to the seventeenth century.
5) *The Philosophy of the Enlightenment:* from Locke to the death of Lessing – 1689–1781.
6) *The German Philosophy:* from Kant to Hegel and Herbart –1781–1820.
7) *The Philosophy of the Nineteenth Century.*

Notes

1 "Introduction" to Wilhelm Windelband's *A History of Philosophy with Especial Reference to the Formation and Development of Its Problems and Conceptions*, trans. James H. Tufts. New York/London: MacMillan, 1926, pp. 1–22. The translation is from the second edition, Strassburg 1900 [1st ed. 1891]. – Ed.
2 Cited in detail in Ueberweg-Heinze, *Grundriss der Geschichte der Philosophie*, I.§ 1. [Eng. trans. Ueberweg's *Outline of the History of Philosophy*, trans. by G. S. Morris. N.Y. 1871.]
3 Herodotus, I. 30 and 50; Thucydides, II. 40; and frequently also even in Plato, *e.g. Apol.* 29; *Lysis*, 218 A; *Symp.* 202 E ff.
4 A conception which it is well known is of much greater compass than the English and French "science." [In this translation the words "science" and" scientific" are used in this larger sense. The term "natural science" will be used for the narrower meaning which "science" alone often has. If it should serve to remind the beginner that philosophy and scientific thought should be one, and that natural science is not all of science, it may be of value. – Trans.]
5 Plato, *Rep.* 480 B; Aristotle, *Met.* VI. 1, 1026 a 18.
6 Plato, *Theaet.* 143 D. Aristotle sets the doctrine "of Being as such" (the later so-called "Metaphysics") as "First Philosophy" over against the other "philosophies," and distinguishes further theoretical and practical "philosophy." In one passage (*Met.* I 6, 987 a 29) he applies the plural *philosophiai* also to the different systems of science which have followed in historical succession as we should speak of the philosophies of Kant, Fichte, Hegel, etc.
7 Cf. the definition of Epicurus in Sext. Emp., *Adv. Math.* XI. 169, and on the other hand that of Seneca, *Epist.* 89.
8 Cf. below, Part I [The Philosophy of the Greeks].
9 Hence Proclus, for example, would prefer to have philosophy called theology.
10 Cf., for example, Augustine, *Solil.* I. 7; *Conf.* V. 7; Scotus Eriugena, *De Div. Praedest.* I. (Migne, 358); Anselm *Proslog.*, ch. 1. (Migne, I. 227) ; Abelard, *Introd. in Theol.* II. 3 ; Raymundus Lullus, *De Quinque Sap.* 8.

11 Thomas Aquinas, *Summa Theol*. I. 32, 1; *Contr. Gent*. I. 8 f., II. 1 ff.; Duns Scotus, *Op. Ox*. I. 3, qu. 4; Durand de Pourçain, *In Sent. Prol*., qu. 8; Raymundus of Sabunde, *Theol. Natur. Prooem*.

12 Laur. Valla, *Dialect. Disp*. III. 9; B. Telesio, *De Nat. Rer. Prooem.;* Fr. Bacon, *De Augm*, III. 1 (Works, Spedding, I. 539, III. 336); Taurellus, *Philos. Triumph*. I. 1; Paracelsus, *Paragr*. (ed. Huser) II. 23 f.; G. Bruno, *Della Causa*, etc., IV. 107 (Lagarde, I. 272); Hobbes, *De Corpor*. I. (Works, Molesworth, I. 2 and 6 f.).

13 Characteristic definitions, on the one hand, in Gottsched, *Erste Gründe der gesammten Weltweisheit* (Leips. 1756), pp. 97 ff.; on the other hand, in the article *Philosophie*, in the *Encyclopedie* (Vol. xxv. pp. 632 ff.).

14 *Critique of Pure Reason*, A. 839; B. 866.

15 Schopenhauer, *World as Will and Idea*, vol. II. ch. 17.

16 Instead of criticizing particular conceptions, it is sufficient here to point to the widely diverging formulas in which the attempt has been made to perform this impossible task: cf., for example, only the introductions to works such as those of Erdmann, Ueberweg, Kuno Fischer, Zeller, etc. All these conceptions thus determined apply only insofar as the history of philosophy has yielded the *result* which they express, but they do not apply with reference to the *intentions* expressed by the philosophers themselves.

17 So in the case of the majority of the philosophers of later antiquity.

18 As for Chr. Wolff; cf. his *Logica*, §§ 29 ff.

19 This is especially the case where philosophy is regarded solely as "science of cognition." Cf., e.g., W. Hamilton in his notes to Reid's works, II. 808. Among the French at the close of the eighteenth and the beginning of this century, philosophy = *analyse de l'entendement humain*.

20 E.g., with Plotinus.

21 So Descartes and Bacon.

22 So, for example, in the Hegelian system.

23 As the influence of astronomy upon the beginnings of Greek [philosophy], or that of mechanics upon those of modern philosophy.

24 The Protestant theology of the nineteenth century stands in this relation to German philosophy.

25 Cf. the opposition of natural science to Schelling's philosophy of nature.

26 *Werthbestimmungen*. Literally, "value determinations" – Ed.

27 This and the next six paragraphs are set in a smaller font; for the purpose of readability, the same font is used throughout. – Ed.

28 H. Diels, *Ueber die ältesten Philosophenschulen der Griechen* in Philos. Aufsätze zum Jubiläum E. Zeller's, Leips. 1887, pp. 241 ff.

29 v. Wilamowitz-Mollendorf, *Antigonos von Karystos* (Philol. Stud. IV. Berlin, 1881, pp. 263 ff.).

30 The Pythagoreans, as is well known, offer a pre-eminent example of this; but sympathies with the Apollo cult are plain enough in the Platonic Academy also. Pfleiderer has lately sought to bring the apparently isolated Heraclitus into connection with the Mysteries (E. Pfleiderer, *Heraklit von Ephesus*. Berlin, 1886).

31 Cf. H. Usener, *Ueber die Organisation der wissenschaftlichen Arbeit im Alterthum* (Preuss. Jahrb., Jahrg. LIII., 1884, pp. 1 ff.), and E. Heitz, *Die Philosophenschulen Athens* (Deutsche Revue, 1884, pp. 326 ff.).

32 Cf. G. Kaufmann, *Geschichte der deutschen Universitäten* I. pp. 98 ff. (Stuttg. 1888).

33 *Schelling* has erected the finest monument to the ideal conception of science in the activity of German universities, in his *Vorlesungen über die Methode des akademischen Studiums* (2. und 3. Vorlesung. Ges. Werke, I. Abth., Vol. 6, pp. 223 ff.).

34 The best evidence for this statement is afforded by just the passionate attacks which Schopenhauer directed against the relation between philosophy and the universities.

35 The next three paragraphs are once again set in a smaller font. – Ed.

36 E.g., in the beginning of the *Metaphysics*.

37 More in detail on these below.

38 Th. Stanley, *The History of Philosophy*. Lond. 1685.

39 J. J. Brucker, *Historia Critica Philosophiae*. 5 vols. Leips. 1742 ff. *Institutiones Historiae Philosophiae*. Leips. 1747.

40 J. G. Buhle, *Lehrbuch der Geschichte der Philosophie*. 8 vols. Göttingen, 1796 ff.

41 G. G. Fülleborn, *Beiträge zur Geschichte der Philosophie*. 12 Studien. Züllichau, 1791 ff.
42 D. Tiedemann, *Geist der Speculativen Philosophie*. 7 vols. Marburg, 1791 ff.
43 De Gérando, *Histoire Comparée des Systemes de Philosophie*. 2d ed. in 4 vols. Paris, 1822 f.
44 W. G. Tennemann, *Geschichte der Philosophie*. 11 vols. Leips. 1798 ff. *Grundriss der Geschichte der Philosophie für den akademischen Unterricht*. Leips. 1812. [Eng. trans. 1833 and 1852.]
45 J. Fr. Fries, *Geschichte der Philosophie*. 2 vols. Halle, 1837 ff.
46 Fr. Schleiermacher, *Geschichte der Philosophie*, from his literary remains in the Coll. Works. III. Abth., 4. Bd., 1 Th. Berlin, 1839.
47 Cf. the introductions of the *Phänomenologie des Geistes*, of the lectures on the *Philosophy of History*, and those on the *History of Philosophy*. Ges. Werke, Bd. II. pp. 62 ff.; IX. pp. 11 ff.; XIII. pp. 11–134. In Hegel's works the *Geschichte der Philosophie*, edited from his lectures by Michelet, occupies Vols. XIII.- XV. Berlin, 1833–36. [*Lectures on the History of Philosophy*, by G. W. Hegel. Trans. by E. S. Haldane in 3 vols. Vol. I. Lond. 1892.] For his standpoint, cf. G.O. Marbach, *Lehrbuch der Geschichte [der] Philosophie* (2. Abth. Leips. 1838 ff.), O. Hermann, *Geschichte der Philosophie in pragmatischer Behandlung* (Leips. 1867), and in part also the survey of the entire history of philosophy which J. Braniss has published as the first (only) volume of a *Geschichte der Philosophie seit Kant* (Breslau, 1842). In France this line is represented by V. Cousin, *Introduction a l'Histoire de la Philosophie* (Paris, 1828; 7th ed. 1872) ; *Histoire Générale de la Philosophie* (12th ed., Paris, 1884).
48 More precisely, this inadequacy, which cannot here be more exactly developed, and which can be fully brought out only in a system of epistemology, consists m the circumstance that that which is given in experience never meets completely the conceptional demands which, in elaborating the same according to the inner nature of the reason, we set up, at first naïvely and immediately, and later with reflective consciousness. This *antinomism* (or failure to meet the laws of thought) can be escaped by ordinary life; or even by experiential science, by working with auxiliary conceptions, which indeed remain problematical in themselves, but which, within certain bounds, suffice for an elaboration of the material of experience that meets our practical needs. But it is just in these auxiliary conceptions that the problems of philosophy inhere.
49 In this way the results of Kant's investigations on "The Antinomy of Pure Reason" (*Critique of Pure Reason*, Transcendental Dialectic, second sec.) might be historically and systematically extended; cf. W. Windelband, *Geschichte der neueren Philosophie*, II. 95 f.
50 This paragraph is in smaller font. – Ed.
51 A. Comte, *Cours de Philosophie Positive* I. 9, with which Vols. V and VI are to be compared as the carrying out of the scheme. Similar thoughts are also found in D' Alembert's *Discours Preliminaire* in the *Encyclopédie*.
52 The following two paragraphs are again in smaller font. – Ed.
53 Kuno Fischer, *Geschichte der neueren Philosophie*, I. 1, Einleitung I.–V.
54 *Urtheile durch ihre Beurtheilungen*
55 This and the next two paragraphs are once again set in a smaller font. – Ed.
56 *Begriffsdichtung*
57 From here until the end of section 2 once again in smaller font. – Ed.
58 The collections of fragments of particular authors are mentioned under the notices of the individual philosophers. It would be desirable if they were all as excellent as Usener's *Epicurea*. Of the fragments of the Pre-Socratics W.F.A. Mullach has published a careful collection, which, however, is no longer adequate in the present condition of research *(Fragmenta Philosophorum Graecorum)*.
59 Plut. *Moralia*,. ed. Dübner, Paris, 1841; Diels, *Dox*., pp. 272 ff.; [Plutarch's *Morals, Miscellanies, and Essays*, ed. by Goodwin, Boston, 1870 ; trans. also in the Bohn Lib.].
60 Ed. Bekker, Berlin, 1847.
61 G. Kaibel, Leips. 1888–90.
62 Ed. Cobet, Paris, 1850.
63 A. Weber, *History of Philosophy*, is to be recommended as a good textbook (5th French ed., Paris, 1891). [Eng. tr. by Thilly, N. Y. 1896.]
64 This applies in every domain of history, in the history of politics and of literature, as well as in that of philosophy.

65 As an example of this it may be noticed that the deserving author of an excellent *History of the Principles of Mechanics*, Ed. Dühring, has developed in his *Kritische Geschichte der Philosophie* (3d ed., Berlin, 1878) all the caprice of a one-sided judgment. The like is true of the confessional criticism passed by A. Stöckl, *Lehrbuch der Geschichte der Philosophie* (2 vols., 3d ed., Mainz, 1889).

66 It is impossible to protest enough against the youthful conceit with which it was for a time the fashion in Germany to look down with ridicule or insult from the "achievements of the present" upon the great men of Greek and German philosophy; this was mainly the haughtiness of an ignorance which had no suspicion that it was ultimately living only by the thoughts of those whom it was abusing and despising.

67 *Moral*.

Chapter 21

"Philosophy of Culture and Transcendental Idealism" (1910)[1]

TRANSLATED BY ALAN DUNCAN

A philosophy of culture can be spoken of in many different senses. Many may expect of it perhaps the positing of an ideal for future culture or the foundation of a universally valid norm for the judgment of actual cultural states of affairs[2]: all, namely, who have been persuaded that the task of a philosopher is not to seek or to understand, but rather to create and to command, values may well tend to demand a sketch[3] for a culture to be *demanded* or *given as a task*[4].

In contrast to this, a philosophy of culture can be restricted to the understanding of a historically *found* or *given* culture. Of course, this will only be a philosophy if the genetic investigations of psychological analysis, sociological comparison and historical development serve only as material for the disclosure of the fundamental structure that all cultural activities have in the timeless, superempirical essence of reason itself.

But numerous mediations are at work between these two types of philosophy of culture. The future image of culture as given as a task, of course, depends upon the conception of the given culture in a more or less conscious way: indeed, this determination is involuntarily all the more decisive, the greater the contrast into which the ideal of past and present are to come; and finally the question must always be put how the realization of that ideal can be developed under the given circumstances. On the other hand, in gaining the philosophical understanding of one's given culture, the perspective toward its future development inevitably arises, for the very reason that the present culture always points beyond itself as something that is in the midst of historical movement.

In all such mediations, though, the antithesis of what is given as a task and what is given[5] asserts itself, adhering to the principal differences of the method in which one does the philosophy of history[6]. Who treats historical development according to the manner of mathematical and conceptual development, in which, after the knowledge of the series' law, the subsequent to each individual member must be inferable, for him, after the law of progress, the end must principally also be given and, in the case of correct insight, must count as predictable. Who, on the other hand, finds the specific essence of historical development precisely in the progressing formation of a conceptually non-determinable, temporally factual occurrence, for him only the tasks of future culture are to be extrapolated from the understanding of things past and present, and in this case the measure of trust in their future realization can no longer be a matter of knowledge, but only of conviction and of worldview.

It would not be difficult to construct the basic types of philosophy of culture possible according to these basic features and combinations thereof, and then to characterize their main representatives, from Rousseau and Condorcet up to the present day. But it seems more important for me to call attention to what they have in common, what they must all fulfill, if they are really to be a *philosophy* of culture, a conceptual science. Whether it be a given culture, or one given as a task, its principles must be revealed in the innermost essence of all active rational activity. For philosophical understanding only begins after the psychological or historical determination of the factual state of affairs, and answers the *quaestio juris* according to no other aspects than those of immanent substantial necessity. But this is, and remains, in my opinion, Kant's critical method, and the fundamental conception that it yields for the understanding of all cultural functions is transcendental idealism.

In the portrayal of the history of recent philosophy I have rendered for the *Culture of the Present Day*,[7] the system of critical philosophy is characterized as an all-encompassing philosophy of culture: I would especially emphasize that it is not Kant's problem in its historical setting that is to be characterized, but his doctrines' meaning with regard to their significance for contemporary intellectual life. Now, it is completely beyond doubt that everywhere in Kant's critical analyses he starts with the question of the justification for the possibility of synthetic *a priori* judgments in the individual consciousness growing out of experience, i.e., such rational functions as are supposed to be universally and necessarily valid for all experience: therein consists what was later called the subjective character of his idealism. But it is also indubitable that, as result of the critique, everywhere it resulted from this the laying bare of the rational grounds for the great structures of culture, from the *Critique of Pure Reason* the fundamental structure of science as Kant found and conceived it, from the *Critique of Practical Reason* and the *Metaphysic of Morals* built upon it the realm of rational ends in morality and right, from the *Critique of Judgment* the essence of art and of aesthetic shaping of life: and only after all this could it be asked, in the spirit of the critical method, how much of those cultural values could be sustained from out of pure reason in the religious form of social life.

This path of Kant's from the problem-setting to the result has been philosophy's progress from the eighteenth to the nineteenth century, from the Enlightenment to Romanticism. In material terms, it was the progress from the natural to the historical human being; methodologically, the exchange of psychology for history as the organon of critique. It was the same path that the development of post-Kantian philosophy took from Fries to Hegel.[8]

But the important question here is: what was the crucial point in this transition? It was Kant's immortal achievement – the discovery of synthetic consciousness. Since the *Critique of Pure Reason*, the days are over once and for all when a mature philosophical consciousness might think of the world as "given" and mirrored in it, as it would seem to the naïve consciousness. In everything we regard as given our reason is already at work: and the justification of our knowledge of things rests only on our first creating them for ourselves. That we must first make the world that we are to experience our own is rooted in the fact that we can only ever experience a selection of it, and the latter only in ordered nexus, and that the principles both for the selection and for the order can only be sought in the structure of our consciousness itself. The world that we experience is our deed. All this up until now is no lofty nor novel bit of wisdom. That from the great, wide world only a small portion enters into empirical consciousness, and that this forms itself in a special way in each individual according to the previous history of his experiencing, has always been the topic of all sorts of considerations, and it was not necessary for Kant to come along and discover this. But indeed, the far-reaching significance of his critical principle rests upon what is basically an astonishingly simple conclusion drawn from this psychological factuality. If there are to be universally valid and necessary judgments at all, as they in fact make up "experience," then they are only possible because amid the empirical associations and apperceptions a transcendental synthesis is at work, a common nexus of the elements rooted in the things themselves and independent of the movements of empirical consciousness. These nexuses of mutual association and belongingness are the forms of "transcendental apperception," and the doctrine that there are no other objects than those yielded by this universally valid synthesis is transcendental idealism.

It is absolutely necessary, not only for the purpose of this enquiry, but for the continued existence and progress of transcendental idealism, on the one hand to stress repeatedly that the Kantian notion of "consciousness as such" is not to be interpreted in the psychological nor in the metaphysical sense, but refers solely to the *factual* preconditions of universally valid judgments, and on the other, to achieve complete and unambiguous clarity about the relation of transcendental apperception to the rational activities of *human* reason. In Kant we find these left in uncertainty, at least with respect to the wording, and thus we come to the most difficult vital question of critical philosophy. For it is subject to far divergent interpretations, as is well known, whether and to what extent those *a priori* forms of reason can be considered as determined by the essence of the human being. In theoretical philosophy Kant upheld the doctrine set forth in the Inaugural Dissertation, that of space and time as the specifically human forms of intuition until the very end, in the literal wording: and just as he had originally deduced their *a priori* validity for all "our" experience precisely from this psychologistically, so too in the *Critique of Pure Reason* did he establish the restriction of the categories to "appearances" solely in that for human beings the manifold that is subject to the categorial synthesis is only given intuitively in space and time: in themselves, the categories should also be valid for other kinds of intuitions, just as the forms of analytic thought ought likewise to be recognized and accepted from the start as rationally valid for any and every content and for all thinking whatsoever. Without attempting to answer the question whether the relation of space and time to "our human intuition" is sustainable in this way, whether Kant himself ultimately would have wanted to ground mathematical truths, which in fact ought to rest on it, on this anthropological basis: it is certain in any case that the deduction of the "Principles" can only gain the systematic structure of *science* – the understanding of this fundamental form of theoretical culture – through the application and simultaneous restriction of the categories to the manifold given to human intuition in space and time.

The case is similar in practical philosophy: only Kant's account goes in the other direction here[9]. While in the analysis of knowledge he ascends from the anthropological, from receptivity and spontaneity, to the universal rational, the categories, he begins (albeit after the analytical preparation in the "*Groundwork*") in the *Critique of Practical Reason* with the law of the pure will, which is valid for "all rational beings," yet takes on the character of this law *qua* categorical imperative only through the relation to dual being of the human as the sensual-supersensual and even the development of the individual duties in the *Metaphysic of Morals* only through the relation of that fundamental imperative to the empirical circumstances of individual or social human life. So here, too, is the structure of the large cultural formations, of morality and law, conceived from the protrusion of a comprehensive, universal world of reason into the human life of reason.

This basic state of affairs, whose correctness is, as far as I can see, principally incontrovertible, yields a clearly defined methodological principle for transcendental philosophy: it amounts, after the discovery of the universally valid preconditions for rational activities, in which everything that we call culture is ultimately rooted, to ascertaining with a substantial analysis how much of this is determined by specifically human, in the broadest sense empirical conditions, and thus extracting the rest, which is rooted in universal and comprehensive rational necessities. This absolute *a priori* is that which is in the strictest sense valid in itself in the Lotzean sense of the *ontos on*: as soon as it enters into empirical consciousness, it is not only colored over by becoming the norm for a function that would cognize, act and create, but also receives the specification that depends upon the determination of empirical consciousness, and this specification also descends in continuous succession from the generic to the spatially and temporally individualized formation. It is in this latter form that we as individuals experience everything that enters into our finite consciousness from world reason, and from this world reason we must gradually regain the universally valid through a process of ascending exclusion[10].

Let me explain these relations with a much debated question in the area of logic. It makes sense to me that for an absolute, only true and (in Spinoza's sense) adequate thought, the negation (in the sense of the quality of judgment) has no meaning; we seek in vain for negation among the constitutive categories, the real relations of objects. But as soon as we enter into the sphere of thought that desires to know, and hence is capable of error, negation and its relation to affirmation gain their essential meaning, and much logical regularity proves to be conditioned by them in this familiar way. Only this entire field applies to every finite consciousness in its movement, and still shows no dependency upon the peculiarities of human thought. We only arrive at this when it comes to certain lingual forms of negation, the expression of distinction (A is not B), and the judgment of exclusion (no S is P) or the so-called negative term (non-A), and so forth. Without the principal distinction of these spheres of meaning the theory of negation falls into the hopelessly entangled net of incomprehensibilities.

With these indications about the methodological execution of the principle of transcendental philosophy alone I have already partially anticipated the revelation of the intimate affinity that exists between it and the problem of a philosophy of culture. For we mean by culture ultimately nothing else than the entirety of what human consciousness by virtue of its rational determinedness makes of the given: and the crucial point of transcendental philosophy is Kant's insight that a synthesis according to the laws of "consciousness itself," according to encompassing, factually valid forms of reason, is already present in what we are accustomed to take as given, as soon as it presents itself as universally valid experience. Kant came to this insight in the critique of science, which, considering his metaphysical desire[11], was a chief priority; on it he built the rejection of dogmatic metaphysics and the foundation of the metaphysics of appearances in the form of "pure natural science": and the principle with which he showed which knowledge is impossible and which is possible, proves to be the perennial foundation of all epistemology, also allowing the individual sciences to distinguish themselves from one another methodologically, as they generate their objects according to their own principles of selection and of order.

This activity of reason, though, which, as science, means a new creation of the world from the law of the intellect, is of the exact same structure as all practical and aesthetic behavior of the cultural human being. Therefore, the substantial unity of transcendental idealism as a philosophy of culture lies here: and only in this sense can a primacy of practical reason be spoken of, as the generation of objects from the law of consciousness is in no other region as much a matter of course and as familiar to everyday consciousness as in this one. For that the moral behavior is directed at reworking the world, given as nature (in the broadest sense of the term, such that it also includes the human life of drives and emotions), by selection and order into a new and higher formation according to the commandment of the will of reason, this is so self-evident that it requires no further explanation: and likewise the system of right[12] creates from rational consciousness a new order of human vital relations, whose ultimate meaning arises in principle from the categorical imperative, in order to guarantee the freedom of the person in the sphere of its social activity. But no less do the basic forms of isolation and synthetic recreation obtain in the entire realm of aesthetic life. All artistic production creates its objects from the activity of consciousness, which Kant has identified as the original and exemplary faculty of imagination of the genius, which thereby becomes capable of general communication; even where the impressionistic artist believes to represent something that is randomly given, he nevertheless has been creatively active in demarcating matter and in the manner in which he has "seen" it. All appreciation of the artwork, however, is nothing but a reliving of that isolating and novel composing, which the artist has enacted originally. Even the appreciation of natural beauty demonstrates in the selection of the standpoint, in the search for the effective lines and relations of all individual moments to one another the synthetic creation of the object. What finally concerns religion, what is valid for science, for morality and right, is valid for it in a modified manner. For religion has no proper realm of rational values: what it contains of them belongs to one of the realms of the true, the good or the beautiful.[13] Religion has its empirical character as a cultural form in the sociological expansion of psychic life beyond the nexus of the empirical subjects towards mythical powers that are experienced in the most different manners, starting from primitive animism up to theological supranaturalism or mystical ineffability. Its special functions, insofar as they derive their rational grounds from the logical, ethical or aesthetic material, partake in their transcendental essence, and the only rational ground that religion can claim its own, consists in the postulate to experience the totality of all rational values in an absolute unity that cannot be encompassed by any form of our consciousness.

These are the substantial reasons that compelled Kant, after the formal schematism of his problem constellations, after having discovered the principle of synthesis as the lawful ground of all science, to apply this principle to all other formations of culture: thus the inner necessity of the subject matter occasioned it that the criticism that was developed according to his method from the problem of science, became, without wanting this, in his achievement a philosophy of culture – *the* philosophy of culture. Culture has arrived at its self-knowledge in the consciousness of creative synthesis: for, according to its innermost essence, it is nothing other than that.

It will always remain peculiar that such a glowing insight, encompassing from the deepest depths the entire wide scope of cultural life, has broken through in such a simple and modest man as the sage of Königsberg. One may have inquired, from time to time, in modern fashion, which personal experience may have made Kant the philosopher of such forcefully peculiar character, the all-crushing, all-penetrating, all-resurrecting thinker: I believe one need not search all too far. If ever a philosopher experienced this creative power of reason in his own innerness powerfully concentrated on itself, then it is Kant. In his labyrinthine development, he went through all philosophical standpoints, without much learned advice or inspiration, from out of his own pondering, and with an original geniality, he built up systems, tore them down and erected them anew, and it was not without reason that he repeatedly measured the formation of philosophical terms against that of mathematical terms, the latter being free to generate its objects, the quantities, purely out of productive phantasy. If he finally concluded that all other science also only knows the world insofar as it creates its own objects out of it according to the law of reason, it was the greatest personal experience in the life of a thinker to listen to him form the objects out of his own depth, not as the professor Immanuel Kant, but rather as the human being conscious of his rational determination, but at last as "a thinking being as such."

The light that thus dawned on the innermost workshop of philosophizing lit the entirety of human cultural life with surprising clarity: and it thus became the source of the modern worldview – the world view of spirit. It had been the boundary of the consciousness of the Ancients to know itself always as merely receptive, as a mirror, to which the highest and the least object, the idea and the sensation, must first be given. And now, from out the long experience of the life of knowledge, in that thinker, so humble for his person, the modern mind dared that proud word: it is the understanding that prescribes laws to nature.

This self-consciousness of creative synthesis must be the central point for the formation of the worldview that our contemporary culture, so obviously multifarious and so at odds with itself, seeks and needs if it is to find a way to great and synthetic accomplishments of its intellectual work, to inner communities of a lasting and fruitful kind. However, such a worldview can never again be gathered together out of the individual's whole mass of knowledge, interests, activities, institutions, achievements and aspirations. For this culture has become too broad and multifarious. Today it encompasses the entire planet; it is a holistic culture, and is such with consciousness, or it would become such. With the rapid progress of technological civilization, the nineteenth century procured the external conditions for the realization of the eighteenth century's ideal of humanity. This ideal, however, is no longer sought in the blurry unity of enlightened cosmopolitanism, but in the strongest differentiation of particular national cultures: and if we hope that this agonistic play of national powers triggered by that same century will exchange the raw forms of rivalry ever more surely, ever more completely, for higher forms, these differentiated forms of culture of the peoples shall yet be retained just as those of the individuals, with whom they have the same duty, and therein the same right. But also the culture of every individual people bears within it a plenitude of activities and states of outer and inner life forms. Who would presume today to command such an overview of them as to weave them all together into a whole in one unified consciousness? This whole no longer exists as a real unity. Shattered into the individual educational and career levels, it only presents a continuum of functional contexts by virtue of the numerous points at which these continuously converge. To spell out a substantial totality out of all these life-contents, though, would be a vain endeavor. The world of our knowledge alone already no longer fits into one head, and the philosophy of bread crumbs and scattered reading that would reap the most universal from all branches of knowledge is a business as fruitless as it is boring. And even if one would once have hoped to have the results of all knowing joined together with the needs of the heart to a well-tempered whole, today this fusion of worldviews would only be able to deliver vague and smudgy contours.

In this respect we have learned to humble ourselves. And furthermore, as all cultural work is the conscious composition of life, we also have need at last for some consistently shared belief. Hence, this belief need not be conscious concretely and at every juncture. After all, it is thus with every individual life activity: with its special functions it is bound and dedicated to the materials, it is impossible and unnecessary to relate each individual detail with complete consciousness to the unity of one's personal life's work at every moment; but this relation must yet be there behind it, if there is to be any value in it, this unity must exist. And all the infinitely different cultural functions are realized in the very same manner, each in the connectedness to its individual content, and their bearers often have only this specific knowledge of them; yet they have their final value only after their merging into one unified system that must have its cohesion in a cultural consciousness, a worldview.

Such a conscious unity can therefore be sought only in grasping the essence of the function, which makes up what is common in all special, however substantially oriented cultural activities; and this can be nothing other than the self-consciousness of reason, which itself creates its objects and, in these, the realm of its own validity. Precisely this is the fundamental doctrine of transcendental idealism.

This philosophy of culture is an immanent worldview, insofar as it essentially humbles itself to what we experience as our own deed. For it, each of the cultural structures, science, order of life, art, counts as a rationally determined segment, a selection and new formation from infinite reality itself; in this respect each represents a sort of "appearance" that in this selection and in this composition only exists for rational consciousness, which has created its own "object" within it, and the last connection of all these "appearances" remains the unfathomable. But this last connection is really nothing other than the whole of what makes up the rational worlds of knowledge, of the order of life, of artistic formation accessible to our activity in individual partial formations. There is only ineffably more, there is vivaciously developed unity there where we have separate pieces, only occasionally referring to one another. But we still have the consolation that every one of these pieces formed anew within us is truly ordered and integrated into that all-powerful context. In this sense transcendental idealism has no more need of "another world", as Kant originally would have deemed necessary in the concept of the "thing in itself"; after all, he himself made us at home in this world afterwards through practical reason, and thus tore down the boundary.

But one thing must be stressed again and again against intentional and unintentional misunderstandings of this doctrine: that the individual must never think of itself as the creative power in the creation of objects; we are involved, inasmuch as genuine cultural values are concerned, never as individuals, nor even as instances of our genus, but act rather as domiciles and hosts of transcendent functions of reason, and therefore functions factually grounded in the essence of things themselves. Only these functions of reason determine the "objects" that are necessarily and universally valid. This participation in a larger world of rational values that nevertheless make up the sense of all the orders upon which our little worlds of knowledge, will and formation are built up, this insertion of our conscious life of culture into rational orders[14] that far transcend us and our entire empirical existence – this is the inconceivable mystery of all spiritual activity. But the entire process of human culture, the strengthening and expansion to which its valuable achievements are subject in history, repeatedly confirms to us this upward growth of our life into rational contexts that mean more than ourselves.

Notes

1   Originally published as "Kulturphilosophie und transzendentaler Idealismus," in: *Präludien*, Vol. II, pp. 279–294. Translated into English for the first time by Alan Duncan.
2   *Kulturzustände*
3   *Entwurf*
4   *aufgegeben*
5   *des Aufgegebenen und des Gegebenen*
6   *die geschichtsphilosophische Methode*
7   *Kultur der Gegenwart*, vol. V, pp. 474 ff., 2nd ed., pp. 521 ff. [This book series appeared between 1905 and 1926, edited by the journalist Paul Hinneberg, and was dedicated to giving a systematic overview of all areas of culture and their scientific treatment. The series was projected to comprise approximately 60 volumes. It was discontinued before its completion due to the Great War and inflation afterwards. – Ed.]
8   See my speech at the Heidelberg Academy [of Science] on the renewal of Hegelianism in the first volume of this collection pp. 273 ff. ["The Renewal of Hegelianism," delivered on April 25, 1910. – Ed.]

9 For more on this, see the treatise by Arnold Ruge, *Die Deduktion der praktischen und der moralischen Freiheit*, Heidelberg 1910.
10 *durch aufsteigenden Ausschluss*
11 *Bedürfnis*
12 *Recht*
13 Cf. the article following in this collection, "The Holy. [Sketch for a Philosophy of Religion]" [pp. 295–332 in Vol. II of *Praeludien*. – Ed.].
14 *Vernunftzusammenhänge*

Introduction

Heinrich Rickert (1863–1936)

BY ANDREA STAITI

Heinrich Rickert was born in Gdańsk (then Danzig, Prussia) on May 25, 1863. His father, Heinrich Rickert Sr. (1833–1902), was a politician and editor in Berlin.

Between 1884 and 1885, Rickert was enrolled at the University of Berlin, where he attended lectures from the philosopher Friedrich Paulsen (1846–1908). In 1885, he moved to Strasbourg (then Straßburg, part of the Prussian *Reich*), where he attended the Neo-Kantian philosopher Wilhelm Windelband's lectures. Windelband (1848–1915) was a major source of inspiration for Rickert's work and he completed a dissertation on *The Theory of Definition* (Rickert 1915) under Windelband's supervision in 1888. In the same year he married Sophie Keibel, a sculptor from Berlin. They had four children.

In 1889, Rickert moved to Freiburg for health-related reasons. Rickert's health was always precarious. After undergoing intestinal surgery in 1896, he suffered lifelong intercostal neuralgia and he developed agoraphobia. In spite of his health problems, Rickert was able to complete his Habilitation under Alois Riehl (1844–1924) in Freiburg, where he was appointed *Professor Extraordinarius* in 1894 and *Professor Ordinarius* in 1896. The dissertation he produced for the Habilitation, *The Object of Knowledge*, is one of his most important works and a milestone in early twentieth-century Neo-Kantianism.

Rickert remained in Freiburg until 1915, when he accepted an offer from the University of Heidelberg to replace his recently deceased mentor Windelband, who had moved there from Strasbourg in 1903. He taught in Heidelberg until 1932, when he retired. He died in Heidelberg on July 25, 1936, and he was buried in Gdańsk.

Rickert had a long and successful academic career. He received several awards and honorary degrees. He taught and in some cases supervised important German thinkers of the next generation, such as Martin Heidegger (1889–1976), Emil Lask (1875–1915) and Walter Benjamin (1892–1940). He had close intellectual exchanges with leading figures of his time, including Wilhelm Dilthey (1833–1911), Georg Simmel (1858–1918), Edmund Husserl (1859–1938), Max Weber (1864–1920), and Karl Jaspers (1883–1969). Although very few of his writings are available in English, in recent years there has been a growing interest in Rickert's work, both to the extent that it influenced other philosophers and as a significant contribution to the discipline in its own right.

Rickert was a very prolific writer and he contributed to virtually every area of philosophy, although he is primarily remembered for his work in epistemology and for his ambitious project to provide the historical sciences with a rigorous philosophical foundation. Besides philosophy, Rickert published critical studies in literature (such as a long interpretation of Goethe's *Faust*.)[1]

Rickert's way of philosophizing is extremely systematic and it revolves around the key notion of 'value.' For Rickert, knowledge is essentially a response to theoretical values (such as 'truth') that exert their normative force on the thinking subject. As he insisted throughout his career (and particularly in the essay *Knowing and Cognizing* included as Chapter 23 in this volume), true knowledge about an object never amounts to a mere depiction or reproduction of that object as it is immediately available in intuition. To know is to produce judgments, in which the object to be known is analyzed into its constitutive parts and re-structured according to a conceptual perspective. This conceptual perspective is never simply extracted from what is given. It is chosen and constructed by the knowing subject. This does not mean that all conceptual perspectives are of equal significance. To *know* is to restructure the immediate contents of our consciousness in obedience to the compelling force of theoretical values, for which the epistemological subject has to be receptive.

If true knowledge is not faithful depiction of immediately given reality but a conceptual restructuring of it, then philosophy can be open to a *plurality* of meaningful ways to produce knowledge. There is no one single way of knowing that simply mirrors reality because knowledge is never a kind of mirroring. In particular, the insight into the restructuring character of knowledge allows Rickert to criticize positivism and scientism, that is, those philosophical positions that only recognize natural science as a source of legitimate knowledge about the world.

This conviction undergirds Rickert's effort to rehabilitate the *sui generis* scientificity of the human sciences, such as history and literary studies. A sample of Rickert's approach to this issue is the central chapter from his *magnum opus Die Grenzen der naturwissenschaftlichen Begriffsbildung*, [*The Limits of Concept Formation in Natural Science*] and also included in this volume (as Chapter 22). Here Rickert wants to show that the way in which the natural sciences build their concepts leaves out of consideration, for essential reasons, the individuality and unrepeatable uniqueness of historical events. Therefore, a different and complementary way of building concepts must be recognized and granted equal scientific dignity. This is the way of forming concepts that is characteristic of the human or, in Rickert's language, historical sciences whose ultimate goal is to deliver knowledge of individuals. Values are a key ingredient in historical conceptualization, in that only individuals (people, events, artworks, etc.) bearing an ostensible relation to historically recognized cultural values (ethical, political, aesthetic, etc.) are *relevant* subject matters for the human sciences.

Further Reading

Beiser, Frederick C., *The German Historicist Tradition*. Oxford/New York: Oxford University Press, ch. 10, "Heinrich Rickert and the Philosophy of Value," 2011, pp. 393–441.

Krijnen, Christian, *Nachmetaphysischer Sinn. Eine problemgeschichtliche und systematische Studie zu den Prinzipien der Wertphilosophie Heinrich Rickerts*. Würzburg: K&N, 2001.

Kuninsky, Milowit, and T. Kadenacy, "The Methodological Status of Cultural Sciences According to Heinrich Rickert and Max Weber," in: *Reports on Philosophy*, 3, 1979, pp. 71–85.

Staiti, Andrea, "Heinrich Rickert", *The Stanford Encyclopedia of Philosophy* (Winter 2013 Edition), Edward N. Zalta (ed.), available online at http://plato.stanford.edu/archives/win2013/entries/heinrich-rickert/ (accessed 16 March 2015) (See also the extensive bibliography in this entry.)

——, *Husserl's Transcendental Phenomenology: Nature, Spirit, and Life*. Cambridge University Press, 2014 (for an account of Rickert's influence upon Husserl and the Phenomenological Movement).

"Concept Formation in History" from *The Limits of Concept Formation in Natural Science* (1902) by Andrea Staiti

What does Rickert mean by "concept formation"? And what does he mean by "history"? As he points out in the introductory section of this chapter, for Rickert a concept is nothing but the "yield" or final product of a theoretical endeavor. When we think hard about something, devise a set of experiments in a science lab or try to decipher old historical documents, what we want to achieve is a *grasp* of the subject matter under scrutiny that makes it intelligible in ideal terms. Philosophers are often inclined to think about concepts as atoms of sense somehow analogous to word-meanings or as murky mental entities that we project onto the world. This is not what Rickert has in mind. To approach Rickert's meaning of "concept," think about the moment when Newton formulated the law of universal gravitation. Rickert would say that this was the moment when he *formed the concept* he had been after from the outset. "The law of universal gravitation" is thus a concept, that is, following the German etymology of *Begriff*, a definitive *grasp* of a subject matter that was previously incoherent or insufficiently understood. Consider the overwhelming mass of natural phenomena related in one way or the other to motion and involving the attraction of bodies that we can observe in our perceptual experience. It was only when Newton finally formed the concept "law of universal gravitation" that the essential trait of all such phenomena was grasped and the overwhelming amount of data was theoretically mastered. Similarly, consider the formidable amount of historical events, personalities, ideas, pamphlets and flamboyant clothing pertaining to what we know as "the French Revolution." It was not until someone formed the concept "French Revolution" that these otherwise largely incoherent data became intelligible from a unitary standpoint.

Both the concept "law of universal gravitation" and the concept "French Revolution" amount to a successful grasp of a large number of intuitively available data. In spite of their similarity in this respect, however, the two concepts differ significantly. The law of universal gravitation is a natural-scientific concept, whereas the French Revolution is a historical concept. Their difference has to do with the *logic* according to which they were formed. As Rickert puts it in a later passage from this selection: "The logical distinctiveness of an empirical science is to be understood in terms of the relationship the content of its concepts bears to empirical reality in its unique and distinctive form." In this sense, we can answer the second question asked at the beginning. *History* for Rickert is a *logical* notion. It is the title for a certain way of forming concepts, which defines an entire province of human knowledge and stands in sharp contrast to *nature* as the province of knowledge characterized by the logically opposite way of forming concepts.

In keeping with Kant's definition in the *Prolegomena*, Rickert understands nature as "the *existence* of things, insofar as that existence is determined according to universal laws."[2] Note that this definition already entails an indication for a fruitful investigation of nature. Natural science will have to seek the universal laws characterizing the existence of things *as* nature. This direction of inquiry towards the universal determines the *logic* of natural science, which Rickert labels "generalizing method." The natural sciences form their concepts by moving *away from* what is merely individual and towards the general. In order to do so, they necessarily disregard the uniqueness of individual occurrences and pay attention exclusively to generally recurring patterns. Newton was not at all concerned with the unique, individual apple that, as the story goes, happened to fall on his head. He regarded that apple exclusively as an instance of a general regularity of nature. This characteristic of natural science makes it impossible for it to deal with individual events. The individual thus marks precisely the limit of natural scientific concept formation, to which the title of Rickert's book alludes. The historical sciences are therefore called to fill in this gap left by natural scientific inquiry. Their *logic* is not generalizing but rather individualizing, that is, the way they form their concepts is geared toward theoretical grasp of unrepeatable and unique events. They do not move away from the individual, but rather precisely toward it. Elsewhere Rickert complains that Western science has been working under the spell of an Aristotelian dogma, namely that the individual is unknowable. This however, is simply not the case. While obviously in order to *know* individuals we still have to use general terms to build our concepts, this does not entail that the use of general terms must necessarily prevent us from knowing individual objects. Upon closer inspection, this is precisely what historians, sociologists, and other people working in the human sciences do all the time. They use general terms such as "French" and "revolution" to try and make unique, unrepeatable events more intelligible.

In a passage not included in this selection, Rickert summarizes his view as follows: "*Empirical reality becomes nature when we conceive it with reference to the general. It becomes history when we conceive it with reference to the distinctive and the individual.*"[3]

The overwhelming bulk of this chapter is devoted to clarifying the notion of historical individual. In fact, while every single bit of empirical reality is individual, in the sense that it is unique and unrepeatable, not every individual is relevant to historical inquiry. As the comparison between the lump of coal and the famous diamond Koh-i-noor attempts to show, only individual entities related to culturally acknowledged values are up for historical investigation. Value-related individual realities make up the domain of *culture*, which Rickert contrasts to the value-free domain of nature. The domain of culture is the ontological sphere in which the individualizing concept formation of history can be meaningfully practiced. We could invest all of our intellectual energies in trying to develop concepts that describe the unique individuality of a stone randomly found on the street. These energies, however, would be wasted and produce completely irrelevant information. If the stone, however, bore mysterious inscriptions made by an archaic civilization, then its status would change completely. It would display an objective relatedness to cultural values from past ages and it would be worth investigating in its unique individuality. The insistence on value-relatedness is important to understand those sections in this chapter where Rickert speaks critically of the phrase *Geisteswissenschaften* (literally, "sciences of the mind"). This label was in vogue in Rickert's time and it had been made prominent by Wilhelm Dilthey, with whom Rickert had a lifelong controversy. Rickert is willing to grant that entities endowed with mental life are central to history. After all trees and rocks do not create history. However, it is not the concept of mental life but the concept of culture as value-related reality (paired with individualizing concept formation) that gives systematic unity to the human sciences.

"Knowing and Cognizing" (1934) by Andrea Staiti

This short but dense piece is the last journal article Rickert published during his lifetime. Here he reiterates a line of criticism that can be found ubiquitously (albeit in less developed form) in his corpus. He labels the contentious position "theoretical intuitionism," that is, an emphasis on intuition as the only legitimate source of knowledge. His goal is to show that true cognition cannot do without concepts and thus inevitably entails more than mere intuition. While the only alleged proponent of theoretical intuitionism mentioned in the text is Rickert's former doctoral student Martin Heidegger, Rickert considered this view widespread in his time. He even considered it common to otherwise very different schools of thoughts, including life-philosophy (Bergson, Dilthey, Simmel), biological vitalism (Driesch, Spengler) and most of all phenomenology (Husserl, Scheler, Heidegger.) This had been the theme of a short book he published over ten years earlier,[4] whose polemical content he presumably regarded as so important to deserve renewed attention in the mid 1930s.

His argumentative strategy is to show that theoretical intuitionism rests upon a conception of cognition as a copy or depiction of reality. He then goes on to show that cognition is never a depiction of reality, thus undermining the logical premise of theoretical intuitionism.

The critique of theoretical intuitionism serves here to introduce a variety of themes that characterize Rickert's mature philosophy, which are given full treatment in his last book, *Grundprobleme der Philosophie* (1934). In particular, Rickert presents a précis of his ontology, which is characterized by a principle of pluralism which refuses to reduce the manifold sense of 'being' to a notion of 'being overall' as Heidegger does in *Being and Time* (1927).

The line of argument in *Knowing and Cognizing* is also an excellent exemplification of Rickert's *heterological principle*, which is arguably the hinge of his philosophy. In order to theoretically master a complex totality (such as, here, "cognition") philosophy has to rely on logically opposite but mutually complementary pairs of concepts that taken together encompass the totality at issue. True philosophical thinking never takes the form of an *either/or*, but of a *both/and*. Here, for instance, the totality of knowledge cannot be understood as consisting of *either* concepts *or* intuition but as a compound of both elements, which must be taken together in spite of their logical opposition.

It is interesting to note that the distinction captured with the German words *Kennen* and *Erkennen* can be found in exactly the same terms in Moritz Schlick's *Allgemeine Erkenntnistheorie* [*General Theory of Knowledge*], and it has elements in common with Bertrand Russell's famous distinction between acquaintance and description.

Moreover, while his name is not mentioned, there are clear indications in the text that the true addressee of Rickert's criticism is Edmund Husserl, who, in his seminal book, *Ideas Pertaining to a Pure Phenomenology and to a Phenomenological Philosophy* (1913), insisted on the intuitive basis of cognition and used precisely the example of a tone to illustrate his conception of eidetic (essential) seeing. Rickert and Husserl have two rather different conceptions of knowledge, in keeping with the different traditions from which they speak. For Rickert, in keeping with Kant, to know is to be able to subsume a particular under a general concept. In order to do so, the concept must be thought of as a necessary ingredient in the very process of encountering an individual. For Husserl, in keeping with Descartes and Leibniz, knowledge is essentially a movement from the obscure to the clear, it is a process of clarifying ideas that have been previously entertained emptily and vaguely. So, whereas for Husserl the moment of *seeing* or *intuiting* crowns the process of knowledge *qua* clarification, for Rickert seeing or intuiting are merely the beginning of a process of knowledge *qua* conceptual subsumption. In spite of their divergent standpoints, there is actually room for mutual enhancement in the two philosophers' perspectives. So, for instance, Rickert takes for granted that we experience tones as tones and that we are able to 'dissect' them into their constitutive components without running into category mistakes. Of a tone, we always try to determine pitch, timbre, intensity, etc. and never, say, its temperature. Why is that? This is the kind of question that Husserl's theory of essence is designed to answer. The things we encounter in experience (as well as our experiences) are structured according to invariant *eide* (or essences) that we can try to make explicit with the aid of a rigorous method ("eidetic variation") culminating in actual *seeing* of the essence at stake. This, however, is the place where Rickert's insistence on the necessity of concepts becomes legitimate. In spite of all emphasis on *seeing*, *vision* and *intuition*, Husserl, too, desires to achieve *cognition* of essence and in order to do so he needs linguistically articulated concepts. Rickert has a good point here: even if we uphold phenomenology's commitment to evidential seeing, *cognition of essence* is always more than mere intuition of essence.[5]

Notes

1. H. Rickert, *Goethes Faust. Die dramatische Einheit der Dichtung* (Mohr Siebeck: Tübingen 1932).
2. I. Kant, *Prolegomena to Any Future Metaphysics That Will Be Able To Come Forward As a Science* in I. Kant, *Theoretical Philosophy After 1781* (Cambridge University Press 2002), p. 89.
3. H. Rickert, *The Limits of Concept Formation in Natural Science* (Cambridge University Press 1986), p. 54.
4. H. Rickert, *Die Philosophie des Lebens. Darstellung und Kritik der philosophischen Modeströmungen unserer Zeit* (Tübingen: Mohr Siebeck 1920.)
5. For a full-scale treatment of this issue see A. Staiti, *The* Ideen *and Neo-Kantianism*, in L. Embree/T. Nenon (eds.), *Husserl's* Ideen, (Dordrecht: Springer 2012), 71–90.

Chapter 22

"Concept Formation in History" from *The Limits of Concept Formation in Natural Science: A Logical Introduction to the Historical Sciences* (1902)[1]

The title "Hellenes" is applied to those who share our culture rather than to those who share a common blood.[2]

Isocrates

Introduction

Up to now, we have come to know the concept of historical science negatively, as that of a task that cannot be resolved by concept formation in natural science. In order to define this concept positively, we will again link the different logical problems it contains to *one* main problem. It must correspond, however, to the problem we placed in the foreground in our elucidation of the character of natural science. In other words, as already noted in the Introduction, here as well what matters is not the path that research takes, and especially not the *search* for the historical material, but rather the form of its *representation*. The entity in which the preliminary or final results of natural science are expressed is called a "concept." Accordingly our task now is to fix the principles of *concept formation in history*. The extension of linguistic usage that lies in this designation is justified by the consideration that the new problem is logically the same as the one that was placed in the foreground in the attempt to develop a logical understanding of natural science. Above all, our task is to understand how the elements of a historical concept are consolidated into a *unity*, or what the scientific validity of historical concepts is based on.

In that case, the solution to the problem may be articulated in the following way. Again, in order to exhibit its logical content as clearly as possible, here too we will begin by bracketing all the substantive particulars of the material of the historical sciences. Thus we will proceed from the limit of all concept formation in natural science, namely, the *individual*, in the most comprehensive sense of the word, in which it designates every unique and individual reality whatsoever. First, not all individual realities are the object of history. Therefore we have to show how a special variety of objects – which we can designate as "historical individuals" in the strict sense, the only objects that are important for a representation of their individuality – are differentiated for historical representation from the infinitely extensive manifold of objects. Second, these historical realities cannot be represented in their complete intensive manifold either. Thus we also have to understand what is differentiated from the content of the manifold of the single historical individual and is consolidated as the individual content of a historical concept. In this way, we will grasp the most general principle of an *individualizing concept formation*, which stands in logical opposition to the generalizing concept formation of natural science. Finally, we will see how mistaken the view is that holds that in the representation of history, it is a question of the mere application of the general conclusions of natural science to the specific case.

As a result of the new mode of distinguishing essential from inessential aspects, the representation of the individual – and thus of the historical, in the logical sense of this term – is shown to be possible. Moreover, it will be shown that the formation of concepts with an individual content – or individualizing concept formation, as we will call it – takes place only through a theoretical "relationship"[3] of historical objects to *values*, a relationship whose nature we will have to define precisely. To that extent, this sort of concept formation could also be characterized as "teleological." However, this historical-teleological moment has nothing to do with the teleological concept of history that appears from time to time and often has been quite justifiably criticized as unscientific. In particular, here it is only a purely *theoretical* principle that can be in question. It is true that, in general, no notice is taken of this principle. However, it is necessarily employed by every historian, regardless of how much he may struggle against every kind of "teleology." Individualizing concept formation, therefore, also proves to be *value relevant*[4], and in this way too, it is opposed to the value-free concept formation of natural science. The concept of *theoretical value relevance*[5] as the genuine logical principle of an individualizing or historical representation requires an exhaustive discussion.

This discussion will be advanced by the consideration that in historical reality, individuals are never *isolated*. All objects of history are rather parts of a larger whole with which they stand in a real nexus. As we have seen, the abstractions of natural science destroy this nexus and isolate instances. History cannot proceed in this way. It becomes the science of the unique, real event only by means of a representation of the *historical nexus*. Concerning this point, it is especially important to note that every individual object is *causally* linked with other individual objects. The causal connections of history, however, should be scrupulously distinguished from the causal *laws* of natural science. Contrary to what is frequently supposed, the representation of causal connections simply does not coincide with a generalizing representation of reality as "nature."

Finally, the fundamental logical principles of concept formation in history are united in the concept of historical *development*. It also holds true, however, that there is no sense in which this consideration implies that the methods of history and natural science approximate each other. First, *historical* development consists of unique and individual processes. And second, these processes fall under historical concepts only by means of the theoretical relationship to *values*. *This* concept of development remains foreign to those representations that, in a logical sense, belong to natural science. Even if this concept plays a role in some parts of the corporeal sciences, that is only because physical reality can also be brought under historical perspectives and represented in an individualizing fashion. This circumstance again proves how inadequate the opposition between nature and spirit is for clarifying the logical problems of history, as long as "spirit" refers to the psychic.

If the concept of developmental history[6] defines the most general logical character of every historical representation, we can turn to the qualifications that must also be made here if our concept is to be applied to historical science as it really exists. We will extend this concept from the absolutely historical – at the outset, the exclusive object of our concern – to the *relatively historical*. In this way, we will become familiar with the *natural scientific aspects of the historical sciences*, which are just as important as the historical aspects of the natural sciences. Here again, we attempt to understand the *interpenetration* and *concomitance* of general and individual factors that are characteristic of *every* empirical science. And yet in spite of all the transitions and intermediate forms with which we will become acquainted, a fundamental logical distinction between natural science and historical science remains. Even though many, perhaps even most, historical concepts have a *general* content in the sense that they comprehend what is common to a plurality of individual realities, in the historical nexus of a unique developmental sequence this generality is always considered as something relatively specific and individual. Just like the absolutely historical, therefore, it must also form a limit for natural science. We will understand how even the general – in other words, what is common to several objects – can be represented in a value-relevant and individualizing fashion. The paradox in this idea is only apparent.

With this demonstration, the *purely* logical work of this chapter is concluded. However, if we want to understand not only the logical nature but also the scientific significance and indispensability of concept formation in history with regard to its substance, ultimately we must also know which specific part of individual reality *requires* a historical representation. This necessity can rest only on specific *material* determinations of certain objects, which then become "historical objects" in the strict sense. Thus we have to inquire into the extent to which there is a connection between the *content* and *form*, or between the *material* and *method* of historical representations. In this way we will also obtain the *substantive* concept of history, which is primarily what we have in mind today when we speak of "history."

At the outset, there is the consideration that the existing historical sciences are not *actually* indifferent to the difference between body and "mind"[7] that was intentionally disregarded at the beginning of our account. On the contrary, they are essentially concerned with mental processes, and *to this extent* they could also be called human sciences[8]. We must ascertain why that is so and whether the historical *method* can also be crucially determined by this circumstance. But it will once again be shown that there is no sense in which the difference between natural science and human science[9] – assuming that "mind"[10] refers only to noncorporeal, real being, or to psychic reality – can be regarded as a determining factor for method, as long as the issue concerns the classification of the empirical sciences into two *materially* different groups.

In opposition to the objects of natural science, it is rather the case that the objects with which the historical sciences in the strict sense are concerned fall under the concept of *culture*. This is because the *values* that govern value-relevant concept formation in history and determine what the object of history is, are always drawn from cultural life, or are *cultural values*. Of course, culture as well, like every reality, can be brought under the concepts of natural science. In other words, it can be represented in a generalizing fashion. But this mode of representation alone is never sufficient for culture. Therefore, it is the *historical sciences of culture* that must be opposed to the natural sciences, with reference to both method and content. They fall under the concept of history that is more than formal, the *material* concept. And yet this concept also remains formal to the following extent: In methodology, we can set up only a formal concept of culture.

Logic can never determine which substantively defined values govern historical representations or what the substantively defined concept of culture consists of. Only historical science itself and a comprehensive philosophy or a theory of *Weltanschauung* oriented to historical science can do that. At best, methodology can make the attempt to fathom the nature of the much discussed process of *historical understanding* by starting from the concept of the cultural sciences. This concept of historical understanding is regarded by some as the true central locus of a theory of the so-called human sciences. But we can begin to solve the problem this concept contains only if we already know *what* is understood by the historian and only if we have grasped the extent to which *historical* understanding must bear an *individualizing* character. In a theory of history, this is also why we cannot *begin with* a distinction such as that between "explanation" and "understanding." Historical understanding cannot only signify the understanding of the real mental or psychic existence of the past. That is because, as a mere real event, it may remain just as unintelligible as corporeal existence. The task of history rather lies in the understanding of culture, which is *more* than a real psychic phenomenon. Thus it makes sense to include history in the human sciences and to employ this latter concept in a "classification" of the sciences that provides more than a superficial schema for the arrangement of the *material* of science only if "mind" refers to something fundamentally different from the real mental life that psychology investigates.

Finally, one further new problem is posed for the logic of history. In every historical representation as well as in every representation in natural science, we employ a series of *presuppositions* that can be designated as the "*a priori*" of scientific concept formation. Insofar as they are relevant here, these presuppositions primarily lie in the concept of the *law of nature* as that of an unconditionally general judgment, on the one hand; and in the concept of the *cultural value* to which every historical object must be theoretically related in order to become a possible object of historical representation, on the other. It is not only possible to pose the question of the *validity* of these presuppositions; because of the special character they have in historical science, the scientific *objectivity* of historical representation – in comparison with natural science – will seem problematic.

In this way, there is another aspect in which history as scientific *knowledge* is again placed in question. Here we finally arrive at the task of comprehending the relationship between natural science and history with reference to their presuppositions as well. This task no longer has any connection with *methodology*, however. In consequence, only the final chapter will deal with the *epistemological* or transcendental-philosophical problems of the *philosophy of nature* and the *philosophy of history* – the problems to which we are led by the question concerning the objectivity of concept formation in history – detached from methodological problems. This will bring our inquiry to its conclusion.

1. The problem of concept formation in history

In order to formulate our new methodological problem precisely, it is necessary that we also look at the *totality* of the questions historical science poses for logic, and then distinguish what we mean by concept formation in history from other forms of thought in historical science.

According to Droysen, the methodology of historical research has four parts: heuristics, criticism, interpretation, and representation.[11] Bernstein also adopts this arrangement. He summarizes the individual principles and operations that constitute applied methodology into four different groups: "*knowledge of sources* or heuristics, which comprehends the collection and apprehension of the material; *criticism*, which is concerned with the sifting of the material and the determination of the facts; the *conception*, which is concerned with knowledge of the significance and the connection of facts; *representation*, which reproduces the facts as known in their connection in a cognitively adequate expression."[12] For the purpose of a synopsis, we can accept this arrangement. We only have to define the meaning of some of the terms a bit more precisely.

As regards its most general meaning, the opposition between material and conception coincides in this context with that between matter and methodological form. We always regard empirical reality as the material of science. In the case of the corporeal world, for example, it consists of a "plurality" of "things." As we have already noted, there is an epistemological standpoint from which this reality – which qualifies only as material for the specific sciences – can already be regarded as formed material. In that case, plurality and substantiality, even reality itself, would be forms that are imposed on the material. This *epistemological* opposition of matter and form must be distinguished from the *methodological* opposition.[13] For an investigation that proposes to represent the forms of historical science in opposition to those of natural science, it can be important to know which forms belong to *every* scientific conception of reality. This is because these latter forms – for example, the form of "reality" – are necessarily *common* to both natural science and history.

Here it is obvious that the boundary is not to be drawn in such a way that we inquire into the *system* of these epistemological forms. On the contrary, we can only undertake the distinction for the specific cases to which the investigation leads us. At the outset, however, it is necessary to note the following: In the ensuing, when we speak without further qualification of forms of scientific conception, general, epistemological, or "constitutive" forms are never intended, but only methodological forms; in other words, the forms that are distinctive to the historical or the natural sciences. Therefore, in a methodological investigation, empirical reality – which, from an epistemological standpoint, is already constituted as the formed material of the empirical sciences – can simply be characterized as material. This will be especially important to the question of the significance of the principle of causality in history.

Even so, the term "material" of historical science is still not unambiguous. This term can refer to *that* material that is directly given to the historian and from which he obtains his knowledge of the things and processes he wants to represent; and it can also refer to these things and processes themselves, which constitute material for methodology only as long as they have not assumed the methodological forms distinctive to historical science. Thus we will call the immediately given material that is not itself an object of historical representation *source material*. The things and processes of empirical reality, on the other hand, that history proposes to represent scientifically we will call its objects; or, to indicate the opposition to the methodological form of history, we will designate them as the *factual material* of history, which falls only under general epistemological forms. In consequence, when we refer to historical material in opposition to historical form, this should never be understood as a reference to the mere source, or to the object that has already been comprehended or analyzed by history, but only to individual historical reality as such.

Finally, with regard to terminology it should be recalled that we do not use the word "representation" merely for the external form of a statement, but for the "conception" as well. In other words, it should be understood as referring to what is meant by knowledge of the "significance" and "connection" of facts. Thus we can formulate our problem with reference to the four groups indicated in the following way: It is concerned not with the first two, heuristics and criticism, but with the last two, conception and representation. We can leave aside the question of how knowledge of the historical facts or knowledge of the reality to be represented is obtained from the sources. Regardless of how interesting it may be to follow in detail the technique of the collection and criticism of the historical material, the differences between the methods of natural science and history that occur here cannot be of such fundamental significance for us as those that appear in the conception and representation of the material that has been ascertained. In the discovery and confirmation of facts, *every* path and detour is equally acceptable and justifiable as long as it leads to the goal. The fundamental methodological differences arise only when *one* group of sciences "conceives" its material as nature and the *other* group "conceives" it as history.

What is to be understood by a "conception," and especially what is meant by the ambiguous expressions "significance" and "connection," will be demonstrated more precisely only in the ensuing. Here it is sufficient to note that our problem begins with the question of how history becomes a science on the basis of established and historically confirmed facts. Or, since we call the scientifically – and, to this extent, conceptually – formed material a "concept" in history as well, how does the historian form his historical *concepts* from his *factual material* (not from his *source material*)? It is only in this way that our problem conforms to that considered in the investigation of concept formation in natural science.

It can also be asked, however, whether in general it makes any sense in history to distinguish, even conceptually, the determination of facts from concept formation. If we examine historical works from the perspective of this issue, then it seems that the historian often represents *everything* that he has taken from the real objects of experience. Quite frequently, moreover, he does not know as much about them as he would like. In that case, the idea that he still had to "simplify" his factual material by a process of selection would never occur to him. Has he not done his work when the facts have been discovered in the sources and criticized? And is it not true that representation is only a form of reportage that, although it may require talent and taste, cannot be regarded as the real *scientific* task? Will not the most faithful and genuine historical representation be the one that explicitly limits itself to the reproduction of the critically confirmed factual material and only "idiographically" narrates "what really happened"? In natural science, it is legitimate to ask what it selects as essential from the infinite profusion of the immediately given real material, and thus to see the focal point of its task in the correct formation of its concepts. But the historical facts obtained from the sources are not infinitely diverse. Therefore, the problems posed for the logic of natural science do not exist for the logic of the historical sciences. As a result, the discrepancy between source material and factual material seems to acquire an essential logical significance.

In fact, a simple reference to the infinite manifold of every empirical reality is not sufficient to exhibit the new problem as clearly as the problem of concept formation in natural science. Of course, we could claim that even if the facts are not given to the historian as an intensively infinite manifold, this still holds true for the *sources*. Thus he always requires a principle of selection to distinguish the essential from the inessential in the sources. On the basis of this consideration alone, however, we would not yet be able to define a problem that can be taken as parallel to the question posed for concept formation in natural science. From the standpoint of logic, that would be a defect. There is no doubt that history is also distinguished from natural science by the manner in which the facts are given to it. Therefore we have to try to understand this difference, insofar as it is germane to the most general logical opposition of nature and history.

In this context, the decisive point is the following. That which the "nature" of reality consists in and what natural science must take cognizance of in order to form its general concepts, is almost always present in a plurality of objects. In particular, the material for the discovery of timelessly valid laws of nature is present at many points. On the other hand, the specific and the individual in which history is interested have existed only on a single occasion – at least this holds true for absolute historical concepts. Thus the knowledge of such a phenomenon frequently is acquired only with difficulty. It follows that the material for the representation of an object in natural science can exist in its entirety. For a historical representation of *the same* object, however, it can be obtained only in an extremely incomplete fashion.

Suppose we return to our problem of concept formation in history. Now we can understand how it is that history, unlike natural science, usually cannot directly experience its facts but must almost always infer them from the traces that are left, and thus why history does not confront its factual material, but rather only its source material, as an infinite manifold. In a few exceptional cases, the object *for* which history forms its concepts is the same as the object *from* which it can form them. Usually the object of direct observation and the object of historical representation – in other words, source and fact – differ. As a result, the view can arise that the historian has to represent *all* the properties of his objects that experience makes available in any way at all. In that case, there seems to be no basis for the claim that concept formation in history can even be conceptually distinguished from the determination of facts.

In spite of this consideration, such a basis can be demonstrated. Initially, of course, the incompleteness of the material of history results in a new difficulty that seems to place the point of our entire enterprise in question. Given the dissociation of sources and facts, it is not clear why the sources should always be available, even for the incomplete determination of precisely *that* factual material that interests the historian. From a logical standpoint, therefore, which processes he is able to represent seems *fortuitous*. This fortuitousness inevitably invests history with characteristics that cannot be derived from its purely theoretical or scientific objectives, and this simply cannot be conceived as logically conditioned. They lend history the appearance of an unstructured material. In understanding the relationship of the logical ideal of a historical representation to the historical sciences that actually exist, this point should be considered most scrupulously. This is because it is much more difficult to bring ideal and reality in conformity here than was the case for concept formation in natural science.

It does not yet follow from this consideration that setting up a logical ideal of historical representation or concept formation is impossible as such. In general, the fragmentary character of the material can be understood as a consequence of the logical concept of history as the science of unique and individual reality. In specific cases, however, this fragmentary character is random. For precisely this reason, we can ignore it in specific cases and employ the fiction that in any given case, the historian can obtain any piece of factual material from the sources. This is because it could randomly happen that all the sources necessary for this have been preserved. Thus we first set up a logical ideal for a conceivable case of this sort, and when the ideal is to be compared with reality, we add the reservations that are typically necessary in view of the usual deficiency in the material available.

But if this fiction can be employed, the *particular* difficulty that arose for our problematic and from which we proceeded is eliminated. To be sure, it is only the source material, and not the factual material of history, that possesses the quality of infinite multiplicity. However, if this signifies nothing more than an *incompleteness* in the factual material, then we need not concede to it any influence on the logical development of a theory of historical representation. This is precisely because the fragmentary character of the material resists logical comprehension in every specific instance. Rather, we can again pose the same question we posed in the elucidation of concept formation in natural science: Why does historical science always attempt to represent only a part of reality in its individual configuration, and which part is this? Assuming that this issue is not governed by caprice, there must be a scientific principle according to which the selection is made. As a result, the logical structure of historical representation and concept formation necessarily depends on this principle.

Although the aforementioned fiction is justified in the interest of logic, it is useful to add that we need it *only* to pose our problem in a perfectly *general* fashion. In actuality as well, there are almost always more facts for the historian to extract from the sources than he represents or incorporates into his concepts. For this reason as well, a principle of selection and simplification is indispensable for him. Concerning this point, we must, of course, distinguish several different cases from one another.

When the sources and the facts coincide, the necessity of a simplification by means of separating the essential from the inessential is self-evident. If the historian can interrogate the persons that form his object, or if he is concerned with geographic arenas of historical events that have been preserved unchanged, or with cultural artifacts such as buildings, works of art, tools, and so on — not only as sources but also as historical facts or objects — then he confronts them, exactly as the natural scientist does, as an infinite manifold. In the same way, he always knows much more than he can and will represent about all the historical events he has witnessed. For example, anyone who has actually seen Bismarck himself knows an inordinate number of facts about him that do not belong in any history, not even in the most exhaustive biography.

The case is not very different for some historical events that lie quite close to us temporally, even though we never experienced them at first hand. Here too on the basis of reliable sources, we could discover a wealth of details that do not have the slightest historical interest. In that case, we will always insist that the historian know how to distinguish the essential from the inessential. That Friedrich Wilhelm IV declined the German imperial crown is a "historical" event, but the question of which tailors made his uniforms remains a matter of complete indifference for political history, even though we could probably acquire precise knowledge of this too. Suppose it is objected against this point[14] that although this fact will indeed always remain inessential for political history, in a history of fashion or haberdashery or prices, it could become historically essential. This is, of course, true, but it proves nothing about the general principle at issue here. It is rather the case that the objection even admits the necessity of a principle of selection for political history. Moreover, facts can easily be cited that are inessential to *every* conceivable historical representation. Of course, the illustrations chosen for this purpose will always seem somewhat "farfetched" because the sources for completely inessential historical facts have usually been lost, and no one has an interest in remembering them. There is no doubt, however, that we could ascertain a multitude of facts about a personality such as Friedrich Wilhelm IV that are historically inessential under all conditions. Simply suppose that a historian possessed a substantial number of letters written in the king's own hand. If he concerned himself with the way the king distributed ink on the page, he could fill volumes with the description of absolutely indubitable facts from the past, but not even the most specialized specialist would maintain that this qualifies as historical science. Thus the "historical concept" of the king certainly cannot consist of *everything* that might be reliably established about him.

The situation seems different when the sources are meager. In such a case, there are in fact circumstances under which we will perhaps omit no individual characteristic that can possibly be discovered. Because of the lack of material, even the most trifling phenomenon acquires a significance here that it perhaps would not have if an ample body of information were available. But can we really say that in these cases the historian represents *everything* that he knows or could know? Here too the mere fact does not yet have any meaning. We can even discover much more about completely "unknown" things than can be incorporated into history. Concerning every person, all that natural science teaches us about bodies and all that general psychology teaches us about mental life can be claimed with confidence. Precisely because he is engaged in a science of individuals, however, the historian is not concerned with this knowledge. Thus even when history knows *too little* about its objects, it still knows *too much* about them. For this reason, it can never confine itself to narrating "what really happened" or to proceeding "idiographically." On the contrary, it always has the task of *separating* the essential from the inessential. For this purpose, however, there must be governing *perspectives*. As principles of historical representation, they should be made explicit. As a result, the problem of concept formation in history clearly emerges, irrespective of the fiction that is justified in the interest of logic.

But does this give us the right to speak of historical representation as a formation of historical *concepts*? Precisely on the basis of our earlier exposition, the following objection could be raised against this claim.

Even if history does not have to report *all* the facts it can ascertain, it remains true that whereas history *substantiates* this or that individual fact as *real*, natural science forms concepts that *hold validly*. Insofar as its concepts are intended to hold validly for reality and only for reality, it is true that *every* empirical science is concerned with real things and processes. If someone proposed to incorporate the products of the imagination into a system of concepts, no one would call that natural science, or a science of any sort. Nevertheless, generalizing natural science, in contrast to history, remains a science of concepts[15] not only in the sense that the more comprehensive or general these concepts become, the less the content of its general concepts resembles the content of individual, empirical reality, but also in the sense that the existence of its objects need not be *explicitly* set out in judgments. Propositions such as "a corporeal world really exists," "water exists," or "there really are living human beings" do not comprise the content, but rather the implicit presuppositions of the natural sciences, which are concerned with the corporeal world in general, water, or human beings. In other words, precisely because such judgments are self-evident, they no longer belong in these sciences. In natural science the crucial point is always the question of the validity of concepts, not the question of the real existence of objects. In historical science, on the other hand, purely existential judgments have a fundamentally different significance. The historian is continually claiming that this was really the case, and that was really otherwise. His main concern lies precisely in the assertion and confirmation of the purely factual truth of such judgments. Contrary to natural science, therefore, the crucial issue is the real existence of objects, not the nonreal validity of concepts. This is why it seems that we cannot posit a historical *concept* formation parallel to that of natural science. In history, the word "concept" must receive a meaning completely different from the meaning it has in natural science. What can be said in response to this objection?

There is, of course, a fundamental difference. Indeed, the purpose of our entire account was to establish this difference. But consider the process in history by which a selection of the essential from the inessential is made, and which determines that a historical representation consists precisely of these and not those existential judgments. The fundamental difference in question cannot prevent us from characterizing this process as concept formation as well. Up to now, of course, we always used the word "concept" in such a way that it designated a nonreal construct with a *general* content. This is because when logic speaks of scientific concepts, it tends to focus almost exclusively on what the distinctive character of the concept of the *natural* sciences consists in. Here we see precisely that one-sidedness that we want to overcome. Unlike the generalizing disciplines, therefore, history does not form general concepts. On the other hand, history can no more incorporate its real objects themselves – for example, Caesar, the Thirty Years' War, the rise of the manors, or Dutch painting – into its representation than natural science can. On the contrary, it is obliged to form "ideas" *of* Caesar or "ideas" *of* the rise of the manors that hold validly and therefore are nonreal. Because the content of these ideas never coincides exactly with the infinitely diverse real processes, they are still "concepts" – even though they have no *general* content – in the sense that in them, what is essential for history is singled out from reality and comprehended, in quite the same way that natural science forms concepts by singling out what is essential to reality and comprehending it.

In addition, it is obvious that the content of historical concepts can be made explicit only if they are reduced to existential judgments that recount the things and processes they represent. As we have shown, however, the transposition into judgments is also necessary to the conception of the content of concepts in natural science. So in this respect, there is no basic difference either. In the one case, it is a matter of judgments that are formed in order to grasp the general, in accordance with the purpose of natural science. In the other case, it is a matter of judgments that give an account of specific and individual reality. But this exhibits only the general difference between representation in natural science and in history. In its most comprehensive meaning, we propose to maintain the term "concept" independent of just this difference. We will use it to refer to every logical construct whose content comprises valid knowledge of objects. Only in this way will we arrive at a truly comprehensive and universal theory of concept formation. In the interest of logic, therefore, it remains just as justified to designate as concepts those constructs in which the historical nature of reality is grasped in an individualizing fashion, as those constructs in which the general nature of things is expressed. In this sense, *all* scientific thought must take place in "concepts," individualizing history no less than generalizing science.

Apart from the use of this unconventional *terminology*, nothing is further from our intention than to invent a *new* method of historical representation that has never been employed and to set it up as the only justified method in opposition to that now in use. As in our investigation of natural science, we are rather guided by the purpose of understanding the scientific activity of the historian as it is really practiced. In other words, our purpose is to become acquainted with the logical structure that *every* historical representation must exhibit. Logic should never have any other relationship to empirical research. Reflection on the distinctive logical features of an investigation can do no more than proceed hand in hand with the investigation itself, and thereby structure it in a more systematic fashion. In the vast majority of cases, however, the sciences are developed to a considerable degree before reflection on their logical structure begins. Even if epistemology questions the basis of certain ultimate "presuppositions" of science and attempts to make their validity problematic in the philosophically justified interest of maximum unconditionality, there is no sense in which it brings into question the distinctive significance of the sciences as specialized forms of empirical research. Thus epistemology does not claim to direct science onto the paths it should take. On the contrary, it proposes only to follow science with a view to understanding it.

This can seem to be so self-evident that it does not need to be said. But it is precisely the logic of the historical sciences that has reason to stress the self-evident. Proposals to finally "elevate history to the rank of a science" by recommending a method it has never employed are still everyday occurrences. These attempts follow a period in which the historical sciences have been developed to an exceptional level. Taken on their own terms, they seem somewhat strange, even reactionary. This is because they invariably have recourse to the ideas of a – happily superseded – distinctively unhistorical or antihistorical philosophy of earlier times. Thus it is even more astonishing that the "modern" methodological constructions are produced not by speculative metaphysicians contemptuous of experience but by philosophers who take pride in their close contact with the empirical sciences, or even by historians themselves who cannot do enough to profess their antipathy to philosophical constructions. In view of these considerations, we can understand why other historians have become suspicious of *all* methodological investigations. Because even the modest philosophy of experience produces such exotic blossoms as the "new historical method," perhaps worse still will be expected from a logic that explicitly stresses that it will begin by proceeding in a "purely formal" way and even places itself in the service of an idealist Weltanschauung. At the outset, therefore, we note that it is the naturalists and the alleged empiricists who are sufficiently remote from an understanding of the existing historical sciences that they demand a "new" historical method. The logic in which we are engaged here, however, can have nothing in view that proposes to inaugurate a new era of historical research. It proposes to understand the logical nature of *that* historical science that actually exists, for only in this way can it assess the significance of history for the theory of *Weltanschauung*.

This obviously does not mean that the logic of history will declare the procedure of an individual historian, such as Ranke, or the special method of a so-called old tendency to be validly fixed for all time and pronounce the introduction of new "points of view" into historical science as unjustified. As an attempt to control the sciences, this would be just as futile as the proclamation of a universal scientific method, or the effort to banish Ranke's work from science. On the contrary, our concept of history must be just as general and comprehensive as our concept of natural science. It cannot exclude the most "modern" endeavors such as economic history, "cultural history," and the geographic and "materialist" conceptions of history, but rather has to understand them logically as well. Precisely for this reason, however, it remains *a priori* impossible for us to reach conclusions that are inconsistent with history as it was written by Ranke or other representatives of the "older" tendency. On the contrary, we believe we can show that the genuinely new perspectives in historical science, such as, for example, the more thorough consideration of economic life – to which logic cannot raise the slightest objection, since it has no judgment at all to offer in a case of this sort – signify the introduction of a new *material* and not the introduction of a new *method*. We also believe we can show that, as long as they write history at all, even the theoretically most radical proponents of the "new method" will always work in practice – even though they may not be aware of this – by employing the method that always has been used in history and always will be used as long as there is a historical science.

A different point, of course, should also be stressed, which will perhaps be regarded as a qualification of the foregoing remarks. Even though the *result* our investigation attempts to establish is "only" an agreement of logical theory with the method of the historical sciences that actually exist, for this reason the *path* on which we will arrive at concepts useful for the logical understanding of historical science cannot consist in a mere *analysis* of existing scientific activity. We even believe that an investigation that proposed to *begin* with such an analysis would never reach logically significant conclusions. We already indicated the basis for this claim in the Introduction. If no science amounts to description – in the sense of a mere reproduction of its material – for this reason, logic cannot qualify as mere "description" either. The sciences themselves are a part of historical reality, which, as we know, cannot be described at all without a principle of selection. The concept of "pure induction" – the name of this slogan, which still has not disappeared – is actually the ideal of a radically "empiricist" form of speculation that proceeds in a purely deductive fashion and has lost all contact with real scientific thought. The attempt to make progress in logic in a purely inductive way will necessarily remain completely fruitless.

The reason for this is obvious. How are we simply to read off the structure of the sciences if the issue concerns the clarification of two methods that are logically, and thus formally, juxtaposed? The division of scientific labor is in the first instance connected not with logical differences but with substantive differences in the material. These differences must inevitably come to the fore as soon as the attempt is made to describe the different sciences "inductively." To gain any sort of perception of the logical oppositions, therefore, we can *begin* only formally, construing them in their most elementary form and without regard to the existing individual sciences. We also find formal constructions of this sort in the work of scientific specialists who have attempted to clarify the method of their own work. Boeckh,[16] for example, in connection with his famous definition of philology as the "knowledge of the known," says the following: "First, it was necessary to formulate an unconditional concept of philology, with a view to eliminating all arbitrary definitions and identifying the real essence of the science." That is what we too will try to do here. Moreover, this is justified if we only keep in mind – again employing the words of Boeckh – the following point: "The more unconditional a concept, the more the conditions must be given in the development."

In the *general* parts of logic, this way of proceeding is regarded as a matter of course. When methodology turns to more specialized forms of science, however, we often find that from the very beginning, the content of the science in question plays the chief role. As a result, investigations of this sort offer more of an encyclopedic survey of the different disciplines than a development of logical concepts. In the ensuing, just as in our account of concept formation in natural science, we will make a scrupulous effort to avoid this encyclopedic tendency – as exhibited, for example, in substantial parts of Wundt's *Logik* – in order really to produce a *logical* methodology of concept formation in history. The empirical material can always occur only as an example for the clarification of a previously established logical principle. Moreover, no one should be troubled if logical principles that at first are developed in a purely formal way must subsequently be restricted when they are applied to the actual praxis of scientific research. As historical facts, the existing sciences cannot be exhaustively reduced to any schema. This provides all the more reason why we need general logical schemata, both to understand the logical structure of the sciences and to distinguish conceptually the different logical components of the sciences that in fact are interconnected.

There is another reason why we are obliged to begin in a formal or "deductive" fashion. Where the theory of science set about its work with previously established concepts, it was usually not aware of this. On the contrary, it conceived the relationship between the general and the particular – as if this were self-evident – in such a way that it considered only the subordination of the particular case under the general concept. As a result, only concept formation in natural science conformed to its schema. Either it was as good as blind to any other possibility, or it attempted to compress everything into its schema. From the outset, our self-consciously deductive procedure considers not only *one* but *all* the conceivable possibilities of the representation of reality. We thereby propose to overcome this one-sidedness and do justice to the sciences that actually exist. Thus we begin by constructing the purely logical concept of a historical method, and we then apply it to empirical science. In other words, our strategy is exactly the opposite of the logical naturalists, who begin by proclaiming a pure empiricism in order to arrive at the purely speculative demand for a "historical science." Assuming that this science is expected to resolve the tasks that fall to history, it can never be realized.

2. The historical individual

As we have seen, the historical in its most comprehensive sense – in which it coincides with the unique, invariably individual, and empirically real event itself – forms the limit of concept formation in natural science. This is due to its perceptual reality as well as to its individuality. The empirical *perception* of reality cannot be represented by any science, because it remains infinitely diverse under all conditions. Thus it cannot be reduced to any concept. But this does not hold true for *individuality*. Although it is given to us perceptually, it does not follow that individuality must remain *identical* with perception. *The problem of concept formation in history, therefore, is whether a scientific analysis and reduction of perceptual reality is possible that does not at the same time – as in the concepts of natural science – forfeit individuality*, and yet also does not produce a mere "description" of facts that cannot yet be regarded as a scientific representation. In other words, we must now ask, From the infinite manifold of the perceptual content of reality, can certain aspects be accentuated and consolidated into scientific concepts in such a way that they represent not what is common to a plurality of things and processes but, rather, only what is present in *one* individual? This is the only way that concepts with individual content will occur that can claim to be historical concepts. It must follow from the foregoing that mere descriptions of individual facts, which obviously are always *possible*, do not yet warrant this name. We propose to reserve the name "concept" for *that* in which a scientific representation finds its conclusion. Therefore we ask, Are individual concepts logically impossible, in the same way that perceptual concepts would be logically impossible?

Obviously we do not contest the indispensability of a *generality* for all scientific concept formation. Even a fleeting glance at a historical representation shows that it too almost always consists of words that have *general meanings*. It could not be otherwise, for these are the only words intelligible to everyone. It is true that historical representations also include proper names, and they seem to constitute an exception. Without further specification of their sense, however, they mean something only to someone who is acquainted on the basis of perception with the individual designated or can reproduce this individual in his memory. The historian should never presuppose knowledge of such individual *perceptions*. If he happens to possess this knowledge himself – which is possible only if factual material and source material coincide – he can communicate it only by specifying its content by means of words that have general meanings. Thus proper names can appear in a historical representation only as proxies for a complex of words with a general meaning; for only then is the representation intelligible to everyone who hears or reads it.

Indeed, we are obliged to claim even more than this. It is not merely this external circumstance that forces the historian to represent everything he wants to express scientifically by using *general* concepts. Earlier we found that every judgment requires a generality and that, for this reason, even the elements with which we form a general concept in natural science are themselves always general. But if this "first generality" – as we propose to call it – is indispensable to all logical thought as such, then it is just as essential to a historical representation as to concept formation in natural science. In the sense that the *elements* of concepts and judgments are general, *all* scientific thought must be articulated in general concepts. So if the task of rendering nothing but individual contents is ascribed to history, then the concept of a historical *science* would in fact be a contradiction in terms.

But does it follow that the *use* of words with general meanings as elements of concepts is possible only in the *one* direction that we find in natural science? Put another way, by using words with general meanings, can unique and individual processes be described only in such a way that the contents of these descriptions can be nothing more than *material* for further conceptual analysis?

Each of the elements of a scientific concept must be intrinsically general. Earlier, however, we saw that considered on their own terms, they still do not qualify as scientific "concepts." On the contrary, only their *combination* is scientifically significant, and this combination certainly does not always have to be undertaken in such a way that another concept with a general content is formed by its means. Rather, it can also follow that the resulting complex of general elements as a *whole* has a content that occurs only in one unique and specific object. Thus it represents precisely that by means of which this object is distinguished from all others. To maintain that the fundamental opposition between natural science and history holds for concept formation too, we do not need more than such a possibility.

As regards the point that all thought requires the general, we can formulate this opposition in the following way. In natural science, the general – which is already present in the most elementary meanings of words – is also what the science endeavors to develop further. In other words, a general concept to which the profusion of specific phenomena can be subordinated is its *purpose*. Even the most restricted law of nature must always hold for an indefinite number of things and processes if it is to deserve the name of a "law." Although history also *uses* the general so that it can think and judge scientifically, the general is nothing more than a *means* for history. In other words, it forms the indirect path on which history attempts to return to the individual as its real object. History employs the general in the same way a description uses it to represent a purely factual individual reality that signifies nothing more than the material of science. The only important point here is to understand the scientific *objective* served by a historical representation of the individual. We propose to characterize the sciences, not with reference to their means but with reference to their objectives. Therefore, assertions such as the claim that all scientific thought employs general concepts are, of course, incontestable. But on this level of imprecision, they are meaningless for the question of whether historical science pursues the same *objectives* as natural science. It must be possible to resolve all concepts into judgments whose ultimate components are indeed general. In their totality, however, these judgments can represent something that is unique and individual as well as something that is general. This is the only issue of importance here.

Therefore our problem does not begin until we pose the question of which principle governs the historical *combination* of conceptual elements? History as a science can never consist in the mere "description" of individual facts. Such descriptions – which we have, for example, in representations of the moon and which can be given for any individual reality at all – are "historical" only in that first quite general meaning of the word, in which it designates the unique and the individual as such. But they cannot serve as examples that clarify the concept of a historical *science*. In history as well, the elements of the concept must form a unity – in the sense of a *coherent* entity[17] – if science is to arise as a self-contained or closed system of ideas. For us, therefore, the tie that binds these elements into one concept with an individual content is the only important matter. This is the only perspective from which we can speak of a *validity* of historical concepts. If such a principle of unity specific to history cannot be discovered, we would have to accept the claim that the representation of everything individual should be regarded as nothing more than a preliminary analysis or a collection of material for a more advanced form of generalizing concept formation. Thus what does the "unity" of historical concepts consist in if the coherence of conceptual elements – unlike the case of a concept in natural science – is not based on the fact that the concept holds generally for all the cases subsumed under it?

To answer this question in principle, suppose we again consider the most comprehensive concept of the historical, in other words, the concept of the real *individual* as such. At this point, we stress that this word does not have only the meaning to which we limited our account in the foregoing, namely, that of the unique, the specific, and the singular. On the contrary, it also includes the *indivisible*. The concept of indivisibility indicates a *unity* that arouses our logical interest. We know that to qualify as singular, every reality must also be composite, for the simple, like the atom, lacks individuality. Thus the following question arises: Is it perhaps more than an accident that combined in the word "individual" are *two* meanings that are interconnected for our problem of the historical concept – that of the unity of a manifold in the sense of a coherence, on the one hand; and that of uniqueness, on the other? It at least seems noteworthy that we also designate as an individual – as that which is indivisible – something that is necessarily manifold. Has the expression "individual" lost its meaning when it is used to designate unique manifolds, and is only the simple atom indivisible? Or are there perhaps individuals also in the sense that their manifold forms a unity – in the sense of a *coherence* – *because of* their uniqueness? If this is the case, here the uniqueness and unity of a manifold are connected with one another in the way that they must be connected in a historical concept if we are to speak of its *validity*. Does the concept of the individual perhaps contain the principle that links the coherent aspects in the historical material and thereby distinguishes them from aspects that are merely contingently related?

We will begin by attempting to establish quite generally whether the concept of indivisibility can be linked with that of uniqueness in such a way that uniqueness forms the basis or presupposition of indivisibility. In this way, we will at least take the *first step* along the path that should gradually lead us to the concept of the historical individual.

Initially, the principle that is the basis of the unity of the indivisibility that arises from uniqueness can be clarified by the comparison of two *bodies*. In this way, of course, we will not yet reach the *final* concept of the historical individual, for there is no doubt that history is primarily concerned with real mental life. Indeed, we must remain with a preliminary concept in this context because we will completely ignore the consideration that all historical reality is an *event* that changes, and because we will consider only the individual as such, insofar as it is autonomous and self-contained, which is never really the case. But if we want to understand logically the method of concept formation in history, we again have to begin by representing the logical principles abstractly to determine them more precisely in the ensuing in a step-by-step fashion.

Consider the principle that alone is at stake at this point and that only concerns the distinction between two kinds of individuals as such. As the bodies with which we will clarify this principle in a logically abstract fashion, let us employ a particular lump of coal and a particular large diamond, such as the famous Koh-i-noor. The point that there is only one particular chunk of coal lying here holds true for it no less than for the diamond, which has a proper name. Like the diamond, its individual properties distinguish it not only from everything else that is differently constituted, but also from every other lump of coal. As regards *uniqueness*, therefore, both bodies are individuals in exactly the same sense. As regards their *indivisibility*, on the other hand, they are quite different. It is true that both *can be* split apart. A blow of the hammer would shatter one individual as well as the other. But while the splitting of a lump of coal is the most indifferent matter imaginable, the diamond will be scrupulously protected from this. Moreover, we do not want to see the diamond split, *because* it is unique. In the case of the diamond, therefore, the unity of its individual manifold is really connected with its uniqueness in such a way that its unity is based on its uniqueness. In the case of the lump of coal, it is true that uniqueness is also present, but it is simply not related as a unity to a possible splitting. The reason is as follows: although another lump of coal can always be substituted for this one, another Koh-i-noor can never be produced. As a result, the difference between the two kinds of individuals must be clear. The unique is always necessarily indivisible as well – or an in-dividual[18] in the strict sense of the word – when its uniqueness acquires an irreplaceable *significance*. In this sense, it is incontestable that not only minds, but also bodies, form individual unities.

There is no doubt that it is only this difference between two kinds of individuals that is applicable to *all* bodies in such a way that, from this perspective, the entire physical world falls into two groups of realities. From the extensively infinite manifold of things, a specific number is differentiated. The vast majority of bodies come into consideration only insofar as they are instances of general concepts. As regards those bodies that are not merely unique but, rather, are also unified in the sense of being indivisible because of their uniqueness, we do not want *just* to subsume them under general concepts. Indeed, we can even claim more than this. If we examine an individual in the strict sense – again, for example, the specific diamond – somewhat more closely, we find that the significance of its individuality does not lie in the *totality* of that which constitutes the content of its manifold. Like the manifold of everything else, this manifold consists of an infinity of determinations. Its irreplaceability can depend on only a *part* of them. It is this part alone that we consider when we "describe" the diamond. The multiplicity of its other properties could be different without thereby modifying or even nullifying its significance. But if the unity the diamond possesses by virtue of its individuality comprehends no more than a part of it, the principle we seek makes it possible not only to regard its individuality as a unity; at the same time, it allows a limited and precisely defined number of its attributes to be consolidated into an individual unity. In addition, this difference between merely coexisting and coherently related "characteristics" must also be found in every body that qualifies as an individual in the strict sense. Thus we see how a certain number of unique *and* – in the sense of indivisible – unified corporeal manifolds, each of which has a specific and determinable content, are discriminated from the totality of the known corporeal world.

Let us attempt to formulate explicitly the general *principle* on which this distinction is based, insofar as this is possible with reference to the example we used. In that case we can say the following: The meaning possessed by the diamond rests on the *value* attached to its irreplaceable uniqueness. The diamond *should* not be split because it is valuable. This must also hold true for all bodies that are in-dividuals. The mode of unity in indivisibility just characterized can arise only if its uniqueness is *related to a value.*

This is not to deny that there are other grounds on which a body is constituted as an indivisible unity. Organisms, for example, cannot be split without ceasing to be organisms, and the same holds true for tools and machines. But *this* sort of unity is not relevant to our discussion, because it does not concern the uniqueness of a specific, singular, individual thing. Our question is only how uniqueness can form the *basis* of unity, and here the answer must be that in-dividuals are always individuals that are related to a value. This and this *alone* is the only point we want to establish for the present. Thus we should again note that this is *not* yet sufficient to define completely the concept of the historical individual and especially that in the Koh-i-noor diamond, we do not yet have a "historical individual" of the *specific* kind that historical science in the strict sense deals with. As a *finished* stone, the diamond has no "history" at all, if for no other reason than because its development is unknown to us. Only if it is brought into connection with persons who value can the diamond acquire a historical significance *in* this connection. We will subsequently become acquainted with the reasons for this. We have made use of the Koh-i-noor diamond and compared it with an arbitrary lump of coal only to clarify *the* difference between two kinds of individuality on the basis of which we shall define the concept of the historical individual more precisely in the ensuing. Thus all objections that amount to the claim that the diamond is not "historical" are unfounded. By means of this example, we want to take *only* the *first* step toward the definition of historical individuality. It is impossible to say everything at once.

At first, we have to ask whether the distinction just made can be carried out for all conceivable empirical reality, and especially whether it can be transposed onto psychic existence. If this is not immediately obvious, the reason is as follows: Among the animate beings with which we are familiar and of which we take note, there are presumably none in whose individual character one part of the determinations is not differentiated from the others and consolidated to form a distinctive individual unity. In particular, we know of no *person* whose individuality does not comprise an essential "core" as the real personality, in opposition to inessential and peripheral processes. Because we find this unity of indivisibility in all human mental life, we are easily led to believe that it is tied to the nature of the psychic itself. But that is a mistake. If we disregard both the epistemological unity of consciousness as such as well as any metaphysical unity of a transcendental mind, the distinction between center and periphery in the empirical manifold of a human mind is based on no other principle than that with which we become acquainted in the comparison of the diamond with the lump of coal. In other words, individual unity as the indivisibility of a personality is grounded on no other consideration but the following: We associate a *value* with this unity, and as a result, the aspects that are irreplaceable or essential with reference to this value form a whole that *should* not be divided. In short, the individual unity or indivisibility of the unique personality is no different from the unity of the individual as such that is related to a value.

On the basis of this consideration, the concept of the "psychic structural nexus"[19] also becomes intelligible. The *historical* unity of a personality is not constituted by an "experienced" unity. On the contrary, as long as we have not grasped its nature, the indivisible unity of the personality that is related to a *value* leads us to the mistaken conclusion that an *individual* unity may already be discovered in the experienced unity of the real psychic structural nexus as such. This becomes especially clear when the structural nexus is also characterized as a *purposive* nexus[20]. That is because a *value* is implicit in the concept of a purpose, and the unity of individuality rests on this value alone. The difference between the corporeal and the mental individual lies *exclusively* in the fact that there is no person whose individuality is so indifferent to us as that of a lump of coal. It follows from this, however, that the indivisible unity of uniqueness is still not tied to the psychic as such. Independent of value, we not only can easily *conceive* a unique mental life that possesses no individual unity – even though it always has to have the unity of the psychic structural nexus; when we consider animals, for example, quite often there is really no "bond" that constitutes uniqueness as the unity of indivisibility – although the unity of the experienced structural nexus cannot be wanting here either, assuming that this unity pertains to the mental as such.

At this point, it is irrelevant why *all* persons are linked with values or are related to values and thus qualify as individuals in the strict sense of indivisibility. It is important to show only that our principle is truly *general*, and therefore that by its means any reality at all – regardless of whether it is physical or psychic – can be analyzed as individuals in the strict sense and the more comprehensive sense. In that case, we also understand why we so easily forget that with reference to uniqueness, *all* realities exist in the same way as individuals in the more comprehensive sense. In the overwhelming number of cases, they are *only* unique. We *take note* of uniqueness and have occasion to become explicitly aware of it only when they are related to a value and thereby become indivisibly unified in their uniqueness, which almost always holds true for psychic individualities. This is why it sounds paradoxical to call leaves or nuts individuals, even though – in the most general sense of this expression – they are exactly as individual as the personalities of history.

Consider, however, the clarification of the principle on which the distinction into two different kinds of individuals rests. What it initially makes explicit is nothing more than the perspective that guides every feeling, willing, and acting person – in short, everyone who takes a position on values, and thus every genuinely "vital" person – in his conception of the world, the perspective on the basis of which the essential and inessential aspects of real existence are distinguished for him. On the one hand, anyone who *lives* – in other words, anyone who sets goals for himself and wants to realize them – can never regard the world *exclusively* with reference to the specific. This is because he can orient himself and act practically in the domain of reality, which is always individual, only by generalizing. Thus he is concerned with some objects only insofar as they are instances of general concepts. On the other hand, many objects will be important for the person who values precisely because of their uniqueness. For him, therefore, they are necessarily indivisible or unified individuals. This distinction is made with such consummate self-evidence that we only rarely take note of its basis and simply do not consider that in such a case, *value perspectives* govern a *selection*. In fact, this is the primordial conception of reality, which is prior to every science. For the real person, therefore – who is always a person who wills, values, and takes positions – reality conceived in the manner just described, as in part generalizing and in part individualizing, actually becomes reality simpliciter. This is why we must explicitly stress that the world of unified individuals – quite like reality as an object of aesthetic perception or as an object of general concepts – is *only* a specific *conception*. As a third conception, we differentiate it in principle from the natural scientific and aesthetic conception. Initially, it can be designated as the world of practical life.

What is the relationship between the prescientific, individualizing conception of reality and the problem of concept formation in historical science?

We have repeatedly stressed that the concept of the *historical* individual in the *strict* sense still cannot be clarified by the concept of the diamond. Our analysis will proceed from the concept of the limits of natural science to the progressive determination of the concept of historical science. At this point, we can say the following: If individual reality as such was identified with the most general concept of the historical *object*, the individualizing conception of reality characteristic of practical life must be designated as the primordial and most comprehensive *historical conception*. Here, however, the "historical" still means nothing more than reality with reference to the unique, the specific, and the individual per se. We have identified the historical interest in this most comprehensive sense with the interest in the individual. Thus those individuals that qualify as in-dividuals for the person who wills and values can be called *historical individuals*, as long as the concept of the historical is regarded exclusively as the concept of the unique and the individual.

Initially even this more narrow concept of the individual still has no significance for the concept of *a scientific* history. Nevertheless it is still important in our methodological context. This is because we can define the most comprehensive logical concept of the historical, which heretofore only comprised a problem, with reference to this concept. In this way, we can at least come *closer* to a solution to the problem. In the foregoing, we designated nature as reality with reference to the general and history as reality with reference to the individual. Although it is true that this formulation comprises the most general concept of natural science, it still has *nothing* to say about the concept of a historical science. Suppose we now claim, in opposition to this formulation, that reality becomes history with reference to the meaning the individual possesses by virtue of its uniqueness for the being that wills and acts. In that case, the *possibility* of a historical *representation* in the logical sense is immediately opened up for us. Because the historical conception or the formation of in-dividuals as just described surmounts both the extensively and the intensively infinite manifold of empirical reality, the perspective that is definitive in this context must also be suited to be the principle for the formation of concepts with an individual content. At the same time, this more precise definition does not alter in the slightest the fundamental logical opposition between nature and history. This is because empirical reality, as the volitional person of practical life would represent it with reference to its uniqueness and singularity, would have to set a limit to concept formation in natural science, just as this holds true for reality itself as an infinite manifold that lies beyond any representation.

But how can the prescientific conception of *volitional* or *practical* life bring us closer to the concept of history as a *science*? At this point that is the crucial question. Does not the prescientific conception remain necessarily opposed to the scientific conception precisely *because* it is the conception of the volitional person? The historical conception, of course, cannot be identical with that of the practical or volitional person. It is true that both share the distinction between individuals in the strict sense and the more comprehensive sense, and both consolidate individual manifolds of this sort into unities – in the sense of entities that have an indivisible coherence. But they also differ in two fundamental respects. We will arrive at the *scientific* formation of in-dividuals only by taking note of these differences.

First, in opposition to the volitional person, the historian as a scientist is not practical but theoretical. Thus his mode of activity is always *representational*, and not *judgmental*. In other words, he shares the perspectives of considering something with the practical person, but not the activity of willing and valuing itself. This can also be expressed in the following way: History is *not* a *valuing* science but a *value-relevant* science. We will establish precisely what counts as "considering" something under value perspectives or the purely theoretical "relation to values," in opposition to volition and practical valuation. Here we only note that this is another reason why we cannot yet regard the Koh-i-noor diamond as a historical individual: We distinguished it from the lump of coal precisely on the ground that, for the person who makes practical valuations, a greater value is ascribed to it than to any lump of coal, which we do not value. The diamond would be intelligible as an individual that is merely theoretically value relevant – and thus as a historical individual in the scientific sense – only in a larger context, which for the time being we cannot yet examine.

At this point, suppose we establish the second difference. In practical life, it always holds true that the volitional person also esteems certain values that qualify as such for him alone. This is why there are many individuals that become in-dividuals for him, even though others have no reason to acknowledge these individual manifolds as necessary unities, in the sense of being indivisible. History, on the other hand, assuming that we want to grasp the concept of the science as well, must always strive for a representation that is valid for *everyone*. That is why only the content of its concepts, but never the principles governing its representation, can be "individual": in other words, valid for only this or that individual person. Thus we are not only obliged to distinguish practical "valuation" from a theoretical "value relationship." We also have to define the value perspectives that are decisive for the theoretically value-relevant formation of historical in-dividuals more precisely than was possible in the comparison of the diamond and the lump of coal.

We will begin with the second point, deferring for the time being the difference between practical valuation and theoretical value relevance. Then the inadequacy of the concept of the historical individual obtained thus far is demonstrated by the fact that in practical life, we regard *all* persons as individuals. There is *no* person whose individuality is as insignificant to us as that of a lump of coal. History, however, never represents the individuality of all persons. What is the basis for limiting it to a part of them?

Obviously it is based on the consideration that history is interested only in what – as we usually put it – has a *general* significance. This must mean that for history, the value with reference to which objects become historical individuals must be a general value: in other words, a value that is *valid for everyone*. All persons become individuals in the strict sense by virtue of the fact that we relate every human individual to some sort of value. On the other hand, suppose we consider which individual life is consolidated as a unity by virtue of its uniqueness and with reference to *general* values. Then we will see that from the totality of persons – just as from the totality of all other objects – a certain number is *set in relief*. In comparing two bodies, we chose the diamond because, with reference to a general value, it becomes an individual that is valued by everyone. If we compare a personality such as Goethe with any average person, and if we ignore the consideration that even the individuality of this average person means something with reference to some value or other, it follows that Goethe is related to such a person in the same way the Koh-i-noor diamond is related to a lump of coal. In other words, with reference to the *general* value, the individuality of the average person can be replaced by any object that falls under the concept of a person. The significance of Goethe, on the other hand, lies precisely in what distinguishes him from all other instances of the concept of a person. There is no general concept under which he can be subsumed. Thus the individual Goethe is an in-dividual in the same sense as the individual Koh-i-noor: His distinctive status as an individual is valued by *everyone* for its individuality. As a result, we see how the relation to a general value makes it possible not only to distinguish two kinds of individuals in every reality whatsoever but also to draw this distinction in such a way that we can expect everyone to acknowledge its validity.

History, therefore, represents objects that become individuals from this perspective by replacing practical valuation with the purely theoretical value relationship. In this way, history as a science distinguishes the essential from the inessential in a *generally valid fashion* and consolidates the essential as a *necessary* unity.

But does this not invalidate the concept of the historical established in the foregoing, and especially the opposition to natural science? Are we still justified in speaking of a science of the distinctive and the individual if the value that constitutes objects as historical individuals is a *general* value?

In addition to the general *elements* of concepts already discussed – which we called the "first generality" – there is a *second generality* in history as well. This circumstance also explains why the difference between natural science and history could be overlooked in discussions about the method of the historical sciences, and why a natural scientific or generalizing method could be proclaimed as universal. It seemed quite self-evident: Science is always concerned with the "*general*." And yet if we make clear what this "second generality of history" signifies, it will be seen that the general value that makes the general validity of a historical conception possible has even less to do with the generality found in natural science than do the general elements of historical concepts. At least as regards their content, historical concepts are general in the same sense as a concept of natural science. In contrast, the general value to which individuals must be related in order to become historical in-dividuals is not supposed to comprehend several individual values as its instances, but rather to be a value that everyone acknowledges, or a value that is *valid for everyone*. And second, if something has a general significance – insofar as it is related to a general value – that does not mean that this thing itself is general. On the contrary, the general significance of an object can even be augmented to the same extent that the differences between it and other objects increase.

Thus, precisely *because* it gives an account of what is related to a *general* value, history has to give an account of the individual and the distinctive. So the historical individual is significant for *everyone* by virtue of that in which it is *different from everything else*. Those who hold that it is never the individual but rather only the general that has a general significance fail to see that it is precisely the most general values that can attach to what is absolutely individual and unique.

Thus it is true that historical representation requires something general as a principle of selection, but this second generality of history is not the *goal* for which its formations of concepts strive, no more than is the case for the elements of concepts. It is rather the *presupposition* on the sole basis of which a generally valid representation of what is unique and individual can be undertaken.

At this point, we will show only that if reality is analyzed into essential and inessential aspects with reference to a *general* value – in other words, a value that is universally acknowledged as such – and if the essential aspects are consolidated as individual unities, the resulting conception of reality is not arbitrary and thus not *a priori* unscientific: On the contrary, it must be acknowledged as necessary by everyone who presupposes the governing values as generally acknowledged; in consequence, it satisfies a necessary condition of the scientific conception.

We have, however, repeatedly identified a second difference between the scientific conception of history and that of the volitional person in practical life. The concept of the historical individual can be conclusively defined only by a thorough clarification of this difference as well. The foregoing exposition is to be regarded as a preliminary account. Whoever proposes to take a position on our concept of the historical individual should rely not on these preliminary definitions but only on the *final* definition, which will now be undertaken.

If the illustrations we used for the concept of the historical individual are considered, the Koh-i-noor diamond and Goethe, it might be supposed that *those* parts of reality become historical individuals when they themselves embody values, or when they are *goods* to which values are attached; moreover, values of a kind that are positively valued by everyone. The concept of a "good," however, is much too narrow to identify the historical individual; nor does it suffice to extend this concept in such a way that negatively valued realities or *bad* things – which is how we draw the opposition to goods are also reckoned among the historical individuals. On the contrary, it is simply not the business of historical science to offer positive or negative *valuations:* in other words, to assert that the individual realities they represent are either good or bad, valuable or antagonistic to value. For in that case, how is history to arrive at *generally* valid value judgments? It is rather the case that we have to scrupulously distinguish what we mean by the "relation" of an individual to a value from the direct positive or negative *valuation* of this individual. Indeed, if our view were conceived as if we held that rendering positive or negative *value judgments* is a task of historical *science*, and thus that history is a *valuing* science, this would be the *most reprehensible of all misunderstandings*. On the contrary, we must regard the dissociation of every "practical" positive or negative value judgment from the *purely theoretical relation* of objects to values as an essential criterion of the *scientific* historical conception. Indeed, insofar as the value perspective is decisive for history, this concept of the "value relation" – in opposition to "valuation" – is actually *the* essential criterion for history as a pure science.

But what does it mean to relate an object to a value theoretically, without valuating it as good or bad, as valuable or antagonistic to values? In order to understand this, let us return once more to the conception of practical life, which always values objects as well, and consider two persons who have pronounced disagreements in what they love and hate – in other words, in what they value. In spite of this, may it not be that with reference to specific values – such as, for example, political values – they both *agree* that reality falls into objects of the following sort: those that if they think about them at all, are regarded as instances of a generic concept, and those they regard as significant because of their individuality?

One of the two may be a radical democrat and a free trader, the other an extreme aristocrat and a protectionist. In that event, there will certainly be few cases in which they agree in their valuations or value judgments about political events of their own time or the past, in their own country or in other nations. In other words, they will regard very different things as good or bad. But does this mean that one of them will be interested only in those individual political events that are indifferent to the other? Of course not. Even among politicians who take the most diverse positions imaginable, *the same* individual events form the object of *interest*. In other words, differences in evaluation must be based on a *common conception of reality*. If such a *common* conception of reality did not obtain, in a case in which two persons are of a different opinion concerning the value of a condition, the antagonists would not even be talking about the same thing. Therefore a controversy over the value of the object in question would be utterly impossible.

Even this example must make it clear that goods and acts of valuation can be regarded not only in such a way that we inquire into the validity of the values that are linked with them and then attempt to establish the justification with which positive or negative valuations are made – in other words, the justification with which things are regarded as good or bad; there is another view of values as well, which is not concerned with the value of things or their lack of value and does not inquire into their quality as being good or bad. This view singles out from the infinite manifold only that which stands in some sort of *relation* to values, so that it somehow *makes a difference* with respect to values. Here we are concerned solely with this sort of value relationship. History as a pure science is not concerned with the justification of valuing objects as good or bad, positive or negative.

Thus whoever is opposed to such valuations in a purely scientific historical context certainly cannot be refuted. A theoretical *relation* of objects to values, however, — by virtue of which they fall into those that are indifferent to values and those that have some sort of meaning with respect to values — cannot be dissociated from the purely scientific perspective of history.

The theoretical value relationship is of such crucial significance for historical science that without it, we would not be able to distinguish historically relevant material from the phenomena of reality that remain historically indifferent. For example, we can regard the personality of Luther as either a good thing or a bad thing. In other words, we can believe that it was a stroke of luck for the cultural development of Germany or that it brought misfortune. On this point, the opinions of historians will probably always be in disagreement. But no one who knows the facts will doubt that Luther had some sort of *significance* with reference to generally acknowledged values, and it can never occur to a historian to claim that Luther's personality is historically *unimportant*. So it cannot be doubted that positive or negative valuation is in principle different from the theoretical relation of objects to values. Valuation is always positive or negative, and the value judgment declares that its object is either good or bad. The purely theoretical relation to values, on the other hand, stands aloof from such an alternative. If an object is essential to this relation, that does not mean we have to consider the character of the object good or bad.

If, in spite of this indubitable difference, the concepts of positive and negative valuation are not distinguished from the concept of the theoretical value relation, the reason perhaps lies in the following consideration. If one event is explicitly judged to be important and another event is explicitly judged to be unimportant, *that* is certainly an act of valuation or a commitment. Such a commitment, however, does not simply coincide with the theoretical relation of objects to values, as a result of which *historical* individuals are formed. It is rather the case that in *all* scientific concept formation, the explicit distinction into essential and inessential features implies a *valuation*. To this extent, natural science is not free of valuations either. Distinguishing the essential from the inessential always presupposes the value of *science*, with reference to which certain components are essential and others are inessential. Where science is not valued as a *good*, a distinction between the essential and the inessential aspects of reality simply cannot be made.

In consequence, the difference between the natural scientific and the historical conception can also be expressed in the following way. If someone regards natural science as a theoretical good and is guided in his thought by the aim of forming general concepts of nature, different factors of empirical reality must become essential and inessential for him than for someone who regards historical science as a theoretical good and distinguishes essential and inessential aspects in empirical reality from one another with reference to the objective of developing a historical science. In methodological investigations, however, we intentionally leave these *logical* values to which the investigator is committed, and which are implicitly presupposed in *all* scientific concept formation, in the background. We are concerned only with the relationship in which the *material* of conceptual representation stands to values, and in this regard we can state the following. It is characteristic of concept formation in natural science that the objects it represents are dissociated and must be dissociated from all relations to values if they are to be regarded as nothing more than generic instances of general concepts. Although it is true that historical science also has to maintain its autonomy from the practical valuation of objects and their evaluation as good or bad, it can never lose sight of the relations of objects to values as such. Otherwise it would be utterly impossible for historical science to distinguish the historically essential from the historically inessential events in empirical reality. The circumstance that *all* concept formation in science presupposes the value of *scientific* objectives should not mislead us concerning the points that the relation of objects to values is distinctive to concept formation in history and that the theoretical value relation must be distinguished from practical valuation.

In any case, we should not confuse diverging positive or negative valuations with the *common* conception of reality by virtue of which only certain objects and not others become historical individuals. For history, the distinction between essential and inessential elements is made in a way that is *independent* of the difference in practical value judgments. On the other hand, the conception that is common to the differing parties also remains "tied" to the "relation" to values. Suppose that by virtue of its individuality, an object acquires political, aesthetic, or religious significance. And suppose it becomes the object of a controversy and appears as historically important or unimportant. In other words, it is set in relief as an individual from the infinite profusion of objects. In that case, we cannot regard political, artistic, or religious life as indifferent or neutral to values, but must rather explicitly *acknowledge some* sort of political, aesthetic, or religious values *as values*. For persons who do not do this, there would be no occasion to ascribe a different *interest* to one individual configuration of specific objects rather than to any other arbitrary configuration. Suppose we designate as the mere relation of reality to values that by virtue of which a conception of reality arises that is *common* to the most divergent value judgments and that, as reality, is neither positively nor negatively valued. In that case, we can rigorously distinguish this relation as purely theoretical from practical valuation. Valuing is always either positive or negative. The relation to values is neither. This consideration alone makes the fundamental difference clear. By means of this mere relation, therefore, a world of individuals is formed for everyone in *the same* way. The value of these individuals, on the other hand, can be assessed quite *differently*. The purely theoretical relation to values has absolutely nothing to say about what is good or bad, valuable or antagonistic to value in such a value-relevant world of individuals.

Now we can understand the following point: Assuming that history proposes to be nothing but a *science*, the *logical ideal* of the historical conception is characterized by the fact that it stands aloof from all practical *volition* concerning objects, and thus it abstracts from all valuation as well; on the other hand, it preserves the mere *relation* to generally acknowledged values in the sense just indicated. For history as a science, therefore, reality is divided into in-dividuals and instances of generic concepts in such a way that even the most radically opposed partisans with their divergent valuations can agree to this conception as held in common.

When we speak in this context of an "ideal" of historical representation, this concept should be guarded from misunderstandings. Like the ideal of the "last natural science," it must also be understood in a *purely logical* sense. In other words, there is no sense in which we claim to impose practical prescriptions on the historian concerning how he *should* proceed. What is at stake here is rather only the question of understanding theoretically what in a scientific representation is purely scientific and what may transcend this. In particular, with the statement of our "ideal," we do not propose to deny that many – or perhaps all – historians *actually* make atheoretical value judgments as well. Finally, it is not our idea to prohibit them from doing this. In that regard we would have little success. We want only to state the following: Although atheoretical valuations, which are always positive or negative, do not belong to the logically *necessary* nature of history as a science, the theoretical relation of objects to values remains *conceptually* inseparable from every historical representation and does not compromise its scientific status in any way. Thus our distinction between practical valuations and the theoretical value relationship would have to be made in the interest of logic even if it could be shown that the historian actually can *never* manage without practical valuations, or even if a purely theoretical representation of history, which abstains from every atheoretical position, were regarded as unacceptable from the standpoint of the interests of the general, *extrascientific* culture. For the statement of a purely *logical* "ideal" of a value-free historical science, even this circumstance is unimportant.

There is another special reason for emphasizing this point. The dominant *state of mind* concerning questions of *value* changes from time to time. *Logic* must hold itself aloof from such a change of mood, which is not based on theoretical grounds. At times, a general mistrust of *every* sort of value factor in science prevails. Then it is most important to point out the minimum value content without which no historical representation of the individual is *possible*. At other times, however, extrascientific interests intrude so powerfully into the foreground that science is required not *only* to provide theoretical truth but also to "be of service to life." Then something else is important for logic. In other words, then a different disposition concerning value questions can easily gain a foothold. It is obvious that every "vital" person is also a *valuing* person, and that abandoning all extrascientific valuations cannot be of service to "life." Where such life interests predominate, the historian will not want to be denied the right to practical valuations.

With regard to this issue, the primary task of logic is to make clear that every practical valuation introduces a factor into history that is no longer purely scientific. It is obvious, however, that this statement itself should not include a valuation in the sense that it disparages *valuative* history in any way. It is rather the case that here as elsewhere, logic only attempts to achieve theoretical *clarity*, and for this purpose alone it requires the conceptual distinction between valuation and the value relation. On the one hand, logic can show in this way that there is no completely value-free science of history. On the other hand, it can stress just as emphatically that in spite of this, a historical representation free of practical valuations is logically quite *possible*, even though it may not be desirable from the standpoint of the interests of a "vital" culture.

Here the principal issue is the theoretical value relation, and we can also make its indispensability explicit in the following way. We may presuppose as given that history is primarily concerned with *persons*, and that within human life not everything has the same importance for history. That, it will be said, is "self-evident." Of course. But there must also be reasons for this. *Why* does history provide an account of one person and remain silent about another? Intrinsically the individual differences between them are no larger than those between all other things. Unless we differentially stress one thing as essential and ignore another as inessential, everything of a specific type differs from every other in infinitely many respects. It is only value relations that determine the "magnitude" of individual differences. They alone are responsible for the fact that we take note of the one event and disregard the other. The more we are inclined to pass over this point perfunctorily as something that is self-evident, the more reason logic has to underscore its self-evidence and stress that without the relation to values, individual differences in the historical life of persons would be just as indifferent to us as are differences in the waves of the sea or leaves in the wind.

Any example we might choose shows what is at stake here. If a historian proposes to write a history of the Renaissance or the romantic school, he can certainly form an ideal of historical objectivity in the attainment of which no one would notice whether his political or aesthetic convictions and the valuations linked with them make him sympathetic or unsympathetic to the Renaissance or romanticism, or whether they appear to him as the ultimate flowering of the development of humanity or as stages of its deepest decline. And even if he does not actually reach this ideal, he can at least regard an abstention from a judgment concerning the value of the objects in question as his scientific obligation. The reason is that, as a historian, a scientifically grounded opinion is possible for him only concerning the empirical process, but never concerning its value. And yet values play a decisive role in his work, for he simply would not concern himself with the unique and individual processes called the Renaissance or the romantic school if they did not stand in a relation to political, aesthetic, or other generally acknowledged values by virtue of their individuality. Thus the belief that we could ever maintain an absolutely value-free standpoint in history – in other words, that we could not only avoid practical positive or negative value judgments, but also theoretical value relations – amounts to self-deception.

Everyone will freely admit that history has to represent only the "essential." When the historian does not follow this rule and incorporates inessential matters into his representations, we raise a serious objection against him. But the word "essential" – and the words "interesting," "characteristic," "important," and "significant" as well, which must always be applicable to the historical – loses all specifiable meaning if there is no relation between the objects designated in this way and some sort of value. Fundamentally, therefore, the claim that every object that falls within the domain of history must be related to a value only articulates in *logically useful* terms the quite trivial truth that everything history represents is interesting, characteristic, important, or significant. The interesting, the characteristic, and the important can be good as well as bad, but the question of whether it is good or bad does not have to be considered at all. To this extent, its *valuation* is unimportant. But everything immediately loses the quality of the interesting, the important, and the characteristic when every sort of *relation* to values is terminated. Thus for this reason as well, valuation and the value relationship should be rigorously distinguished.

At this point, let us have another look at the foregoing. The definition of the concept of the historical individual has proceeded in three stages. At first, the historical was the unique and distinctive reality simpliciter, which is always individual in the sense of being singular. This concept was sufficient to clarify the limits of concept formation in natural science. Second, the historical was whatever a volitional being associated with a value, at the same time being a real entity unified in its uniqueness, for example, the Koh-i-noor diamond. Here we became acquainted with the conception of reality characteristic of practical life. Finally, we were able to define the historical individual as the reality that is consolidated for everyone as a singular and unified manifold by means of a purely theoretical relation to a general value – a reality that insofar as it breaks down into essential and inessential aspects from the perspective of this theoretical conception, can also be represented scientifically by history. It is only here that we arrive at the concept that comprehends the historical as the object of the historical *sciences*.

Now, the first two stages of the definition of the concept have no further interest for us. In particular, we must eschew examples such as the Koh-i-noor diamond in order to avoid the misunderstanding that it qualifies as an example of a "historical" individual in the strict sense. The first two stages only form the path on which we gradually attempted to reach the concept of the true historical individual. In the ensuing, when we speak of historical individuals or in-dividuals without further qualification, it is always the concept of the third stage of the definition that is intended.

It is obvious that this concept also remains, for the present, formal; thus in comparison with the substantive concept of history, it is still much too *broad*. Logically, however, the concept of history can now be formulated as follows. It is a science *of reality* insofar as it is concerned with unique, individual realities as such, the only realities of which we have any knowledge at all. It is a *science* of reality insofar as it adopts a standpoint in which we merely consider something, a standpoint that is valid for everyone; thus it is solely by means of a relation to a general value that history constitutes significant or essential individual realities or historical individuals as the object of its representation. It is only owing to this definition that the concept of a science of reality is no longer merely a problem, as it was at the outset, and no longer includes a contradiction, insofar as the real – *exactly* as it exists independent of every conception – does not enter into *any* science.

Perhaps it is not superfluous to point out that linguistic usage is also quite compatible with the three stages of our definition of the concept. *First*, we use the ambiguous word "historical" to designate mere facticity, as was conventional in the linguistic usage of earlier times, in the philosophy of the Enlightenment, for example. Thus when we say that Galileo's frequently cited remark "And yet it moves" is not historical, we mean only that Galileo did not really say this. Here, "historical" has exactly the same meaning as "*real*." Therefore we also understand why all rationalists take a negative view of merely factual truths as truths that are "merely historical." This first sense of the word "historical" was our first concept.

Second, we speak with emphasis of a "historical moment," meaning that an event possesses great significance by virtue of the fact that it is a good to which a value is attached. Indeed, we regard ourselves as important if we are allowed to experience such a historical moment. This significance can arise only by the association with a value that is then transferred to us. Thus the second meaning of the word "historical" coincides with the second stage of our concept.

Third and finally, we say that this or that has "become historical," or better – because this can easily be understood as the negative value judgment that it is antiquated – that it "belongs to history." By this claim, we again intend something different. We want to say that an event of the past no longer has any positive or negative value for contemporary life. Thus it is dissociated from what we want. Some philosophers, for example, wish that Kant would finally become "historical" in this sense. In other words, they want to eliminate him from the philosophical controversy of the present. On the other hand, regardless of how "historical" Kant had become, he would still remain in certain relations to scientific values, and only because of these relations would he belong to history. So we see how the third meaning of the word "historical" coincides with the last concept we were obliged to add to the concept of the individual in order to obtain a concept of the historical individual that is useful to the theory of science.

In short, as regards the three different meanings of the word "historical" – namely, real, significant, and what has been withdrawn from controversy – we can claim that we could take them all into account in the same way or "sublate" them in our concept. This may at least provide a small contribution to the justification of our exposition.

3. Value-relevant concept formation

Now that we know what a historical individual is, the *principle of concept formation in history* will no longer be in doubt, at least as regards the absolutely historical and single individuals that have not yet been drawn into the stream of events, which is all we are concerned with at this point.

What falls under historical concepts is what is set in relief from reality and consolidated as individual unities by means of the purely theoretical relation of an object to generally acknowledged values. No further discussion is needed to show how both the extensively and the intensively infinite manifold are overcome in this way in a manner that differs in principle from the mere description of an arbitrarily selected aspect of reality. Only a small part of the extensive manifold of different configurations falls under historical concepts. In the same way, only a small part of the intensive manifold of a single historical individual forms the essential content of the historical concept. As regards simplification, therefore, the product of this sort of concept formation is analogous to that of natural science. As regards the substantive result of concept formation, however, they are logically antithetical. The concept of natural science comprises what is common to several individual configurations. What belongs to single individuals alone is excluded from the content of the concept itself.

When the concept is formed *on the basis* of a single individual reality, however, the historical concept includes precisely what distinguishes the different individuals from one another. Either it completely disregards what is common to them, or it retains this only insofar as that is indispensable to the definition of their individuality. Thus we meet a kind of conceptualization in which the content of science does not become increasingly remote from the individuality of reality, which was the case for the sort of simplification produced by concepts of nature. On the contrary, by its means the content of science is formed in such a way that it expresses the individuality – even if not the perceptuality – of empirical existence.

In order to clarify the sense in which this solves the most general logical problem of historical representation, we must again explicitly note that the principle of value relevance thus obtained serves to surmount both the extensively infinite as well as the intensively infinite manifold of reality. It might be supposed that value relevance comes into play only when specific objects are set off in relief from the *extensive* manifold of things as essential for history. The representation of the *intensive* manifold of the single historical individual, on the other hand, would be independent of the principle of value relevance. As a result, the significance of this principle for concept formation in history would be considerably restricted. We would be obliged to say the following: Although the question of which objects in general are essential does indeed depend on values, this means only that the historian has to discriminate some objects or other from the infinite manifold to represent them historically. His real scientific work would begin only after the selection was made. Under this condition, if the principle of value relevance extends no further than the selection of historically essential objects in general, then it could not be called a principle of historical *concept formation*.

This view is untenable, however. If the principle of value relevance has an important role in historical science, it must be decisive for surmounting both the extensive and the intensive manifold. It is only *because of* the individuality of an intensive manifold that the object in question comes to have importance for the general value. Thus it is only with reference to the individuality of its infinite manifold that the single individual can be differentiated as a historical individual from the infinite multiplicity of other individuals. Therefore the principle of value relevance is just as crucial for the representation of intensively infinite content as it is for the selection of the object in question from the extensive infinity of things and processes in general.

Insofar as the unity of the historical individual is always based on a value relation, it can be called a *teleological* unity, and historical individuals can be called teleological individuals. This is connected with the consideration that the concept of purpose is conceived as the concept of a future *good* that is to be realized. In other words, it is linked with the concept of a value that is attached to it. In consequence, we generally call every way of thinking in which values play a decisive role "teleological." In that case, concept formation in history, which has to conform to this sort of teleological formation of in-dividuals, can also be seen as *teleological*. Accordingly, concept formations in history can be distinguished from those of natural science as teleological *concept formations*. If it were permitted to coin a philologically unjustified term, the historical individual could also be called "what is not to be divided"[21], and concept formation in history could be called the "formation of entities that are not to be divided"[22]. But wherever it is indicated that an individual is understood as a teleological individuality – in other words, an individuality that *is not to be divided* – it will be better to employ the term "in-dividual"[23], even though it does not express the teleological moment of what *should* not be divided.

Nevertheless, the expression "teleological" certainly arouses suspicions in the minds of many. In particular, whoever makes any reference to teleology in the historical sciences must guard himself against misunderstandings. It is precisely historical teleology that has such a bad reputation, and justifiably so since there is in fact an unscientific historical teleology. Thus we should define precisely the exclusive sense in which value-relevant concept formation can be called "teleological."

It often happens that the concepts "causal" and "teleological" are opposed to each other. In that case, all teleology is regarded as untenable because it seems to be incompatible with the conception of causality. Terminologically, of course, this antithesis is not a particularly happy one. Assuming that the teleological conception is meant to exclude the causal, the difference intended here can consist only in the following. In the causal conception, the effect is conceived as produced by causes that precede it temporally. In the teleological conception, on the other hand, the effect as purpose is supposed to have the capacity to act before it is realized. Thus *both* conceptions are really "causal," for the fact that the effect is regarded as a purpose and is linked with a value makes no difference to causal relations as such. So we should speak of an opposition not between causality and teleology in general but, rather, between two different *kinds* of causality, as this is expressed in the "efficient cause" and "final cause." If we disregard all value perspectives, the final cause remains an *efficient* cause. The difference intended, therefore, consists only in the following: In the teleological conception of causality, the temporal sequence of cause and effect is *reversed*. In other words, in the one case there is a sense in which the cause thrusts the effect forward; in the other case, however, the final objective with which the value is linked – that is, the purpose – has the capacity to draw to itself the means by which it is realized.

Regardless of these considerations, for an empirical conception of reality, it is in fact always the first kind of causal concept alone that is applicable. So in historical science as well, the struggle against *that* form of teleology that amounts to a temporal reversal of the causal relationship insofar as it assumes operative purposes is quite justified. Causes that function before they really exist can never be given to us as historical facts. Thus the question of whether reality is influenced by causes that have the capacity to draw to themselves the material for their own realization cannot arise for a history that qualifies as an empirical science. The problem of a teleological causality in the sense at issue here – assuming that it is a problem at all – belongs rather in metaphysics. We propose to call this kind of teleology – which must take into account causes that lie beyond all empirical reality – *metaphysical teleology*, to place it at a distance from historical science.

And yet a certain reversal of the temporal sequence of cause and effect also seems to obtain when a conscious being has an objective in view and reaches it by his volitionally governed actions. Indeed, perhaps the concept of metaphysical teleology would not have arisen if it could not have been formed in an analogy with processes of this sort. Nevertheless, it is clear that this teleological conception must be distinguished from the metaphysical teleology of causality. It does not require a reversal of the sequence of cause and effect that is inconsistent with an empirical science. The *idea* of the objective, not the objective itself, is operative, and the idea also temporally precedes the intended effect. A teleological process of this sort, therefore, conforms completely to the only concept of causality that is valid for empirical reality.

This sort of teleology is germane to historical science to the extent that it *can* in fact be used to understand historical processes. If things occur that obviously fulfill some purpose, and if this purpose cannot be identified as the motive of an agent, then to explain such events, an inference will be made to the activity of a being whose actions are guided by a conscious and purposive will. This mode of thought can be generalized to all human life; in other words, conscious intentions and purposes will be sought *everywhere*. There have been times when history has done this as well. In that case, it can comprehend the course of historical events only by showing what value historical constructs have for persons. On this basis, it infers that they were always intentionally produced by rational beings who had this value in view. In such a case, therefore, history also proceeds in a fundamentally "teleological" fashion. We propose to call this sort of teleology *rationalistic teleology* because, on this view, historical events are shown to be intended consequences produced by rational and purposive beings. The role this sort of teleology has played in history is well known. Human beings allegedly created language because they needed it for mutual understanding. They supposedly founded the state in order to regulate their lives, arrange matters auspiciously, and so forth. By means of presuppositions of this sort, the content of every historical representation must assume a rationalistic-teleological character.

Do we have this teleology in mind when we speak of a value relevant method of historical science? There is no doubt that the essential aspects of some historical events have been influenced by persons who acted rationally according to conscious purposes. The aim of making rationalistic teleology into the general *principle* of history is quite out of the question, however, because historical individuals in our sense certainly do not always have to be beings that set purposes for themselves and act on them; on the contrary, bodies as well can become historical individuals. Like metaphysical teleology, therefore, rationalistic teleology lies outside our province.

We also have another reason to stress this point. Namely, it can be claimed that the rationalistic teleology of history is "individualistic." Those who see the setting of a conscious purpose and the conduct that follows from it as the motive force of all historical movements, and in consequence regard purpose as the explanatory principle of history, must not only see individual personalities as the chief object of history – because the setting of conscious purposes can be confirmed in them alone; as a result of this, they must also take the view that single individuals *make* history, so that everything becomes a product of individual intention. But we are far from advocating an individualistic conception of history in this sense. If we see the individual as the object of historical representation, this does not mean that we regard individual *wills* as the determining factor in the historical process. On the contrary, it means only that history is concerned with the individual as the unique and the distinctive. As a purely logical claim, this idea remains compatible with the most varied views imaginable as to what the genuinely operative factors in the historical process are. The determination of these factors cannot be the task of logic, but only the task of history itself. At this point there is no sense in which we are concerned with the question of whether the setting of individual purposes ever occurs in the *factual material* of history. Consider the extent to which there are necessary relations of logical significance that obtain between the governing values with reference to which the essential aspects of a historical concept are linked to form a unity and the distinctive characteristics of history that follow from the fact that it is concerned, among other things, with personalities who set purposes. This is, of course, a question that eventually can be posed as well. But it is one of those problems that results from the distinctiveness of the historical *material*. In this context, therefore, we are obliged to disregard it completely.

Thus the "teleological" character of history is not determined by purposes that appear in the historical *material*, but rather by value perspectives with reference to which historical *concepts* are formed. This is why we should not be surprised if nothing of teleological import is to be found in the content of many historical representations and if, as a result, many historians believe that they remain detached from all value relations. In most cases, the elements of the historical concept that cohere with reference to the governing value are simply placed *next to one another*, as if something purely factual were stated. Thus their unity – which consists in the fact that for the historian, they *alone* form what is essential to a process – need not be linguistically expressed at all. Rather, their coherence, which obtains with reference to the value, is exhibited only by the fact that they appear in the representation at all. The mere fact that they are spoken about sets them off as essential. For this reason the logical structure of a historical representation must first be explicitly investigated. Indeed, we should not expect to be able to prove what we have in mind with regard to *every* statement in a historical work. There are historical representations in which the governing value perspectives of concept formation can be discovered only in the context of the whole. In that case, an exhaustive and detailed analysis would be required to identify the value-relevant principle. We only occasionally find passages in historical writings that clearly exhibit, even on superficial examination, what we have in mind here. This will hold true especially when the historian needs to explicitly justify the representation of an event that may perhaps seem inessential to many. In that case the presupposition that is usually taken as self-evident – that only the essential has a place in the representation – must become problematic and explicitly formulated. These cases are exceptional, however. In history, "what matters" is what in this sense is essential or teleologically necessary with reference to the leading value. That is why there is an account of it, but not of other matters. It is in this sense alone that we can say that there has never been a historian who would not proceed in a value-relevant or "teleological" fashion.

In the natural sciences, the validity that is more than empirically general is most clearly exhibited in the possibility of discovering laws of nature. In historical concept formation, we also encounter an analogous problem; namely, the validity of the historical representation must depend on the validity of the values to which historical reality is related. Thus the claim that historical concepts have an unconditionally general validity presupposes the acknowledgment of unconditionally general values. We have shown in detail – and we cannot exaggerate the importance of this point – that this acknowledgment does not imply the possibility of a consensus concerning the *valuation* of historical objects. However, it remains necessary that values in general be acknowledged on which we all – even as scientists – take a position and to which reality must be related. This is the only condition under which its individual, unique course can never be completely indifferent to us, and thus a representation of its individuality can never seem purely arbitrary or superfluous to us.

Therefore it is not sufficient that we rule out purely individual values and designate as the governing principles of a historical representation those values that are common to all members of a certain community. On the contrary, if history is to compete with the kind of general validity that natural science claims in stating laws of nature, we must not only assume that certain values are in fact acknowledged by all the members of certain communities; we must also assume that the acknowledgment of values in general can be required as indispensable for every scientist, and thus that the relation of unique and individual reality to *some* values that have a general validity that is more than empirical is *necessary*. Scientific necessity can be ascribed to a historical representation only under this condition.

We will not consider the question of what is to be understood by the validity of unconditionally general values and how they are connected to the problem of value-relevant concept formation until Chapter 5. We can understand the sense in which the claim of the historical sciences to "objectivity" depends on the validity of unconditionally general values only when the logical structure of the historical sciences has been exhaustively clarified and we are better acquainted with the values that in fact govern concept formation in these sciences. Here our sole purpose was to point out the *problem* in historical science that corresponds to the problem of the supraempirical, unconditional validity of natural laws. In the foregoing, we did not answer the question about the validity of natural laws either. We presupposed without any further basis that it makes sense to make judgments of a generality that is more than empirical. Thus all we showed was the following: In the investigation of reality as nature, a formation of concepts that is more than arbitrary is possible only *if* there are unconditionally general and valid laws. Here too we will limit ourselves to the following claim: An investigation of reality as history that is more than arbitrary is possible if and only if the acknowledgment of the validity of values in general and the relation of individual reality to them cannot appear as arbitrary from any scientific standpoint. The issues of whether and with what justification we may speak of unconditionally general laws of nature, on the one hand, and a scientifically necessary relation of reality to unconditionally general values, on the other, are no longer purely methodological questions.

Of course, we do not deceive ourselves concerning the fact that although the use of unconditionally general values as a scientific presupposition of history encounters the greatest suspicion, the question of whether there is anything such as an unconditionally general law of nature can be regarded as a rather superfluous epistemological speculation. But prejudices of this sort are connected with the one-sided conception of the nature of "science," opposition to which is the goal of this entire investigation. At the outset, at least, an unbiased conception should treat the question of the unconditional validity of values as just as open as the question of the unconditional validity of natural laws. In *both* cases, a supraempirical factor is inescapable. For the present, we can let the matter rest with this statement.

4. The historical nexus

Nevertheless, even if we disregard all problems of value, what we have said thus far about the representation of individual realities by history is still not sufficient to define the logical concept of historical science. To articulate the concept of the historical individual in its simplest form, we must first conceive the objects of history as configurations that are not only individual but also – in a certain sense – self-contained and thus *isolated*. But we should not regard the individual or the singular as what is isolated. In the real events of the empirical world, nothing is ever isolated. Not even history as the science of the individual process of empirical reality can be "individualistic" in the sense that it analyzes its material into *isolated* individuals or "gestalts." From the perspective of our presuppositions, isolation would be unhistorical. It is only generalizing conceptualization that is tied to an isolating form of abstraction. In history, it is true that there are descriptions of states that ignore the connection between the objects described and other things and processes, but historical science will not regard its task as exhausted by isolating representations of this sort. On the contrary, its work is done only when it places every object that it considers in the *nexus* in which this object actually exists.

What follows from this for the logic of history? First, it seems that this further step again places in question the correctness of the concept of the historical developed earlier. In opposition to the single historical individuals, the nexus in which they belong must be called *general*. In light of the consideration of this nexus, therefore, does not history cease to be a science of individuals?

Here again, we in fact encounter a "generality," and in addition to the general *elements* of concepts and general values, it is the *third generality* that appears in every history. It can easily be shown, however, that the historical representation of an individual object in its general *historical* nexus and the subsumption of the same object under a general concept of *natural science* are two intellectual formations that have a fundamentally different, even a mutually exclusive, logical significance. The "general" historical nexus is a comprehensive *whole*, and the single individuals are its parts. Generality in the sense of natural science, on the other hand, is the general content of a *concept* under which single individuals are subsumed as *instances*. It should not be necessary to prove that the relationship of the parts to the whole differs from that between the instances and the general concept under which they are subsumed. Whenever the "individualistic" conception of history is contested with the claim that each individual belongs to a "general" nexus and for this reason the historian must proceed – as the preferred expression has it – in a "collectivistic" fashion, and *thus* on the basis of natural science or generalization, these two relationships are confused with one another. It is not merely the generality of the natural scientific *concept* and the generality of the *value* that we have to distinguish; we must also scrupulously distinguish these two generalities from a third: the generality of the historical *nexus* as the comprehensive historical *whole*. Thus the historical individual considered in the foregoing is always articulated in a historical whole. But there is no sense in which such an articulation coincides with *subsumption* under a general concept or a natural law.

The distinction is so clear and self-evident that we are obliged to ask how confusion on this point was ever possible. It can arise only in the following way. The whole, whose part is the single historical individual, forms a *group* whose parts can all be brought under *one* general concept. In consequence, this whole has the same *name* that is usually used to designate each of its parts. In that event, the whole is called a *class*[24]. If a historical individual as a part of such a class is given the general class name, it looks as if it is thereby subsumed under the general class concept. Thus it seems to be comprehended in a natural scientific, generalizing fashion. However, we should not forget that the word "class"[25] refers not only to the general concept of natural science, but also to a concrete *plurality of individuals*, and from the fact that something is a part of a concrete class, it does not follow that it can be seen only as an instance of the class concept. On the contrary, the concrete class, the nexus – or however we propose to describe a historical *whole* – is individual and distinctive, just like each of its parts. In other words, it is more comprehensive and extensive, but not conceptually more general, than the single individuals of which it consists. The Italian Renaissance, for example, is just as much a historical individual as Machiavelli, the romantic school just as much as Novalis.

Suppose we want to know whether a part of a whole is considered from the standpoint of what it has in common with other parts of this whole, in which case it becomes essential only as an instance of a general concept; or whether it should be grasped in its individuality, the basis on which it is distinguished from all the other parts of its class. In that event, we will always speak, in the first case, of the *instance* of a class concept and, in the second, of the individual *constituent* of the concrete class or collectivity. For history, therefore, Machiavelli and Novalis are not instances but constituents. Their inclusion in the "general" historical nexus of the Renaissance or romanticism signifies the inclusion of one individual in another more comprehensive individual. That this intellectual operation does not coincide with the subsumption of an object as an instance under a general concept can be doubted only by someone who has not learned to distinguish the general *content* of a concept from its general *extension*. That should pose difficulties only for beginning students in logic – even though their number is not inconsiderable among the "modern" theoreticians of history who propose to make history into a natural science.

They should take note of the following. The content of a concept is general because it comprises what is common to a plurality of individuals, or because it applies to an indefinite plurality of individuals. Its extension is general because it comprehends *all* members of a plurality of individuals in an individual nexus or whole. Thus if history is obliged to consider every historical object as a constituent of a "general" – in other words, a relatively comprehensive – nexus, this does not mean that the historian no longer proceeds in an individualizing fashion. He represents even the "general nexus" as an individual and unique construct. Insofar as the whole or the collectivity is relevant to history as a unique and individual reality, there is no *logical* opposition between the individualizing historical method, as we understand it, and the only kind of historical method that can be regarded as "collectivistic."

In short, we see that the principles of historical conceptualization are not altered by the inclusion of the single individual in the general – that is, more comprehensive, but in other respects still individual – nexus. Since the relationship of the part to the whole remains relative, it cannot be otherwise. In other words, every extensive manifold of parts can also be conceived as an intensive manifold, and thus every individual must be conceived both as a constituent of a whole and also as a whole that has its own constituents.

Precisely for this reason, however, one point seems to pose difficulties. If we place every individual within a new whole, ultimately we must reach a whole that no longer belongs to a nexus that is even more comprehensive. This "ultimate whole," therefore, would necessarily have to be an isolated entity – in other words, something whose existence history does not admit. In fact, however, this poses no new problem for us. From a logical standpoint, the ultimate historical whole would be the actual universe. As long as there was a "universal history" in the true sense of the word, as was the case during the Middle Ages, its most comprehensive nexus, which lay between the Creation and the Last Judgment, in fact had to be an isolated individual. The world as a whole was bounded by nothingness or the nonworld. But we no longer regard the real "cosmos" as an object of possible experience. As we could show, there is not even a generalizing science of the cosmos as a whole. Thus this concept no longer has any significance for a logic of history. Of course, it is always true that the "ultimate" *historical* whole can be placed as a constituent in a more extensive nexus, which actually is an individual as well. But in the final analysis, this more comprehensive nexus can no longer have significance as a whole, but only through the uniqueness of one of its parts. In consequence, it possesses historical individuality only in this respect. Therefore, its other parts come into question only as instances of natural scientific concepts, in the way we have already shown. If we consider the cosmos in the strict sense, natural science has to form concepts of it, but only in the sense that these concepts are valid for all of its aspects. History, on the other hand, underscores one of its aspects, because of the significance the individuality of this aspect has with reference to values. In this aspect, history sees the *ultimate* whole with which, as history, it is still concerned. Therefore, this aspect of the cosmos, conceived in an individualizing fashion by means of value relevance, is the "ultimate" or the most comprehensive *historical* nexus conceivable.

To make this quite clear, suppose we attempt to elucidate the concept of the ultimate historical whole and the relations between the historical constituent and the historical nexus with some examples. We begin with a historical personality. It is an individual whole and at the same time an individual constituent, an extensive as well as an intensive historical manifold. It forms a unified whole insofar as it comprehends everything that is historically significant to it. Each of its acts and every aspect of its fate are individual. Insofar as its acts and its fate are historical individuals, the personality is constituted for history by its acts and its fate as its parts. These parts unite in the personality to form a unity with reference to the significance the personality as a whole possesses for the governing value. At the same time, however, such a personality is a constituent of a more extended whole – a family, a generation, a people, an age – to which it is related in the same way that each of its parts is related to it. This is because each of the more comprehensive nexuses can also be seen as a unified individual whose components are formed by personalities, families, or peoples that belong to it as its essential constituents. This whole, then, is included in a still more comprehensive individual whole, and so on, and so on.

In the final analysis, the ultimate historical whole can be the culture of humanity, or humanity itself. In that case, the culture of humanity would be a constituent of humanity. The latter, however, would also be a constituent of the organic world. Or does the organic world form a historical individual as well? In other words, among its parts, is it not merely humanity that is conceived as a historical individual? On the contrary, can its other parts also be regarded as historical individuals? Finally, can the limit perhaps be extended further still? Can our planet qualify as a historical individual, and is it the ultimate historical whole? Or must it be seen as a constituent of a more comprehensive nexus, the solar system, and is it only the latter in which we would have the most comprehensive, "ultimate" historical individual? In any case, we have to stop with the solar system. This is because we know too little of the other parts of the whole of which it is a constituent in order for them to become historically significant on the basis of their individuality as well. For the present, at any rate, they come into question only as instances of general concepts. This is logically fortuitous, however, for without knowledge of the content of the governing values of the selection, the concept of the ultimate historical whole cannot be substantively defined. Here it is essential to note only that at some point, the most comprehensive historical whole is included in a still more extensive nexus that is no longer a historical individual. On the contrary, its other parts are of interest only for a generalizing science.

For the rest, the chief purpose of our reflections was to show how historical science, even when it links its objects to the "most general" – that is, most comprehensive – cosmic nexuses, still does not cease to be a science of the individual, the unique, and the specific.

---

5. Historical development

In another respect, the idea of the causal nexus is even more important.[26] We need only recall a famous saying of Schopenhauer's, that causality is not a taxi we can halt at will, for it to seem that the firm bond the theoretical relation to a value imposes on a process, thereby consolidating it into a necessary unity, is again broken. Every individual cause we ascertain is itself an individual effect that also has its own individual cause. If we consider that no historical object would be as it is without the individual character of another individual cause, then the relation to the value that constitutes a process as a historical development is transposed onto the individual configuration of events that is causally connected with this process, even though the content of this configuration need not be essential or significant for the value. Then it is first of all the case that every developmental sequence must be traced into the past. And second, it seems that if our requirement of causality is to be satisfied, every developmental sequence must be extended not only longitudinally but also laterally, for every stage of a historical process is causally determined both by past events and by events that are contemporaneous with it.

Thus we will have to introduce another new concept to completely understand the logical structure of the representation of historical developmental sequences. Indeed, it is necessary to distinguish two kinds of historical in-dividuals. The first has a direct relation to the governing value, the second an indirect relation *mediated* by the causal nexus. As a result, we can speak of *primary* and *secondary* historical individuals.

It will not always be easy to specify in detail which historical objects belong to one kind and which to the other. It can happen that an individual with a primary historical significance from one governing value perspective has only a secondary historical significance – or no historical significance at all – from another perspective. Friedrich Wilhelm I, for example, can have only a secondary interest for the history of *philosophy*, insofar as he influenced the destiny of Christian Wolff. For the *political* history of Prussia, on the other hand, he can be an eminently primary historical individual. There are only a few individuals who can be claimed to have a primary historical significance from every perspective, but there are many of whom it can be said that there is no perspective from which they have a primary historical significance. For example, Schiller's father is considered only in the history of German literature, and here he can be regarded only as a secondary historical individual, in other words, as a man who would have no interest for us had he not been Schiller's father. In any case, the division of primary and secondary historical individuals is conceptually clear as soon as we set down the following. For a given governing value perspective, one kind of object is consolidated as a historical in-dividual directly as a result of the peculiar character of the content of its manifold. In the case of the other kind of object, the historical interest in it arises only by means of the intermediate link of the causal connection that obtains between it and the directly essential or primary historical individual.

6. The natural scientific components of the historical sciences

The foregoing analyses were intended to work out the difference between historical and natural scientific concept formation as rigorously as possible. Thus attention was focused on what we call the *absolutely* historical. In consequence, it was necessary for us to exaggerate the logical opposition of natural science and history, in other words, to set up a logical ideal to which science, in part, cannot even aspire. We know, however, that such an "exaggeration" belongs to the methodical principles of our investigation, and it is harmless as long as the necessary restrictions are not absent. Thus the restrictions that follow should not be regarded as "concessions" that would again weaken the clearly articulated logical principle. Now the point is rather to show how the logical principle takes shape when *applied* to the actual *praxis* of science. Its application would not be possible had we not previously overstated the principle in working it out in its pure state.

The reason why the concepts developed earlier require further determination in order to be employed for the understanding of historical science as it actually exists should be clear from the foregoing analyses. When we set up the most general form of the opposition of natural science and history by means of the difference between the general and the individual, we saw the extent to which the different parts of natural science form more or less general concepts and thus, in our terminology, also exhibit components that are more or less historical. As a result, the concept of nature became relative.[27] Because the purely logical concepts of nature and history are interdefinable, it follows that just as there are historical components in natural science, so there are natural scientific components in history. Thus the concept of the historical must become relative as well. But as long as the concept of historical *representation* remained purely problematic, we could only allude to this consequence without saying exactly what should be understood by a *concept* that is relatively historical. Now that we are acquainted with the principle of historical concept formation in its most general form as individualizing value relevance, we have to define it in such a way that it can be applied to the relatively historical. Only then will it be possible to understand the logical structure of the historical science that actually exists, for there is no historical representation that employs concepts that are only absolutely historical.

We arrive at the problem that concerns us here only when a concept with a content that is general in the sense of natural science also produces an exhaustive historical representation, or when *generalization* is also capable *of individualization* in such a way that nothing which is historically essential with reference to value relevance is lost. This will always be the case where historical meaning attaches to a complex of characteristics that occur not only in a single real object but also in several individuals that otherwise are quite different from one another. Then these individuals not only comprise a group; a group concept can also suffice for their historical representation. As always, the group as a *whole* is unique and individual, consisting of nothing but individuals. But since none of these individuals exhibit historically essential characteristics that are not also shared by all the other individuals that belong to the group, history need not form an absolute historical concept of such a historical whole. In other words, it need not represent its individual parts for their own sake. On the contrary, in such a case, the historian too sees the individuals that make up the group as *equivalent*. By virtue of these same characteristics, every individual is both a member of a historical whole as well as an instance of a general concept. As a result, individualizing historical concepts are formed by means of value relevance. And yet they have a general content: In other words, they comprehend what is common to *all* the individuals of a group. This common feature is, then, what is essential with reference to the governing value of the representation, and it also adequately exhibits the individuality of the group.

At this point, suppose we take a look back. The logical distinctiveness of an empirical science is to be understood in terms of the relationship the content of its concepts bears to empirical reality in its unique and distinctive form. The fundamental difference between natural science and history is that natural science forms concepts with a general content, whereas history forms concepts with an individual content. Or, the former generalizes and the latter individualizes. But this does not mean that the particular has *no* significance for natural science and the general *no* significance for historical science. Not only are the concepts of the general and the particular relative, but no science at all is possible without general concepts. Nevertheless, the vague formulation that history requires the "general" says little about its method of concept formation. Moreover, there is certainly no sense in which the idea of a universal method based on natural science can be justified in this way. First, the "general" does not always refer to a concept with general content. And even in the case of general concepts, what is important is the position they occupy in the totality of a science and the principle that consolidates their elements into a unity.

Above all, we must distinguish the following four kinds of generality in history.

First, the *elements* of all scientific concepts are general. Only natural science forms from these elements concepts that themselves have a general content. History forms from them concepts with individual content.

Second, history cannot represent all individuals, but only those that are essential with reference to a *general value*. Nevertheless the relevance to this value does not make the content of concepts general. On the contrary, the general significance of historical objects attaches precisely to their individuality.

Third, historical science never regards individuals in isolation, as the generalizing sciences do, but in a *general nexus*. Again, this is not a concept with a general content, but rather an individual reality. The incorporation of an individual into the "general" whole to which it belongs cannot be confused with its subsumption under a general generic concept. In the last two cases, therefore, we cannot even speak of natural scientific components within a historical nexus of ideas.

Only in the fourth and last case, when history comprehends a *group* of individuals so that each qualifies as equally significant, does history form concepts with a general content. But even in this case, it does not employ a natural scientific *method*, for concepts that are relatively historical do not have the purpose of articulating the "general nature" of the objects subsumed under them. Their content is intended rather to represent the historical individuality of a group of objects that all become historically essential by means of the same characteristics. Thus they are "historical" concepts – in other words, formed in an individualizing fashion through value relevance – not only because their general content, in comparison with an entity even more general, is particular and is regarded explicitly with reference to this particularity, but also because precisely these and no other components are linked by means of a "teleological" principle to form a unity, as a result of which the conceptual elements are connected in a *coherent* fashion.

In view of the foregoing, it should be clear what we mean both by natural scientific components in history and by relatively historical concepts. We should emphatically reiterate that these amplifications of the concept of the historical as we first set it up are indispensable to the logic of the historical sciences. It would never occur to us to maintain that natural science is concerned *only* with the general and history *only* with the individual. Even a cursory glance at representations in natural science and history shows that this would be mistaken. Natural science always proceeds from the unique and the individual, and history is continually in need of general group concepts. The only point was to show what significance the general and the individual have in the natural sciences and the historical sciences. However, a logic of the sciences will never ignore the fact that in *all* scientific disciplines, the general and the particular are *connected* with each other in the most intimate fashion.

7. Historical science and mental life

Nevertheless, we have still not finished.[28] In addition to logical and formal differences, there are *material* differences that no one will deny, and logic must obviously be concerned with them as well. In fact, the theory of historical science will be *complete* only by examining *both* principles of differentiation. We know why we were obliged to *begin* with purely logical oppositions. Now that we are acquainted with them and have developed the differential logical structure of conceptualization in both history and natural science, we are compelled to consider the question of whether and to what extent a methodologically significant *connection* between the *formal* and the *material* differences of the sciences is demonstrable. Only by answering this question can we obtain a *substantive* concept of history that must be more limited than the previously established formal concept and that we can eventually link with what is generally understood by a "historical science."

We now turn to this new problem. Suppose that on the basis of the logical distinctions developed in the foregoing, we now show that the actually existing material differences between the sciences – which we intentionally disregarded at first and which are usually employed to distinguish the sciences from one another – can also be understood as logically necessary. This demonstration does not signify a softening of our position; nor does it even represent a "concession" to the usual way of proceeding in these problems, which is not rigorously logical. On the contrary, it forms the necessary conclusion of our logical theory, its real *confirmation* and culmination. This is because it is only by considering material differences that we can show how our logical concepts can be made *fruitful* for the entire theory of science. As regards the opposition of formal and material – and this point must always be stressed – it is a question not of "either/or" but of "both/and." To give precedence to form, as we were obliged to do, is not to *ignore* content completely.

We have already considered the material differences between objects in the distinction between nature and "spirit." This distinction becomes most obvious in the consideration that history is in fact primarily concerned with *mental* or *psychic* processes. Of course, if one takes the "materialistic" philosophy of history seriously, it might seem as if this were placed in doubt. In truth, however, this doctrine has virtually nothing to do with the question of whether historical objects are psychic or physical. Even if it were true that all historical movements are determined by "material" interests – in other words, by the aspiration for things that preserve and advance corporeal existence – *endeavors* oriented to "material" goods remain volitional acts, and thus mental processes. A "materialist" history is concerned with them as well. Thus we are obliged to pose the following question: How is the fact that the material of history is *mental life* – even if not exclusively, but at least in part, and often primarily – relevant to the logical structure of historical conceptualization?

The first and most general concept of the historical had its source in the concept of the limits of the natural sciences. This is why, from a logical point of view, we were obliged to reject "human science" as the name for history. In addition, value-relevant and individualizing conceptualization also seemed indifferent to the distinction between mind and body. The *first* concept of the historical individual was even developed by comparing two material objects and was then applied to mental individuals without requiring the addition of anything new in principle. In the further course of our investigation, we were also able to develop logical principles without considering the substantive characteristics of the psychic. When reference to examples made the discussion of human mental life unavoidable, a concept formed in this way was still not *exclusively* applicable to representations of psychic existence. We must now, however, attend to the fact that most historical sciences are predominantly concerned with mental processes. This raises two questions of logical importance.

From this fact, can we perhaps derive further previously unnoticed distinctive logical features of the historical method that would force on us another definition of the concept of historical science? And, assuming that this question is to be answered in the negative, is the predominance of the psychic in the material of history quite arbitrary methodologically, or can it be understood on the basis of the logical nature of historical conceptualization? The second question is not resolved with the first. Even if further logical properties specific to historical representation cannot be established on the basis of the concept of the psychic, it is still possible that mental life has properties as a result of which it *requires* a historical representation by means of a value-relevant, individualizing conceptualization to a greater extent than holds true for physical existence.

Even if we begin by contesting the view that completely new logical *principles* definitive for historical representation can be established on the basis of the concept of real psychic existence, this does not mean that we overlook the fact that a fundamental difference obtains in the *investigation* of mental and corporeal material and that this difference would have to be taken into account by the parts of methodology concerned with the determination and the *critical analysis* of *the factual material* of history. Bodies are immediately given to us all through sense perception. As regards the totality of psychic processes, on the other hand, our direct knowledge based on sense perception is limited to our own mental life. In representing a real mental process, therefore, the historian lacks access to the object of immediate experience. However, does anything of significance for establishing the logical ideal of a historical *representation* follow from this?

We know why the difference between the physical and the psychic just mentioned implies no fundamental methodological differences for the natural scientific or generalizing mode of analysis. A natural scientific concept never attempts to comprehend the individuality of an object. This is why the psychologist who generalizes on the basis of his own directly accessible mental life can develop material for the formation of concepts that are valid for *all* psychic existence. At most, the inaccessibility of third-person mental life, as a result of which it cannot be directly experienced, creates difficulties for this psychologist in that he cannot bracket the individual on the basis of a direct comparison. On the contrary, it is often only by means of a complicated chain of inferences that he learns whether this or that psychic characteristic is generally distributed or purely individual. In historical conceptualization, on the other hand, are matters not fundamentally different? It is precisely from the perspective of its individual qualities that the historian represents third-person mental life. Thus he is concerned with what is inaccessible to immediate observation under all conditions. This is why it seems that the historical representation of psychic processes is actually linked with difficulties that differ in principle from those that would be posed by the representation of directly observable bodies. In the final analysis, therefore, does not the concept of "human science"[29] acquire a fundamental logical significance, even if — or precisely if — what we understand by "mind"[30] is nothing other than the temporal course of real mental existence?

Because this question is of interest for us only insofar as it bears on the problem of whether additional essential *logical* modifications should be introduced into the opposition developed earlier, between generalizing and individualizing conceptualization, our answer can be negative. Consider the difficulties posed for the historian by the inaccessibility of third-person mental life. Disregarding the importance they acquire for the process of research and *investigation* — which is irrelevant to our inquiry — they are essentially included among the factors that follow from the disparity between source material and factual material that is necessary to all history. *Logically*, therefore, they signify nothing more than the *incompleteness* of the factual material of history, which can almost always be confirmed. It is true that the historian needs the capacity — as this is often put — to "place himself in" the mental life of another person or to "recreate" other individualities in his own experience. In this case, he practices a variety of theoretical activity known neither to the physical scientist nor to the generalizing psychologist. This activity, of course, poses interesting problems concerning the mutual "understanding" of individuals. But this consideration does not show that the distinctiveness of so-called historical understanding has any importance in principle for the *logical* structure of historical *representation*, which is our only concern here.

Thus we only have to answer the other question. Can the fact that psychic realities are more frequently represented in the unique and individual development than holds true for corporeal realities be understood on the basis of the logical nature of historical conceptualization, or must this remain logically fortuitous?[31]

But, so it will be asked, can we even pose such a question in light of the foregoing considerations? Suppose that the distinction between the physical and the psychic that is necessary to the natural scientific interest is unimportant for history. And suppose that the concept of the spiritual that history would have to form in order to retain the concept of a unified world that can be represented historically remains undefined. In that case, does the claim that history is primarily concerned with "spiritual" or "mental" processes qualify as an unequivocal proposition? Is it not rather the case that without a *line of demarcation* between the physical and the psychic — and one that is also acknowledged by history — our question about the basis of the privileged status of mental life loses its sense?

This is in fact the case. Even if we ignore this point and provisionally propose to retain the natural scientific distinction between the physical and the psychic, it would immediately be clear that we could never understand why that which falls under the concept of what occupies space should be less significant for a historical representation than that which does not occupy space, which holds true for everything that is psychic. As regards the psychic in this sense, an individualizing representation can be no more necessary than it is for the physical. Thus we must try to identify a distinction between body and "spirit" that differs from the one usually employed in the generalizing sciences. Only in this way can we hope to understand why it is actually the case that mental life is more often represented in an individualizing historical fashion than holds true for corporeal existence.

If we begin with empirical reality that has not yet been analyzed by natural science, we can clearly differentiate in it processes in which a way of acting on the basis of alternatives is expressed – in other words, acknowledgment or refusal, approval or disapproval, desire or abhorrence, affirmation or denial: in short, *taking a position on a value* – from processes that are indifferent to all values. This difference is of fundamental significance for us in the following respect: Without encountering a contradiction, we will always characterize all realities that – in the sense just indicated – take a position or valuate only as mental processes, and never as corporeal processes. The converse of this proposition is, of course, not true: The act of valuating cannot be ascribed to everything that qualifies as mental or psychic. If, for example, we claim that we only "conceive" something, we exclude valuating from mental life but include conceiving. So there may be much more in the domain of real existence that does not valuate, and yet still should be included in mental life. In consequence, this concept of the mental would be too narrow. It is sufficient, however, if the only point is to know what *always* qualifies as mental – and thus not corporeal – with a view to posing an unambiguous question about the relationship between mental life and history.

In these considerations, we even have an indication of the direction in which the question must be answered. Since the concept of value is connected with the concept of the historical in such a way that the only reality represented historically is reality as related to a value, and since the concept of the mental is linked with the concept of value in such a way that only mental beings[32] are valuating beings, then *the concept of value also establishes the relationship between the mental and the historical*. Moreover, the value-relevant moment of historical conceptualization must make it clear why real mental life stands in a different and more intimate relationship to historical science than does real corporeal existence. So from the *formal* concept of historical method, we finally arrive at the *substantive* character of the historical *material*.

Of course these remarks alone do not yet say very much about the nature of such a relationship. In the first place, it seems that the objects of history are connected with a psychic existence insofar as they are objects for a *subject* that distinguishes their essential from their inessential aspects with reference to a value. It could be shown that even the scientific subject must take a position and valuate; thus it must also be a mental being in the sense explained. Even though this consideration is quite important for the objectivity of the sciences, there is *no* science that lacks such a relationship of its objects to a mental being that forms concepts. If this fact were decisive for the methodical character of a scientific representation, natural science would also have to be described as a human science[33] on the grounds that it is also inconceivable without a "mind"[34] that distinguishes the essential from the inessential. So if our purpose is to discover the special connection that obtains between historical method and mental life, we should begin by completely disregarding the cognitive *subject* of science and concern ourselves exclusively with the *objects* of history. In other words, we should consider only the question of why it is primarily real mental existence that is found in *the factual material* of history.

In every case in which reality is related to a value, the objects with which we are acquainted fall into two fundamentally different classes: those for which this relationship is merely possible, and those that not only *signify* something for the value by virtue of their existence but also *take a position on this value*. Objects belonging to the first class can be mental as well as corporeal. Objects of the second class, on the other hand, which are essential because of the position they take on the value, are necessarily mental. We should consider this point first. Suppose that in an empirical reality to be represented in an individualizing fashion or in the factual material of history, there were such beings who also take a position on the values that govern their individualizing representation. In that case, these beings would have to occupy the *central focus* of the material represented. In other words, all other objects would not only qualify as historically essential insofar as they become historical individuals with reference to the governing values of the *subject* of the scientific representation – that is, the historian; they would also qualify as historically essential insofar as their individuality has a significance for the real mental *objects* whose volitions and actions are represented. Thus history would link these other objects to the governing values of the representation, and it also would connect them with the mental beings represented, the beings that take a position, valuate, and are present in the *material* of history. In this way, a concept of historical representation more *limited* than the previous concept is developed. As long as we did not reflect on a specific historical material, we were concerned solely with *one* kind of historical object. But if we presuppose mental objects of the kind just indicated, or historical personalities that *valuate*, they must be distinguished from other objects. In particular, all bodies in such a representation become essential only in the following way: because of what links them to the governing values of the cognitive *subject*, the historian, as well as because of the way they influence the volitional and valuational *objects* – that is, the mental processes of the historical personalities represented – or because of the manner in which they are the object of the volitions and actions of these personalities. Consider, for example, a history of Italy that is governed by the perspective of the value attached to art. Here it must above all be the volitions and actions of *artists* that are essential. It is their individuality that is significant from the standpoint of the governing value, and all other real existence will be connected to this *mental* phenomenon of volition and action.

In order to make the paramount significance of mental beings within the historical material explicit, we propose to designate as *historical centers* all historical objects that themselves take a position on the governing values of the representation and that must always be mental entities. Then we will see that if such centers are present in the material of the representation, history necessarily relates everything else to them. According to the foregoing, however, it is only *possible* that there are such centers in the material of history. Even by this point, therefore, our concept of history remains *substantively* undefined. Indeed, in light of the foregoing exposition, it does *not* seem necessary that such mental entities are *always* present in the historical material. Finally, it is not clear why these entities have to take a position concerning precisely *those* values that govern the historical representation. In other words, it is not clear why they are always historical centers. Thus we must move beyond the mere possibility, which is all we have established up to this point, and show why some sort of mental life *necessarily* belongs to all historical material.

This will be managed without difficulty as soon as we consider the only conditions under which a reality can *give us occasion* to represent it in an individualizing fashion, and when we further reflect that not every arbitrary value can become the governing perspective of a historical representation. The results of this consideration will then be, first, that every historical object must be related not only to values in general but also to a real valuating – and thus mental – entity; second, that the presence of these mental entities in the material of history is not logically fortuitous; and, third, that we have occasion to represent a reality in a historical or individualizing fashion only under the following condition: Among these mental entities, there are some that themselves take a position on the governing values of the representation. In consequence, there is in fact *no historical representation without a real mental center*.

At this point, we do not need to show why an explicit justification of this fact – which is probably self-evident to every historian – is not superfluous from the standpoint of methodology. This is the only way it is possible to understand the logical structure of the historical "human sciences." Finally, it is also the only way we can see why the concept of the human sciences has been so tenaciously held to be important for methodology.[35]

In regard to the necessary relationship of every historical object to a valuing mental being, we will return once more to the prescientific conception of reality characteristic of practical life, from which our definition of the concept of the historical individual began. The agreement between historical conceptualization and the prescientific conceptualization of the active and volitional person consisted in the fact that for both, the individuality of things acquires significance. The fundamental difference between the two lay in the fact that the historian does not take a volitional and valuational position on things, but rather relates them to a value by considering them theoretically. Thus although historical objects are also detached from every valuating, volitional, and active being in the sense that they can no longer be objects of a direct valuation, the values to which they are related cannot – as this might be put – "remain suspended in space." In other words, they cannot merely "hold validly" as "pure" values. On the contrary, if we are concerned with a *historical* science of reality, they must be values appraised by a real volitional, valuating – and thus also mental – being. But this implies that to qualify as the object of a historical individualizing representation, an entity must not only stand in a general logical relationship to values, but must also have a *real* connection to an actual valuating being. It follows that there is a certain sense in which the concept of a psychological life and the concept of a historical individual that is conceived in a value-relevant fashion are inseparable.[36]

This insight is not sufficient for our purpose, however. Valuating mental beings always appear as mental beings in the historical *material* as well. It seems that the preceding considerations have not yet made this understandable. To demonstrate the extent to which this is necessary, we should not reflect on a representation that is restricted to a *part* of a historical development. On the contrary, we must consider the most comprehensive historical nexus or the "ultimate historical whole," as we have called it: the whole that still possesses a historical individuality for the governing value perspectives of the representation, and to which all objects, which are merely its parts, can be interrelated as constituents. For example, one might think that historical biology is not at all concerned with mental life. But that holds only as long as we confine ourselves to one of its aspects. The historical whole of biological development includes man – insofar as he represents its "peak" – as a mental entity too. Otherwise we could not speak of "progress." And, as we have seen, the entire sequence must be related to man to qualify as a *historical* "development."[37] In the same way, psychic realities, with which all historical individuals must be brought into a real connection, also belong to every historical whole. Thus it follows that in a comprehensive historical whole, all historical objects stand in some sort of historical connection with mental entities.

There is, of course, a special case that creates difficulties in this context. The real mental being to which historical development is related – and that, in consequence, necessarily belongs to the real historical nexus as a constituent – may possibly be a *single* individual, namely, the historian. This seems to be an exception to the foregoing position, which requires that we abstract from the cognitive subject. But suppose we examine this case more closely. If no mental entity other than the historian is present in the historical material to be represented, the historian comes into question not *only* as a cognitive subject but also as an *object* in a historical nexus with the other individuals. As a constituent, therefore, he is necessarily incorporated into the most comprehensive object of historical representation, or the whole of the value-relevant sequence of development. This entails that in the ultimate historical whole, there is always at least *one* mental entity.

Finally, why should this mental entity always constitute the historical *center* as well? When the historian himself is not only the cognitive subject, but must also be included in the most comprehensive historical nexus of the objects represented, the answer to this question is obvious. This is because the governing values of the representation are necessarily those on which the historian takes a value position. We have mentioned this possibility only to show that there is *no* conceivable case in which a mental entity fails to appear in the historical material. In fact, the historian almost always represents developmental sequences to which he himself does not belong as a historical constituent, sequences in which only other mental entities are present. Why should these mental entities include those who themselves take a value position on precisely the values that govern the historical representation?

This is in fact the decisive issue. Here too, however, the answer is not difficult. Suppose that the values of the narrator himself, on which he takes a value position, are not held by any of the mental beings that belong to the most comprehensive historical nexus. Nevertheless, to understand these beings, he must at least be able to "get the feel" of their values. This is because whenever a reality stands in no relationship either to us or to valuing beings whom we can understand, we will see that reality solely as "nature." That is, in science, we will try to subsume it under a system of general concepts. For a historical representation, this leaves only two possibilities open. On the one hand, the values of the mental beings that belong to the historical material are the same values with reference to which historical individuals are formed for the narrator as well. In that case, the matter is simple, for it is self-evident that these "spiritual" beings will also be historical centers. In a history of art, for example, the value of art with reference to which historical concepts are formed for the historian is the same value on which artists take a real value position. Thus the artists in question must necessarily become historical centers. Or, on the other hand, the values of the mental beings are not those of the narrator, as will be the case for events that are spatially or temporally remote from him. Then he must get the feel of these mental beings to the extent of being able to understand them. As a result, suppose that the unique and individual actions and passions of these valuating mental beings have become interesting to him. In that case, as long as he conceives these mental entities in a strictly historical fashion – in other words, as long as he proposes only to relate them to values theoretically – he can do no more than the following: In distinguishing the essential from the inessential in a representation of these beings based on value relevance, he is obliged to employ the values on which they take a real value position. This is because it would make sense to employ for concept formation values totally different from those found in the historical material itself only if the objects were not to be represented historically in a value-relevant fashion on the basis of a standard of value but were, rather, to be valuated. And we know that this cannot be the task of the historian who proceeds in an "objectively" scientific way.

So at least as regards those historical representations that are fundamentally restricted to a theoretical value relationship, and thus in no sense take a practical or extratheoretical value position as well, it is clear why we cannot speak of a purely fortuitous coincidence between *those* values that govern the representation and those that determine the valuative conduct of the mental beings represented. In a representation that is purely scientific in the sense at stake here, the values governing conceptualization are always to be derived from the historical *material itself*. That is, they must always be values in regard to which the beings or centers themselves – the objects of the representation – act in a valuative fashion. To understand this result, it is necessary for us always to keep in mind that it holds exclusively for the *logical ideal* of an "objective" historical representation. Thus it cannot hold true for a historical science that goes beyond the theoretical value relationship to the practical valuation of its material.

Therefore we come to the following result. First, every historical individual is related to real beings that valuate and thus are mental. Second, these mental beings must be included among the objects from which the ultimate whole of the historical representation is constituted. And third, these beings must also be the mental historical centers, with which all other objects are to be brought into a real historical nexus in a value-relevant fashion. So the *stricter* concept of history, which in the foregoing was obtained as a mere possibility, has become the *substantive concept of history in general*. At the same time, we approximate much more closely what the empirical sciences regard as history in the stricter sense than was possible by means of the purely formal concept of history. The linguistic usage that is tied to substantive rather than logical differences will call "historical" only those representations in which mental beings constitute their center.

As we now see, this is quite legitimate. For this reason, we should not dream of contesting the view that history in the strict sense, as a special science, must always be concerned with mental objects too; to *this extent*, therefore, it can be called a human science. At the same time it is again clear why a logical investigation cannot *begin* with the concept of human science as a science of real *mental life*. The fact that history is a science of mental entities does not determine its logical structure, for mental processes can also be represented in a natural scientific or generalizing fashion. Rather, the converse is true: On the basis of the logical structure of historical science – in other words, from the nature of an individualizing and value-relevant conceptualization – it can be understood why history primarily takes a certain kind of mental life as the object of its investigation.

Thus we can understand quite well how it happened that almost all theories of historical science attempted to obtain the decisive criterion for its differentiation from natural science by means of the substantive opposition of body and spirit. The foregoing discussion explains the broad currency of views of this sort and even lends them a *relative* justification. All students of the disciplines that do not fall within the natural sciences – the theologian, the jurist, the philologist, the historian, and the economist – feel that, in comparison with natural scientists, they belong together. If we inquire into the reason for this, we will always be disposed to regard the concept of the "spiritual" – in other words, the concept of the psychic – as the bond that ties the nonnatural scientific disciplines together into a unified whole. In fact, their objects are and must be predominantly mental. Thus it is easy to understand why anyone who proposes to survey the entire domain of scientific activity and its differences would divide the sciences into natural sciences and human sciences, or sciences of mental phenomena. Finally, suppose that in the attempt to develop a theory of the human sciences, the volitional and *valuing* subject is taken as the starting point. Because natural science – including psychology, but in contrast to history and the other "human sciences" – must always detach its objects from every valuing subject, the starting point chosen is not false. It can even bring much to light that is valuable for the characterization of history and its opposition to natural science.

The detailed pursuit of this matter would carry us too far. Moreover it is not needed, for even at this juncture the following point must be obvious: Despite the necessary connection between history and mental life, whoever wants to understand both the *logical* and the *substantive* differences between natural science and history will not succeed by *beginning* with the mental and the concept of human science. We no longer need to show that in this way, the logical oppositions of method are more obscured than clarified. Even if we construe the concept of "mind" so narrowly that only volitional and valuing beings fall under it, we must always emphasize that like any other reality, they can also be subsumed under the concepts of natural science or treated in a generalizing fashion. From a logical standpoint, therefore, wherever the understanding of the nature of *historical* science is at stake, the term human science remains as vacuous as ever.

In addition, it should also be explicitly pointed out that nothing can be achieved even if we employ the concept of the spiritual as a specific *kind* of psychic phenomenon in order to define the substantive concept of history. In that case, the concept will be too narrow in a certain respect and much too broad in another. The concept is too narrow in the sense that only the historical center must be a being that takes a value position, and thus a mental being as well. Even the historical center is never represented by history in its "spirituality," which is achieved exclusively by conceptual isolation. In other words, it is never represented as a mental being, but rather always as a complete mental and physical reality. The concept is too broad in the sense that not *all* volitional and valuing mental beings are also objects of historical science. Thus another concept of mind would have to be formed even if it is only the central material of the historical sciences that is to be defined by its means. As a result, the fact that a necessary relationship between mental life and history obtains to the limited extent that valuing beings are always psychic beings, shows just how *little* can be learned from these considerations, even for the problem of defining a substantive concept of history.

If the word "mind" is used in a sense still more restricted than that just indicated, its meaning becomes arbitrary. In a methodological investigation, therefore, it would be most advantageous to drop the concept of human science[38] in which "mind"[39] continues to be understood as a real psychic being. There is only one reason why the expression has become entrenched: Formerly what was understood by "mind" was different from what is meant today. It actually stood in opposition to what is merely psychic. Nothing but misunderstandings can result from the retention of expressions that not only have forfeited their earlier meaning but are even expressly employed in a sense different from that of their former use. The danger of such misunderstandings is particularly acute in the case of the word "mind." This is why the polemic against the term "human science" is more than a verbal quibble. We can terminate the controversy only when we are again in the habit of understanding by "mind" something different from the psychic. In that case, it would be especially important to distinguish this concept from what J.S. Mill has in mind when he speaks of a "logic of the human sciences." Indeed, this word should be used only on the assumption that everyone knows quite well that the spiritual[40] is juxtaposed not only to the corporeal but also to the purely psychic. The concept of the spiritual as the psychic remains totally inadequate under all circumstances for the characterization of historical method, as well as for the definition of the historical material. This will become quite clear when we find out what actually constitutes the material of the so-called contemporary human sciences.

8. The historical sciences of culture

Suppose we want to determine those aspects of reality for which a natural scientific, generalizing mode of treatment can never suffice, and thus which *material* not only makes a historical, individualizing representation possible but also demands it. In other words, suppose we want to arrive at a complete *substantive* concept of history on the basis of a more precise determination of the logical principles explicated in the foregoing. In that case, we are obliged to employ the concept of the *values* that govern historical concept formation. The issue of which material becomes historically *essential* and which does not depends on these values. In particular, a more precise determination of their content must identify the content of the historical *center*. This is the preeminent issue for – to the extent that this is possible in logic – a substantive concept of the historical center also implies a substantive concept of the historical in general.

It is obvious that the further development of this line of thought is possible only by ascertaining *facts* that can no longer be deduced as logically necessary. The circumstance that a value as such governs historical representation made it understandable that the historical center is always a valuing entity. Thus it is also a mental entity and in this sense "spiritual"[41]. But even this point could be determined only by reference to the fact that valuing beings in the empirical world as we know it are never *merely* corporeal beings. This demarcation, which is basically not much more than negative, was the *first* step along a path we will now pursue further. If we propose to restrict the concept of history, *which is still too broad*, then we must successively adduce the various facts from which something germane to the substantive concept of history can be derived.

The *second step* we have to take along such a path follows from the consideration that every putatively scientific historical representation must relate its objects to a value that is a value *for everyone*. In the first place, this refers to all those for whom the historian's representation is intended. But this *generality* of the value can have a twofold sense. It is either the value that is really esteemed by everyone, and thus accepted by them; or it is demanded of everyone as a value that should be esteemed and accepted. In other words, it can have either a *factual* or – as we propose to put it – a *normative generality*. Provisionally, however, the concept of the normative in our case should still be differentiated from the idea of a supraempirical element of *objective* "validity." Even as regards the normative, we will remain within the domain of the factual in the following sense: We will call values "normatively general" when their recognition is in fact *required* of all members of a certain community.[42]

Suppose we consider what follows from this as regards a more exact determination of the governing values of the historical representation. A look at the facts shows that every general value germane to historical science must be a value that is either acknowledged by or required of *human beings*. In the case of normatively general values, this is obvious. And even values that are in fact acknowledged as general can only be values that human beings recognize. For the historian to identify them, they must be open to empirical determination, and this is possible only in the case of human beings. It follows that human beings will always stand in the center of the reality that is the object of a historical representation. We have a historical interest in a reality only if it is truly connected with mental entities who themselves take a position on general human values. And human values, as far as we can tell, are held only by human beings. Thus we have obtained a concept of the historical center – and therefore a concept of history as well – that already comes another step closer to what empirical science in fact regards as "history." The principal object to which existing historical scholarship relates everything else is always the development of *human mental life*.

Even this concept is still too broad, however. The next and *third* step on the path to the definition of the concept of history is taken when we reflect on the following fact: General values – and this holds true for values that are in fact generally acknowledged as well as for normatively general values – obtain only among human beings who live together in some sort of *community*, in other words, *social* beings in the broadest sense of the term. We know that there are no isolated individuals at all in empirical reality. Moreover, human mental life that has developed to the point of recognizing general values can only be a life with other human beings, or a social life.

As regards factually acknowledged general values, the concept itself implies that they are values of a human community. Even when we regard a value as normatively general, however, it is always demanded of a real community of human beings. Concerning the word "community," we should think not only of social groups whose members are situated in spatial and temporal proximity, but also of communities that are held together solely by an "ideal" bond, for example, the communities consisting of all those who take a position on science, on art, and so on, and whose members may be widely dispersed in both space and time. If we call the general values of such communities "social values," we can say that the values governing a historical representation are always human social values. Here again, it follows that there must be human beings in every reality that is a possible object of a historical representation. By virtue of the individuality of their volition and action, they constitute in-dividuals with respect to social values. It also follows that the mental life of a human community, which is significant because of its singularity, stands at the center of every historical representation. Even individuals as apparently isolated and detached as Spinoza should be seen as social beings with regard to the scientific community or the *societas philosophorum* to which they belong, and must belong in order to acquire a historical significance.[43]

Thus the central historical process is always either the development of a single human mental life in an individual social nexus or else an individual social whole whose individual constituents are combined into groups. These individual constituents need be brought only under a relative historical concept because each single constituent is historically essential by virtue of the same volitional acts and the same conduct as all the others. In that case, all other objects are related to these social individuals because they stand in a real historical relationship with them.

Consider, therefore, the principles of value-relevant historical concept formation and the three foregoing facts: the fact that valuing beings are mental beings; the fact that general values are human values; and the fact that for the historian, general human values are social values in the most comprehensive sense of this term. On this basis, we arrive at a concept of history that from a substantive standpoint, already is quite often regarded as exhaustive and is used to distinguish history from natural science. Nature, on the one hand, and human social life, on the other – these are the two groups of facts, so it is supposed, into which the two main groups of sciences are divided. Now we see how such a view acquires a relative *justification* in our investigation.[44]

Only one further point should be noted. This concept of the historical is frequently linked with the idea that "social" life cannot be represented "individualistically." Here again the atom is confused with the individual, and the social totality is confused with the general class concept. That is why we deliberately speak of an "individual social nexus" and of "social individuals." Such a verbal juxtaposition can sound paradoxical only to someone who does not see that the real historical nexus of a society is always something individual and that it is precisely the subsumption of individuals under a general concept that would detach them from the social and historical totality in order to constitute them as abstract atoms. As we have seen, generalizing concept formation necessarily remains connected with a more or less isolating – and, in this sense, atomizing – concept formation.

Nevertheless, even the concept of history we have now obtained is still not sufficiently precise for our purposes. Indeed, the decisive feature is still missing, for on its basis we still do not understand why the purely natural scientific treatment of human social *mental life* should be less *satisfactory* than such a treatment of another real object; in other words, why a generalizing sociology cannot answer all the scientifically essential questions the life of human society poses for us, and why there is also an individualizing history of human society. So to arrive at an even more limited concept of history, we must define the concept of the general value that governs the historical representation more precisely.

In this context, the following point is crucial. The factually general recognition of values with reference to which objects are supposed to become historical in-dividuals cannot rest exclusively on a so-called natural drive. That is, it cannot coincide with the propensity of any given individual, as is the case, for example, in goods such as the appeasement of hunger or satisfaction of the sexual drive. Regardless of how "general" the values may be that are linked with these goods, their realization in goods remains, at least in part, an affair of single individuals. To the extent that this is the case, a formation of individuals that is valid for everyone can never develop with reference to these values. It is only social organizations, created by the members of a society for the satisfaction of their needs, that in their individuality have a significance for everyone conjointly. Thus we can say that the general values governing historical concept formation also must always be a common concern of the members of a community. In that event, the difference between factually general and normatively general values disappears, for under these conditions factually general values must also appear as requirements for all members of the community. In this sense, they can be seen as normatively general values, which is the case, for example, for the values of the church, the nation, law, the state, marriage, the family, economic organization, religion, science, art, and so on. Thus only human beings who become in-dividuals with respect to goods of this sort and the values attached to them are possible historical centers for the science of history. This is because only a representation that gives an account of them can presuppose acknowledgment of its governing values by everyone for whom the representation is intended. In consequence, only such a representation can make a claim to general validity.

Suppose we try to find a common *name* for these values that are attached to goods of this sort, values we have only illustrated thus far. In that case, we will best reconsider the concept *of nature* in order to see what, in addition to the purely logical or purely formal concept of history, stands in *opposition* to it. Here again, we can proceed only from a concept of nature that includes psychic as well as physical existence but that still has a sense different from the sense "nature" bears when it designates reality with respect to the general. Suppose we also consider that by nature we understand all real objects in which we bracket every value relationship – the necessary consequence of subsumption under general concepts. We are not introducing a novel concept of nature. On the contrary, we are simply making explicit the value indifference of the concept of nature already established, which comprehends reality with reference to the general.

Thus there are two groups of concepts that can appear in *opposition* to the concept of nature as understood in this way. Earlier we mentioned pairs of concepts such as nature and art, and nature and morality, as well as pairs of concepts such as nature and God. We could also include nature and mind under this second type – where "mind," however, would not be understood as the empirical material of psychology. *The* common feature of both pairs of concepts would lie in the fact that they juxtapose to the natural as the value free, something that has value as a supranatural, supraperceptual, transcendent entity. It is obvious, however, that here, where we are concerned with determining the principles of an empirical science, metaphysical oppositions such as nature and God or nature and "mind" cannot be employed. In contrast to the supraperceptual, the historical is also "natural." Thus only *that* group of concepts remains that includes the pairs nature and art, nature and morality, and so on; and the name for what is juxtaposed to nature in this way can only be culture. This expression, therefore, will be important for us.

This word, originally used for the cultivation of the soil, is now conventionally employed as the name for *all* those goods that the members of a community take seriously, or whose "cultivation" can be required of them. For this reason, the normatively general social values we have discussed should be designated as *cultural values*, and the opposition of nature and culture finally makes it possible to develop conclusively the *substantive* concept of historical science in opposition to the *substantive* concept of natural science. Culture is the common concern in the life of peoples. Thus it is also the good with reference to whose values individuals acquire their *historical* significance as something that everyone acknowledges. In consequence, general cultural values that are attached to this good govern historical representation and concept formation in the selection of what is essential.

In this context, we will leave open the question of whether there is a relationship between cultural goods and supraperceptual and transcendent goods whose necessity can be demonstrated by philosophy. As an empirical science, history is not concerned with this question. Here the only issue is to demarcate a domain of normatively general entities that are objects of valuation and cultivation from *those* realities we regard as indifferent to values – indeed, realities we must regard in this way if we propose to conceive them as "nature," that is, as mere instances of general concepts that can be replaced by other such instances.

But if normatively general cultural values are the governing principles of every historical representation, we have gone one step farther in the definition of the concept of the historical *center*. In the first place, it is self-evident that *those* persons become preeminently important for history who themselves have taken a real value position on the normatively general social values of the state, law, the economy, art, and so on,[45] persons whose individuality has acquired essential significance for the real course of history in this way. All other real existence remains historical only to the extent that its individuality has an influence on human cultural activity and its results. But this concept of the historical center is still not entirely sufficient for our purposes. The "general" historical nexus is of relevance not only insofar as every historical individual is linked with a more extensive social whole of which it is a constituent. On the contrary, we also have to consider that history – to the extent that this is possible – always has to represent the development of its objects, that is, *sequences of change*, whose successive stages are fundamentally different from each other.

A community of the following sort is, of course, conceivable. In their volition and action, its members take a position on values to which they ascribe normative generality. They may even work unceasingly for the realization of normatively general goals without noticing any essential changes in the character of their activity and its results as time passes. In this case, it seems that history is limited to the representation of a continuous state. Even in such a case, however, the focus of the interest would concern the question of how the continuous state was gradually attained as the result of a unique development. Indeed, if there really were no longer *any* sense in which changes were essential, such a community would no longer have a "history" that still required a distinctive representation. This is because everything of significance in the end product – which no longer undergoes development – must already have been present in the history of its previous unique development. Regardless of this consideration, it is doubtful whether there are many *constant* cultural communities in the sense under consideration here. And in any case, culture, in the sense of the word that has become conventional today, obtains only if, at least earlier, the life of communities has occurred in such a way that the activity of each stage presupposes the activity of the previous stages, or continues to build on their foundation in such a way that an essential and individual *difference* between the various stages can be identified with respect to general values.

In other words, real culture exists only where value-related or historical-teleological *development* either exists or has existed. Thus we see an even more intimate connection between culture and history. It can also be clarified in another way by employing a concept that has been the subject of much discussion. We speak of "natural peoples"[46] and juxtapose them to "historical" peoples as well as to "civilized" or "cultural peoples"[47]. Again we can leave undecided the question of whether there are absolutely unhistorical beings who have no culture at all. But if a people really exhibits no historically essential changes in the entire course of its known development, then in fact we could subsume it only under general concepts of recurrence. In this respect, therefore, we could conceive it only as "nature," in the logical sense. A people exhibits historically essential changes only if it manifests a historical development with reference to its cultural values. On the basis of this consideration, we see that there is only one respect in which it makes sense to speak of natural peoples. We also see the relationship between this concept and the concepts of cultural and historical peoples. As a result, it is again clear that historical peoples must always be cultural peoples, and culture can exist only in historical peoples. The concepts of culture and history condition each other reciprocally. In a certain sense, they are interdependent: It is cultural values alone that make history as a science possible, and it is historical development alone that brings forth real cultural goods to which cultural values are attached.

Now we have finally defined the concept of the *central processes of history* to the extent that this seems necessary for our purposes. The governing perspectives of every historical representation must be values of normatively general validity. These values are realized in the goods to which they are attached only within a historical development. As the historical center, the material that should be historically essential with reference to such values must include the development of human cultural life, to which the other aspects of this material can be related.

Obviously this concept of the historical material as the concept of historical cultural life is also *formal* in a certain respect. It comprises only the members of a historically developing community who have volition and act. The actions of these members become essential by virtue of their individuality when they are related to their own normatively general values and also to the values governing their representation, where the latter values are in agreement with the former. Therefore, the specific *content* of these values and actions remains undetermined and does not concern a logical investigation as such. As was previously the case, the different cultural values mentioned here and the objects that correspond to them should be regarded only as examples. The concept of history that remains formal in relation to culture will suffice to answer the questions we still have to pose. The fact that we call the concept of history obtained in this way both *substantive* and *formal* cannot be a cause for misgivings. It is substantive – and, in this sense, more than formal – in comparison with the *purely* logical concept of reality considered from the perspective of its individuality. But it remains formal in comparison with the concept of a representation that is concerned with a historical material substantively defined in terms of *specific* cultural goods and cultural values. Only in what follows can we show the extent to which the normatively general governing cultural values of an "objective" historical representation must remain formal, in the sense indicated, under all conditions. At this point, we are concerned only with ascertaining the *name* that must be most appropriate for the governing values of history and, in consequence, also for the material that is historically essential with reference to these values. Concerning this point, there can no longer be any doubt.

As a result, we can conclude the purely logical exposition of the structure of concept formation in the historical cultural sciences. The distinctive problem of this book, which was formulated in the Introduction, seems to be solved. We have identified the logical nature of the kind of scientific representation that begins at the limits of concept formation in natural science, as regards both its *method* and the most general character of its *material*. We have also seen the extent to which this representation can fill the lacunae in our knowledge of the real world that must always be left by natural science, no matter how comprehensive it may be. The elucidation of these theses was the chief purpose of our enterprise.

Notes

1 Ch. 4, "Die Historische Begriffsbildung," in *Die Grenzen der Naturwissenschaftlichen Begriffsbildung: Eine logische Einleitung in die historischen Wissenschaften*. Ed. Paul Tillich. Tübingen, 1902. Ed. and trans. Guy Oakes. Cambridge/New York: Cambridge University Press, 1986, pp. 61–138. This is an abridged translation (section 9 of this chapter is omitted). Where the translator has skipped passages in the running text, this is indicated with "…" – Ed.
2 In Rickert's text, the epigraph from Isocrates is quoted in Greek. – Trans.
3 "*Beziehung*"
4 *wertbeziehende*
5 *Wertbeziehung*
6 *Entwicklungsgeschichte*
7 *Geist*
8 *Geisteswissenschaften*
9 *Geisteswissenschaft*

10 *Geist*
11 See *Grundriss der Historik*, 2nd ed., 1895.
12 See *Lehrbuch der historischen Methode*, 5th and 6th eds., 1908, pp. 250 seq.
13 On this point, see my book *Der Gegenstand der Erkenntnis*, 6th edition, 1928, fifth chapter: "Das Problem der objektiven Wirklichkeit" and "Konstitutive Wirklichkeitsformen und methodologische Erkenntnisformen."
14 As Eduard Meyer has done in *Zur Theorie und Methodik der Geschichte*, 1902. See also my book *Kulturwissenschaft und Naturwissenschaft*, 6th and 7th eds., pp. 89 *seq.*
15 *Begriffswissenschaft*
16 *Enzyklopädie und Methodologie der philologischen Wissenschaften*, 1877, p. 20.
17 *Zusammengehörig* literally means "belonging together." *Zusammengehörigkeit* is a state in which things belong together, for example, a state of contiguity, unity, solidarity, or coherence. – Trans.
18 *In-dividuum*
19 *des psychischen Strukturzusammenhanges*
20 *Zweckzusammenhang*
21 *Individuendum*
22 *Individuendenbildung*
23 *In-dividuum*
24 *Gattung*
25 *Gattung*
26 In the foregoing part of section 5 that is not translated here, Rickert distinguishes seven different concepts of development. His aim is to identify the concept of historical development required by his idea of historical individuals that are connected in a causal nexus. – Trans.
27 This refers to the discussion in chapter 3, section 3 (*Die Grenzen*, pp. 237–258), which is not included in the translation. Here Rickert argues that the extent to which concept formation in natural science abstracts from the perceptual and individual properties of reality is a matter of degree. This means that there are historical components of the various natural sciences, for example, a historical biology or a natural history of the organic world, as well as a natural science of biology. – Trans.
28 In the two paragraphs immediately preceding section 7, Rickert makes the following observations: "Thus we come to the following result. It is not only the case that in our prescientific forms of knowledge there are two conceptions of reality that are different in principle, the generalizing and the individualizing. Corresponding to them, there are also two forms of the scientific treatment of reality. In their ultimate objectives as well as their final results, they differ from one another logically and in principle. That should not be understood as the principle for the *real division* of scientific labor. A logical classification or articulation is not a real division. The *formal* opposition of nature and history cannot and should not serve as the actual division. This is because the latter is linked with *substantive* differences in the material, not with logical differences. Here we are concerned only with the conceptual differentiation of two different general orientations in the sciences that quite often, or even always, may actually function conjointly. But their conceptual differentiation would still be necessary even if, with respect to their ultimate *objectives*, two kinds of scientific conceptualization could not be distinguished from each other in the way we have shown. Even if no science is possible without the help of the general, the fundamental logical difference between natural science and historical science remains unaffected, in spite of all the relativity of natural scientific and historical concepts. In both disciplines, the path sometimes moves through the particular, at other times through the general, and the general is always employed as an instrument. But the goal of one discipline is the representation of the more or less general; the goal of the other, the representation of the more or less individual. All borderline cases and intermediate forms can alter nothing with regard to the logical opposition between these two *orientations*.

With these considerations, we can conclude our investigation *of the purely logical* forms of historical science and their relation to those of natural science." – Trans.
29 *Geisteswissenschaft*
30 *Geist*

31 Not infrequently, the following exposition, which develops the concept of the "historical center," has been virtually ignored in the criticism of my views (recently, this holds true even for Troeltsch). For this reason, I should like to point out that it is of *decisive* importance for my *total conception* of history. Without it, what I understand and mean by "history" in the *stricter* sense — that is, the sense that is *more* than formal-logical – remains unintelligible.

32 *Seelische Wesen:* This expression, which is used repeatedly throughout chapter 4, section 7, designates a creature that has a mind, or a being to which the mental acts of willing, thinking, judging, valuing, and so on can be ascribed. – Trans.

33 *Geisteswissenschaft*

34 *Geist*

35 In view of this statement of the problem and the ensuing attempt to solve it, I cannot understand how Bernheim (*Lehrbuch der historischen Methode*, 5th and 6th eds., p. 3) can maintain that I "did not adequately recognize the logical connection between the historical object and the principle of the historical mode of thought." I think, rather, that precisely the *logical* connection between human science [*Geisteswissenschaft*] and historical science – as well as the logical connection between cultural science and historical science considered in the next section – is clarified for the first time in this book. That is because it could be understood only on the basis of insight into the value-relevant character of individualizing conceptualization. I must also stress this point in opposition to critics such as Troeltsch, in order to repudiate the view that I was concerned *only* with formal differences. The contrary is the case. I have considered material differences just as scrupulously as the formal. It was only necessary that I *begin* with formal differences since it is a *logic* of the historical sciences that is presented here.

36 This will be shown more precisely in section 9 [Nonreal Meaning Configurations and Historical Understanding].

37 This thesis is defended in Rickert's discussion of concepts of historical development (*Die Grenzen*, chapter 4, section 5), material that is not included in the translation. – Trans.

38 *Geisteswissenschaft*

39 *Geist*

40 *das Geistige*

41 *geistig*

42 At this point, I do not intend to consider the different kinds of "validity" of values in any more detail. This issue arises only in Chapter 5. On this matter, see also my *System der Philosophie*, I, pp. 132 *seq*. Here it should also be noted that general values should not be confused with general concepts of these values. What is meant by "generality" in this sense – namely, the fact that it is valid for everyone – can itself be something individual.

43 The concept of the social can also be taken in a narrower sense. In that case, social goods such as marriage, the family, the state, and the nation are juxtaposed to asocial goods such as art and science. On this point, see my *System der Philosophie*, I, pp. 370 *seq*. We cannot consider this issue here. Asocial goods such as art and science are of relevance to *history* only insofar as they are situated in a real social nexus. Philosophy, which attempts to interpret their *transhistorical meaning*, can – indeed, must – conceive them differently.

44 Critics who find that I have not given the *substantive* characteristics of the material of the historical sciences in the stricter sense their legitimate place have paid insufficient attention both to these and to the ensuing remarks, and to my concept of the historical center as well. Otherwise the charge of "formalism" would not make sense. Of course, the facts on which I base my position here are so trivial that one might suppose it is not worthwhile to make them explicit. What is at stake here, however, does not concern new and interesting *facts*. Indeed, it would fare badly for my line of thought if the facts I adduce were not trivial or self-evident. Here as everywhere in a logic of history, my task has been to demonstrate the *connection* between the characteristics of the factual material of history, with which everyone is familiar, and the logical structure of their historical representation. Not everyone is familiar with this connection. The "formalism" with which I am reproached lies in its analysis. None of my critics have been able to explain how a logic of history can employ a procedure that is not formal in this sense and still remain logic. The opposition to my formalism can be explained only by the fact that although we have "theories of the human sciences," we have no logic of the disciplines that do not fall

within the natural sciences. The purpose of this book is to establish the basis for such a logic, and this is the sole perspective from which it should be judged.
45 In a sense that later will be further specified, instead of "taking a position" we can also say the following: Those persons (whether as individuals or as groups) are included in the historical centers of a historical material of the past in whom the cultural values of their time were "truly vital." This is why they become historically essential.
46 *Naturvölker*
47 *Kulturvölker*

Chapter 23

"Knowing and Cognizing. Critical Remarks on Theoretical Intuitionism" (1934)[1,2,3]

TRANSLATED BY JON BURMEISTER

Epistemology and the science of the whole

The problem of cognizing is not particularly popular in philosophy today. Many thinkers believe that instead of deliberating about the nature of cognizing, we should immediately tackle the "matter itself," and in philosophy this means: we should only ask what the world as a whole *is*, not how it is *cognized*.

But in a journal with the name "Kant Studies," one should always be allowed to reexamine the problem of cognition. Everyone reading this knows that, in the discipline today called "epistemology[4]," Kant contributed an entirely new position within the whole of philosophy. But those reading this also know that the question which Kant's "transcendental philosophy" put in flux regarding the problem of cognition should by no means be considered settled. On the other hand, everyone (hopefully) also knows that Kant never thought epistemology should be viewed as the sole or even the most important philosophical discipline. This is the case not only when we consider the various parts of his philosophy such as (where this goes without saying) the *Critique of Practical Reason*, the *Critique of Judgment*, and *Religion within the Bounds of Pure Reason*; it is also the case with the *Critique of Pure Reason*, which should not be viewed as a *merely* epistemological work. It belongs to the worst mistakes of some (but not all) of the representatives of so-called "Neo-Kantianism" that they have allowed this view to arise, and have even strengthened it. The days in which a view like this is possible are, hopefully, forever a thing of the past. Even in his "theoretical" philosophy in the *Critique of Pure Reason*, Kant treated philosophy not as a specialized discipline but as a *science of the whole*. He tackled the old question of the being of the world[5] with a new method, thereby practicing metaphysics or ontology *in his particular manner*. For him, epistemological investigations were never anything more than a *means* to gain an answer, in his unprecedented and utterly singular way, to the question of what the world as a whole is.[6]

However, the following remarks are not explicitly about Kant. Apart from any systematic connection with his thought, we can point out that the question which is popular today – "epistemology or metaphysics (or ontology)?" – is based on a false dilemma. Those who, as metaphysicians or ontologists, strive to comprehend the *being* of the world as a *whole* are precisely those who must concern themselves with the cognizing of the world. Otherwise, the result would be a philosophy that is highly fragmentary in its theoretical side, one with nothing to say about how it, within the world it believes to have cognized, is able to come to a cognition of this world. To be sure, there have been systems concerned with the being of the world which do not consider it necessary to take on the problems arising here, but in the long run these systems have had no scientific endurance. One need only consider materialism, which was never able to say how, in a merely material world, it was able to come to the cognition that the world consists only of matter. In this inability, materialism is perpetually a failure as philosophy, and the same is true with every system that is not able to solve the problem of cognition.

To put it generally, we can say that whoever attempts to cognize the essence of the world in its totality must also comprehend how, within the world, a cognizing of the world as a whole is achieved. Only in this way does one *think* in a truly universal or world-encompassing manner. Looking into the past, we find that Kant was not the first thinker to assign the theory of cognizing a fundamental significance within the entirety of the science of the world. Disregarding still older forms of thought, Plato's thoughts cannot be understood unless we recognize that epistemological considerations (arising in connection with Socrates' doctrine of the concept, as presented to us by Aristotle) played within them nothing less than a decisive role. With virtually all philosophers of lasting significance, epistemological thoughts and universal-ontological or metaphysical thoughts are intimately associated with one another. It is a misleading claim that philosophy only recently, with "Neo-Kantianism," wrongfully shifted the emphasis of its investigation by not beginning straightaway with the cognizing of the world, but instead placing the concept of cognizing first. Realistically, there is no *either-or* but rather a *both-and*; that is, only a union of epistemology and ontology can lead us to the world as a whole.

In any event, discussions about the being of the world today must be intimately connected with epistemological considerations. The cognizing subject or "I" belongs to the universally cognized world just as much as the cognized object does. Only both in unison make up the world as a whole which philosophy is to investigate. In this respect, an ontology which concerns itself only with the cognized object always remains one-sided and thus "unphilosophical." To a philosophy that is genuinely comprehensive and that wishes to be a science of totality, it is necessary to add a theory of the cognizing subject as an essential component.

Theoretical intuitionism and Copy Theory[7]

Yet we do not need to further justify the following remarks as being "truly" philosophical through any additional general discussions. Instead, we can turn our attention to our particular question. The goal we have in mind here is only to confront a view that is widely held today about the essence of cognizing, and to show why it is unsustainable. In doing so, the intimate relation of epistemology to the question of ontology will still not become completely clear. Only at the end will a few suggestions about this be possible, and here at the outset we set ourselves a modest task which is limited to a very specific point. We wish merely to discuss a commonly held concept of cognizing in its problematic character, and to at least negatively demonstrate that it is impossible for critical thinking to be content with this concept. Only when it is seen as untenable does it make sense to proceed to the cognizing of the being of the world in its totality.

In cognizing, one often places the greatest importance on *intuition*, emphasizing this in particular over against the concept as that which the truth-seeker must above all, and indeed exclusively, come to attain. In this view, it is necessary to grasp objects immediately or intuitively, as they are given in intuition. When one adheres to this, one will not enter into "constructions" in one's cognizing which distance the truth-seeker from the intuitively-given material of cognition and thereby lead to falsehoods. For many, this view seems to be simply obvious. This epistemological point of view which places all the importance on intuition can be succinctly referred to as *theoretical intuitionism*, and our concern here is with one specific aspect of it: can it be carried out? In particular: is there a merely intuitive cognition of the whole being of the world?

In order to arrive at an answer to this question, we must realize above all what necessarily emerges for the essence of cognizing as a *consequence* of the reduction of cognizing to mere intuiting. Given the indicated premises, the task of cognition is evidently to be viewed as that which has *mirrored* as faithfully as possible what is given to us in intuition; one must then see in the "adequate" or "true" cognition something like a copy[8] of the existing objects that are to be cognized. It is from this point that we wish to tackle the problem, and we have good reason to do this. Since mere intuiting (which of course does not need to be seeing in an actual sense, but can equally can be a hearing or a tasting or something similar, provided it has to do with the world of sense) is supposed to be something other than a representing capacity, it cannot be thoroughly comprehended. Copy theory is necessarily linked to intuitionism, in that the latter stands or falls with the former.

It was Heidegger[9] who was able to go the farthest in this regard (and with gratifying consistency that is always instructive). He held that, in cognizing, it is essential above all to "discover" the existing object in the literal sense of the word, and so to remove the potential cover which hides the object or makes it invisible to immediate intuition. Finding the truth would thus be essentially a liberation from a veiling or enshrouding error, and in this sense it would be something negative. If one merely clears away all the obstacles which stand in the way of intuiting the matter at hand, the truth then becomes visible on its own and must show itself as unconcealed. Heidegger attempted to etymologically connect the Greek concept of *a-letheia* with the concept of dis-covering[10]. Let us leave this to one side. What is crucial is this: according to theoretical intuitionism, the true would be nothing other than the intuitively unconcealed, the unveiled.

What stance should we take toward this view of cognizing? Regarding Heidegger in particular, one cannot claim that it is easy to stand by his view of truth-finding as that of a "discovering" and *at the same time* to stand by the claim that what is essential in cognizing is simply the immediate intuition. For, the process of discovering must be understood as a *method*, and it can potentially require considerable *conceptual* work which would take us far afield from what we would otherwise designate as immediately and intuitively given. But the main point is this: if one deems the un-veiling of the intuitively given to be the method which leads from error to cognition, one must implicitly admit that there are *two* completely *different kinds* of intuition, the veiling kind and the true kind. Then the question immediately arises which of the two is the true intuition to which we must adhere when we wish to cognize. This certainly cannot be decided from the intuition *alone*.

However, this side of the problem which theoretical intuitionism in its systematic form presents to us will not be dealt with here any further. We are only asking about whether it is possible to reduce cognizing in general to mere intuition and, consequently, to determine the concept of cognized truth such that all that is present within it is the immediacy of an intuitability not falsified by any construction.

First of all, no one would deny that at least in many cases – and indeed always, when it is a question of the sensible world – immediate and "un-veiling" intuition *also* belongs to cognition. Neither would anyone deny that science's cognition thus has the task of being in some sense "adequate" or "similar" to the intuited objects which it wants to cognize. But that is still not *sufficient* for an adherence to intuitionism. Rather, both the role that the intuitive moment plays in science and the concept of the adequation of the precise determination are required; otherwise, we will be drawn into disastrous errors which completely delude us about the relation which we as theoretical humans have to the world, and which thus at the same time introduce untenable elements into our overall "worldview." In order to find some solid ground on the matter, we wish first and foremost to ask: do we achieve *scientific* cognition of an object if all that we obtain from it is an unveiled intuition? Here we intentionally limit the concept of cognizing to that of science because, as with the meanings of most words common in practical life, it would otherwise be too indeterminate and ambiguous to be useful for the short investigation that we have in mind.

At the same time, we can specify the concept of cognizing in another way in order to separate it from a concept with which it is often confused. If such a confusion occurs, one will not be able to come to a clear decision about the meaning of theoretical intuitionism. Let us draw on a statement from Hegel. Beneath his portrait by Wilhelm Hensel, he wrote, "Our knowledge should be cognition. Whoever knows me will cognize me herein." Without needing to affiliate ourselves in a substantial way with Hegel, we can say that *knowing* is not yet the scientific *cognizing* which interests us here. Consequently, we can add that mere intuiting can indeed lead us to what we call "knowledge" of an object, but this by no means decides the question as to whether – within science, which strives for *cognition* – one can remain with such a knowing that is achieved through mere intuiting. Through this separation of knowing from scientific cognizing, the problem at hand can now be formulated in an unambiguous way.

Cognizing and the meanings of words

We know that the problem we are concerned with here is a comprehensive one which should be approached from various angles; in our remarks we must confine ourselves to clarifying the questions that emerge here only in a particular manner, as opposed to the other kinds of clarification that might be possible. We will proceed on the assumption that all scientific cognizing necessarily takes a *linguistic* form. We will also assume that, at least in the vast majority of cases, and in general where copies[11] are not necessary for understanding a scientific work, the only factors which are essential for cognizing are those that have (as one says) found their "expression" in language. Without words, a scientific cognition that is communicable to other researchers would simply be impossible. As a result, linguistically formulated cognition must already contain everything that is significant for scientific cognizing, in order to make it into cognizing. We must therefore take this as a starting point and attempt to determine the essence of cognizing in it, at least so far as is necessary from this point onward to achieve clarity about the question of whether cognizing dissolves into mere intuition or into a knowledge gained through intuition.

Naturally, language comes under consideration here not simply as a perceived part of the world of sense, for cognition cannot be contained in audible or visible words themselves. These remain something "external"; that is, on their own they provide no true or false cognition. They must instead, as we often say, bring something to expression, something which they themselves as words are not, but which rather (if one will allow the metaphor) only "adheres" to them, and which – as something fundamentally other – supervenes on the merely sensuous existence that they have as words. But in what does this "something other" consist?

Everyone differentiates the words which he *understands* from those which remain unintelligible to him, and the intelligible words are separable from the unintelligible ones by the fact that the former are connected with *meanings* that one thinks one understands. Thus, the essential moment for cognition must be located not in the words, but in the meanings of the words. To take the simplest case: when the cognition of the world of sense is in question, can the meanings of words be designated as representations of sensuous, perceptible objects? And can one claim that the cognition of these objects in this regard is based on their mere intuition?

When we say, e.g., that a leaf is green, if it were the case that the meaning of the word "green" were itself green, we would be able to see in this cognition an intuitive copy of the sensuous being. But this is precisely what is not at issue. The meaning of the word "green" is not even sensuously perceptible like the word "green" is, let alone like the green leaf, and thus under no circumstances can it be considered a copy of the cognized green object. With the help of the meaning of the word "green," a representing[12] cognition of the green object consisting *merely* of intuition is supposed to be achieved, yet it remains completely unintelligible; theoretical intuitionism thus already fails in those cases where one could be most inclined to adhere to it.

This simple consideration also has ontological significance.[13] Specifically, it points to the fact that the meanings of words which we understand through cognition not only cannot be placed in the bodily sphere, but also cannot be placed in the mental[14] sphere of the being of the world. As bodies, they would need to be intuitively perceptible, and clearly they are not. But the meanings of words cannot thus be counted as falling under mental life, because it belongs to the essence of *all* mental existence that it is directly accessible in the same way only by *one* individual, *respectively*. My mental life is never that of *another* person, and he, likewise, is my "neighbor." But when the meanings of words appear in cognition, they are understood by *any number* of different individuals in the *same* way, and in this regard the meanings should not be regarded as mental. From this we can conclude: not only materialism, but also the view which holds the world in its totality to be merely a "psycho-physical" reality, i.e., which wishes to recognize as "existing" nothing other than mental and bodily processes, will never amount to a satisfactory theory of the world as a whole.

However, we do not wish to follow these ontological thoughts any further, and we will instead limit ourselves to the epistemological side of things. In this regard we can say that sensuously-perceived objects, on the one hand, and the comprehensible and non-perceptible meanings of words with whose assistance we cognize the objects, on the other hand, lie in two *completely different regions of being*. In this respect, they are totally dissimilar to one another. Consequently, the concept of an adequate cognition as that of an approximating cognition – as theoretical intuitionism necessary represents it – is already entirely problematic. The sensuous objects which are to be cognized are *perceived* in intuition as having color, sound, etc. The meanings of words with which we cognize them, by contrast, are not perceived but rather *understood*, and no one can say that what is understood can be either set over against what is perceived as its adequate *copy*, or designated as *resembling* it. Thus, the claim that the simple cognition "the leaf is green" contains nothing more than the "unveiling" intuition of the green leaf is a claim which remains, for anyone who has carefully considered the matter, both entirely unclear and theoretically unsatisfying.

In saying this, we are of course not disputing that at least occasionally, and indeed in every case when it involves the world of sense, one must have intuitively perceived an object and thus known it in order to understand the meanings of the words with which it is cognized. But the *content* of the understood meanings of words nevertheless remains, with respect to *intuiting, quite distinct* from the content of the perceived objects. Since the meaning of a word is neither colored nor otherwise in any way sensuously perceptible, it does not make sense to call a cognition consisting of the meanings of words a copy of an object. For it does not at all resemble an object as a copy resembles the original, and this reveals that theoretical intuitionism – which wishes to reduce all cognizing to mere intuiting – is wholly problematic. At the same time, this also means that the concept of true thinking as that of dis-covering and the concept of truth as that of the unveiling or unconcealment of intuition both become untenable.

Cognizing and assertions

Yet we can go one step further. Even if one wanted to believe that the single word "green" meant something like a copy of the color green, which as a result is "dis-covered" in intuition, it must also be noted that the *single* word, along with its meaning which refers to the object to be cognized and which indeed is indispensable for cognition, nevertheless never suffices on its own for the act of cognizing. Rather, cognizing finds its complete expression within science only in *propositions*, i.e., in complexes of words. And if they are true and thus able to supply cognition, propositions must assert their meaning or their sense in accordance with something about the object.[15] But the content of a true assertion cannot be comprehended as the copy of the intuited object. Intuitionism thus completely fails here for additional reasons, as soon as one attempts to think it through.

Several more remarks about this should be made, the first of which is to point out an affliction that the orientation toward language can carry into epistemology. As fruitful as it can be to adhere to the linguistic expression which science necessarily uses, we must nonetheless equally guard against viewing *grammatical* form in its linguistic character as invariably epistemological. For this reason, we should not simply orient ourselves without further ado toward the grammatical form of our assertions. It is an old saying that the logician has to guard against grammar, and this warning is a justified one. This becomes apparent particularly in the much-discussed linguistic entities which, by virtue of just one word, are already capable of expressing a truth. Although it cannot be shown here in more detail, such entities are to be understood from an epistemological point of view simply as *abbreviations* of linguistic expression, and they do not have an essentially positive epistemological meaning which corresponds to them as such. Moreover, they play no role in science and for this reason can here be passed over.[16]

Next we can say: each cognizing true assertion, and thus each expression of cognition – when it is linguistically fully developed so that its epistemologically significant structure also manifests itself grammatically – consists (as one says in grammar) of a subject and a predicate. Or, to put it in Greek terms, it consists of a *hypokeimenon* and *kategoroumenon*. More specifically, there is the subject, which perhaps can be perceived in a direct, intuitive, and "unveiled" manner and is then designated as "this." To this subject is attached a predicate which means something *other* than the subject word. Otherwise one cannot speak of an "objective" cognition. So-called identity propositions, or (speaking with Kant) "analytic judgments" which present no distinction of subject and predicate, do not provide any legitimate cognition. To the logically adequate linguistic expression of every scientific truth thus belong at least *two different linguistic meanings*, and the claim that these two stand in a relation to each other which eludes every mere intuition demands no specific proof.

As soon as one understands this, one will see clearly that the concept of scientific cognition contains problems which are unsolvable by means of a copy theory necessarily linked to the claim that cognizing is intuiting. One will also see that theoretical intuitionism therefore remains perpetually inadequate as epistemology.

In principle, everything that is essential for our discussion has now been said. But because what is at stake here is the repudiation of a widespread "dogma," it will be beneficial in closing to further illuminate these thoughts with a particular example. To those who mistrust purely conceptual considerations, this example will also make it, so to speak, "intuitively" clear that a true cognition never can be reduced to mere intuition. To this end, we can once again limit ourselves to the simplest conceivable cognition, the cognition of a sensuous object. It is precisely with this kind of cognition that it can be best shown why it does not make sense to equate cognizing with mere intuiting.

Let us assume that, via intuition, we have heard a tone. We can then claim that we *know* it. But we cannot stop with this if we want to achieve *cognition* of the tone. If the tone is to be communicable to other people, we must assert something about it which we differentiate from the intuitively heard tone itself. In fact, such an assertion – no matter how "simple" the heard tone may be – can move in *various* distinct "directions," i.e., it can find expression in various predications which all share the commonality of containing a true cognition of the tone. In the event that cognition of the tone is purported to be more or less complete, various assertions about it are indispensable. We cannot remain with something so "simple" as the merely intuited hearing, no matter how unveiled the tone might be in this. This is something that should be pursued more precisely in its details.

First of all, we cognize that the tone is "real," and this being-real cannot be equated with the intuition of the tone. Indeed, the being-real does not in any way appear in the mere intuition. What then from the intuition of the tone is the meaning of the word "real" expected to portray? Which of its features should it resemble? Regarding the meaning of the word "real," there is absolutely nothing in the mere intuition that could be viewed as its "original," nothing to which the cognition would stand in an intuiting relation. Already with this, then, every copy theory fails, and thus every intuitionism as well. The meaning of the word "being-real" cannot in any sense be situated in the realm of the *merely* intuited entity.

However, we do not need to limit ourselves to the cognizing assertion that the tone is actual. We also want to know of what or how the tone is *constituted*, and this question undoubtedly brings the intuition of the tone into consideration. But in what way? When we cognize the tone, we can specify by means of assertions *either* its duration, *or* its strength, *or* its pitch, *or* its timbre. It is within these different assertions, then, that the content of cognition must be found and understood. How does it display itself? With various words referring to the apparently distinct "sides" of the tone cognized as actual, we assert something else true about the tone each time, and only the unison of the different assertions results in a complete cognition of the tone: it "has" first this duration, second this pitch, third this strength, fourth this timbre. The tone which "with a single blow" is perceived in intuition as something "simple" thus, in cognition, transforms itself into a *multiplicity* of "characteristics" or "moments."

Yet we must ask once again: can such assertions which in their plurality dissect the intuition of the tone still count as representations of the tone? With the cognition of the tone, does it make some sort of sense to speak of its mere intuition? That is something no one would want to claim. The mere intuition of the tone gives "everything all at once." Cognition does not do this, and cannot do this. Instead, it dissects the tone which we perceive in intuition as a "whole" by means of several assertions in a sequence of "moments," moments which only immediately and intuitively combine in perception but which, in cognition, must be detached from each other and predicated singularly and separately.

This shows once again that only our "thinking" which is something other than intuition is capable of separating out that which is bound together in intuition, and only through the fact that it does this can we even cognize the familiar tone that is given in intuition. In so doing, we necessarily grant a separate existence to the moments of the tone which exist together in the perception, and indeed in a manner in which they do not appear in intuition. In consideration of this fact, how could one still wish to claim that cognizing is equivalent to mere intuiting?

This immediately leads us still one step further. If we have *thought* the intuitively "simple" tone as a multiplicity, then we can say that *each* sensuously actual tone "has" both duration and strength, as well as pitch and timbre. In this and *only* in this do we find the universal "essence" of the intuitively perceived tone, or only with this have we cognized the tone *as tone*, which we previously only knew intuitively. Then we have with our cognition once again gone far beyond intuitive knowledge. Such a process which opens up the "essence" of a matter can be in absolutely no way conceived of as a kind of representation through intuition. Rather, through our cognizing we necessarily reconfigure[17] the material of cognition given to us in intuition in a manner for which there is no "pre-figure"[18] in intuition itself. Such a reconfiguring is indispensable for all cognizing which seeks to penetrate to the universal "essence" of a matter, and through this the intuition-theory of cognizing is once again demonstrated to be entirely untenable.

In summary we can say: a cognizing which is more than mere knowing can so little be conceived of as a representing act of intuiting[19] that we must rather understand it as a complete *transformation* of the given intuition through non-intuitive factors that, by means of science, are brought to expression linguistically through sentences. In multiple ways, then, we have seen that such sentences or assertions or judgments (or whatever other term one wishes to use) cannot be true in the sense that they represent the intuition, or are themselves simply an intuition. But strangely enough, the conclusion is sometimes made that assertions in cognizing are not what give the truth of cognition. Indeed, some have written that assertions or judgments are nothing less than the "death of truth." Such views appear "ingenious" to some. However, the thinkers who take them seriously forget that these views *themselves* invariably carry out assertions or judgments which entail the claim to be true, and they also forget that there has never been a scientific work whose truth content did not consist of assertions or judgments. Thus, if assertions or judgments do not lead to truth, there is no way for humans in general to scientifically cognize the truth. Only assertions or judgments carry the character of truth in science, and if one does not believe that they have capacity to cognize what is true, one would do well to give up not only all cognizing but also all epistemology[20]. For, in order to be true, the theory of cognizing[21] also must consist of assertions.

The *problem* which epistemology must therefore necessarily pose is how a cognition can be true *even though* it is never a mere representation of the object to be cognized, and in this respect invariably contains more than a mere intuition. That intuiting on its own does not suffice for cognition has been known even by those who otherwise refuse "to think about thinking," who would thus not engage in epistemology. Goethe certainly placed the greatest value on intuition in his scientific work. But even in his color theory, where he could never dispense with intuition, he said, "The mere observation of the matter at hand cannot help us." In keeping with this idea, we can say that theoretical intuitionism – rejected even by Goethe, the "eye man" – should be abandoned as a comprehensive epistemology once and for all.

An ontological prospectus

At this point, the main issue that we wished to address with these critical remarks on theoretical intuitionism can be considered complete. In closing, we will attempt to indicate at least briefly the general philosophical significance our findings have not only in an epistemological respect, but also in an ontological one.

To do this, we wish to take up once again the example of the cognition of a tone. With this it has already become apparent that the cognizing of the intuition, which contains "everything all at once," proceeds to a conceptual *multiplicity*, and indeed to such a kind which, as such, does not exist in the pure intuition. Now a tone obviously belongs to the simplest entities which are known to us in intuition, and consequently the cognition of it will likewise be relatively "simple." If, on the other hand, we consider the task of philosophy to be that of cognizing the world in its *totality*, it is clear from the outset that it involves a much more complicated task. As we can easily recognize[22], the world which we know is already given to us in intuition as an immense *manifold*. Thus from the outset it is clear that in philosophy we cannot hope to do theoretical and cognitive justice to the familiar multiplicity of the world if we attempt to depict it in cognition as "simply" as possible. In our thinking we should not distance ourselves so far from intuition that we allow its multiplicity to go completely unobserved. And if the cognizing of a relatively "simple" tone moves in a pluralistic direction, we can then say of the cognition of the world that it allows the being of the world to be grasped theoretically only if it possesses an extensively pluralistic character. In any event, philosophy as a science of totality seeks merely a "unity" of the *manifold of the world*, and how far it must go in its striving for unity cannot initially be said, so long as it wishes to proceed in an unbiased manner.

Naturally in such a brief, concluding prospectus we can only provide a few suggestions, and it is impossible to give a detailed account either in substance or in content of the aspiration to grasp the manifold of the world by means of cognition. We wish to limit ourselves to *one* point, and in the process to again consider one particular dimension of the problem of cognition which we have already confronted in the cognizing of a tone. When it is a question of the tone's *mode of being*, we will always say that the tone which is made familiar by being heard in intuition is "real." We also know that precisely with this word we mean a sensuous reality which certainly cannot be brought to expression *intuitively* and immediately through cognition, but is "experienced" immediately and intuitively and in this respect is familiar. From this we can make a cognizing assertion about the being of every tone which in this case, so to speak, "goes without saying," and the general mode of being of the intuitively heard tone is in this respect not a problem for science. Every given tone that we hear is sensuously real. This is something straightforward and not disputed.

But how do things stand with the being of the world in its *totality*? Here we are immediately confronted with *questions*. For we can easily see that there "are" objects in the world which we wish to cognize, and to which the predication that they are "sensuously actual" is not appropriate. The triangle, for example, which mathematicians are concerned with, does not belong in the same mode of being as the heard tone. It is not sensuously perceptible and in this respect should perhaps be called "non-actual." Nevertheless, we would still say that it somehow "is."

The difference of the triangle's mode of being from that of the tone is obvious. When the mathematician claims of the triangle that the sum of its angles is the same as two right angles, this is never strictly the case for a sensuously actual triangle. Thus, when it makes its cognizing statements, mathematics does not have objects in view which (in their manner) "are" as the heard tone is. With this it therefore becomes apparent: for an all-encompassing theory of the world in its *diversity*, even the *being* of objects becomes a problem.

Another example might further illuminate these thoughts. We have already indicated that, to every scientific cognition which is communicable to others, there belong the intelligible meanings of words. Even they are a part of the world and must, in the cognition of totality, be taken into account as something "existing." However, perhaps many thinkers who ontologically still remain trapped in psycho-physical dualism are inclined to believe that they can categorize the meanings of words as *mental* entities. Such entities would, indeed, not be spatially extended like bodies, but they would nonetheless take place within time, i.e., have a specific beginning and a specific end, and in this respect they could easily be included in spatial-temporal, psycho-physical reality.

Yet this opinion does not stand up to examination. It is not correct to say that the meaning of a word which we understand begins temporally and ends temporally in the way that a psychological process does. This would be true only of the mental acts with which the single individual accomplishes an understanding of the meaning of the words. The being of the meanings of words themselves, however, is of an entirely different sort. It has no temporally specific beginning and no temporally specific end. We have already indicated that the meanings of words in their being are not grasped as individual mental processes, but rather can be understood as the *same* by any number of individuals at any given time. What they, on the one hand, have in common in this regard with mathematical entities, and how they, on the other hand, differentiate themselves from them will not be further investigated here. At any rate they are also not in this manner "sensuously real" like all the components of psycho-physical reality, and in this respect we can recognize in them a new example of the truth that the general being of the world can be theoretically-ontologically grasped only by a cognition which moves with a *pluralistic* tendency.

These examples could easily be multiplied. It follows from them that, in order to span with sufficient comprehensiveness the scope in which the philosopher's cognizing of the being of the world is to move, the first step which the philosopher as *ontologist* must take is this: through the indication of the final ontological predicate which he applies to the world as a whole, he must bring the whole *expanse* of the being of the world to consciousness. In so doing he certainly *also* needs intuition so as to get to *know* the different modes of being which confront him in the world. But with equal certainty it is impossible that he, as a cognizer, will remain with the pure knowledge supplied to him by intuition. If he desires to come to a science of the world as a whole, he must transform the manifold of the world, which already shows him the most general being of the world, into a pluralistically shaped cognition of this being. To this end, in his thinking he must once more go far beyond all the immediately and intuitively given entities. In this way it can become clear, at least in principle, which consequences of our epistemological considerations also hold for the configuration of a general ontology.

One last remark should be added to our discussion to avoid the appearance that, in a cognition of the world which necessarily carries itself out in multiple ontological predications, we are led into the limitless. This remark will also serve to avoid the appearance that our epistemological claims imply the impossibility of even *approaching* the cognition of the world as a whole. A merely *individualizing* exposition of the world would present us with a task that is, in principle, unsolvable. We will never be able to think the plenitude of individual configurations in their totality. However, ontology necessarily proceeds in a *generalizing* fashion.[23] In the formation of its *general* concepts of the different modes of being, it does not need to come to the point at which it is always engaging in the further ontological fragmentation of the intuitively given manifold, such that it then must say to itself that an advance in the universality of the generalizing cognition (which involves a striving toward an *end*) is permanently excluded.

Thus the situation is not hopeless, because our thinking possesses not only the capacity of fragmenting but also that of *synthesizing*, and because this capacity allows us to bring the manifold of the world under a system of general ontological predicates such that it no longer confronts us as wholly incalculable and limitless. In particular, our thinking has the ability – one which pure intuition never has – to form what we will call *alternatives*, and these lead us to totality. This is, briefly put, what is essential: we are able to so order a manifold which we know that we can bring a group of objects under the one general concept, and then can say that *everything* which *cannot* be found in this group necessarily belongs to *another* group, *only* a group whose content can likewise be positively determined. In general, wherever this is possible we may assume that the entirety of the objects to be cognized falls either under the one concept or under the other, and in so doing we have also gained the concept of the unified whole. This concept arises such that the objects of both the one group and the other fall under it. On this understanding, *the one and the other taken together* must be the whole.

One should not confuse these thoughts with the dialectic usually undertaken in connection with Hegel. Pure *negation* would not lead us the smallest step forward toward an ontological determination of the world. "The other," which together with "the one" forms the whole, may not be simply determined as the *"not-one"* but must be designated *positively* as "the other." Otherwise our thinking would remain "empty," and this should be the case just as little (speaking with Kant) as our intuition should be allowed to remain "blind." To be sure, we can always say that "the other" which forms the whole together with "the one" is *not* "the one." But this negation never suffices on its own for a determination of "the other," which must "complete" "the one" in the actual sense of the word. Whoever believes that it does pays homage to a "rationalism" that precisely lacks an understanding of the meaning of intuition which holds for the positive configuration of our concept.

Thus, with the cognizing of totality we must not think dialectically or "antithetically." Such ambiguous expressions about the world consisting of "opposites" are simply unhelpful. To master the manifold of the world, we must rather engage in a *heterothetical* thinking which always seeks to ascertain how the positively determined "one" and the positively determined "other" in their unity necessarily result in the whole.

To penetrate through to totality with the help of alternatives, we will also, indeed, make the attempt at such an advancing cognition precisely where it is a question of the different kinds of being of the world, i.e., in ontology. This cannot be further carried out here in any substantial way. Our last remarks merely served to indicate that the pluralistic tendency – one that is necessarily connected with cognizing and that sets it in contrast with any merely intuitive grasping of an ostensible unity of the world – does not necessarily lead to our cognizing thinking being faced with an insurmountable task, when it turns toward the world as a whole and ascertains its kinds of being. Rather, we can say once more: pure intuiting would stand helpless before the manifold of the being of the familiar world. Conceptual thinking, on the other hand, which fundamentally differentiates itself from all pure intuiting, may hope – in conjunction with intuition – to master the multiplicity of the world in cognition.

Notes

1   "*Kennen und Erkennen. Kritische Bemerkungen zum theoretischen Intuitionismus,*" Kant Studien 39 (1934), pp. 139–155. Translated for the first time into English by Jon Burmeister. Rickert's excessive use of *Sperrdruck*, reproduced here by italics, has not been followed in each case. – Ed.

2   The thoughts in the following short essay are drawn in large part from a book which I intend to publish with J.C.B. Mohr (Paul Siebeck) Tübingen under the title *Grundprobleme der Philosophie: Methodologie, Ontologie, Anthropologie*. [The book appeared in 1934. – Ed.]

3   The title in German is *Kennen und Erkennen*. The main theme of this essay turns on the wordplay between these two terms and between their cognates, *Kenntnis* and *Erkenntnis* and the verbs *kennen* and *erkennen*. In everyday German, the verb *kennen* means "to know" in the sense of "being familiar or acquainted with," as in the way that one knows a friend. The verb *erkennen*, on the other hand, has the stronger and more scientific meaning of "objectively comprehending," as in the way that one knows the distance from the earth to the sun. In this essay, "*kennen*" will be translated as "to know," and "*erkennen*" – following the Kantian tradition (e.g., the Guyer/Wood translation of the *Critique of Pure Reason*) – will be translated as "to cognize." Accordingly, the nouns *Kennen* and *Erkennen* are translated here as "knowing" and "cognizing," and *Kenntnis* and *Erkenntnis* as "knowledge" and "cognition." – Trans.

4   *Erkenntnistheorie*

KNOWING AND COGNIZING   395

5   *Weltsein*
6   Cf. on this my book, *Kant als Philosoph der modernen Kultur. Ein geschichtsphilosophischer Versuch*, 1924, and "Die Heidelberger Tradition und Kants Kritizismus," 1934.
7   *Abbildtheorie*
8   *Abbild*
9   Cf. *Sein und Zeit*. First half, 1927, pg. 32 ff. Naturally the following remarks refer only to Heidegger's "discovery"-theory and are not directed against his philosophy in general. Radical intuitionism appears in Heidegger only in those places where he attempts to justify the relationship with phenomenology. Incidentally, and fortunately, he did not at all work in accordance with his own "method." The scientific worth of his "fundamental ontology" is here not called into question.
10 *Ent-decken*
11 *Abbildungen*
12 *abbildende*
13 Cf. my essay: "Die Erkenntnis der intelligiblen Welt und das Problem der Metaphysik." *Logos*, Vol. XVI and XVIII, 1927 and 1929.
14 *seelisch*
15 On the following, cf. my book *Der Gegenstand der Erkenntnis. Einführung in die Transcendentalphilosophie*. 1892, 6th ed. 1928.
16 Cf. on this my book: *Die Logik des Prädikats und das Problem des Ontologie*, 1930. There it is shown in detail why apparently monomial logical entities possess only linguistic and not epistemological relevance.
17 *umbilden*
18 *Vorbild*
19 *abbildendes Anschauen*
20 *Erkenntnistheorie*
21 *die Theorie des Erkennens*
22 *erkennen*
23 The generalizing and the individualizing methods are dealt with in several of my books. They are treated in detail in *Die Grenzen der naturwissenschaftlichen Begriffsbildung. Eine logische Einleitung in die historischen Wissenschaften*, 1896–1902, 5th edition, 1929. More briefly, they are dealt with in *Kulturwissenschaft und Naturwissenschaft*, 1899, 7th edition, 1926, and additionally in *Die Probleme der Geschichtsphilosophie*, 1905, 3rd edition, 1924.

Introduction

Emil Lask (1875–1915)

EMIL LASK WAS BORN IN 1875 IN WADOWICE, then Galicia (now Polish territory), as a son of Jewish parents. He began his studies in 1894 in Freiburg, drifting back and forth between jurisprudence and philosophy. He studied under Max Weber and Alois Riehl, before joining the circle of students around Rickert, who would be his main influence. After three semesters in Freiburg, he switched to the University of Strasbourg, where he studied especially under Windelband, who became his "second teacher in philosophy," as he later said. He returned to Freiburg in 1898 and finished his dissertation under Rickert in 1902 with a thesis on "Fichte's Idealism and History". His interest in jurisprudence continued between then and 1905, when he took his Habilitation in Heidelberg.[1] In Heidelberg, he belonged to the circle around Max Weber. Until 1913, he taught at the University of Heidelberg as *Privatdocent* (an unsalaried professor), and he was named *Professor Extraordinarius*, a salaried position, in 1913, to assist the ailing Windelband. In this time, he wrote his two seminal works, *The Logic of Philosophy* of 1911 and *The Doctrine of Judgment* of 1912, which were conceived as merely the opening writings of his philosophical system. In 1908, he presented a paper at the third international congress for philosophy in Heidelberg, whose rhetorical title, "Is there a 'Primacy of Practical Reason' in Logic?," makes plain that he takes issue with a main staple of the Southwest School. Contrary to Rickert's claim, Lask emphasizes the objectivity, or objective validity, of cognition, departing from any primacy of the practical or the acting subject. This main idea was to come to fruition in his *magnum opus, The Logic of Philosophy*, from which passages have been selected here.

Shortly after the outbreak of the Great War, Lask volunteered as soldier and was killed in Turza Mala, in his native Galicia, close to where Wittgenstein was working on his *Tractatus*, also as a soldier in the trenches. His collected works, consisting of his dissertation, his two books and a few articles and book reviews, were published in 1923 and 1924 by his student Eugen Herrigel.

Lask is considered one of the most gifted thinkers of the Neo-Kantian movement altogether, who had a significant influence especially on Heidegger and also Lukács, but who was also influential for his mentors, Windelband, Rickert, and Weber. He was considered by many "the greatest hope of German philosophy."[2] His few writings are all extremely dense and "formidably difficult, not only in substance but also in style" (Beiser). He was widely considered an up-and-coming star. His career was cut short due to his untimely death in the trenches of the Great War, before receiving a proper professorship. One can only imagine how the philosophical scene in

Germany would have looked had Lask survived and had he become, as was largely expected, an *Ordinarius*, carrying on the legacy of Neo-Kantianism in his idiosyncratic manner.

Further Reading

There is very little literature on Lask in English. For an account of his philosophy, cf. the book by Glatz (below), which contains an extensive bibliography. Beiser's masterful account of 2008 is, at less than 10 pages, a good place to start.

Beiser, Frederick C., "Emil Lask and Kantianism," in: *The Philosophical Forum*, 2008, pp. 283–296.

— —, "Emil Lask and the End of Southwest Neo-Kantianism," in: *The German Historicist Tradition*, Oxford/New York: Oxford University Press, 2012, pp. 442–466.

Glatz, Uwe, *Emil Lask. Philosophie im Verhältnis zu Weltanschauung, Leben und Erkenntnis.* Königshausen & Neumann, Würzburg 2001.

Rentsch, Thomas, "Emil Lask," in: B. Lutz, ed., *Metzler Philosophenlexikon*. Stuttgart: Metzler, 2003, pp. 394–397.

The Logic of Philosophy and the Doctrine of Categories (1910): Announcement, "The Logic of the Ontic Categories. Logic as Philosophy of Validity," and "The Unboundedness of Truth"

As mentioned, Lask is considered one of the profoundest and also one of the most difficult philosophers of the entire Neo-Kantian movement. This is in part so because he can be seen as stretching "Kantianism," whatever one may understand that to be, to the absolute limit. The question to open up a discussion of his philosophical position can be put as follows: In what way can one consider Lask a Kantian at all? Lask's starting point, in *The Logic of Philosophy*, is, as he himself puts it, "to apply Kant's Copernican Turn to the object of philosophical cognition." But already his understanding of what the Copernican Turn amounts to is quite idiosyncratic: "the transference of transcendental forms to the object, the constitutedness of theoretical objects through categories," quoting from the announcement of his work. What is striking in this reading of the Copernican Turn is precisely the emphasis on the object and its being constituted by categories. Lask, thus, espouses an anti-subjectivist reading of Kant's transcendental turn. To some interpreters, such as Beiser, this is already a break with the Kantianism of the traditional sense. Furthermore, Lask's attempt at applying the Copernican Turn to the "object of philosophical cognition" also means that Lask espouses a distinction that is a staple of the Southwest School, going back to Lotze: between the realm of reality or being and that of validity. The object of philosophical cognition belong to this latter sphere, along with other objects of validity. In limiting cognition to objects of experience only, Kant missed a whole region of "entities" (or, more precisely, "non-entities," since they do not have to exist to "be" valid) and neglected to account for it. Thus, the metacritique of the Kantian critique entailed at the same time the *quaestio iuris* for the sphere of validity, of objects that need not exist, but are valid nonetheless. In insisting on this sphere of validity, which exists no matter if a human being, angels or God experience or intend it, Lask finds in Husserl his closest ally. Thus, Lask attempts to find and account for the categories that apply to these "things." Thus, both the being of the sensible and that of the valid is ultimately bound to his notion of the "boundlessness of truth, of the all-encompassing scope of the dominion of logic and on the conviction that everything, insofar as it is a something and not a nothing, is affected by categories and stands in logical form." In this way, Lask arrives at a Neo-Platonist-inspired "panarchy of the logical," which has also been called a "logical mysticism" (Rentsch), when Lask writes that "the dominion of the logical in itself is boundless" and that thereby "not panlogicism but rather the panarchy of the logos must be restored to its glory."

Interpreters such as Crowell have pointed to the important relevance of this idea of Lask's to current debates concerning the inherent conceptuality of putatively non-conceptual content. Regarding Lask's Kantianism, it is indeed hard to see how this radically anti-subjectivist extreme position can be Kantian at all. As Beiser summarizes, "There are three general reasons why it is necessary to regard Lask as [only] a nominal Kantian: He violates Kant's critical doctrine that all knowledge is limited to experience, he revives a correspondence theory of truth contrary to Kant's transcendental idealism, and he endorses a theory of immediate knowledge that borders on mysticism."[3] But perhaps it is more appropriate, rather than to accuse him of making a total break with Kant's principles, to say that Lask's philosophy is more the expression of an ambiguity. On this reading, Lask's philosophy tends to an extreme ontological thinking, on the one hand, and on the other "could not and did not intend to completely renounce the epistemological ideal of an aprioristic-subjectivistic thinking."[4] For the traditional Kantian, the move towards a doctrine of categories of validity clearly violates Kant's very principle that we can have cognition only with respect to objects of experience. However, if the sphere of validity is itself something that has a direct bearing on our life, that our life is meaningful because it contains (or instantiates) values, then Lask's attempt to account for this sphere in the framework of transcendental philosophy is perhaps understandable and even admirable for its daringness. It is certainly an avenue of philosophy, Kantian or not, that has not been explored to the extent that it deserves.

A word on Lask's philosophical style. His struggling attempts to bring to language new figures of thought, rendered into admirable English by the translator, have led him to utilize a somewhat "expressionistic" style that operates with metaphors and neologisms. In having this obvious linguistic force at his disposal, he follows in the footsteps of Fichte and Hegel, and the peculiar language that Heidegger later used clearly owes a great deal to Lask. In his seeming reversal of the (allegedly) subjectivistic Copernican turn and the overcoming of substance ontology, Heidegger, too, stands in the tradition of Lask.

Notes

1   Accounts differ on this. Ollig claims that his work in jurisprudence resulted exclusively in the piece "*Rechtsphilosophie*" in the Festschrift for Kuno Fischer and that his Habilitation thesis was on the same topic as his dissertation. According to other accounts, such as Beiser's, "*Rechtsphilosophie*" *was* his Habilitation thesis, which, given its length of some 55 pages, is rather unlikely, unless it was a shortened summary of the thesis submitted to the university.
2   Quoted in the entry by Rentsch, p. 395.
3   Beiser, "Emil Lask and Kantianism," p. 294.
4   Malter, quoted in Ollig, p. 71.

Further Reading

Crowell, Steven, "Husserl, Lask, and the Idea of Transcendental Logic," in: *Husserl, Heidegger, and the Space of Meaning*. Evanston: Northwestern University Press, 2001.
— —, "Transcendental Logic and Minimal Empiricism: Lask and McDowell on the Unboundedness of the Conceptual," in: *Neo-Kantianism in Contemporary Philosophy*, R. M. Makkreel & S. Luft, eds., Indianapolis: Indiana University Press, 2009, pp. 150-175.
Emundts, Dina, "Emil Lask on Judgment and Truth," in: *Philosophical Forum* 39.2 (2008): 263–281.
Mohanty, J. N., "Lask's Theory of Judgment," in *Phenomenology on Kant, German Idealism, Hermeneutics and Logic*. Ed. O. Wiegand, R. J. Dostal, L. Embree, and J. J. Kockelmans. Dordrecht: Springer, 2000, pp. 171–188.
Motzkin, Gabriel, "Emil Lask and the Crisis of Neo-Kantianism. The Rediscovery of the Primordial World," in: *Revue de Métaphysique et de Morale*, (2)1989, pp. 171–190.

Chapter 24

"Announcement" of *The Logic of Philosophy and the Doctrine of Categories* (1910)[1]

TRANSLATED BY ARUN IYER

In this text an attempt is made to acquire for logic and in particular the theory of categories a new region of investigation with a reflection on the logical presupposition of philosophical cognition. There will also be an attempt to draw consequences for logic from the scientific and cognitive character of philosophy. The text postulates a logic that is centered on philosophy and a doctrine of categories. In this way the extension of the sphere of the tasks of logic should come together with a heightened understanding of the essence of philosophy.

    Central to this project is the fundamental idea of Kant's Copernican turn: the transference of transcendental forms to the object, the constitutedness of theoretical objects through categories. The text's main thesis runs as follows: *To apply Kant's Copernican turn to the object of philosophical cognition*. Only the strictest sensualism would have grounds to resist the extension of the domain of objectively logical and the constitutively logical and the transcendental structure of objects exemplified by the division into categories and category material, to include non-sensual objects, for instance, to the valid form. That is because so long as in everything that can be thought there exists alongside the sensible-intuitive portion a non-sensible portion that is independent of the former and different from it – something that even Kantianism does not contest – the related categorical content must have an equal constitutive significance. If one were to call the non-sensible part just an abstract figure of merely methodological relevance that is artificially separable, then the same generalization could be made about the sensible material. In this respect the sensible has no priority over the non-sensible. The latter can be categorically raised to the status of an object just as well as the former. To philosophize is also to cognize and this cognition has an object. Even this object is to be interpreted as something transcendentally and categorically logical in accordance with the Copernican thesis. Philosophy is, first of all, legitimized as a cognition in logic. For this reason we need to expand epistemological logic[2] and the doctrine of the categories beyond the limits into which Kant and the whole of Kantianism has forced it up until this time. The reduction of the categories to sensible intuitive material and to the sensible-intuitive realm is to be resisted in accordance to the very principles of Kantianism itself. *Not a panlogism but rather the panarchy of the logos and the all-encompassing dominance of the categorical form must yet again be advocated*. This results in a splitting up of the whole system of categories into two distinct realms and a doubling of the categorical content as it constitutes the sensible and the non-sensible objects of knowledge.

It is on such an expanded foundation of the dominion of constitutive forms that the theory of the "reflexive-general," the universally applicable, and the categories directed towards any random entity as such is to be built. It is to be shown in this way that primarily through the extension of the categorical concepts to the realm of philosophy, the essence of philosophical cognition and the difference between "cognition" and "life" can be rigorously characterized.

In the concluding chapter that is historical in character an overview of the previous approaches to liberating the categories from the restriction to sensible and natural categories towards a theory of categories of non-sensible philosophical objects of cognition will be provided. As a result of this overview it is found that in Aristotle, the categories are intended without any distinction and uniformly for both the sensible and the non-sensible world. It is Plotinus who for the first time presents the categorical forms for the *mundus sensibilis* and the *mundus intelligibilis* separately becoming, as a result, the theoretician of categories of the Platonic-Aristotelian two-world theory. The entire middle ages are dominated by the impetus to provide a comprehensive picture of a system of categories encompassing the entire universe of objects. The chapter devotes a detailed presentation to Kant's stance towards the question of the dominion of the categories. It ends by examining the sporadic traces of the universal systems of categories in the nineteenth century that include the philosophical object.

Notes

1 "Selbstanzeige," in: *Sämtliche Werke,* vol. I. Wuppertal: Dietrich Scheglmann Reprintverlag, 2002, pp. 330–332. Translated for the first time into English by Arun Iyer. – Ed.
2 *erkenntnistheoretische Logik*

Chapter 25

"The Logic of the Ontological Categories" from *The Logic of Philosophy and the Doctrine of Categories* (1911)[1]

TRANSLATED BY ARUN IYER

Theoretical philosophy, logic, the doctrine of categories is a branch of the philosophical science of validity[2]. The object of this enterprise belongs to the sphere of validity. In the introduction we set the spheres of what is and what is valid in opposition to one another. Then – especially in the second section we assigned to both spheres their respective types of knowledge, namely, the scientific and the philosophical. Now the theory of knowledge as a philosophical discipline is under all circumstances, thus even the theory of knowledge applied to the realm of being, concerned with something that is not, with something that is valid, with the validity of knowledge, with theoretical validity. Now that we have entered into logical investigation, what was established before for the sphere of validity as for the philosophical object in general, also holds for the object of logical investigation. Yet earlier we used the sphere of truth simply as an example of the realm of sense. Moreover we already indicated in passing that the rough division, within the realm of what can be thought, between what is and what is valid lead to assigning even for the object of *theoretical* philosophy and logic, a transcendental space within the totality of what can be thought. It is only by explicitly transposing the logical into the sphere of validity that we can wrench logic out of its isolation. All the derivatives of the concepts of validity and those of the guiding concepts of this entire sphere of validity such as the concepts of meaning, of sense, and above all of value will from now on find their home in the realm of the logical. Without this clear integration of the logical into one of the spheres of what is thinkable the whole reawakening of theoretical transcendental philosophy, of Kantianism in the second half of the nineteenth century, the wresting of theoretical philosophy from scientific psychology, on the one hand, and from the metaphysics of the supersensible, on the other, still does not appear as a state of complete awakening. Even when we are given assurance that logic is not about the origin but about the "concept," not about the causes but about the "reasons" of experience, not about cognition in a subjective sense but in an "objective" sense, not about psychological but about "logical" characterization, it is still ultimately a stammering of words and a groping in the dark. A primitive[3] magic surrounds the word "logical." This word "logical" is passed off as ultimate, incomparable and uncoordinatable, beyond which one cannot investigate. The logical is precisely logical and thus neither metaphysical nor psychological. Of what kind is it then and has it nowhere its equal, no place in all that is thinkable? It was a decisive step on the part of contemporary validity and value theory to have brought the logical unequivocally, unquestioningly and uncompromisingly under the roof of the two-sphere theory, under the duality of being and validity[4] and to have given it the place to which it belongs. One must certainly halt one's investigation when one has arrived at something that is ultimate. But even the logical is not something that is ultimate. The two-world theory has the capacity to subordinate the logical under ultimate concepts that are more comprehensive and to put it into an illuminating relationship with the other philosophical disciplines.

Thus logic, theory of knowledge, theoretical transcendental philosophy have to do with theoretical validity[5], with one section of the sphere of validity[6]. But the Kantian theory of knowledge deals exclusively with the knowledge pertaining to the realm of being and the whole of the first part that follows will be restricted to this chapter of theoretical philosophy concerning the realm of being.

Now as before the sphere of validity in general and so also the theoretical content of validity must, for the time being, continue to be left completely undetermined. The first section deals with the relationship between the sphere of the validity of knowledge[7] and the object of knowledge and thus the sensible-intuitable region of being, which Kant introduced into the history of thought. It does so independently of any precise characterization of transcendental structures and *a priori* unities of validity. Even though the Kantian concept of *form* is never to be really separated from his theoretical transcendental philosophy and his Copernican turn, we must, for reasons pertaining to the way in which we break the problem down, come back later to address the formal character of the theoretical in the second section.

Section 1. Kant's Copernican turn

The universal historical place of Kant in the development of the theoretical philosophy is based on his Copernican turn. However much one mixes in his overthrow of the concepts of truth and knowledge of the previous millennium along with his metaphysical two-world theory and his distinction between appearance and the thing-in-itself into the historical shape of his system, his revolutionary achievement in the theory of truth and knowledge still stands out of this mix as something independent. It is because of *Kant's* Copernican turn that theoretical speculation through all the ages can be divided into a dogmatic and a critical epoch. However the fact that he grasped the problem of knowledge not as a psycho-genetic problem but as a critique of pure speculative "reason" still does not explain his unique place and make him the founder of a new epoch. The great rationalists of all time were his predecessors in this regard. And if the uniqueness of his critique lay in that undertaking of testing cognition itself before one investigates the objects of cognition, something that was constantly advanced for that purpose, his doctrine would have lacked originality and *Kant* would be reduced to the position of an imitator of *Descartes* and *Locke*. That is because the still not so major move of privileging and prioritizing of the philosophical problem of knowledge over the philosophical problem of being does not lead one beyond the dogmatism that is common to all pre-Kantian approaches. What is totally new and unheard of, what had not yet "occurred to" anyone, consisted rather in the conversion of the concept of being into a concept of transcendental logic.[8]

The whole pre-Kantian dogmatism of the rationalist, empiricist, and skeptical modes of thinking, with respect to the relationship between the theoretical sphere and the object of knowledge, has its common essence in the fact that it asserted in general yet another relationship between, a separation, a *duality*, of object and truth, "being" and "knowing," being and transcendental content of knowledge. It posits an objectivity beyond that of the "understanding," beyond what is theoretically graspable, outside of logical validity-content[9].

The true overcoming of every kind of "dogmatism" that Kant had achieved (in the narrow epistemological sense) is seen in the abolishing of this metalogicity, this "transcendence" over the logical, in the abolition of this independence of being over and above the logical sphere, in the destruction of the ancient separation of the object and its truth-content, in the recognition of the transcendental logicity or "understandability"[10] of being.

It is thus simply not a question of the relationship between the knowing subject and the object, not about the subject-object duality, but rather of a relationship between the transcendental-logical *content* of knowledge[11] and the object. Moreover *Kant's* originality seems to indeed consist in the fact that for him objectivity is displaced into a subjectivity that is necessary and universally valid. That alone ultimately results in the objectivity of the object[12] being led back into the objectivity[13] that somehow resides in a subject and, in addition, to the objectivity[14] that belongs to the theoretical realm of the subject or reason and thus to theoretical objectivity[15] or the objectivity[16] of knowledge. Thus the separation of objectivity[17] and theoretical validity is abolished. In this regard, the Copernican achievement finally comes down to the fact that every duality[18] of objectivity[19] and logical validity is destroyed; logical content is grasped as that which establishes or constitutes objectivity[20] and thus as constitutive transcendental-logical content; the objectivity of the objects is understood as something that is to be accounted for in terms of logical validity.

Kant advocated this identification of objectivity[21] and logical validity-content for the object of cognition pertaining to being and the cognition pertaining to "nature" and for the reality of sensible-intuitable actuality. What lies then in those expressions such as being, reality, actuality, existence? Here Kant – and herein lies his highest and plainly most tremendous achievement – had wanted to extract a sense from out of all these words that the millennia before him had simply overlooked. He aroused philosophical reflection to give thought, for once, on the sense that confronts us in all these expressions when we utter them more or less emphatically. Then one discovers: something is *actually* so, something is *really so*, that indeed means nothing else than: it is indeed in *truth* so.[22] The character of actuality and reality of something means nothing other than: it has its objective matter and its truth therewith. The objective existence, the stability and independence of reality and "nature," the necessity and persistence of what happens are nothing other than the necessity and the inevitability of the valid[23] truth. Further, objectivity[24] is nothing other than validity, nothing than being unconditionally valid and correct[25], the objectivity of being nothing other than absoluteness of being valid. Objective necessity, being, existence is just the transcendental-logical validity-content of the sensible-intuitable. That is what the Copernican turn means when one grasps it as the act of transcendental logic: the logical validity-content is not turned towards the objects. It is not functionally dependent upon them. It is not bound to them like a shadow accompanying them. It is not a truth about objects as if to mean: the more the objects, the more the truths about them. Rather the inverse is the case: the objects are turned towards logical validity, in the objects there is a turn towards logical validity, and their objectivity *is* the valid truth[26]. So actuality is as much existing in truth; tangible and causal cohesiveness of reality is as much *belonging*-together in truth.[27] In objectivity, being, existing, and perdurance, we are confronted with a logical validity[28] that makes a corresponding demand upon us. The "object" is: the truth that "confronts" subjectivity with a corresponding claim to validity[29]. It is a truth that "stands face to face" with subjectivity. Accordingly, objectivity at the same time implies that what is valid in this case is already conceived as a thinkable object relating to the subject. The "object" is the transcendental-logical content, if it is already posited as the "object" in correlation to the cognizing comportment of the subject.

The sense of the Copernican thesis is: reality, tangibility, and causal connection contain theoretical content and nothing else. We are here not just content to say: but that happens to be the case only from one-sided epistemological-logical "perspectives." Rather, with the revelation of its theoretical character as validity *the* very essence of being, objectivity, and reality is disclosed and there is no perspective from which this essence would appear otherwise.

Section 2. The insertion of the concepts "form" and "sense" into the Copernican thesis[30]

The logicizing of objectivity must immediately lose its paradoxical nature for the popular as well as the dogmatic consciousness as soon as it is noted that only the objective *character in* the object should be surrendered to the logical, but the objects in their concrete totality should in no way be branded panlogistically as just nothing but logical content. This logicizing concerns only that aspect in the objects, beings, realities, things, causally connected events that stands out as the mere character, moment, epithet, predicate, "category" of objectivity, of being, of reality, of tangibility, of causal connectedness from the density of their remaining content[31]. What can be accounted for by the logical content emerges as a mere moment of *objectivity*[32] in the fullness of what is concretely objective[33]. The realm of objects splits itself into the moment of objectivity and what is objective, into being and the content of being, or in short into being and beings, into thingliness and things, into causal necessity and what is causally bound. The logical stands as a mere moment over an a-logical mass.[34]

With this clarification of the position that the transcendental-logical content assumes, our presentation unavoidably hits upon the necessity of a first decisive revision of fundamental concepts, which completely overturns the prior accounts of the structure of the sphere of validity. With one stroke the entire previous doctrine of the sphere of validity is rectified and it is precisely because of this that the current special doctrine of the theoretical validity-content and the Copernican overthrow is rendered more precisely. The introduction had to still concern itself with its form of non-sensibility, its resemblance to validity and its timelessness in general. Now on the contrary we raise the question, the most important one that we can come up with: whether any "realm" presents us with a prototype of pure validity-content, a uniquely pure mass having the form of something valid and timeless or if perhaps the stuff pertaining to the timeless character of validity simply makes up one of its moments in a whole and which gives the whole its form. From now on the structure and the constitution of the objective "realm" will be our main focus.

Our decision to focus on the structure and the constitution of the objective realm is simple and foundational. This is because the general doctrine of the structure of the sphere of validity has revealed to us the proto-relationship[35] that governs the elements of a concrete whole having the form of validity. The objective realm is in reality always articulated! It is no quasi-amorphous, no formless mass! It has "form"! And in addition what is valid is the "form" of this objective realm. *Only* the form needs to have the mode of eternal validity. What is valid *only* plays the role of the *form* in the realm of objective concreteness. The validity is in accordance with its position and its quasi-functional essence the form-content[36].

With this we have arrived at the fundamental principle, which has to occupy the peak of the entire philosophical science of validity and by consequence the whole of theoretical transcendental philosophy. This fundamental principle can be expressed in the following way. When one considers something determinate, for example, logical content, one will be aware that the validity-content does not fulfill its sense by itself, does not rest on itself, does not constitute a "world" for itself, but rather points beyond itself towards something foreign outside of itself in the manner of something that is in need of something else that fits tightly with it, like something that is in need of completion. There is no validity that were not a validity concerning, that were not validity *with regard to*, that were not a validity *of*[37]. There is no marked off region of sheer validity-content that is self-sufficient, self-standing, not in need of support, that does not point to something outside of itself and cut off from everything else. One can denote this non-independence, this inescapability from being attached to something else and being for something else, in accordance with well-respected terminology as the *form*-character of validity. The validity-content is a mere empty form awaiting fulfillment from "matter" or "content." Everything that is of the nature of validity is a validity that is directed towards that entity from which the valid form anticipates fulfillment by way of content[38]. Everything that has validity always concerns something else and is in need of matter, which is what is affected by form. Just as one may denote the validity character[39] figuratively as "form," so can the situation of that to which validity pertains and which it requires for its fulfillment be denoted as "content" or "matter." For a preliminary illustration of this fundamental relationship one could pick out random individual forms of logical content! Identity is incomprehensible without an entity, a content which is identical and clothed in a valid form of identity. Identity points beyond itself to an entity that is identical. In the same way difference, this logical relation, this relationship, this logical between is incomprehensible without a between-what, without the members of the relationship, between which there is a relationship. Relationship points to the members and the members stand in a relationship. But since relationship is an example of a logical form, it means that: form always points towards content in being valid "*with respect to*" that particular content[40], and contents stand under that form. Now in so far as the Copernican thesis tells us being, tangibility, causality also represent theoretical validity-content, the relationship of being to beings is of the same nature as that of the aforementioned relationship of identity to that which is identical. In the case of the relationship of tangibility[41] and causality, the connection to what is tangible and causally connected matter is of the same nature as the relationship of difference to those that differ. Being, tangibility, causality are the form or, as the theoretical form should from now on be called, the category. The discussion of the Copernican thesis has now advanced towards the concept of form which was also decisive for *Kant*. With the insertion of the concept of categories the Copernican thesis will henceforth mean the following: objectivity in the objects is a category that coincides with the categorical form in its relation to the realm of truth.

However, before a more precisely articulated sense of the Copernican thesis is further pursued, a moment must first be devoted to the revision that has been witnessed in the entire doctrine of the sphere of the validity and with it also in the "realm of truth." The realm of the truth will from now on indicate the homogenous type of structure that is constituted of form and matter. It is then obvious that alongside the concept of the form we now also need a term for the whole [comprised of form and matter]. This intertwining, this fusion of form and matter, this whole, in which the form that is in itself empty and in need of completion emerges together with its fulfillment granted to it by the content, should be denoted as *sense*.[42] The objective realm and also the realm of truth, which was mentioned in the introduction, is the realm of "sense." The sense consists not of sheer validity-content as it must have previously seemed to us; rather the validity-content constitutes only the form of sense. The sense is distinguished from the mere form through the fact that it also contains the fulfillment that is granted to it by the content, which is already implicitly demanded by the form. The unity that encompasses the elements of sense, however, coincides precisely with what is already implied by the character of the mere form to be always valid with respect to something else[43]. The valid content, for example, the specific theoretical content, which gives its imprint to the sense as a whole, rests entirely and indivisibly in the form of the sense. Matter, in being affected by validity-content is, so to speak, simply coupled [to the form]. Only the form, and not the whole structure of sense, should therefore be regarded as that which resembles validity[44]. The affected matter could then, for example, be a *non*-valid[45] entity if we take into account the truths in relation to the sensible being of matter, that is to say, where the sensible being is rendered valid by the theoretical form. Sense is therefore as a whole neither something along the lines of validity that is timeless, nor is it something along the lines of non-validity that is temporal, but rather a fusion of the two: a sensible-temporal being that is affected by timeless form, a validity-content taken together with that in relation to which it is valid. We have ultimately done away with the realm of uninterrupted, undivided timelessness.

This portends a tremendous rectification of the earlier representation of the sphere of validity that we must now undertake. According to the earlier formulation of the two-world theory it would appear as if on the one side there stood a region that was constituted through and through by the validity-content, as if there were in this region structures composed entirely and indistinguishably of the stuff of eternity, such as, for example, timeless truths. Now it has become apparent that in these so called timeless truths the species that is timelessly valid is simply their form. The truths as a whole are not timeless *simpliciter* but timeless in relation to that which is non-timeless and affected by the timeless. In the realm of truth, i.e., in the realm of theoretical sense, that which does not resemble validity, namely, the sensible-being as matter, as something affected, also has its place and remains undiminished within [the whole]. Of that one can be easily convinced. That is because when the truths that green is different from yellow and sweet from sour, that a is the cause of b and c is the cause of d, should be multiple, they cannot be so on account of the general category of difference or causality, but on account of the varying sensible matter. The latter [sensible matter] thus is included here in the determination of individual "timeless truths." It grounds the differentiation of *sense*. The sense of one sentence is thus different from that of the other despite the similarity of category. Now one becomes aware that it is simply the radiance of the valid form that pours its gleam over the whole individual sense-structure and transforms it into an image of the "timeless truth." From this sense-structure that is imprinted by form, we must recover what we previously established about the essence of timelessness. From now the sense of all the expressions that were used in the introduction becomes clear. It becomes clear that the truths about what is blue, what is spatial, what is temporal, what is sensible are not themselves blue, spatial, temporal, and sensible truths. At that time it still appeared as if the sensible blue was mirrored in a realm of truth that consisted of sheer timelessness, in the purified form of an ideal blue, in an ideal unity of meaning "blue" as if as a member of the species that is timelessly valid, as a blue, it signified the timeless blue embedded in a comprehensive structure of pure timelessness. In that prior formulation we still acceded to the idealizing of sensible contents into the timeless existence of a prototype that went back to *Plato's* doctrine of ideas, which, by way of example, is currently found in *Lotze* and *Husserl*. It must actually be said that *Lotze* had indeed clearly worked out the notion of validity but without recognizing that it is only the form that is valid. As opposed to it the a-logical-sensible element can neither be valid nor "mean" anything, but only stand *under* a valid form, *in* the logical sphere. It can be affected by the categorical form through which the glory of the timeless form of meaning[46] appears to hover over the whole content[47]. Blue, inserted into the realm of truth, means nothing else than the non-valid-sensible and a-logical blue. It remains what it is by being enveloped and rendered valid by the timelessly valid, categorical truth-form. The truths about what is spatial, temporal and sensible are non-spatial, timeless, unsensible, formal validity of truth[48] with respect to the spatial, temporal, sensible, which is the matter that is affected [by the categorical form]. It is only in the theoretical form that one can find the timelessness and unsensibility of the whole realm of truth. That is what rationalism was from the very beginning mistaken about: that the a-logical material is able to indeed stand in the logical, but without thereby transforming into something logical.[49]

One will even then find the concept of sense that has been advocated just now unsatisfactory and inadequate. It is hardly immediately obvious that the unity and self-contained nature of sense should consist in nothing further than the intertwining of form and matter. Nevertheless this conviction regarding the ultimate and most extreme simplicity of the structure of all sense cannot be more precisely grounded. We can only immediately admit so much that despite everything the theoretical sense, which has been treated by logic from time immemorial and which can be abstracted from propositions, expression and judgments, is a sense, which must always be either positive or negative as well as correct or incorrect and that it exhibits a more complicated structure than the mere interlocking of form and matter. If we stay, despite this, with this simple model of sense we are guided by an insight that could be proved in connection to a systematic logic. This is the insight that richer and more complex structures indeed betray a very articulated construction and are in that sense fabricated. Moreover, what we have presented here is the unfabricated sense with a simple structure that lies at the basis of all these complex constructions. It is not unintentional if no further complexity is admitted into the prototype of sense. Even in what follows too we will be time and again discussing only this simple prototype of sense. In addition we will simply skip over the simplicity of half of this prototype of sense. This is the half, which can be immediately separated from the sense-carrying structures of knowledge and which constitutes the *proteron pros hemas*. But this move is completely unobjectionable, because in this study we will be concerning ourselves not with the further development of the doctrine of sense but only with the theoretical doctrine of form, the doctrine of categories.[50]

We have now taken the decisive step beyond indeterminate ideas pertaining to the objective realm of reality, for instance, theoretical reality or truth. We have stated the dominant, we can even say, the only dominant structure of all reality, namely, its organization into form and matter. The realm of truth, just as the realm of aesthetic sense, can be nothing other than a content ruled by form, in so far as one admits that the entire a-logical content can enter into the theoretical sphere as matter in the same way as the whole extra-aesthetic state of affairs can enter into the aesthetic sphere as "stuff"[51]. The a-logical and the extra-aesthetic do not stop being a-logical and extra-aesthetic. They are only *couched* in a logical and aesthetic form. The fact that any particular truth and any particular beauty is still truth and beauty in every instance, irrespective of the infinite multiplicity of matter, is due to the sameness of the sense-bestowing form. It makes no sense anymore to insist on the "merely" formal character of theoretical content when any sense consists in nothing other than matter that is imprinted with form.

When we have thereby really encountered the way in which all sense is articulated we become clear as to the fundamental significance the concept of form must attain in the whole philosophy of validity. From this it follows that the doctrine of categorical form must occupy the highest position in theoretical philosophy and in logic. The specificity of theoretical sense or truth is based on the specificity of the theoretical form. Thus the primary concern of logic will be the separation of the pure content of logical form from all the other content and the determination of the share of the logical aspect in the entirety of the content as well as the establishment of the boundaries between the logical and the a-logical. The logician surveys the whole of existence in accordance to the specific logical content that pertains to existence. He isolates the prototype of the logical form, the logical or the logos from its involvement with the a-logical. He separates the logos and in doing so he pursues a critique of pure logos. If one understands the term category to mean the logical form in the widest sense then the concept of category must become the highest concept of logic. That follows from our last presuppositions that logic is the philosophical knowledge of validity and all validity-content manifests itself as form.

When we apply the concepts of form and sense to the theoretical realm of validity, we can grasp the concept of truth in a precise way. We can bring it down to its simplest form by means of the following two propositions. The first: the realm of truth must be marked off from everything that does not have such a character on the basis of a specific theoretical or logical validity-content and a universe of logical meanings of validity[52]. Truth cannot be something random but it must be distinguished by a theoretical character. And the second: Truth as a whole cannot, on the other hand, be singular sheer validity-content or an instance of pure logical meaning. This follows from the form-character of the specific logical content which necessarily implies a division into the form and the matter of the truth. It follows from these two propositions that truth must always be about a form-matter complex. It must always concern matter that is affected, encompassed and rendered valid by a logical form. We can now discover an ambiguity in the concept of truth. We can understand by "truth" merely the specific logical content of truth that bestows upon the realm where truth is to be found the status of a realm *of truth*. But we can distinguish the truth in *concreto*, the truth in conjunction with matter from the formal content of truth, from the merely empty categorical form of the truth. That is to say we can distinguish the "realm" of truth or theoretical sense in the whole comprising of that which is constituted by categorical form of truth and matter that is affected by it. The instance of truth in *concreto* is the instance of matter standing under a categorical form. This individual truth – of which there are many – is the individual categorical matter standing under a theoretical form. By truth plain and simple one should always understand the theoretical or the true sense and against which the merely categorical form as truth-form or the formal truth-content should be explicitly identified. For this reason, the truth-form and theoretical form, true sense and theoretical sense should be taken to be synonymous here and in what follows.

By simply introducing the concept of form into the sphere of validity we have not decisively overcome two-world theory that was presented in the introduction. We have simply shown that the sphere of validity does not consist of just that which resembles validity but is also made up of form and matter. Conversely, the idea of the co-existence of two independent regions side by side was still not shaken up by this. However, this much has already been established, namely, that in the realm of sense the entire sensible content of the realm of the objects has once more found a voice. However, if we did not pay heed to this, the realm of objects and the realm of truth could indeed remain two separate spheres existing side by side with only this peculiarity that they had the sensible component in common, which latter would find two voices, one in each of the two realms. So, to persist with the earlier example, the sensible blue of the blue objects would at the same time appear in the other realm – the realm of truth – and would function there not as the timeless meaning of blue but rather as the sensible matter. But this possibility is immediately ruled out if one were to bring the Copernican thesis to bear anew on the previous discussion of the concept of sense. This is because the Copernican thesis implies that the allegedly separated realms of objects and theoretical sense also coincide with respect to their formal components since, according to this thesis, the objectivity of the objects is identical to the form in the realm of sense. But since the sensible component is duplicated on both sides, the formal components are in the same way shown to be identical. The Copernican thesis receives a more precise formulation when one introduces the concepts of form and sense into the undifferentiated formulation of the thesis in the previous section. The unified formulation simply says: The object coincides with the theoretical. The formulation that is divided according to form and matter goes: the objectivity of the objects coincides with the theoretical form, the whole that is constituted by the objects with the theoretical sense.

It is now possible to formulate the Kantian philosophy of identity with respect to the relationship between the object and the logical content in such a way that it can be distinguished more sharply from panlogism: The objectivity of the formal aspect pertaining to the objectivity of the objects coincides with the categorical truth-form, the whole constituted by the objects, the objectivity of the material aspect, the realm of objects coincides with the whole of the theoretical sense. Objectivity is identical to the categorical truth-form and the objects are identical to the theoretical sense. The objects that concretely exist are certainly not pure logical contents but rather a-logical matter couched in logical validity-content. Spatio-temporal objects also mean: non-spatial and timeless objects with regard to what is spatial and temporal. Just as the objectivity of the spatio-temporal objects *is* the non-spatial and non-temporal truth content[53], so *are* spatio-temporal objects "spatio-temporal" a-logical matter affected by non-spatio-temporal formal truth-content.[54] Or one could instead say individual objects are individual theoretical configurations of sense, individual "truths." This is because truths in the sense of particular items of theoretical sense encompass in addition to the timeless content of validity also non-valid[55] matter that is affected by the latter. One may therefore say without hesitation that: spatio-temporal objects *are* spatio-temporal truths, physical objects are physical truths, astral objects are astronomical truths, psychical objects are psychological truths and so on. They are certainly truths, particular instances of sense, not cognitions, judgments, propositions. In addition, they are truths in the non-fabricated world, not in the situation that is completely free of all scientific laws!

We must therefore reject any alleged parallelism, any binding-together of the *ordo et connexio rerum* and the *ordo et connexio veritatum*, according to which there is a whole set of non-spatial and timeless truths "about" the whole set of objects and states of affairs that occupy space and persist in time and that the former somehow corresponds to the latter and is associated to the latter as an accompanying shadow. In our time, this separation of object and truth, object and "sense," object and "meaning" is advocated in a particularly emphatic manner by *Bolzano* and *Husserl*. It is now clearly apparent that in such a position objectivity and truth-form, objects and truths are made independent of each other, while in truth the two realms of objects and truths about the objects merge together into one region of objects that is identical to the whole of the truth, the alleged shadow of truth falls in with the objects themselves, which supposedly cast this shadow.[56]

This alleged dualism of the two realms, of the object and the truth about the object, reveals itself as a doubling that is doubly unjustified. For one, the categorical content repeats itself on the opposite side, namely, in the realm of the object as a meta-logical, meta-categorical objectivity, in relation to which the truth turns into a relationship of mirroring and shadowing. But conversely a-logical matter makes a detour again in a transfigured form into the shadow-realm of the truth, where everything has to be a singular pure timeless whole of validity. In place of the duality of the logical form-element and the a-logical material-element, the two together constitute the singular realm of theoretical sense. In this realm we have the comprehensive reign of the duality of a meta-logical realm, in which the logical appears in a meta-logical guise, on the one hand, and on the other hand a pure logical realm, where the a-logical is displaced into the heaven of the timelessly valid meanings. The Copernican interpretation destroys the duality of both realms, but erects the opposition between categorical form and the matter of the categories inside a single realm of truth, and which for the very same reason is the realm of the objects. There is no "about"-relationship between the two realms[57]. But there is inside one single realm the relationship of being-in-reference to, and the being-affected by between two structural-*elements*. There is the formal validity of truth in reference to a matter that is affected by this formal validity of truth. In place of the mirroring of truth in relation to the object the form-matter, duplicity is the only thing decisive for the concept of truth.[58]

We can here only hint at where lies the fundamental explanatory ground for the persistent sundering of truth and object, for the mirroring-relationship, in which one brings truth and sense to concretion. It lies in the fact that one constantly starts out from a fabricated sense of proposition and judgment, which however does not coincide with the object, but which can either hit or miss the object. As a result one does not understand that even the object is itself nothing other than sense, namely the authentic prototypical[59] sense – and that the gap between sense and object amounts to a distance between one sense and another. Everything that one attributes to the mirroring relationship between truth and object applies, however, to the relationship between fabricated and prototypical sense.[60] We will go into the other reasons for why the object and the truth have been set apart in the second section. In that section, we will first of all give the Copernican doctrine of identity our fullest attention and we will subject the entire formulation of the two-world theory to a renewed examination. (Compare 2nd part, chapter I, 2nd section, "The Two-Object Theory and the Copernican Thesis.")

In grasping objectivity as a logical form, the Copernican interpretation simultaneously leads to the creation of a "transcendental logic." This is because certain logical-categorical forms again receive an immediate objective meaning, even being recognized as objectivity itself. Even in dogmatism the logical was already granted a meaning that extends outward towards the realm of the object and beyond what is merely formal and subjectively immanent. But always in the sense of some kind of correspondence, harmony, mirroring between the real and the "ideal" or logical, between the object and "the act of cognition." The logical had to be the logical moments of a conceptual expression and mirror-image of real relations. Thus the reality of a trans-subjective actuality was always already solidly bound up with the objectivity of logical moments. The rejection of a transcendental actuality always already involved the denial of the transcendental validity of logical concepts and vice versa. But through Kant the real and the logical, which were up until now only related to one another and only occasionally connected, come to coincide with one another. The opposition between the real and merely logical meaning will through him fall away and reduce to an opposition inside the logical. Reality is drawn into the logical and the logical extends into objects as their being, thingness and causal necessity. We may thus speak only of an extension of the logical into objectness, but not of a dominance "over" it. Otherwise objectness and theoretical validity content would yet again seem to exist as separate dimensions, between which some kind of the relationship prevailed. We must, however, consider doomed *all* the theories of correlation, whether they assert the existence of a dominance or a dependence of the logical in relation to being, apriority of being over validity or of validity over being. Just as we must fight every version of truth that is characterized by mirroring and shadowing, so also conversely, we must fight any assertion of a dependence in the opposite direction, apriority of theoretical validity, of the "demand," of the "ought" before being.[61][62]

What we have gained up to now allows us to declare: The formal nature of any given validity-content, the structure of sense has been discovered, and with the help of the Copernican thesis the coincidence of the realm of the object and the realm of truth has been grasped. Corresponding to these discoveries two errors of the two-world theory that emerged in the introduction have been revealed. Firstly, the introduction treated the sphere of validity as a realm that was self-enclosed, not form-like and pointing beyond itself and so granted the theoretical realm an independence from the realm of the objects and so was guilty of a comprehensive reduplication of the two realms.

Section 3. The sensible as that which is not valid[63] and which is foreign to validity[64]

The scope of the Copernican revolution comes to the fore even more starkly if the reversal that it affected in the two-world theory formulated in the introduction is now pursued even further. The two regions comprising of objects and truths that were held separately from each other in the introduction merge into one single "realm." Should there indeed yet be a duality, in some sense two spheres, that of temporal beings and that of timeless validities[65], then they can at most be two spheres of *elements* or factors which compose one region, namely, the realm of the object that coincides with the realm of theoretical sense. The region of being, and so also the realm of theoretical sense that is identical to it, are constructed out of the "sphere" of the theoretically valid[66] and the sphere of the non-valid-sensible[67], which can be seen as form and matter respectively. Just as the non-sensible and valid[68] form finds its way into the objective region of being so also the non-valid[69] sensible matter is to be conversely found in the realm of sense that is identical with the objective region of being. The two-world theory is to be reformed into a two-element theory.

This simultaneously leads to a further and more general realization. From the fact that the valid, namely, the categorical content emerges in the very midst of the realm of the being, we have to deduce that if one wished to sever the valid[70] from the non-valid[71] in everything that gives itself to thought, one would, on the one hand, have no realm of being at all. This is because the realm of being is still something that contains validity. It contains in it theoretical validity-content. We must therefore first extract the validity-content that is embedded in the realm of being and banish it to the other side, if we really want to preserve on one side the mass that is non-valid through and through purified of *all* and any theoretical-categorical stuff pertaining to validity. Now it becomes apparent that it is the Copernican thesis that helps us arrive at this true orientation and correct demarcation of these spheres. It first acquaints us with the comprehensive whole of that which is valid, in that it grasps the categorical moment of being also as validity-content. On the other hand, it makes it possible for the first time to uncover the non-valid free of all foreign accretions and extract the categorical content of being from the sphere of the non-valid. This is the same categorical content of being that combines unnoticed with the matter of being to form the unity of the realm of being.

The boundary between the non-valid and the valid runs right through the middle of the realm of being. And even the specific epithets or predicates which allow us to give the whole realm of being its name, namely, being, thingliness, etc. fall out the sphere of the non-valid as logical moments. It is precisely these constituents of the sphere of being that are placed on the side of non-beings. It is not accidental that these "epithets" or "predicates," which are now revealed as "categories," were already picked out in the earlier presentation as something peculiar. They are in fact of another kind than all the remaining parts of being[72] taken together.[73]

We must henceforth formulate more precisely what we mean. It is not the *region of being*, but only a *being*, that means that which stands under the category "being," but *sans* this its categorical form itself. It is not reality, but the real, that is to say that *which* is affected by the categorical form and first give rises to reality. This is what forms a hemisphere comprising the non-valid. In the realm of being everything is a being. In contrast to being the categorical content of being is itself a validity. The being of beings already belong to the valid and so to non-being. In the same way the reality of the real already belongs to the non-real. Being is valid[74], what is non-valid is first and foremost matter, in relation to which the categorical form of validity[75] comes to be called "being." This categorical matter exists. But its "being" grants it validity. One may call any matter "a being" only with regard to the fact that it stands under the category "being." It is therefore ambiguous to speak of being in the first place. This is because one can understand under that term either the whole region of being and with it the bulk content that stands under the categorical form "being" along with the form of being itself, or the mere something that is *can be* affected by the category "being." Only in this latter sense of mere matter of being is a being to be separated from what is valid. One may, for this reason, no longer calmly continue to designate the non-valid as the realm of being but rather as a being. One must, in this regard, only make clear that with this mode of expression one is already not stuck anymore at the level of the merely non-valid[76] but already pays heed to what the non-valid[77] is in itself and still more reflects on the role that it plays in the framework of theoretical sense. We characterize being according to the situation in which it is opposed to the categorical form. In the following presentation "a being" will always be meant in the sense of the matter of being.

We must thus distinguish between a being or the matter of being, between the being of beings or the category of being and the region of being or the sense that is constituted out of matter and category; and in the same way between the real, between the categorical character of reality and reality. We could also separate in a threefold way, what is object-like[78] or the object-matter, objectivity or the object-form and the realm of objects, the concrete whole[79] of objects or objective sense[80].

Now, for the first time, we have succeeded in arriving at the ultimate components out of which the entirety of something is built up. Every kind of ultimate schism and heterogeneity exists not between distinct regions, but between distinct elements of what is thinkable, which the introduction aptly characterized as the incommensurability between the sphere of being and validity. The totality of what is thinkable appears from now on as something cleanly split into two spheres of ultimate elements. In exactly the same way, with regard to the decision concerning what is to be placed in which of the two hemispheres, in every specific case we can say the following: Once one knows that in general there is what concretely is and what is valid[81], then it can be established that everything that is thinkable encloses this heterogeneity in some way or the other and that generally speaking a being cannot, for the same reason, be validity[82] and vice versa. Each sphere is to be determined by a negation of the specific mode of objectivity[83] that is characteristic of the other. Validity[84] is simply the positive expression for that which is not a being[85] in the same way as a being is for that which is not valid[86]. Just as validity is non-spatial, non-temporal and not a being[87] so must a being be non-valid[88] and if we take our cues from the way in which that which resembles validity must manifest itself, a being must not resemble value or meaning.[89] If we wanted to allocate in some way even a trace of meaning[90] to the stuff that pertains to a being, we would be guilty of complete senselessness for allowing a validity[91] to pass under the banner of being. That which is immediately encountered, the "reality" of everyday experience that is staggered variously with sense and value appears no longer as what is ultimate and indivisible. Out of this everyday reality what is merely a being and what is only-real must first be specifically extracted by the removal of every accretion that resembles validity and value. With this, the concrete whole that is purified of all the additional elements pertaining to what is not, a being merges with the stuff that pertains to beings. It remains to be seen in what manner that which is valid[92] may be bound to that which is not[93] and from what kind of [94] entanglements the knowledge of being has to first extract its material in order to obtain it in its purity. How many [of its materials] will claim to be beings, for example psychic beings, into which, truly speaking, value and meaning is snuck in. In that case one is immediately aware of having before oneself not a pure mass of reality but being and validity in some combination. So the negative requirement of being completely meaningful becomes very clearly a criterion of a being, of a psychophysical being, of a psychical as well as a physical being.

But only now does one procure for this whole realm of being itself, for reality, for the whole comprising of all existing objects its transcendental topography, so to speak. It is revealed as the residue available after having abstracted from everything that resembles value and validity. It is simply the non-valid[95] *sans* anything resembling value[96] while including only the categorical truth-content. It is what is ultimately stripped of all divinity, value and meaning in which the validity of truth is the only thing that still remains as the sole validity-content. But the rest of this whole that is throughout and without exception not valid is just a being or the matter of being[97].

However by excluding the sphere of validity, the matter of being[98] was characterized merely negatively, as what remains, as the other, as the non-valid. But it belongs to the very essence of things that the philosophical characterization of the matter of being[99] cannot happen in any other way except negatively. The matter of being[100] belongs before the tribunal of the ontological cognition[101]. It can never directly be the object of the philosophical reflection, but at most, indirectly through its relationships to the object of the philosophical cognition, namely, the sphere of validity. Whenever one deals, as we are doing here, with the sphere of non-validity as is the case with "a being" or the "matter of being"[102], one does so in connection with a logical investigation of the categorical content and it is a matter here of a setting-into-relationship of the non-valid entity with the appropriate categorical form "being." It is thanks to this situation that one has the possibility of subsuming matter somehow under a philosophical perspective. But it is still a one-sided determination which is undertaken in order to simply set the non-valid in a relationship to a specific theoretical, categorical content.

If one wanted to also take into consideration its functional position [of the non-valid] in relation to every kind of validity-content and thus in relation to every kind of form then one could indicate it simply as "the material" ("matter"). But that would still not be an unambiguous case if it were to be shown that in addition to the entity that simply exists even the form itself can take up the position of matter. Even if it were the case that only what is valid could play the role of form, it does not need to be the case that what is valid only plays the role of form. Perhaps there is – what appears at this point to be only as a playful possibility – also the form of a form. Then the valid form would end up in the position of matter vis-à-vis another form. In that case not only beings, but also validity could be "matter." This could possibly give rise to a comprehensive structure of forms in which any form when indeed seen from below would be a form and seen from above would be matter. Despite this, one must simply not separate the functional essence of the form's mode of being from validity and even when it takes the place of matter it still does not lose its form character. Therefore, in any structure of forms the matter cannot always be a form-matter, pointing beyond itself into infinity. There needs to be a terminus that does not point beyond itself anymore: a matter that is not form anymore, but only matter.[103] Since all that is valid is form, this position of matter will be occupied by what is not valid, by being. If the validity-content is in accordance with its essence an empty form, then it already means that this empty form is ultimately juxtaposed to something that is itself in accordance with its essence, only matter. Thus the functional opposition of matter and form leads to the absolute opposition of the valid and the non-valid. Now if it is considered functionally, that which is non-valid can be unambiguously characterized not just as matter *per se*, but rather as what is only-matter, the primordial matter[104], the fundamental matter, the mere "stuff," the mere "matter," the *prote hyle*. It is, as will be emphasized still more clearly in the second part, a symptom of the general restriction of logical research to the sensible matter of being[105] that the structural concept of "content" seems to coincide simply and unreflectively with that of a being and that it is only a being that counts as the content or the matter. As opposed to this, one can grasp the ancient concept of "matter" from the concept of the primordial matter[106]. Then one is able to recognize the following in the ancient philosophy of the primordial elements[107] constituting the objects of thought: the part, which in accordance to their essence is non-sensible, resembling value and validity, and the accompanying part, which is sensible, not resembling value and validity, are brought into the functional relationship of amorphous *hyle* to intangible form. From now on, one also grasps that the merely functional and thereby figurative distinction of form and matter[108] is connected to the essential distinction between that which resembles value and that which does not.[109]

With this concept of primordial matter[110], it would be possible to provide a philosophical definition of matter that is drawn exclusively from the functional relationship of the non-valid to the whole of the validity-content. With such a definition, however, nothing positive is said about the content itself that is non-valid[111]. Even from a philosophical perspective we would remain without a positive characterization of matter. We find ourselves dependent upon a merely negative characterization, upon the specification of its otherness and what it is not. There exists for this sphere no other philosophical designation than that which is found in Greek philosophy: *me*, *heteron*, matter.[112] In order to be cautious we may also hint at the following: that it be may be the case that the non-valid is placed before our discerning cognition, it stands there, in a manner that cannot be overlooked, as something no longer simply unaffected and untouched by logic and also no longer a merely unadulterated non-valid something. Categorical moments, and among other things, even the symptoms of comparative reflection have infected it in such a way that we simply cannot also avoid speaking of it as a something, a content, a state of affairs, a concrete instance, a manifold among other things. What all this means from the logical standpoint will be discussed later (in the second part, in the first and second section of the second chapter).

We have to thus be content with a negative, diagnostic characterization, which however delimits the matter of being with absolute precision. However there are also positive expressions, which when understood broadly enough are appropriate for the whole of the sphere of the non-valid. It is all those designations in which a being is understood as sensible or sensible-intuitable, as that which is given only to feeling and intuition, sensible-experienceable and perceivable. Now all these are most definitely positive expressions, but strictly speaking they are just names coined by the ontological cognition, mere words which are philosophically capable of saying even less, just like the words blue and sweet, vitriol and sugar. They simply hint at psychophysical processes of the lived experience and psychophysical organs of lived experience, at the "senses," feeling, intuition. If we accept that they are adequate names, that the non-valid consists of just matter pure and simple that is given to feeling, they are still however philosophically speaking completely mute designations for the mode of being of the non-valid. How could it be otherwise with these positive expressions for what is not of the order of meaning[113]? They are designations in which even the slightest indication of the essence of this whole sphere is not included. If one still believes that one is somehow able to understand such expressions as "sensible" already in their philosophical significance, then one has to surreptitiously endow the positive expression with the negativity of that which is not of the order of meaning[114]. This is what generally happens when the positive expression almost always appears as one of the opposing members of pair of antonyms such as sensible–non-sensible, sensible–supersensible, sensible–intelligible among others. We can therefore keep the inessential and obscuring secondary connotations of all these expressions at bay only if we, from the very outset, invest these expressions with the sense of that which does not resemble validity[115]. Only through this negative delimitation does one grasp why in the concrete instance of what is thinkable such a hemisphere of the something delimits itself.

One should not designate what is not of the order of value and meaning[116] as worthy and meaningful[117]. Such expressions would suffer from an annoying multiplicity of meanings. Meaningful[118] and meaningless would seem to stand in opposition to each other like worthy[119] and worthless, with both terms gaining value and meaning in the process. In that case only such a being would be meaningless of which one could also say that is meaningful. In this sense one calls a being meaningful and meaningless to exclusively imply that it is carrier and site of the experience of value[120], always cognizant of the fact that something resembling validity and value is "realized" in a being itself. One can therefore ascribe these qualities only to beings understood as the carriers of experience and to forms of the subject or their symbolic representations (such as propositions, lectures, books etc.).[121] We seem to have described here only the specific mode of existence of beings themselves, but only negatively through a comparison with that which resembles value without in any way conceding that validity could be realized in a being. Only the otherness of a being in contrast to what is valid should be emphasized here and no other ("constitutive") relation between the two spheres comes into question. In order to express more precisely the whole foreignness of being in relation to the whole sphere of validity and nothing but this, one should designate being as "foreign to meaning"[122] instead of what is meaningful[123] and also as "foreign to value and validity"[124],[125] Insofar as a being is seen to be foreign to meaning there is no question of it lacking anything. There is also no question of it being plagued by the unjustified demand to be meaningful. The designation of the foreignness is also meant to emphasize its indifference [to value]. We ascribe indifference – what correspondingly counts as neutrality – quite frequently to a being, again with the awareness that it is to be the carrier of value, and also the fact it is capable of being willed according to whether it is worthy and worthless. It is in this way that volitions are morally indifferent. One can even call non-voluntary theoretical behavior indifferent with regard to moral rightness and wrongness. A being merely "compared" to the sphere of value is foreign to value and meaning. When it is only thought of as a substrate in relation to the sphere of value, it can be also called meaningless, indifferent and neutral.

We need to justify no more that the foreignness to value has anything to do with worthlessness, that foreignness to validity has nothing to do with invalidity and that foreignness to meaning has nothing to do with meaninglessness. The opposition pertaining to value is a division *within* the sphere of value. A being is however foreign to value, that is to say it is foreign to the whole sphere of value and thereby foreign to worthlessness as much as worthiness, foreign to invalidity as much as validity. There actually does not exist a difference of value between the two spheres of being and value precisely because there exists between them a difference of value and non-value. For this reason, one may also not designate the rift between the non-sensible and the sensible, strictly speaking, as "opposition" insofar as "opposition" should express the completely incomparable relationship between worthiness and worthlessness[126]. Such opposition can occur within the realm of the non-sensible but not between that which resembles value[127] and that which is foreign to value. When every now and then expressions such as "primordial opposition"[128] could not be avoided in this text, it was exclusively meant as an emphatic designation for difference which is this bland and abstract relationship for its own sake between two members of a relationship. Foreignness to value, the sensible for itself, still conceived independently of any association with the sphere that lies over and above it, should not be conceived along the lines of the "matter" of many systems as the principle of worthlessness or somehow as a lower sphere. Although we have not developed it more precisely here, we can attribute "incompleteness," "conditionedness," "finitude" not to what is foreign to value as such but only to something in relation to value. Nothing other than foreignness exists between the two spheres. Hence there is neither an opposition of values nor a disparity or a hierarchy of some kind between the two in this case. All the oppositions between the conditioned and unconditioned, relative and absolute, finite and infinite, incomplete and complete are to be rejected as formulations of the two-world theory because they express a disparity of values.[129]

It is more precise to designate the sensible as the a-logical or the irrational stock of the thinkable.[130] A-logicity and irrationality alone would only be synonymous with foreignness to the meaning if in accordance with the terminology of the intellectualism of the ancients, one understands under logos *and ratio* validity-content and sense in the widest sense and not merely theoretical *logos* and intellectual *ratio*. On account of the sometimes wide and sometimes narrow meaning of *logos* and *ratio* and the logical and rational will, one must avoid these terms here. It is always the narrow meaning of *logos* and *ratio* that best constitutes the basis of the expressions a-logical and irrational. But the sensible is not only a-logical or irrational. It is not only that which is logically impermeable. Lying not only outside the region of logical content, but also outside the whole sphere of validity and meaning the sensible is also equally foreign to the ethical and aesthetic[131] sphere of values as it is to the theoretical. In any case foreignness to meaning implies irrationality but irrationality does not imply foreignness to meaning. With the customary reduction of theoretical philosophy to the realm of being today this distinction is anyway irrelevant. This is because the sensible is *the* a-logical here and another kind of a-logical is never in question. The a-logical here, in accordance with its *scope*, coincides simply with foreignness to meaning. Contrary to this, if one had the intention, as in this investigation, to pursue logical content over and beyond the realm of being, then one would have every reason to sharply distinguish between foreignness to meaning and irrationality. Considering that the non-sensible as irrational material can also stand in opposition to logical content, the scope of the irrational perhaps extends beyond the sphere of the sensible. It may very well be the case – the second part will shed more light on this – that in the light of the schism that was brought out by the latest rift between [sensible and the non-sensible] what is of the order of meaning may equally well have a place alongside what is foreign to meaning within the sphere of the irrational. We can appropriately say that the sensible is something irrational, which cannot be conceptually presented and which cannot be construed, something that is not logically accessible and which cannot be illuminated with clarity. We can also appropriately say that when it comes to the sensible we can only appeal to immediately intuited experience, that it is indescribable and immediate, that it can only be "passively" taken in and "experienced."[132] But merely this amenability to immediately lived experience and intuition is still not enough [to characterize the sensible]. This is because the sensible shares this quality of being unreachable for the "understanding" and this foreignness to understanding perhaps with something that is both a-logical and resembles meaning. Even the object of ethical, aesthetic and religious surrender[133] may be a-theoretical, irrational and "foreign to thought"[134]. A-logicity is no adequate distinguishing mark of the sensible. The sensible character must be still more specifically described. The sensibility that transcends mere a-logicity, a-theoretical immediacy or "intuitability" consists in nothing other than a comprehensive foreignness to meaning that surpasses mere irrationality. The sensible is in the concrete instance of what is experientially livable the obscure residue and sediment of what is not only theoretically ungraspable, but also comprehensively unclarifiable and incomprehensible. It is that into which lived experience cannot plunge as it can do in the case of meaning that stands opposed to the sensible in being valid[135] and possessing value[136]. The sensible is that which does not confront us as a thing demanding surrender[137]. It is something which lacks essence or rather is foreign to essence. It is what is just brutally there, tells us nothing and remains mute, the region of impression robbed of sense and meaning. This is "sensibility," which is "in us" and equally "outside us" – a difference which simply makes no sense here when it is simply the case of the foreignness to meaning of certain state of affairs[138].

If it is the sensible and not the realm of being that is to be isolated as one hemisphere of the thinkable in accordance with the revised understanding of the two-world theory by way of the Copernican thesis, then one must comprehend what stands on the other side [of the sensible] on account of its otherness as the non-sensible, which then encompasses the unsensible[139] and the supersensible[140]. This latter distinction within the thinkable can be articulated as that between the sensible and the non-sensible.

When we focus on the sensible that is foreign to meaning[141] we end up focusing on the whole realm of being. This is because the sphere of being can now be defined as the realm of theoretical sense, whose matter is sensible. The categorical content of being is characterized simply as *the* theoretical form, under which what is sensible-intuitable stands as matter. "Being" is even the specific theoretical validity-content for the non-valid, the sensible. What "being" means is to be understood only with the help of the sensible, which is foreign to validity and meaning but not vice versa. One cannot understand the sensible through the concept of being. This is because "being" as a completely *determinate* categorical form receives its particular meaning only from its matter, and thus through that which is foreign to meaning.

The Copernican insight now receives its well-known formulation: the realm of being is not an a-logical mass that is foreign to meaning, that is sensible-"*a posteriori*" through and through, merely "to be experienced." It does lie completely outside the logical and the "understanding," but it extends into the logical form and results from "reality" that is sensibly clothed. When they are affected by categories sensible masses of content, they are raised to the realm of the things and causally connected happenings. The realm of sense consists of more than just merely sensible stock. It consists, for example, of the sensible that is already permeated and dominated by unsensible, "*a priori*" forms of the understanding.

Up until now the insertion of the concept of form into the Copernican thesis has simply resulted in a shift of the two-world theory with which we originally began, and in its reformulation into a two-element theory. While till now the concept of theoretical form was only introduced in a completely general way, at this stage the Copernican interpretation of the realm of the being must be supported by a somewhat more fundamental treatment of the doctrine of the categories. Certainly even here, as always, it was done only in a sketchy way and without ultimate systematic grounding. But at least all the concepts have had to clearly emerge – the concepts of category, objectivity, irrationality, cognition whose most precise recapitulation will occur later in the philosophical theory of categories and the philosophical theory of knowledge.

Notes

1 *Gesammelte Werke*, vol. II, pp. 23–49. Translated into English for the first time by Arun Iyer. – Ed.
2 *Geltungswissenschaft*
3 *uralter*
4 *das Geltende*
5 *Gültigkeit*
6 *Geltungssphäre*
7 *Erkenntnisgültigkeit*
8 The following interpretation of Kant's theory of knowledge will be supported by the historical treatment of the concluding chapter [ch. 4, "The Philosophical Categories in the History of Theoretical Philosophy."].
9 *logische Geltungsgehalt*
10 "*Verstandes*"-*artigkeit*
11 *Erkenntnisgehalt*
12 *gegenständliche Objektivität*
13 *Objektivität*
14 *Objektivität*
15 *Objektivität*
16 *Objektivität*
17 *Gegenständlichkeit*
18 *Doppeltheit*
19 *Gegenständlichkeit*
20 *Gegenständlichkeit*

21 *Gegenständlichkeit*
22 [Later marginal note by Lask:] And not merely lived through, *as* object (and) this *thought*.
23 *geltender*
24 *Gegenständlichkeit*
25 [Later marginal note by Lask:] Due to this it has its "correctness."
26 *geltende Wahrheit*
27 [Later marginal note by Lask:] Objectivity encompassing many contents = objective connectedness! Reformulated as theoretically valid content!
28 *logisches Gelten*
29 *entgegengelten*
30 One must not forget that the whole intent of this work in connection with the recapitulation of such fundamental logical concepts had to be left in a completely rudimentary state.
31 *Inhaltlichkeit*
32 *Gegenständlichkeit*
33 *Fülle des Gegenständlichen*
34 [Later marginal note by Lask:] extends into objects
35 *Ur-verhältnis*
36 *Formgehalt*
37 *Hingelten*. Lask uses the term "*Hingelten*" instead of "*Gelten*" to show that validity is always a validity of something and that there can be no validity in itself. The prefix "*hin*" is supposed to indicate the intentional nature of validity in that it is always directed towards something beyond itself. Wherever possible I will try to indicate the prefix "*hin*" with an appropriate English construct such as "validity of" or "validity with respect to." But wherever it becomes exceedingly cumbersome to do so I will simply translate "*Hingelten*" as validity and put the German in footnote. In other words, the hylomorphism that Lask is propounding in this essay, whereby validity becomes of the form of a concrete matter corresponding to it, compels him to modify the German *gelten* into *hingelten* to indicate that validity always corresponds to a concrete matter that is valid and that it never exists independent of matter. – Trans.
38 *ein inhaltliche Erfüllung erwartendes Hingeltendes*
39 *Hingeltungscharakter*
40 *weist hingeltend auf Inhalt hin*
41 *Dinghaftigkeit*
42 Sense is used here in an absolute sense and not in the sense of "sense of." In the case of this linguistic usage the true or theoretical sense in the absolute sense is first and foremost the sense of judgment or proposition. On the subject of "sense" ["*Sinn*"] and "meaning" ["*Bedeutung*"] compare Husserl, *Logical Investigations, II*, 1901 [presumably Investigation I of Part II, "Expression and Meaning" – Ed.].
43 *Hingeltungscharakter*
44 *Geltungsartig*
45 *nichtgeltendes*
46 *Bedeutungsartigkeit*
47 *Inhaltlichkeit*
48 *Wahrheitsgelten*
49 [Later marginal note by Lask:] For the first time with the help of my terminology ("truth," "sense") one can express the fact that the categories, although identical to the form of the object and the objectivity itself, are still a specific logical form [*Logizität*]. Contrary to the metaphysical doctrine of the categories, the significant portion of whose core is the constitutive [categories]!
50 My plan to base the objective domain of factualness [*Sachlichkeit*] in logic on the sense that is separable from acts of cognition and sense carrying symbolic signs was decisively influenced by the strong impetus to revise the fundamental concepts of logic that comes from Husserl. A more detailed work on the fundamental problems of logic that will come later will provide more precise information on this topic.
51 *Stoff*
52 *Geltungsbedeutungen*
53 [Later marginal note by Lask:] Theoretical form-content

THE LOGIC OF THE ONTOLOGICAL CATEGORIES 419

54 [Later marginal note by Lask:] Theoretical form-content
55 *nichtgeltende*
56 [Later marginal note by Lask:] This is really oblique! I have really not at all duly considered the distance that actually exists between object and the immanent realm of valid truth. I have done so only casually, as for example 35 above. Even in Part II, chapter I, section 2 it is not attended to adequately! Against that in the doctrine of judgment I explicitly justify the about-relationship!
57 *Hinsichtlichkeit*
58 I am simply speaking here of the supposed mirroring-relationship between sense and object, theoretical form and objectivity. The relationship of the knowing subject's comportment towards sense or towards the object remains completely untouched by this [discussion].
59 *urbildlich*
60 One can agree with Rickert when he stipulates an about-relationship between the sense of the propositions and the object: "I build a true proposition about or from an ideal being but the sense of this proposition coincides just as little with the ideal being itself as the sense of a proposition about real being is identical with this real being." Rickert, "*Zwei Wege der Erkenntnistheorie*," Kantstudien XIV, 1901, 35/6
61 This doctrine of priority which for example is advocated by Rickert in "*Gegenstand der Erkenntnis*" will however be addressed first in Part II, in section 2 of Chapter I ["The Two-Object Theory and the Copernican Thesis"].
62 [The editor of the German edition, Herrigel, quotes here from a letter by Lask to Heinrich Rickert from the November 27, 1910; first printed as a note in this place in the text in *Gesammelte Schriften* II, p. 272. This lengthy passage is not reproduced here. – Ed.]
63 *Nichtgeltende*. Lask's use of the verb *gelten* [to be valid] in adjectival form *geltende* [valid] gives it a very peculiar transitive sense in this text. *Gelten* is strictly speaking intransitive. But Lask's hylomorphism imbues the verb *Gelten* with a transitive sense that comes close to "validate." The reader would do well to keep this in mind when reading this text. – Trans.
64 *Geltungsfremde*
65 *geltende*
66 *Geltenden*
67 *Nichtgeltend-Sinnlichen*
68 *geltende*
69 *nicht-geltende*
70 *das Geltende*
71 *das Nicht-Geltende*
72 *Seinsmasse*
73 [Later marginal note by Lask:] Consequently it is to be noted that here I am considering *only* what is *valid* and what is sensible. I would be extending this argument if I were to say that for all objects their objectivity is logical form, thus of the order of validity. Following this the supersensible cannot be a realm of objects but only an *element* of the object or a *factor*!
74 *geltend*
75 *Hingeltungsform*
76 *bloßen Nicht-Geltenden*
77 *das Nicht-Geltende*
78 *Gegenständliches*
79 *Inbegriff*
80 *gegenständlicher Sinn*
81 *Geltendes*
82 *Geltendes*
83 *Gegenständlichkeitsart*
84 *Geltendes*
85 *Nichtseiende*
86 *das Nicht-Geltende*
87 *unseiend*
88 *nicht-geltend*

89   [Later marginal note by Lask:] To be inserted: ...must be that which does not provide sense impression...
90   *Bedeutungmäßigkeit*
91   *Geltendes*
92   *das Geltende*
93   *das Nicht-Geltende*
94   Reading *weichen* as *welchen* – Trans.
95   *Nicht-Geltendes*
96   *Nicht-Wertartiges*
97   *Seins-Material*
98   *Seinsmaterial*
99   *Seinsmaterial*
100 *Seins-Material*
101 *Seins-Erkennens*
102 *Seinsmaterial*
103 [Later marginal note by Lask:] Thus: not matter that resembles form
104 *Urmaterial*
105 *Seinsmaterial*
106 *Urmaterial*
107 *Urelemente*
108 *Stoff*
109 In this regard it is certainly worth pondering whether, in line with models of past of metaphysics, the valid form simultaneously actualized a power of constituting itself into a transcendent being [*überseienden gestaltenden*] thereby making itself independent. The metaphysical concept of form in this way essentially deviates from our concept of a mere dependent form of validity directed towards something [*Hingeltungsform*], compare also what is under part II, chapter I beginning ["The Transposition of the Problem of the Categories to the Non-Sensual Sphere"].
110 *Urmaterial*
111 *Nichtgeltungsgehalt*
112 However, in this regard the relationship between otherness and negation may be completely uncertain. Actually the more precise characterization of the logical uniqueness of such a philosophical characterization of the non-philosophical objects of knowledge has to be left out here.
113 *Nichtbedeutungsmäßige*
114 *Nichtbedeutungsmäßigen*
115 *Nicht-Geltungsartigen*
116 *Nichtwert- und Nichtbedeutungsartige*
117 *wert- und bedeutungsbar*
118 *Bedeutungsbar*
119 *wertbar*
120 *Wertartigen*
121 That one may also use it to indicate the sense that is detachable from the substrate of lived experience is not in question here.
122 "*Bedeutungsfremde*"
123 *Bedeutungsbare*
124 "*Wert- und Geltungsfremde*"
125 This expression is used precisely to broaden the term "foreign to thought" ["*denkfremd*"] coined by J. Cohn. See *Voraussetzungen und Ziele der Erkenntnis* [*Presuppositions and Goals of Knowing*], 1908, p. 106.
126 *Unwert*
127 *Wertartigen*
128 "*Urgegensätzlichkeit*"
129 It may be noted here that in contrast to this, in the first great system of two-world theory, the Platonist system, the authentic opposing pole of the supersensible, the principle that is ultimately in opposition to the supersensible is in no way *genesis* but what remains behind in relation to

genesis when everything is abstracted from it, what is in relation to *genesis* the image of the idea. Consequently the principle of so-called "matter" is not understood as something that is lacking in value but as that which is foreign to value and meaning. First of all, it is out of the mixture of the supersensible, which lies beyond the worthy and worthless and the sensible, which lies within the scope of worthy and worthless, that *genesis* emerges. It is the site of incompleteness and is in opposition to both worth and worthlessness. So it is fundamentally even in Aristotle in whose work this point is explicated nowhere more beautifully than in Book 12 of the *Metaphysics*.

130 [Later marginal note by Lask:] First and foremost a-logical = what remains behind after the abstraction of categorical form.
131 [Later marginal note by Lask:] and the religious-supersensible
132 [Later marginal note by Lask:] cf. already the Kantian aposteriori, *empirical*, receptivity; cf. impression.
133 *Hingabe*
134 *denkfremd*
135 *entgegengeltende*
136 *werthaft*
137 *ein Hingabe Heischendes*
138 *Bestand*
139 *das Unsinnliche*
140 *das Übersinnliche*
141 *Sinnlich-Bedeutungsfremde*

Chapter 26

"The Boundlessness of Truth" from *The Logic of Philosophy and the Doctrine of Categories* (1911)[1]

TRANSLATED BY ARUN IYER

The extension of the problem of the categories beyond the sensible is ultimately based on the fundamental idea of the boundlessness of truth, of the all-encompassing scope of the dominion of logic and on the conviction that everything, insofar as it is a something and not a nothing, is affected by categories and stands in logical form.

This makes it necessary for one to also consider at least in passing the sphere of the supersensible. Again the legitimacy of the supersensible[2] and of metaphysics as science is absolutely not in question. What is rather in question is only the argument that *if* in any case metaphysics is possible and justified as a science alongside the philosophical science of validity[3], then here too we cannot avoid moving a step forward towards acknowledging the existence of the category for the supersensible in exactly the same way that the category for the unsensible[4] is inseparably connected with the cognition of validity.

At this point, however, the following must be established as a matter of principle to prevent troublesome misunderstandings. A doctrine of the categorical form for the supersensible cannot be metaphysics, but only logic, just as the doctrine of the categorical content of being[5] was not a knowledge of the sensible, but logic. Just as little as the categories *for the* sensible are sensible, so also are the categories for the supersensible not supersensible. Just as someone on account of the doctrine of the categories pertaining to being is hardly a sensualist, so is someone on account of a doctrine of the categories pertaining to that which is beyond being[6] hardly a metaphysician. For all regions the category is uniformly the logical form and therefore it is everywhere unsensible[7] belonging to the sphere of validity, whether the matter be sensible, unsensible[8] or supersensible[9]. It is true that the category manifests a semantic encumbrance coming from the different kinds of matter but the category does not *become* the matter from which it only receives the trace of a reference to matter. In both the realm of being and the realm of that which is beyond being, the category differentiates itself as a mode of validity compared to the sensible[10] and the supersensible[11] kind of matter. In fact, in the realm of that which is beyond being, the category shares the non-sensibility[12] of its matter. By contrast, in the realm of validity, the situation is such that the category and the material of the category belong to the same sphere: the sphere of what is valid and unsensible[13]. For logic the question is exclusively about the division between the category and the matter pertaining to the category. One must never mix in metaphysics with the doctrine of categories, even with that for the supersensible[14].[15]

If thus the doctrine of the categories should not stray into metaphysics, the doctrine of categories for its part cannot provide any ammunition for the destruction of metaphysics. The formal objectivity, the objective content, which has to do with matter in all realms, is generally resolved into categorical content according to the Copernican interpretation. However it does not mean that the sensible, unsensible and the supersensible matter that is left to the side receive the stamp of sheer logicity in a panlogic fashion. Whether there is a metaphysics as a science depends solely on the legitimacy and the knowability of the a-logical supersensible that is stripped of everything logical.

The Copernican insight on its own completely destroys a metaphysics that is directed towards the sensible realm. That is because the entire existence of such a metaphysics is based on a pre-Copernican-dogmatic delusion, which makes the forms of the object, e.g. substance and causality, independent of the forms of truth and cognition, exaggerating the former into the theme of a separate science. It never does this, by the way, without stealthily letting – for how could it be otherwise – a glimmer of the radiance of truth fall on the metalogical necessity of being[16]. As long as the philosophy of nature wishes to be something other than a doctrine of categories, it will find its life being ultimately snuffed out by the Copernican discovery. This is because nature as a distillate of the sensible realm of being consists, similar to the sensible realm, in nothing but semantically alienated matter[17] and categorical form. Cognition of being[18] and "theory of knowledge"[19] will from now on have to share in the tradition of such problems as that of psychophysical beings. The clarification that we have provided so far heralds the Copernican turn in that by including the allegedly meta-logical themes of a natural philosophical metaphysics in the logical, it lets an ontology of the natural philosophical kind disappear without a trace into logology. It understands all philosophical problems, as long as they do not fall under the metaphysics of the supersensible, uniformly as problems of validity. It thereby eliminates the dogmatic ontology of the sensible realm, which is the only apparent exception to it.

Only such a metaphysics that under the guise of metaphysics engages in categorical logic, without itself being aware of this, can be affected by the Copernican tendency. Now there is no doubt that the metaphysics of the supersensible can also suffer from pre-Copernican dogmatism. It would then not be able to disentangle the a-logical and categorical moments pertaining to its objects, namely, the metaphysical "state of affairs." It would also not be able to advance towards its own object-matter, namely, the supersensible that is untouched by the logical. Perhaps it would include all those things under the metaphysical problem of substance, which would have to be rightfully transferred to the categorical logic pertaining to the supersensible. One realizes that the pre-Copernican standpoint leads to an intellectualistic burdening of the non-logical whereby it becomes necessary from this standpoint for metaphysics to labor with logical contents in disguise. This is because the pre-Copernican standpoint is not in a position to identify the categorical addendum as such and shift it into logic. But such a metaphysics could be purified of its pre-Copernican-dogmatic components and it would be rendered null and void in a manner similar to the metaphysics of the sensible realm of being. If the excess pertaining to categorical content were to be eliminated, what would remain would be just the essential metaphysical object matter[20], namely, the supersensible matter pertaining to these categories[21], which is to be distinguished from this excess of categorical content. Even if all of metaphysics were to be a deception and a delusion, some type of epistemological reflection is, in any case, powerless to convince us of this. Theory of knowledge or logic, or the doctrine of categories is just not the thing that could decide on this question. Only in the case where metaphysics seeks to seize for itself the task of the doctrine of categories usurping in the process the problems of the validity, can the doctrine of categories object to its being used in such objectively illegitimate "hypostasizing"[22].

The extension of the problems of the categories, which are actually dealt with in logic, to the metaphysical sphere depends upon the *cognizability* of the supersensible[23]. But the question of the boundlessness of the truth is in itself not synonymous with the question of the cognizability [of the supersensible]. Up until now we focused relentlessly on the categorical content encountered in cognition, which constitutes a self-presenting object of logical investigation and therefore on the categorical content that could be found in the ontological cognition[24] and in the philosophical cognition of validity[25]. The scope of the categorical form investigated by logic extends as far as legitimate cognition. But this proposition cannot be reversed: cognition need not extend as far as the categorical form itself.[26] Behind this requirement of logical research to secure in its complete breath and comprehensiveness the categorical form that extends into the whole of cognition, lies the axiom of the universal dominion of the logical. This axiom is to be distinguished from, and is independent of, the question of the capacity of the logical to be actually encountered in cognition. The dominion of the logical in itself is boundless, although the domain of the logical that is accessible to cognition is perhaps bounded. The axiom of truth simply means: all categorical matter, so to speak, are couched in the same inescapable truth-form. Nothing is exempt from being affected in this way [by a truth-form]. It was also established that truth does not accompany things like their inseparable shadow. We have to give up the idea of a separated region of truth consisting purely of timeless validity-content, an idea by way of which the boundlessness of the truth was almost exclusively interpreted up until now. Yet one may certainly speak of a realm of the truth in itself in a modified sense. This is because any entity[27] stands as matter under a corresponding categorical form of validity[28] that is appropriate for it.[29] Truth in itself is the sense that is analyzed into form and matter whereby the matter in itself is affected by the categorical form.

It is useless to dispute the all-encompassing dominion of the truth. It is also completely nonsensical to admit, for instance, the existence of an entity[30] shorn of everything logical, but to deny that it is in itself capable of being affected by categories. One can snare such a misology like all skepticism in the well-known trap of the performative contradiction. When it has been asserted that an entity is impervious to being affected by the categories, such an entity already stands in the grip of categories as soon as one reflects upon it, even in those reflections that deny this to be the case. It is only in the event of an "immediate," unreflected, theoretically untouched surrender to an entity[31] that it stands shorn of all logic in a pre-objective state. As opposed to this, it is always already confronted in reflection as an object. With this, we have already hinted at a cognizability that goes even beyond categorical affectedness in itself[32]. However, there needs to be only a minimum of objectivity in the case of such a [non-categorical] reflection. Matter needs to be theoretically legitimated only as a "something," as the "it is." What precisely this merely "reflexive" category of the "it is" entails remains, for the present, unresolved. In any case, we have already thereby advanced towards encapsulating the entity in categories. And further: as it should have already been anticipated, its follows from the still unfamiliar essence of the reflexive category that something may stand clothed purely and exclusively in the reflexive category even before it is given to reflection. It also follows that it cannot in itself be something merely general, but it exists first and foremost as the specific sensible, unsensible or supersensible entity. That is to say this something must in itself be affected by constitutive categories. Yet this whole argument is simply a detour and it is only meant to show how full of contradictions the disputing skeptic is. When all is said and done this argument again leads to the axiom of truth. If one has conceded that entities in themselves have the capacity to be affected by categories, then one must, in accordance with the doctrine of the differentiation of meaning, also concede all the distinctions of the constitutive categories in themselves right up to the most individual and the smallest.

An a-logism and irrationalism which wanted to advocate for some entity the exceptional position of being unaffected by logic would be plainly wrong. But it is one thing to talk about the capacity of being affected by categories or the "applicability" of the categories in itself, and quite another thing to talk about the applicability of categories for us. It may be possible for us to experience something completely shorn of everything logical without our needing to know it. We are perhaps granted an "immediate" experience of it without it being possible for us to have a moment of categorical "clarity" about it. We are never in a position to drag it before the tribunal of reflection, to find a categorical epithet for it, to know it. With regard to the supersensible, for example, it could be the case that the most general constitutive category of this realm will never disclose itself to us. With the expression "beyond-being", we would have simply acted in accordance with the categorical axiom of truth and indicated our conviction that there exists a constitutive realm of categories that is simply not accessible to us. Yet one does not have to interpret this state of affairs in this fashion. Whoever admits to metaphysical knowledge will claim that it is only for the category of the supersensible that we lack a felicitous expression similar to the term "validity"[33] that Lotze coined for the category of the unsensible. Yet the constitutive regional category is always simply composed of the theoretical form and a moment of meaning. This moment of meaning always refers to the sensible, unsensible, or supersensible matter which cannot be compared to one another. If we talk of the existence (and thus the objectivity) of God, for example, then we are already "talking" of the supersensible; we already know about the supersensible. In that case religious behavior, "faith" is already permeated by "knowledge," by the "knowledge of God" and not only do we experience the supersensible but already the truth that concerns the supersensible.

Just a sideward glance at metaphysics is enough to explain the standing of the contemporary doctrine of the categories which is essentially influenced by Kant. The thinker, who introduced a whole new development of the doctrine of categories, believed that the knowledge of the supersensible had to be eliminated. As a consequence, he abolished the category for the supersensible as something that transcends *our* cognition. The *Kantian* two-world theory takes the prototype[34] of an entity as something that is resolved into the duality of the sensible and supersensible, a duality that has enjoyed such unconstrained recognition since antiquity among the non-sensualistic thinkers. It is now our job to clarify that Kant – spellbound by these alternatives – never inquired into a second region of the non-sensible and ignored in his theory of knowledge his own theoretical critique of knowledge and his own recognition of the unsensible transcendental forms. Otherwise he would have come to recognize that it is not possible to deny *all* cognition of the non-sensible. As will be borne out more precisely in the concluding historical chapter, the sphere of validity does not simply count for Kant, so to speak, as an object of his own transcendental philosophy. In recent times, however, what "counts" as an independent object of philosophical investigation has separated itself from everything else. We have realized that we have indeed fallen into the vicinity, but not perhaps into the realm of the metaphysics of the supersensible itself. In opposition to *Kant's* denial of the cognition of the non-sensible[35] we have literally granted to philosophy its own unsensible[36] field of research in explicitly recognizing a duality of the sensible and the unsensible[37] objects of the knowledge. *Kant* restricted the categories to the realm of the sensible-intuitable because he wanted to abolish knowledge of the supersensible in order to make place for faith. Does philosophy today want to abolish knowledge of the things that are eternally valid in order to make place for atheoretical immediate surrender[38] alone? Is it really of the view – to borrow the words of *Windelband* – that the light of eternity shines not in science[39] but only in conscience?[40] Do we then stand even today before the same alternatives that confronted Kant that the categories be permitted either only for the sensible or also for the supersensible? Only the all-powerful authority of *Kant* can make it somehow explicable to us that despite the changed circumstances, we have still not drawn the consequences of the existence of a philosophical science of validity[41] for a doctrine of categories. In logic and theory of knowledge, the sphere of validity and the knowledge of validity[42] simply fall into oblivion because we still stand under the influence of the exclusive opposition between the sensible and the unsensible that dominated the past. We still know only the alternatives of a doctrine of categories for the sensible and the supersensible realm of objects. Earlier we had suggested that the separation of the unsensible and the supersensible is of the greatest significance for the understanding of the whole contemporary situation precisely in the doctrine of the categories. That suggestion now stands vindicated.

Behind the postulation of an extension of the problem of the categories there lay two demands. First and foremost, the demand to reflect on the all-encompassing dominance of the logical. The other demand can be expressed as follows: As long as an object is cognizable there exists a categorical form available prior to cognition and that through the recognition of the existence of the categorical form, we become aware of the task confronting us, namely, of grounding this categorical content[43].

It is only through the fulfillment of these demands that the fundamental elements for the system of theoretical forms can be uncovered in their true scope and a true universal doctrine of categories according to the principle of Kantianism, i.e., of transcendental-logical formalism can be erected upon them. *Not panlogicism but rather the panarchy of the logos must be restored to its glory.* It is critical transcendental-logical formalism becoming consciousness of its own universal meaning. It is a Kantianism itself that rebels against the constraints into which *Kant* and the Neo-Kantians (in the broadest sense) squeezed it in and through its historical representation.

Notes

1 From *The Logic of Philosophy*, pp. 105–111. Translated into English for the first time by Arun Iyer. – Ed.
2 *übersinnlich*
3 *Geltungswissenschaft*
4 *unsinnlich*
5 *Seinsgehalt*
6 *Überseinskategorien*
7 *unsinnlich*
8 *unsinnlich*
9 *übersinnlich*
10 *sinnlich*
11 *übersinnlich*
12 *Nichtsinnlichkeit*
13 *Unsinnlich-Geltenden*
14 *Übersinnliche*
15 This distinction separates fundamentally and most acutely the standpoint that is represented here from that of thinkers such as E. v. Hartmann, to whom in a later place the greatest merit will be conferred for his insight into the scope of the problem of categories.
16 *Seinsnotwendigkeit*
17 *bedeutungsfremde Masse*
18 *Seinserkennen*
19 *Erkenntnistheorie*
20 *metaphysische Objektsmaterial*
21 *übersinnliche Kategorienmaterial*

22 "*Hypostasierung*"
23 *übersinnlich*
24 *Seinserkennen*
25 *Geltungserkennen*
26 [Later marginal note by Lask:] Even if all forms are ultimately immanent; because reflection only creates the ground.
27 *etwas*
28 *Hingeltungsform*
29 [Later marginal note by Lask:] the more the entities, the more the truths about them.
30 *ein etwas*
31 *Hingabe*
32 *kategoriale Betreffbarkeit an sich*
33 *Gelten*
34 *Inbegriff*
35 *nichtsinnlichen*
36 *unsinnlich*
37 *unsinnlich*
38 *Hingabe*
39 I have taken the liberty to translate *Wissen* as "science" rather than "knowledge" in order to convey the homonymous relationship between the German *Wissen* and *Gewissen* which strictly translated would be "knowledge" and "conscience," respectively. Lask is here playing with the homonymous relationship between the German words for knowledge and conscience, *Wissen* and *Gewissen*, respectively. – Trans.
40 *Praeludien*, 3rd ed., p. 460.
41 *Geltungswissenschaft*
42 *Geltungserkennen*
43 *kategorialer Gehalt*

Introduction

Hans Vaihinger (1852–1933)

FOR WANT OF A BETTER LOCATION, Hans Vaihinger is placed at this position in this volume. Hence it must be emphasized at the outset that Vaihinger was *not* a member of the Southwest School (although he hailed from Swabia in the Southwest of Germany). Since he was, in his time, one of the most famous representatives of Neo-Kantianism in Germany and beyond, the editor has opted to include him and passages from his famous *Philosophy of the As-If* here.

Hans Vaihinger was born in Nehren, close to Tübingen, the son of a Protestant minister. He studied in Tübingen, first theology, then switching to philosophy. He further studied in Leipzig and Berlin. In 1877, he received his Habilitation in Strassburg under the positivist Ernst Laas (under whom Natorp had also studied and written his dissertation). His *Habilitationsschrift*, "Logical Investigations. The Doctrine of Scientific Fictions," deals with the topic that would remain his main philosophical interest during his lifetime: the role of fiction. In 1884, Vaihinger was recruited to the University of Halle, where he stayed until his early retirement in 1906 due to an ailment of his eyes that led to complete blindness. He remained active as a scholar nonetheless.

Indeed, Vaihinger owed his eminent position in the Neo-Kantian movement to his impressive scholarship. His commentary to Kant's First Critique (1881/1892) in particular was a much-consulted guide, translated into many languages and is still used today. He also helped establish what was to become the bulwark of the Neo-Kantian movement through the founding of the journal *Kant Studien* (in 1897) and the *Kant Gesellschaft* in 1904, the centennial of Kant's death. It is one staple of the Neo-Kantian movement in general to bring philological-historical scholarship to a new level. Vaihinger is mainly responsible for this achievement as a scholar and as a teacher of an entire generation of scholars.

Vaihinger's *magnum opus, Die Philosophie des Als-ob* (*The Philosophy of the As-If*) was written between 1876–78 but remained unpublished until 1911. The 800-page book went through ten editions between then and 1938, and it was published in twelve languages. It was one of the most popular books, in terms of sales and dissemination, of the entire Neo-Kantian movement. Although he has been nearly forgotten by philosophers, there has been a continued interest in his thoughts in literary studies and psychology.

Further Reading

Fine, Arthur, "Fictionalism," in: *Midwest Studies in Philosophy* 18 (1), 1993, 1–18.
Stampfl, Barry, "Hans Vaihinger's Ghostly Presence in Contemporary Literary Studies," in: *Criticism*: Vol. 40: Iss. 3, Article 5, 1998.
Gregory, Frederick, "Questioning scientific faith in the late nineteenth century." in: *Zygon*, Volume 43, Number 3, September 2008, 651–664(14).
Pollard, Stephen, "'As if' Reasoning in Vaihinger and Pasch," in: *Erkenntnis*, Volume 73, Number 1, July 2010, 83–95(13).

"General introduction," "The Atom as fiction," and "Things-in-themselves," from the *Philosophy of the As-If* (1911)

Vaihinger's basic question is, "how is it possible for us to attain truth by way of deliberately false assumptions?" The answer is, essentially, that we produce useful fictions in order to attain knowledge. Knowledge, to Vaihinger, is the comparison of the unknown with the known, in order to reduce the unknown to a minimum. We do so by creating fictions in our minds that help us navigate the world. As he says, "the human representation of the world is an enormous web of fictions full of logical contradictions, i.e., of scientific figments for the sake of practical purposes and of inadequate, subjective pictorial representations, whose correspondence with reality is ruled out *a priori*" (from Ch. II of the "General Introduction," which is not included here). These contradictions cannot be eliminated but are, in fact, constitutive for the generation of knowledge. If we understand that they are but fictions, their problematic character vanishes. They are useful fictions created to deal with our contradictions in our representation of the world. In this sense, "in the psyche there takes place not merely a mechanical play of ideas, but the movement of ideas fulfills to a great extent the demands of utility by its continual modification. All psychical processes are *useful* in the sense mentioned." We thus produce "useful fictions," that exist "as if" they are true. This cognitive living in the mode of "as if" is, thus, not a special mode of existence, but our normal *modus operandi*, since we do not know what things "in themselves," apart from our representation of them, really are. This was something that, to Vaihinger, Kant exposed for the first time in his philosophy. These fictions are, thus, a pragmatic way of navigating the world as representation in the way we "adapt and accommodate" ourselves to circumstances and objects for the fulfillment of a given purpose. Accordingly, thought is an organic function like all other functions. One could call this an original synthesis of pragmatism, transcendental idealism, and Schopenhauerianism (the world as our representation). Prime examples of useful fictions are the atom and things in themselves. Regarding the atom, whether it is "an hypothesis or fiction," it is made up of a "group of contradictory concepts which are necessary in order to deal with reality." Likewise, the idea of a *Ding an sich* is "not an hypothesis but a fiction," which was missed by many interpreters of Kant, who believed it was this, that, or the other; whereas Vaihinger claims, its contradictory character is constitutive for the very function it has. In truth, it is nothing but "an x to which a y, the ego, as our organization, corresponds." Therefore, it is a fiction, but a necessary one that "cannot be dispensed with in philosophy, any more than can imaginary numbers in mathematics." This interpretation of Kant's transcendental idealism once again indicates Vaihinger's original reading.

The *Philosophy of the As-If* was, as mentioned, a bestselling philosophical work, read mainly by a non-academic audience, and was, consequently, used mainly as a critical target by most contemporary philosophers. For instance, Husserl's phenomenological investigations into the "as if" modes of consciousness (e.g., in fantasizing) are terminologically indebted to Vaihinger, but radically reject Vaihinger's overall philosophical stance.

Further Reading

Aquila, Richard, "Hans Vaihinger and Some Recent Intentionalist Readings of Kant," in: *Journal of the History of Philosophy*, 41(2), 2003, 231–250.

Schaper, Eva, "The Kantian Thing-in-itself as a Philosophical Fiction," in: *Philosophical Quarterly*, 16, 1966, 233–243.

Chapter 27

"General Introduction" to *The Philosophy of the As-If* (1911)[1]

Chapter I. Thought, considered from the point of view of a purposive, organic function

Scientific thought is a function of the psyche. By the term "psyche" we do not understand a substance, but the organic whole of all so-called "mental" actions and reactions; these never come under external observation, but have to be partly inferred from physical signs, partly observed by the so-called inner sense. Psychical actions and reactions are, like every event known to us, necessary occurrences; that is to say, they result with compulsory regularity from their conditions and causes. If we would compare psychical processes with some group of external phenomena, the physical and in a narrower sense mechanical processes are less suitable than the functions of the organism. This statement is confirmed by the fact that so-called empirical utility is found in the psychical functions as well as in the organic functions of the bodily sphere. This utility is manifested here as there in a ready adaptation to circumstances and environment; in the maintenance of a striving and successful reaction of the physical or psychical organism to external impulses and influences; and in the adoption and acceptance or the repulsion of new elements. In the psyche there takes place not merely a mechanical play of ideas, but the movement of ideas fulfills to a great extent the demands of utility by its continual modification. All psychical processes are *useful* in the sense mentioned; above all the so-called theoretical processes of apperception. Scientific thought consists in such apperception-processes and is therefore to be considered from the point of view of an organic function.

Thus we would compare the logical or thought-processes with the organic creative processes. The appropriateness that we observe in growth, in propagation and regeneration, in adaptation to environment, in healing, and so on, in the sphere of the organic repeats itself in the psychical processes. The psychical organism also reacts fittingly to stimuli. It is not merely a receptacle into which foreign matter is simply poured, but may be compared to a machine with a chemical retort, which uses foreign matter most fittingly for its own maintenance and the maintenance of its motion, and appropriates it through assimilation, not through pure juxtaposition, And similarly consciousness is not to be compared to a mere passive mirror, which reflects rays according to purely physical laws, but "consciousness receives no external stimulus without molding it according to its own nature." The psyche then is *an organic formative force*, which independently changes what has been appropriated, and can adapt foreign elements to its own requirements as easily as it adapts itself to what is new. The mind is not merely appropriative, it is also assimilative and constructive. In the course of its growth, it *creates its organs* of its own accord in virtue of its adaptable constitution, but only when stimulated from without, and *adapts them to external circumstances*. Such organs, created by the psyche for itself in response to external stimuli, are, for example, forms of perception and thought, and certain concepts and other logical constructs. Logical thought, with which we are especially concerned here, is an active appropriation of the outer world, a useful organic elaboration of the material of sensation. Logical thought is therefore an organic function of the psyche.

Just as the physical organism breaks up the matter which it receives, mixes it with its own juices and so thus makes it suitable for assimilation, so the psyche envelops the thing perceived with categories which it has developed out of itself. As soon as an external stimulus reaches the mind, which rapidly responds to it as though provided with delicate feelers, inner processes start, a psychical activity begins, the outcome of which is the appropriation of the thing perceived for some purpose.

To Steinthal is due the merit of having established and worked out this view of the organic function of the logical movements involved in knowing; we go a step further, in attempting to consider the organic thought-functions from the point of view of *purposive activity*. Sigwart and Lotze begin their Logic with this teleological point of view. Just as it is the purpose of the eye to transform the various ether-waves into an ordered system of fixed sensations, and, through refraction, reflection and so on of rays, to make reduced "images" of the objective world; and just as that organ is suitably arranged for the fulfillment of this purpose and is able to carry out independent movements of accommodation and modifications according to circumstances – so the logical function is an activity which suitably fulfills its purpose and *can adapt and accommodate itself to circumstances and objects for the fulfillment of this purpose*. It is the purpose of the organic function of thought to change and elaborate the perceptual material into those ideas, associations of ideas, and conceptual constructs which, while consistent and coherent among themselves are, as the phrase goes and as we can also say provisionally, "clothed in objectivity."

Since, however, we do not know objective reality absolutely but only infer it (and this is also an ordinary scientific view) we must revise our statement and say that thought has fulfilled its purpose when it has elaborated the given sensation-complexes into valid concepts, general judgments, and cogent conclusions, and has produced such a world that objective happenings can be calculated and our behavior successfully carried out in relation to phenomena. We lay most stress on the *practical* corroboration, on the experimental test of the utility of the logical structures that are the product of the organic function of thought. It is not the correspondence with an assumed "objective reality "that can never be directly accessible to us, it is not the theoretical representation of an outer world in the mirror of consciousness nor the theoretical comparison of logical products with objective things which, in our view, guarantees that thought has fulfilled its purpose; it is rather the practical test as to whether it is possible with the help of those logical products to *calculate events that occur without our intervention* and to realize our impulses appropriately in accordance with the direction of the logical structures.

[2]It is interesting to observe how Lotze in his *Logic* withdraws his first definition,[3] of the truth of thought, that is to say its final purpose: "Truth consists in the agreement of ideas and their associations with the objects presented and their own relations," and modifies it to: "Connexions of ideas are true, if they are in accordance with those relations in the matter of the ideas, which are the same for all consciousness, and not the mere occurrence and

juxtaposition of impressions, which are different for each individual consciousness." But when Lotze claims as the final function of thought a general world-image that shall be the same for all[4] he overlooks that such a general agreement would still offer no guarantee of the "truth" of combinations of ideas. Only the practical test is the final guarantee; but even here we can only conclude that combinations of ideas fulfill their purpose, and have been rightly formed. From the standpoint of modern epistemology we can therefore no longer talk about "truth" at all, in the usual sense of the term.

Helmholtz too, in several places in his works, as in the Optics, and particularly in his lecture entitled "Logical Principles of the Empirical Sciences" assigns the principal value to the practical proof demanded above.

We will not at this point settle the question, deeply rooted in metaphysics and in our whole practical outlook, whether the logical function, or, to put it otherwise, whether the theoretical activity is or should be an end in itself for man, or whether all theoretical functions have arisen solely from our impulses, and have therefore ultimately to serve only practical ends.

[5]Schopenhauer in particular has taken this latter view in modern times. As the will, according to him, is the only metaphysical principle, and a will that is blind and illogical, so the brain with all its ideas is in his opinion essentially nothing but a tool, whose function it is to serve the will and preserve the life of the individual. The intellect occupies a subservient position in regard to the will. That Herbart adopted a very similar position is less well-known, but it is a natural conclusion from the relation of the psychical monads to the organism, which can well exist without them. He therefore calls the mind a "parasite of the body," exactly as Schopenhauer does; it serves chiefly to facilitate the preservation of the organism. They both regard the theoretical activity, consciousness, therefore, as a tool of the organism and a means to self-preservation. It is not, as such, essential to our subsequent enquiry how the relation of thought, of the theoretical and conscious thought-processes to the life of the instinct and will is understood; but, as we proceed, the treatment of thought as an instrument may prove useful in securing the right orientation. If thought only exists on account of the will, or as we may say with Fichte, on account of action, then knowledge is not the ultimate purpose of thought; it cannot, therefore, be an end in itself but only a by-product, something emerging incidentally, as it were, from the workshop of thought. The practical value of thought would then rank first, and "knowledge" would only be a secondary and incidental motive, as Schopenhauer also assumes. This point may be of interest in the course of our enquiry, when we come to treat of conceptual structures whose intellectual value is as questionable as their practical value is obvious. Steinthal pertinently develops the same view: "We need knowledge of the world of things, and of ourselves, and of the connection of things with each other and with ourselves, in order to be able to live." He mentions, quite in accordance with the modern attitude, three chief tasks for which knowledge is required: the search for food, cultivation, and protection from the elements. "Knowledge is therefore a necessary factor in Nature's economy. It combines with physical and chemical operations to render the existence of the human race and the animal kingdom possible; it facilitates the material conditions which are essential to life." Thought, then, must be regarded as a mechanism, as a machine, as an instrument in the service of life; and this way of treating it is more important for logic than appears at first sight.

For our more limited purposes we may be content with the definition given above, according to which the test of the correctness of a logical result lies in *practice*, and the purpose of thought must be sought not in the reflection of a so-called objective world, but in rendering possible the calculation of events and of operations upon them. For us the purpose of the logical function of thought is to keep us constantly in a position to deal with things so that, with given conditions, relations, stipulations, and circumstances, we may receive an exactly ascertainable sense-impression (for every determination of objective data ultimately rests on that, and can be scientifically established in no other way); and so that, by such and such an impulse under certain conditions, we may produce an exactly ascertainable effect, which in its turn cannot be observed except by means of certain sensations. Only through the reduction of the concepts "thought, action, observation," etc., to elements ultimately physiological, to sensations, do we obtain a correct standard for the valuation of logical work, which converts elements of sensation into logical structures. These latter again, in the last resort, exist to be converted into sensations, or to serve to control impressions and adjust will-impulses, that is to say, nerve-impulses.

[6]All purposeful activity manifests itself in seeking out, collecting, or producing the necessary and serviceable means for the attainment of its object. The organic activity of thought also manifests its purposeful nature in exerting itself to attain its aims by all the means at its command.

If sensations are the starting-point of all logical activity and at the same time the terminus to which they must run, if only to render control possible (and as we remarked above, it must remain undecided whether we must regard the logical functions between these two points as having some inherent purpose), then the purpose of thought may be defined as the elaboration and adjustment of the material of sensation for the attainment of a richer and fuller sensational life of experience.

In order to attain the purpose of its activity as completely and quickly as possible, namely, to deal with independent events and to render them possible for or dependent on our will, thought or the logical function employs the most diverse means.

Thought is bent on continually perfecting itself and thus becomes a more and more serviceable tool. For this purpose it expands its province by inventing instruments, like other natural activities. The arm and the hand do the same, and most ordinary instruments are to be regarded as elongations and extensions of these organs. The natural function of thought, which we spoke of above as a tool, also expands its instrumentality by the invention of tools, means of thought, instruments of thought, one of which is to form the subject of our enquiry.

Thought undertakes ingenious operations, invents brilliant expedients, is able to introduce highly complicated processes. The material of sensation is re-modelled, re-coined, compressed, it is purged of dross and mixed with alloys from the fund of the psyche itself, in order to render possible a more and more certain, rapid, and refined solution of the problem of the logical function. All these very different and highly complicated processes and operations are governed by very few and simple laws, just as the complicated work of the physical organism and its apparently very different organs is reducible to remarkably simple, regular elementary forms and processes. It is the business of logical theory to reduce the complicated logical processes to such simple elementary processes, to a few, definite mechanical events. The rich life of the spirit, as it expands with its countless variations in the vast field of science, rests in its most complicated forms and processes on simple, primitive laws. It arises only as a result of the extraordinarily ingenious modification and specialization of these few elementary types and laws, which partly under the pressure of external causes and circumstances, and partly in obedience to immanent processes of development, expand into that rich and infinite system of knowledge of which man is so proud. Just as *Meleagrina margaritifera*, when a grain of sand gets beneath its shining surface, covers it over with a self-produced mass of mother-of-pearl, in order to change the insignificant grain into a brilliant pearl, so, only still more delicately, the psyche, when stimulated, transforms the material of sensation which it absorbs into shining pearls of thought, into structures. By means of these structures the logician follows the adaptable, organic, purposeful, logical function into its most secret processes, its most delicate forms of specialization. In both cases it is the ingenuity of the *purposive activity* which arouses our wonder and attention. We deliberately emphasize the utility of the organic function of thought, because we shall subsequently be dealing with logical structures in which this purposiveness is strikingly manifested.

So far in our exposition we have not yet touched on an aspect which is of great importance for the right understanding of the logical function: the fact, namely, that the organic function of thought is carried on for the most part *unconsciously*. Should the product finally enter consciousness also, or should consciousness momentarily accompany the processes of logical thought, this light only penetrates to the shallows, and the actual fundamental processes are carried on in the darkness of the unconscious. The specifically purposeful operations are chiefly, and in any case at the beginning, wholly instinctive and unconscious, even if they later press forward into the luminous circle of consciousness, which in course of time is able both as regards the individual and the general history of culture to bring under its control ever wider areas of psychical activity. Logic is especially concerned to throw light on the dark and unconsciously working activity of thought, and to study the ingenious methods and devices which that unconscious activity employs in order to attain its object.

However we may conceive the relation of thought and reality, it may be asserted from the empirical point of view, that the ways of thought are different from those of reality, the subjective processes of thought concerned with any given external event or process have very rarely a demonstrable similarity to it. We make this observation in order to emphasize that the logical functions are subjective but useful efforts which thought makes to attain the objects we have already described. Whatever objective reality may be, one thing can be stated with certainty – it does *not* consist of logical functions, as Hegel once thought.

[7]The Hegelian system offers historically the most glaring and typical example of this general error of philosophy: the confusion of thought-processes with events, the conversion of subjective thought-events into objective world-events. (That the Hegelian dialectic is, however, based on a correct insight into the nature of logical development, we shall have occasion to remark later.)

Actually the greatest and most important human errors originate through thought-processes being taken for copies of reality itself[8]; but the ultimate practical agreement of our ideas and judgments with so-called "things" still does not justify the conclusion that the processes by which the logical result has been obtained are the same as objective events. On the contrary *their utility is manifested in the very fact that the logical functions, working according to their own laws, do constantly coincide in the end with reality.*

Chapter II. Thought as an art, logic as technology (a collection of technical rules of art)

We have spoken of thought as an organic function. Every natural faculty, and this applies to all organic functions, can, through practice, development and hereditary transmission, be raised to an art. Only in this sense can thought be an art. Logic is sometimes called a technology.

Whoever calls logic technology must consider thought as an art.

It is inaccurate to consider logic itself as an art. Thought is an art, but logic is a science, and a technology in particular.

It need hardly be stated that in this use of the word and concept "art" we are taking the meaning in which the aesthetic side is not emphasized. We are not concerned with an artistic activity, but with an ingenious dexterity. So long as the organic activity of thought remains in the sphere of the unconscious (the "hypo-psychical" according to Laas) we call it preferably *purposeful*, just as we attribute a similar purpose without hesitation to all organic functions, without thereby raising the metaphysical problem of teleology; but when the organic activity leaves the sphere of the unconscious for more wakeful activities, when consciousness seizes the rudder, we choose to call this organic activity *technical*. The more the natural faculty of thought, the instinctive activity of the logical functions is improved and refined – the more the logical operations are specialized, and the finer logical functions fall to the lot of special individuals in consequence of the division of labour in the economy of nature – the more do these terms find justification in this fact. If thought is a wide-spread activity, acquired by the individual in the course of his development, as so many other arts which are *necessary* to human existence, then the more difficult part of the logical problem is carried out by single individuals, specially gifted and developed for that purpose; but as soon as a common natural faculty becomes specialized in such a way that particular individuals practice it with particular dexterity, we call it an art. Certain technical rules are developed: the totality of these rules is called the technology; and such is logic, whose chief task is to present and establish the technical rules of thought.

Chapter III. The Difference between the Artifices and the Rules of Thought

Methodology, as hitherto employed, has endeavored to collect the technical rules of thought in their completeness and to employ them systematically. It has succeeded in registering, analyzing and systematically establishing those technical operations and manipulations which are the most frequent, regular, and important. It is the operations whose skillful application, intelligent realization, and rational improvement are essential to the progress of modern science which have been raised from practice into theory and reduced to the simple and primitive forms of the logical function. The admirable methods of the empirical sciences, methods adapted to their object with an astonishing flexibility, and able to utilize and conform to all circumstances, as in the case of organic beings – these methods found a worthy and completely suitable expression in modern methodology, which has its most brilliant representatives in England, France, and Germany.

Meanwhile, as it seems to me, there are methods employed in scientific practice which have up till now not been duly considered and recognized in theory.

[9]I refer to the methods employed less in natural science than in mathematics and the ethico-political sciences, that is to say, in the most exact science and in fields where exactitude is definitely excluded. It is quite natural that since the methods of the natural sciences had been given a great deal of attention, the methods employed in other branches of science and neglected in natural science should demand examination. In modern logic natural science is given undue prominence at the expense of the sciences mentioned, and to the disadvantage of logic. Mill pays scarcely any attention to the special methods of mathematics, and the methods of the moral sciences are too briefly treated. But the remarkable utility of the logical function is displayed in these two fields to far greater advantage than in the simpler methods of the empirical natural sciences, if only because in those fields the logical function encounters disproportionately greater difficulties and phenomena of a much more complex character than those of natural science. Just at the points where the empirical method of natural science converges on the methods of exact mechanics and abstract physics, and where on the other hand they approach the complicated phenomena of social life, the insufficiency of purely inductive methods is clearly manifest. It is here that methods begin which present a higher synthesis of deduction and induction, where, that is to say, both these methods are united in the endeavor to solve difficulties which can only be overcome indirectly.

The methods to which we refer may be described as irregular in contrast to the regular methods of ordinary induction. In other spheres also, however, the regular are systematically employed before the irregular, and the latter are left on one side. But where the methods in question have so far been met with, they have either been used too little and too superficially, or in the wrong place and the wrong systematic connection; or they have been confused with other similar forms, as is customary in every science; or, finally, they have been treated with timidity, as everything irregular is treated at first. In logic too a veil of secrecy was woven about such forms.

We make a distinction between *rules* and *artifices* of thought. In other functions also this distinction is of value; the *rules* are the totality of all those technical operations in virtue of which an activity is able to attain its object directly, even when more or less complicated. In logic too we call such operations, and in particular those of induction, "rules of thinking". The artifices, on the other hand, are those operations, of an almost mysterious character, which run counter to ordinary procedure in a more or less paradoxical way. They are methods which give an onlooker the impression of magic if he be not himself initiated or equally skilled in the mechanism, and are able indirectly to overcome the difficulties which the material in question opposes to the activity. Thought also has such artifices; they are strikingly purposive expressions of the organic function of thought. And as in certain arts and handicrafts such artifices are kept secret, so we notice that this is also the case in logic. We will give only one remarkable instance by way of illustration. When Leibniz by an ingenious artifice of this sort (which we shall later take as our typical example and as one of the chief subjects of our analysis) discovered an amazingly simple and skillful solution of problems which up till then had passed for insoluble, he anxiously tried for a long time to keep this artifice secret; and those to whom he communicated it astonished mathematicians not yet acquainted with it by the solution of different problems. Newton acted similarly; and so too, we are told, did the school of Pythagoras.

Chapter IV. The transition to fictions

We are therefore dealing with a peculiar kind of logical product, a special manifestation of the logical function. We have already seen that this peculiar activity is expressed in what we call artifices, that its products are artificial concepts. We would here, anticipating the outcome, substitute other terms for these expressions: our subject is the fictive activity of the logical function; the products of this activity – *fictions*.

The fictive activity of the mind is an expression of the fundamental psychical forces; *fictions* are *mental structures*. The psyche weaves this aid to thought out of itself; for the mind is inventive; under the compulsion of necessity, stimulated by the outer world, it discovers the store of contrivances that lie hidden within itself. The organism finds itself in a world full of contradictory sensations, it is exposed to the assaults of a hostile external world, and in order to preserve itself, it is forced to seek every possible means of assistance, external as well as internal. In necessity and pain mental evolution is begun, in contradiction and opposition consciousness awakes, and man owes his mental development more to his enemies than to his friends.

Meanwhile, in the interests of greater clearness and intelligibility we may premise the following remark:

By fictive activity in logical thought is to be understood the production and use of logical methods, which, with the help of accessory concepts – where the improbability of any corresponding objective is fairly obvious – seek to attain the objects of thought. Instead of remaining content with the material given, the logical function introduces these hybrid and ambiguous thought-structures, in order with their help to attain its purpose indirectly, if the material which it encounters resists a direct procedure. With an instinctive, almost cunning ingenuity, the logical function succeeds in overcoming these difficulties with the aid of its accessory structures. The special methods, the by-paths of which thought makes use when it can no longer advance directly along the main road, are of many different kinds, and their explanation is our problem. They often lead through thorny undergrowth, but logical thought is not deterred thereby, even though it may lose something of its clearness and purity. It is relevant also to remark here that the logical function, in its purposeful instinctive ingenuity, can carry this fictive activity from the most innocent and unpretentious beginnings on through ever finer and subtler developments right up to the most difficult and complicated methods.

Part I

Basic principles

General introductory remarks on fictional constructs

The normal and most natural methods of thought always have as their primary object the formation of those particular apperceptions that are of a final and definitive character; and only such ideational constructs are formed as can be shown to correspond to some kind of reality. It is in fact the essential object of science to develop only such ideas as have an objective correlate and to eliminate all admixture of the subjective.

Such a task is, however, not easily accomplished, for many difficulties are encountered. The ideal, in which the world of ideas consists exclusively of congruous, well-ordered and non-contradictory constructs is only to be attained slowly and with difficulty. The way to this ideal is through methodology.

The first and the natural task of methodology is to suggest in what direction representations possessed of real validity are to be sought.

Our natural tendency is to adjust all our representations, to test them by comparison with reality, and to render them free from contradiction. This is the most natural and obvious method, and it appears to be the only way of advancing a scientific theory of knowledge. This would hold true even if our mental constructs were direct reflections of reality. But the customary modes and results of thought already contain so many subjective and fictional elements that it is not surprising if thought also strikes out along other lines. It must be remembered that the object of the world of ideas as a whole is not the portrayal of reality – this would be an utterly impossible task – but rather to provide us with an *instrument for finding our way about more easily in this world*. Subjective processes of thought inhere in the entire structure of cosmic phenomena. They represent the highest and ultimate results of organic development, and the world of ideas is the fine flower of the whole cosmic process; but for that very reason it is not a copy of it in the ordinary sense. Logical processes are a part of the cosmic process and have as their more immediate object the preservation and enrichment of the life of organisms; they should serve as instruments for enabling them to attain to a more complete life; they serve as intermediaries between living beings. The world of ideas is an edifice well calculated to fulfill this purpose; but to regard it for that reason as a copy is to indulge in a hasty and unjustifiable comparison. Not even elementary sensations are copies of reality; they are rather mere gauges for measuring the changes in reality.

Before entering on our task it is necessary to make a distinction that will subsequently assume considerable importance. Ideational constructs are in the strict sense of the term real fictions when they are not only in contradiction with reality but self-contradictory in themselves; the concept of the atom for example, or the "Ding an sich" [*thing-in-itself*]. To be distinguished from these are constructs which only contradict reality as given or deviate from it, but are not in themselves self-contradictory (e.g. artificial classes). The latter might be called half-fictions or semi-fictions. These types are not sharply divided from one another but are connected by transitions. Thought begins with slight initial deviations from reality (half-fictions), and, becoming bolder and bolder, ends by operating with constructs that are not only opposed to the facts but are self-contradictory.

Notes

1   *Philosophy of the As-If*, K. Ogden, trans., London: Routledge, 1965, pp. 1–16. – Ed.
2   The next two paragraphs are indented and printed in a smaller font than the main text, both in the original and the English translation. – Ed.
3   *Logic*, p. 4.
4   Cf. Laas, *Analysis der Erfahrung*, pp. 95, 127: the objective world in "consciousness in general."
5   This paragraph is indented and printed in a smaller font than the main text, both in the original and the English translation. – Ed.
6   This paragraph is indented and printed in a smaller font than the main text, both in the original and the English translation. – Ed.
7   This paragraph is indented and printed in a smaller font than the main text, both in the original and the English translation. – Ed.
8   Cf. Kant, *Prol.*, § 40: "All illusion consists in holding the subjective ground of judgment to be objective." Reason falls into error "when it mistakes its destination, and refers transcendentally to the object what only concerns its own subject and its guidance in all immanent use." Cf. *Proleg.*, § 55.
9   This paragraph is indented and printed in a smaller font than the main text, both in the original and the English translation. – Ed.

Chapter 28

"The Atom as Fiction" from *The Philosophy of the As-If* (1911)[1]

Our task of revealing the ultimate bases of the framework of thought has not yet been fully accomplished, for there are still some fictional ideas and expedients to be examined, and in particular the atom. This is a modification of the general concept of matter to which it bears the same relation as does the fiction of the differential to the fiction of the length of a curve; matter being conceived as made up of infinitely small constituents. A lively controversy has arisen in connection with the atom, the point at issue being whether it is an hypothesis or fiction. This is our own description of the problem, for the disputants themselves are, for the most part, not clear what it is all about. The opponents of the atom are generally content to point to its contradictions and reject it as unfruitful for science. A rash form of caution, for without the atom science falls. And yet, with it, true knowledge and understanding are impossible. It is a group of contradictory concepts which are necessary in order to deal with reality. Of late it has been recognized that the atom is a fiction, a fictional counter, as has been clearly shown, among others, by Liebmann.

[2]O. Liebmann, *Zur Analysis der Wirklichkeit*, pp. 290 ff., particularly p. 295. "The atom is a transitional idea whose provisional character is obvious. Its imaginary conceptual existence is due to a conceptual equilibrium of a peculiarly unstable character." Cf. also what he says, page 296: "It is true that the atom is a mere theoretical counter, a provisional fiction, an interim-concept, but for the present it is an exceedingly useful interim-concept." Whether the concept can be dispensed with entirely is an open question. To judge from the present state of the problem, apparently it cannot; and to-day, at any rate, the atom is used by both the chemist and the physicist for the co-ordination of their laws, which they cannot yet formulate in a purely abstract manner.

The fiction of a simple element, of the atom, is still retained, in spite of the fact that the "material" has long since "evaporated into energy" (as von Hartmann puts it). Cf. Cooke, *Die Chemie der Gegenwart*, 1875. This book is based entirely on the atomic theory, and yet the author is not a believer in the atom. Cf. for the chemical concept of the atom, Lothar Meyer, *Die Moderne Chemie*, p. 15.

For the opinion of scientists themselves about the atom, cf. Lange, *History of Materialism*, and the same author's *Beiträge*, p. 51, where he says that atoms are a means to an empirical treatment of nature and to orientation.

All this only becomes valuable in relation to our general principle, which has deprived many another concept of its dignity as an hypothesis and shown it to be fictional and subjective. The dispute about the atom will also provide an instructive and exceedingly interesting theme for subsequent treatment, for it involves the whole of the modern philosophy of nature.[3] For the most part, the participants adopted a wrong method of attack. The defense was always anxious to show that the alleged contradictions were only apparent and that the concept therefore possessed objective validity and could be applied. Their opponents, on the other hand, demonstrated the contradictions and so refused to allow the concept any legitimate place in science; in other words, they poured out the baby with the bath, while the defense accepted it – unwashed. The final result was always that the idea persisted in spite of all criticism, but its contradictions invariably called forth fresh contradictions.

The recognition that there is right and wrong on both sides generally comes at the end of a discussion – the concept in question is contradictory, but necessary: for most of the fundamental concepts are of this character. It is remarkable that in the course of time the realization that these contradictions exist becomes blunted through the use of the concepts. We need only note the extent to which mathematicians and physicists have accustomed themselves to differentials and atoms and no longer notice the contradictions inherent in them. Yet though the contradictions in ideas to which we have grown accustomed are no longer noticed, they are at once recognized in new constructs. The introduction of the infinite, of differentials, gave rise at one time to the same opposition as that which the introduction of an n-dimensional space encounters to-day at the hands of competent thinkers. The irrational and imaginary numbers had the same fate in mathematics.

Notes

1   *Philosophy of the As-If*, Chapter XV, pp. 70–72.
2   The next three paragraphs are indented and printed in a smaller font than the main text, both in the original and the English translation. – Ed.
3   In general, we may say that many important controversies in the history of science have been concerned with the question whether a given concept was an hypothesis or a fiction, with the result that both sides grew weary and the disputed construct was, for the time being, accepted.

Chapter 29

"Things-in-Themselves [as Fiction]" from *The Philosophy of the As-If* (1911)[1]

Before turning to the idea of the absolute we must discuss one other idea, the thing-in-itself. From all that has preceded it is fairly clear what our attitude must be – that the "thing-in-itself" is not an hypothesis but a fiction. By the use of this formula we have solved many of the difficulties hitherto encountered. Kant is the originator of this concept, which is a product of the logical function as an imaginative activity. The first point which arises from this is the historical understanding of Kant himself. All the ambiguity that Kant developed in connection with this concept was due essentially to his hesitation, his wavering between the thing-in-itself as an hypothesis or a fiction. Thus in the first edition of his *Critique of Pure Reason,* Kant in one place calls it "a mere idea," i.e., a fiction. In constructing this concept Kant was throughout hardly clearer than Leibniz with his differentials. The term *limiting concept* also receives an important elucidation from the above; for as a fiction the notion of a thing-in-itself represents a limiting concept in the same sense in which we speak of the method of limits in mathematics, the limit being elevated by a fiction into something real and treated as such. Thus the whole controversy about the thing-in-itself in the early days of Kantian philosophy, as conducted by Reinhold, Schulze, Maimon, Jacobi, Fichte, and others, and renewed recently during its second efflorescence, at once becomes clearer. It is simply a question whether the concept is a fiction or an hypothesis. It was Maimon who realized this most clearly. Schulze saw the contradictions in the idea and rejected it; Maimon saw the contradictions and retained it as a fiction. We must certainly follow his example. To Maimon also is due the brilliant comparison of the things-in-themselves with imaginary numbers, i.e., with $\sqrt{-a}$. $\sqrt{-a}$ is the symbol of a mathematical fiction, the unjustified extension and transference of a mathematical operation to a case where the nature of the material forbids its application and renders it meaningless. Nevertheless, mathematics often requires this idea, and proceeds with it *as if* it symbolized a reality, a number that could be expressed; but, be it remembered, this fiction always drops out as valueless at the end of the procedure.

This is what also occurs in the case of the thing-in-itself.

It arises from the unjustified application of a logical operation. The illegitimate extension of the mathematical operation in the formula $\sqrt{-a}$ is the extracting of a root, and here the parallel logical operation consists in the application of the categories, *thing* and *attribute* (and causality) to what makes their application meaningless, namely to actual and ultimate *reality*. If it be admitted that all categories are merely subjective, then this category, too, cannot be applied to actual reality. But, as we know, there is another category involved here, the category of *causality*. This, too, is unjustifiably applied to a something where its application is not legitimate, namely, to actual reality. If, with Kant, we agree that this category is subjective, then it is a contradiction to ascribe it to actual reality. Such an application belongs to the group of illegitimate transferences or extensions where a quite different case is brought under some unsuitable construct. The analogy of this illegitimate extension of mathematical operations is particularly illuminating here, for in this case also the extension is to an unsuitable field, to actual reality. Only within the limits of discursive thought do these categories possess a meaning and a justification, for here they serve to introduce logical operations. Only within the world of our ideas are there things, things that are causes; in the real world these ideas are but empty echoes.

[2]The idea of causality is entirely inapplicable to reality itself. Actual reality will not tolerate this category. If sensations are, in fact, essential reality, then their reduction, together with space, matter, etc., to the impact of some unknown object, is an unjustified extension of the concept of cause and effect.

But everything that is reduced to this category seems to be grasped, and the thing-in-itself allows the category of causality to be applied to actual reality. This, on our view, is the world of sensation. When, therefore, Kant reduces sensations, together with space, time, etc., to the system of co-ordinates of cause and effect, object and subject, the whole world appears to be understood as an effect.

The fiction of the thing-in-itself would thus be the most brilliant of all conceptual instruments. Just as we introduce into mathematics and mechanics ideas which facilitate our task, so Kant introduces a device in the form of the concept thing-in-itself, as an *x* to which a *y*, the ego, as our organization, corresponds. By this means the whole world of reality can be dealt with. Subsequently the "ego" and the thing-in-itself are dropped, and only sensations remain as real.

From our point of view the sequence of sensations constitutes ultimate reality, and two poles are mentally added, subject and object.

In spite, then, of its numerous contradictions the idea of the thing-in-itself cannot be dispensed with in philosophy, any more than can imaginary numbers in mathematics. If we wish to speak of the real world at all, we must use some category, for otherwise it is not only unthinkable but even inexpressible.

The result of our whole inquiry is that the subjective and fictive method culminates in the thing-in-itself. In order to explain the world of ideas which exists within us, Kant assumed that the actual world consisted of things-in-themselves, mutually interacting, and on the basis of this interaction he explained the genesis of sensations. We must, however, remember that Kant only had the right to say, and in the first instance only wanted to say, that we must (compelled thereto by reason of our discursive thought) regard real existence *as if* things-in-themselves really existed, as if they influenced us and thus gave rise to our idea of the world. In actual fact this is all he had the right to say according to his own system; and in that case the thing-in-itself was a necessary fiction, for only thus can we imagine actual reality or think and speak of it at all. Kant, however, did not adhere to this definite standpoint, but his thing-in-itself became a *reality*, in short an *hypothesis*, and hence his hesitating discussion of the concept.

Notes

1   *The Philosophy of the As-If*, Chapter XVII, pp. 74–76.
2   The next four paragraphs are indented and printed in a smaller font than the main text, both in the original and the English translation. – Ed.

Part 4

Responses and critiques

Introduction: Moritz Schlick (1882–1936)

IN HIS REVIEW OF CASSIRER'S BOOK ON EINSTEIN (*Einstein's Theory of Relativity*), Schlick, the founding father of logical positivism and the Vienna Circle, focuses on the central question that modern physics poses to Kant's philosophy and by extension every philosopher committed to Kant's central tenet, the claim of synthetic *a priori* cognition. The problem is the following: If Einstein's revolution in physics overcomes Newton's scientific paradigm, and if it is the case – as the members of the Marburg School emphasized – that Kant's philosophical system is the product of a meditation on Newton, *how can Kant's central claim be upheld*? If it cannot, it would seem that the entire critical system would be devalued on that account. It was precisely this claim that Cassirer intended to reject in his philosophical interpretation of Einstein's work. What is at stake is nothing lesser than Kant's crucial claim as to the existence of synthetic judgments *a priori*, and by extension the *a priori* itself, understood in the proper (Kantian) sense. To this end, Cassirer claims, as Schlick points out, that he "has made it his object to prove that the philosophical foundations of relativity theory can be found only in the field of critical philosophy." Cassirer maintains that the overall philosophical framework to accommodate Einstein's standpoint can only be "logical idealism," the stance of the Marburg School, in other words. It is this claim that Schlick takes issue with in his review. Schlick's strategy is to question Cassirer's either/or: that an interpretation of modern physics need be either empiricist or critical. In order to establish a third alternative, Schlick argues it suffices to salvage the Kantian view that we insist on the "necessity of constitutive principles for scientific experience." To accept such principles, in Schlick's view, is compatible with an empiricism. Empiricism, then, is the rejection of the synthetic *a priori* alone, not of constitutive principles for the experience of nature; these are, however, mere conventions and not "apodeictic," which would be Kant's criterion. Cassirer, however, believes he can salvage the synthetic *a priori* by going beyond Kant, when he insists on, as one could call it, a two-tiered *a priori*. The first would be the insistence on constitutive principles for the scientific experience of nature that accord with a certain scientific paradigm or viewpoint (Newton's *or* Einstein's). The second and more fundamental one is, as Schlick quotes Cassirer, "only the idea of the 'unity of nature', that is, of the law-abiding character of experience in general." Indeed, Cassirer's letter to Schlick of October 23, 1920 (reacting to a letter by Schlick, not the present text), deserves to be quoted at some length; for as becomes obvious, Cassirer did not see his position refuted through Schlick's critique.

"I, too, feel – although I do not want to downplay the difference [between us] – that there exist nonetheless between *your* version of empiricism and my view of the critical method strong connections and that both can go together for a good stretch. ... The point of difference between us, it seems to me, lies in the *concept* of the *a priori*, which I understand somewhat differently than you: namely, not as a constant stock[1] of material 'intuitions' and concepts that remains the same once and for all, but instead as a function that is lawfully determined and that therefore remains identical with itself in its *direction* and its form, but that can experience, in the course of the progress of knowledge, the most different characters in terms of content[2]. I would call '*a priori*' in the rigorous sense only the idea of the 'unity of nature' or the 'distinctiveness of attribution'[3]. ... This principle of distinctiveness itself is, to me, more than a mere 'convention' or a 'inductive generalization': it is, to me, an expression of 'reason', of Logos itself."[4]

There is a long history of rejecting the synthetic *a priori* in the twentieth century. It is, in this light, to be seen whether Cassirer's position can still find supporters besides Friedman (cf. Friedman 2001).

Notes

1 *Bestand*
2 *inhaltlich die verschiedensten Ausprägungen*
3 '*Eindeutigkeit der Zuordnung*'
4 Cassirer 2009, pp. 50 f.

Further Reading

Cassirer, Ernst, *Ausgewählter wissenschaftlicher Briefwechsel*. Hamburg: Meiner, 2009.
Friedman, Michael, *The Dynamics of Reason*. Stanford: CSLI Publications, 2001.
Heidelberger, Michael. "From Neo-Kantianism to Critical Realism: Space and the Mind-body Problem in Riehl and Schlick," in: *Perspectives on Science: Historical, Philosophical, Social*, 15(1), 2007: 26–48.

Chapter 30

"Critical or Empiricist Interpretation of Modern Physics?" (1921)[1]

REMARKS ON ERNST CASSIRER'S EINSTEIN'S THEORY OF RELATIVITY (1921)

An indelible, inalienable feature of critical philosophy is the way in which it is rooted in exact science. Just as Kant himself, according to a well-attested view (particularly upheld by Hermann Cohen) was pursuing, in his critique of knowledge, the goal of providing a philosophical justification for the Newtonian principles of nature, so the neo-Kantian schools endeavor to prove the truth of the basic ideas of the critical philosophy by seeking to demonstrate its usefulness and fertility for present-day physics as well. It has not been difficult for neo-Kantianism to keep pace with the development of natural science, as it passed from the mechanical to the energetical, and finally to the electrodynamical view of the world; but does it also have sufficient power and elasticity to share in the leap whereby physics in our own day has set out on a new path? At a time when there were only quite few attempts to assimilate the special theory of relativity to the critical point of view, and when the general theory had not yet been completed at all, I thought it necessary to answer this question in the negative. It seemed to me that the principles needed for a philosophical illumination and vindication of that theory could be drawn far more readily from the empiricist than the Kantian theory of knowledge[2]; and even on subsequent occasions I found no reason to abandon this position, more especially since the successful completion of the general theory, which took place soon afterwards, brought victory to an idea that had arisen from the soil of extreme empiricism (namely the positivism of Mach). But, given the importance and difficulty of the question, it is a duty to test the matter once more at every serious opportunity. Such an opportunity is provided by the appearance of Ernst Cassirer's book[3], and I therefore gladly accede to the request of the editors of *Kant-Studien*, that I make a renewed examination of the problem in the light of this book; an examination, to be sure, which for external reasons can be made only in a comparatively brief form.

Cassirer, in his book, has made it his object to prove that the philosophical foundations of relativity theory can be found only in the field of critical philosophy, and more precisely in that form of the critical viewpoint which he is pleased to label logical idealism. He sets himself the task of deciding, by epistemological analysis, "whether the theory in its origin and development is to be taken as an example and witness of the *critical* or of the *sensualistic* concept of experience".[4]

But in light of this formulation, doubts are immediately bound to arise: Is the problem really reducible to these alternatives? Do we have here a *tertium non datur*? There is certainly an empiricism that is distinct from sensualism and cannot be reduced to it, as can easily be discerned both historically and in terms of subject-matter. So if it is shown (as it is not hard to do) that the theory of relativity cannot be made out upon purely sensualist premises, this alone does not prove either the necessity or even the admissibility of the critical interpretation of the theory, unless the concept of logical idealism has been taken so broadly that the above alternative is in fact permitted. But then it runs the risk of losing its bold coloring, and hence its philosophical value; the most heterogeneous opinions could be brought in under it. At some points Cassirer does actually seem inclined to such general formulations that the borderlines of his critical viewpoint threaten to become unclear. We must try to trace the boundaries here.

In order to establish a firm basis for the considerations to follow, I must state briefly the indispensable features that I take to be associated with the concept of criticism. Such a foundation is absolutely necessary for any discussion of the compatibility of relativity theory with the critical theory of knowledge, for only so do we avoid the tiresome intrusion of questions concerning the interpretation of Kant; the discussion remains unprofitable, so long as everyone can resort to the not uncommon argument, that his opponent is not giving a correct account of the Kantian view.

So let us lay down the following preliminaries. All exact science, whose philosophical justification undoubtedly forms the prime goal of the theory of knowledge founded by Kant, rests upon observations and measurements. But mere sensations and perceptions are not yet observations and measurements; they only become so by being ordered and interpreted. Thus the forming of concepts of physical objects unquestionably presupposes certain principles of ordering and interpretation. Now I see the essence of the critical viewpoint in the claim that these constitutive principles are *synthetic a priori judgments*, in which the concept of the *a priori* has the property of apodeicticity (of universal, necessary and inevitable validity) inseparably attached to it. I am convinced, indeed, that this explanation is a correct account of Kant's own view, but even if neither he nor his followers had ever professed this type of criticism, the factual truth or falsity of the following assertions would be quite unaffected thereby, and this is all that matters in an inquiry directed to systematic rather than historical questions.

The most important consequence of the view just elaborated is that a thinker who simply perceives the necessity of constitutive principles for scientific experience should not yet be called a critical philosopher on that account. An empiricist, for example, can very well acknowledge the presence of such principles; he will deny only that they are synthetic and *a priori* in the sense described above.

Cassirer recognizes that "empiricism and idealism meet in certain presuppositions.... Both here grant to experience the decisive role, and both teach that every exact measurement presupposes universal empirical *laws*".[5] But in then addressing himself to the pressing question of "how we reach these laws, on which rests the possibility of all empirical measurement, and what sort of validity...we grant to them"[6], he contrasts the critical viewpoint only with the sensualist one, under the name of 'strict' positivism. He quite rightly condemns the attempt sometimes made by Mach, to treat even analytico-mathematical laws like things "whose properties one can read off by immediate perception",[7] but that does not prove the truth of logical idealism, it merely refutes the sensualist theory. Between the two we still have the empiricist viewpoint, according to which these constitutive principles are either *hypotheses* or *conventions;* in the first case they are not *a priori* (since they lack apodeicticity), and in the second they are not synthetic. How fares it with the proof that the principles of Einsteinian physics do not have this character, but are to be claimed as synthetic *a priori* propositions?

There can be no doubt that Kant himself included among the synthetic *a priori* principles constitutive of objects the axioms of Euclidean geometry and Galilean kinematics. And even after the mathematical discovery of the non-Euclidean geometries, the majority of Kantians have clung to the Euclidean view of nature as the only possible one, declaring (quite openly, for example in the case of Alois Riehl and Richard Hönigswald) that Euclidean geometry in fact has the *intuitive* necessity attributed to it by Kant, whereas the other geometries possess only conceptual thinkability, which does not conflict with the Kantian view.

Now the special theory of relativity is incompatible with the principles of Galilean kinematics, and the general theory is also irreconcilable with the propositions of Euclid. Anyone who accepts Einstein's theory must reject Kant's theory in its original form; as Cassirer himself often stresses, we have to take a step beyond Kant. But that is by no means our concern here. The critical viewpoint, as above defined, could nevertheless maintain and preserve itself in face of the new theory, and even celebrate still greater triumphs; all that would be needed is for the ultimate foundations of the theory to disclose themselves as synthetic propositions of absolutely necessary validity for all experience. What are these propositions?

For this must assuredly be noted: anyone who upholds the critical claim, must, if we are to accord him credence, also really set forth the *a priori* principles which must form the solid basis of all exact science. For transcendental philosophy, as Cassirer rightly says, space and time are not things, but 'sources of knowledge'.[8] We therefore have to demand a statement of the cognitions of which space, for example, is the source. The critical idealist must designate them as definitely and clearly as Kant was able to point to the geometry and 'general theory of motion' which alone were known and recognized in his day. All those who have judged relativity theory from the Kantian standpoint have pointed out that it is concerned with *empirical* time (that is, time measured by physical methods) and *empirical* space, and to these they contrast the Kantian 'pure intuition' of space and time as that which first makes these empirical constructions possible, and so must remain quite undisturbed by any advance in physics, which can invariably refer only to the empirical. By this turn the state of the problem is not altered, but merely expressed in another way, for pure intuition is simply the cognitive source of those *a priori* principles that are needed for the construction of empirical time and empirical space; for many it is simply a comprehensive term for the essence of those principles themselves. In each case the existence of a 'pure space' and 'pure time' can be demonstrated as such only by actually pointing out the system of the relevant synthetic *a priori* principles, or at least giving an unambiguous indication of how it is to be found. It cannot be sufficiently emphasized that an adherent of the critical philosophy can vindicate himself only by producing such a system of judgments. Every attempt to reconcile Einstein with Kant must discover synthetic *a priori* principles in the theory of relativity; otherwise it must be regarded from the outset as a failure, since it has not even got to the point of stating the problem correctly.

Cassirer, of course, sees the problem in its proper light, and at two places in his book seems to give closer definition to the content of the pure intuition proclaimed by logical idealism. In the first passage[9] he sees it in the concept of the coincidence of 'world-points', to which the general theory notoriously reduces all laws of nature. But this 'coincidence' simply cannot, in my view, be regarded as the sheer essence and nodal point of *a priori* propositions, being initially just representative of a *psychological* experience of coming together, much as the word 'yellow' designates a simple color-experience that cannot be further defined. Only so can it play the intermediary role between reality and scientifico-conceptual construction that the theory attributes to it. In other words, we are confronted with an *empirical* intuition.[10]

A second answer to the question of what synthetic *a priori* propositions about space are now left standing is given by Cassirer on p. 101 [p. 433], where he says:

> For the *a priori* of space...involves...no assertion concerning any definite particular structure of space in itself, but is concerned only with that function of 'spatiality' in general, that is expressed even in the general concept of the linear element...as such, quite without regard to its character in detail.

But this formulation, which seeks to affirm that there simply has to be such a thing as a linear element in the description of nature, can hardly satisfy. For what is the set of axioms that is supposed to be included in this claim? It cannot be the axioms of constancy, for the possibility, already envisaged by Riemann, of discontinuous determinations of space, has been brought within arm's length by modern quantum theory. And whatever other axioms one might choose, there is no seeing why just these should constitute the one necessary structure of space, since others that are no less 'self-evident' have fallen victim to the progress of physics.

Any claim about content, however general it may be, already seems too special here, and it is perfectly consistent to reply to the question, as to what the ultimate synthetic *a priori* principles of all science may be, with the answer (which I take from a kind letter of Cassirer's), that they "really consist only of the idea of the 'unity of nature', that is, of the law-abiding character of experience in general, or, more briefly perhaps, of the 'univocal nature of coordination'." But this seems to me to involve the inescapable intrusion of the danger that I described above as the inevitable consequence of too great an extension in the range of the critical conception. For it would now no longer be possible ever to claim of a physical theory that it confirmed the critical philosophy: the latter would have, rather, to be compatible with *every* theory, in the same way, and without possibility of selection, so long as such a theory satisfies the mere conditions of being scientific. Unitary obedience to natural law is assuredly the *conditio sine qua non* of science, since, as Cassirer himself says,[11] "the general doctrine of the invariability and determinateness of certain values...must recur in some form in *any* theory of nature." Even for the empiricists, as Cassirer acknowledges,[12] laws are "what is truly permanent and substantial"; even the empiricist believes in the unity of nature, in the law-abiding character of all experience; all he holds is that its validity and objective necessity cannot be proved by a transcendental deduction or in any other way. Here the critical philosopher can appeal to no physical theory, for each of them proves by its verification in experience only the factual, not the necessary validity of the principle of the unity of nature.

Like a scarlet thread there runs through Cassirer's book the demonstration, conducted by a brilliant use of the finest historical and philosophical scholarship, that the theory of relativity not only does not contradict the ideal that has guided the development of exact science from Plato to the present day, but represents, on the contrary, its currently most perfect fulfilment; that the relativity of measurements laid down by the theory in no way signifies a renunciation of strictly univocal objective lawfulness, but provides, on the contrary, the way to attain to the most universal laws and to discover the ultimate invariants. A more recent essay of Cassirer's (in the December number of the *Neue Rundschau*) is essentially devoted to the same argument. However necessary and valuable it was to counter by such considerations the natural lay misunderstandings of Einstein's theory, and to set it at a proper remove from any sophistical 'relativism' of the skeptical type, this only serves to confirm that the theory of relativity, precisely because it is a scientific theory, naturally represents an *establishing*, not an *abolition*, of the most universal, objectively valid laws. The Einsteinian world-picture allows the unity of nature to emerge more perfectly than the Newtonian, not, however, because it is in better accord with the critical philosophy, but because, even when measured by the physical conception of knowledge, and regardless of its ultimate philosophical interpretation, it represents a higher stage of knowledge.

The question whether Cassirer's so deeply thought-out logical idealism has succeeded in proving the correctness of the claim, that only on the basis of the critical epistemology can the theory of relativity be philosophically founded and justified, is one to which, in virtue of the foregoing, we are unable to give an affirmative answer, precisely on the decisive point: the doctrine of synthetic *a priori* judgments as the constructive principles of exact science obtains no unambiguous confirmation from the new theory. Cassirer's observations appear to me to provide no convincing evidence of how we may deal the wound dealt to the original Kantian viewpoint by the over-throw of Euclidean physics. But that is not yet to say that the relation between transcendental philosophy and relativity theory has now been shown to be a purely negative one; on other points significant contacts may occur between the two viewpoints, and important common elements be disclosed.

It is very natural to seek in the critical doctrine of the *ideality* of space and time a close natural affinity with the ideas of relativity theory. The insubstantiality which seems to distinguish the space of Einstein's theory of nature from the fixed space of Newton (and so, too, with time), has in fact been seen as a welcome confirmation of the Kantian philosophy. Cassirer also takes this view. With reference to my statement that, on the general theory of relativity, only an indissoluble unity of space, time and matter still possesses the predicate of reality,[13] he observes that this insight "belongs to the fundamental doctrines of critical idealism";[14] and goes on: "the ideal separation of pure space and pure time from things (more exactly, from empirical phenomena), not only permits but demands precisely their empirical 'union'".[15] This latter is true enough, for as forms of intuition space and time are no more separable from the formed matter in them than the matter, conversely, can exist without a form. But the 'union' proclaimed by relativity theory, which I was trying to specify in this remark, is a far more intimate one than the unity of matter and form on which transcendental philosophy has nowhere made any advance. So when Cassirer goes on: "This union the general theory of relativity has verified and proved in a new way...", the stress has to be laid entirely on the word *new*. This novelty is utterly misconstrued by E. Sellien, who says:

> For the factual determination of space and time in experience, space, time and bodies belong together. This proposition is no achievement of Einstein's theory, as Schlick maintains with such emphasis; it has long been known, and in no way refutes Kant's doctrine *of pure* time, since it simply does not touch it.[16]

It is, however, a quite fundamental misunderstanding of general relativity theory to think it possible to construe my above-mentioned observation as though it merely denied in a negative way the separate existence of time and space in contrast to matter (and vice versa); that would certainly be a long familiar triviality. In Einstein's theory, the mutual dependence of space, time, and matter goes far deeper than that; it is, for example, impossible on that theory to speak of the measurements of a spatial configuration without reference to the manner of its material occupancy. That in *this* way the theory of space becomes a branch of physics, deserves to be dwelt on with great emphasis. Only Riemann has anticipated this idea with complete clarity; it was not only at a far remove from the critical philosophy,[17] but seems to contradict it, since it makes it impossible to view space and time as mere forms in the traditional sense, whose laws are to be dealt with independently of their content. When Einstein remarks on the working-out of general relativity that it takes from space and time "the last remainder of physical objectivity", Cassirer thinks "that the theory only accomplishes the most definite application and carrying through of the standpoint of critical idealism within empirical science itself".[18] But if – which Cassirer rightly insists[19] as the first task of the epistemologist – we set out in full clarity the meaning of the term 'physical objectivity', we again run into the aforementioned finding, to which the doctrine of the ideality of space and time can do justice only on its negative side; for it turns out that with this denial of 'objectivity' we do indeed deny to space and time any independence of whatever kind from matter, but that the residue which *then* remains of the physically spatial and temporal, in combination with matter, also enjoys the same reality as the latter. Einstein himself has at times declared that, even according to general relativity, physical space has reality, but no independent reality. Thus the spatial and temporal retain a meaning in which they can no longer be regarded merely as 'forms' in the usual sense, but now belong to the physical determinants of bodies; the 'metric' does not just mean a mathematical measuring of the physically real, but itself gives expression to the presence of this. Space and matter, as Cassirer most aptly puts it, "no longer occur as different classes of physical object-concepts".[20] So when it is supposed that Einsteinian physics "in this respect displays fewer contradictions to the Kantian transcendental aesthetic than any earlier physics",[21] this seems to me to harbor a misapprehension of the positive aspect of Einstein's theory of space and time. It would also be extraordinary if the Kantian theory of knowledge were held to stand in such clear contradiction to the Newtonian view of nature, whose philosophical vindication was one of its principal goals.

But even though critical principles may fare ill in correctly evaluating the most general form of relativity (covariance under *any* substitutions, in the language of the theory), they could yet perhaps furnish a viable basis for Einstein's theory, insofar as they at least stand in a favorable relation to the principle of the relativity of all *motions* (covariance under a certain group of substitutions). It cannot, of course, be demanded of a philosophical system that it carry through this principle as a theory, but the principle can very well derive from it, qua indispensable postulate. If even this is too much to ask, we may at the very least expect that the principle, once established on other grounds, will at once be recognized as congenial and taken up with maximum vigor by the system. On its own premises, the critical philosophy would in fact have been very well placed to do this; yet in its historical manifestations it has satisfied none of the requirements just stated. On the contrary, it was the positivist Mach who first emphatically elevated the general principle of relativity into a postulate for the description of nature. He demanded – and this actually on philosophical grounds – a formulation of natural laws such that the rotation of the earth against the fixed stars, for example, could be viewed with equal justice as a contrary revolution of the firmament about the earth. To discover Kant's attitude to this view – which was just as possible in his own day – we must read the *Metaphysical Foundations of Natural Science*,[22] where in the Observation following Principle I in the first chapter, and in Proposition 2 and the General Observation on Phenomenology in the fourth, he discusses the problem. Like Leibniz, Huygens and others, he there feels definitely called upon to maintain the relativity of *all* motion. But while Newton recognized that this was inconsistent with *his* mechanics, and so logically (though maybe not altogether cheerfully) postulated absolute motion for the latter, Kant seeks a way out by positing, in addition to the antithesis of relative and absolute, that of 'true' and 'apparent' motion[23]!

In his *Substanzbegriff und Funktionsbegriff*[24] (1910), Cassirer has already dealt with the question of the relativity of rotation[25]. It is extremely notable with what acumen he then reviewed the consequences of the Machian view. For he says:[26]

> The positivistic scruples against the 'pure' space and the 'pure' time of mechanics thus prove nothing because they would prove too much; logically thought out, they would also have to forbid every representation of physically given bodies in a geometrical system in which there are fixed positions and distances.

Thus here, and in the developments preceding the passage cited, we find rejected in essence from the critical standpoint precisely those consequences to which science now finds itself compelled.

Cassirer is certainly correct in his view that confirmation of the Machian relativity thesis still provides in itself no compelling proof of the necessity for an empiricist interpretation of Einstein's theory[27] – but it remains nevertheless an extremely significant indication of this, and not, I think, a misleading one. For the epistemological motive which, (rightly or wrongly) led Mach and Einstein to the postulate of the relativity of all motions, was the principle *that differences in reality may be assumed only where there are differences that can, in principle, be experienced*. This fundamental rule has often been enunciated, even by such metaphysicians as Leibniz, with whom it actually appears in two forms, namely as the principle of the identity of indiscernibles, and as the principle of observability (Cassirer also introduces it in the latter form);[28] but it is still a large step from stating the rule to a consistent upholding and enforcement of it. Yet if the principle is recognized and evaluated in its true significance, it can, I believe, be elevated to the supreme principle of all empirical philosophy, to the ultimate guideline which must govern our attitude to every question of detail, and whose ruthless application to all special problems is an exceedingly fruitful procedure. If this view is correct, the connection of relativity theory with the empiricist theory of knowledge would then be seen, anyway, as an intimate, strictly factual, and not merely external or contingent one.

In the final chapter of his book, Cassirer stresses emphatically that the space and time of relativity theory are just the space and time of *physics*, not of reality as such, so that the space and time *of psychology*, say, stand contrasted to them as something of an altogether different kind. It is, in fact, of the greatest importance to be always clear about the fact that we can speak of space and time in totally different senses – and most important of all precisely for anyone who is ultimately interested in discerning the connection between these different senses. When I elsewhere[29] set psychological space (and time), as the purely intuitive, in contrast to physical, as a purely conceptual construction, I was well aware that Kant defines 'intuition' in quite a different way. On this point I have been misunderstood by a succession of critics. Cassirer declares[30] Kant's pure intuition to be a specific 'method of objectification', which indeed it is *as well*, but its nature is not exhausted by this. Kant certainly wanted to purge it of everything psychological – but I shall never be able to persuade myself that he succeeded. For no such success is possible,[31] without employing the sole method which permits us to separate the purely conceptual elements of geometry from the psychologically intuitive, namely, the method of implicit definition, first framed in modern mathematics.[32] Without it we cannot even grasp the idea of a pure concept, or understand this in abstraction from all psychological elements. Kant's space of pure intuition therefore necessarily contains such elements as give the concept of space that content without which he would consider it 'empty'. He does indeed regard his space as identical with that of Newton (Cassirer is also of this opinion, which I have always shared myself; though Sellien,[33] whom Cassirer otherwise quotes with approval, appears to contradict it); but Newtonian space, for Kant, is simply an intuitive one, not yet purified of the elements which *we* must still describe as psychological. So Kant's pure intuition – corresponding as it does to the received view of space and time – is a halfway house between the purely conceptual and the psychologically intuitive; and since I consider it one of the most important findings of the modern theory of exact science (Henri Poincaré having made an especial philosophical contribution on this point), that there simply *is no* such hybrid or halfway house, I have had on the one hand to deny the existence of a pure intuition like that of Kant[34] and have ventured to speak of a confusion of the physical concept of space with its sensory representatives;[35] while on the other hand I have had to declare that there is a core of truth to be found in the doctrine of purely subjective forms of intuition, precisely insofar as they are still not wholly divested of psychological elements. So these views I am unable to abandon.

Pursuit of the changes of meaning in the terms 'space' and 'time' through the various fields of intellectual life gives Cassirer the opportunity to range his view of relativity theory in broad terms within a wider context, and to direct upon it, not only the light of the specialized critique of knowledge, but also the radiance of systematic philosophy. Thus the book concludes with a survey whose breadth conforms to the high level of the standpoint adopted. But we are left with the impression that this standpoint already transcends the region of critical philosophy proper, and that only in virtue of this has Cassirer succeeded in doing the degree of philosophical justice to the theory of relativity that is achieved in this intelligent and thoughtful book.

I gladly comply with the invitation of the *Kant-Studien* editors, to report in brief at this juncture on two other books about Einstein's theory, since the writings in question are such as to repay discussion. The first, written by Max Born,[36] gives a brilliant, comprehensive account of Einstein's theory from the physicists' point of view. It fills in most appropriate fashion a very palpable gap in the Einstein literature, for while the layman's introductions to the theory so far available have confined themselves to bare essentials in the treatment of its basic physical concepts, in Born's book the theory appears for the first time without detachment from its natural background; on the contrary, great emphasis is explicitly laid upon its place in the system of physics, and the connections from which it has actually arisen are made clearly apparent. For the non-physicist it is of the greatest value to be initiated into these connections, since it is through them that the natural road to understanding leads. Born not only levels this road by avoiding all higher mathematics; even logarithms and trigonometrical functions are absent. But the main thing is, that the book is through and through the work of a philosophical mind. This is shown, not by the fact that Born interrupts the course of his exposition with philosophical glosses and asides, but in the high level of the viewpoints that determine the structure, and in the deep thought that is everywhere manifest in the treatment of the subject. It is shown above all, moreover, in the brief philosophical introduction, which strikes one as positively classical in the warmth and pregnancy with which it expounds the basic idea: that the absolute can be found only in the realm of the subjective, and that the thinking mind can penetrate into the sphere of objective validity only by sacrificing the absolute, in order to exchange it for knowledge of the relative. A fundamental insight indeed, which is not only evident in theoretical science, but also holds good, I am convinced, in practical philosophy as well.

The second work is the monograph *Relativitätstheorie und Erkenntnis a priori* by Hans Reichenbach (Berlin 1920). It undoubtedly represents a great advance in the logical interpretation of Einstein's theory. Using a sort of axiomatic method, Reichenbach probes, by a very acute and original analysis, into the logical foundations of relativity theory, and in so doing, by uncovering certain more hidden principles (he speaks, for example, of a 'principle of the approximable ideal', a 'principle of normal induction' etc.), he makes a valuable contribution to the logic of exact science as such. He reaches the conclusion that Einstein's theory is incompatible with the original doctrine of Kant, and proposes a transformation of the concept of the *a priori*, such that relativity theory will no longer contradict it, and the most important thesis of the Kantian philosophy will remain, as he thinks, intact. This thesis he professes to find in the insight that all knowledge becomes possible only through the logical presupposition of certain principles, which first constitute its object as such. Such principles he calls *a priori*, but dispenses with the mark of apodeicticity; hence they are not necessary, and the progress of experience can provide motives for modifying them. "*A priori* means '*prior* to knowledge', but not 'for all time', and not 'independently of experience'".[37] In view of my earlier remarks, this strikes me as a total departure from the basis of the critical philosophy, and I should designate Reichenbach's *a priori* principles as conventions, in Poincaré's sense. Thus I cannot commend the author's terminology, but in substance I agree entirely with him on most of the essential points. Even in those questions about which he takes issue with me in the book, there is really no profound difference of opinion, as an elucidation of our positions by correspondence has subsequently disclosed. But for a reader averse to these positions, the book is still of value, for a piece of philosophy so marked out as this is by originality, clarity and acuteness of argument must offer him pleasure and profit, even when it provokes him to dissent.

Notes

1   'Kritizistische oder empiristische Deutung der neuen Physik?', in: *Kant-Studien* 26 (1921), pp. 96–111. Translation taken from *Philosophical Papers* I, Dordrecht: Reidel, 1979, pp. 322–334. Translated by Peter Heath. – Ed.
2   'Die philosophische Bedeutung des Relativitätsprinzips', *Zeitschrift für Philosophie und philosophische Kritik* 159 .
3   Ernst Cassirer, *Zur Einsteinschen Relativitätstheorie. Erkenntnistheoretische Betrachtungen*, Berlin 1921 [Engl. by W. C. Swabey and M. C. Swabey in *Substance and Function and Einstein's Theory of Relativity*, Chicago 1923. Page references to both editions are given in the text – Trans.].
4   *Einstein's Theory of Relativity*, p. 26 (English, p. 367).
5   *Einstein's Theory of Relativity*, pp. 94 f. (p. 426).
6   Ibid.
7   Ibid.
8   *Einstein's Theory of Relativity*, p. 78 (p. 411).
9   *Einstein's Theory of Relativity*, p. 84 (p. 417).
10 This is also the true meaning of my remarks in *Raum und Zeit in der gegenwärtigen Physik*, 3rd ed., 1920, p. 83.
11 *Einstein's Theory of Relativity*, p. 45 (p. 384).
12 *Einstein's Theory of Relativity*, p. 95 (p. 427).
13 Ibid. p. 67.
14 *Einstein's Theory of Relativity*, p. 93 (p. 425).
15 *Einstein's Theory of Relativity*, p. 94 (p. 426).
16 *Die erkenntnistheoretische Bedeutung der Relativitätstheorie*. Dissertation, Kiel 1919, p. 37; also published as supplement (Ergänzungsheft) no. 48 to *Kant-Studien*.
17 On this point too, there have been attempts to portray Kant as a predecessor of Einstein. On the basis of some remarks in Kant's first work, *Gedanken von der wahren Schätzung der lebendigen Kräfte*, Ilse Schneider observes (*Das Raum-Zeitproblem bei Kant und Einstein*, Berlin 1921, p. 70): "Thus Kant is the first to point out the connection of geometry and physics, especially gravitation". But Kant's attempt to bring the three-dimensional character of space into relation with the formula of Newton's law of gravitation can by no stretch be regarded as a premonition of the unification of geometry and physics in the epistemological sense, and has, on the contrary, nothing at all to do with it. One might point here with equal justice to the Cartesian identification of substance and extension, which Cassirer also mentions (p. 60 [pp. 395 f.]), though without in fact exaggerating its true significance.
18 *Einstein's Theory of Relativity*, p. 79 (p. 412).
19 On p. 13 (p. 356).
20 Cassirer, p. 61 (p. 396).
21 Ilse Schneider, *op. cit.* p. 65.
22 [Engl. by J. Ellington, Chicago 1970, tr. of *Metaphysische Anfangsgründe der Naturwissenschaft*, 1786.]
23 Ilse Schneider, *op. cit.* p. 14, cites the relevant passage in Kant with approval, since she makes him out to be an opponent of absolute motion; but she forgets that, precisely from the standpoint of relativity theory, these distinctions represent a monstrosity.

24 Engl. *Substance and Function*. Page references to German and English editions are given in the text. – Trans.
25 *Substance and Function*, pp. 230 ff. (pp. 170 ff.).
26 *Substance and Function*, p. 246 (pp. 185 f.).
27 *Einstein's Theory of Relativity*, p. 97 (pp. 428 f.).
28 Ibid., p. 37 (p. 380).
29 *Raum und Zeit*, 3rd ed., 1920, p. 81 [Engl. present vol., no. 9, p. 261] and *Allgemeine Erkenntnislehre*, p. 301 [1st ed., 1918; Engl. by A. E. Blumberg, *General Theory of Knowledge*, New York 1974, p. 353].
30 *Op. cit.* pp. 123, 124 n. [see note 2; Engl. *op. cit.* p. 451 n.].
31 As can be seen, for example, from Sellien's remarks, *op. cit.* p. 40 [see note 5].
32 Cf. *Allgemeine Erkenntnislehre*, pp. 30 ff. [1st ed.; Engl. *op. cit.* pp. 31 ff.].
33 *Op. cit.* p. 16. The reference there is to time; but the arguments apply similarly to space.
34 *Allgemeine Erkenntnislehre*, pp. 300 f. [1st ed.; Engl. *op. cit.* pp. 352 f.].
35 *Raum und Zeit*, 3rd ed., 1920, p. 83 [Engl, present vol., no. 9, p. 262].
36 *Die Relativitätstheorie Einsteins und ihre physikalischen Grundlagen, gemeinverständlich dargestellt*, with 129 illustrations and a portrait, Berlin 1920.
37 *Einstein's Theory of Relativity*, p. 100.

Introduction

Rudolf Carnap (1891–1970)

BY MICHAEL FRIEDMAN

The selection presented here is the final section of Rudolf Carnap's doctoral dissertation, *Space: A Contribution to the Theory of Science*, which appeared in *Kant-Studien* in 1922. This was an interdisciplinary dissertation, comprising mathematics, physics, and philosophy, directed by the neo-Kantian philosopher Bruno Bauch at Jena. Carnap aims to sort out the conflicting views of the nature of space held by mathematicians, (largely neo-Kantian) philosophers, and physicists by carefully studying the relationships among three different types or meanings of space: formal, intuitive, and physical space. The first is what we would now call a purely formal-logical (uninterpreted) order structure (relational structure) with no intrinsically spatial meaning. The second is something like a form of intuition in the sense of Kant (Carnap appeals to Husserl's notion of "essential insight"[1] as well), which does have an intrinsically spatial and perceptual meaning. The third is typified by space as described in Einstein's recent (1915–16) general theory of relativity – which space, in particular, is no longer considered to be Euclidean. Yet Carnap also follows Poincaré and others in taking the metrical structure of physical space to be determined by a stipulation or convention, constrained by the perceptually given "factual basis[2]" of merely topological (intuitively) spatial structure. Carnap therefore sharply distinguishes between the "necessary form" of topological intuitive space and the "optional[3] form" of metrical physical space. His conclusion is that only such necessary form counts as a condition of the possibility of experience – and, indeed, only that given by topological intuitive space of arbitrarily many dimensions (together with that of the corresponding type of formal space).

Notes

1 *Wesenserschauung*
2 *Tatbestand*
3 *wahlfrei*

Further Reading

Carus, André W., *Carnap and twentieth-century thought: explication as enlightenment.* Cambridge: Cambridge University Press, 2007.

Caton, Hiram., "Carnap's First Philosophy," in: *Review of Metaphysics, 28*, 1975: 623–659.

Friedman, Michael, and Richard Creath, eds. *The Cambridge Companion to Carnap.* Cambridge University Press, 2007.

Chapter 31

"Space as a Condition of Experience" from *Der Raum* (1922)[1]

According to Kant, space is the condition for the possibility of any (outer) experience whatsoever. Is this true for the spatial features of all the systems we have distinguished? To decide this, consider which spatial features are necessarily encountered in *every* (outer) experience, even when it has not yet, on the basis of freely chosen stipulations, been given a *particular* spatial form that goes beyond the necessary form. Experience, insofar as it is represented only in the unambiguous necessary form containing no arbitrary stipulation whatever, we have called the "factual basis[2]." Only the spatial features inherent in the factual basis, then, can be conditions for the possibility of experience. And these, as we have seen, are only the topological, not the projective, and above all not the metrical relations.

The transformation of a statement belonging to the factual basis from one metrical spatial form into another – e.g., from the Euclidean into one of the non-Euclidean – has been aptly compared to the translation of a sentence from one language into another. Now, just as the genuine sense of the sentence is not its representation in one of these linguistic forms (for then its representation in the other languages would have to be regarded as derived and less basic), but, rather, only what they all have in common, so too the sense of a statement belonging to the factual basis is not one of its metrical representations, but what they all have in common (the "invariants of topological transformations") – and that is precisely its representation in merely topological form.

In treating this question it has often been correctly pointed out that this "transcendental function" of space – the grounding of experience – can be attributed only to an unambiguous spatial form, and that therefore the non-Euclidean spatial forms could not be considered for this role. From this correct assertion it may not, however, be concluded that therefore only Euclidean space can assume this role. For it is on a par with the others and possesses as little or as much uniqueness as any of the non-Euclidean spaces, such as the one with a constant curvature of -20. The correct inference from that premise can arrive only at topological space, for it alone is both superordinate to those others and also completely unambiguous: the factual basis of experience cannot appear in several different topological forms.

The topological spatial relations that form the condition of the possibility of every object of experience cannot be those of physical space, since it is not independent of the factual basis of experience but represents only the actual, not the necessary, findings [of observation]: e.g., this particular physico-spatial figure has a particular topological relation to that one (of contact, connection, inclusion, etc.). The features of topological intuitive space, in their independence from experience and in the universal validity attributable to them in virtue of their cognitive source – and consequently also those of formal topological space, that general relational structure of undetermined things of which topological intuitive space forms a particular special case – can alone have this experience-constituting validity.

The much-disputed question whether the three-dimensionality of space belongs among those features that are the condition of every object of experience is to be answered in the negative. As we have seen in our construction of intuitive space, it emerges as a datum of intuition that the spatial figures of the intuitive realm have up to three dimensions. However, in the extension of this realm to the global space it turns out that, if we have a figure of k dimensions, although it can be concluded that the global structure to which it belongs has at least k dimensions, the upper limit to the number of dimensions of the global system cannot be inferred. From this finding of intuition it thus follows only that the global intuitive space has at least three dimensions. Even less can it be safely concluded from the knowledge of physical space, which possesses no necessity but only experiential probability, or from that of formal space, for which the number of dimensions is obviously not limited, that it is a condition of the possibility of any object of experience to have at most three dimensions. And the view that this latter conclusion can be arrived at by arguing that only the three-dimensionality of spatial forms guarantees the unique identification of experience is likewise off the mark. Rather, the situation is precisely the reverse: spatial determination becomes ambiguous, corresponding to the many different possibilities for such limits, if we allow an upper limit to the number of dimensions. And to avoid this equivocation, the unlimited number of dimensions has to be postulated as a possibility, so that arbitrarily many dimensions for an object of experience are consistent with its possibility as such an object.

It has been frequently discussed, by mathematicians as well as philosophers, that Kant's contention concerning the significance of space for experience is not shaken by the theory of non-Euclidean spaces, but must be transferred from the three-dimensional Euclidean system, the only one known to him, to a more general one. But to the question which this is to be, the answers are either indeterminate, as only isolated properties of the three-dimensional Euclidean structure are proposed as requiring generalization, or contradictory, chiefly because of a failure to distinguish the different meanings of space and insufficient clarity about the conceptual interrelations among the kinds of space themselves – especially the relation of the metrical to the superordinate topological ones. According to the above reflections, the Kantian conception must be endorsed. The spatial system possessing experience-constituting significance, in place of that suggested by Kant, can be precisely specified as topological intuitive space with indefinitely many dimensions. With that, not only the attributes of this system, but at the same time those of its order framework, are declared to be conditions of the possibility of any object of experience whatsoever.

Notes

1 The translation is largely the work of Michael Friedman and A. W. Carus. It also appears in the *Collected Works of Rudolf Carnap, Volume 1: Early Writings*, edited by A. W. Carus, Michael Friedman, Wolfgang Kienzler, and Sven Schlotter (Open Court Publishing Company, 2012). It appears here with the permission of Open Court Publishing Company. – Trans.
2 *Tatbestand*

Introduction

Edmund Husserl
(1859–1938)

HUSSERL'S RELATION TO HIS FELLOW NEO-KANTIANS IS DIFFICULT TO CHARACTERIZE. This is in part the case because, on the one hand, Husserl wanted to maintain cordial and professional relations with his contemporaries in Marburg and Southwest Germany. Indeed, Husserl was a personal friend with the Natorp family and, as Rickert's successor in Freiburg, Husserl took over the students Rickert had left behind (among others, Heidegger, who had written his Habilitation thesis under Rickert). On the other hand, Husserl pitted his school, the "Phenomenological Movement," deliberately against the Neo-Kantian Movement. He was keen to show how, in general, the artificial approach "from above" (deductively), which the Neo-Kantians advocated, could be rejected by the direct approach "from below," which the phenomenological approach suggested. This "from below" vis-à-vis "from above" was a general critique that Husserl, rightly or not, leveled against the Neo-Kantians on many occasions. In the present text (not published until 2002), Husserl was to offer a modification of this critique in the form of his assessment of the Neo-Kantian (Southwest) account of the respective sciences of nature and spirit. The following is an especially interesting discussion, because it takes place against the background of Husserl's own discussion of nature and spirit. Husserl's account of nature and spirit as two strata of constitution on the part of consciousness is known from *Ideas*, book II. The constitution of nature is the lowest level of constitution; on this rests the constitution of the spiritual world. Nature and spirit as products of constitution are respectively accessed by two different attitudes: the natural and personalistic attitude. These two attitudes do not yield two different sciences, as for instance natural science and human or cultural science that deal with different spheres of reality. Instead, studying these attitudes is, in part, the task of the original phenomenological research program. In this sense, Husserl's phenomenological account of the constitution of these different spheres of experience undercuts, or is much more basic than, the account the Neo-Kantians offer when they talk about nature and culture as regions of existing reality. This is at least Husserl's assumption when he tackles, in this fairly late lecture of 1927, the Neo-Kantian-Southwest distinction between nomothetic and idiographic sciences that is known from Windelband's famous "History and Natural Science" (in this volume, Chapter 19). Husserl interprets the idiographic move towards the individual as just another extension of Kant's Copernican Turn, according to the two moves of the human spirit towards the universal on the one hand and the individual on the other. What both accounts overlook is the specific manner in which the world gives itself to us *as a lifeworld* in all peculiarity that makes demands on us and that we have to heed rather than making demands on the world. The account that phenomenology offers, as starting from the prescientific lifeworld and from there moving to a scientific account of the world, either as natural or as spiritual, is thus, to Husserl, the true transcendental account that starts "from below" rather than covering up the lifeworld with a "shroud of ideas" from above. This figure of thought anticipates Husserl's interpretation of the crisis of modern science in his last book, the *Crisis of the European Sciences*. But it is clear that his previous critique of the Neo-Kantian approach prefigures this later critique, which Husserl could not have conceived without working through this Neo-Kantian distinction. This discussion also shows how Husserl construed his own phenomenology as fulfilling Kant's true intentions.

Further Reading

Jalbert, John E., "Husserl's Position Between Dilthey and the Windelband-Rickert school of Neo-Kantianism," in: *Journal of the History of Philosophy* 26.2, 1988, 279–296.

"A Critique of Windelband and Rickert on the Classification of the Sciences" from *Nature and Spirit* (1927)[1,2]

TRANSLATED BY ELIZABETH A. BEHNKE

Windelband and Rickert on the classification of the sciences in methodological terms[3]

Windelband's distinction between nomothetic natural sciences and idiographic historical sciences

A full exposition that would make the general ideas just indicated[4] completely comprehensible requires a critical consideration of the second and opposing tendency we previously mentioned, i.e., the second interpretation of the fundamental distinction underlying the conflict between the natural and the human sciences: namely, the tendency associated with Windelband and Rickert. It is an opposing tendency insofar as it does not take the division into two great provinces of the world – "nature" and "mind qua psyche" (a division it does not deny as such) – as the distinction that could fundamentally resolve the conflict over the correct relationship between the natural and the human sciences. Its particular focus is that the conflict is above all concerned with the supposed reform of the human sciences through natural-scientific method. Thus Windelband's theory has recourse to a universal logical *distinction of method* that plays no role in the opposing tendency, where it is not considered essential.

The proponents of naturalism, who in the manner previously discussed, only consider distinctions of provinces to be important, think that in each world-sphere the universal-logical must recur in the same methodological forms, such as individual and general description, induction of laws, and explanation via laws. Natural science has progressed the furthest in this regard, and as is well known, it is the model for the sciences dealing with the mental in the world. Holding this view, the proponents of naturalism think that human science is a new type of science only with respect to its province, not with respect to the sort of method it uses: when *method* is the determining factor, all sciences of the factual are natural sciences.

This methodological "naturalism" is exactly what the Windelband–Rickert theory is opposed to, offering instead a theory of a type of scientificity that is necessarily specific to history in contrast to natural science. A critical consideration of this theory will prove to be very useful, and will also reveal a fundamental and much more serious naturalism inwardly governing Windelband's and Rickert's theories as well.

A remark is appropriate at the outset. I am addressing the Windelband–Rickert theory in my treatment of interpretations of the distinction between the natural and the human sciences, even though their theory rejects the concept of "human sciences" (a move whose justification will become obvious as we proceed). The sense of this rejection will immediately become clear from Windelband's critique of the traditional opposition between nature and mind, a critique that already implies a critique of the division of the sciences according to their provinces.

According to Windelband,[5] the division goes back to the prevailing Cartesian dualism that divides the universal, objectively real sphere of being into material reality and mental or psychic reality. The sciences are subsequently divided according to these spheres of reality. One would then count psychology and the sciences of the social-historical world, including all types of culture (art, science, law, morals, etc.), among the human sciences. For Windelband, however, this division is far from satisfactory: on closer examination, *psychology* should not be lumped together with all of the other "human sciences"[6]. To the extent that mind[7] is another word for psyche, then considered in terms of its object, psychology might well be regarded as a human science on terminological grounds, and might even be characterized as the "foundation" of all the other human sciences. But from beginning to end its methodological stance is entirely that of the natural sciences, and is completely different from that of the other so-called human sciences. In fact, psychology can even be characterized as a "'natural science of inner perception'" – and let me add that Waitz, a follower of Herbart, has written a textbook on psychology as a natural science, a work that was well received in its time.[8] A division burdened with such difficulties could never hold up. It is true that each particular province has a particular method determined by it. But in general, the methodological "distance between psychology and chemistry" is, as Windelband expressly states, "hardly greater than the distance between mechanics and biology."

Where we find a truly radical distinction of universal method is between the disciplines usually termed natural sciences (but including psychology), on the one hand, and on the other hand, the historical disciplines, including most of the disciplines usually termed human sciences – obviously, those concerning the social-historical world, which belong to the historical disciplines precisely due to their methodology. What is distinctive about each of these types of science? Or as we ought to say, what determines the *methodological idea* of *nature*, quite apart from the question of divisions of provinces, and on the other hand, what determines the *methodological idea* of what Windelband does not want to call "mind,"[9] rejecting this word in favor of "*history*" as the more characteristic term? The answer is that the natural-scientific type is aiming for the general, the lawful. Natural sciences are defined as nomothetic sciences. In the sphere of mechanics, the laws are laws of mechanisms; in the sphere of biology, they are biological laws, and in the psychic sphere, psychological laws. On the other hand, as their name already indicates, the historical sciences are concerned with the unique event as a "more or less" temporally extended process, and the methodological goal would be to bring this event to actual and "exhaustive" presentation in its unique reality.[10] This is the case whether the event belongs to this or that province – e.g., whether it is a matter of a single factual political event or "a coherent sequence of acts or occurrences," of "an individual person or an entire nation; the definitive properties and the development of a language, a religion, a legal order," a literary or artistic tradition, a scientific theory and a science, etc. Here the cognitive aim is always to reproduce such an "artifact of human life" in its unique facticity, describing it and making it comprehensible. Thus the *nomothetic* sciences stand in contrast to *idiographic* sciences: the former are directed toward general laws, the latter toward historical facts. Windelband also speaks in Germanic coinage of

Gesetzeswissenschaften, or sciences of laws, and *Geschehniswissenschaften*, or sciences of occurrences or incidents. (And he makes an even sharper distinction, saying that the former lead to apodictic-general propositions, the latter to assertoric propositions.)

In Windelband's theory, then, the concept of "*natural science*" as a science whose sphere of objects is that of nature and "*human sciences*" as sciences whose sphere of objects comprises themes related to the mental is abandoned: these are merely *methodological titles*. He explicitly tells us that the same objects can become the theme "of both a nomothetic and an idiographic investigation" – he even thinks (which follows from this) that "in a certain respect, the distinction between the invariable[11] and the unique" is a *merely relative* distinction: what "undergoes no immediately perceptible change within a very large span of time," and may therefore be treated nomothetically with regard to its unchangeable forms, can still turn out "from a more comprehensive perspective" to be valid only "for a more limited time-span," i.e., it finally turns out to be something "unique." Thus language is governed in each case by "formal laws" that "remain the same throughout all changes of expression." On the other hand, this language is precisely a particular language, a historically factual "transitory phenomenon" with its temporary formal laws. It is similar for law and morals, but also for the provinces of biology and astronomy, for all of the sciences of organic nature. Hence even the sphere of the material world (nature in the narrower sense) can be considered historically, and not merely "nomologically." As a systematic scientific taxonomy, Windelband says, biology has a nomological character; under the aspect of greater time spans and astronomical distances, however, this is merely relative. During "the last few thousand years" of human observation, "invariable types of organisms" have presented constant lawful forms. But there is a developmental history of the species; in addition, any such set of laws is relative to the earth – and who will dare to assume the same laws on other planets, etc.?

Windelband then goes on to display the specific tendency of this entire exposition: namely, a vindication of (human) history as a science, and moreover, as a science fully equal to the natural sciences. He points out that ever since antiquity, the prevailing tendency in the sciences has been to overestimate the value of the search for laws while underestimating the importance of research into the unique – Aristotle already limited his concept of science to knowledge of the general, and is not willing to call history a science. This simultaneously means that the sciences place a higher value on *abstraction* at the expense of *intuition*. But in the end, history, along with its entire conceptual apparatus, serves to establish intuitions, "images" of human beings and human life in their "full and vital individuality." In contrast, no matter how intuitive the starting points of natural-scientific cognition may be, the ultimate aims of such cognition are theories – "in the final analysis," mathematically formulated sets of laws "whose timeless immutability governs all events." Thus "from the colorful world of the senses, the natural sciences construct a system of…concepts" in which "the true nature of things" lying behind the appearances can be grasped, "a silent, colorless world of atoms," etc.

For Windelband, what serves to ground the legitimacy of historical science – quite apart from the fact that historical-scientific research directed toward unique individuals is in *practical* terms as useful and indispensable as natural-scientific research into laws – is the old idea (already clearly worked out by John Stuart Mill) that knowledge of the factual world is not possible on the basis of the knowledge of laws alone. Each application of a known law to explain the facts presupposes ascertaining the facts. And if the explanation relies on causal laws to trace the facts that are given back to previous facts of which they are the lawfully necessary consequences (and these in turn to still earlier facts), we can never get around the need to ascertain individual facts. Windelband could have additionally noted not only that it is impossible, and indeed, unthinkable to posit "first" world-facts from which all temporally later facts are lawful causal consequences, but that even such first causes would still have to be ascertained in their individuality in order to be able to explain the world to come on their basis.

Windelband also touches on a problem that was treated by Dilthey as well (although in a completely different sense): that of the *significance* of historical facts. For Dilthey, this is a concept that belongs in principle to history as a human science[12], as a science of social-historical reality. But this cannot be the case for Windelband, even though he is only explicating the history of the mental[13], since his concept of history is, after all, a purely methodological concept and is thus valid for the physical world as well. Hence for him the problem of significance becomes a formal problem of choosing which of the endless plurality of experiential facts the scientist will single out as facts of historical science. His example: "In the year 1780, Goethe had a door bell and an apartment key made," etc., and there is "documentary proof" of this in a locksmith's bill – but this is not a "historical fact." Yet just what does comprise the historicity of a fact? Without posing and answering this question in any clearer terms (as Rickert later did, making it the focus of his systematic discussions), Windelband nevertheless takes the underlying principle of selection to be what Rickert later called *value relevance* or *relation to values*.

"Every interest and evaluatory judgment, every ascription of human value" is related to the individual and unique; thus all of our feelings of value[14] "are grounded in the uniqueness and incomparability of their object." Here he is alluding in particular to the uniqueness of personality and of a historical process in its entirety. It is "the inalienable 'metaphysical' right of historiography" to "maintain the past in its unique and unrepeatable reality" for human recollection.

Windelband says "metaphysical" because for him, the problems of metaphysics are linked with uniqueness.

I should immediately add that Rickert has carried Windelband's presentation of this point to its conclusion and supplemented it in his own fashion – namely, by introducing a distinction between *valuation or value judgment*[15] and *value relevance or relation to values*[16]. According to what Windelband says, it could seem as if in ascertaining "historical" facts by choosing facts with a more significant value, historiography itself is involved in feelings of value, or to put it even more strongly, that it would have to be partisan. But history is supposed to be non-partisan, objectively unmoved in ascertaining the facts.

According to Rickert,[17] history in the customary sense of human history deals with "human beings, their institutions, [and] their deeds," and indeed, does so "as an individualizing science of culture."[18] Culture is a title for *objects of value*. Under such subordinate titles as morals, church, law, art, economy, etc., human beings strive for objects that they value and about which they form or observe ideas of value. Thus the historian treats objects as related to values. But they are the values of the human beings with whom the historian is concerned, humans who are bearers and creators of culture. Hence the historian him/herself does not necessarily take a stance on the basis of these humans' ideals; the historian does not need to take up their values into his/her own actual feelings of value and write history from the point of view of an interested party. The historian *can* do this, and need not be partisan in the pejorative sense in doing so. Be that as it may, however, it is not necessary and essential that a historian do so.

It is the relation of the historical object to its value in a given case, then, that determines its significance, or determines what about it is a historical fact, and what is significant for the value concerned is what is individual about it. Everything else is not in question historically, and in this sense is without significance.

Rickert's transcendental theory of the correlative methodologies of the natural and the historical sciences as ways for cognition to overcome the infinite manifold[19] of the world

Rickert's[20] major work on *The Limits of Concept Formation in Natural Science* attempted in general to supplement the only short presentation Windelband made of his theory in his inaugural address as rector of the University of Strasbourg in 1894 ("History and Natural Science"), giving it a deeper systematic justification while constantly defending it against actual and possible objections. This does not yield a new theory; Rickert retains Windelband's basic framework as a whole, and his additions merely flesh out and ground Windelband's own thinking.

Especially conspicuous in this respect is the theoretical notion running through the entire work and systematically knitting it together: namely, the idea of *using the two correlative routes of generalization and historical individualization* (i.e., what Windelband calls nomothetic and idiographic work) to "overcome" the infinite manifold of the world to be known. Rickert's theory is clearly rooted in Kantian transcendental idealism; it is a modified transcendental theory. Kant proceeded from the fact of the pregiven objective sciences through which the world of experience[21] is scientifically known in an objectively valid manner. He asks how this achievement is possible. All of these sciences – in particular, mathematics and natural science, along with metaphysics insofar as it is supposedly a science – operate with *a priori* presuppositions, or even claim, as mathematics does, that they themselves hold good *a priori* for the world of experience. How, he asks, is the possibility of knowledge that is *a priori*, yet holds good for all possible experience, to be understood – and with it, the possibility of a rigorous, objectively valid scientific knowledge of the facts of this world of experience? The solution to his problem takes the form of a so-called *transcendental deduction*. That is to say, if a world is to be objectively cognizable on the basis of sensuous experience at all, this is only conceivable if this world has an intuitive formal structure deriving from the knower, if it has a conceptual structure – and if judgments about it stand under precisely those *a priori principles* of which all objective sciences make use. It is this "being provided with form"[22], then, that first makes a world of sensuous experience cognizable at all, i.e., objectively determinable for everyone.

Rickert[23] reduces this basic idea to a *formal theory* (although this formal theory is not purely carried out) – one that is, to be sure, infinitely simpler than Kant's own theory, a cross all Kantians have to bear.

He[24] takes as his starting point the given world and its extensive and intensive infinity. How can cognition overcome this double-sided infinity? Direct experience is only possible for individual objects and finite groups of such objects. But new infinities continually open up before us. Even the individual object bears within itself its own ("intensive") infinity that no experience (representation) could ever master. It is only through the concept that the "finite…human mind" can do away with or overcome the "extensive and…intensive manifold" of intuitive givens, which is "impossible to survey" as a whole. At the same time, this accomplishes a cognitive simplification of the intuitively given, a simplification that is ever greater the more general the concepts are. The concept selects particular determining moments from the fullness of the concretion as a whole. But cognition does not get very far with the intended overcoming if the concepts are *merely empirical*, drawn from intuition through abstraction based on comparison, or if it stops with *merely classificatory descriptive judgments*. Classification is necessarily confined to the intuitive surroundings, and there is no guarantee that the open infinity will always and everywhere fall into the classes found. How could we even conceive of a complete classification for an infinity that could never actually be intuitively surveyed as such? It is clear that if we can "capture" and overcome the infinity through cognition at all, this can only take place through *unconditionally general concepts and judgments:* "unconditionally general judgments" are "laws of nature." As the science whose goal is overcoming the infinite manifold through cognition, natural science has as the final goal of all its concept formations not empirical generalities, but "insight into the necessity of things" according to the "laws of nature." All of its classificatory, merely descriptive concept formations are guided by this ultimate goal; all of its summaries of characteristic features are minimum preliminary stages for those concepts "in which a necessary nexus of laws of nature comes to expression."

But even this is not enough – conceptual laws alone are not sufficient. If the laws always and everywhere holding good in unconditional generality were to consist of an open plurality of laws lacking any connection with one another, this would itself be an unsurveyable manifold, and the goal of natural-scientific cognition would not be attained. Hence the laws must comprise a system of laws that is, despite its infinity, a "surveyable series" in such a way that this series itself once again has a law of its own – a cognizable law – so that we can acquire knowledge of the totality of particular laws as a totality we can keep track of and master. Thus in the end, there lies in the essence of a natural science, and its aim of overcoming the infinite extensive and intensive manifold, a necessary striving toward an "ideal" – that of an "ultimate natural science" with "ultimate things" that no longer have anything individually intuitive about them, and that stand in a relational nexus thought in terms of absolutely valid laws of nature.

Further on we shall attempt to show that the looming possibility of an infinite manifold of shifting qualities of these ultimate things must still be overcome through the requirement that all ultimate things and their relations must be, qualitatively, absolutely of one species, and finally, must also be absolutely indivisible in quantitative terms. Thus a formal-logical consideration of the possible cognizability of the infinite manifold results in the transcendental construction of atomism and of the mechanistic conception of the world, carried out first of all for physical nature. But in essence this continues to hold good for the psychophysical world as well if this infinite world is to be cognizable at all.

Following Windelband, then, Rickert constructs – on formal methodological grounds – a *natural science* as a science that must (not contingently, but as a matter of principle) aim at the general, the lawful, if it wants to subject the infinite manifolds to the power of cognition.

At the same time, this notion opens the way toward the correlative methodology, that of *history*. Natural science designates a theoretical process from which individual concretion and intuition (for Rickert, as well as Windelband, these are equivalent) are completely purged. Individuality and intuition have completely vanished from ultimate natural science. Yet there is also a theoretical interest directed not toward overcoming the infinities, but precisely toward individuality. This too does of course have its own intensive infinity. The latter, however, does not need to be overcome if the theoretical interest is constrained by a principle of selection that is necessary rather than arbitrary – and this is the principle of value relevance, of relation to values.

As clever and impressive as Rickert's theoretical foundation is, it arouses serious doubts. Formal constructions of this type are quite dangerous, for the evidence that initially makes them seem obvious may very well be specious. Our only defense is to ascend, in rigorously ordered processes, from the most concrete intuition to the abstractions arising in the course of the construction. This takes a genuinely concrete epistemology, or better, a phenomenological foundation that draws these lofty formal generalities from their intuitive origins.

Here I can merely suggest some readily accessible points for critique. First of all, in my opinion, Rickert violates the pure style of the transcendental deduction by importing a *pragmatic tendency* (in a broadened sense) into his concept formation, although in contrast to the usual pragmatism concerned with the utility of customary *praxis*, he is carrying out a theoretical pragmatism. In the broader sense, theory too is indeed a *praxis*; generalizing, forming concepts and laws, and ultimately producing exact, completely non-intuitive concepts as well as strict laws of nature are to be the *means* to make the infinite cognizable. But we could now say: must the infinite do us the favor of complying with our conceptual products, of being cognizable via concepts and laws? Why would the infinite world have to be concerned with our cognitive interests and requirements at all?

A conceptually *calculable* world may certainly suit us. And we may see that this presupposes the possibility of constructing a complete set of rigorous laws with correspondingly rigorous concepts. But why would the world have to do us the favor of corresponding to a mechanistic ideal? In the end, it doesn't do so at all. Moreover, has it actually been made evident that a scientifically cognizable world would have to be conceptually calculable *idealiter* in every detail? Is the mechanistic ideal perhaps only valid for the physical world-structure, and countersensical beyond this?

One thing first of all: the discussion cannot be allowed to proceed as if what is meant here is that an infinity exists, but would not be cognizable if it did not stand under concepts and laws – hence it must stand under them. The deduction may not proceed as though concepts were merely useful instruments for us finite human beings to be able to realize the goal of attaining knowledge of a world that obviously exists in advance, as though there were somehow a world truly existing for us cognitive subjects prior to cognition, and again, as though something like cognition somehow already had its own goal in advance, prior to such instrumental arrangements.

Cognition, theoretical cognition, aims at objective truth, at ascertaining what any cognitive subject can ascertain with insight as truly existing, and can do so equally well as any other cognitive subject. Cognition of any sort is unthinkable without both *intuition* and *concept* – which means first of all that it is not conceivable without some relation to a preceding experience. But mere experience does not ascertain anything objectively; the judicative legitimation achieved by cognition is necessarily carried out in concepts. When cognition truly and conceptually ascertains the being and being-thus of an entity, however, this very entity is itself conceptual. Concepts are not merely the affair of us cognitive subjects, and the entity does not exist in itself with all concepts foreign to it. Furthermore, when conceptual cognition brings us insight into laws, we are not legislators who provide these laws for things that have no laws in themselves; instead, the laws belong to the world itself as an existing world, and in their being they are inseparable from this world.

And there is still more to say in connection with these insights (which are themselves drawn from a concrete eidetic investigation of cognition). One cannot begin with a world of infinite manifolds existing in itself prior to cognition – indeed, a world that is still completely unknown – in order to inquire afterwards into the subjective means through which subjective human interests termed "theoretical" are to be satisfied: a world existing in itself with infinite manifolds of ontic determinations existing in themselves first has any possible ontic sense at all through certain performances that are cognitive performances. The true being of such a world means nothing other than its correlative *cognizability in principle*.

Perhaps one will object that things – and an entire infinity of things – can still be given through sheer experience (individual and communal experience), even for animals and prescientific human beings. But we must now attend to what this means, and what in fact comprises and maintains its good sense.

Critique of Rickert's construction of formal requirements by confronting it with Kant's procedure. The necessary task of an exploration of experience and of the essential correlation between the world of experience and the scientifically true world

In the final classes before the break, we were dealing with Windelband's theory, which attempts to replace the contentual contrast between nature and mind with a methodological distinction that can more properly be designated as a contrast between nature and history. The methodological idea of nature determines the specific character of all those sciences that are accordingly to be termed natural sciences. They are nomothetic; they aim toward the general, the lawful. In contrast, the historical sciences are directed toward the unique, the individual, aiming to present it in its unique reality; they are idiographic. Seen in terms of content, however, the same objects and provinces of objects can be subjected not only to nomothetic but also to idiographic method, becoming themes for the natural sciences in the one case and the historical sciences in the other. We can thus say with Windelband that everything has its nature and everything has its history.

Rickert's comprehensive systematic justification of Windelband's theory speaks of generalizing and individualizing method or concept formation. As we indicated, he outlined a type of transcendental theory arguing for the necessity of this most fundamental contrast, which necessarily runs through our entire world-cognition and must be decisive for any theory of science.

How can our cognition overcome the infinite manifolds of the world? With sheer experience, we are entangled in external and internal infinities. We are led *in infinitum* from single particulars to single particulars, from objects to ever new objects, and with the same object, from features to ever new features. If the finite human mind is to overcome these infinities, this is only possible through concepts and laws. Instead of focusing ad infinitum on the individual and pursuing the unreachable goal of an exhaustive determination of it, the mind directs its gaze toward the general, toward what is everywhere the same. It begins with descriptive-classificatory concept formation. But this does not truly overcome the infinities completely, since we are once again caught in open infinities. For it to be possible to overcome the infinities, we must overcome the merely descriptive classification by searching for rigorous laws. Entailed in this is the following: if the striving for cognition is not to be aimless, if it is going to be possible to overcome the infinite manifolds, then the world must be a rigorously lawful world. But even this is still not sufficient – there could be infinitely many laws with no relation to one another, lacking any systematic unity. If overcoming infinities is truly to be the goal – or (which for Rickert is the same thing) if a cognition of the world is to be possible – then the infinite manifolds of laws must themselves be encompassed by one single, cognizable set of laws. This is how the necessary ideal of ultimate natural science arises. It must likewise follow from this that all of the objects in the world not only stand under this set of laws, but must be of a single type as far as their qualities are concerned, and must ultimately be quantitatively indivisible. This is the ideal of ultimate objects.

In the end, this deduction can be summarized in the following result. If it is to be possible to overcome the infinite manifold of the world, then the world must be the world of determinism: a world that is cognizable absolutely rigorously on the basis of a single, fundamental set of exact laws. Moreover, it must correspond – in a psychic as well as a physical respect – to precisely the atomistic-mechanistic ideal that has guided classical physics since Galileo, an ideal that this physics has continued to develop, even if only with respect to the physical side of the world. It is certainly the case that modern science has not been as successful with the psychic side. But here too it is necessary to maintain the ideal of an ultimate science of laws and of ultimate psychic objects conceived in analogy to physical atoms: the psychic as given in intuitive experience must be substructively replaced with ultimate non-intuitive elements – the so-called sensations.

Thus the task of the natural sciences (or taken together, of a universal natural science, a natural science related to the universe) is deduced as a task that must necessarily be undertaken if any cognition that can overcome the infinities of the world is to be possible at all. We can even say that natural science is defined as a science that has this overcoming as its goal. And the method deduced *a priori* from this goal – the method of progressive, stepwise generalization – provides the definition for natural-scientific method, accounting for the methodological commonality of the various sorts of sciences of physical and psychophysical nature.

Everywhere the descriptive disciplines – e.g., those of natural history, or on the psychic side, descriptive psychology, as well as the morphology of concrete human characters (characterology) – are mere subordinate levels, transitional stages toward the corresponding exact sciences: ultimate natural science is always the guiding aim at every moment.

One of the main ideas running throughout this deduction is that natural-scientific method does indeed proceed from experience, from concrete intuition, but as it progresses to ever higher abstractions that are ever more empty of content, it becomes ever more distant from the intuitive concretion. For Rickert, this is equivalent to being ever more distant from individuals. For him, *generalization* is *de-individualization*, since he also takes natural-scientific method to be uninterested in the individual from the very beginning; instead, it is exclusively interested in generalities.

Can there be yet another science besides natural science, one whose goal is the individual, the unique? As we have seen, Rickert's response (which here too essentially follows Windelband) is his theory of the "limits" of natural-scientific method, or – which is the same thing – his theory of value relevance, of relation to values. Objects need not be of interest as natural objects, i.e., the goal does not have to be cognitive mastery of the infinite manifolds lying in them. The infinity is immediately restricted when an object or a sphere of objects touches our feelings through its individual particularity. It is of value to us as this individual or is related to a pregiven universal value, as when we consider our surrounding world in terms of universally valid values of art, state, religion, etc. – i.e., as "related to values." It is only when all of the value-interests pertaining to the matters themselves (presented as individuals) remain out of play, or are deliberately set out of play, that overcoming infinities arises as the sole remaining interest. And this is the natural-scientific interest, or in other words, the interest *in infinitum* to determine the objective entity as it is, irrespective of its value. *Nature is the world considered as value-free*. As soon as the world is considered from the point of view of values, new scientific goals arise – those of history.

We had already begun to formulate our *objections* to a theory that is so beautifully crafted, yet on closer examination less satisfactory. Our objections first of all concerned such a seemingly radical justification of natural-scientific methodology, a justification that we characterized as a modification of Kant's transcendental methodology.

In his work, Rickert repeatedly mentions that there is no reason for his scientific-theoretic deduction to take epistemological issues into consideration. But for my part, I do not understand how such a deduction could be possible – and could be grounded – any way other than epistemologically. Kant's transcendental deductions are of this type. As genuinely epistemological, they move within the framework of a concrete, although universal, consideration of our experience and our world of experience, as well as of our sciences of this world of experience – sciences like mathematics and natural science, which are capable of actually evident achievements, or sciences such as metaphysics, which merely pretend to produce such achievements. Here – thus always remaining within the framework of a concrete total intuition – is where Kant poses his questions and outlines his deductions.

We believe that what we are experiencing is the existing world; it seems that all we have to do is to bring something we already have to "expression" through description in descriptive concepts, judgments, statements. Yet *experience needs thinking*, an entirely different kind of thinking: in order to grasp what is experienced in its *true being*, experience needs *objective science*. What does the latter accomplish? How are we to understand the cognition arising through science as a labor of the human mind – a cognition of the being of the world, of its being and being-thus in "objective" truth? How are we to understand that a science of the world is tied *a priori* to a certain set of fundamental concepts – fundamental concepts and judgments that "precede" experience and prescribe a norm for it?

We can only experience an objective world in universal experience, we can only say that it is objectively valid, when scientific thinking can be built up on the basis of experience in such a way that for every member of the cognitive community, it becomes evident with compelling validity that what is merely intuited, without concepts, in the experience in question, and brought to expression via description, is not objective as described. This experience is nevertheless the basis upon which the cognitive achievement of science first exhibits, discloses, and displays the *"objectively"* true being lying in what is intuitively experienced. That experience can support "scientific" thinking is the only thing that allows an "objective" truth-content – objectively true being under the title of "world" – to be ascribed to it. But when is experience able to support scientific thinking, and conversely, when is a thinking truly scientific, truly disclosing objectively valid experiential truths? Are not the conditions for the possibility of such experiential cognition expressed in the fundamental *a priori* concepts of genuine science? And what forms must experience itself take with respect to the world of intuitively experienced things in order for this world to be conceptually, judicatively graspable in accordance with scientific truth, etc. – graspable as objective, as valid in itself?

Kant proceeds in this way, leading us to see that an existing world is not a fact given in advance in someone's sheer experience. Nor is the cognitive activity of science some kind of subsequent fiddling around with this fact – one that would merely construct a more complete (individual or general) picture of the real world itself than prescientific experience can afford us. Instead, he provides the insight that the world that exists for us only exists for us at all in our cognition; it is nothing other for us than what is formed in our experience and our thinking under the title of objective cognition. The objectively *true* world is then an ideal to be exhibited, in us and for us, as legitimately true with intersubjectively valid necessity: it is not a contingent individual matter, but is given in insight in cognitive communalization.

Kant does indeed take as his point of departure the fact of universal experience and the science of experience, and the naive validity with which we accept them. However, since he is inquiring into the sense and the possibility in principle of this fact (and of any such fact whatsoever as a possibility), the fact loses the character of an abiding presupposition holding good without question; the task of making its possibility in principle comprehensible leads to its being "bracketed."

As for Rickert, he presupposes the world as a pregiven fact – one that remains in ontic acceptance for him – and begins by pointing to the extensive and intensive infinities in which our direct experiential cognition are entangled. His basic question is then: how can we finite human beings overcome these infinities through cognition? As we heard, Rickert deduces ever new requirements that must be fulfilled for the possibility of overcoming such infinities.

Against this we raised the following objection: why must the world care about our requirements? Perhaps what we perceive of it, and whatever we can ever intuitively experience of it, is merely contingent, and can only be grasped in descriptive classifications of the sphere of experience closest to us. Perhaps the matter rests there; perhaps there are no unconditionally general natural laws at all, and certainly no ultimate natural science with ultimate objects in the sense of an atomistic-mechanistic ideal of nature.

We do of course have a Galilean physics, which in its further development as so-called "classical physics" does presuppose such an ideal and has continued to work it out with great success. But this certainly did not happen on the basis of formal cognitive requirements that were imposed upon the experiential world so that we could "overcome" it. Instead, it was being immersed in researching the character of the experiential world, with its concrete-general contents, that impelled natural scientists toward their own ideal formations. And this eventually made them aware of the ideal itself as the ideal point of intersection, as it were, of their concrete, and methodologically informed, cognitive labors. Natural science thus arose in the naiveté of a life of experience and thought that is concretely directed toward nature.

As a philosopher, Kant adopted a higher vantage point from which he could survey the typical universality of this life. From this standpoint he posed questions of his own that were still relevant to concrete understanding, but concerned a deeper sense and possibility of its achievements and of the legitimacy of its goals and its universal normative ideals. Rickert, however, leaves concrete life and science behind, posing formal requirements and constructing formal necessities with the goal of cognitively overcoming infinities. This construction is indeed nominally related to the world of our actual and possible experience, but even the very idea that it is the world of possible experience is not concretely drawn from experience itself.

Nominally, Rickert's construction relates to the world that has attained its individually determined ontic sense from our actual and possible experience, and continues to attain ever new ontic sense while concordantly preserving its sense-structure. That this ontic sense is experientially verifiable for anyone (and for us communally), and that it simply lies ready to be read off from the world, is never placed in question. But this very constitution of the world of experience as our common world – as a world with a concrete experiential sense that is constituted and confirmed for us individually and as a community – is itself never taken into consideration philosophically. In other words, the world as, first of all, a unitary experiential sense (and unitary across every structural form and manifold) remains unquestioned – or rather, what remains unquestioned and unexplored is the universal experiencing life as the life constituting this sense of unity (or as we are also accustomed to say, as bringing about the concordant, sense-bestowing, synthetic achievement of sense).

Thus "world-experience" remains an empty word whose concrete ontic sense has never been explicated or clarified with insight, and any requirement set for this emptily thought world is accordingly an empty requirement. This is carried over to a higher level that must necessarily be distinguished, the level specifically explored by Kant: how does thinking overcome the relativity of sensuous experience? Or how is it to be understood that experience, in its infinitely various possible experiences and possible experiential syntheses, bears within itself a true world as an (objective) world "in itself," one that is "definitively" and "scientifically" true? When are we to understand that experience does this, and what the conditions of possibility are for it doing this? What achievement can come about from the side of thinking, of scientific theorizing, and if this is to be an achievement of the form, "truth in itself" along with "being in itself" (being objective), what distinctive governing rules are implied for the universal structure of the experience in which all individual experience is unified into intersubjectively concordant experience? What governing rules of objective experience (i.e., an experience in which objectivity is legitimately demonstrated, or for which a theoretical achievement must be effected as its basis) are expressed in the basic forms of objective theory, and expressed in a particular manner for each region of being, as "categories" of objectivity and fundamental categorial axioms? Or even: the experiential unity, world (the sensuous, everyday world), is supposed to bear a scientifically true world within itself, one that is "logically" determinable, objectively determinable in a scientific manner. The world of experience (of experience in the common sense) is supposed to be able to be "made logical," and experience in the common sense is supposed to be scientific experience (i.e., a *logos*). Such experience would not merely aim at true being in a vaguely anticipatory way; instead, the universality of possible experiences bears true being within itself throughout and "*a priori*," as necessarily making scientific determination possible by virtue of the universal structure of this experience. The sensuous world in its presumptivity is supposed to be a legitimate anticipation of a true world – a world that is true in a logically exact sense. How and when is this to be understood? What essential structures pertain to the correlation between the sensuous world (appearance) and the true world (science)?

What really remains *entirely unquestioned* in Rickert's systematic deductions is the *essential sort of experience* (and the thinking that is to refer to it) through which the world has a concretely determined sense for us, a sense through which it is not an empty infinite manifold. Instead, this world, with such-and-such sense-structures pertaining to it *a priori*, is the only meaningful world we have. Rickert does indeed speak of physical and psychophysical nature, of space, time, and causality; he likewise speaks of things in their infinity of progressive qualitative and quantitative experience, of describing them, of the formation of exact concepts, of inquiry into laws – but all this in an empty formal manner that is far removed from the matters concerned.

If rational cognitive requirements that are valid *a priori* are to be placed on the world, and are to be deduced in their validity, we would still *first* concretely have to *show that* the only meaningful world for us – the world of our experience and of the theoretical thinking that gradually discloses it – poses these requirements to our cognition; that it does so because it is itself, precisely as what it is, a world of experience and cognition; and that as such a world, it has certain intuitively demonstrable structures that constrain us, thus placing requirements on our predicative thinking. In other words, we must carry out an intuitive exploration of the essential correlation between the world of experience and the world of scientific truth in their concrete-universal structures. We must give the word "world" its full, concrete sense and show that an infinite manifold of this essential sort ("world") can only be cognitively actualized as "true" and existing in the "objective" sense in such-and-such forms of cognition, in sciences of such-and-such methodological forms. Then the requirements to be posed for rational cognition are not merely something we arrive at by empty formal deduction once we are determined to overcome infinite manifolds, without ever asking whether their sense allows such an overcoming. Instead, the requirements to be posed are those that *the world itself* (and first of all, the sensuous world) *places upon us* through the sense proper to it, to the extent that this first original sense (the sensuous world) intrinsically has its own possibilities of, and tendencies toward, idealization as "objective." But the sense proper to the world is first of all nothing other than the sense that confronts us as experiencers, in the concordance of our experience, as the intuitive presumption of an existing world – a sense that is to be theoretically disclosed in new sense-bestowing idealization taking the forms of predicative truth and science, a sense that is to be constituted by us as theorizing cognitive subjects in specific cognitive labor. We must therefore bear in mind that the being of the world, which was taken as a matter of course right at the beginning and remained unquestioned, has, as we can easily see, a thoroughly presumptive character.

It is only by proceeding in this way, hence only by proceeding epistemologically in the genuine sense, that we can deduce the radical norms and forms of a possible science of the world and of an existing world as its correlate. This is essentially the path that Kant was the first to embark on. And even if we cannot follow him completely, this is only because he had not yet found a sufficiently concrete-intuitive way in which to explore the world in its correlation with the subjectivity that lives in and knows the world.

Notes

1. Edmund Husserl, *Natur und Geist. Vorlesungen Sommersemester 1927.* Ed. Michael Weiler. *Husserliana* 32. Dordrecht: Kluwer Academic Publishers, 2001 (subsequently cited as Hua 32), pp. 78–102. Translated into English for the first time by Elizabeth A. Behnke. – Ed.

    As the editor of Hua 32 points out (p. xvi), these lectures offer what may well be Husserl's most explicit philosophical critique of the work of Wilhelm Windelband (1848–1915) and Heinrich Rickert (1863–1936). The selection translated here (§§15–16) comes from Part I ("The philosophical problem of a classification of the sciences"), Chapter 3: "Material-contentual *(sachhaltigen)* classifications of the sciences" (§§13–16). Section titles within pointed brackets, as well as notes identified with the abbreviation "Hua Ed.," have been supplied by the editor of Hua 32. –Trans.

2. "*Geist*" is typically translated as "mental" below, but as is usual, it is always translated as "human" in the term "*Geisteswissenschaften*" (human sciences), where "*Geist*" refers to the sphere of human cultural meanings in general—Trans.

3. On §§15–16, cf. Supplement XVII: "On the critique of the 'matter of course' presupposition of the opposition between a science of laws and a science of individuals. Contra Rickert-Windelband" (Hua 32, pp. 224–229); on §15, cf. Supplement XVIII: "Comments on excerpts from Rickert's texts" (Hua 32, pp. 230–233)—Hua Ed.

4. In §13, Husserl moves beyond the classification of the sciences in sheerly formal terms (the topic he treated in Chapter 2) and distinguishes classifications based upon the regions of the world that become their provinces from classifications based upon method. In §14, he addresses the first of these tendencies, using as his example the Cartesian dualism that divides realities into two classes—"physical" and "psychic"—and pointing out that the sciences based on this division take it for granted that "science" means "objective science," purified from anything "merely subjective"; the "mind" or "psyche" is then unreflectively assumed to be analogous to physical realities, so that the goals and methods of a science of physical nature come to be applied to a "naturalized" subjectivity as well.—Trans.

5. In what follows, Husserl is for the most part paraphrasing Wilhelm Windelband's inaugural address as Rector of the University of Straßburg (1 May 1894): *Geschichte und Naturwissenschaft. Rede zum Antritt des Rektorats der Kaiser-Wilhelms-Universität Straßburg* (2nd, unaltered ed., Straßburg, 1900); see "History and Natural Science," in the present volume—Trans.

6. "*Geisteswissenschaften*"

7. *Geist*

8. Here Husserl is referring to Theodor Waitz, *Lehrbuch der Psychologie als Naturwissenschaft* (Braunschweig, 1849)—Hua Ed.

9. *Geist*

10. Cf. Windelband 1900, p. 10 – Ed. (= 1980, p. 174/reprinted in this volume as text above; the point about the name of the historical sciences refers to the etymological link between *Geschichte* [history] and *Geschehen* [events]—Trans.).

11. *Immergleichen*

12. *Geisteswissenschaft*

13. *Geisteshistorischen*

14. *Wertgefühle*

15. *Wertung*

16. *Wertbeziehung*

17. Here Husserl is referring to Heinrich Rickert, "Geschichtsphilosophie," in *Die Philosophie im Beginn des zwanzigsten Jahrhunderts*, ed. Wilhelm Windelband, 2nd rev. and enl. ed. (Heidelberg, 1907), pp. 321–422; in what follows, he refers above all to Rickert's *Die Grenzen der*

> *naturwissenschaftlichen Begriffsbildung. Eine logische Einleitung in die historischen Wissenschaften*, 2nd rev. ed. (Tübingen: Mohr, 1913); see Hua 32, p. xiv—Hua Ed.
18   Cf. Rickert 1907, p. 370; with regard to this paragraph and the next, cf. also Rickert 1913/1986, Ch. 4, "Concept Formation in History"—Hua Ed.
19   Husserl scholars normally translate "*Mannigfaltigkeit*" and "*Mannigfaltigkeiten*" as "multiplicity" and "multiplicities"; given the Kantian background of Rickert's discussion, however, here the singular and plural forms of the noun "manifold" will be used instead (as in the English version of Rickert's work), even though what is at stake is precisely an infinite multiplicity of possible experiential givens—Trans.
20   Rickert's transcendental deduction [Husserl's marginal title—Trans.].
21   For the sake of consistency, the word "*Erfahrung*" and its cognates will be translated throughout by "experience" and its cognates; hence in the present case, the phrase reads "world of experience" rather than "empirical world." This is not only to preserve Husserl's rich and distinctive sense of the term "experience," but to forestall any possible misunderstandings based on Kant's and Husserl's different approaches to key philosophical distinctions: whereas the typical Kantian contrast is that between the "transcendental" and the "empirical," Husserl contrasts the empirical with the eidetic (essential) and the transcendental with the mundane. In the present text, "empirical" always translates Husserl's "*empirisch*"—Trans.
22   *Formung*
23   Rickert's transcendental theory of natural-scientific methodology [Husserl's marginal title—Trans.].
24   In what follows, Husserl paraphrases part of Ch. 1, "Conceptual Knowledge of the Conceptual World," from Rickert 1913, especially pp. 30–118—Hua Ed.

Introduction

Martin Heidegger (1889–1976) and Ernst Cassirer

THE DAVOS DISPUTE BETWEEN HEIDEGGER AND CASSIRER – an up and coming German philosopher who was to become a leading Nazi philosopher in 1933 and the established "Olympian" philosopher of Jewish origin – has taken on an almost mythical place in twentieth-century philosophy. There is probably no historical event that has been considered more important than this "faceoff" (cf. the authoritative account by Gordon 2010) due to this historic constellation. The *Davoser Hochschultage* were an annual event, and in 1929 it was dedicated to the philosophy of Kant, and hence the two leading philosophers of Germany had been invited to present their views on Kant at this year's venue. Both Cassirer and Heidegger, however, used this meeting to showcase their own philosophies. According to most accounts, the atmosphere was friendly and professional, and both philosophers had met several times before and were on friendly terms. Also, to both of them, this event did not seem overly important and neither reported to having "gotten" much out of it. Indeed, knowing their respective philosophies, what both offer here is more or less a summary of their own thoughts. Hence, this meeting would by no means have become as important as it has become in hindsight, after the events taking place as of 1933, when Heidegger assumed the presidency of the University of Freiburg and publicly joined the Nazi party, and Cassirer left Germany, preempting his certain dismissal, to spend the rest of his life in exile. Although Cassirer was to continue publishing after 1933 and Heidegger had yet to perform his famous *Kehre*, this dispute deserves to be the final coda of this volume. For at the time, it appeared to many listeners that an era had come to an end – the era of Neo-Kantianism – and a new one began, both philosophically as well as politically. As of this time, it is true, Neo-Kantianism ceased to be considered a living philosophical movement, while newer philosophical trends flooded the scene.

Philosophically, it is worth pointing out that Cassirer is, as always, the more conciliatory philosopher when he tries to frame their opposition merely in terms of emphasis and direction. In Cassirer's presentation, both agree on the finite factical existence of the human being; but they differ in that, to Heidegger, this is the *terminus ad quem* of his thinking: it is the goal to be achieved in gaining an understanding of what the human being really consists in. Cassirer acknowledges the finite *Dasein* as a starting point, as a *terminus a quo*, but the *terminus ad quem* is, to him, the world of symbolic formation of which finite Dasein can partake in order to leave behind the shackles of finitude and mortality. Heidegger is perhaps more radical in his assessment of their respective difference, when he claims that there *is* no place in Cassirer's thought for what Heidegger calls "*Dasein.*" In other words, Heidegger criticizes Cassirer for neglecting to account for the individual in the universe of symbolic formation. This debate leads Heidegger to compose his *Kant and the Problem of Metaphysics*, to appear later in that year, which is perhaps one of the most curious Kant interpretations, since Heidegger uses Kant himself as the one raising the issue of, but in the end recoiling from, human finitude. Whether or not one will find this interpretation convincing, it is beyond a doubt that Heidegger's Kant interpretation is meant to refute the prevailing Kant interpretation on the part of the Neo-Kantians, of whom Cassirer was one of the last living defenders.

Further Reading

Friedman, Michael., *A Parting of Ways: Carnap, Cassirer, and Heidegger*. Chicago: Open Court Publishing, 2000.

Gordon, Peter Eli., *Continental Divide: Heidegger, Cassirer, Davos*. Cambridge/Mass.: Harvard University Press, 2010.

Lynch, Dennis A., "Ernst Cassirer and Martin Heidegger: The Davos Debate." in: *Kant-Studien* 81.3, 1990, pp. 360–370.

Chapter 33

The Davos Dispute (1929)[1]

Cassirer: What does Heidegger understand by Neo-Kantianism? Who is the opponent whom Heidegger has in mind? The concept "Neo-Kantianism" must not be defined substantially, but functionally. What is at issue is not the character of that philosophy as a dogmatic doctrinal system, but a way of formulating the question.

Heidegger: If I am to begin by naming names, I will mention Cohen, Windelband, Rickert, Erdmann, Riehl. What is common to every form of Neo-Kantianism can only be understood in terms of its origin. This is the embarrassing dilemma of philosophy before the question of what still really remains to it [as a field of inquiry][2] within the totality of knowledge. There appeared to remain only the knowledge about science, not of "that-which-is"[3]. It was this point of view that defined the movement back to Kant. Kant was seen as the theoretician of the mathematico-physical theory of natural science, but to show the problematic of metaphysics, more specifically of ontology. My intention is to work this essential content of the positive basis of the *Critique of Pure Reason* into ontology. By reason of my interpretation of the Dialectic as ontology, I believe that the problem of Being[4] in the Transcendental Logic, seemingly only negative in Kant, is really a positive problem.

Cassirer: Cohen is only understood correctly if he is understood historically, not simply as an epistemologist. I do not conceive of my own development as a defection from Cohen. The positioning of the mathematical sciences of nature is for me only a paradigm, not the whole of the problem. – Heidegger and I are in agreement on one point: for Kant the productive imagination is of central significance. I have been led to this through my work on the symbolic. The imagination is the relation of all thinking to intuition, *synthesis speciosa*. The synthesis is the fundamental power of pure thought. What matters for Kant is the synthesis which makes use of the species. And this leads to the heart of the image-concept,[5] of the symbol-concept. – Kant's major problem is how is freedom possible. Kant says that we conceive only that freedom is inconceivable. And yet there is the Kantian ethics. The categorical imperative ought to be such that the moral law holds not only for men, but all rational beings in general. The moral as such leads beyond the world of appearances. What is at stake here is the breakthrough to the *mundus intelligibilis*. In the ethical realm a point is reached which is no longer relative to the finitude of the cognizing being. – And this ties in with what Heidegger has done. The extraordinary importance of the schematism cannot be overestimated. Yet in the ethical realm Kant suppresses the schematism. For he says our concepts are "senses of..."[6] (not cognitions), "senses of..." which can no longer be schematized. There is at most a typology, not a schematism, of Practical Reason. For Kant the schematism is a *terminus a quo*, not a *terminus ad quem*. Kant's point of departure is the problem posed by Heidegger. However, the circle widened for Kant. Heidegger has made the point that our cognitive power is finite. It is relative and confined. But how does such a finite being attain knowledge, reason, truth? – Heidegger formulates the problem of truth and says there cannot be any truths in themselves, or eternal truths, but truths are always relative to *Dasein*. For Kant, on the other hand, this was exactly the problem. Granted this finitude, how can there be necessary and universal truths? How are synthetic *a priori* possible? That is the problem which Kant exemplifies with mathematics. Finite cognition involves itself with truth, but this relationship again works into a "merely" [i.e., is qualified] (?) Heidegger has said that Kant has given no demonstration of the possibility of mathematics. But this problem is posed in the *Prolegomena*. Once more, then, this pure theoretical question, how does a finite being come to a determination of objects which as such are not limited by finitude, must first of all be clarified. – My question now is this: Does Heidegger wish to renounce this complete objectivity, this form of absoluteness, which Kant has stood for in the realms of the ethical and the theoretical and in the *Critique of Judgment*?

Heidegger: To begin with the question of the mathematical sciences of nature. In Kant, nature does not mean an object of the mathematical science of nature, but rather the totality of "that-which-is" in the sense of the present-at-hand[7]. Kant means "that-which-is" as such without limitation to a determinate area of "that-which-is." What I want to show is that the Analytic is not an ontology of nature as object of natural science, but a general ontology, that is, a critically based *metaphysica generalis*. Kant himself says that the problematic of the *Prolegomena* is not the central theme. This is, rather, the question concerning the possibility of a *metaphysica generalis*, more exactly, of its realization. – Cassirer wants to show further that finitude is transcended in the ethical writings. There is something in the categorical imperative which exceeds the finite being. Yet precisely the concept of imperative displays in itself the inner relation to a finite being. Even this transcendence still remains within itself and cannot escape from itself into an eternal and absolute of practical reason. One goes astray in the interpretation of the Kantian ethics if one does not see the inner function of the Law for *Dasein*. Certainly there is something in the moral law which goes beyond sensibility. However, the question is, What is the character of the inner structure of *Dasein* itself? Is this structure finite or infinite? There lies in this question a really central problem. Just in that which one puts forward as constitutive infinity, the character of the finite comes to light. Kant designates the imagination of the schematism as *exhibitio originaria*. This power of origination is, it is true, in a certain way, a creative power there, but as *exhibitio* it cannot dispense with receptivity. Man is never infinite and absolute in the creation of "that-which-is" itself[8], but he is infinite in the sense of the understanding of Being[9]. This infinity of the ontological is by its very nature bound to ontic experience, so that one must say just the opposite: this infinity which breaks forth in the imagination is precisely the most acute argument for finitude. Ontology is an index of finitude. God does not have it. [i.e., ontology] – Thereupon Cassirer's next question with reference to the concept of truth arises. At the most profound level truth itself is at one with the structure of transcendence through the fact that *Dasein* is "something-which-is" which is open to other "things-which-are" and to itself. We are "something-which-is" that keeps itself in the unhiddenness of "that-which-is." To keep oneself in this way in the openness of "that-which-is" is what I call Being-in-the-truth[10]. And I go further. Because of its finitude man's Being-in-the-truth is at the same time a Being-in-the-untruth. Untruth belongs to the inmost core of *Dasein*. I believe that I have found only here the root which establishes a metaphysical explanation for what Kant called "metaphysical illusion," – To take Cassirer's question concerning universally valid eternal truths. When I say truth is relative to *Dasein*, that is no ontic statement in the sense that what is true is always only what the individual man thinks. The proposition is metaphysical. Truth as such can only be as truth if *Dasein* exists. Only with the existence of something such as *Dasein* does truth first come about. But now to the question: What about the validity, the eternity of truth? One commonly formulates this question in terms of the problem of validity, i.e., in terms of the asserted proposition. The problem must be broached differently. Truth is relative to *Dasein*. The transsubjectivity of truth, this breaking-out of truth beyond the individual, signifies the Being-in-the-truth means to be given over to and to be taken up with "that-which-is." What can here be separated as objective knowledge, taking into account the particular matter-of-fact individual existence, has a truth content which says something about "that-which-is." This is however, badly interpreted if it is said that over against the flow of experience there is something permanent, the eternal, the meaning and concept. At this point, then, I pose the question: What does eternal really mean here? Is this eternity not merely permanence in the sense of the *aei* [the "forever"] of time? Is it possible only by reason of an inner transcendence of time itself? What do all those expressions of transcendental metaphysics, *a priori, aei on, ousia*, mean? They are only to be understood and are only possible through the fact that time itself has the character of horizon, so that I have always conjointly in an anticipatory remembering stance, a horizon of present, futurity, and pastness, and, consequently, there is given a transcendental-ontological time determination within which alone something such as the permanence of substance is constituted. – My entire interpretation of temporality is to be understood from this point of view. The whole problematic in *Sein und Zeit*, which treats of the *Dasein* of man, is no philosophical anthropology. It is much too limited and much too sketchy for that. Here there is a problematic which has not as such hitherto been broached. The question [of *Sein und Zeit*] is in terms of this. The analysis of death is intended to expose in one direction *Dasein*'s radical futurity, and not to furnish a final and metaphysical teaching concerning the essence of death. The analysis of dread[11] has the sole function of preparing the question: On the basis of what metaphysical meaning of *Dasein* itself is it possible that man as such can be put before such a thing as Nothing[12]? Only if I understand Nothing or Dread do I have the possibility of understanding Being. Only in the unity of the understanding of Being and Nothing does the question of the origin of the "why" suddenly arise. The central problem of Being, of Nothing, and of the Why, is the most elementary, the most concrete problem. The entire Analytic of *Dasein* is directed toward this. At the same time I pose a further question of method. In what way must a metaphysics of *Dasein* be initiated? Is there not a definite over-all view of life[13] at its basis? It is not the task of philosophy to provide such an over-all view of life, though certainly such a view is already the presupposition of the activity of philosophizing. The over-all view of life which the philosopher provides is not a direct one in the sense of doctrine, but rests in this, that in the act of philosophizing it comes about that the transcendence of *Dasein* itself, i.e., the inner possibility possessed by this finite being to be in relation to "that-which-is" in its totality, is made radical. The question, how is freedom possible, does not make sense because freedom is not an object of theoretical comprehension, but an object of the act of philosophizing. That can mean nothing else than that freedom is, and can only be, in the act of freeing. The sole adequate relation which man has to freedom is [in terms of] the act by which freedom sets itself free in man.

Questions Addressed to Cassirer (by a student of philosophy)

1) What way can man find to infinity? In what fashion can man participate in infinity?
2) Is infinity to be achieved as a privative determination of finitude, or is it a domain in its own right?
3) To what extent should it be the task of philosophy to effect a liberation from dread, or is it its task to hand man over quite radically to dread?

Cassirer: Ad 1. In no other way than through the medium of Form. The function of Form is such that man, while he changes his existence[14] into Form, i.e., while he has to transform everything which is in him as experience into some kind of objective structure, does not, it is true, thereby become radically freed from the finitude of the point of departure (for this is still definitely related to his finitude), but insofar as his existence develops out of finitude, his existence leads finitude out of itself into something new, immanent infinity. Man cannot make the jump out of his own finitude into a realistically understood infinity. However, he can have, and must have, a *metabasis* which leads him from the immediacy of his own existence into the region of pure Form. "From the chalice of this realm of spirits, infinity pours forth for him."[15] The realm of spirits is not a metaphysical realm of spirits. The realm of spirits is just that spiritual world which he himself has created. That he could create it is the seal of his infinity. – Ad 2. It is not only a privative determination, but is a domain in its own right. Not, however, a domain that is won only in conflict with finitude, but rather infinity is precisely the totality, the perfect fulfillment of finitude itself. And this fulfillment of finitude is just what constitutes infinity. Thus Goethe's "Wouldst thou stride into the infinite, thou hast but to go in the finite in every direction."[16] Ad 3. That is a question which goes right to the roots, and one can answer it only with a kind of profession of faith. Philosophy has allowed man to become free just so far as he can become free. Thereby it frees him radically, to be sure, from dread as a pure state of feeling. The aim is liberation in this sense: "Cast the anxiety of the terrestrial from yourselves." That is the position of Idealism which I have myself always professed.

Heidegger: In his first lecture Cassirer has used the expressions *terminus a quo* and *terminus ad quem*. One could say that the *terminus ad quem* is a complete Philosophy of Culture in the sense of clarification of the wholeness of the Form of a structure-creating consciousness. The *terminus a quo* in Cassirer is completely problematical. My position is the opposite: the *terminus a quo* is my central problematic. The question is whether the *terminus ad quem* is just as clear for me. This, I hold, consists not in a complete Philosophy of Culture, but in the question: *ti to on* [What is Being]? The problematic of a metaphysics of *Dasein*, for me, grows out of this question. Or, to come once again to the heart of the Kant interpretation, I attempted to show that to start from a concept of the *logos* is not quite such an obvious procedure, but, on the contrary, that the question of the possibility of metaphysics requires a metaphysics of *Dasein* itself, in such a way that the question, what man is, doesn't have to be answered so much in the sense of an anthropological system, but that this question must first of all be really clarified with respect to the perspective in which it will be posed. Are the concepts *terminus a quo* and *terminus ad quem* only a heuristic formulation of the question or are they based in the essence of philosophy itself? This problematic does not seem to me to be clearly worked out in Cassirer's philosophy up till now. What matters first of all for Cassirer is to expose the different Forms of the form-giving activity and then, subsequently, to push forward from there into a certain dimension of the form-creating powers themselves. Now one could say it follows that this dimension is still basically the same as that which I call *Dasein*. This would be wrong, however. The difference appears most clearly in the concept of freedom. I have spoken of an act of freeing in the sense of the setting free of the inner transcendence of *Dasein*, entering directly into the thrownness[17] of *Dasein*. I have not given freedom to myself although I can be the self that I am only through being free. The self that I am, however, now not in the sense of an undifferentiated ground of explanation, but in the sense that *Dasein* is the really fundamental event in which the act of existing of man, and with that, every problematic of existence as such essentially comes about. – I believe that what I designate with the term *Dasein* cannot be translated by one of Cassirer's concepts. What I call *Dasein* is essentially characterized not only through that which is designated as "spirit," or as "life," but rather it is the original unity and the immanent structure of the relatedness of a man who, in his shackledness to the body, stands in a special boundness with "that-which-is," in the sense that *Dasein* as free, thrown in the midst of "that-which-is," effects a breaking-into "that-which-is," a breaking-into which is always historically in the final sense fortuitous; so fortuitous that man exists at the highest point of his own possibility only in a very few moments of *Dasein*'s duration between life and death. – In all my philosophical work I have completely left out of consideration the traditional form and division of the philosophical disciplines, because I believe that orienting oneself in terms of these constitutes the greatest snare in the way of getting back to the inner problematic of philosophy. Neither Plato nor Aristotle knew anything about such a division in philosophy. This was an affair of the Schools. Effort is required to break through these disciplines and to come back again to the specifically metaphysical mode of Being of the respective areas [underlying these disciplines]. Art is not merely a Form of the form-creating consciousness, rather art has itself a metaphysical sense within the fundamental even that *Dasein* itself is. – I have intentionally stressed these differences. The work that really has to be done is not helped by smoothing them over. For the sake of clarity I would like to place our entire discussion once more under the sign of Kant's *Critique of Pure Reason*, and once more to fix upon the question, what man is, as the central question. This question need not be put anthropocentrically, but it must be shown, through the fact that man is the being who transcends, i.e., is open to "that-which-is" in its totality and to himself, that by means of this eccentric character man is also at the same time put into the totality of "that-which-is" as such. The question and the idea of a philosophical anthropology has this meaning, not that of investigating man empirically as a given object. Rather it has to be motivated out of the central problematic of philosophy itself which must lead man back beyond himself into the whole of "that-which-is," in order to make manifest to him, for all his freedom, the nothingness of his *Dasein*. This nothingness is not an inducement to pessimism and dejection, but to the understanding of this, namely, that there is genuine activity only where there is opposition and that philosophy has the task of throwing man back into the hardness of his face from out of the softness of one who merely lives off the work of the spirit.

Cassirer: I believe it has already become clearer in what the opposition consists. It is, however, not fruitful to stress this opposition repeatedly. We are at a point where little is to be gained through purely logical arguments. It seems, then, we are condemned here to some sort of relativity. However, we may not persist in this relativity which would place empirical man in the center. What Heidegger said at the end was most important.

His position cannot be anthropocentric either. And then, I ask, where now lies the common center in our opposition? We do not need to look for this. For we have this center, and we have it indeed because there is one common objective human world in which, although the differences of individuals are in no way cancelled, a bridge is built from individual to individual. That I find again and again in the primal phenomenon of language. Everyone speaks his own language, and yet we understand one another through the medium of language. There is something such as *the* language, something such as a unity over and above the endlessly different ways of speaking. Therein lies the decisive point for me. And therefore I start from the objectivity of the symbolic Form because here "the inconceivable is achieved."[18] That is what I should like to call the world of objective spirit. There is no other way from one existence[19] than through this world of Form. If it did not exist, then I would not know how such a thing as a common understanding could be. Cognition, too, is therefore simply only a basic instance of this position, because an objective assertion is formulated which no longer takes into consideration the subjectivity of the particular individual. – Heidegger has correctly said that the fundamental question of his metaphysics is the same one which formed Plato and Aristotle: What is "that-which-is"? And he has said further that Kant once again took up with this question. However, here an essential difference seems to me to obtain, which is in fact what Kant called the Copernican revolution. The question of being seems to me, I admit, to be in no way eliminated as a result of this revolution. However, the question of being acquires a much more complicated form. In what does that revolution consist? The question of how objects are determined is preceded by a question about the constitution of the being of an objectivity as such. What is new in this revolution seems to me to lie in this, that there is now no longer a single such structure of being, but rather that we have completely different structures of being. Each new structure of being has new *a priori* presuppositions. Kant shows how every kind of new Form always bears upon a new world of objectivities. In that way a whole new multiplicity enters into the problem of the object as such. By that means the old dogmatic metaphysics becomes the new Kantian metaphysics. The being of the old metaphysics was substance, that *one* which underlies. In the new metaphysics being is in my language no longer the being of a substance, but the being that proceeds from a manifold of functional determinations and meanings. And here appears to me to lie the essential point of distinction of my position in opposition to Heidegger. – I hold to the Kantian formulation of the question of the transcendental. The essential of the transcendental method lies in this, that it begins with a given. Thus I inquire into the possibility of the given called "language." How is it conceivable that we as one existence[20] to another can understand each other in this medium? Or, how is it possible that we are able to see at all a work of art as an objective determinate thing? This question must be solved. Perhaps not all questions in philosophy are to be solved on this basis. I believe that only if one has posed this question does he gain access to Heidegger's formulation of the question.

Heidegger: To repeat Plato's question cannot mean that we fall back upon the answer of the Greeks. Being itself is splintered into a multiplicity, and a central problem consists in gaining a position from which to understand the inner diversity of the ways of Being out of the idea of Being. – Just reconciling differences will never be really productive. It is the essence of philosophy, as a finite affair of man, that it is limited within the finitude of man. Since philosophy is concerned with the whole of man and the highest in man, this finitude must show itself in philosophy in a completely radical manner. – What matters to me is that you retain this one thing from our confrontation: don't fasten on our differences as the disagreements of individuals engaged in philosophy, but rather come to feel that we are once again on the way towards taking seriously the central question of metaphysics. What you see here on a small scale, the difference of individuals engaged in philosophy within the unity of the problematic, is also to be found, though quite differently, on a large scale; and that is just the essential thing in confronting the history of philosophy, to see how it is precisely the differentiating of standpoints which is the root of philosophical work.

Notes

1. The following piece is a translation of "*Arbeitsgemeinschaft Cassirer-Heidegger*" (printed in Guido Schneeberger, *Ergänzungen zu einer Heidegger-Bibliographie*, Bern, 1960, pp. 17–27), translated by Frances Slade, in: N. Langiulli (ed.), *The Existential Tradition: Selected Writings*. New York: Doubleday, 1971, pp. 192–203. This text is a record of the discussion between Cassirer and Heidegger which took place at Davos, Switzerland, in March 1929 during the second Davoser Hochschulkurse. Since this record was made by two auditors of the discussion, the statements contained in what is here translated under the title "A Discussion Between Ernst Cassirer and Martin Heidegger" do not represent the written statements either of Cassirer or of Heidegger. The translator wishes to thank Joseph Carpino and Thomas Prufer for their many comments and suggestions during the course of the preparation of this translation. He would also like to acknowledge the generosity of Willi Schmidt who read parts of this translation and made suggestions for its improvement. – Trans.
2. Material enclosed within brackets [] has been inserted by the translator. Material enclosed within parentheses () appears in parentheses in the German text. Page numbers in brackets are the page numbers of the German text. – Trans.
3. *das Seiende*
4. *Sein*
5. Reading "*Bildbegriffes*" for "*Bildungsbegriffes*" as emended by Guido Schneeberger in a letter to the editor. – Trans.
6. *Einsichten*
7. *das Ganze des Seienden im Sinne des Vorhandenen*
8. *des Seienden selbst*
9. *des Seins*
10. *In-der-Wahrheit-sein*
11. *Angst*
12. *das Nichts*
13. *Weltanschauung*
14. *Dasein*
15. The German text reads: "*Aus dem Kelche dieses Geisterreiches strömt ihm die Unedlichkeit.*" Cf. Schiller's poem "*Die Freundschaft*," lines 59–60; and Hegel's *Phänomenologie des Geistes*, concluding lines. – Trans.
16. "Gott, Gemüt und Welt," *Sprüche in Reimen*.
17. *Geworfenheit*
18. The German text, in quotation marks here, reads: Weil hier "*das Unbegreifliche getan*" ist. It seems intended to recall "Das Unbeschreibliche, Hier ist's getan" in *Faust*, Part II. – Trans.
19. *Dasein*
20. *Dasein*

Main Neo-Kantian Works in German

Ernst Cassirer

Das Erkenntnisproblem in der Philosophie und Wissenschaft der neueren Zeit. Three volumes. Berlin: Bruno Cassirer, 1906–1920. Fourth, posthumous volume: *Das Erkenntnisproblem in der Philosophie und Wissenschaft der neueren Zeit. Vierter Band. Von Hegels tod bis zur Gegenwart (1832–1932).* Edited by Birgit Recki. Leipzig: Felix Meiner Verlag, 2000.
Substanzbegriff und Funktionsbegriff: Untersuchungen uber die Grundfragen der Erkenntniskritik. Berlin: Cassirer, 1910.
Zur Einsteinschen Relativitätstheorie. Erkenntnistheoretische Betrachtungen. Berlin: Bruno Cassirer, 1921.
Philosophie der Symbolischen Formen. Three volumes:
    Erster Teil: Die Sprache. Berlin: B. Cassirer, 1923.
    Zweiter Teil: Das Mythische Denken. Berlin: B. Cassirer, 1925.
    Dritter Teil: Phänomenologie der Erkenntnis. Berlin: B. Cassirer, 1929.
    Vierter Teil: Zur Metaphysik der symbolischen Formen (posthumous). Edited by John M. Krois et al. Leipzig: Felix Meiner Verlag, 1995.
Determinismus und Indeterminismus in der modernen Physik. Göteborg: Göteborgs Högskolas Årsskrift 42, 1936.
Zur Logik der Kulturwissenschaften. Göteborg: Göteborgs Högskolas Årsskrift 47, 1942.
Gesammelte Werke (ECW). Hamburger Ausgabe. 26 Volumes. Edited by Birgit Recki. Leipzig: Felix Meiner Verlag, 1995–2009.
Nachgelassene Manuskripte und Texte (ECN). Edited by John Michael Krois et al. Leipzig: Felix Meiner Verlag, 1995–2014.

Hermann Cohen

Kants Theorie der Erfahrung. Berlin: Dümmler, 1871 (1st ed.), 1885 (2nd ed.).
Das Prinzip der Infinitesimal-Methode and seine Geschichte: Ein Kapitel zur Grundlegung der Erkenntniskritik. Berlin: Dümmler, 1883.
System der Philosophie. Three volumes:
    Logik der reinen Erkenntnis. New York: Olms, 1902.
    Ethik des reinen Willens. New York: Olms, 1904.

Aesthetik des Reinen Gefühls. Berlin: B. Cassirer, 1912.
Religion der Vernunft aus den Quellen des Judentums. Leipzig: Fock, 1919.
Werke. Edited by Helmut Holzey. Hildesheim: Georg Olms, 1977ff.

Hermann von Helmholtz

Handbuch der physiologischen Optik. Volume Nine of *Allgemeinen Encyclopädie der Physik.* Edited by Gustav Karsten. Leipzig: Leopold Voss, 1867. Second revised edition 1896, Leipzig: Leopold Voss.
Wissenschaftliche Abhandlungen. Three volumes. Leipzig: Johann Ambrosius Barth, 1882, 1883, and 1895.
Vorträge und Reden. Fifth edition. Two volumes. Braunschweig: F. Vieweg u. Sohn, 1903.
Schriften zur Erkenntnistheorie. Edited by Moritz Schlick and Paul Hertz. Berlin: Julius Springer, 1921.

Friedrich Albert Lange

Geschichte des Materialismus und Kritik seiner Bedeutung in der Gegenwart. Second revised edition. Iserlohn: J. Baedeker, 1873–75. New edition by Alfred Schmidt. Frankfurt: Suhrkamp, 1974.
Logische Studien. Ein Beitrag zur Neubegründung der formalen Logik und der Erkenntnistheorie, Iserlohn: J. Baedeker, 1877 (posthumous).

Emil Lask

Fichtes Idealismus und die Geschichte. Tübingen, 1902.
Die Logik der Philosophie und die Kategorienlehre. Tübingen: Mohr/Siebeck, 1911.
Gesammelte Schriften. Three volumes. Edited by Eugen Herrigel. Tübingen: Mohr, 1923–24. Reprinted in Jena: Schleglmann, 2002.

Otto Liebmann

Kant und die Epigonen: eine kritische Abhandlung. Stuttgart: Carl Schober, 1865.
Philosophische Tradition. Straßburg: Trübner, 1883.
Gedanken und Thatsachen: Philosophische Abhandlungen, Aphorismen und Studien. Two volumes. Straßburg: Trübner, 1904.
Zur Analysis der Wirklichkeit. Eine Erörterung der Grundprobleme der Philosophie. Straßburg: Trübner, 1911.

Rudolf Hermann Lotze

Mikrokosmus: Ideen zur Naturgeschichte und Geschichte der Menschheit, Versuch einer Anthropologie. Three volumes. Leipzig: Hirzel, 1856, 1858, 1864.
Logik. Leipzig: Hirzel, 1874. New edition by Gottfried Gabriel. Hamburg: Felix Meiner Verlang, 1989.
Metaphysik. Leipzig: Hirzel, 1879.

Paul Natorp

Sozialpädagogik. Theorie der Willensbildung auf der Grundlage der Gemeinschaft. Stuttgart: Frommann, 1899 (1st ed.), 1922 (5th ed.).
Die logischen Grundlagen der exakten Wissenschaften. Leipzig: Teubner, 1910 (1st ed.), 1921 (2nd ed.).
Philosophie. Ihr Problem und Ihre Probleme. Einführung in den iritischen Idealismus. Göttingen: Vandenhoeck & Ruprecht, 1911 (1st ed.), 1929 (4th ed.). New edition by K.H. Lembeck. Göttingen: Edition Ruprecht, 2008.
Allgemeine Psychologie nach kritischer Methode. Tübingen: Mohr/Siebeck, 1912. New edition by S. Luft. Darmstadt: Wissenschaftliche Buchgesellschaft, 2013.
Sozialidealismus. Neue Richtlinien sozialer Erziehung. Berlin: 1920 (1st ed.), 1922 (last ed.).
Platos Ideenlehre: eine Einführung in den Idealismus. Hamburg: Felix Meiner, 1921. Reissued 1994.
Vorlesungen über praktische Philosophie. Erlangen: Philosophische Akademie, 1925.
Philosophische Systematik. Edited by Hans Natorp. Hamburg: Felix Meiner Verlag, 1958. Reissued 2000.
Editor's Note: There is no Collected Works of Natorp. A near-complete bibliography can be found in the entry on Natorp by Alan Kim on SEP.

Heinrich Rickert

Der Gegenstand der Erkenntnis. Einführung in die Transzendentalphilosophie. Tübingen: Mohr/Siebeck, 1921.
Kulturwissenschaft und Naturwissenschaft. Sixth and seventh expanded editions, Tübingen: Mohr Siebeck, 1926. New version by Reclam, 2001.
Die Grenzen der Naturwissenschaftlichen Begriffsbildung. Eine logische Einleitung in die historischen Wissenschaften. Sixth improved edition. Tübingen: Mohr/Siebeck, 1929.
Die Logik des Prädikats und das Problem der Ontologie, Heidelberg: Carl Winters, 1930.
Grundprobleme der Philosophie. Methodologie, Ontologie, Anthropologie, Tübingen: Mohr Siebeck, 1934.
Philosophische Aufsätze. Edited by R.A. Bast. Tübingen: Mohr Siebeck, 1999.
Editor's Note: There is no Collected Works of Rickert. A nearly complete bibliography can be found in the entry on Rickert by Andrea Staiti on SEP.

Hans Vaihinger

Die Philosophie des Als-Ob. Leipzig: Felix Meiner, 1911 (1st ed.), 1922 (7th ed.).

Wilhelm Windelband

Über die Gewißheit der Erkenntnis: Eine psychologisch-erkenntnistheoretische Studie. Berlin: Henschel, 1873. Reprint: Hamburg: Adlibras Verlang, 2005.
Präludien: Aufsätze und Reden zur Philosophie und ihrer Geschichte. Tübingen: Mohr/Siebeck, 1883 (1st ed.), 1924 (3rd ed.).
Über Willensfreieheit. Tübingen: Mohr, 1905.
Der Wille zur Wahrheit. Heidelberg: Winter, 1909.
Die Prinzipien der Logik. Tübingen: Mohr, 1913.
Die Geschichte der neueren Philosophie. Leipzig: Breitkopf & Härtel, 1919.
Einleitung in die Philosophie. Second edition. Tübingen: Mohr, 1920.

Translation of Neo-Kantian Works in English

Ernst Cassirer

Determinism and Indeterminism in Modern Physics: Historical and Systematic Studies of the Problem of Causality. Translated by O. Theodor Benfey; preface by Henry Margenau. New Haven, CT: Yale University Press, 1956.

An Essay on Man: An Introduction to a Philosophy of Human Culture. New Haven, CT: Yale University Press, 1944. Reprinted 1972.

The Individual and the Cosmos in Renaissance Philosophy. Translated with an introduction by Mario Domandi. New York: Harper & Row, 1963.

Kant's Life and Thought. Translated by James Haden; introduction by Stephan Körner. New Haven, CT: Yale University Press, 1981.

Language and Myth. Translated by Susanne K. Langer. New York: Dover Publications, 1946.

The Logic of the Cultural Sciences: Five Studies. Translated and with an introduction by S.G. Lofts; foreword by Donald Phillip Verene. New Haven, CT: Yale University Press, 2000.

The Logic of the Humanities. Translated by Clarence Smith Howe. New Haven, CT: Yale University Press, 1961.

The Myth of the State. Translated by Charles William Hendel. New Haven: Yale University Press, 1946. Reprinted 1979.

"Nature and Natural Science". In *Knowledge and Postmodernism in Historical Perspective* Edited by Joyce Appleby et al. New York: Routledge, 1996.

The Philosophy of the Enlightenment. Translated by Fritz C.A. Koelln and James P. Pettegrove. Princeton, NJ: Princeton University Press, 1979.

The Philosophy of Symbolic Forms. Four Volumes. Translated by Ralph Manheim; preface and introduction by Charles W. Hendel. New Haven, CT: Yale University Press, 1953–1996.

The Platonic Renaissance in England. Translated by James P. Pettegrove. Austin, TX: University of Texas Press, 1953.

The Problem of Knowledge: Philosophy, Science, and History since Hegel. Translated by William H. Woglom and Charles W. Hendel; preface by Charles W. Hendel. New Haven, CT: Yale University Press, 1950.

The Question of Jean-Jacques Rousseau. Edited and translated with an introduction and a new postscript by Peter Gay, New Haven, CT: Yale University Press, 1989.

The Renaissance Philosophy of Man. Edited by Ernst Cassirer, Paul Oskar Kristeller, and John Herman Randall, Jr., in collaboration with Hans Nachod [and others]. Chicago: University of Chicago Press, 1948.

Rousseau, Kant, Goethe: Two Essays. Translated by James Gutmann, Paul Oskar, Kristeller, and John Herman Randall, Jr. Princeton, NJ: Princeton University Press, 1945.

Substance and Function and *Einstein's Theory of Relativity*. Translated by William Curtis Swabey and Marie Collins Swabey. New York: Dover Publications, 1953.

Symbol, Myth, and Culture: Essays and Lectures of Ernst Cassirer, 1935–1945. Edited by Donald Phillip Verene, New Haven, CT: Yale University Press, 1979.

The Warburg Years (1919–1933): Essays on Language, Art, Myth, and Technology. Translated with an introduction by S.G. Lofts with A. Calcagno. New Haven, CT: Yale University Press, 2013.

Hermann Cohen

Ethics of Maimonides. Translated with commentary by Almut Sh. Bruckstein; foreword by Robert Gibbs. Madison, WI: University of Wisconsin Press, 2004.

Religion of Reason: Out of the Sources of Judaism. Translated with an introduction by Simon Kaplan; introductory essays by Leo Strauss; introductory essays for the second edition by Steven S. Schwarzschild, Kenneth Seeskin. Atlanta, GA: Scholars Press, 1995.

Reason and Hope: Selections from the Jewish Writings of Hermann Cohen. Translated, edited, and with an introduction by Eva Jospe. Cincinnati, OH: Hebrew Union College Press, 1997.

The Significance of Judaism for the Progress of Religion: An Address. Berlin: Protestantischer Schriftenvertrieb, 1911.

Hermann von Helmholtz

"Goethe's Presentiments of Coming Scientific Ideas." In *Science and Culture: Popular and Philosophical Essays*. Edited by David Cahan, 393–412. Chicago: The University of Chicago Press, 1995.

Hermann von Helmholtz. Epistemological Writings. The Paul Hertz/Moritz Schlick Centenary Edition of 1921. Translated by Malcom Lowel; edited by Robert S. Cohen and Yehuda Elkana. Dordrecht: D. Reidel Publishing Company, 1977.

"On the Conservation of Force," in *Scientific Memoirs*. Translated by John Tyndall, 114–162. London: Taylor and Francis, 1853.

"On the Interaction of the Natural Forces." In *Science and Culture: Popular and Philosophical Essays*. Edited by David Cahan, 18–45. Chicago: The University of Chicago Press, 1995.

"On the Relation of Natural Science to Science in General." In *Science and Culture: Popular and Philosophical Essays*. Edited by David Cahan, 76–95. Chicago: The University of Chicago Press, 1995.

On the Sensations of Tone as a Physiological Basis for the Theory of Music. Translated by Alexander J. Ellis from the fourth (1877) edition. New York: Dover Publications, 1954.

"The Recent Progress of the Theory of Vision." In *Science and Culture: Popular and Philosophical Essays*. Edited by David Cahan, 127–203. Chicago: The University of Chicago Press, 1995, 127–203.

Selected Writings of Hermann von Helmholtz. Edited with an introduction by Russell Kahl. Middletown, CT: Wesleyan University Press, 1971.

F. A. Lange

The History of Materialism and Criticism of its Present Importance. Three volumes. Translated by Ernest Chester Thomas, London: Trübner & Company, 1880–1881.

Rudolf Hermann Lotze

Logic. Translated by B. Bosanquet et al. Second edition. Oxford: Clarendon Press, 1887.
Metaphysic. Translated by B. Bosanquet et al. Second edition. Oxford: Clarendon Press, 1888.
Microcosmus: An Essay Concerning Man and his Relation to the World. Two volumes. Translated by E. Hamilton and E.E. Constance Jones. Edinburgh: T. & T. Clark, 1885.
Outlines of Aesthetics. Translated and edited by G.T. Ladd. Boston: Ginn, 1885.
Outlines of Logic. Translated and edited by G.T. Ladd. Boston: Ginn, 1887.
Outlines of Metaphysic. Translated and edited by G.T. Ladd. Boston: Ginn, 1884.
Outlines of Philosophy of Religion. Translated and edited by G.T. Ladd. Boston: Ginn, 1885.
Outlines of Practical Philosophy. Translated and edited by G.T. Ladd. Boston: Ginn, 1885.
Outlines of Psychology. Translated and edited by G.T. Ladd. Boston: Ginn, 1886.

Paul Natorp

"On the Objective and Subjective Grounding of Knowledge." Translated by L. Phillips and D. Kolb. *Journal of the British Society for Phenomenology* 12, no. 3 (1981): 245–266.
Plato's Theory of Ideas: An Introduction to Idealism. Edited with an introduction by Vasilis Politis; translated by Vasilis Politis and John Connolly; postscript by Andre Laks. Sankt Augustin: Academia, 2004.

Heinrich Rickert

The Limits of Concept Formation in Natural Science: A Logical Introduction to the Historical Sciences. Edited and translated by Guy Oakes, Cambridge, UK: Cambridge University Press, 1986.
Science and History: A Critique of Positivist Epistemology. Translated by George Reisman; edited by Arthur Goddard. Princeton, NJ: Van Nostrand, 1962.
"The Theory of Definitions." In *Essays on Definition*. Selected and edited by Juan C. Sager; introduction by Alain Rey. Amsterdam: John Benjamins Publishing Co., 2000.

Hans Vaihinger

The Philosophy of "As if." Translated by C.K. Ogden. London: Routledge and Kegan Paul Ltd., 1924.

Wilhelm Windelband

A History of Philosophy: The Formation and Development of its Problems and Conceptions. Translated by James H. Tufts. London: Macmillan, 1901.
An Introduction to Philosophy. Translated by Joseph McCabe. London: T. F. Unwin, Ltd., 1923.
"The Principles of Logic." In *Logic: Volume 1 of the Encyclopedia of the Philosophical Sciences*. Edited by Henry Jones; translated by Ethel Meyer. London: Macmillan, 1913
Theories in Logic. New York: Philosophical Library, 1961.

Index

A History of Philosophy With Special Reference to the Formation and Development of Its Problems and Conceptions (Windelband) 269, 299–316
a posteriori concepts 40, 43–4, 50–1
a priori concepts 28–30; cognition critique 105; concept formation 334, 341; connection between science and theory of cognition 103; critical/genetic method 275, 281, 285; culture and transcendental idealism 318–20; Euclidean/Non-Euclidean geometry 237–8, 242–3; *Hermann Cohen and the Renewal of Kantian Philosophy* 222, 224–5, 229–31; history of philosophy 295, 307, 334, 341; "logic of origin" 94; logic to physics relationships 120, 121, 124–5; materialism 69; modern physics 448–51, 454–5; naturalism 295; ontological categories 417; response and critique 472, 474; scientific logic 199; "the synthetic principles" 107–11, 114; *The World of Ideas* 91; thing-in-itself 40–1, 43–4, 49–53
absolute differential calculus 244
Absolutism 74
abstraction: *Kant and the Marburg School* 183; objective and subjective grounding of knowledge 170–1; response and critique 465
acceleration 123
action: at a distance 124, 127; historical concept formation 371; of reason 282
activity 165–6, 172, 432, 434–6
actuality 132–3
aei kata tauta hosautos echon 241
Aenesidemus 47–50

aesthetics: critical/genetic method 276, 281; *Hermann Cohen and the Renewal of Kantian Philosophy* 231–2; *Kant and the Marburg School* 185–6; symbolism 254–5, 256, 261–3
affect, fellowmen 154
affirmation 85–6
afterlife 150–1
aggregates 18, 112–13
agnoia 53–6
agroikos sophia 246–7
algebraic geometry 14
Analysis der Wirklichkeit (*Analysis of Reality*) (Liebmann) 37
analytic directions of thought 200–2
analytic judgments, *Kant and the Marburg School* 181–2
analytic methods, logic to physics relationships 117
analytical cognition, scientific logic 205–6
analytical geometry 18, 118–19
anamnesis 205–6
Ancient Philosophy 308
angles 11, 15
Anhypotheton 192, 194, 203–4
Anticipations 121, 123
antinomy of Kantian reason 43
Antiquitates Ebraeorum (Grotius) 144
apagogical proof 210
apathy 152, 153
apparent depiction 125
appearances 42–3; culture and transcendental idealism 319, 323; objective and subjective

grounding of knowledge 165, 171–2; scientific logic 205–6; "the synthetic principles" 112
applied mathematics, "the synthetic principles" 114
aprix taiu chetoin 248
Archimedes 122
architectonic connections 263
argumentation 29–30
Aristotle 88–91, 93, 108, 122; critical/genetic method 272; division of philosophy and of its history 311; history/naturalism 292; name and conception of philosophy 299; objective and subjective grounding of knowledge 173–5, 176; scientific logic 200–1, 205
artifices of thought 436–7
as-if philosophy 429–43
assertions 389–91
Aster, E. von 189, 192
astronomy, symbolism 257
asylum ignorantiae 45
The Atom as Fiction 429, 440–1
atomism: as-if philosophy 429, 438–9; fictions 440–1; logic to physics relationships 122–4, 127, 128; response and critique 470–1
authority 171, 173, 176
autonomy/autotely 230–1
awareness, *see also* consciousness
axioms: critical/genetic method 273–83; principle of intuition 110–14; response and critique 473–4; "the synthetic principles" 110–14; theory of cognition 104

Bacon, F. 48, 288
being: boundlessness of truth 423; Euclidean/Non-Euclidean geometry 238, 243; *Hermann Cohen and the Renewal of Kantian Philosophy* 227–8; *Kant and the Marburg School* 183, 192, 193; language and myth 249–50; logic to physics relationships 121, 122; ontological categories 402, 411–12, 415, 416–17; response and critique 473–4; *The World of Ideas* 87–91; theoretical intuitionism 384–5
belief, critical/genetic method 277
Beltrami, E. 16, 17, 19, 22–4, 28, 32
bias, history/naturalism 293–6
"binding forces" 242–3
biographical history of philosophy 309
Boileau, N. 46
Bolzano, B. 224, 409
border concepts, *see also* thing-in-itself
border conflict, intuition/thought 102
Born, M. 454
brotherhood, fellowmen 140, 141–2, 145

Brouwer, L.E.J. 255
Bühler, K. 258

Carnap, R. 457–60
Cassirer, E. 214–64, 450–2; *Euclidean and Non-Euclidean Geometry* 216–17, 236–45; *Hermann Cohen and the Renewal of Kantian Philosophy* 215–16, 217–19, 221–35; main works 486; response and critique 477–85; *The Place of Language and Myth in the Pattern of Human Culture* 217–19, 246–53; *The Problem of the Symbol and Its Place in the System of Philosophy* 219–20, 254–64; translations 489–90
categorical axioms, response and critique 473–4
categorical imperatives, thing-in-itself 56
categories, doctrine of 399–400, 422–7
categories of being, logic to physics relationships 122
categories of causality, thing-in-itself 49, 52–3
categories of substantiality, thing-in-itself 52–3
category mistake *see* thing-in-itself
causality: historical concept formation 332, 357–8, 364–5; thing-in-itself 49, 52–3
center of gravity 122
central process of history 379–80
certainty 223
chief doctrine and chief mistake, Kant 38, 40–62
children, thing-in-itself 52–3
choris para ta kath' hekasta see particular, the...
choris para ta katholou see universal, the...
choris ton onton 87, 89
Christianity 71–2, 144
Christoffel, E. 244
Church: name and conception of philosophy 300, *see also* religion
circles 15
citizens, fellowmen 138
classification of sciences 463–76
co-operation 68
co-ordinates 19–20
cognition 12–13; boundlessness of truth 423–6; connection with science 103; considerations against theory 103–4; critique 104, 105; distinction from logic 102; grounding of the infinitesimal 105; *Hermann Cohen and the Renewal of Kantian Philosophy* 223, 227; historical precondition of critique 105; Infinitesimal Method 101–5; *Kant and the Marburg School* 183–4, 186–8; "Knowing and Cognizing" 328–9, 384–95; of the object in general 110; ontological categories 410; response and critique 467–9; scientific logic 202–8, 210–11; thing-in-itself 44, 48–55, 57–8

Cohen, H. 95–106, 180–4, 188–9, 192, 207–8, 215–16, 221–35; *Kant's Theory of Experience* 96; main works 486–7; *Religion of Reason out of the Sources of Judaism* 98–9, 137–57; *The Principle of the Infinitesimal Method and Its History* 95, 101–6; translations 490
coherence: historical concept formation 344; scientific logic 207
collectivity, historical concept formation 362–3
collision, logic to physics relationships 118
"commitment to the generic" 295–6
common conception of reality, historical concept formation 351, 353
community, historical concept formation 376, 378–9
concealed masses, logic to physics relationships 129–30, 131
conception of philosophy 299–303
conceptions and problems 299–316
concepts: culture 375–80; development 364–5; formation 327–8, 331–83, 467; freedom 144, 230–1; *Hermann Cohen and the Renewal of Kantian Philosophy* 230; individuality 342–56; language and myth 248–9, 251; mental life 367–75; nexus 361–4; of a principle of mechanics 125–6; problems 334–42; thing-in-itself 56; value-relevant 356–61, *see also different concepts*
conceptual knowledge, fellowmen 138
conclusion 12, 13
concomitance, historical concept formation 332–3
conditio sine qua non of science 450
conditionedness, ontological categories 415
confrontation 210–11
congruence 21, 30–1, 34–5
connectedness, scientific logic 204–6, 207
connection 68, 167, 335–6
conscience, fellowmen 144
consciousness 34; as-if philosophy 431–2, 435–6; critical/genetic method 275–6, 280–3; culture and transcendental idealism 318–23; distinction between logic and theory of cognition 102; Ethical Materialism 73–4; fellowmen 149, 152; *Hermann Cohen and the Renewal of Kantian Philosophy* 224, 228; *Kant and the Marburg School* 183; logic to physics relationships 132–3; objective and subjective grounding of knowledge 166, 176; "the synthetic principles" 113; theory of cognition 103; thing-in-itself 44
consequence, critical/genetic method 282
The Conservation of Energy 1–2
constellations, symbolism 257
construction problems 13–14

constructive direction of knowledge 177
constructive objectification 176–7
content: historical concept formation 333; objective and subjective grounding of knowledge 165–6, 172
conventions, modern physics 448
convex mirrors 22
Copernican philosophy 402–10; boundlessness of truth 423; Euclidean/Non-Euclidean geometry 242–3; language and myth 249; ontological categories 409–10, 417; symbolism 263
copy theory 385–7
correctness, logic to physics relationships 125, 126–7, 131
correlations, scientific logic 208
cosmological problems, division of philosophy and of its history 311
cosmos 44
counterforce, logic to physics relationships 126
creative synthesis, culture and transcendental idealism 321–2
Critical or Genetic Method? (Windelband) 267, 271–86
critical philosophy 267, 271–86, 307–8; historical concept formation 334; history of philosophy 310; idealism 190; interpretations of modern physics 447–56; thing-in-itself 43, 48, 57
Critique 108–9, 120, 184
Critique of Judgment 227
Critique of Practical Reason 230
Critique of Pure Reason 38, 42, 47, 230; critical/genetic method 271; culture and transcendental idealism 318–19; theoretical intuitionism 384
critiques 445–6; Carnap 457–60; Cassirer 477–85; classification of sciences 463–76; Heidegger 477–85; historical reason 279–80; Husserl 461–2; modern physics 447–56; Rickert 463–76; space and experience 459–60; Windelband 463–76
culture: chief doctrine 50; concept formation 333–4, 337–8, 341, 352–4, 364; critical/genetic method 279–80; fellowmen 148–52, 156; historical sciences 375–80; idealism 70–1, 76–8; language and myth 217–19, 246–53; transcendental idealism 269–70, 317–24

daphne 247
De jure naturali et gentium juxta disciplinan Ebraeorum (Seiden) 144
"*de omnibus rebus et de quibusdam aliis*" 304–5
de-individualization 471

death 150–1
deductio iuris 182
deduction 12; as-if philosophy 436; critical/genetic method 274–5, 282; *Kant and the Marburg School* 185–6; response and critique 470–1; scientific logic 199–200; thing-in-itself 47, 57
definition 132
Deipnosophistae of Athenaeus 308–9
Deism 68, 71, 72, 74
Democritus 45
density, logic to physics relationships 126
depiction, logic to physics relationships 125–31
Descartes, R. 117, 118, 119, 122, 260, 402
determination, objective and subjective grounding of knowledge 177
determinism, response and critique 470–1
deutera ousia 89
dialectical method, critical/genetic method 282
Dilthey, W. 466
direction 10–11
distance 9, 124, 127–8
distinction between types of energy, logic to physics relationships 128
diversity, theoretical intuitionism 391–2
divine names 252
division of philosophy and of its history 311–13
docta ignorantia 56
dogma: boundlessness of truth 423; name and conception of philosophy 300; ontological categories 402–3; theoretical intuitionism 389–90
Doppelgänger, history/naturalism 296
Droysen, J. 334
dualism, symbolism 257
dynamic conceptions of nature 122–3
dynamic theory 129

ecclesiastical organisations *see* religion
Egoism: materialism 68, 72–3, 75; objective and subjective grounding of knowledge 171
Einstein, A. 134, 236–45, 450–3
Eleatic school 122
electrical forces 124, 261
elemental common feeling 154
eleos 153
emotions: history/naturalism 296, *see also* feeling
empirical consciousness, critical/genetic method 280, 283
empirical reality, thing-in-itself 40–2
empirical sciences, history/naturalism 289–90, 291, 294
empirical treatment of axioms, critical/genetic method 276–7

empiricism: *Hermann Cohen and the Renewal of Kantian Philosophy* 225; historical concept formation 341; *Kant and the Marburg School* 187, 194–5; modern physics 447–56
energy, logic to physics relationships 122, 127–8, 131–4
energy conservation 133–4
Epicurus 122, 153–4
epigones 37, 38
epistemology: historical concept formation 334, 335, 340; modern physics 451–3; ontological categories 403–4; theoretical intuitionism 384–5, 389
equal objects 6–7
equality 34–5; border conflict between intuition/thought 102; fellowmen 141, 145, 146, 147; limit method 101–2; transcendental geometrical axioms 30–2
equilateral triangles 35
Erdmann, B. 111
error of formalism, scientific logic 199–200
essential relations, logic to physics relationships 125
established fact 172
estimates, history of philosophy 307–8
eternal covenants 140
ethics: division of philosophy and of its history 312; fellowmen 137–8, 152; *Hermann Cohen and the Renewal of Kantian Philosophy* 228–31; idealism 75, 76; materialism 73–4; *The World of Ideas* 83
etiam oblivisci interdum expedit 46
Euclidean geometry 13–24, 35, 216–17, 236–45; *a priori* concepts 28–30; "the synthetic principles" 114; transcendental geometrical axioms 32
Euclidean and Non-Euclidean Geometry 216–17
eudaemonism 150
Events 86
existence *see* being
experience: critical/genetic method 277; culture and transcendental idealism 318–19; *Kant and the Marburg School* 181; language and myth 249–50; logic to physics relationships 120, 126–7; materialism 72; modern physics 447, 449; objective and subjective grounding of knowledge 165–6; response and critique 470–5; space 459–60; "the synthetic principles" 108–9; thing-in-itself 40–1, 42
"explanations", language and myth 250
extensive quantities, "the synthetic principles" 112–13
external position, name and conception of philosophy 302
eye for an eye 145

fact-of-being conscious (*Bewusstheit*) 228
factors of motion 2
factual material, historical concept formation 335–6, 359
factual validity, critical/genetic method 275, 278
fallacia falsi medii 47
Faraday, M. 123–4, 226
Faraday–Maxwell theory 124
feeling 57–8, 154, 262, *see also* sensation
fellowmen 137–57
Fichte, J.G. 46–7, 72–3, 121–2, 189, 281–2
fictions 429, 437–43
"fields of force", Euclidean/Non-Euclidean geometry 242–3
finitude, ontological categories 415
first form of Kant's doctrine 42
Fischer, K. 42, 111, 306
fitness to the purpose 127
flat space 19, 21–3
fluxion calculus 118
force 8, 21, 122–7, 130, 242–3, 261
foreigners, fellowmen 141, 142
foreignness to validity 410–17
form: Euclidean/Non-Euclidean geometry 241, 243; historical concept formation 333; *Kant and the Marburg School* 185; logic to physics relationships 121, 128; objective and subjective grounding 165; ontological categories 404–10; symbolism 257–8
formal logic 164, 199–200, 310
freedom: of conscience 144; *Hermann Cohen and the Renewal of Kantian Philosophy* 230–1
fundamental proposition 111
fundamental theory of natural science 123
fundamentally synthetic forms of unity 241

gait, *Kant and the Marburg School* 183
Galileo, G. 111–14, 122–3, 288, 473
Gauss, C.F. 15–16, 130, 244
Gawronsky, D. 132
generality/generalization: historical concept formation 343–4, 349–50, 360–6, 376–9; history/naturalism 294–6; response and critique 467–8, 471; theoretical intuitionism 393
genetic methods 267, 271–86, 307–8
genetic views of cognition 202
geodetic lines 14–15
Germanic peoples 302
gestalts 361
"*Glaube*" 277
God 68, 71–4, 138–44, 147–53, 156
Goethe, J.W. 117, 262, 349
governing perspectives, historical concept formation 338

Grassman, H. 255
gravity 122
great circles 15
Grotius, H. 144
grounding: critical/genetic method 272; of knowledge 164–79
Grounding of Ethics 229
Groundwork for a Metaphysics of Morals 230
guest-friends 139
guilt 152–3

Hamilton's principle 21
harmony 67, 69
heavy matter, logic to physics relationships 120
Hegel, G.W.F. 45, 74, 189–90, 192; as-if philosophy 435; critical/genetic method 284; history of philosophy 304–5
Heidegger, M.: response and critique 477–85; theoretical intuitionism 386
Hellenistic period 299–300, 302
Helmholtz, H. von 1–2, 120, 222, 240; as-if philosophy 433; main works 487; translations 490
henades 88
Heraclitus 82–3
Herbart, J.F. 44, 45
Herbartian 242
Hermann Cohen and the Renewal of Kantian Philosophy (Cassirer) 215–16, 221–35
Hertz, H. 124–32, 226, 255–6
heterogeneity 243–4
heuristics 334–7
Hilbert, D. 255, 258–9
historical concept formation 327–8, 331–83; culture 375–80; development 364–5; individuality 342–56; mental life 367–75; naturalism 365–7; nexus 361–4; problems 334–42; value-relevant 356–61
history 269; conceptions and problems 299–316; critical/genetic method 278–81, 284–5; *Hermann Cohen and the Renewal of Kantian Philosophy* 226–7; natural science 268, 287–98; response and critique 463–9; thing-in-itself 57
The History of Atomism (Lasswitz) 133
History of Materialism (Lange) 64, 96–8, 117–36
History and Natural Science (Windelband) 268, 287–98
hodos ano kato mie 244
homaloid space 19
homogeneity 6–8; *Hermann Cohen and the Renewal of Kantian Philosophy* 232; *Kant and the Marburg School* 191
human science 367–75, *see also* naturalism
Humboldt, W. von 249

Hume, D. 41, 47–50, 108, 277
Husserl, E. 224, 258, 406, 409, 461–2
hylogenous moments 34
hypo-psychical 435–6
hypokeimenon, theoretical intuitionism 389
hypostasizing, boundlessness of truth 423
hypotheses, modern physics 448

idealism: critique of cognition 104; *Hermann Cohen and the Renewal of Kantian Philosophy* 232; historical concept formation 353–4; *Kant and the Marburg School* 187–8, 190, 193–5; logic to physics relationships 121, 132; objective and subjective grounding of knowledge 174; ontological categories 410; standpoint of 66–78; symbolism 263; transcendental 317–24
ideas 82–92
identity: *Kant and the Marburg School* 181–2, 186–7; limit method 101
idiographic historical science 463–6
idiographic sciences 291–2
idol worship 141–2
ill, fellowmen 151
imaginability 29
imitation 90
immanent criticism 310
imperatives, thing-in-itself 56
incompleteness: historical concept formation 337; ontological categories 415
indifference 149, 415
individuality/individualization 137; historical concept formation 331–4, 342–62, 365–6, 371–2, 377; history of philosophy 307; response and critique 467, 471; theoretical intuitionism 393
indivisibility, historical concept formation 344
induction, as-if philosophy 436–7
inductive proof 210
inference: critical/genetic method 272; symbolism 256
infinite: *Hermann Cohen and the Renewal of Kantian Philosophy* 225–6; historical concept formation 337; logic to physics relationships 118–19, 123, 131, 133–4; response and critique 467–9; scientific logic 204–6
infinitesimal method 95, 101–6
"inner perception": history/naturalism 290, *see also* awareness; consciousness
instances, historical concept formation 361–2
intellect 54–6
intellectual fruitfulness, history of philosophy 310
intellectualist idealism, logic to physics relationships 121

intellectus ipse 118
intelligence, *The World of Ideas* 88
intentional misinterpretation, logic to physics relationships 121–2
interpenetration, historical concept formation 332–3
interpolation, history/naturalism 293
intuition 32–3; border conflict with thought 102; culture and transcendental idealism 319; *Kant and the Marburg School* 185, 186; "Knowing and Cognizing" 384–95; logic to physics relationships 118, 120; mathematics 255; modern physics 449, 453; principle of the axioms 110–14; response and critique 465; scientific logic 198–9; "the synthetic principles" 110–14
"is in the same state" 241
isolated individuals, historical concept formation 332, 361
Israelites 137–57

Jacobi, F.H. 45, 277
Judaism 137–57
judgment: concept formation 343, 360–1; critical/genetic method 275; culture and transcendental idealism 320; *Hermann Cohen and the Renewal of Kantian Philosophy* 223, 225; history 296, 343, 360–1; *Kant and the Marburg School* 181–2; naturalism 296, 343, 360–1; ontological categories 409–10; response and critique 466, 467–8; scientific logic 208–9; "the synthetic principles" 108–10, *see also a priori* principles; valuation
The Judgment of Reality (Gawronsky) 132
juridical institutes, fellowmen 143

Kant and the Marburg School (Natorp) 161, 180–97
Kant und die Epigonen (*Kant and His Epigones*) (Liebmann) 37, 38
Kant's Theory of Experience (Cohen) 96
kategoroumenon, theoretical intuitionism 389
Kautzsch, E.F. 145
kenologein 91
Kepler, J. 288
killing, fellowmen 146
kinesis 189
kinetic form, logic to physics relationships 128
"Knowing and Cognizing" (Staiti) 328–9, 384–95
knowledge: as-if philosophy 433; boundlessness of truth 423, 425–6; concept formation 334; critical/genetic method 272–3; division of philosophy and of its history 311–12; fellowmen 138, 155, 156; history 290,

294–6, 297, 334; "Knowing and Cognizing" 384–95; modern physics 449–51; naturalism 290, 294–6, 297; objective and subjective grounding 164–79; ontological categories 402–3; scientific logic 209–11; of what always 241

Laas, E. 435–6
Lagrange, J.-L. 126
Land, J.P.N. 3–4, 27, 29–30, 32–3
Lange, F.A. 63–78, 96–8, 108–9, 117–36, 222; *History of Materialism* 64, 96–8, 117–36; main works 487; *The Standpoint of the Ideal* 64–78; translations 490
language 85–7, 217–19, 246–53; critical/genetic method 279–80; historical concept formation 373–4; history/naturalism 297–8; theoretical intuitionism 387–9
Lask, E. 396–427, 487
Lasswitz, K. 133
lateral direction 10–11
lateral translation 10
law: fellowmen 142, 144–8, 156; *Hermann Cohen and the Renewal of Kantian Philosophy* 231; *Kant and the Marburg School* 182, 187; objective and subjective grounding of knowledge 165, 172, 173, 177; symbolism 263
law of the infinitely small 131
laws of the exchange of energy 127
laws of motion 21
laws of nature 90–1
laws of thought 126
least action principles 130
Leibniz, G.W. 44–6, 117–19, 122, 255, 260; as-if philosophy 437; history/naturalism 297, 298; modern physics 453
Lemmata concepts 6–7
lenses 23
Lessing, G.E. 263
Liebmann, O. 37–9, 222; *Analysis der Wirklichkeit* (*Analysis of Reality*) 37; *Kant und die Epigonen* (*Kant and His Epigones*) 37, 38; main works 487; *Vier Monate vor Paris* (*Four Months Before Paris*) 37
life-value 193
light and electricity 261; symbolism 261
limit method 101–2
"limiting the unlimited" 203
The Limits of Concept Formation in Natural Science (Rickert) 327–8, 331–83, 467
lines 9–23
Lingua universalis 260
linguistics *see* language
Lipschitz, R. 21

Lobachevsky, N.J. 17, 30
Locke, J. 103, 118, 260, 402
locomotions 9–10
logic 162–3, 198–213; as-if philosophy 432–6, 437–8; border conflict between intuition/thought 102; boundlessness of truth 422–7; concept formation 327–8, 331–83; critical/genetic method 275–6, 280, 282–3; distinction from theory of cognition 102; division of philosophy and of its history 311–12; foundations of the exact sciences 198–213; *Hermann Cohen and the Renewal of Kantian Philosophy* 225, 229; history of philosophy 288, 293, 297–8, 305, 310, 327–8, 331–83; *Kant and the Marburg School* 191, 192, 194–5; language and myth 252; naturalism 288, 293, 297–8; objective and subjective grounding of knowledge 165, 167–8; ontological categories 397–421; of origin 94; response and critique 473–4; symbolism 256; to physics relationships 117–36
The Logic of the Ontic Categories. Logic as Philosophy of Validity 397–8
logistics, *Kant and the Marburg School* 181–2
logos: *Kant and the Marburg School* 182, 191; language and myth 252; ontological categories 415–16; scientific logic 202–4
Lotze, R.H. 79–92; as-if philosophy 432–3; boundlessness of truth 426; critical/genetic method 273; culture and transcendental idealism 320; main works 487; ontological categories 406; *The World of Ideas* 80–92; translations 491
love, fellowmen 144, 146

Mach, E. 453
macrocosm/microcosm 44, 54
magnitudes 7–8, 9–23, 30–1
Maimonides 142–3
Marburg School 93–100; Cassirer, E. 214–64; Euclidean and Non-Euclidean Geometry 216–17, 236–45; fellowmen 137–57; *Hermann Cohen and the Renewal of Kantian Philosophy* 215–16, 221–35; *Kant and the Marburg School* 161, 180–97; logic to physics relationships 117–36; Natorp, P. 158–213; *On the Objective and Subjective Grounding of Knowledge* 159–60, 164–79; "the synthetic principles" 107–16; *The Place of Language and Myth in the Pattern of Human Culture* 217–19, 246–53; *The Principle of the Infinitesimal Method and Its History* 95, 101–6; *The Problem of a Logic of the Exact Sciences* 162–3, 198–213; *The Problem of the Symbol and Its Place in the System of Philosophy* 219–20, 254–64

mass, logic to physics relationships 126–32
mass appeal, critical/genetic method 278
material bodies/points 9
materialism 96–8; Deism 68, 71, 72, 74; *Hermann Cohen and the Renewal of Kantian Philosophy* 229–30; historical concept formation 334–7, 341, 343, 352, 359, 367–8, 372–3; history/naturalism 293–4; logic to physics relationships 121; ontological categories 413; *The Standpoint of the Ideal* 64–78
mathematics 9; cognition 101; critical/genetic method 273–4; *Hermann Cohen and the Renewal of Kantian Philosophy* 223, 225–6; history/naturalism 289–90; *Kant and the Marburg School* 194–5; logic to physics relationships 117, 119–20, 132–3; objective and subjective grounding of knowledge 168; scientific logic 198–200; symbolism 255; "the synthetic principles" 113–14; theory of cognition 104
mathesis anamnesis 54
matter 8, 10; Euclidean/Non-Euclidean geometry 242–3; *Kant and the Marburg School* 185; logic to physics relationships 120, 121, 124; ontological categories 407, 413–15; symbolism 257, 261; theory of cognition 103; thing-in-itself 44–5, *see also* thing-in-itself
maxims of interpolation 293
Maxwell, C. 18, 124, 261
meaning of words 387–9
measure of curvature 15–16, 18–19
mechanics: logic to physics relationships 123, 124, 125–6; symbolism 255–6
Medieval Philosophy 308
Mendelssohn, J. 263
mental life, historical concept formation 367–75, 376
mental structures, fictions 437–43
"merely thought" 129–30
metabasis eis allo genos see thing-in-itself
Metaphysic of Morals 319–20
Metaphysical Foundations of Natural Science, modern physics 452
"metaphysical need", name and conception of philosophy 300–2
metaphysics: as-if philosophy 433; division of philosophy and of its history 311; historical concept formation 358; history/naturalism 288–9, 290; response and critique 466; theoretical intuitionism 384–5
method of limits 101–2
method of natural science *see* mathematics
Michaelis, J.D. 144

Middle Ages 313
Mill, J.St 436
mirrors 22
misery 154
misinterpretation 121–2
misunderstanding in question 86–7
modal relations, scientific logic 207
modality, *Kant and the Marburg School* 185–6
modern logistics, *Kant and the Marburg School* 181–2
modern periods: division of philosophy and of its history 313; history of philosophy 308
modern physics 447–56
momentum 126
monades 88
monotheism 138–9, 142–4, 149, 153, 156
morality: culture and transcendental idealism 319–20; division of philosophy and of its history 312; fellowmen 143–4, 147–9, 153–6; logic to physics relationships 119
Mosaic Law (Michaelis) 144
motion 2, 9–10, 21; *Hermann Cohen and the Renewal of Kantian Philosophy* 225–6; logic to physics relationships 123, 124–7, 128; modern physics 452
movement of thought, *Kant and the Marburg School* 183
Müller, J. 222
Müller, M. 247, 248, 249
multiplicity: historical concept formation 337, 345–6; ontological categories 414–15; theoretical intuitionism 391–2
murder, fellowmen 146
myth 217–19, 246–53
mythology 246–53

name of philosophy 299–303
Natorp, P. 158–213; *Kant and the Marburg School* 161, 180–97; main works 488; *On the Objective and Subjective Grounding of Knowledge* 159–60, 164–79; *The Problem of a Logic of the Exact Sciences* 162–3, 198–213; translations 491
natura non facit saltus 131
natural history, *Hermann Cohen and the Renewal of Kantian Philosophy* 226–7
Natural Law and the Gentile Peoples of the World According to the Hebrew Teaching (Seiden) 144
natural necessity, critical/genetic method 278
naturalism 64, 68–9, 268, 287–98; culture and transcendental idealism 320; Euclidean/Non-Euclidean geometry 243–4; *Hermann Cohen and the Renewal of Kantian Philosophy* 222–3, 226–7; historical concept formation 327–8, 331–83; logic to physics relationships

123; modern physics 452; response and critique 463–9; *The World of Ideas* 90–1, *see also* mathematics
navigare necesse est 193
necessities of thought 21
necessity, critical/genetic method 275, 277–8
negation: culture and transcendental idealism 320; theoretical intuitionism 394
negative concepts, thing-in-itself 38, 40–62
negative valuations, historical concept formation 351–2
neighborly love, fellowmen 144
new historical method 340
Newton, I. 107, 114, 118–20, 126, 242, 261
"next man" concepts 137–8, 147
nexus causalis 48, 50–1
*n*fold extended aggregates 18
Noachides 139–44
noetic knowledge 311–12
noetos huperouranios topos 88
nominalism 173–4
nomothetic sciences 291–2, 296–7, 463–6
non-ego 68
non-Euclidean geometry 236–45
non-sensible 425–6
non-validity 410–17
nonsense 42
normative generality, historical concept formation 376–9
"nothing"/non-concepts/non-things (*metabasis eis allo genos*) 38, 40–62, 207–8, *see also* thing-in-itself
noun concepts, language and myth 251

objectivity: as-if philosophy 432; boundlessness of truth 423; grounding of knowledge 164–79; historical concept formation 334, 343–4, 352–3, 360–1, 376; *Kant and the Marburg School* 182–3; modern physics 451–2; ontological categories 403–4, 408–9; response and critique 472–4; symbolism 262, *see also* transcendental origins of geometrical axioms
objects: culture and transcendental idealism 323; historical concept formation 333, 336–7, 370–2; language and myth 249–50; ontological categories 409, 410–11
occurrences 86
omne simili claudicat 49–50
omnis determinatio est negatio 239
On General Physical Concepts (Hyder) 6–11
On the Objective and Subjective Grounding of Knowledge (Natorp) 159–60, 164–79
On the Origin and Significance of Geometrical Axioms (Hyder) 2–4, 12–26

ontic views of cognition 202
ontological categories 384–5, 391–4, 397–421
ontos on 80–1, 87, 320
"opposing man" concepts 147
opposition: historical concept formation 378; ontological categories 415
Optimism 67, 69
ordo et connexio rerum/ordo et connexio veritatum 409
organic nature 292
organon 103
orientation of symbolic form 257–8
origin 133; critical/genetic method 272; history of philosophy 307–8; *Kant and the Marburg School* 183–4; principle of 206–8; scientific logic 206–8, 211
The Origin and Meaning of Geometric Axioms 2–4, 27–36
ousia 89

pain, fellowmen 152
paradigms, symbolism 257
parallel lines 15
"*paronymia*" 247
participation 90
particular, the, objective and subjective grounding of knowledge 172–5
Pasch, M. 258–9
passion 154
passive reflex action, fellowmen 155–6
past perceptions 7
peoples, fellowmen 138–9
perception: concept formation 342; history 290, 342; logic to physics relationships 129; naturalism 290, 342; symbolism 256; *The World of Ideas* 83–4
perceptions 7–8, 44; historical concept formation 343; transcendental geometrical axioms 34–5
permissibility, logic to physics relationships 125, 126, 130–1
personalities, history of philosophy 307, 309
perspectives: historical concept formation 338; ontological categories 403–4
Pessimism 67, 69
"petites perceptions" 44
Phaedrus 246
phenomena: Euclidean/Non-Euclidean geometry 241–2; history/naturalism 291–2, 295; objective and subjective grounding of knowledge 171–3, 176–7; unequivocally determinate 177
The Philosophy of the As-If 442–3
Philosophy of Culture and Transcendental Idealism (Windelband) 269–70
physical geometry 2–4, 31–2, 35

physical objectivity 451–2
physical reality in space 240
physically equivalent space-magnitudes 31
physically equivalent topogenous moments 34–5
physics 117–36, 447–56
physiology, *Hermann Cohen and the Renewal of Kantian Philosophy* 223
pity 153–6
The Place of Language and Myth in the Pattern of Human Culture 217–19, 246–53
Placita Philosophorum 308–9
Planck, M. 133–4
planes 16, 17, 22
Plato 53–6, 80–93, 117; history/naturalism 295–6; *Kant and the Marburg School* 189, 191–3; language and myth 246–8; name and conception of philosophy 299; objective and subjective grounding of knowledge 174–5; ontological categories 406; scientific logic 203; symbolism 257, 263
plausibility 278
plurality: fellowmen 137; historical concept formation 334–5, 362; "the synthetic principles" 111; theoretical intuitionism 393
poetry: history of philosophy 307; materialism 67, 70, 71; symbolism 262
Poincaré, H. 236–7
politics, fellowmen 144, 146–7, 156
polytheism, fellowmen 148, 153, 156
position 85–6
positive valuations, historical concept formation 351–2
positivism: history/naturalism 296; objective and subjective grounding of knowledge 173–4, 175–6
"possibilities", Euclidean/Non-Euclidean geometry 243–4
potential form, logic to physics relationships 128
poverty, fellowmen 147, 149–52, 156
practical life, historical concept formation 348
practical problems, division of philosophy and of its history 312–13
pragmatism: history of philosophy 305, 306; response and critique 468–9
pre-critical idealism 232
precision, history of philosophy 307
prejudice *see* judgment
present perceptions 7
presupposition: of limit method 101–2; of mathematical cognition 101; theory of cognition 103–4
"primeval enigma of existence" 305
primordial conception of reality 347–8
primordial matter, ontological categories 413–14

Principia 118
principle of the Anticipations 121
principle of the axioms of intuition 110–14
The Principle of Conservation of Energy (Planck) 133–4
The Principle of the Infinitesimal Method and Its History (Cohen) 95, 101–6
principle of origin 206–8
principle of *vis viva* 122
Principles of Mechanics 255–6
'Principles of the Understanding' 91
Prinzhorn, H. 262
pro jure mundi 144
problem concepts 209–11, 299–316
The Problem of a Logic of the Exact Sciences (Natorp) 162–3, 198–213
The Problem of the Symbol and Its Place in the System of Philosophy 219–20, 254–64
process, scientific logic 203
projection 211
Prolegomena 43, 108–9
proof 210, 272, 280
prophetic teachings, fellowmen 149–51, 156
propositions: critical/genetic method 272–3; ontological categories 409–10; thing-in-itself 49
prote ousia 89
proteron pros hemas 407
proteron te physei 262
proton pseudos 38
providence 151
pseudogeometries 243–4
pseudospherical space 19, 21–4; *a priori* concepts 28–9; transcendental geometrical axioms 31–2
pseudospherical surfaces 16, 17
psychic processes 367–8
psychic structural nexus 347
psycho-genetic knowledge 311–12
psychological deductions 47, 57
psychologism, *Kant and the Marburg School* 182–3
psychology: division of philosophy and of its history 311; modern physics 449; objective and subjective grounding of knowledge 168; theory of cognition 103–4
pure, mathematics 113–14
pure activity, fellowmen 155
pure concepts 48; empiricism 194–5; experience 277; geometry 31; induction 341; intelligence 88; intuition 120, 198–9, 453; logic 333, 380; natural science 320; space 449; subjectivity 176; thought 118, 120, 123, 182, 198–9
purposeful/purposive activity 432, 434–6
Pythagoras 111–12

quality: *Kant and the Marburg School* 191; scientific logic 207
quantity: border conflict between intuition/thought 102; *Kant and the Marburg School* 191; limit method 101–2; scientific logic 207; "the synthetic principles" 111–12, 113, *see also* extensive quantities
question concepts: scientific logic 210–11; *The World of Ideas* 86–7; theory of cognition 103–4; thing-in-itself 53–6

Rafael 57–8
Ranke, L. von 340–1
ratio: *Kant and the Marburg School* 182, 187, 191; ontological categories 415–16
ratio ignava 45
rationalism 70; *Hermann Cohen and the Renewal of Kantian Philosophy* 225; historical concept formation 358–9, *see also* logic
realism: Euclidean/Non-Euclidean geometry 242; logic to physics relationships 132
reality: as-if philosophy 432; historical concept formation 331–2, 335, 339–40, 351, 353, 355; history/naturalism 290, 295; logic to physics relationships 132–3; ontological categories 412–13, 417; *The World of Ideas* 86–9, *see also* transcendental origins of geometrical axioms
'Realm of Shadows' 71
realms of truth 407–8, 410–11
reason: critical/genetic method 282; *Kant and the Marburg School* 182, 185–6; objective and subjective grounding of knowledge 171, *see also* logic
reciprocal action 152
recognition: *Kant and the Marburg School* 186; scientific logic 205–6
redemption 71
reflex action, fellowmen 155–6
Reichenbach, H. 454–5
relations, objective and subjective grounding of knowledge 173
relations of thought, distinction between logic and theory of cognition 102
relative nothing, scientific logic 207–8
"relative truth", history of philosophy 306
relatively historical concept formation 332–3
relativism: critical/genetic method 277–8; Euclidean/Non-Euclidean geometry 241
Relativitätstheorie und Erkenntnis 454–5
relativity, theory of 236–45
religion: culture and transcendental idealism 321; division of philosophy and of its history 312; fellowmen 137–57; language and myth 252; logic to physics relationships 119;

materialism 70–6; name and conception of philosophy 300, 302; symbolism 254–5, 256
Religion of Reason out of the Sources of Judaism (Cohen) 98–9, 137–57
Renaissance 308, 354–5
representations 14, 17, 22–3, 27–8; of a determinate space 112; fellowmen 150–1; historical concept formation 331, 334–5, 337, 348–9, 352, 365–6, 369; logic to physics relationships 118, 125; thing-in-itself 40–2, 48, 50; transcendental geometrical axioms 33
responses and critiques 445–6; Carnap 457–60; Cassirer 477–85; classification of sciences 463–76; Heidegger 477–85; Husserl 461–2; modern physics 447–56; Rickert 463–76; space and experience 459–60; Windelband 463–76
retribution, fellowmen 148
rhythm, symbolism 262
rich and poor, fellowmen 147, 149–52, 156
Rickert, H. 190–1, 325–83; *The Limits of Concept Formation in Natural Science* 327–8, 331–83, 467; main works 488; response and critique 463–76; *The Limits of Concept Formation in Natural Science* 327–8, 331–83; translations 491
Riemann, B. 3, 18–21, 242, 244
righteousness 149
rigid system of points *see* solid bodies
Roman period 302, 308–9
romanticism 354–5
Rosenkranz, J.K.F. 42
rotations 20
rules of thought 436–7
rules of the understanding 241–2
Russell, B. 260

sacrifice, fellowmen 146
Schiller, F. 70, 71, 117, 232, 275–6, 365
Schleiermacher 72, 74, 272, 277
Schlick, M. 445–6
Schopenhauer, A. 222, 230–1; as-if philosophy 433; chief doctrine 42, 47, 54–6; fellowmen 154–5; historical concept formation 364; history/naturalism 296; "the synthetic principles" 109
Schulze, G.E. (Aenesidemus) 47–50
science: concept formation 348; connection with theory of cognition 103; critique of cognition 104; of the eternally existent 241; logic 198–213, *see also* history; naturalism
Science of Knowledge 46–7
secularisation 73–4
Seiden, J. 144

seisachtheia 156
Seneca 46
sensation 7–8, 57–8, 154, 262; critical/genetic method 272–3; *Kant and the Marburg School* 184, 186; logic to physics relationships 120–1; response and critique 470–1; theory of cognition 103, *see also* perceptions
sensationalism, symbolism 260
sense, ontological categories 404–10
sensibility: boundlessness of truth 422–6; *Kant and the Marburg School* 185–6; logic to physics relationships 118, 131; ontological categories 410–17
"sets" of successive parts 112–13
shegagah 146
shortest lines 11, 13, 15, 18–20, 22–3
sickness 150
sicuti apparent/sicuti sunt 107
significance of historical concepts 335–6, 466
Sigwart, Ch. von 432
sin, fellowmen 146, 148
singularity, fellowmen 137
social misery/suffering 152, 153, 154
social relations, name and conception of philosophy 302
social values, historical concept formation 376–7
sociology, division of philosophy and of its history 312
Socrates 52–6, 83, 156, 291, 302
Sodom 140
sojourners: fellowmen 142, 145, 146, *see also* stranger-sojourners
solid bodies 20, 22
Solomon 142, 146
sources of knowledge, modern physics 449
Southwest School 265–70; *A History of Philosophy With Special Reference to the Formation and Development of Its Problems and Conceptions* 269, 299–316; boundlessness of truth 422–7; *Critical or Genetic Method?* 267, 271–86; cultural philosophy 317–24; *History and Natural Science* 268, 287–98; "Knowing and Cognizing" 328–9, 384–95; Lask 396–427; ontological categories 397–421; *Philosophy of Culture and Transcendental Idealism* 269–70; Rickert 325–83; *The Limits of Concept Formation in Natural Science* 327–8, 331–83; transcendental idealism 317–24; Vaihinger 428–43
space 27–8; Euclidean/Non-Euclidean geometry 237–40, 241–3; experience 459–60; intuition 32–3; *Kant and the Marburg School* 194–5; logic to physics relationships 124, 126, 127, 128–9; magnitudes 7–8, 9–23, 30–1; modern physics 449–54; ontological categories 409; symbolism 256; "the synthetic principles" 112; thing-in-itself 40–2; transcendental geometrical axioms 30–1
speculation 67
speech 85–7, *see also* language
Spencer, H. 247
spheres 15–17, 19, 21–4, 28–9, 31–2
spherical mirrors 22
spherical representations 22–3
spherical space 19, 21–4; *a priori* concepts 28–9; transcendental geometrical axioms 31–2
Spinoza 45, 154–5, 320
spirit: historical concept formation 367–75; impoverishment 70; suffering 152
stable motion 2, 10
Steinthal, M. 432
stimulus, theory of cognition 103
stoicism 149, 152, 153–4
straight lines 11, 13, 14–15, 16, 18–20, 22–3
stranger-sojourners 142, 145
strangers 139, 141–2, 144–6
Strauss 70
subjectivism, *Kant and the Marburg School* 187–8
subjectivity: as-if philosophy 438; grounding of knowledge 164–79; historical concept formation 370–1; symbolism 262
substance, logic to physics relationships 131–3
substance in force, logic to physics relationships 122
substantiality, thing-in-itself 52–3
substantive concept of history 333, 367, 373–5, 378, 380
Substanzbegriff und Funktionsbegriff 452–3
suffering 151–3, 156
sum of the angles of a triangle 15
supersensibility, boundlessness of truth 422–6
surface-beings 14–15
surfaces 9–10, 13, 15–19
syllabein eis hen 167
symbolic form 217–20
symbolism 219–20, 254–64
synthesis/synthesizing: culture and transcendental idealism 321–2; *Kant and the Marburg School* 191; of knowledge 297; ontological categories 393–4; scientific logic 205–6, 208–9
synthetic consciousness, culture and transcendental idealism 318–19
synthetic directions of thought, scientific logic 200–2
synthetic forms of unity, Euclidean/Non-Euclidean geometry 241
"the synthetic principles" 107–16

"systasis", scientific logic 207
"system", scientific logic 207
system of validity, *Hermann Cohen and the Renewal of Kantian Philosophy* 227

Tait, P.G. 126
tautological propositions, thing-in-itself 49
teleological concepts: critical/genetic method 275, 281–3; historical concept formation 332, 357–60, 367; idealism 80
Thales 45
thaumazein 53–6
The Atom as Fiction 429, 440–1
The Conservation of Energy 1–2
The History of Atomism (Lasswitz) 133
The History of Materialism 64
The Judgment of Reality (Gawronsky) 132
The Limits of Concept Formation in Natural Science (Rickert) 327–8, 331–83, 467
The Logic of the Ontic Categories. Logic as Philosophy of Validity 397–8
The Origin and Meaning of Geometric Axioms (Hyder) 2–4, 27–36
The Philosophy of the As-If 442–3
The Place of Language and Myth in the Pattern of Human Culture 217–19, 246–53
The Principle of Conservation of Energy (Planck) 133–4
The Principle of the Infinitesimal Method and Its History (Cohen) 95, 101–6
The Problem of a Logic of the Exact Sciences (Natorp) 162–3, 198–213
The Problem of the Symbol and Its Place in the System of Philosophy 219–20, 254–64
The Standpoint of the Ideal (Lange) 64–78
"the synthetic principles" 107–16
The World of Ideas (Lotze) 80–92
theocracy 143–4, 146
theology 76
theoretical intuitionism 384–95
theoretical meaning of philosophy 299–300
theoretical pragmatism, response and critique 468–9
theoretical problems, division of philosophy and of its history 311–12
theoretical value relevance, historical concept formation 332
theory of cognition: connection with science 103; considerations against name 103–4; distinction from logic 102
theory of knowledge 423
theory of light and electricity 261
theory of relations 239
theory of relativity 236–45
theory of signs 255

thing-in-itself (*metabasis eis allo genos*) 38, 40–62, 429; as-if philosophy 438–9, 442–3; culture and transcendental idealism 323; fellowmen 155; logic to physics relationships 121; objective and subjective grounding of knowledge 166–7, 175; symbolism 254
Thomson, W. 126
thought: as-if philosophy 431–7; border conflict with intuition 102; *Kant and the Marburg School* 182, 183, 185, 186–7; logic to physics relationships 118, 120, 122–3, 126, 129–30, 131; ontological categories 416; scientific logic 198–9, 200–2; *The World of Ideas* 87–8
"threshold of consciousness" 44
time 7–8; Euclidean/Non-Euclidean geometry 241–2; *Kant and the Marburg School* 194; logic to physics relationships 124, 126, 127, 128–9; modern physics 449–54; ontological categories 409; thing-in-itself 40–2
topogenous moments 34–5
totality: fellowmen 137; historical concept formation 345–6; "the synthetic principles" 111; theoretical intuitionism 391–2
Transcendental Aesthetic 41, 42, 43, 185–6
Transcendental Analytic 41
Transcendental Deduction 185–6
Transcendental Dialectic 272
Transcendental Logic 41, 121
transcendental philosophy: chief doctrine 57; concept formation 334; Euclidean/Non-Euclidean geometry 240; *Hermann Cohen and the Renewal of Kantian Philosophy* 223–5, 227; history 296, 334; idealism 40–2, 187–8, 193–4, 317–24; intuition 32–3; *Kant and the Marburg School* 180–4, 189–90, 192; logic to physics relationships 127; naturalism 296; ontological categories 403, 410; origins of geometrical axioms 30–5; response and critique 467–9; scientific logic 198–9, *see also a priori* concepts
transitory phenomena 291–2, 437–8
Trendelenburg, F.A. 2
triangles 15, 35
truth: boundlessness of 422–7; history of philosophy 306; objective and subjective grounding of knowledge 167–8; ontological categories 407–8, 410–11, 412–13; response and critique 470–5
Two-Object Theory 409–10

Überzeugungsgefühl 277
ultimate authority 171, 173, 176
ultimate historical whole 364, 372–3
ultimate objective unities 177

unconscious: as-if philosophy 435–6; symbolism 256
understanding: Euclidean/Non-Euclidean geometry 241–2; historical concept formation 333–4, 337; ontological categories 417; theoretical intuitionism 387–9
undulation theory 120
unequivocally determinate "Phenomena" 177
uniform motion 2
unities: culture and transcendental idealism 322–3; Euclidean/Non-Euclidean geometry 241–2; fellowmen 147; *Hermann Cohen and the Renewal of Kantian Philosophy* 224; historical concept formation 331, 344, 346–8, 350, 357; history of philosophy 304; *Kant and the Marburg School* 188; objective and subjective grounding 164; objective and subjective grounding of knowledge 165, 167, 177; scientific logic 206, 208–9; "the synthetic principles" 111, 113–14; world of ideas 88
universal characteristics, symbolism 255
Universal conception 83
universal constants, logic to physics relationships 134
universal history, historical concept formation 363
universal language, symbolism 260
universal propositions, critical/genetic method 272–3
universal suffering, fellowmen 156
universal, the, grounding of knowledge 172–5
unsensible 425–6
Usener, H. 252

Vaihinger, H. 428–43, 488, 491
validity: boundlessness of truth 422, 424–6; critical/genetic method 274–80, 283–4; culture and transcendental idealism 323; *Hermann Cohen and the Renewal of Kantian Philosophy* 227–8, 232; historical concept formation 334, 339–41, 344, 350, 376; objective and subjective grounding of knowledge 166, 168–70, 172–3; ontological categories 397–421; symbolism 257; *The World of Ideas* 86–8, 90–1
valuation: concept formation 348–9, 356–61; historical concept formation 332–3, 346–7, 351–2; history/naturalism 296; response and critique 466, 471, *see also* history
venture of the hypothesis 185
verb concepts, language and myth 251
vérités éternelles/verités de fait 297, 298
Vier Monate vor Paris (*Four Months Before Paris*) (Liebmann) 37
villains 149
virtue of knowledge, fellowmen 156
vis viva principles 122
Vischer, F.T. 254
vital force, *Kant and the Marburg School* 193–4
volition, historical concept formation 348, 353, 371, 374
vowels, symbolism 259–60

Waehner, A.G. 144
well-being and ill, fellowmen 149–50
well-being and woe, fellowmen 149
Weltanschauung 307, 340
Werner, H. 259
Weyl, H. 255
Wilhelm, F. 338, 364–5
Windelband, boundlessness of truth 425–6
Windelband, W. 265–86; *A History of Philosophy With Special Reference to the Formation and Development of Its Problems and Conceptions* 269, 299–316; *Critical or Genetic Method?* 267, 271–86; *History and Natural Science* 268, 287–98; main works 488; *Philosophy of Culture and Transcendental Idealism* 269–70; response and critique 463–76; translations 491
"*Wissenschaft*" 299
"*Wissenschaftslehre*" 282
woe, fellowmen 149, 151–2
Wolff, C. 364
Wolffian 46, 205
words *see* language
world of ideas 82–92
"world of values" 193
worshippers of idols 141–2

Young, T. 18

Zeus xenios 139

eBooks
from Taylor & Francis
Helping you to choose the right eBooks for your Library

Add to your library's digital collection today with Taylor & Francis eBooks. We have over 50,000 eBooks in the Humanities, Social Sciences, Behavioural Sciences, Built Environment and Law, from leading imprints, including Routledge, Focal Press and Psychology Press.

Choose from a range of subject packages or create your own!

Benefits for you
- Free MARC records
- COUNTER-compliant usage statistics
- Flexible purchase and pricing options
- All titles DRM-free.

Benefits for your user
- Off-site, anytime access via Athens or referring URL
- Print or copy pages or chapters
- Full content search
- Bookmark, highlight and annotate text
- Access to thousands of pages of quality research at the click of a button.

Free Trials Available
We offer free trials to qualifying academic, corporate and government customers.

eCollections
Choose from over 30 subject eCollections, including:

Archaeology	Language Learning
Architecture	Law
Asian Studies	Literature
Business & Management	Media & Communication
Classical Studies	Middle East Studies
Construction	Music
Creative & Media Arts	Philosophy
Criminology & Criminal Justice	Planning
Economics	Politics
Education	Psychology & Mental Health
Energy	Religion
Engineering	Security
English Language & Linguistics	Social Work
Environment & Sustainability	Sociology
Geography	Sport
Health Studies	Theatre & Performance
History	Tourism, Hospitality & Events

For more information, pricing enquiries or to order a free trial, please contact your local sales team:
www.tandfebooks.com/page/sales

www.tandfebooks.com

Printed in Great Britain
by Amazon